GW01571754

EVERYWHERE MEANS SOM_____ ___ SOMEONE

STRANGE CARGO

Commissioned for the Folkestone Triennial 2011
'A Million Miles From Home'
www.folkestonetriennial.org.uk

Photography by Ben Hills

Folkestone Triennial

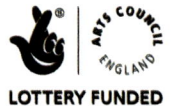

LOTTERY FUNDED

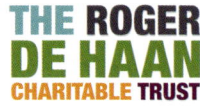

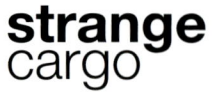

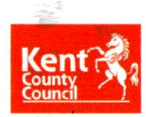

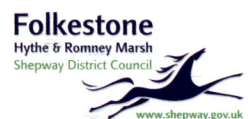

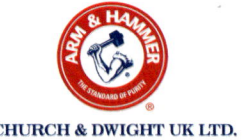

CHURCH & DWIGHT UK LTD.

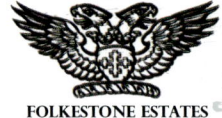

FOLKESTONE ESTATES

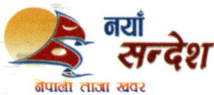

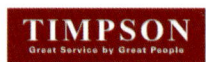

Strange Cargo

Georges House
8 The Old High Street
Folkestone · Kent · CT20 1RL

T: +44 (0)1303 244533

www.strangecargo.org.uk
info@strangecargo.org.uk

Strange Cargo is a Registered Charity, No.1068396

Photography by **Ben Hills**
www.benhills.co.uk · ben@benhills.co.uk

Design & Illustration for project by **Scarlett Rickard**
www.scarlettrickard.co.uk · design@scarlettrickard.co.uk

FOREWORD

At last – a book about real travelling. Going on a journey isn't about clocking up the miles, but adopting a state of mind. It's about looking very, very carefully. This is what this wonderful collection of moments forces you to do – see Folkestone afresh. Whether you're a longterm resident or a visitor on a daytrip, it will reveal new details and stories about the cobbled high street, the mishmashed waterfront, the beaches and the higgedly-piggedly roads and buildings stretching up to the gentle hills.

Travel is always as much about another time as another place, and it's startling how many of the contributions are about memories of what *was* there, rather than records of what *is*. We all long to time travel – back to our youth, in our grandfather's footsteps, or simply to a place we believe was better than today. This book takes you to that magical lost land, reminding us of what once was.

When I moved to Folkestone twenty years ago, my friends in London thought I was mad. How could I leave the excitements of a big city for a seaside town that had seen better days? It was like going to live with an elderly aunt who was once a beauty, but no longer shone. It didn't even have a pier (or so I thought, until I read this book.) But Folkestone was full of small discoveries – the rope and tyre swing in the woodland by Little Switzerland, the fossil I found one late long-shadowed afternoon under the cliffs, a café called Paradise selling eggs sunny-side up. I felt like an explorer. I had found a new place and, as a result, my whole world was bigger.

When I now give talks about travel writing around the country, I ask the audience if they've ever been to India. Often, half the well-travelled crowd raise their hands. Then I ask how many have been to Folkestone. Sometimes, someone has. I do this to prove that the places that appear most ordinary are sometimes the least known. Folkestone, for most people, is a more faraway place than Goa.

I no longer live in Folkestone. I am writing this on an island off the west coast of Ireland, where I spend much of my time. But the many years I spent in Harvey Street still linger in my writing and inform my imagination. While living in my pink-painted house, I wrote two books about the sea. Today, I can see the waves from my Irish desk. Folkestone wedded me to the water. And I return to the town often, to sit on a dedicated bench and look out over the grey to France. Next time, it will be with this book in my hand, to unearth new treasures.

So here we have Folkestone – exotic, enticing, little known. But not for much longer. This beautiful book will put it on the traveller's map. Enjoy your own journey.

Dea Birkett

www.deabirkett.com

INTRODUCTION

Everywhere Means Something to Someone. Strange Cargo has been commissioned by Andrea Schlieker for the 2011 Folkestone Triennial.

Folkestone is where Strange Cargo lives and works, and we are in the unusual position of being the only artists making work for this Triennial who are not *'A Million Miles from Home'*. The People's Guidebook to Folkestone has been made in collaboration with local people with the intention of making visitors feel as if they are being shown around the town by a good friend, someone who is able to pass on those small and sometimes inconsequential pieces of information about the town that only locals would know.

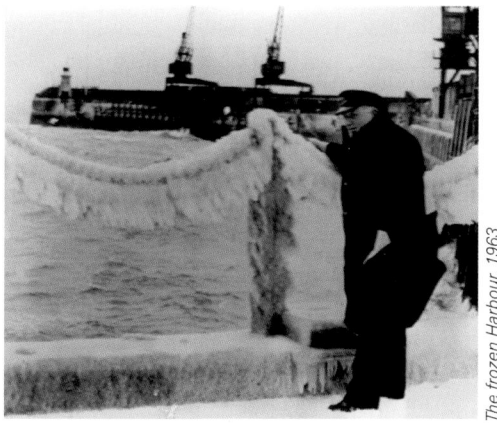

The frozen Harbour, 1963

Strange Cargo has actively pursued getting to know local people and, because the way we work often invites others to play a central role, we have developed a relationship that makes working together uncomplicated and mutually significant. In this instance we spread the word about what we were doing and waited for individuals to come forward with their contributions.

We did not set hard and fast rules about what type of information should be in the book, choosing instead to let it find its own form from what people chose to contribute. It has grown into an eclectic mix of information, not a regular guidebook, but an assortment of instructions, trivia, memories, facts and whimsies. By overlaying the geography of Folkestone with personalised local knowledge, they are presented with a glimpse of what it is that makes Folkestone home to the people who live here.

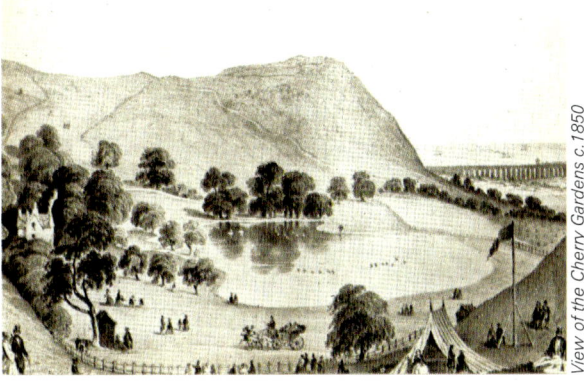

View of the Cherry Gardens c.1850

Everywhere means something to someone; even if only small traces remain that indicate earlier use or occupation, such as an evocative road name, a strangely out of context object, or an emotional trace relating to an incident invisible to most people; a significance will often be able to be recalled or interpreted by someone.

The ability to read these ambiguous fingerprints is mostly the preserve of locals, who have the capacity to serve as arbitrators for place-based knowledge. Folkestone is changing, and this is inevitable and should be embraced, but acknowledging the depth of people's attachment to places is equally important; distinctiveness authenticates a place, and this characteristic should remain integral to the processes of renewal.

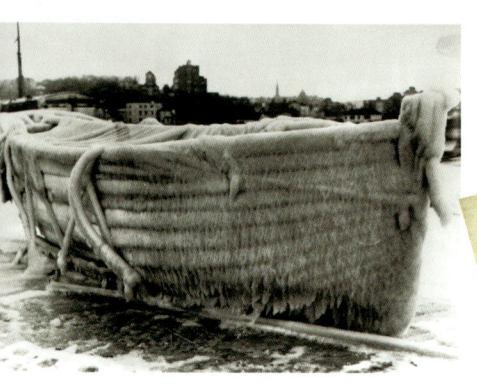

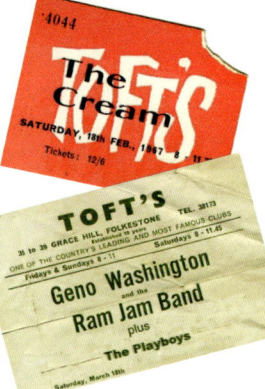

As individuals struggle to find their place in society and feel truly engaged, recognition and connection to a place – the vernacular of the *local* – is one of the few things that many people in a community have in common. Articulating personal knowledge of a location can create a language of place, a bond that truly excites people, constructing an occasion where people can sense kinship, feel engaged and connected, to each other, and to their community.

Welcome to our home.

Brigitte Orasinski *Artistic Director, Strange Cargo*

EVERYWHERE MEANS SOMETHING TO SOMEONE

सर्वत्र, मतलब केहि चिज कसैको लागि

फोक्सटनमा प्रत्येक तीन वर्षमा आयोजना गरिने खुल्ला कला महोत्सवको (Triennial outdoor art festival) सुभ अवसरमा Strange Cargo ले एउटा कलात्मक सृजनाको रुपमा यो स्यानो उपयोगी पुस्तकको तयारी गरेको छ । Strange Cargo फोक्सटनका स्थानिय रङ्ग कर्मिहरुको एउटा समूह हो जसले वारम्वार यहाँका स्थानिय वासिन्दाहरुलाई आमन्त्रण गरेर आफ्नो सृजनात्मक कार्यमा सहभागी गराउने गर्दछन् । यो पुस्तक तयार गर्नको लागि उनीहरुले स्थानिय वासिन्दाहरुलाई फोक्सटनमा भएका घुम्न र हेर्न योग्य ठाउँहरुको जानकारी उपलब्ध गराउनको लागि अनुरोध गरेका थिए । सयौंको संख्यामा प्राप्त भएका यस्ता सूचनाहरु मध्ये धेरैलाई सम्पादन गरेर यस पुस्तकमा समावेस गरिएको छ ।

घरवाट लाखौ माईल टाढाको वसाई भएपनि फोक्सटनमा रहेको Strange Cargo ले भूगोलको विभिन्न ठाउँवाट फोक्सटनमा घुम्न आउने आगन्तुकहरुलाई आवश्यक सूचनाहरु सरल किसिमले उपलब्ध गराउने प्रमुख उद्धेश्यले यो पुस्तकको तयार गरि एको हो ।

वास्तवमा यो एउटा परम्परागत पुस्तक नभएर यसमा फोक्सटन वरपर भएका सम्पूर्ण ऐतिहासिक स्थलहरु, आनन्दमय विश्राम गर्ने र आफ्नो इच्छानुसारको खाने तथा पिउने ठाउँहरुको फोटोहरु समेत समावेस गरिएको छ । यसको अतिरिक्त यसमा उल्ले खित रमणिय ठाउँहरुमा सजिलै पुग्न सकियोस भन्ने आशयले प्रत्येक ठाउँहरुको सचित्र वर्णन र त्यहाँ जाने वाटोको विस्तृत जानकारी समेत समावेश गरिएको छ ।

हामीलाई आशा छ, तपाईहरु फोक्सटनमा आइ विभिन्न स्थानको भ्रमण गरेर सक्दो मनोरञ्जन लिनुहुनेछ !

बृजीट ओरसिन्स्की
निर्देशक

EVERYWHERE MEANS SOMETHING TO SOMEONE

PEOPLE WHO HAVE CONTRIBUTED STORIES FOR THIS GUIDEBOOK

Adam Philpott
Adam Smith
AJ Charlie
Ajay Deshar
Alan Curd
Alan E Clough
Alan Taylor
Alex Clayton
Alia Sanger
Alice Neate
Amanda Beckett
Amanda Oates
Amber
Ana Philpott
Anah
Andrea Calgolari
Andrew Green
Andy Jarrett
Angela Sonnen
Ann Barns

(nee Procter)
Ann Berry
Ann Finney
Ann Saxby
Anne Mortimer
Anthony Wilson
Barbara Witham
Barbara Wood
Barry Bergin
Baz Hodson
Becky Burton
Becky Ingelbretch
Belinda Cripps
Ben Hills
Ben Johnson
Bernard Bushell
Beryl Wood
Bev McLellan
Brandon
Brian Balderstone

Brigitte Orasinski
Cameron McGhie
Carmela Calgolari
Carol Clark
Casey Pearson
Castle Hill CoE
Primary School
Chandiraj Rai
Charles Newington
Charlie
Charlie Osbourne
Chelly Surrell
Cheryl Papasian
Chris Capon
Chris Davis
Chris Phillips
Chris Ruddle
Chris Smith
Christine Judge
Christopher Curd

Claire Angel
Clive Weatherhogg
Cremilla Catt
Damian Collins
Damon
Dan Desborough
Dan Stockman
Daniel Addison
Darren Blyth
Darryl Osbourne
Dave Allen
Dave Thompson
David Bratton
David Bricknell
David Crocker
David Crocket
David Dickinson
David East
David Gray
David Martin

David Noble
David Springett
Debbie Faulds
Debbie Munnelly
Deborah Crofts
Denis M. Langley
Dennis Fristy
Derek
Di Burns
Diana
Diana Crampton
Diana Hartley
Dizzy Hayter
Don Fagg
Doreen Burton
Doreen Butcher
Eamonn Rooney
Edward Neate
Eileen Harris
Eileen Martin

Eileen Nicholls
Elena Philpott
Elisha Ryan
Elisse Whitby
Elizabeth Burton
Elizabeth Ellis
Elsie MacDonald
Emily Ghassempour
Emily Rogers
Ethan Coates
Eva Billings
Eve McBride
Evelyn Joyce
Chipperfield
Evone Hobson
Fiona Parker
Cabache
Fran Addison
Fran Grellier
Francis

Fred Hall
Gary Calver
Gerry Jenkinson
Gillian White
Grandad
Greg Stevens
Gwen Powell
Harkaraj Rai
Hayley Sanders
Helen Derry
Helen Mayer
Iain Neilson
Ian Fell
Ian Gordon
Imitations Dance
Theatre
Ingrid Goodchild
Jack
Jack Doolan
Jackie Hindle

Jackie Luckman
Jacquie Brown
Jake Baker
James Marsh
Jan Barker
Jan Gearing
Jan Holben
Janden Miller
Jane Walters
Janel Whitby
Janine Gray
Jasmyne
Jason Ritchie
Jayne Baxter
Jean McKenna
Jeff Daly
Jemi Bayliss
Jenny Coleman
Jessica Graham
Jo Miller

Jo Molby
Joan Bonus
Jodie Booth
Joel Snowman
John Bailey
John Creasey
John Dean
John Sims
John Sonnen
John Sussams
John Walters
Jonathan McCabe
Joseph Bleach
Josephine Gray
Joshua Carter
Joshua Oz
Josie Frost
Jules Boyd
June Howkins
Karen Rennie

Kathleen Margaret
Pritchard
Kathy Globe
Kay Hull
Kay McLoughlin
Kaye El-Shama
Keith Holland
Kelly Thomas
Kelvin Pawsey
Ken Molby
Kerry Bartle
Kevin Gorett
Kevin Harvey
Kim Walker
Kyle
Laura Edison
Laura Pinkham
Laura Jacobs
Layla Boyd
Lesley Bryan

Lesley Hardy
Lesley Whybrow
Liam at The Shed
Linda Blomquist
Linda Harris
Lisa Oulton
Liz Gibbons
Liz Timmins
Lore Boyd
Louis Fidge
Louise Gamberini
Louise Kedwell
Louise Long
Lucy Davies
Lucy Gibson
Luk Tourlouse
Lynda Daniells
M Brown
Mamata Gurung
Mandy Graham

Marc Thorin
Margaret Pratt
Margaret Wart
Marie Gibson
Marika Woods
Mark
Mark Sutherland
Martina Godesova
Marty Ratcliffe
Maryanne Grant-
Traylen
Maureen Criddle
Megan
Megan Latham
Megan Webb
Melanie Jacobs
Melanie Wrigley
Melita Godden
Michael George
Michael Leatherdale

Michele Brailsford
Michelle Charlton-
Taylor
Mick Orasinski
Mike Edison
Molly
Monty Ratcliffe
Mr Jarman
Mr P Lodgedoc
Mrs Godden
Mrs Tia Star Bartlett
Mrs W Fisher
Muriel
Muriel Joan Taylor
Nadine Dakin
Nathan White
Neil Kelly
Nellie Prentice
Nicholas Perry
Nicholette Goff

Nick Adams
Nick Blanchet
Nick Ewbank
Nick Grant
Nick Jacobs
Nick Spurrier
Nick Wesley
Nicky Vines
Nigel Harland
Pam Tonothy
Paola Dionisotti
Pat Neal
Pat Weedon
Paul Fristy
Paul Greenstreet
Paul Harris
Paul Rennie
Paul Seward
Paul Wimsett
Pauline Fitzpatrick

Peggy Brisley
Pete Geoghegan
Peter Bamford
Peter Jurzynski
Peter Neate
Peter Richards
Peter Smith
Peter Watchous
Phil Cross
Philip Lee
Ray Duff
Rhearina Chopping
Rhia Williams
Richard Doran
Rita from the
Portofino Restaurant
Rita White
Rob Clark
Rob Prentice
Robert Mouland

Robert Perry
Roger Joyce
Roly Lovell
Ron Butcher
Ron Chambers
Rosalind Ryan
Rose Brown
Rose E Denton
Rosemary Blakemore
Rosie Smith
Roy Cheesemur
Roy Ingleton
Ruth Parkinson
Ruth Tyler
Sally Penfold
Samuel Bricknell
Sandra Booth
Sandra Perry
Sandy Buckley

Sarah Calver
Scarlett Rickard
Selma
Shane Record
Shelly Lewis
Simon
Simon Byatt
Simon Everett
Sindy Mills
Sinead Fost
Slim
Sonya Latham
St. Augustine's RC Primary School
St. Peter's CoE Primary School
Stella Maris RC Primary School
Stephen Emery
Steve Thompson

Steven Smith
Sue Harrison
Susan Clarke
Susan Triffitt
Susan Webb
Sylvia Evans
Tahlia
Tamasin Jarrett
Tania Bartlett
Tanya Henton
Terry Hindle
Theresa Smith Thomas
Thomas Clark
Tim Warner
Tom Capon
Tom Miller
Toni Brenchley
Tony Butcher
Tony Hulse

Tracey Stanley
Tracy
Tracy Kyle
Trinity
Una Kennedy
Val Murton
Valerie Redding
Veronica Moorbed
Vince Sharp
Vince Williams
Warren Chambers
Will Jennings

We received more stories that we had space to include, so to acknowledge everyone equally for their participation, we have included a full list here of everyone who has contributed to this guidebook. Thank you all very much.

.

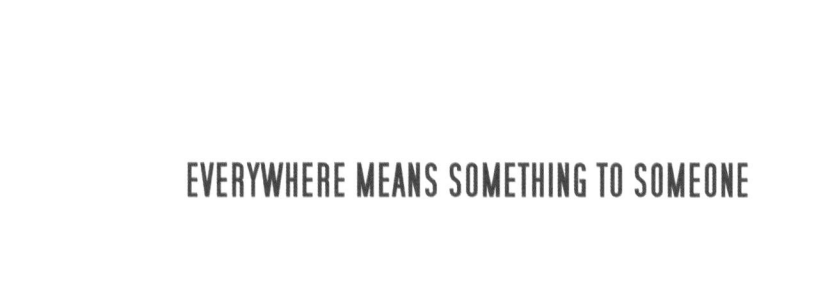

This guidebook includes practical suggestions for good eateries, helpful walking tours, and knowledge of those special places to sit and ponder. There are recollections of natural disasters, fisticuffs, and significance attached to places because of past events. Dogs, rats, cows and dolphins are all mentioned, and there is even a recipe and a poem. Some places such as the Spider Museum, the exquisite little light switch in the ladies' loo at the Portifino restaurant, or the mahogany wheelhouse from an old cross-Channel steamer that now serves as a garden shed, were not able to be included but are still, none the less, just as important as everytthing else. We do feel that it should become general knowledge however, that Sandgate was the birthplace of Hattie Jacques. We have learned that Buffalo Bill set up camp in Folkestone in 1904, the Rolling Stones played here several times, and Jimi Hendrix used to live in a caravan on the beach just up the road. Also, that the Bolshoi Ballet danced an impromptu performance for the Russian Ambassador at the Metropole Hotel in the 1950s. We cannot offer our guarantee that all of the facts are accurate, but then that is not the point of the guidebook. What is most important is that these are home truths and are the common currency of local people. Some of the stories are an invitation to venture further into the district.

We have included descriptions in Nepalese as there is a significant Nepali community in Folkestone, the soldiers and families of the resident regiment of the Royal Gurkha Rifles at Sir John Moore Barracks at Shorncliffe. Every story has a co-ordinate which refers to the map at the end of the book.

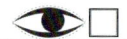

There is a little rocky pool with a trickling waterfall surrounded by flowers and moss, on the path that runs along the stream in lower Radnor Park. When we were children we used to play there and dip our hands in the water and catch newts. As a small child I thought it was such a magical place, you could really imagine fairies playing there.

त्यहाँ एउटा ढुंगाले बनेको सानो झरना र ताल थियो । मलाई बाल्यकालमा लाग्थ्यो कि यो एउटा जादु नगरी हो र त्यहाँ अप्सर हरु खेल्ने गर्दथे ।

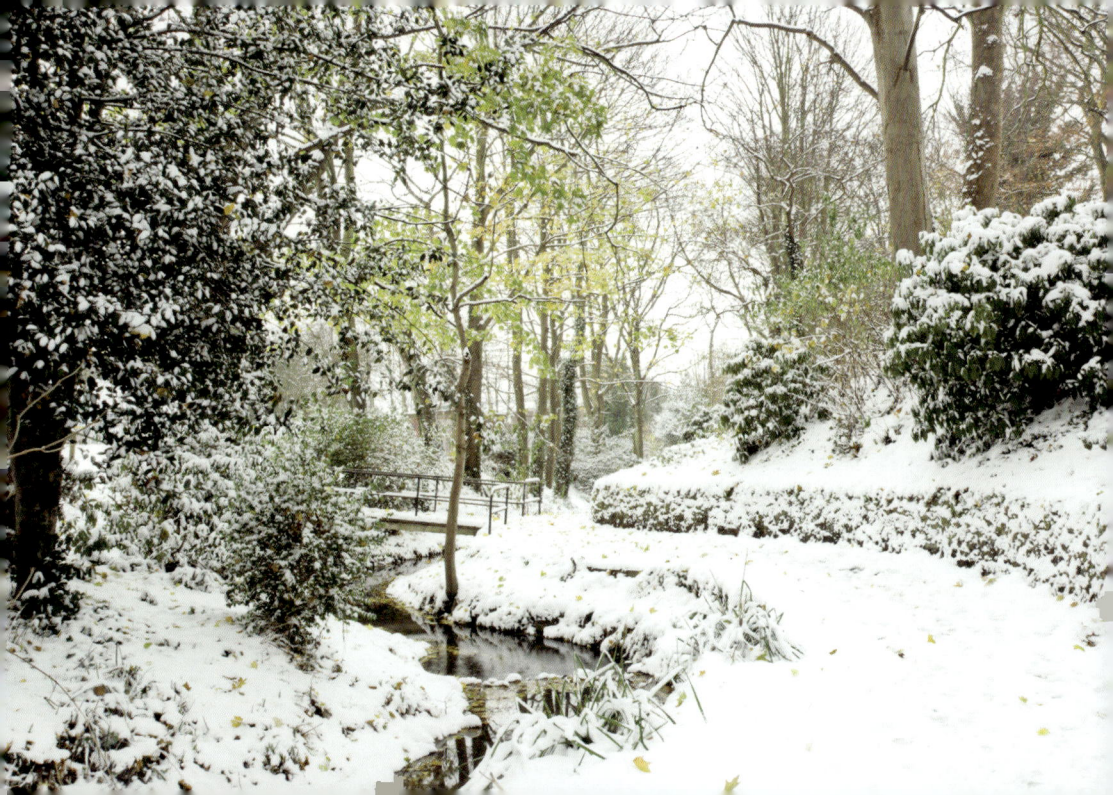

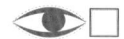

J. Thompson in Geraldine Road is one of the oldest family-run garage businesses in the town. It was started by Joe Thompson in 1968, when he bought the business from Tony Shepherd, a motorcycle engineer and dealer. The garage has a vintage petrol pump outside, which no longer pumps fuel, but is a distinctive local landmark. The building has had a varied history; in 1926 a taxi firm occupied the premises and for a time afterwards, it was a soft drinks factory. After the war it became a garage, started by Peter Mazzetti, with a gratuity from the army. He went on to run a Rootes car dealership in Park Road, now called Geraldine Motors.

Joe is retired and Thompson's is now run by his son Dave and his grandson Adam, but despite being 80 this year, Joe still comes in most days to help out.

यो शहरको Geraldine Road मा भएको J. Thompson सवैभन्दा पुरानो एउटा परिवारले चलाएको मोटर मर्मत गर्ने व्यवसाय हो । त्यसताका यसको छेउमा पुरानो पेट्रोल पम्प थियो । यो हाल त्यहाँ छैन तर पनि यसलाई स्थानिय वासिन्दाहरुले राम्ररी चिन्दछन् ।

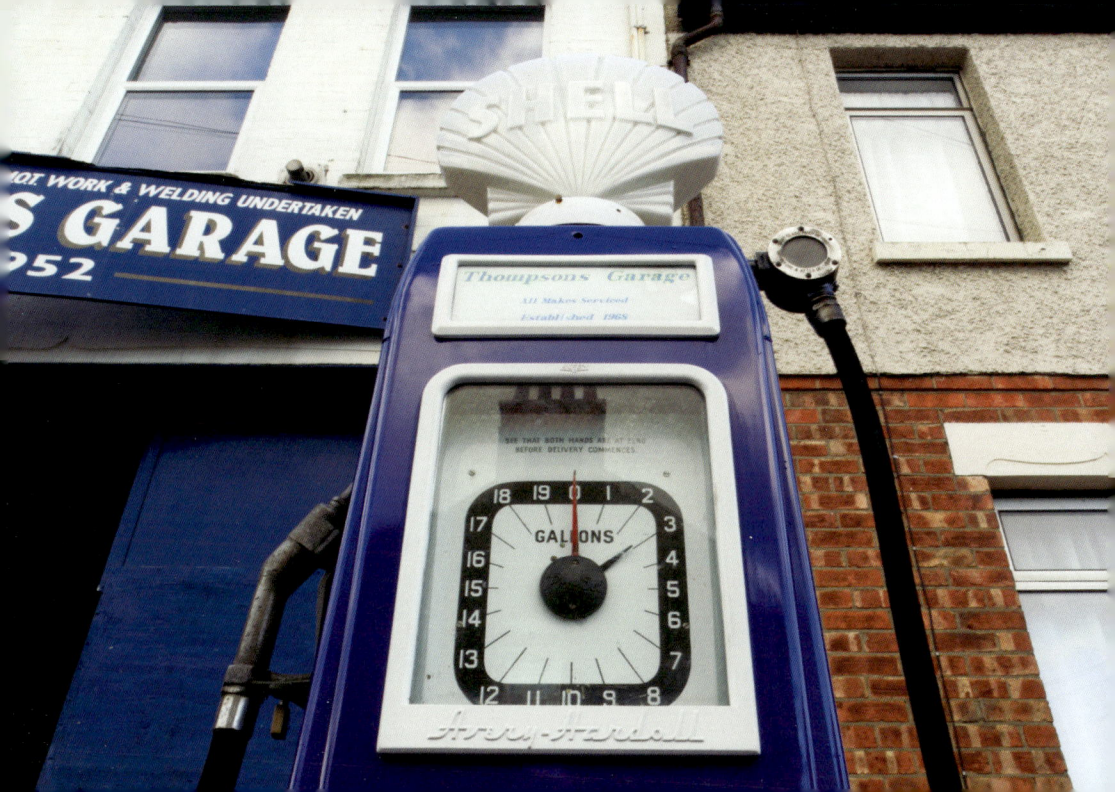

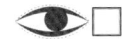

As a young lad, I had a misspent youth and I knew every path along the cliff top in Folkestone. My parents had a hotel in Clifton Crescent. At the top end of the Leas not too far from the Martello Tower, there were the remains of a water lift, just like the one that's still there at the other end of the Leas. The tracks and winding gear were abandoned and left to rot after the War, and if you climbed up the bank you could see it in the undergrowth.

Leas को माथिल्लो भागमा पानीले चल्ने लिफ्ट थियो । युद्ध पछाडि यसको प्रयोग बन्द गरियो त्यसपछि यो खियाले मक्कियो। यदि ढिस्को माथि चढेर हेर्नें हो भने अभै यसको अवशेष झाडिमुनि देख्न सकिन्छ ।

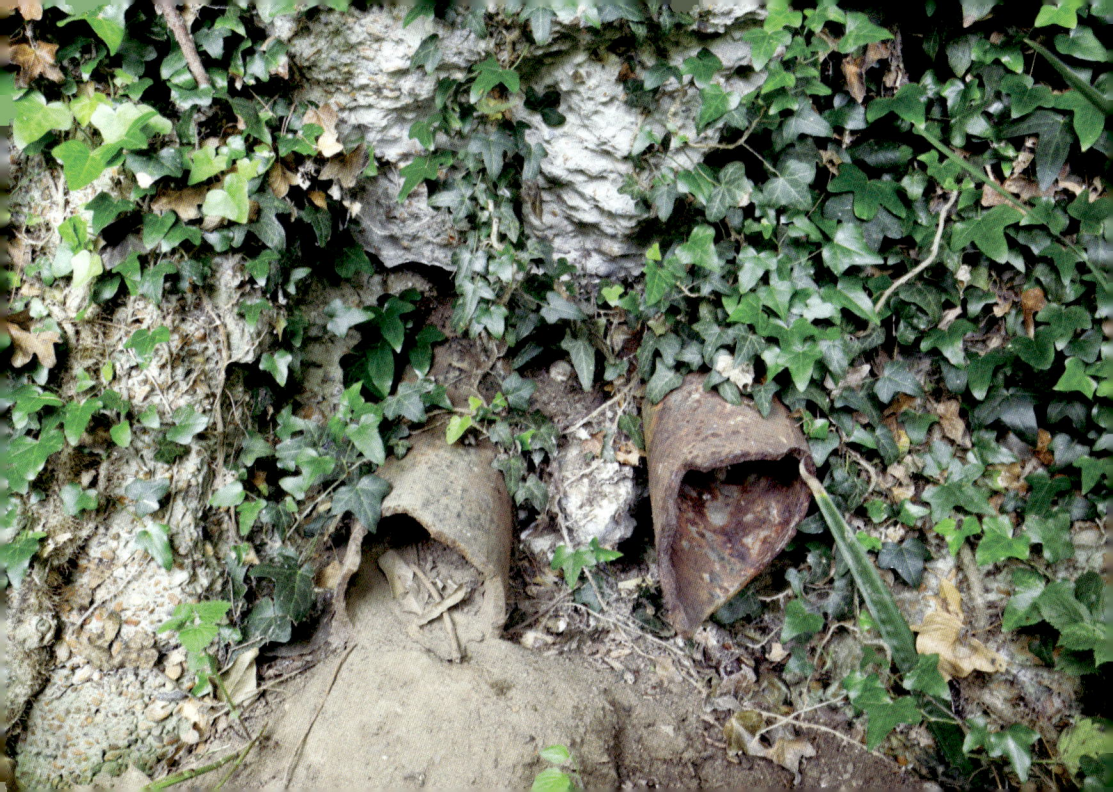

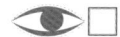

A leaning, rather out of context hawthorn tree is the last remaining fragment of the sweeping driveway leading to the Pleasure Gardens Theatre. There used to be a semi circular tree-lined driveway for carriages and cars bringing people to the theatre, and every time I see the tree I am taken back to the times when the magnificent Pleasure Gardens was on that site.

अर्ध गोलाकारको अन्तिममा एउटा hawthorn को रुख थियो, जस्को वाटो भएर मानिसहरु आ-आफ्ना सवारी साधन मार्फत Pleasure Gardens Theatre मा आउने गर्थे ।

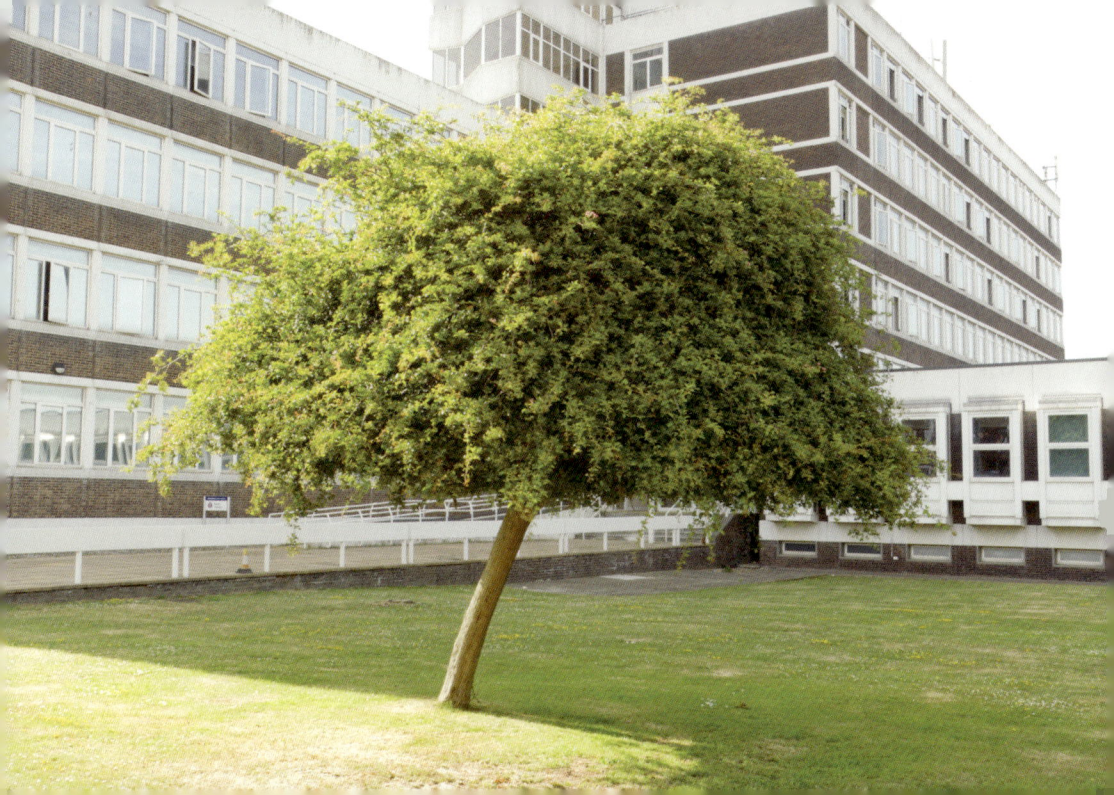

The last remaining fragment of the Folkestone's Victorian pier – a singular rusting girder indicates where the pier started. The concrete arches marked the entrance to it.

फोक्स्टनमा भएको भिक्टोरिया बन्दरगाहको अन्तिम अवशेषले यहाँबाट बन्दरगाह शुरु भएको कुरा बुभिन्छ । त्यहाँ भएको सिमन्टले बनेको प्रवेश मार्गबाट बन्दरगाह भित्र जान सकिन्थ्यो ।

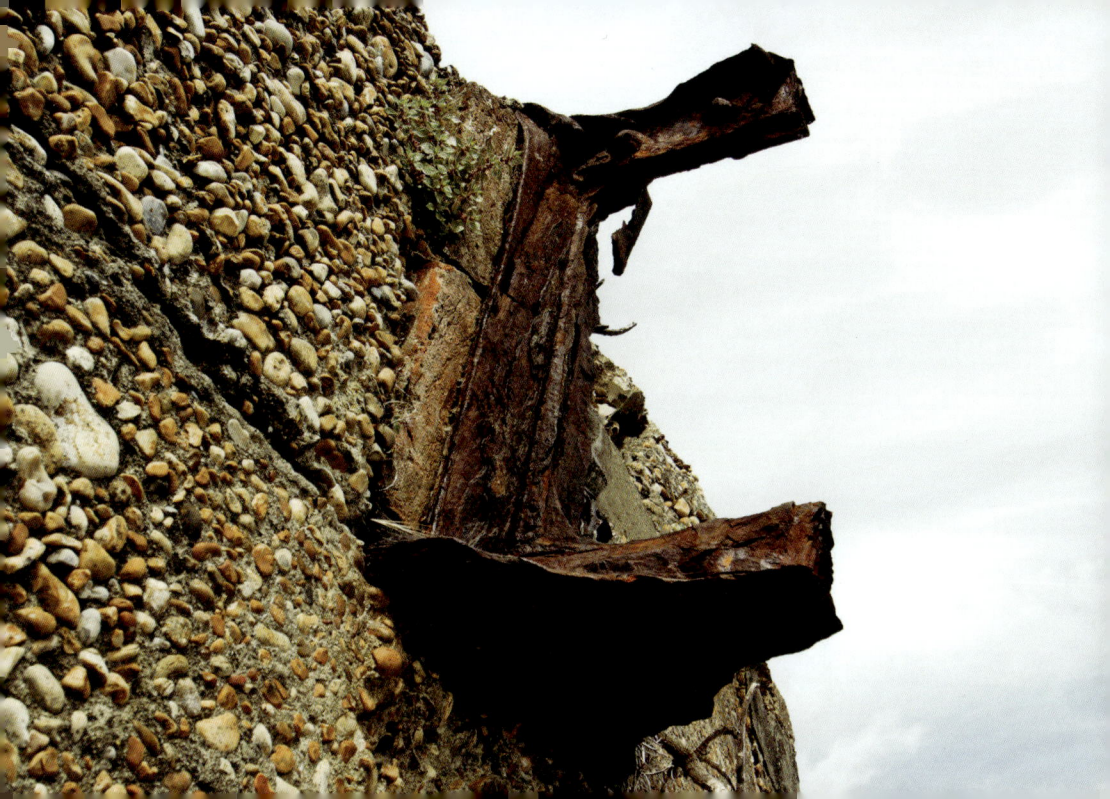

On the Canterbury Road between Crete Road East and where the road descends in to Folkestone, two rusty pipes can still be seen coming down the steep, chalky bank.

I was told by my father, and have also read somewhere some years ago, that the pipes were installed to prevent a German tank advance out of Folkestone towards Canterbury. High up on the bank a large tank of petrol was sited and it was the duty of the army, or more probably the Home Guard, to open the valve on the tank and release petrol on to the road in front of the advancing invaders. A grenade would then be thrown to ignite the petrol.

Of course the invasion did not happen so this weapon was never used.

भिरालो भित्तामा भएको दुईवटा खिया लागेको पाईपहरु युद्धको बेलामा क्यान्टवरीको सुरक्षाको लागि दुश्मनहरुको ट्यांकरलाई रोक्न धराप बनाईएको थियो । एउटा ठूलो पेट्रोल ट्यांकी बाटो भन्दा माथि राखिएको थियो । दुश्मनहरुको ट्यांकर त्यो बाटोमा आए भने सुरक्षामा खटिएका सैनिकहरुले पाईपको सहायताबाट उनीहरुलाई पेट्रोल खन्याईदिने र हाते बमको प्रयोग गरेर आगो लगाईदिने योजना बनाईएको थियो । अभाग्यवश दुश्मनहरु यो बाटोमा आएनन् र त्यो हतियारको प्रयोग कहिले पनि भएन ।

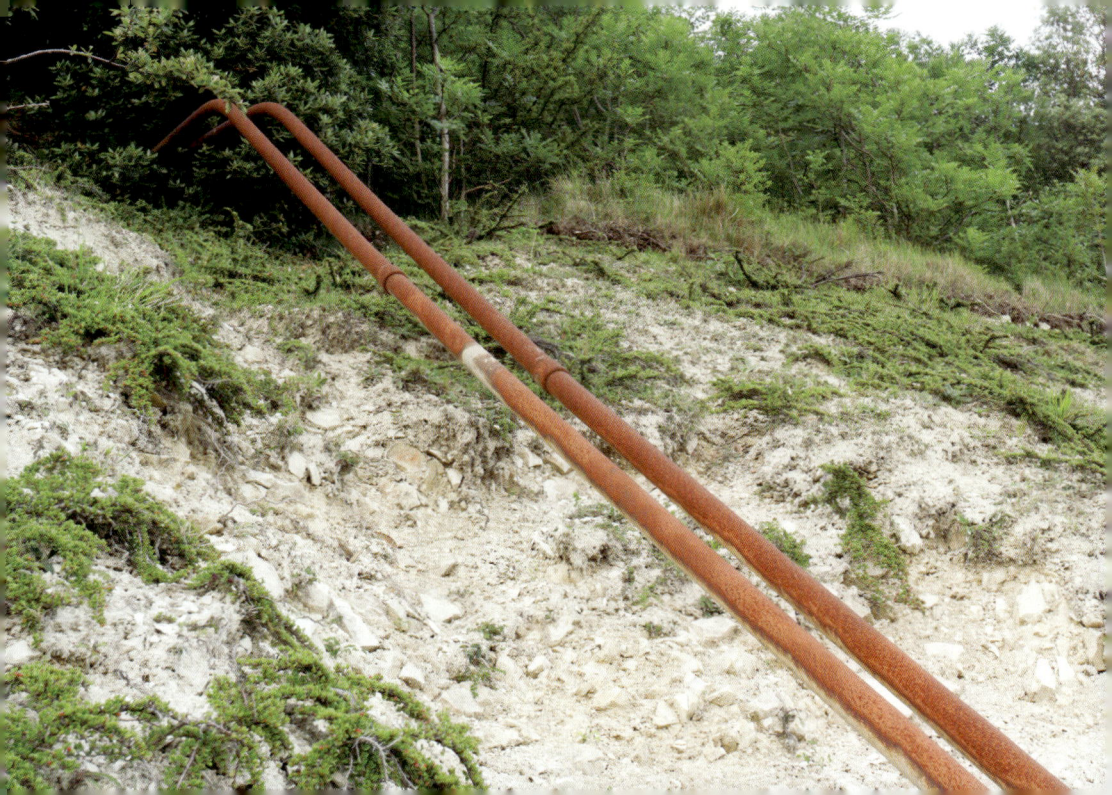

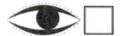

The gates of the University used to be the entrance to the old hospital and Pickfords removal store and there are traces of where, as a young man, I used to run the axle of my delivery hand-cart over the surface as I was parking it. It was big and it had iron-clad wheels. The scratches are near the brick wall and every time I see them, I am transported back to the days when I worked there.

आफ्नो उमेरमा म फर्निचर ओसार-पसार गर्ने काम गर्दथें र सामान भएको ठेलागाडी विसाउनको लागि प्रायजसो पर्खालमा गाडीको पांग्रा अड्याउने गर्दथे । त्यतिबेला ठेलागाडीको पांग्रा गुड्दा पर्खालको ईंटामा कोतारिएका धर्साहरु आज घण वर्ष पछ्याडि पनि म देख्दैछु ।

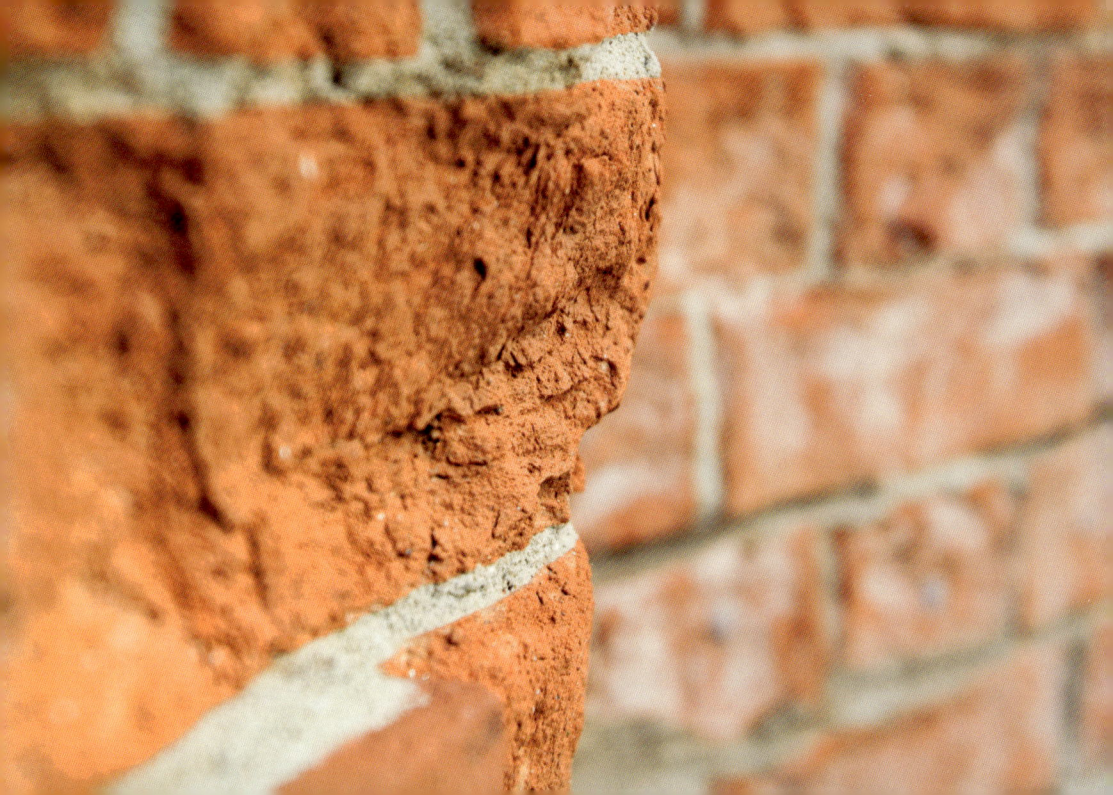

People talk about 'The Bomb' on the Sunny Sands. I have never known it as the Bomb. I didn't come to Folkestone until I was sixteen and, although I must have seen 'The Bomb' a lot before I was nineteen, my first real memory of it was of strolling along the wall at high tide with a boyfriend on our way home after the pub one night. The water was lapping up and down around the artefact and my friend pointed at it and said, "By Neptune's helmet!" Yes, he was being slightly rude, but it tickled me so much I was giggling all the way home and have never forgotten it to this day. I still think of it as Neptune's Helmet...

समुन्द्रको सतह बढेको बेलामा म समुन्द्री किनारमा हिँडिरहेको थिए । पानीको बहाव तलमाथि हुँदा एउटा धातुको सामान हल्लि रहेको देखिन्थ्यो । मेरो साथीले त्यस वस्तुलाई देखाउँद Neptune को टोपी हो भन्थ्यो । उ अलिक अशिष्ट स्वभावको व्यक्ति थियो तर म बाटो भरी सँधै उसलाई हाँसेर टारिदिने गर्थें ।

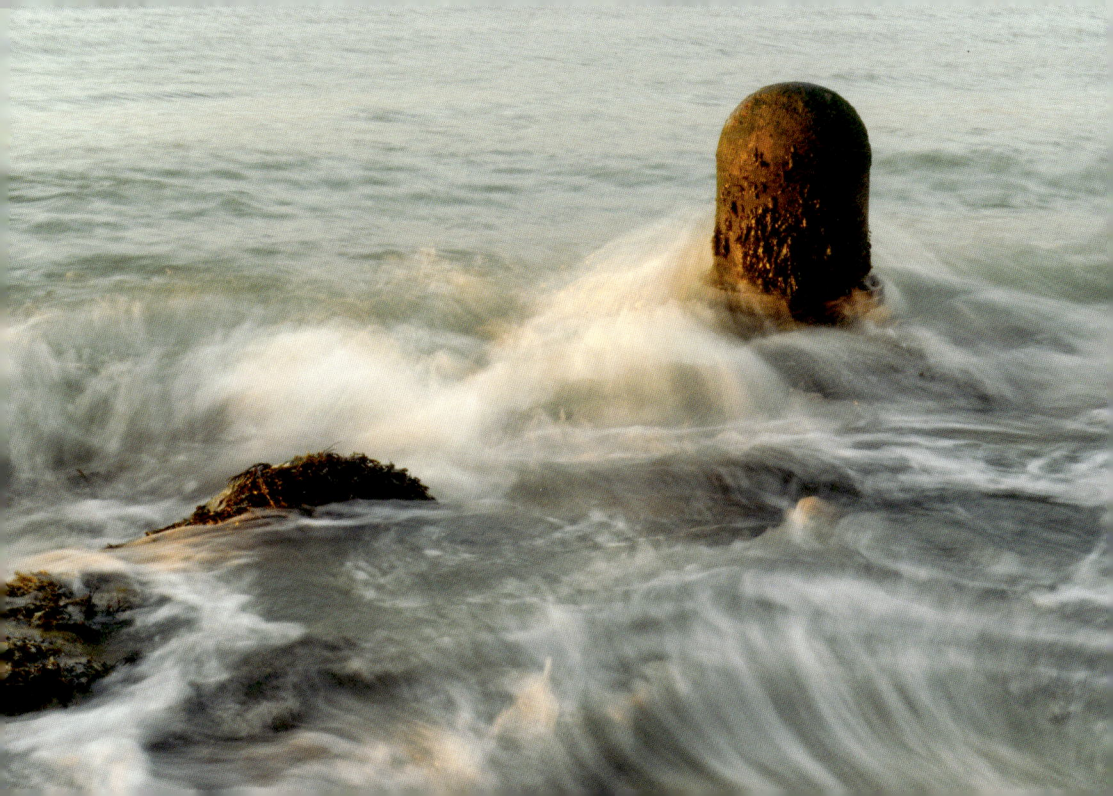

Blossom Fight Corner – where Radnor Park Avenue and Radnor Park Road meet is a corner where the blossom from the trees collects on the path.

One year, we had a blossom fight there: like a snowball fight, but a good deal more gentle. Now, every week, from the first crocus until the blossom is ready to drop, my youngest daughter asks "When can we have a blossom fight?"

पार्कको कुनाको बाटोमा रुखहरुबाट झरेका फुलहरु जम्मा हुन्छन् । एक पटक त्यहाँ हामीहरु मिलेर झरेका फुलहरु जम्मा पारेर हिउँको डल्लो जस्तो बनाएर खेलेका थियौं । वसन्त ऋतुको प्रत्येक हप्ता मेरी छोरीले 'हामीहरु फुलको खेल खेल्ने हो ? भनेर सोच्ने गर्छिन् ।

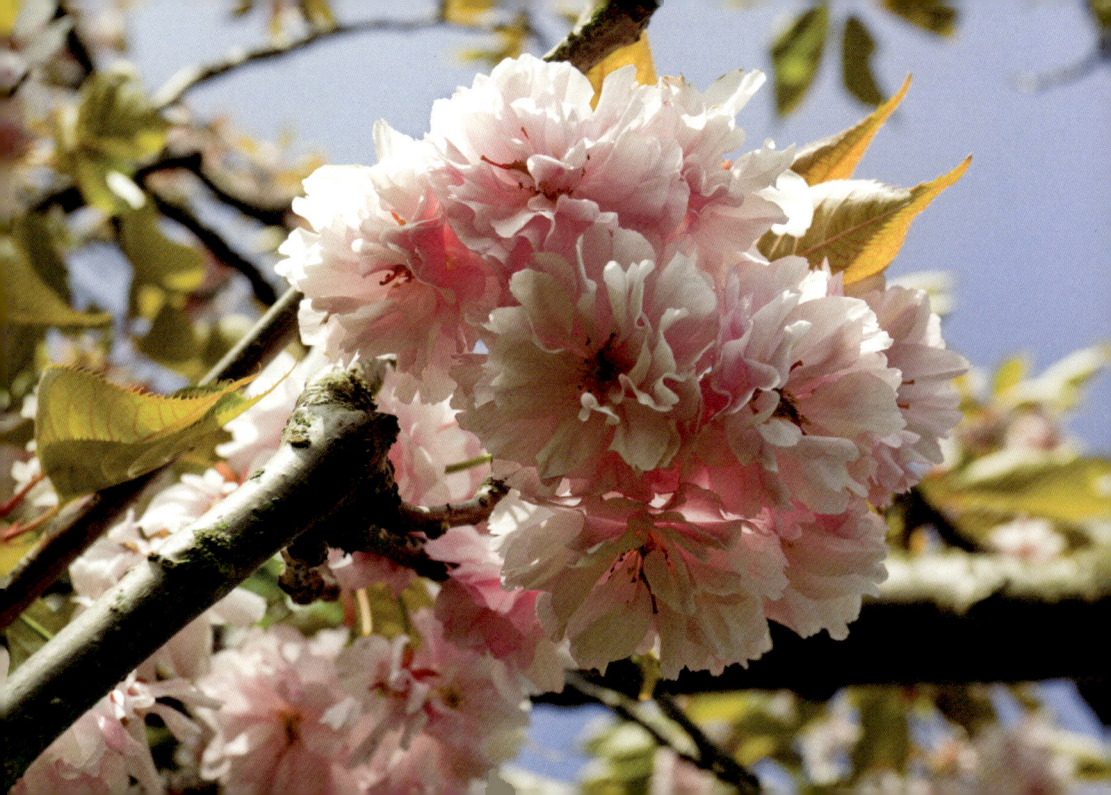

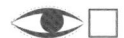

My boyfriend used.to work at the Rotunda amusements on the seafront and I used to trot down the '100 steps' (although I think there were 116) from the Road of Remembrance, nearly every day, to see him at lunch and back up again. I even did it several times when I was expecting!

The other set of steps I remember as being very evocative are now closed. When going down them, you would get about half way and then go through a sort of enclosed part where there was a sort of roof made (if I remember correctly) of wire-meshed glass. It was pretty derelict-looking the few times I walked through it, but it always made me wonder what it was and what it might have been like in its day. I always imagined it would have been a very romantic place in the evenings, possibly with entertainment. But that would have been well before the 80s when I became familiar with it! Folkestone must have been such a very splendid place once upon a time.

म प्राय हरेक दिनको खाना खाने वेलामा ११६ वटा खुडकिला तल झरी मेरो केटा साथीलाई भेट्न Rotunda रमाईलो पार्कमा जान्थे किनभने उ त्यहाँ काम गर्दथ्यो । त्यस पछी पून फर्केर माथी आउँथे । गर्भवति भएको वेलामा समेत मैले यसो गर्दैथ्ये ।

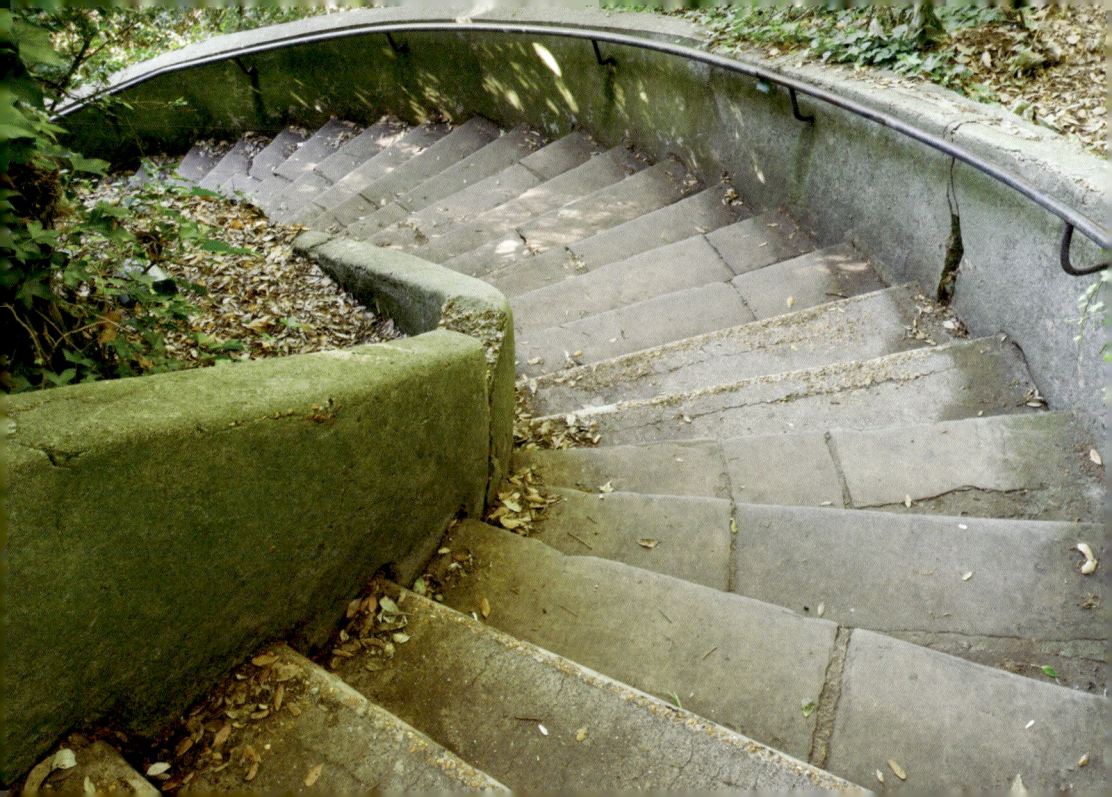

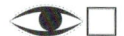

From memory there are usually 3 to 5 lads who carry the cross. There's a short church service, then the crowd walk through town following the cross. When they reach the top of Sugar Loaf Hill there is another service and prayer for Folkestone. The vicars/priests/pastors from the churches across Folkestone take turns to lead at both services, and musicians play. Often people submit prayers on slips of paper during the service, and after the crowd has gone some will stay and read the prayers out in front of the crosses, which has been known to go on through the night! On a nice day it is a lovely walk, with a really friendly crowd, and has the most amazing views over Folkestone and the surrounding area.

An artist I know made a piece of work called *Did Jesus die in Folkestone?* showing the crosses on Sugar Loaf Hill. He told me that when he was a young boy, he came with his mother on a car journey from their home in Dover. When he saw the crosses on the hill, this is the question he asked her. It's one of my favourite artworks ever.

Easter को पर्वमा फोक्सटन भरिका मानिसहरु Sugar Loaf Hill को शिरमा अचयककभक चढाउन गिर्जाघरमा भेला हुन्छन् । मानिसहरु कागजमा प्रार्थना लेख्छन् र विशेष दिनमा डाँडा माथि लगेर पढ्छन् ।

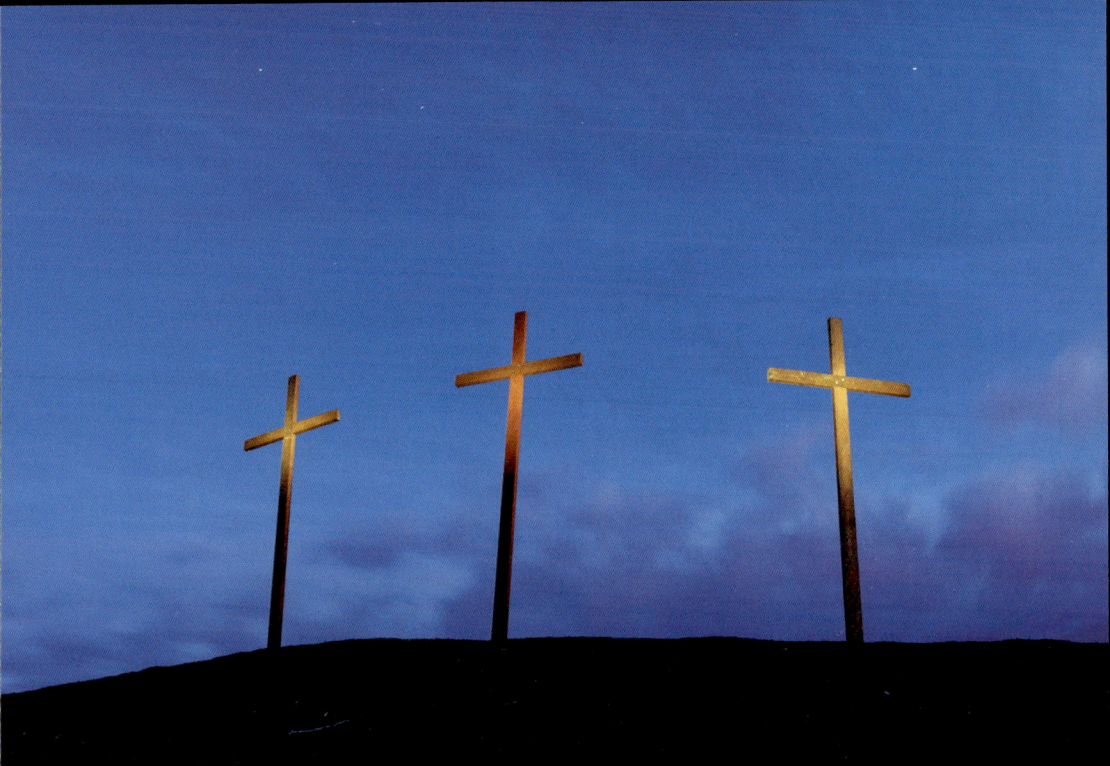

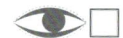

When the hospital was built in 1846, coins were put into the concrete pillars in the entrance hall. Every time I go in there I know that I am one of the few people that knows about them.

A lot of royalty have visited and my Dad has stood on the steps with the Duke of Edinburgh. It was where I was born. My Dad said to him, "My wife is expecting a baby," and the Duke said, "So is mine." I was born in this hospital, but I'm not sure about Prince Charles.

There was a statue outside in the grounds of a lady; it was hit by a bomb and lost one of its arms, and my Mum always said to me, "That's what happens when you bite your nails."

१८४६ सालमा अस्पतालको निर्माण भएपछि प्रवेश द्वारको छेउमा भएको सिमेन्टको खम्बा भित्र सिक्का हाल्ने प्रचलन थियो । प्रत्ये क पटक म त्याहा जाँदा मलाई लाग्दछ कि यसको बारेमा जानकारी भएका थोरै मानिसहरु मध्ये म पनि एक हुँ ।

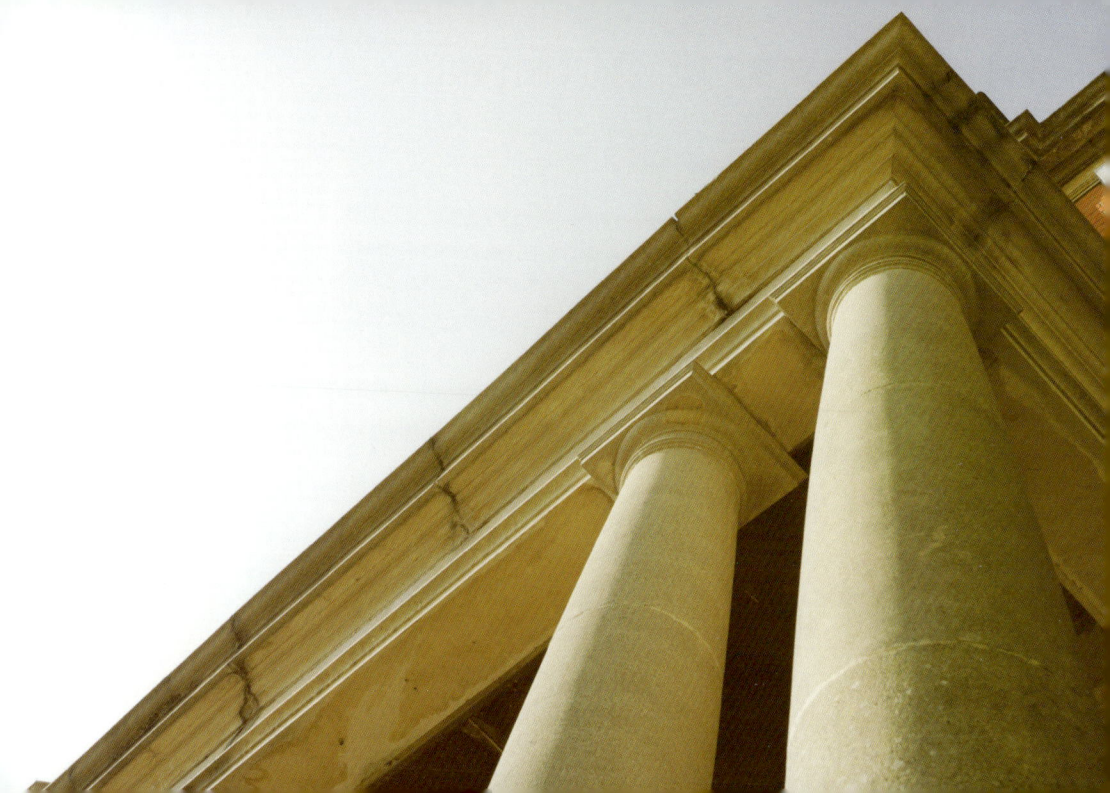

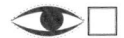

The viewpoint on Crete Road East is perhaps even better than the view from Castle Hill.

A lot of people who visit the town love to walk, and I would suggest heading for the hills and Folkestone Downs where there is the Holy Well. It's the most picturesque and beautiful scenery you could imagine – particularly when you reach the top near Hawkinge. It's somewhere unusually lovely to visit.

How many people know the origin of the name of this spring and its importance to early settlers? The site of an Iron Age hut was excavated close to the spring, demonstrating its vital importance in ancient times. I am sure this must rank as one of the most important sites in the area, hidden away in the fold of the Downs, it continues to flow, first out from under the chalk, and then back into the ground, before emerging as the Pent Stream, which in its turn disappears into a culvert and emerges as an unspectacular outlet on the beach.

फोक्सटनको भ्रमणमा आउने धेरै मानिसहरुलाई म डांडातिर र फोक्सटनको तल होली वेल भएको ठाउँतिर घुम्न जाने सल्लाह दिने गर्दथें । त्यहाँ तपाईंहरुले सोचे जस्तै सुन्दर दृश्यहरु हेर्न पाईनछन् ।

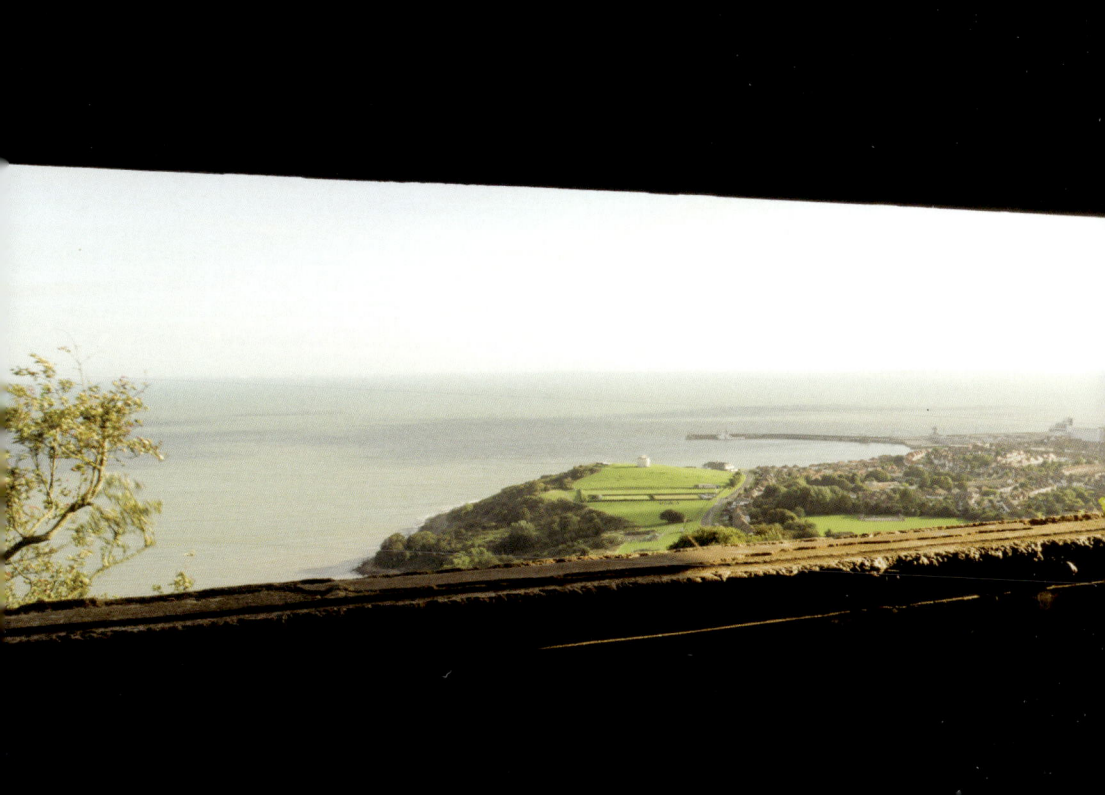

When I was younger during the war, I worked in Bobby's department store as a hairdresser. It was such a beautiful salon. Our restroom balcony was on the first floor. It overlooked the road, opposite the old Post Office and in 1943 I remember all the girls, in their pretty pink uniforms, used to stand on the balcony and wave to the soldiers as they marched up from Bouverie Square, which was a proper grassed square in those days, towards the Road of Remembrance to embark for France. There must have been a big push on somewhere, as there were always army cars and hundreds of soldiers in the road; I particularly remember the Durham Light Infantry. Our boss was a miserable old devil called Herbert Bobby, and he always made us come in. His brother Wilfred was a floorwalker at Bobby's and was a bit of a rascal, but Herbert was the brains.

आजकाल Debenhams भएको ठाउमा पहिलो विश्व युद्धको समायमा Bobby's department store थियो जाहा म केश सिंघारको रुपमा काम गर्थे । गुलाफी कलरको सुन्दर कपडाहरु लाएका यूवतिहरु यसको बरण्डामा उभिएर सिपाईहरुलाई हात हल्लाउने गर्थे । ति सैनिकहरु Bouverie Square देखि Road of Remembrance सम्म कवाज खेल्ने गर्थे ।

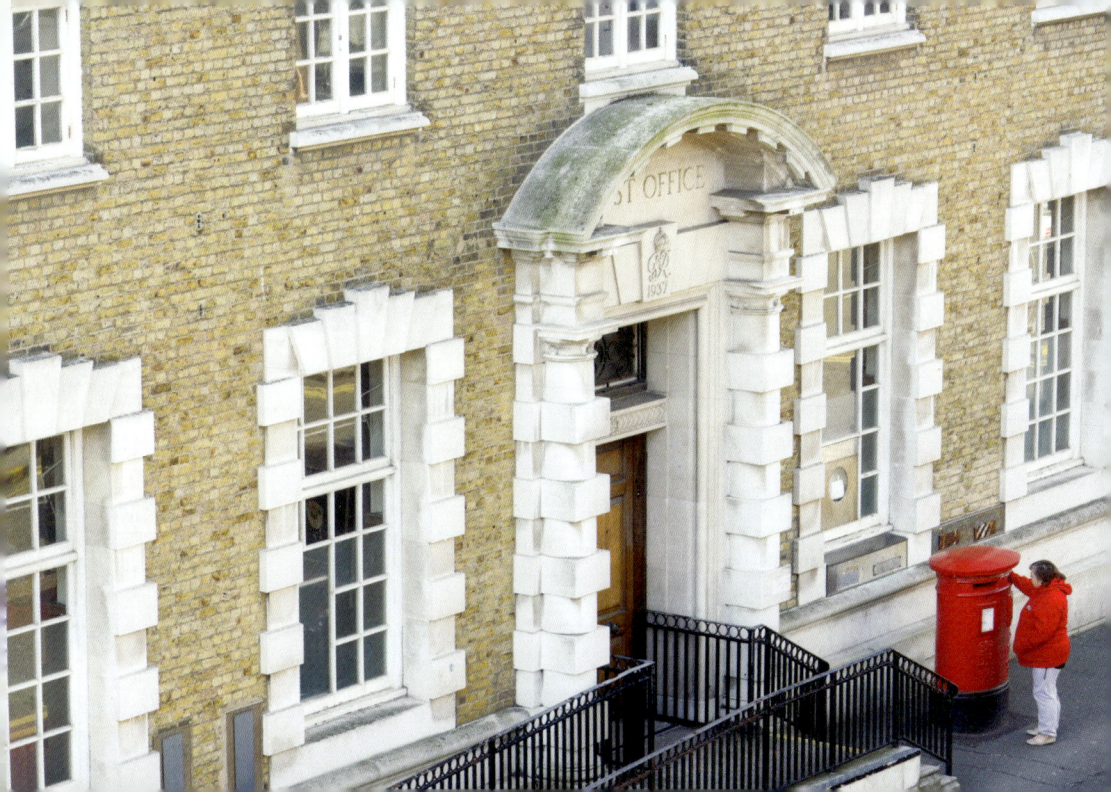

I was born in Yorkshire, where Mackeson stout was a very popular drink, and always assumed it came from the north. I can be forgiven because ads and posters at the time used to proclaim 'Mackeson, heart of the North'.

I moved to Hythe in 2002, which is where I discovered Mackeson was originally created and brewed in the town. Apparently the original brewery dated back to 1669, and by the early 1800s it was a booming business, thanks to the thirsty soldiers and labourers working on the Royal Military Canal at the time. Brewery records show that the famous 'Milk Stout' was first produced in 1907 and ceased brewing at Hythe in 1968. The old 'Malt House', at the beginning of Hythe High Street, still exists as an antique collectors' market. I'm pleased to see that the Brewery Taps frontage has been preserved, allowing it to be appreciated by anyone that passes by; long after the company's demise it recalls the national success of a local brewery and I'll drink to that.

Mackeson को वियर भट्टीको सुरुवात सन १६६९ मा Hythe बाट गरेका थिए भने सन १९६८ मा आएर यो बन्द भएको थियो । यस Brewery Tap को छानोहरु अझै सम्म सुरक्षित रहेकोमा म खुशी छु किनभने यो भवन असाध्यै राम्रो छ ।

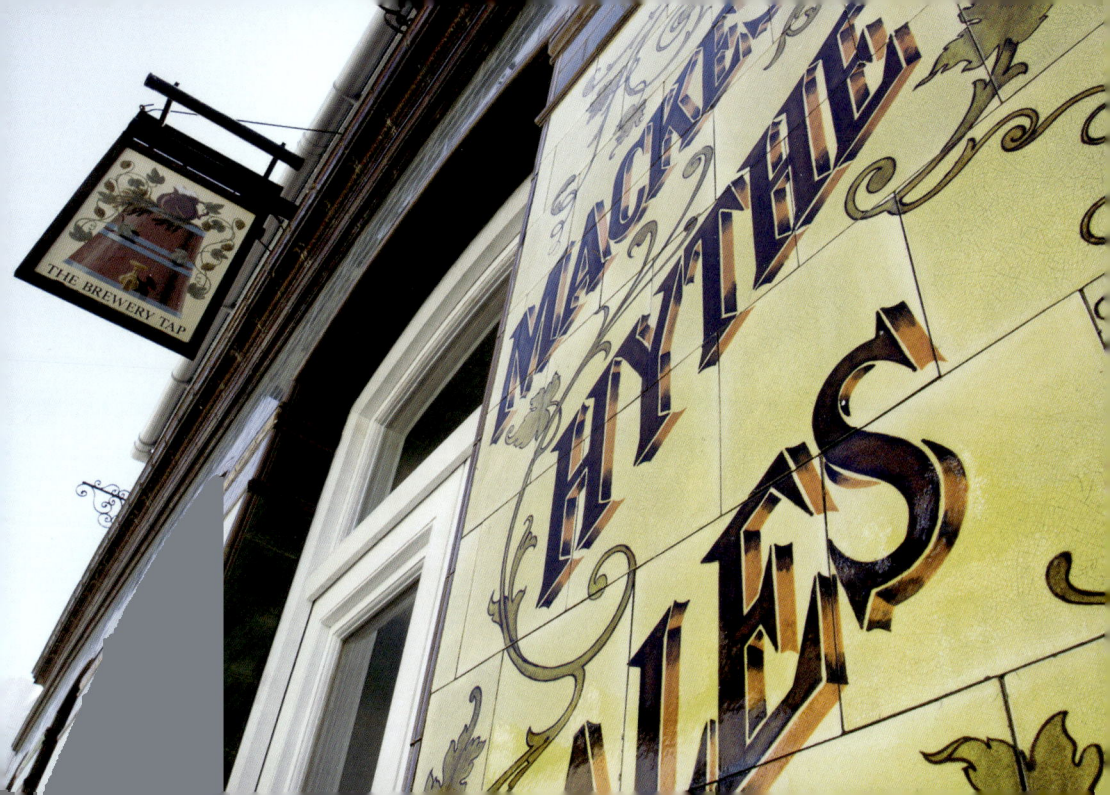

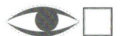

In the late 50s through to the 70s, on the ramp at the side of the Leas Cliff Hall, there was a small garden where flowers were planted. These were accompanied by Braille plaques for blind people to identify what was growing there. These are sadly long since gone.

A bit further down were the old steps, which linked the Leas to the Lower Sandgate Road. These have also now been closed. I well remember them as a child running to and fro from where my family lived in Shakespeare Terrace to the lower area where me and my friends would spend the sunny days (and some of the better winter ones) rummaging around the bushes and across the small bridges etc. I remember also blind people with their families feeling the plaques and touching the plants on the bank.

सन १९५० मा Leas Cliff Hall को छेउमा फूलहरु रोप्ने एउटा सानो बगैंचा थियो । त्यहाँ भएका फूलहरुको बारेमा जानकारी गराउन दृष्टिविहिनहरुको सुविधाको लागि अन्धलिपि पनि राखिएको थियो । दुःखको कुरा हो, हाल यो बगैंचा छैन ।

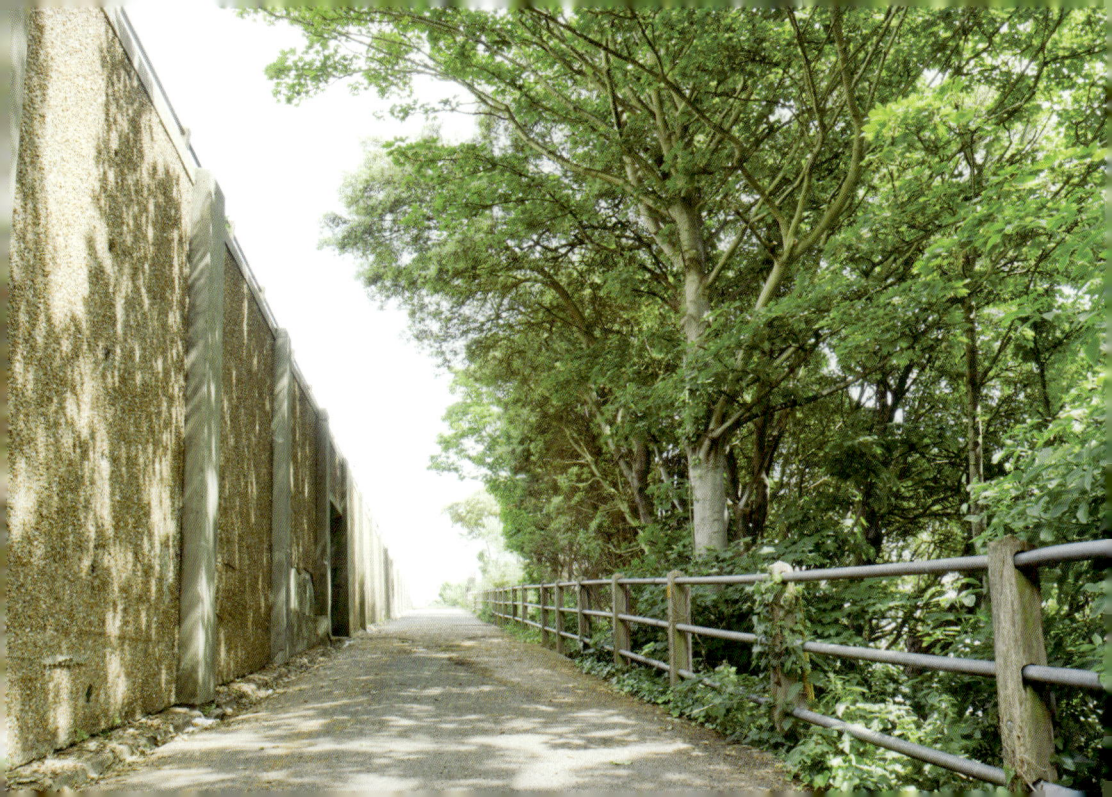

After WWI, Folkestone wanted to commemorate its dead and details were requested from bereaved relatives. Mrs Butcher replied, believing her son had been killed in action. She received a municipal Certificate of Glory and his name was inscribed on Folkestone's War Memorial, where it can still be seen. In fact, Private Frederic Butcher of the East Kent Regiment refused to go over the top with a raiding party and was tried by Court Martial. His excellent service record saved him, but sadly it happened again and on 27 August 1918 Private Butcher was shot at dawn by firing squad. Probably his mother never realised how he had died. It may not have been unique for a disgraced soldier to be included on a memorial, but it was very rare.

Thankfully, all these wronged men have now been given a full pardon and are officially included on memorials alongside the names of their comrades.

पहिलो विश्व युद्धमा विरगति पाएका विर योद्धाहरुको नामावलि फोक्सटनमा राखिएको छ, जसमा Private Frederic Butcher को नाम पनि समावेस छ । वास्तवमा लडाई गर्न अश्विकार गरेकोले उसलाई सजाय स्वरुप Court Martial गरी बेलुकी पख गोली हानि मारिएको थियो । यो सिपाहीहरुको लागि दुःख लाग्दो कुरा हो यद्यपी यस्तो घटनाहरु कमै मात्र हुन्छन् ।

यस्ता सजाय पाएका सिपाहीहरुलाई मरनोपरान्त आम माफि दिएर उनीहरुको नाम सम्मान स्वरुप अन्य व्यक्तिहरुको नामावलि सँगै राखिएको हो ।

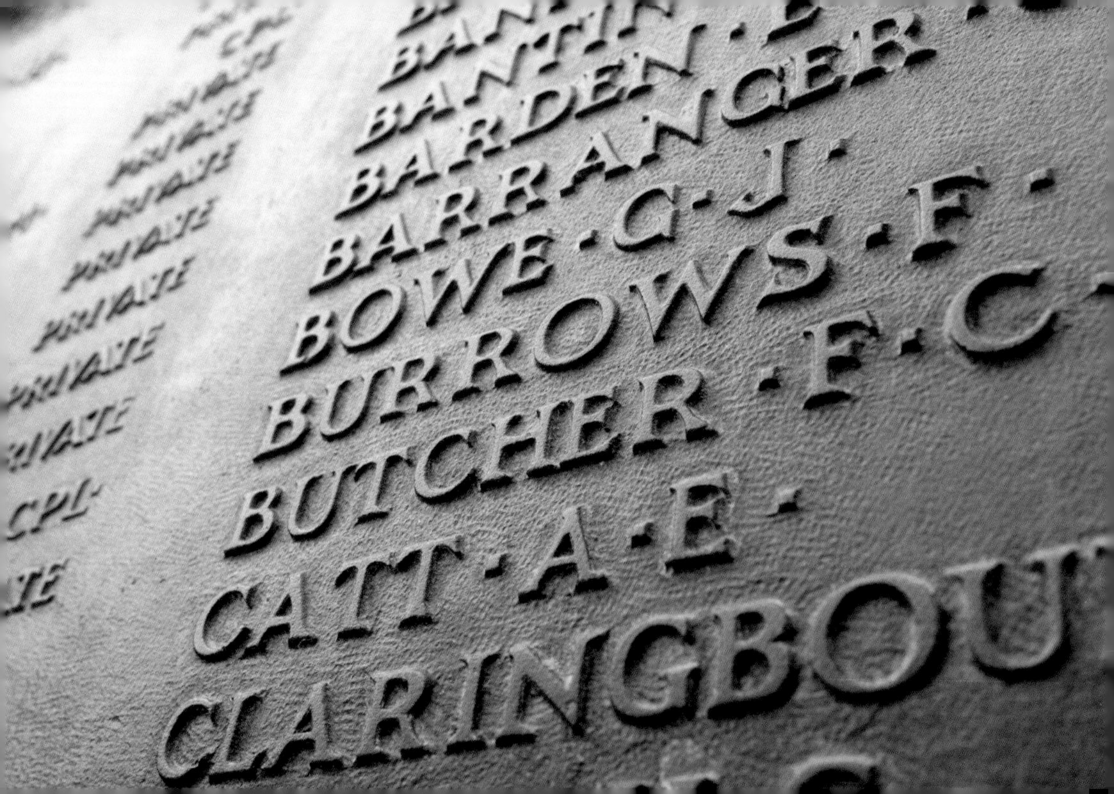

PRIVATE

PRIVATE

PRIVATE

PRIVATE

PRIVATE

PRIVATE

CPL·

BANTIN·

BANTIN·

BARDEN·

BARRANGER

BOWE·G·J·

BURROWS·F·

BUTCHER·F·C·

CATT·A·E·

CLARINGBOU

As a boy in the 60s, over the back fence of my house was the old corporation dump off Biggins Wood: fields, an old clay brick pit and the Downs. All bar the last are now under the motorway and Channel Tunnel site. The clay pit had a tin hut, which served as HQ for our games, and on the woods side there was a small ledge, just above the pit side, that I personally liked as a quiet 'escape' area, especially on sunny days.

On the Downs there is the old Saxon Shore way, and as you got to the end bit, up on top by the fence next to the waterworks, before Crete Road West, there is an area where we used to just sit and survey our childhood 'kingdoms'. This bit is still there.

There are a few other such places along the footpath just above the perimeter fence, where I used to take a packed lunch and catch or watch butterflies (the rare Adonis Blue flits across this area still). We would wander further beyond the unfenced Caesars Camp hill to the Elham Valley Railway track, dodging military movements and ending up eventually, though only sometimes, on the other side of the old tunnel.

सन १९६० मा बाल्यकालमा यो क्षेत्र मेरो खेल्ने ठाउँ थियो । हामीहरु डाँडाको छेउमा बसेर त्यो बाल्यकालको खेल्ने ठाउँतिर हेनें गर्दथ्यौ । यो ठाउ गाडीको बाटोको मुनि र Channel Tunnel को छेउमा पर्दछ ।

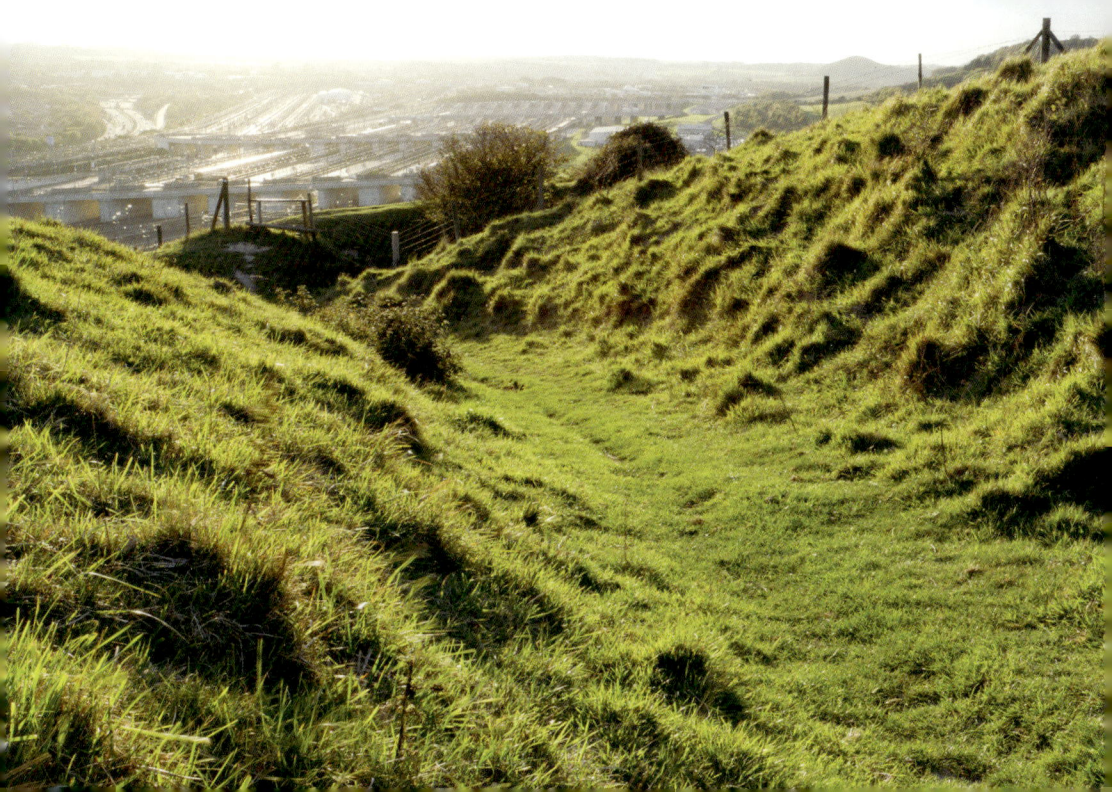

My neighbour David Martin is 90 years old and when he was a boy his parents were landlords of the True Briton pub at Folkestone Harbour.

David remembers famous people coming to the pub, and when he inherited his late sister's book of her handwritten poems, he found a newspaper article linking comedian Max Miller and the 6th Earl Wellington to the True Briton. He also found a letter from Max's wife to his sister dated 1 August 1962 (It appears that Max was ill at the time and the letter was written after his final broadcast), and a ten page typed document titled 'Memories of Folkestone from 1925' and numerous hand written pages about life in the True Briton.

मेरो छिमेकीको बाल्यकालमा फोक्सटन त्यावरमा भएको True Briton pub को स्वामित्व उसका अभिभावकहरुमा थियो । यसको स्वामित्व उसले प्राप्त गरेपछि उसको दिदीले लेखेको कविताको किताबमा एउटा अखबार भेट्रायो । यो अखबारमा Max Miller and 6th Earl Wellington Wellington to the True Briton बारेमा लेखिएको थियो ।

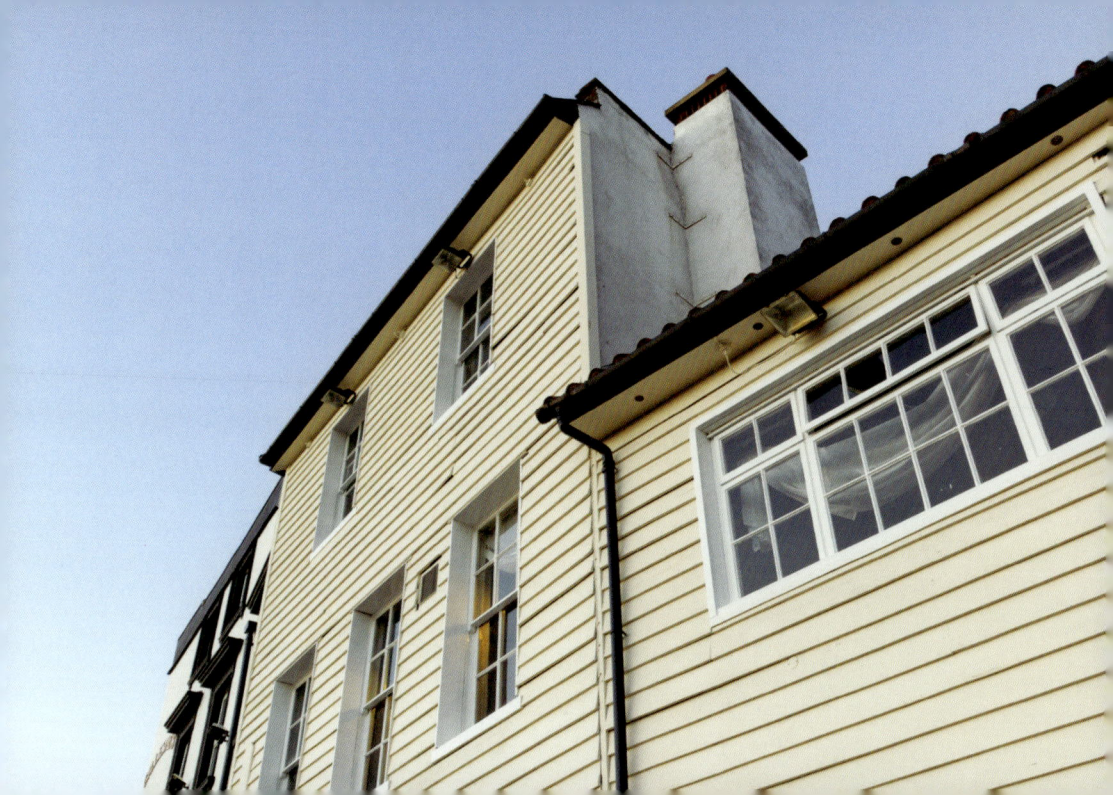

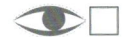

This square piece of concrete is all that remains of a shelter where me and my husband used to meet when we were dating. It was 1953, we got married in 1955. He used to live in Cheriton and I used to live in digs. We would meet there in the evenings and sometimes he would go there with his band after a gig at then East Cliff Pavilion.

We celebrated our Golden Jubliee five years ago.

He died two weeks ago.

सन 1953 सालमा म र मेरो श्रीमानको विवाह हुनु अघि सिमेन्टले बनेको चारपाटे खालि स्थानमा भेटने गर्दथ्या । सन १९५५ सालमा हामी दुवै दम्पतिले विवाह गयौं । मेरो श्रीमान Cheriton मा वस्नुहुन्थ्यो र म चाहीं digs मा बस्थें । हामी दुवै प्राय जसो साँझ पख भेट्ने गर्दथ्यौ र कहिले काहीं भने मेरो श्रीमान उनको व्याण्ड East Cliff Pavilion सँग जाने गर्नुहुन्थ्यो ।

५ वर्ष अगाडी हामी दुवै दम्पतिले हाम्रो Golden Jubliee मनायौं । वहाँको दुई हप्ता अगाडि मृत्यु भयो .

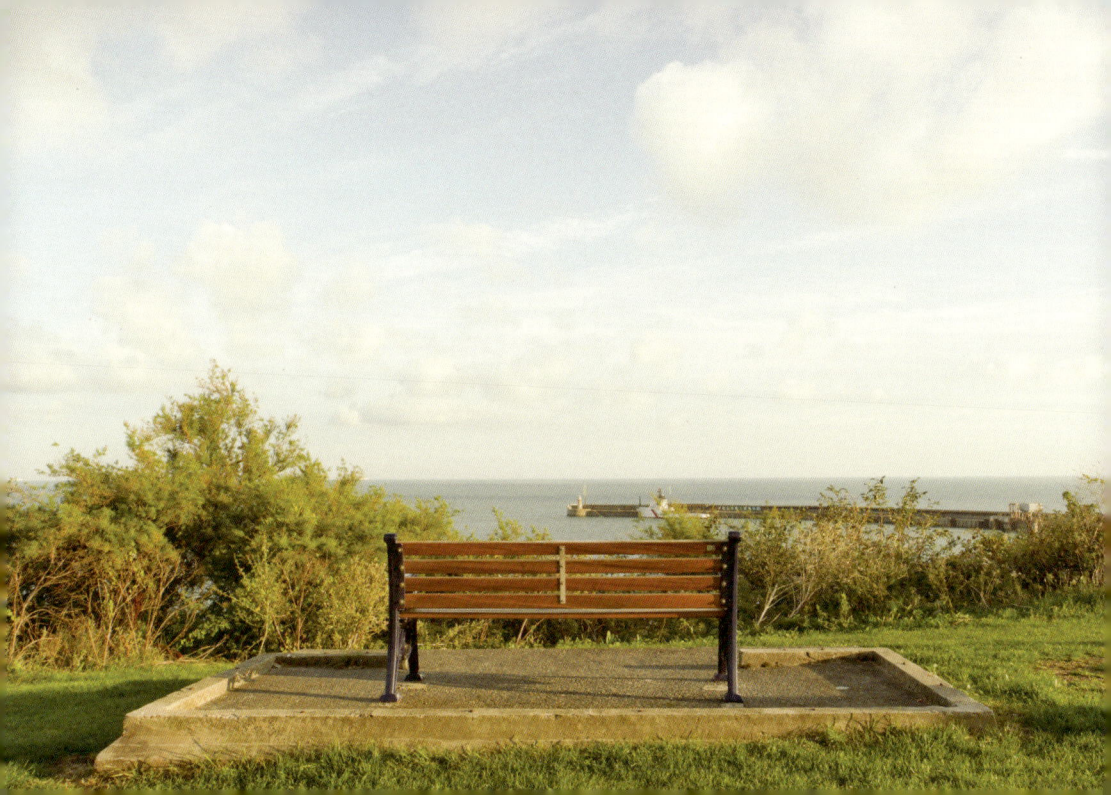

When I first came to Folkestone in 1963 with my dad, the first thing that struck me was the amazing flowerbed in the middle of the road by Central Station. I had never seen anything like it before. Folkestone's such a great place and no matter how much it costs to do these flower displays I hope they can always find the money.

सन १९६३ कुरा हो जब म युवा अवस्थामा थिए,, फोक्सटनमा पहिलो पटक आउँदा Central Station को बाटोको मध्य भागमा फुलका अति सुन्दर गमलाहरु सजाएर राखिएको थियो । मैले यस्तो राम्ररी सजाएको कहिले पनि देखेको थिईन ।

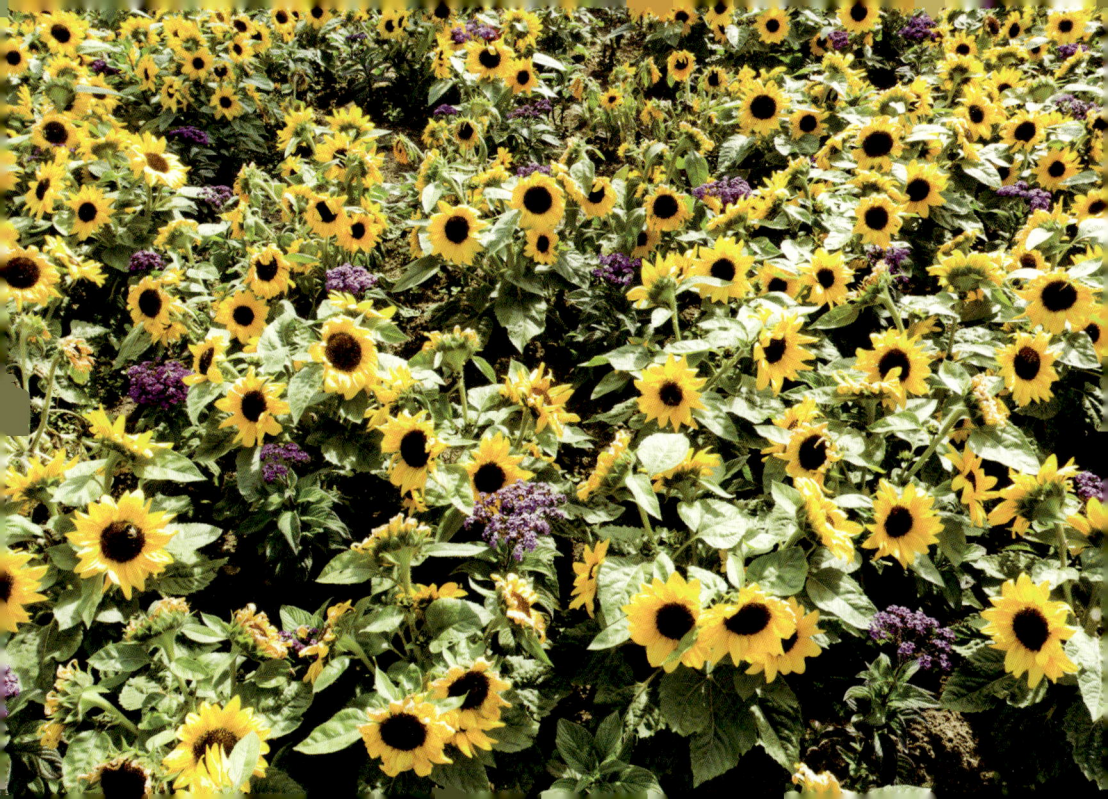

Shangri La is the name of the imposing house at the seaward end of the Bayle Parade with an eagle facing out to sea near the top of it. Rumours abound about the house, and it is popularly believed to have been a German Embassy before World War I. Local researchers have found no evidence for this, but people still insist it was the case.

There are examples of marvellous pargetting around the top of this line of buildings in the Bayle Parade.

This building was the German Embassy and was an operative signalling base to across the Channel. A man was discovered, suspected of spying, and he was taken out into the garden and shot. His ghost now haunts the garden.

Shangri La एउटा घरको नाम हो । यो घर Bayle Parade को छेउमा छ । यसको माथिल्लो भागमा एउटा चिल समुन्द्रतिर फर्काएर राखिएको छ । यो घर विश्व युद्ध भन्दा पहिले जर्मनी राजदुतावासको थियो भन्ने जनविश्वास थियो तर यसको कुनै तथ्य भने छैन ।

यो घर जर्मन राजदुतको थियो । च्यानल पार गर्नको लागि जर्मनीहरुले यस घरबाट संकेत निर्देशन दिने गर्थे । त्याँको संकेत दिने व्यक्तिलाई पत्ता लगाएर वगैचामा लगी गोली हानी मारिएको थियो । हाल यस वगैचामा मृतात्मा डुल्छ भन्ने भनाई छ ।

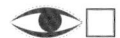

Unless it has been removed, there is a small plaque with the inscription along the lines of 'This wing was built with the help of the Cheerful Sparrows' with, I think, a date of 1929. It is on the wall just inside the door.

I think the Cheerful Sparrows were a group of local businessmen who raised funds for good causes, or maybe just for the hospital. I remember being taken as a child to a Cheerful Sparrows Fete at the top of the Leas in the 1930s.

त्याँहा सन १९२९ मिति भएको एउटा सानो सुचना पाटी छ, जसमा 'This wing was built with the help of the Cheerful Sparrows' भनेर लेखिएको छ । यो पाटी ढोकाको भित्र पटी भित्तामा राखिएको छ । Cheerful Sparrows भनेको स्थानिय व्यवसायीहरुद्वारा गठन गरिएको एउटा संस्था थियो । यो एक परोपकारी संस्था भएकोले सहयोग रकम जम्मा गर्दथ्यो ।

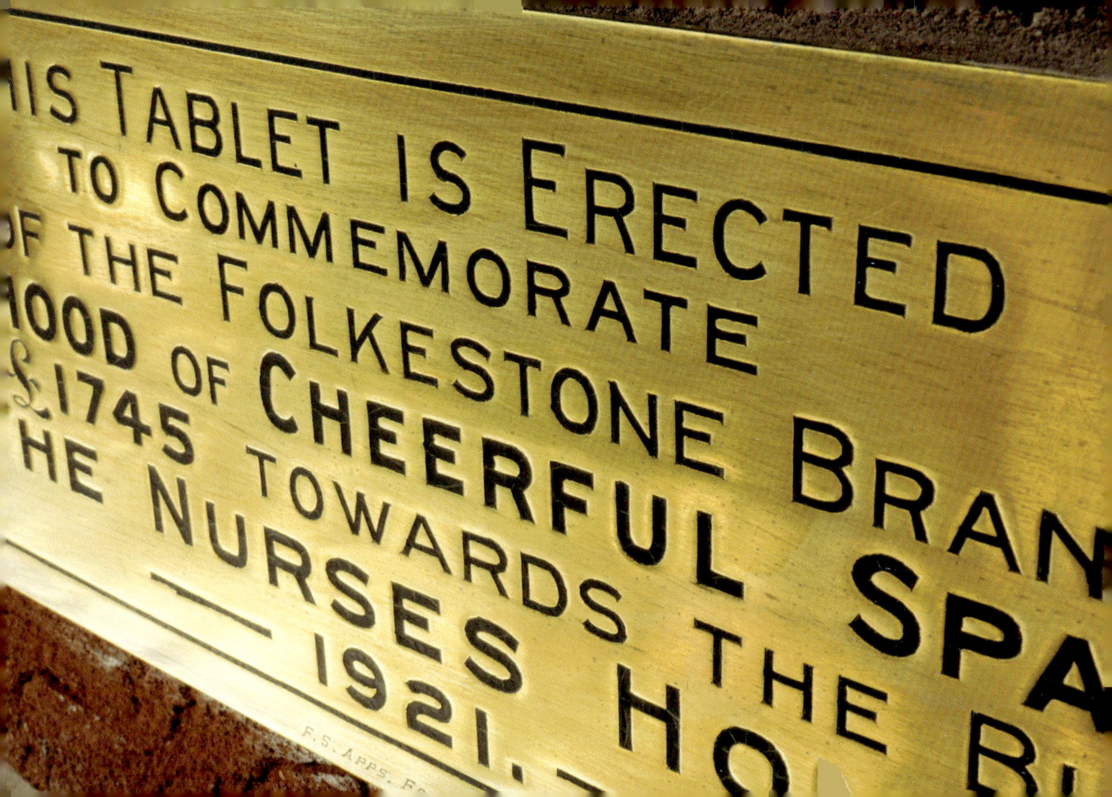

THIS TABLET IS ERECTED
TO COMMEMORATE
OF THE FOLKESTONE BRAN
HOOD OF CHEERFUL SPA
£1745 TOWARDS THE B
HE NURSES HO
1921.

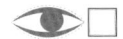

Memories of Folkestone in the 1930s, by Kathleen Margaret Pritchard (nee Sharp), dictated to her daughter Linda Blomquist for email submission:

"I was brought up in North Street, Folkestone. My best friend, Peggy Ford, lived a few doors away and we grew up more like sisters than neighbours, as our families were friends too. In those days St Peter's church, St Andrew's Nunnery and St Peter's school dominated North Street, The Durlocks and the fish-market areas of the town. The nuns at St Andrew's were a familiar sight and, as a little girl, I was convinced that they had wheels under their habits and they glided along, rather than walked! One of my earliest memories is of being sent with Peggy to buy a basin of dripping from the convent kitchens. We had to walk down what seemed an endlessly long, dark corridor in order to reach the kitchens, and I held Peggy's hand very tightly, as it scared me. St Andrew's was used as a hotel after the convent closed and now has been converted into private flats. The building also houses St Peter's school hall and dining room. Peggy and I are still best friends, our friendship having lasted for well over 70 years."

मेरो बाल्य कालमा North Street मा बस्थे र मेरो मिल्ने साथि Peggy भन्ने अलि पर्तिर बस्दथ्यो । एकदिन आमाले हामीहरुलाई St Andrew's convent मा गएर खाना पकाउने तेल लिएर आउनु भन्नु भयो । तर त्याहां वस्ने स्त्री पुजाहारीहरुको पैरन दे खेर हामीलाई असाधै डरलाग्दथ्यो । Peggy र म ७० वर्ष पछि अहिले पनि उस्तै मिल्ने साथि छौ ।

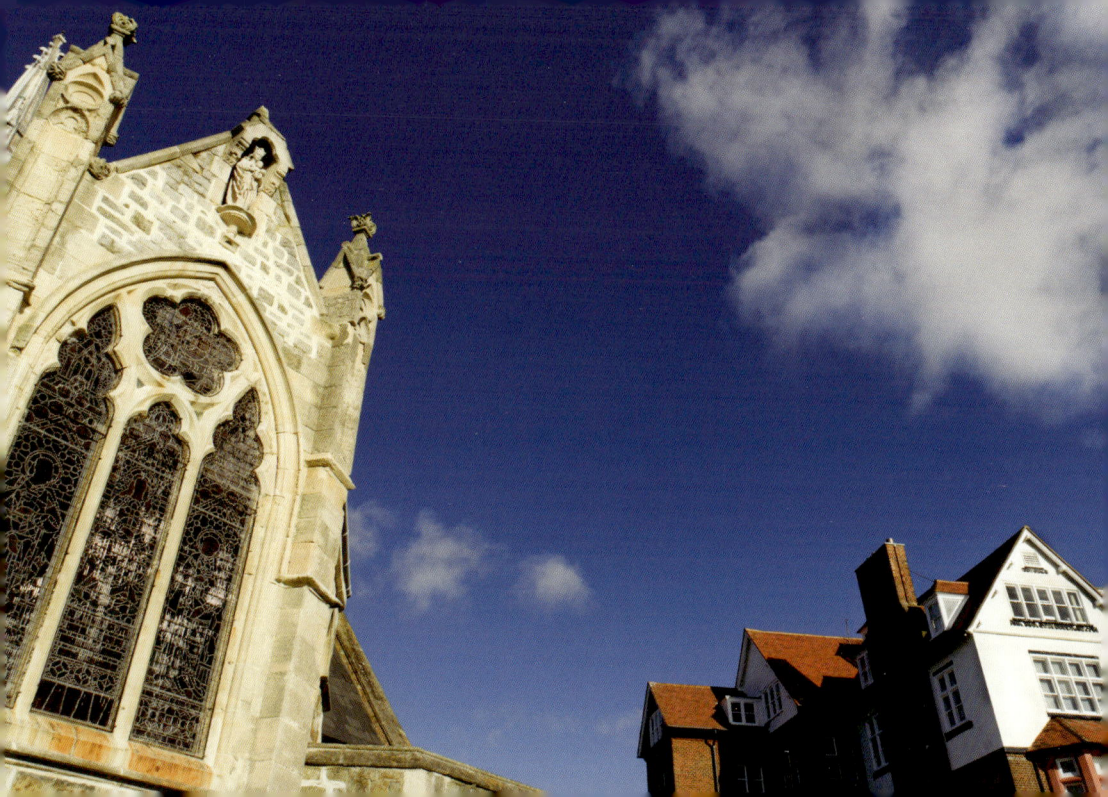

When I was seven or eight my father took me down to the Lower Sandgate Road on the Leas Lift. This would have been about 1949 or 1950. We walked across the road and stood looking out to sea where stood the derelict Victorian Pier.

Originally built in 1888 it was used for variety shows, concerts, dances, and the world's first beauty contest. It closed during the Second World War, when the centre section was demolished for defence purposes. It was then destroyed by fire in 1945 and finally demolished in 1954.

सन १९५० सालमा म बाबासँग भक्तिएको बन्दरगाह हेर्न Victoria जाने गर्दथ्यौं ।

यो बन्दरगाहको निर्माण सन १८८८ सालमा भएको थियो । विभिन्न प्रकारको मनोरञ्जनात्मक कार्यक्रम, कन्सर्टहरु, नाचहरुको लागि यसको प्रयोग गर्ने गरिन्थ्यो र यहाँ पहिलो विश्व सुन्दरी प्रतियोगिता पनि सम्पन्न भएको थियो । विश्व युद्धमा सुरक्षाको दृष्टीकोणले यसको विच भागलाई भत्काईएको थियो । सन १९४५ सालको आगलागीले गर्दा सवै जलेर ध्वस्त भए पछि सन १९५४ सालमा पूर्ण रुपले भत्किएर यसको अवशेष मात्र बाकी रहेको छ ।

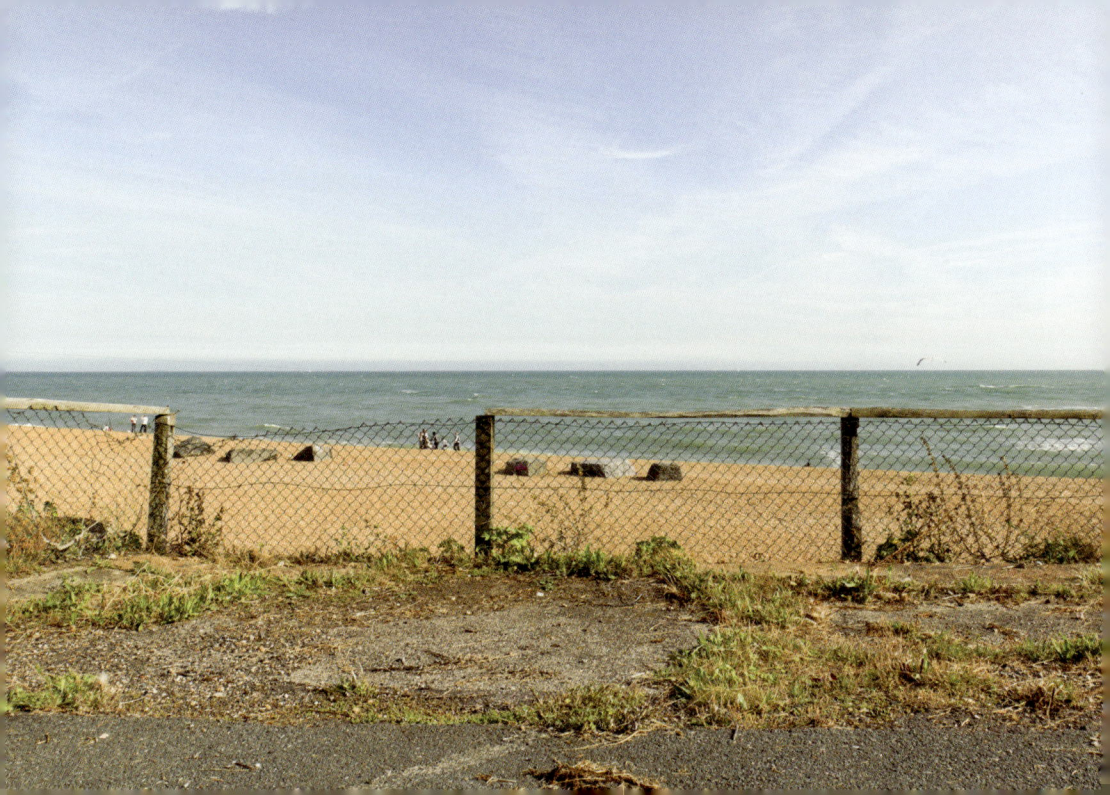

The objects protruding from the ground by the Coastwatch lookout belie the existence of an underground bunker. In the event of nuclear war, it would have been manned by six ROC members. They would have lived in bunk beds, breathed filtered air, eaten dried food and carried out measurement of nuclear blast locations, intensity and windspeeds, communicating their information to Government agencies involved in evacuation, infrastructure repair, etc. communicating by landline phone. As 1960s teenagers we watched men on exercise go into the underground bunker down a vertical ladder. We guessed this was some secret installation. In my 20s I worked for the ROC and saw the inside of a similar bunker (cliff erosion meant this one had been abandoned).

Above ground you can see the bunker entrance, air filter housing and structures for attaching measuring equipment. The ROC disbanded at the end of the Cold War in the early 1990s.

Coastwatch ले रेखदेख गर्ने ठाउँ अगाडिको जमिनमा सिमेन्ट र धातुले बनाएको वस्तु निस्केको देखिन्थ्यो । त्यो जमिन मुनि भएको घर भित्र पस्ने ठाउँ थियो । सन १९६० मा परमाणु युद्ध भएमा सुरक्षित रहनको लागि त्यो घरको निर्माण गरिएको थियो । यो Royal Observer Corps लाइ ४ देखि ६ जना सदस्यहरुद्वार संचालन गर्ने योजना थियो ।

सन १९९० सालमा Cold War को अन्त्य भएपछि या Royal Observer Corps पनि निस्कृय भयो ।

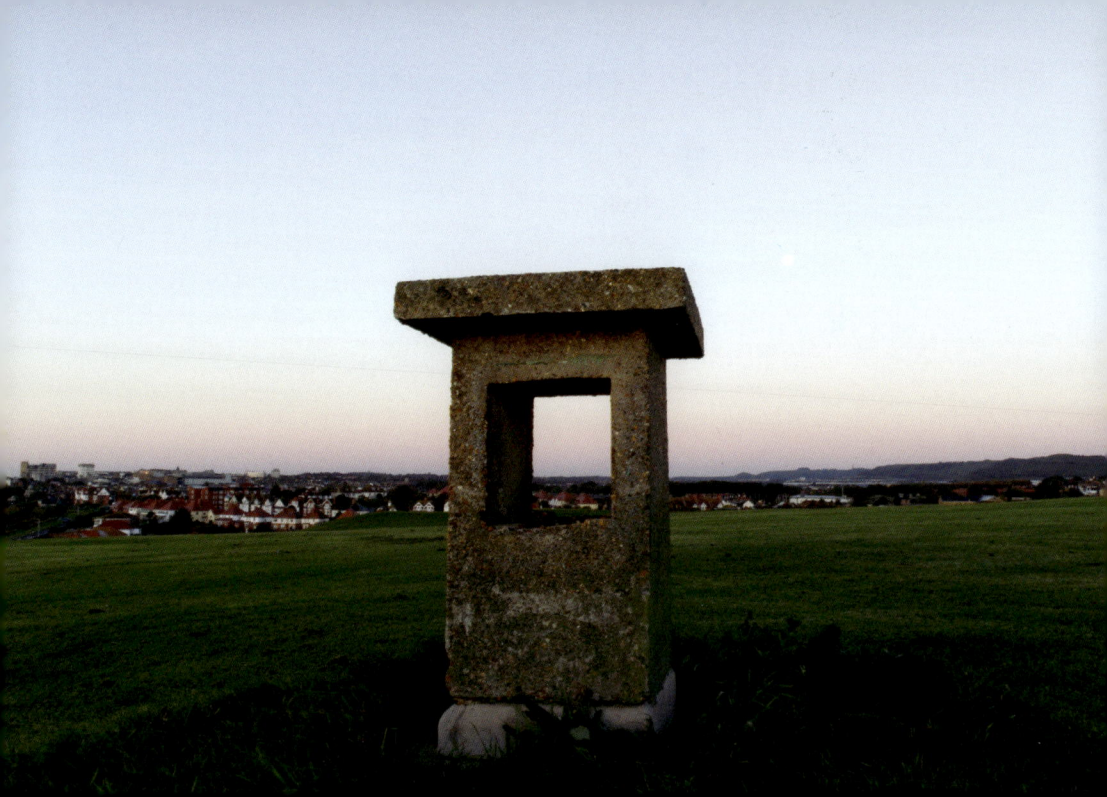

These boat-shaped structures are on the beach just near the old outfall pipe at Copt Point, which is the name for the headland of the East Cliff, midway between the Sunny Sands and the Warren. They were featured on the front of the 2008 Folkestone Triennial catalogue, but what are they?

Southern Water, who are responsible for the piping and the structures at Copt Point, haven't any idea.

यस्ता अनौठो सिमेन्टले बनेको डुंगा आकारको चौतारहरुको बारेमा कसैलाई पनि केही थाहा छैन । यी चौतारहरु घमाईलो वगरको केही परतिर छन ।

EVERYWHERE MEANS SOMETHING TO SOMEONE

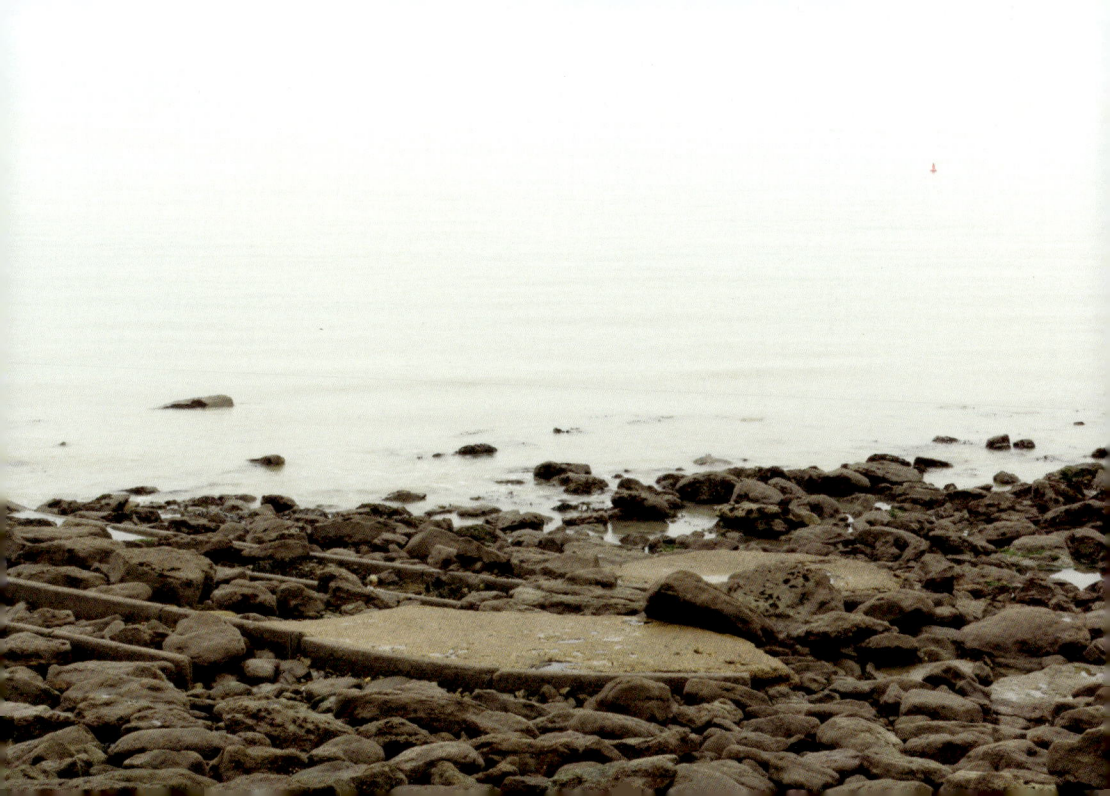

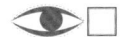

Built circa 1805, the walls are eight feet thick landward side, 13 feet thick seaward. It was built as a defence against Napoleon but used again in the 1940s as a wartime lookout, and by the Coastwatch in 2003.

I worked for five summers here as a custodian. A quiet job but interesting, you could sit out in the sun at the top of the steps all day, eat your sandwiches, enjoy the news, read and chat with the occasional visitor. The most pleasant and relaxing job I ever had.

The Tower closed as a Visitor Centre in 2004 as a result of budget cuts by Shepway District Council. Ah well, all good things come to an end!

Napoleon को हमलाबाट सुरक्षाको लागि सन १८०५ मा जमिनको सतहमा ८ फिट र समुन्द्रतिर १६ फिट चौडा भएको पर्खालको निर्माण गरिएको थियो । यसको प्रयोग सन १९४० सालमा लडाईको समयमा रेखदेख गर्न र Coastwatch को लागि सन २००४ मा प्रयोग गरिएको थियो ।

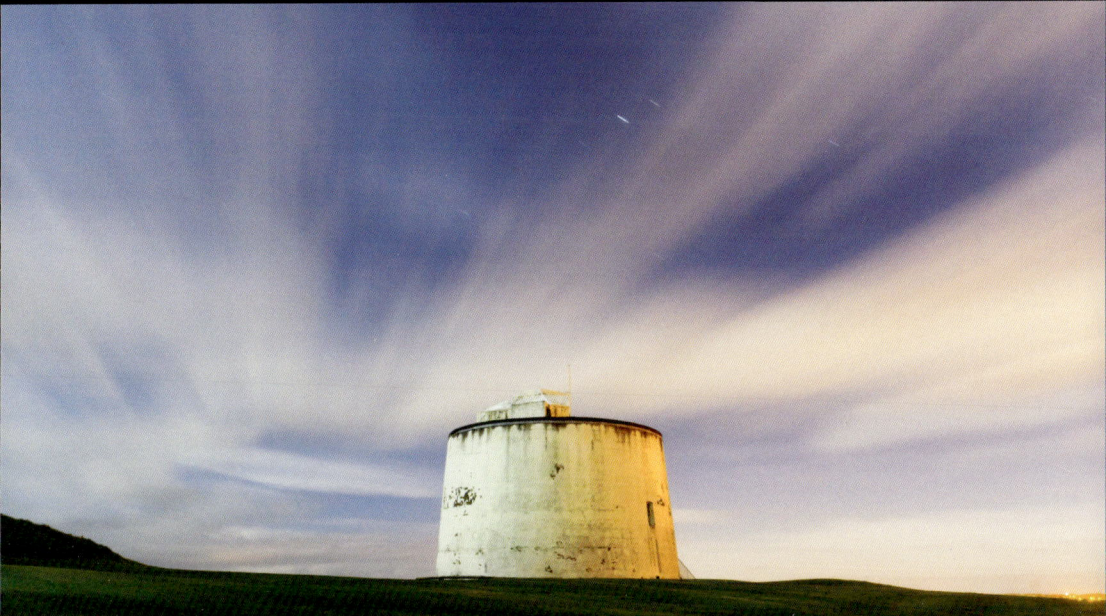

The roundabout at the end of Churchill Avenue, where you come off the M20, used to be a pond where I would go fishing. I think of this every time I go round the roundabout.

चर्चहिल एभेन्युको अन्तिम जहा M20 जोडिन्छ, आजकाल त्यहाँ एउटा Roundabout छ तर त्यो भन्दा अगाडी त्यहाँ एउटा स्यानो पोखरी थियो र म त्यहाँ बल्छी खेल्न जान्थे । जब म त्यो Roundabout मा पुग्छु, सधै यो सम्फने गर्दछु ।

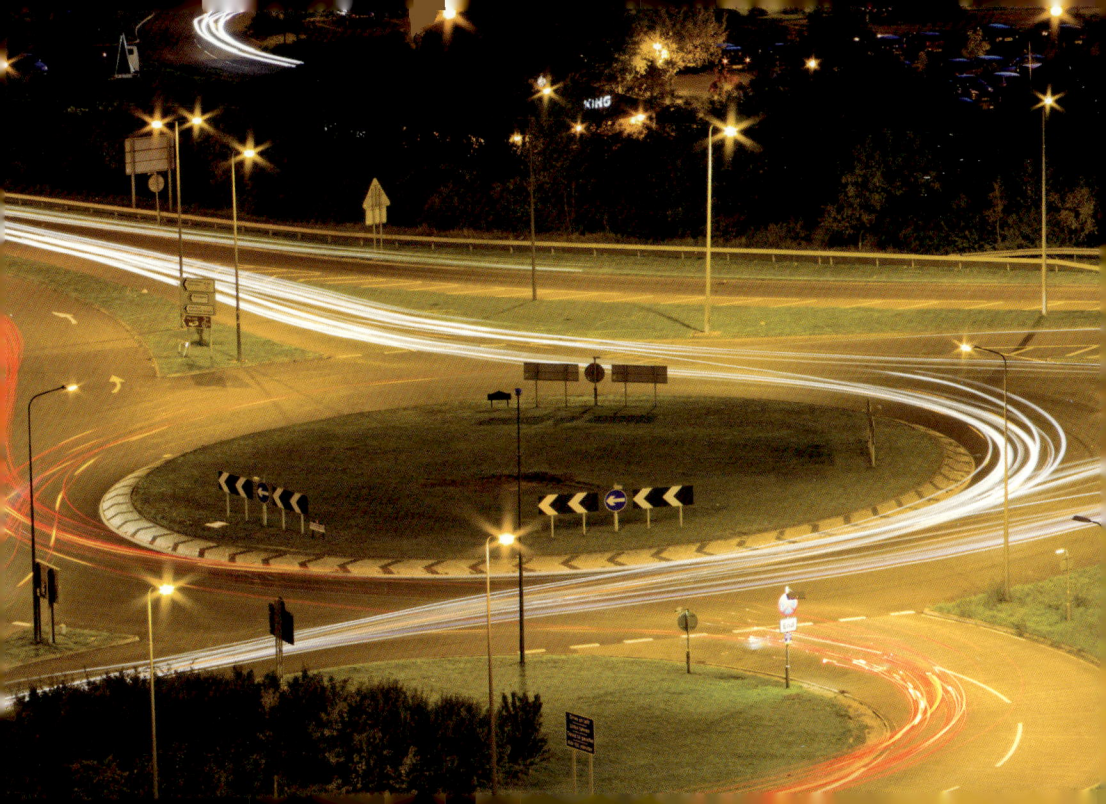

I thought people would like to know the history of the site on which our two properties stand. I researched the books in the Reference Library and it makes very interesting reading.

1763 – Tenements and Stables; 1830 – Wesleyan Chapel; 1847 – Appolonian Hall: Dancing, Concerts; 1851 – Police Station and Cells, Rate Office, Sessions Hall; 1868 – Museum; 1887 – School of Science and Art; 1889 – Borough Rate Office; 1891 – Sale by Police Action; 1892 – Walter Stroud: Printer, Stationers, Book Binders; 1898 – E.W. Southey: Decorator, Plumber, Picture Frame Maker; 1904 – Unoccupied; 1907 – Harpers: Pianoforte and Music Saloon; 1908 – Unoccupied; 1909 – The London & Paris Glove Company; 1911 – Parnell's Glove Company; 1912 – Unoccupied; 1913 – Parsons; 1913 – Marks and Spencer Penny Bazaar; 1930 – Marks and Spencer; 1952 – Buffs and St Mary's Club; 1974 – Conversion to shops

सन 1763 सालमा निर्माण भएको यो दुईवटा घरहरु विभिन्न प्रकारका व्यवसायीक प्रयोजन जस्तै पुलिस चौकी, गिर्जाघर, संग्राहलय, पियानो प्रशिक्षक, पञ्जा बनाउने, छापाखाना, Marks & Spencers, Off Licence को लागि प्रयोग हुँदै आईरहेको छ ।

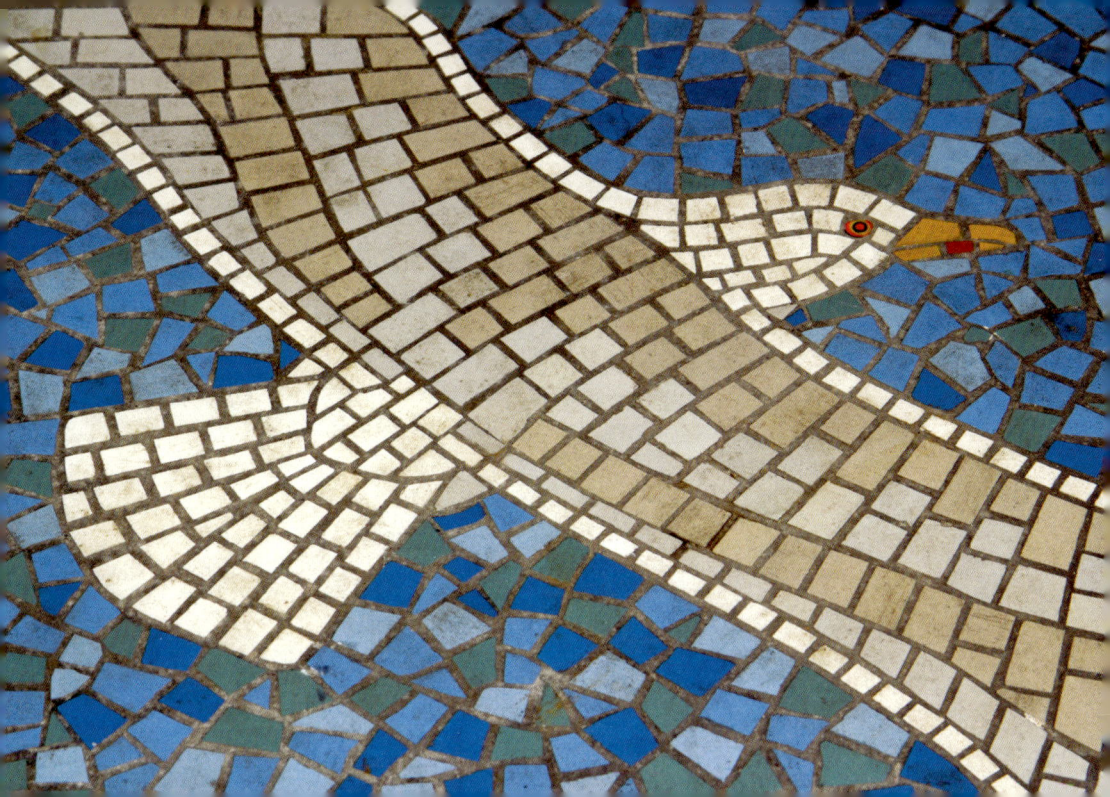

This name has for many years been applied to the area of small valleys and springs that lie between Sugar Loaf Hill and the A260 road to Canterbury. Legend has it that this was the site of a holy well, sometimes called Lady Well or St. Thomas' Well. Certainly such an area as this would be a prime candidate for an early sacred spring, and it would indeed be surprising if it were not regarded so in ancient times. The names mentioned above refer no doubt to later Christian tradition, 'St Thomas' referring to a belief that this spring was used by pilgrims en route from the continent to the shrine of Thomas Becket in Canterbury. The curious round stone with the hole is all that remains, which I first thought was a milling stone, but it turns out that there is a similar stone at Glastonbury where one places a cup where the hole is, to receive a spout of water from the spring, so perhaps Holywell operated in a similar way a hundred years ago.

Holywell Spring को गोलाकार ढुंगाको बाँकी भागमा प्वालहरु छन् । Glastonbury मा पनि त्यस्तै खाले ढुंगा छ । त्यहाँ एउटा प्वाल भएको ठाउँमा पिउने पानीको एउटा कप राखिएको छ ।

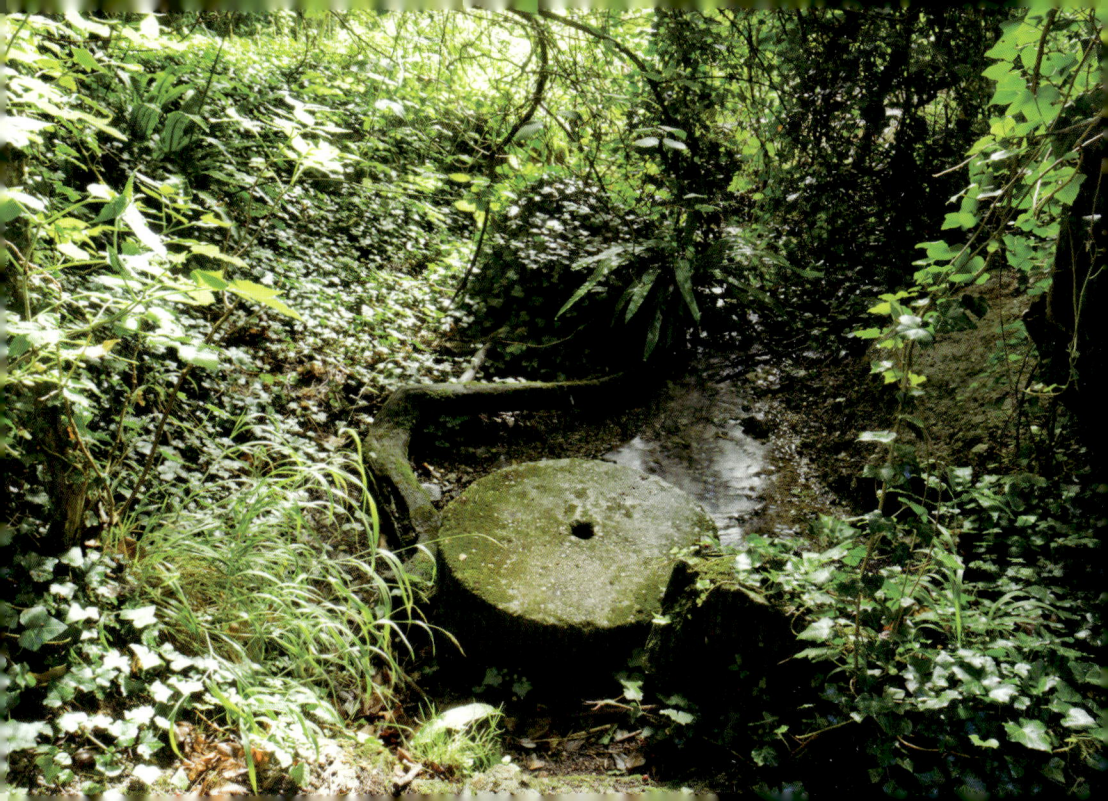

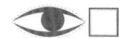

During a recent visit to the Fishmarket, I was amused to see the Health & Safety signs about not removing the chains along the quayside – and absolutely *No Swimming*. Amused, because that is exactly what we young lads used to do in the late 40s. We would remove one of the chains and take a running leap into the somewhat smelly water of the harbour. It was, in fact, our favourite swimming place, as swimming between the fishing boats and other obstacles was much more interesting than the Sands (they were not yet 'Golden') or the beach.

The jump (we were not so silly as to try diving) off the edge of the quay into the water about ten feet below (we only did it at or near high tide) was our version of Extreme Sports.

माछा बजारमा 'पौडी खेल्न शक्त मनाही छ' भन्ने सूचना टाँसेको देखेर मलाई हाँस उठ्यो ।

सन १९४० सालतिर हामी युवाहरु चेन तानी दगुरेर गन्हाउने पानीमा हाम फाल्दथ्यौं । यो हाम्रो असाध्यै मनपर्ने पौडी स्थान थियो किनभने यो माछा मार्ने डुंगाहरुको विचमा भएकोले अन्य स्थान भन्दा रमाईलो थियो ।

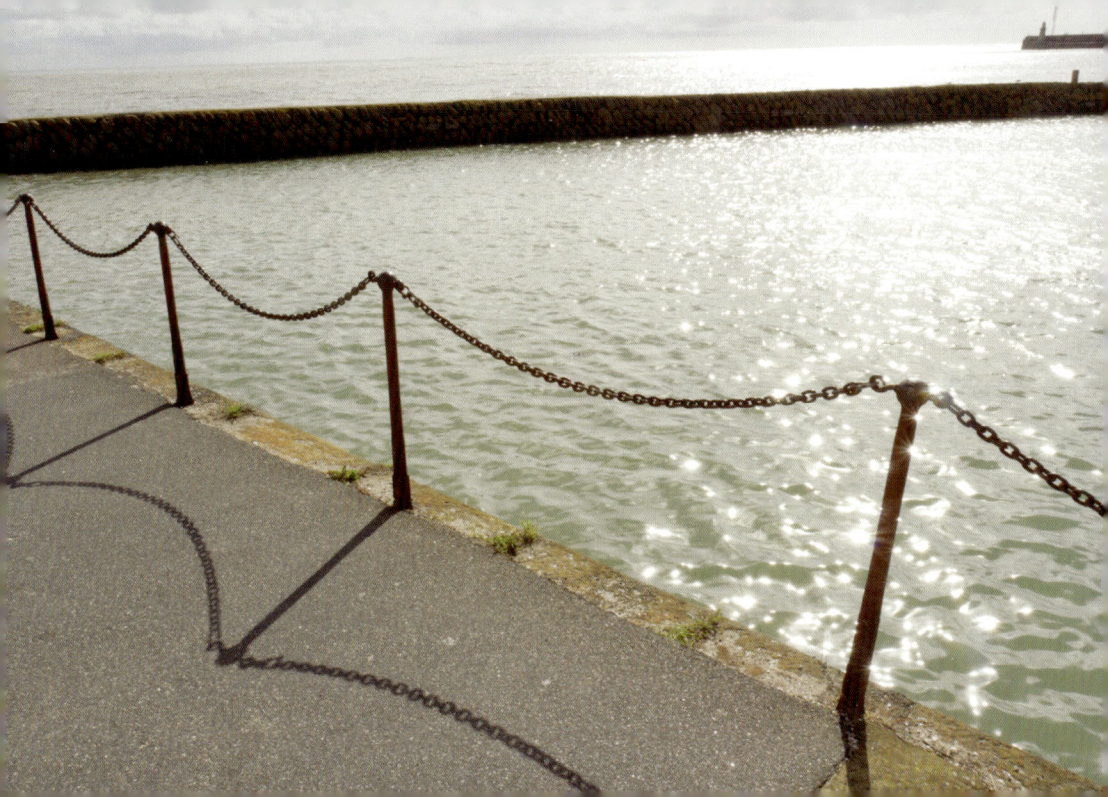

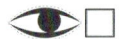

I worked at the 'Mini Golf Course' at Marine Gardens for seven years for Shepway District Council. I had a free pass to travel on the Leas Lift, so I used it every day to get to work. The land was then bought by Jimmy Godden and I lost my job. After this I joined Kent Police.

I loved it down there and met lots of people.

मैले ७ वर्षसम्म Marine Garden का 'Mini Golf Course' काम गरेको थिए । मलाइ Leas Lift मा निशुल्क प्रवेश गर्ने सुविधा भएकोले प्रत्येक दिन काममा जान-आउन सजिलो थियो । Jimmy Godden नाउँ गरेको व्यक्तिले उक्त जग्गा किने पछि मैले आफुनो जागिर गुमाएँ । त्यसपछि Kent Police मा भर्ति भएँ ।

त्यो काम मलाई असाध्यै मन पर्थ्यो, किनभने धेरै मानिसहरुलाई भेट्ने अवसर मिल्यो ।

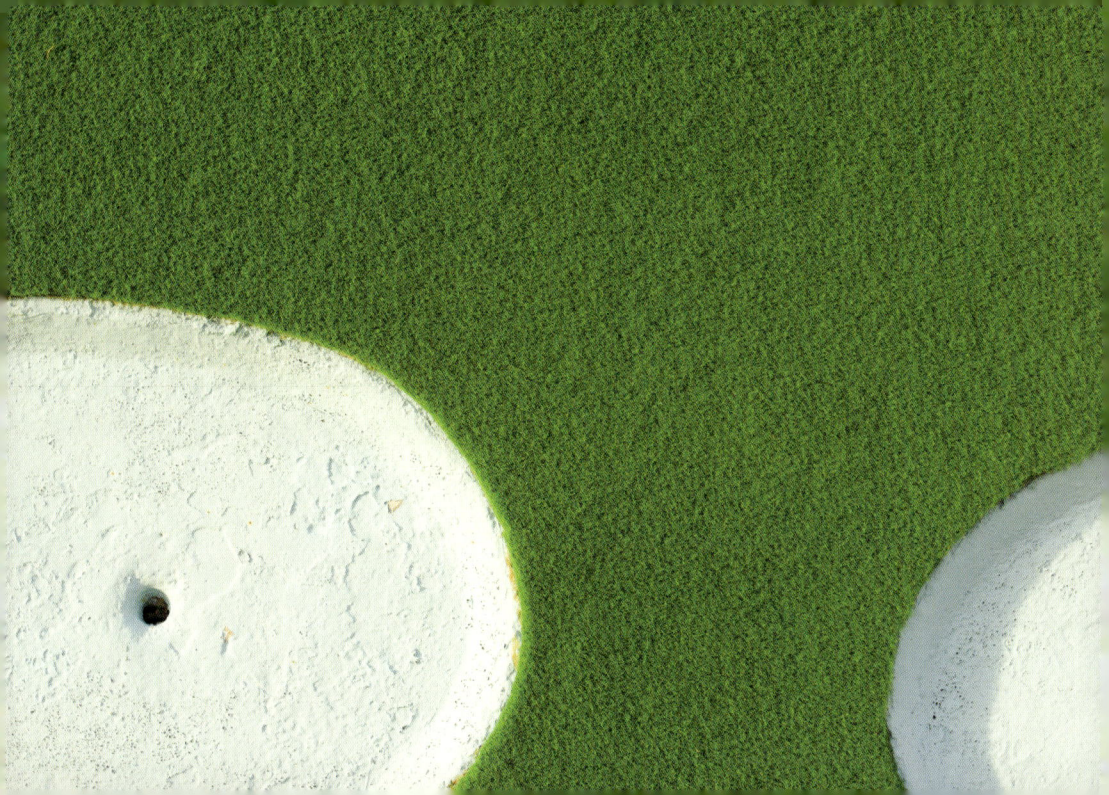

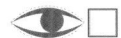

I attended St Peter's church, under the ministration of Father Pickburn. My brother Dennis was an altar boy and he would swing his incense burner violently when he neared my friend Peggy and I. This would make us cough and splutter and earn us a ticking off from the adults. I think he did it for the perverse pleasure of seeing us told off. My three great-grandchildren were all christened at St Peter's church and my grand-daughter and eldest great grand-daughter were at St Peter's school. Whenever I see the church, the school and the St Andrew's building, wonderful memories of my childhood come flooding back. There is a plaque in St Peter's church dedicated to Father Pickburn and in one of the staff rooms at the school there is a plaque of remembrance for pupils who died in the First World War. One of the names is Victor Tumber, an uncle of mine whom obviously I never met as I was not born until 1933.

स्कुलमा भएको एक कर्मचारी कोठामा पहिलो विश्व युद्धमा मारिएका व्यक्तिहरुको सम्झना स्वरुप एउटा नामावलि सुचि राखिएको छ । त्यो सुचि मध्येको एक Victor Tumber मेरा काक थिए । उनलाई मैले कहिले पनि भेटिन । किनभने म सन १९३३ सम्ममा जन्मेकै थिईन ।

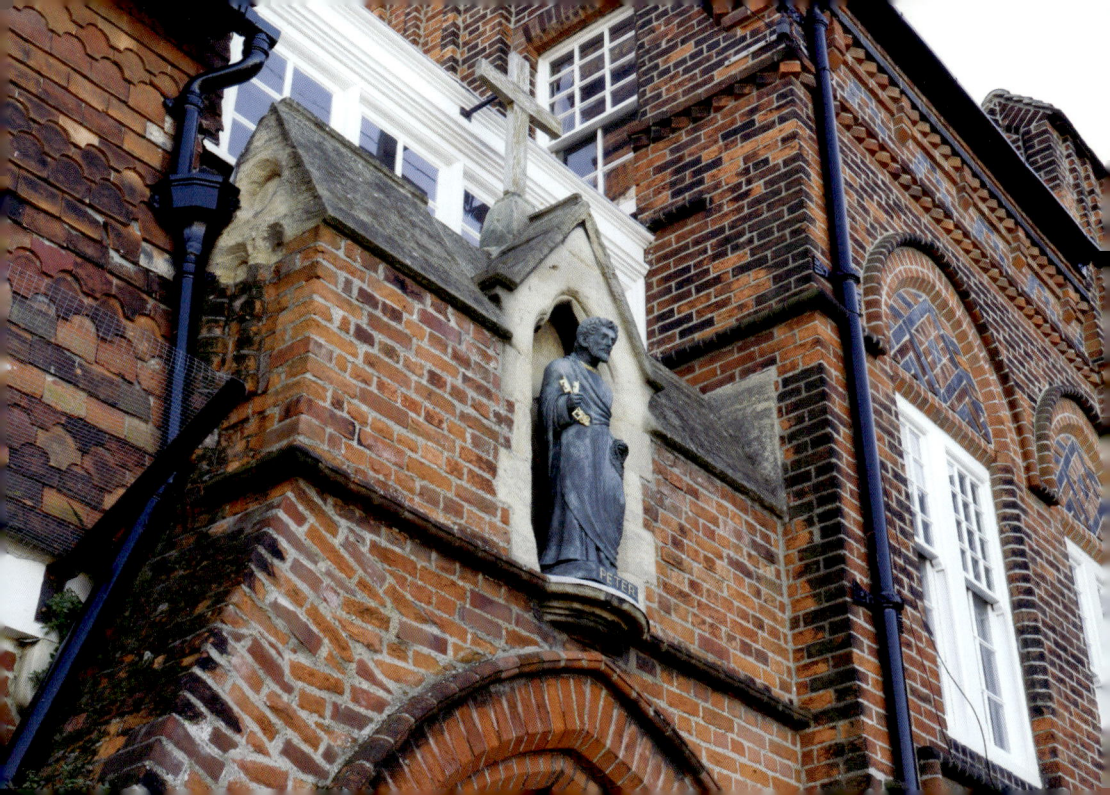

PETER

Emin is a legend, he looks like the guy from *Everybody Loves Raymond*. All the skaters and bikers from the Shed get their sweets and energy drinks from Emin. On his birthday he brought drinks over to the skate park for us all. There is even a sign on his shop saying 'no bikes on the wall'.

Emin एउटा महात्मा हो । सबै स्केट खेलाडी र वाईकल चलाउनेहरुलाई चकलेटहरु र अन्य पेय पदार्थहरु Emin ले नै उपलब्ध गराउथ्यो । उसको जन्मदिनमा उसले हामी सबैको लागि पेय पदार्थहरु किनीदिएको थियो ।

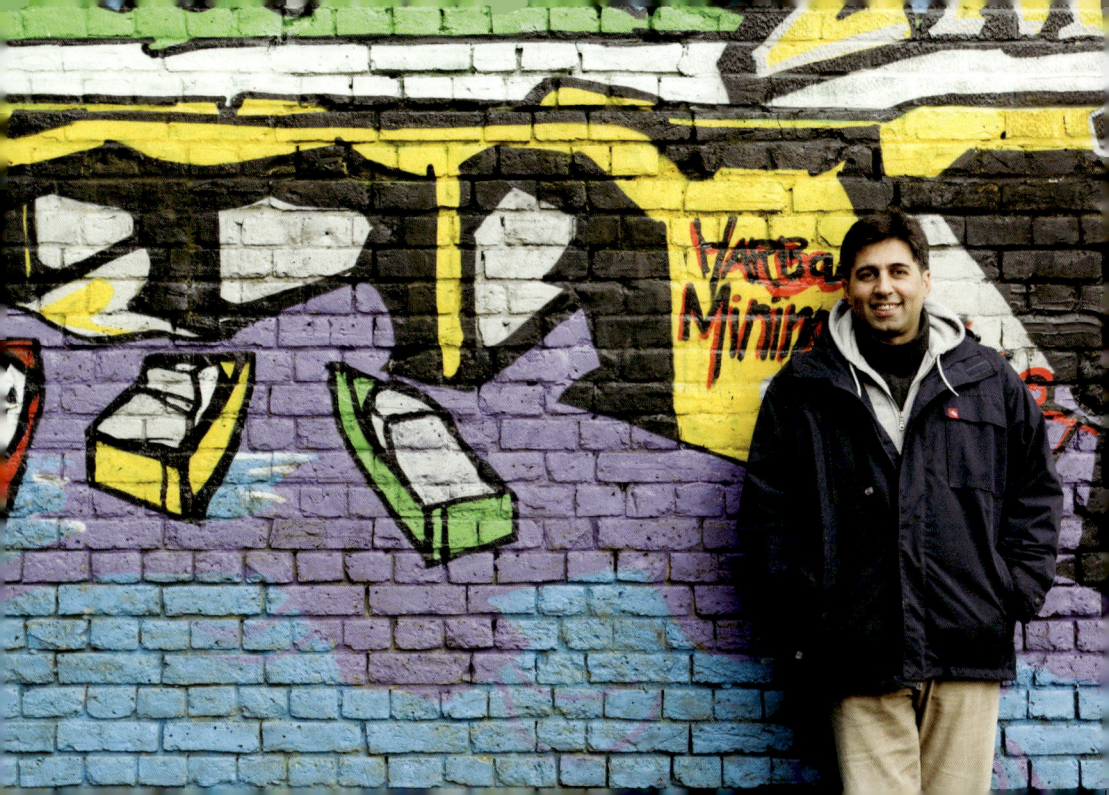

Everyone who lives in Folkestone knows about the arches under the prom on the Sunny Sands. They used to be far higher inside, before they filled up with sand, but they still have the same damp smell of seawater and seaweed that they have always had. The concrete steps that lead up from the beach to the walkway above are relatively recent addition, but before they were built, you used to be able to walk the whole length of the beach under cover.

Children still have lots of fun running through them, they are good for sheltering from the wind and unexpected showers, or fierce sunshine. As the tide comes in they become the last place to retreat to avoid the waves. They provide privacy to wrestle yourself in and out of wet and sandy swimming costumes and they have seen many a romantic assignation – there must have been more than one baby named Archie over the years who was the result of a night (or day) of passion under the arches.

वगरमा भएको arches मा केटाकेटीहरु कुदेर रमाईलो गर्ने गर्दथे । हावा पानी आएको वेलामा उनीहरुलाई ओत लाग्नको लागी पनि यो उपयोगी थियो । यसबाट छलिएर त्याँ मानिसहरु पौडी खेल्दा लगाउने लुगाहरु फेर बदल पनि गर्दथे ।

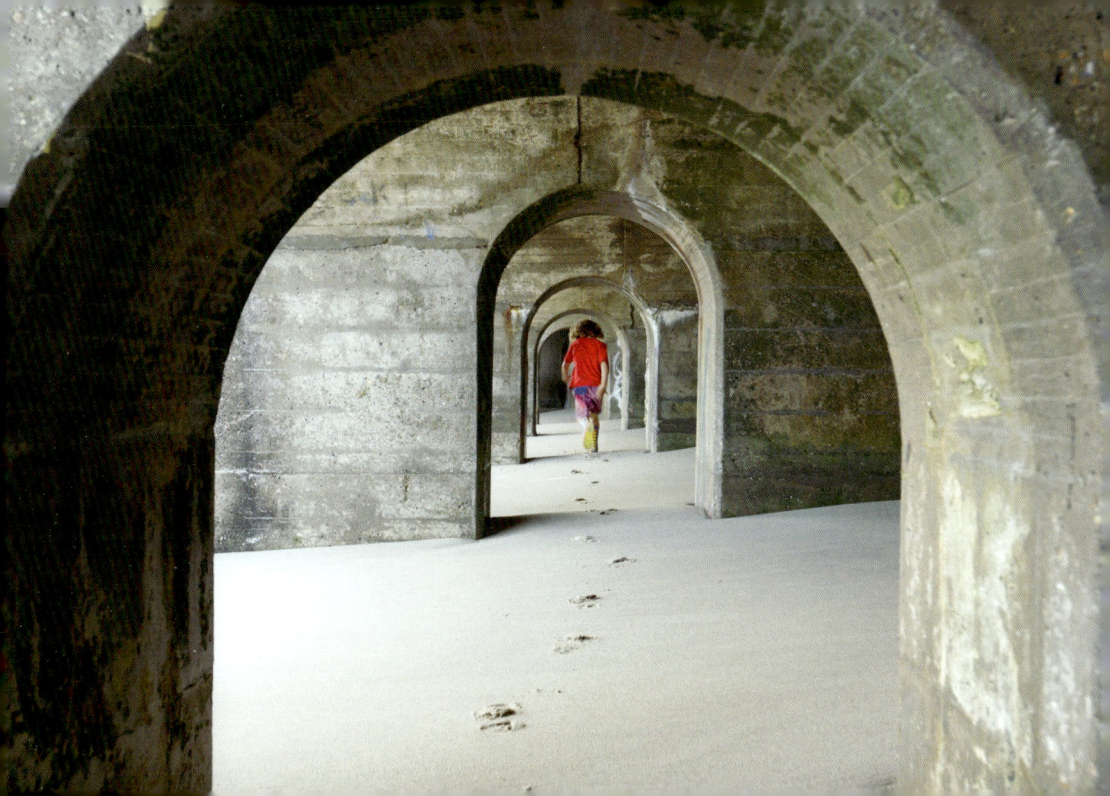

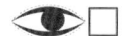

When I have been away it is always nice to come over the hill on the M20 and, as you approach the Channel Tunnel, the lights always make me feel like I am home.

Before the Tunnel was built, it was always the street lights that snake up Dover Hill in the distance that would welcome you home.

म बाहिर गएको वेला सँधै माथि डाँडाको बाटो भएर M20 सम्म राम्रो लाग्छ ।त्यस पछि Channel Tunnel तिर जादा त्यहाँ भएको बत्तिहरुले मलाई घरमा नै भएको महसुस हुन्छ ।

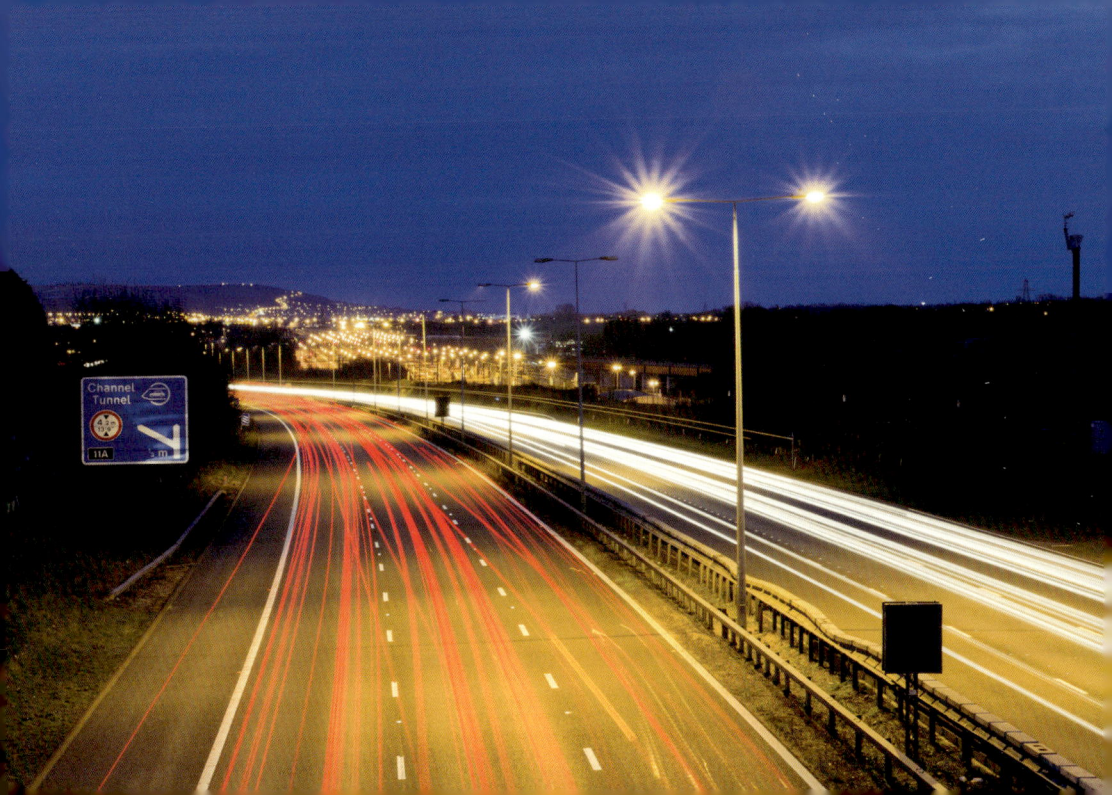

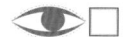

The thing I remember most from before the War is the weeping ash tree in Kingsnorth Gardens. When I was a schoolboy in the 30s, my friends and I often went to look at the goldfish and other creatures in the two ponds in the gardens. On going from one pond to the other we would pass under the tree and on hot days would sit on the seat and enjoy the shade. This was before we knew of its history.

One of my friend's fathers started work just after the First World War with his father who was a builder and plumber. At a job in Cheriton Road they were asked to dispose of a tree in the front garden. They didn't want to destroy the little tree, so they dug it up and replanted it in the middle of the old brickfield. In the 19th century, before it became Kingsnorth Gardens, this used to be the brickfields where they made the bricks to build the viaduct. When the gardens were designed and constructed, they kept the little tree and it is now the centrepiece of the gardens.

मेरो र साथिको बाबाले पहिलो विश्व युद्ध सकिए लगत्तै पानिको धारा र घर बनाउने काम शुरु गरे । एक पटक चेरिटन सडकमा भएको बगैंचाको अगाडि पट्टीको रुख काटने जिम्मा उनीहरुलाई दिईएको थियो । उनीहरुले त्यो सानो रुखलाई मास्न चाहेनन् । त्यसैले उनहिरुले त्यो रुखलाई खनेर पुरानो brickfield को मध्य भागमा सारिदिए । यो अभैपनि Kingsnorth बगैंचामा छ ।

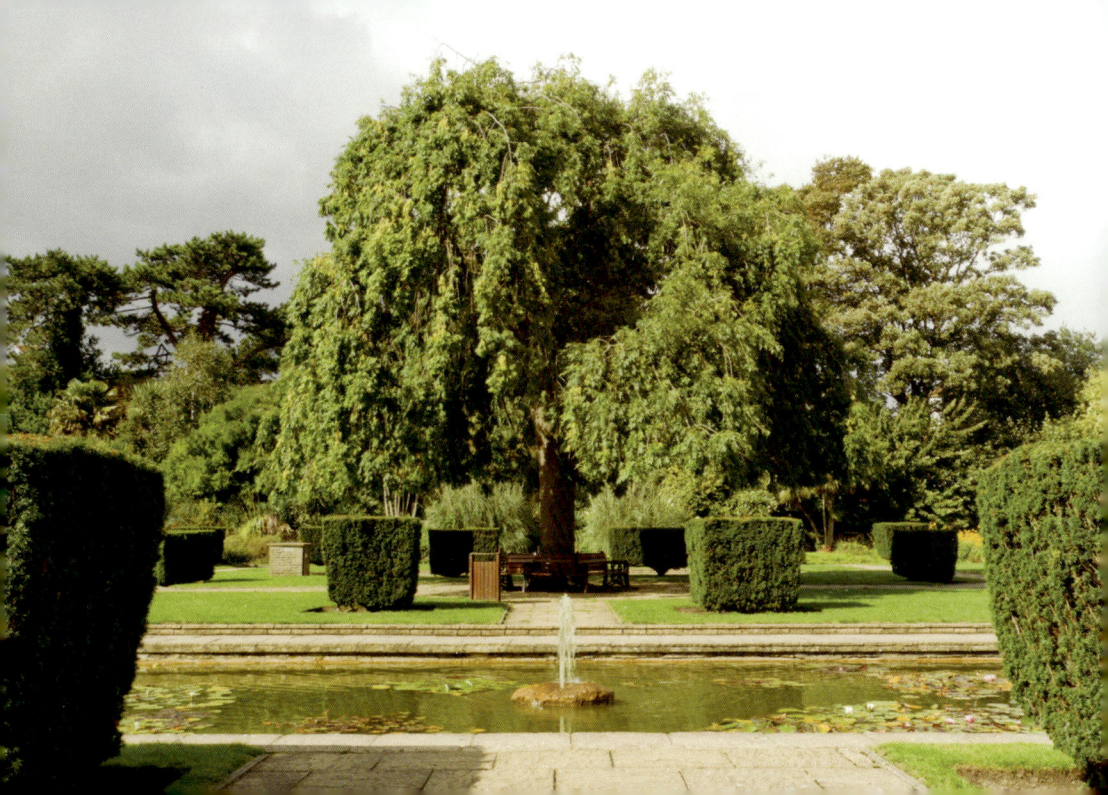

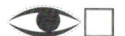

There is an old derelict building down on the Fishmarket that is painted blue and has decorative windows. It was not always like this. Some years ago a film crew gave this building a make-over and it was used in the making of a television drama called *Moon and Son* starring Millicent Martin. It was quite novel to walk around the town about your daily business and bump into a film set, although I personally, did not see any of the famous actors.

When the weekly drama came to television it became compulsive viewing, attempting to recognise places in Folkestone. Some places had been disguised – such as the beach huts down Lower Sandgate Road. It almost fooled me that it must have been filmed in France or in a studio, for they had decorated them with hanging baskets and then made them look like apartments that people live in. If only! I might have been in the queue to purchase one.

After the series ended it gave me a real sense of pride in my birth town. I really love Folkestone and I hoped it would make people want to visit.

धेरै वर्ष पहिले यहां रहेको भवनमा टेलिभिजनका कार्यक्रमहरु छायांकन गरिएको थियो ।

EVERYWHERE MEANS SOMETHING TO SOMEONE

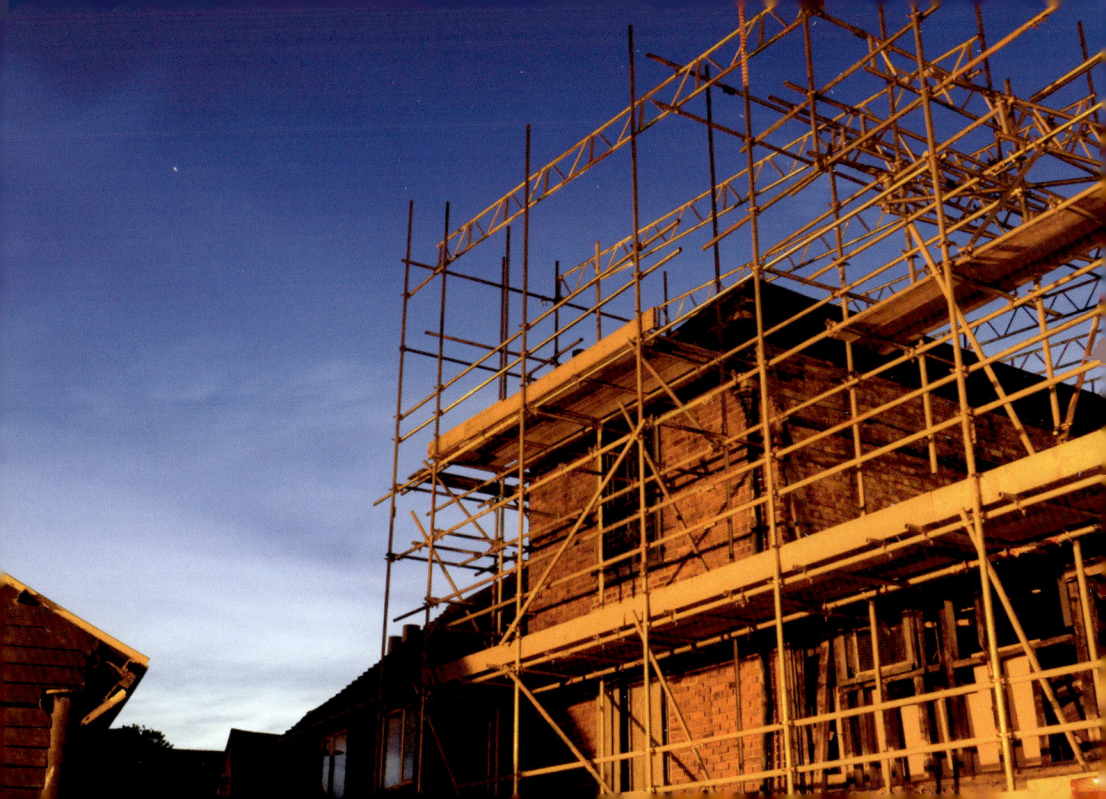

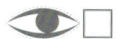

I love the fact that at different times of the year odd things pop up in Radnor Park. From the Moscow State Circus to boot fairs, they all look great as you come upon them. I also always can't help but look at the view as you drive along Cheriton Road looking across the park toward the hospital. The scene reminds me of one of those old 3D postcards, as the foreground buildings float strangely in front of the distant backdrop of the hills, which are several miles away.

When the Queen Mother died, Admiral the Lord Boyce took over as Lord Warden of the Cinque Ports, and to commemorate the occasion he planted an oak tree in the gardens of Radnor Park. The significance of this is that he is a Naval man and oak was historically used to build ships.

चेरिटन सडकमा गाडी कुधाउँदा पार्कको दृश्य हेर्न मलाई रामो लाग्छ । अस्पताल तिर हेर्दा यसको पछ्छाडी धेरै माईल टाडा भएको डाँडाहरुमा अस्पताल तैरिरहेको जस्तो देखिन्छ ।

रानीको आमा Cinque Ports को विशिष्ट संरक्षक थिए । उनको मृत्यु पछ्छाडी रेडनर पार्कको वगैचामा एक विषेश किसीमको रुखको विरुवाहरु रोपियो जुन रुख चाही ऐतिहासिक रुपमा पानीजहाज बनाउने काठको लागी प्रख्यात थियो ।

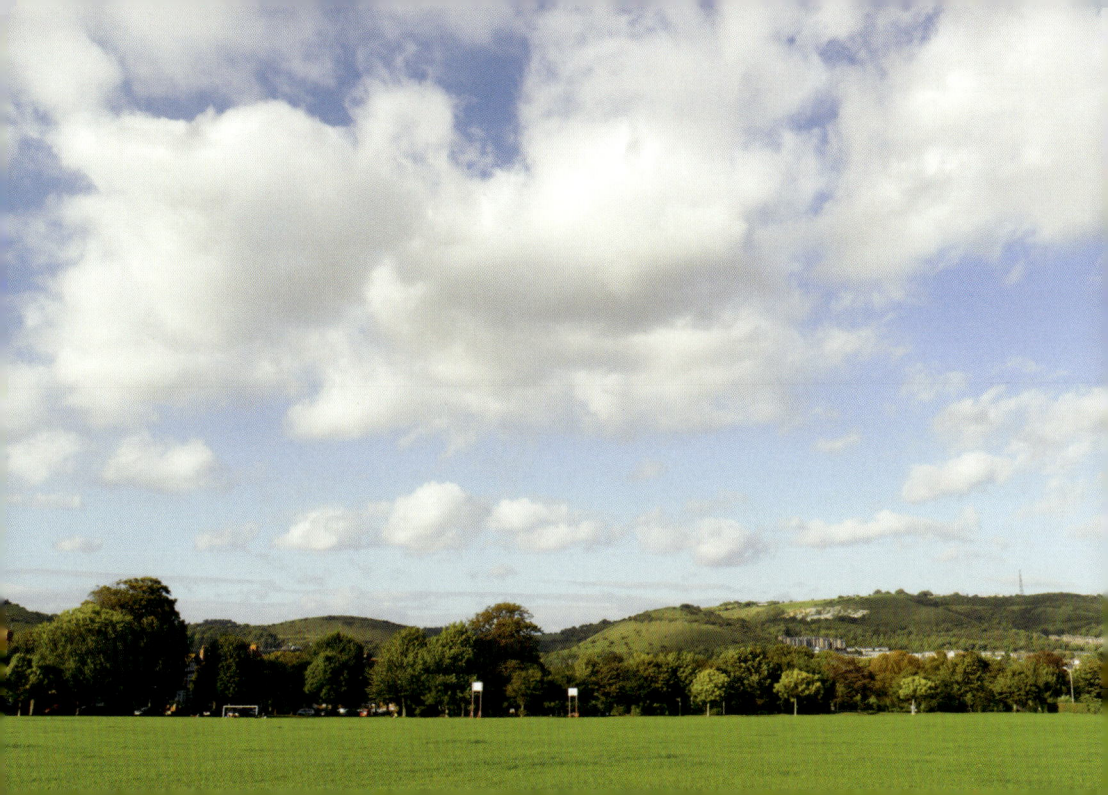

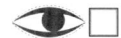

The Cabin Café was demolished a few weeks ago – my favourite greasy spoon and last bastion of spotted dick and Horlicks.

Folkestone is being slowly paninified.

Will the replacement eatery live up to expectations?

केही हप्ता पहिले त्यो भोजनालय भत्काईएको थियो । त्यो मलाई मनपरेको पुरानो शैलीको खाना किन्न पाईने एउटा ठाउँ पनि थियो । के अब त्यसको सट्टामा बन्ने अर्को रेष्टुरेन्ट पहिलेको जस्तै असल हुन सक्छ ?

EVERYWHERE MEANS SOMETHING TO SOMEONE

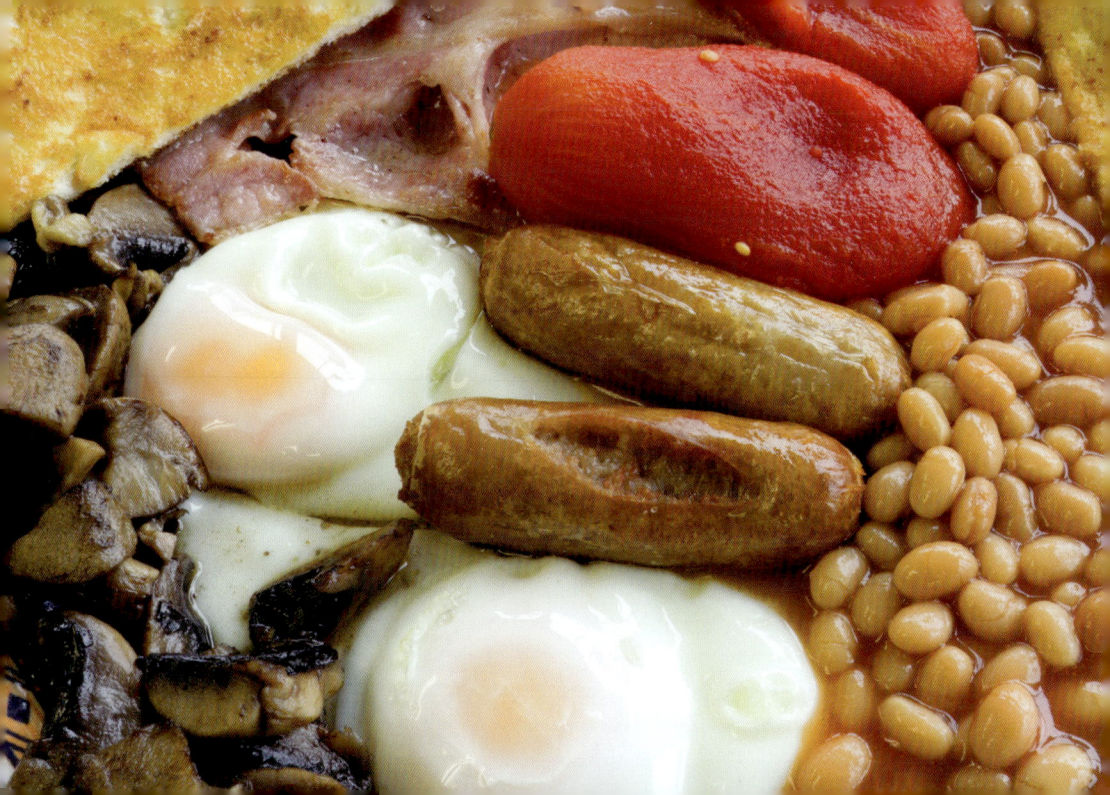

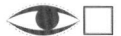

The famous British artist John Constable, who painted *The Haywain,* sent his two eldest sons to school at The Priory in Folkestone. They didn't enjoy it and only stayed for a year, but as a result he painted several paintings of the harbour, some of which are very well known.

Folkestone Harbour is a constant source of inspiration for local artists. Each year without exception, for the summer exhibition of the Folkestone Arts Society, artists will submit paintings of Folkestone Harbour.

वेलायतको प्रशिद्ध चित्रकार John Constable ले 'The Haywain' को चित्रण गरेका थिए । उनका दुई छोराहरु Priory in Folkestone मा अध्ययन गर्दथे । उनीहरुलाई त्यहाँ रमाईलो नभएकोले एक वर्ष मात्र त्यहाँ बसेका थिए । तरपनि उनले फोक्सटन बन्दरगाहको धेरै चित्रहरु बनाएका थिए । ति मध्ये केही चित्रहरु प्रख्यात छन् ।

स्थानिय रङ्ग कर्मिहरुको लागी फोक्सटन ह्यावर उनिहरुलाई उत्सहित गर्ने एउटा क्षेमताको मुहान हो । फोक्सटन कलाकार संघले प्रत्यक वर्ष summer exhibition को आयोजना गर्दछ जसमा प्रतियोगीहरुले फोक्सटन ह्यावरको चित्र प्रसतुत गर्दछन ।

EVERYWHERE MEANS SOMETHING TO SOMEONE

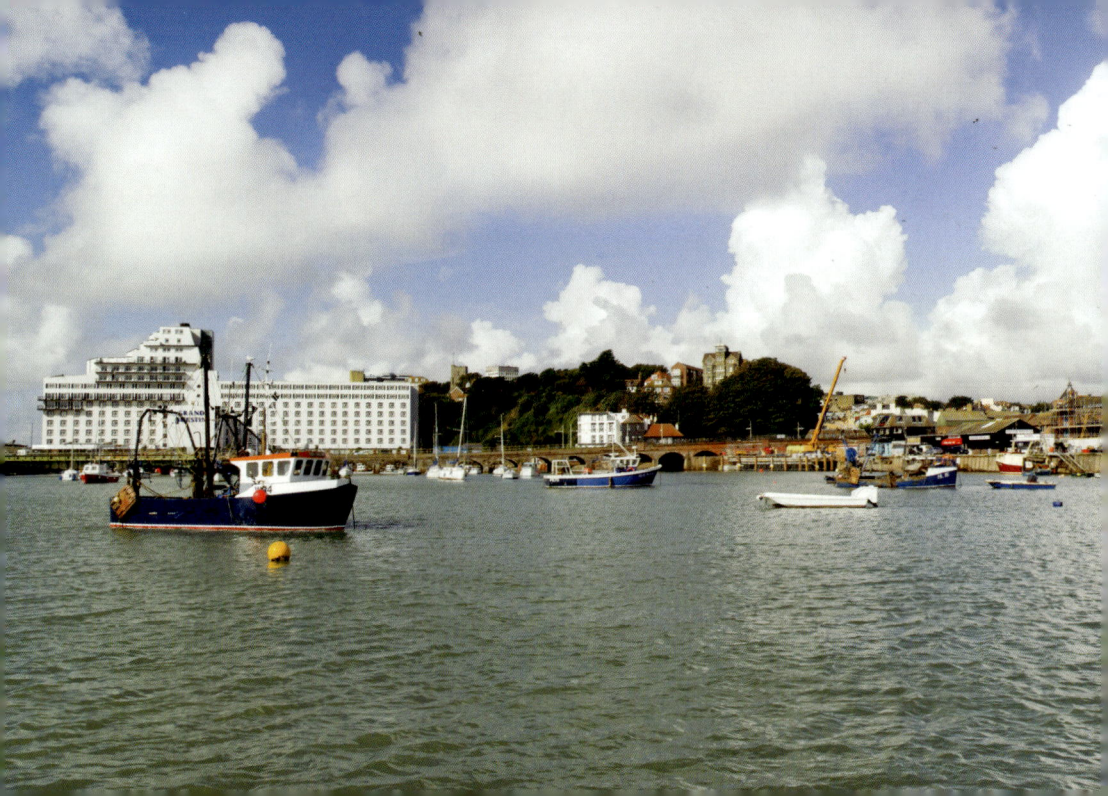

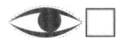

Anthony Ashley Cooper, the 7th Earl of Shaftesbury, died at 12 Clifton Gardens in Folkestone on 1 October 1885. He was a major Victorian social reformist and a prominent politician and philanthropist. He was widely known as the 'reforming Lord Shaftesbury' in the 19th century, and he fought for the rights of children and the abolition of slavery.

सन १ अक्टोबर १८८५ मा 7th Earl of Shaftesbury, Anthony Ashley Cooper को १२ Clifton Gardens फोल्कस्टनमा मृत्यु भएको थियो । उनी भिक्टोरियाको पालामा सबैले मानेका समाज सेवी राजनीतिज्ञ र दार्शनिक थिए । उसलाई १९ औं शताब्दीमा समाज सुधारक Lord Shaftesbury भनेर चिनिन्थ्यो । उनले बालश्रम र दासत्वको खिलाफ आवाज उठाएका थिए ।

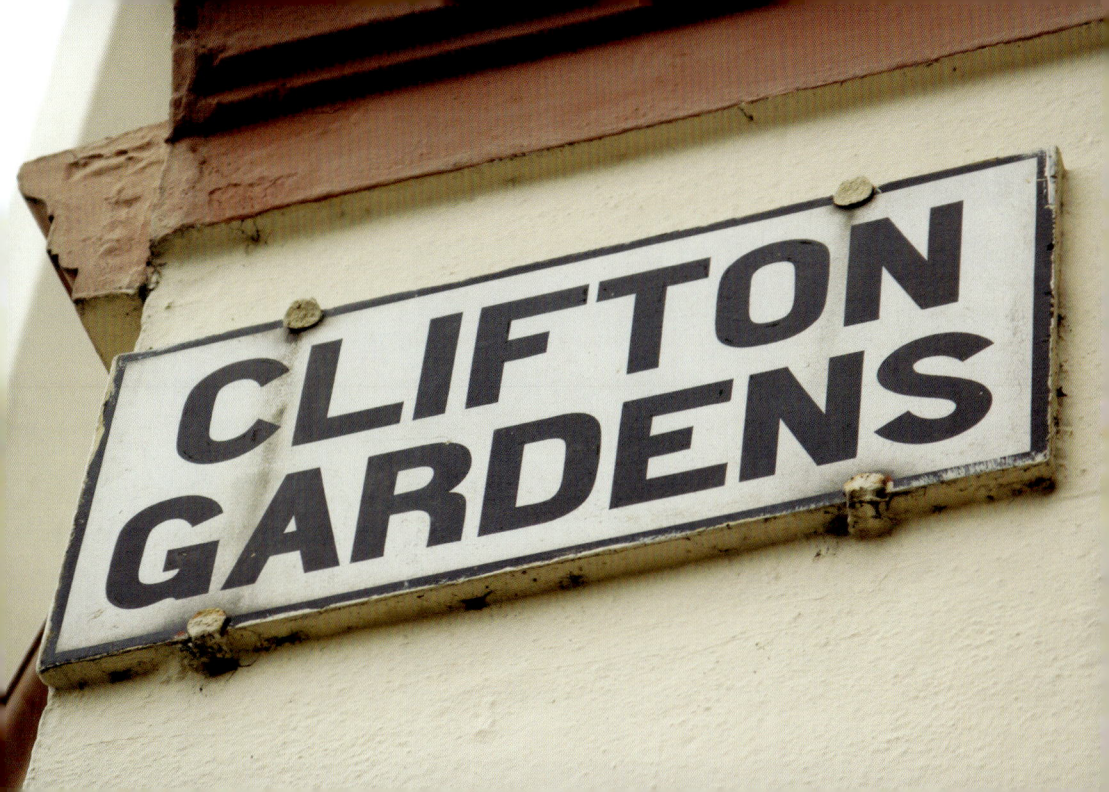

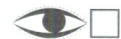

Samuel Beckett, the famous playwright, married his lifelong companion Suzanne Descheveaux-Dumesnil on 25 March 1961, in a secret civil ceremony in Folkestone. It is said that he married mainly for reasons relating to French inheritance law and it was to make sure that if he died before her, she would inherit the rights to his work, since she was French and there was no common-law marriage under French law. It would be nice to think that it was also because he loved her. To comply with British law, Beckett was obliged to be in residence in Folkestone for minimum of two weeks, in order for him to be married in the registry office here.

Samuel Beckett एउटा प्रख्यात नाटककार थिए । उनले २५ मार्च १९६१ मा फोक्सटनमा गोप्य समारोहमा Suzanne Descheveaux Dumesnil लाई जीवन साथिको रुपमा विवाह गरेका थिए । श्रीमती भन्दा उनको मृत्यु पहिला भएमा उसको सबै सम्पतिको सर्वाधिकार श्रीमतीलाई इच्छा पत्र दिएका थिए ।

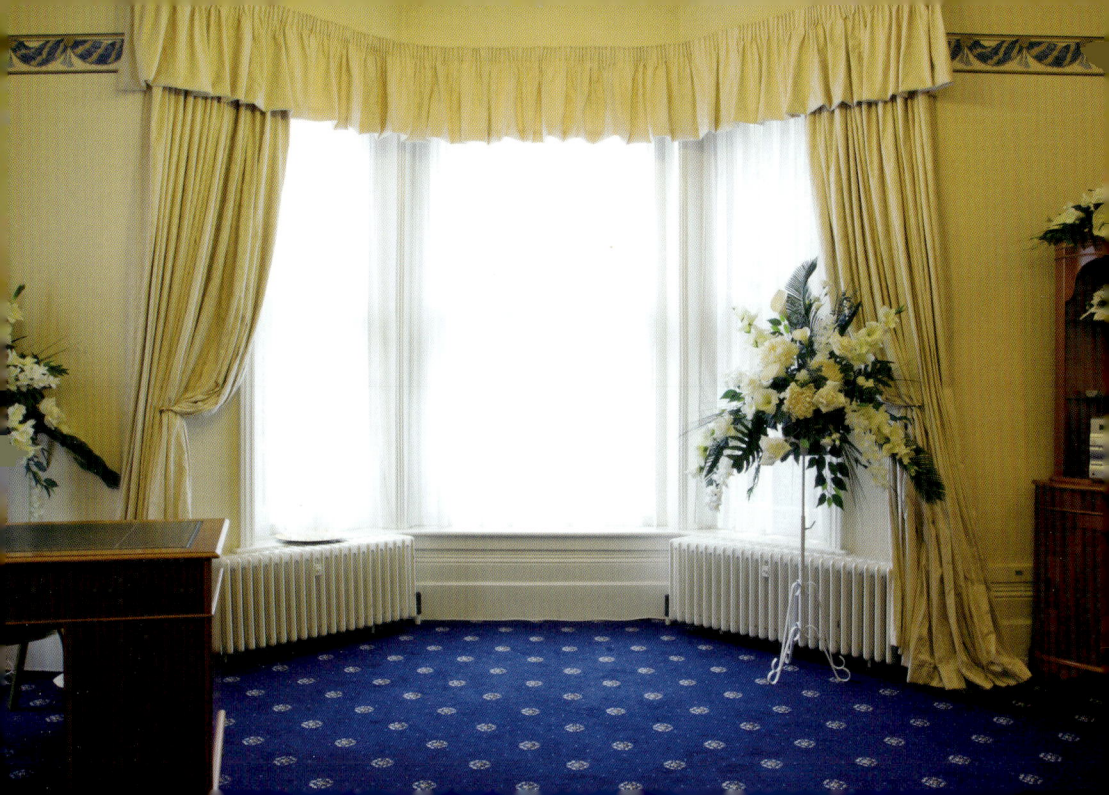

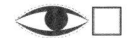

On the Warren, just past Copt Point, the fossil beds are the second biggest in the UK, only second to the Jurassic Coast in Dorset. The rest of the world's fossils beds are measured from Folkestone's records. As the cliffs erode, which they do quite rapidly, the fossils just drop into the sea and are washed up in the rock beds. There is really good crabbing there too.

बेलायतमा भएको दोश्रो ठूलो Fossil Beds Warren हो । अन्य विश्वको fossil beds फोक्सटनको अभिलेख द्वारा मापन गरिएका छन् । तटको भिर निरन्तर रुपमा कटान भएर fossil हरु समुन्द्रमा खस्छन त्यस पछी ढुंगे वगरतिर समुन्द्रले बगाएर लान्छ ।

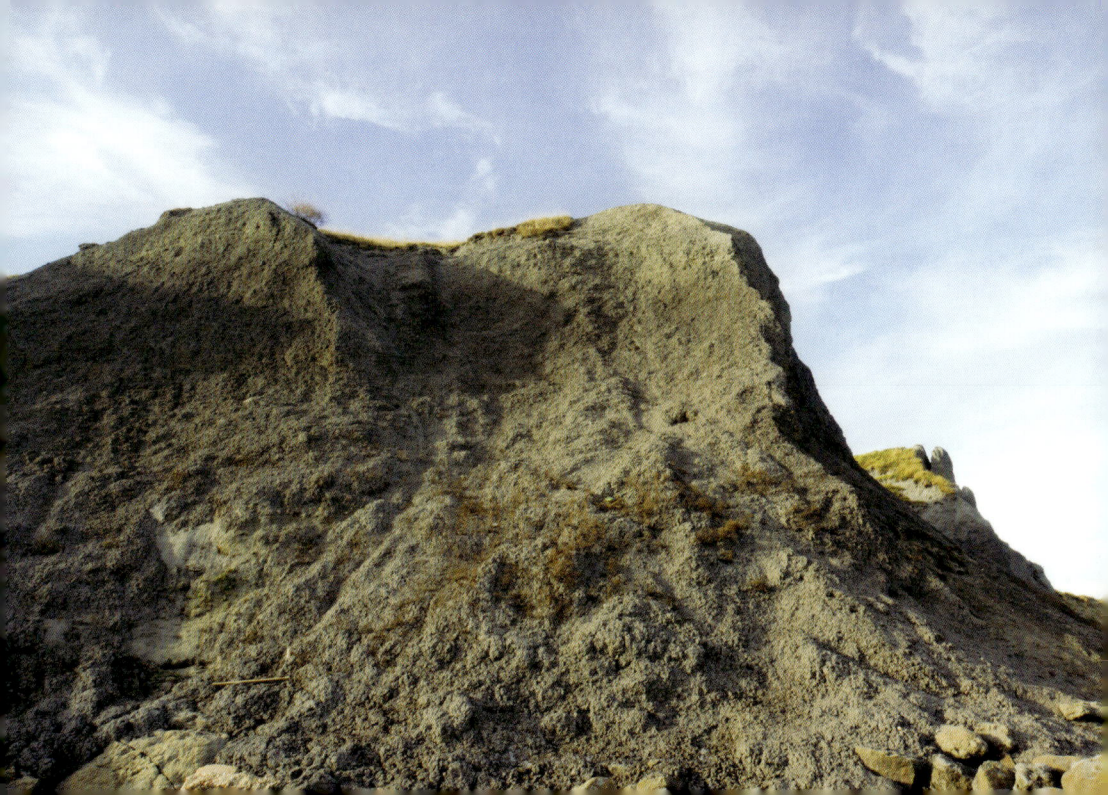

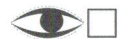

The Coastal Park is lovely and it's free! There are places all over it that you can have a barbeque, and if you are feeling lazy, like me, you can go to the Mermaid Café for a jacket potato. It's formal at one end and wild flowers at the other. It's got everything, I often go there.

The cycle route from Hythe to Folkestone is magnificent, on a sunny day you could easily be anywhere in the South of France. The colour of the sea is great and changes depending on the light.

यो कोस्टल पार्क रमाईलो र स्वतन्त्र ठाउँ हो । यो पार्कको सबै ठाउँहरुमा हिड्डुल गर्न, साईकल चलाउन र बार्विक्यु गर्न सकिन्छ ।

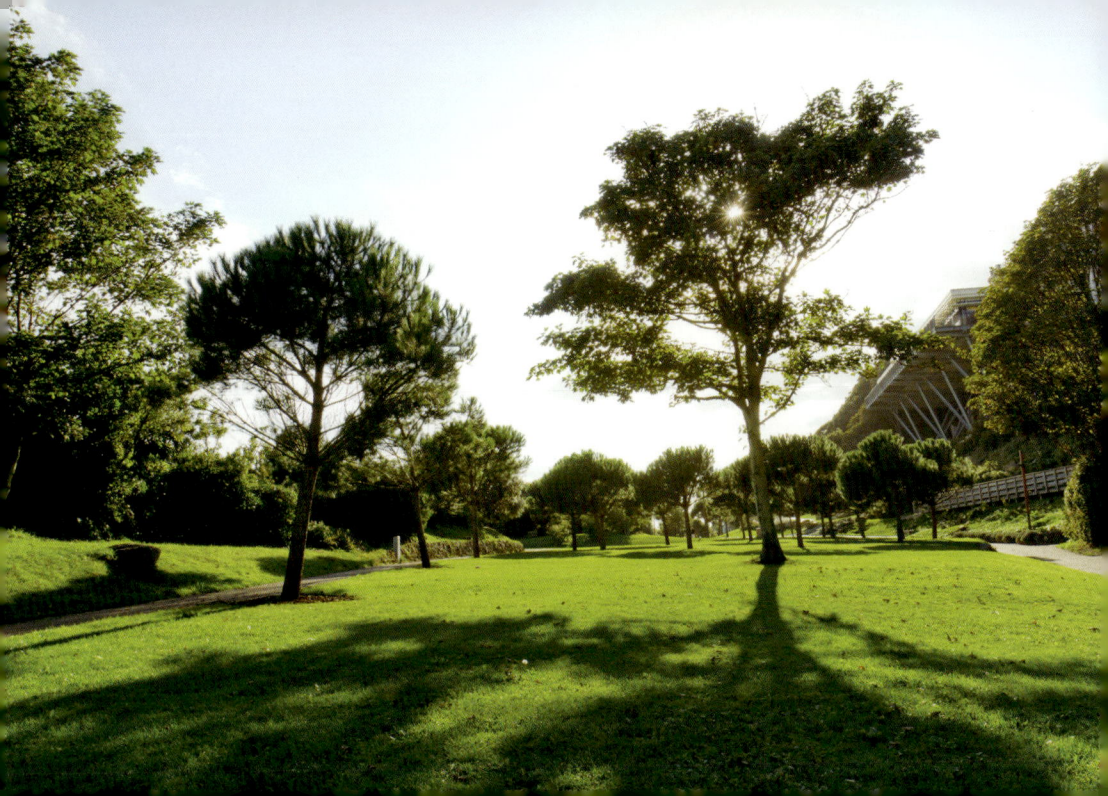

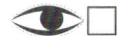

When I was a child, my family used to visit Folkestone beach and seafront for a day out and one of the best parts of the day was riding in the Leas Lifts. It was always so exciting. I live nearby now, and make a point of taking my nephews and nieces on it. It's not a long journey, but wonderful and seems strangely scary, it's definitely a fantastic thing to experience.

फोक्सटन शहरको भ्रमणमा सबैभन्दा राम्रो ठाउँ Leas Lift मा चढ्नु हुन्थ्यो । यसमा चढ्दा संधै रमाईलोको अनुभव हुन्थ्यो । यो त्यति लामो यात्रा होईन तर रमाईलो अनि केही डरलाग्दो पनि थियो । वास्वमा यसमा अतिनै राम्रो अनुभूति हुन्छ ।

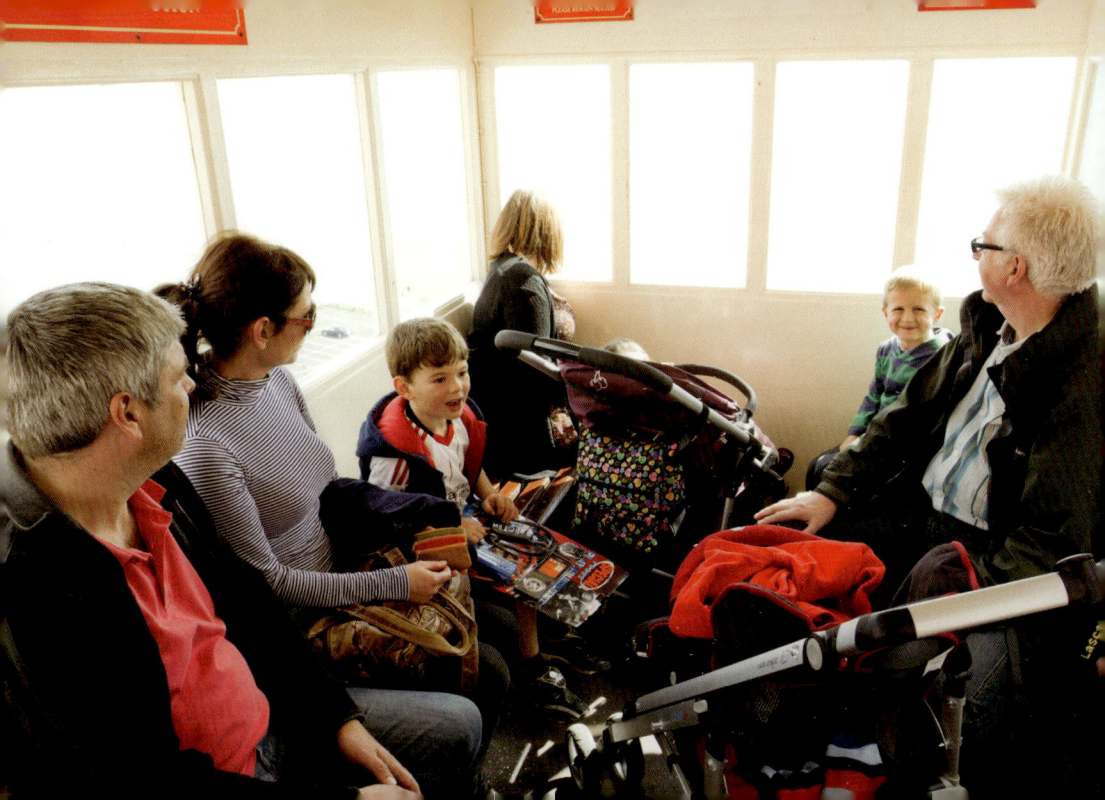

Down in Seabrook is Sandy Lanes – continue to follow the track into the woods at the bottom of Hospital Hill, where the road bends and goes up hill. This is where lots of kids go BMXing, there are lots of WWI trenches and WWII pillboxes, which are all overgrown. This is where soldiers used to train during the wars before they were sent off to fight in Europe.

Sandy Lanes in Seabrook जहाँ केटाकेटीहरु BMX साईकल चलाउँछन, त्यहाँ पहिलो र दोस्रो विश्वयुद्धका पालाका खाडलहरु छन् । यो ठाउँमा त्यसताका सेनाहरुलाई युरोपको लडाईमा जानु पूर्व तालिम गराईन्थ्यो ।

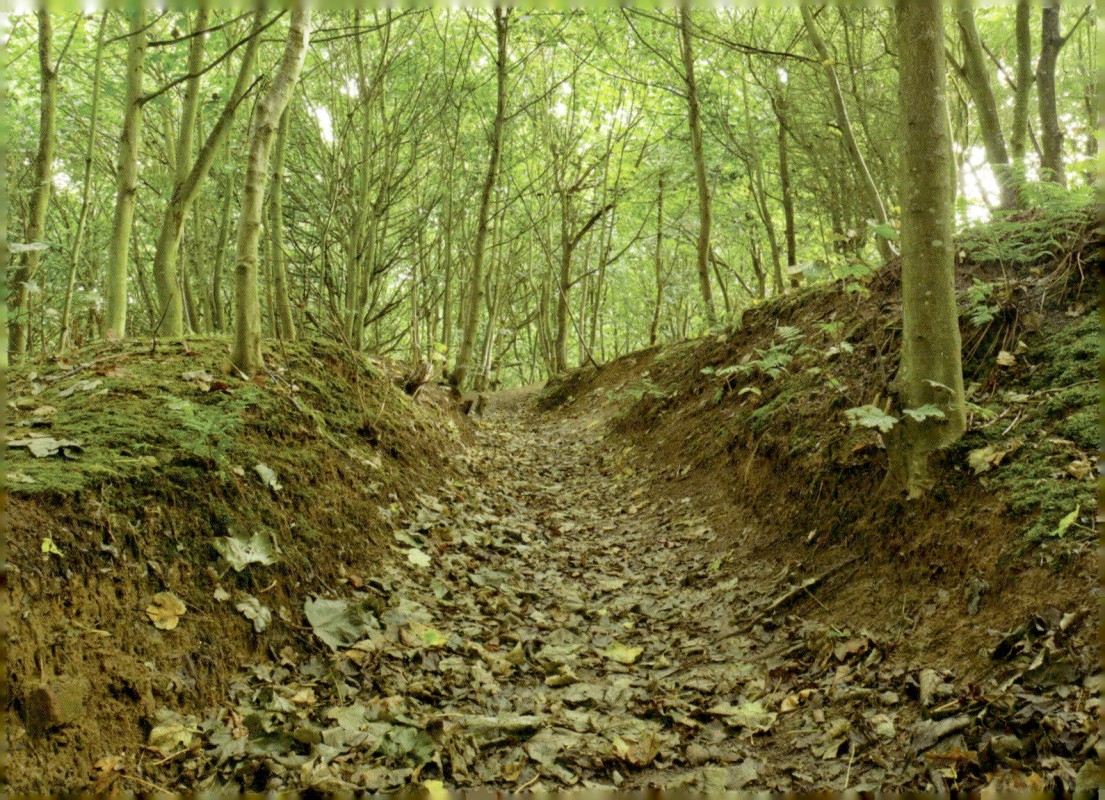

English comedian, writer, composer, actor and singer George Grossmith lived in Folkestone. His performing career spanned more than four decades and he created 18 comic operas, nearly 100 musical sketches, around 600 songs and piano pieces, three books and both serious and comic pieces for newspapers and magazines. He created many memorable characters in the comic operas of Gilbert and Sullivan, including Sir Joseph Porter in *H.M.S. Pinafore*, the Major-General in *The Pirates of Penzance* and Ko-Ko in *The Mikado*. He also wrote, in collaboration with his brother Weedon, the 1892 comic novel *Diary of a Nobody*. He retired to Folkestone, a town that he had visited for many years, in the first few years of the new century, where he went on to write his second volume of reminiscences *Piano and I* in 1910. He died at the age of 64 at his home in Manor Road in Folkestone on 1 March 1912.

फोक्सटनको Manor Road मा अंग्रेज हास्य कलाकार, लेखक, रचनाकार, अभिनेता तथा गायक George Grossmith बस्ने गर्दथे । उनले यस क्षेत्रमा ४ दशक भन्दा वढि समय विताएका थिए । उनले १८ वटा रमाईलो गीतिकथा, झण्डै १०० वटा संगीत सृजना, लगभग ६०० वटा गीतहरु र पियानोका धुनहरु, ट वटा किताबहरु र समाचारपत्र तथा मासिक पत्रिकाहरुमा हृदय विदारक र रमाईलो लेखहरुको रचना गरेका थिए ।

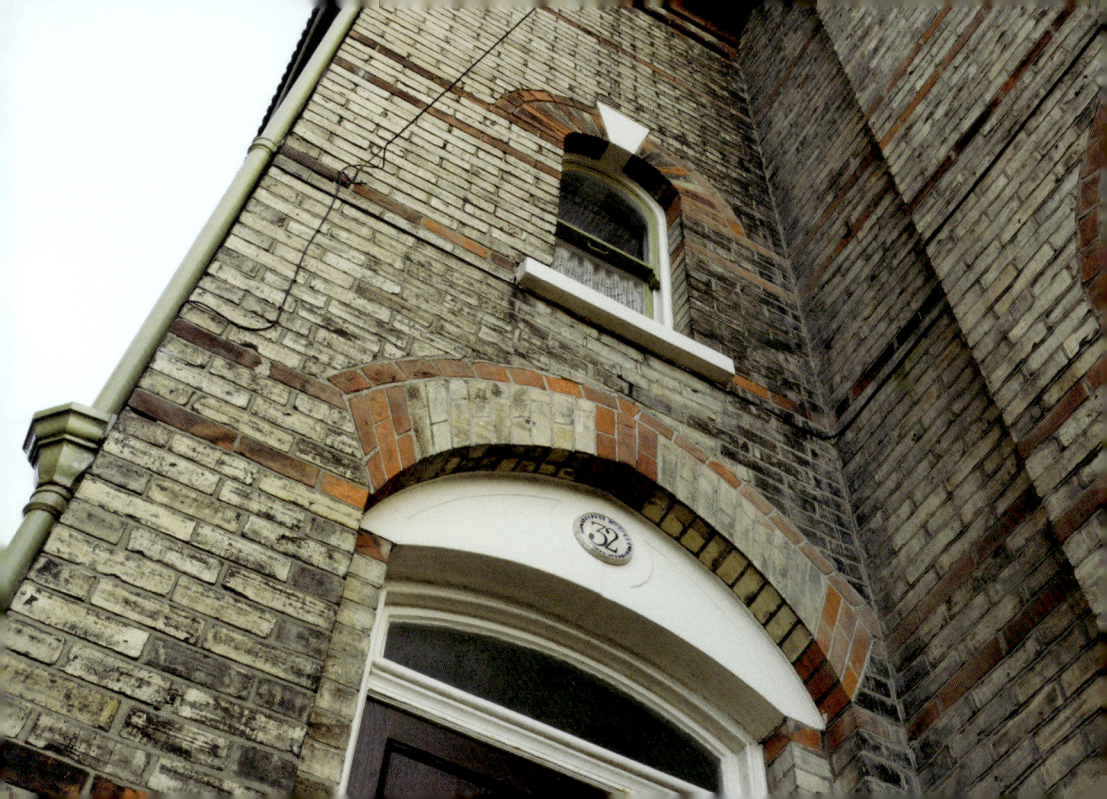

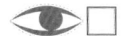

One of my favourite places in Folkestone is the renovated gardens within the Italian sunken pond on the Bayle. It is a beautiful oasis of clam with water lillies and a Tracey Emin artwork. I was fascinated to discover that this is a place of miracles as the water actually flows uphill. It was the place of an ancient abbey that was demolished in the dissolution, the stones were then reused by Henry VIII to build Sandgate Castle for defence in the 16th century.

मलाई मनपर्ने फोक्सटनको रमणिय ठाउँहरु मध्ये Bayle को पुरानो ईटालिको कुवा एक हो । वास्तवमा यस ठाउँको पानी उकालो बग्छ भन्ने अचम्मको कुरा थाहा पाउँदा म ज्यादै खुशी भएको थिएँ । अति पुरानो यो गिर्जाघरलाई Henry VIII ले १६ औं शताब्दीमा भत्काएर यसको ढुंगाहरुलाई सुरक्षाको लागि पुन: प्रयोग गरी सानगेट किल्लाको निर्माण गरेका थिए ।

EVERYWHERE MEANS SOMETHING TO SOMEONE

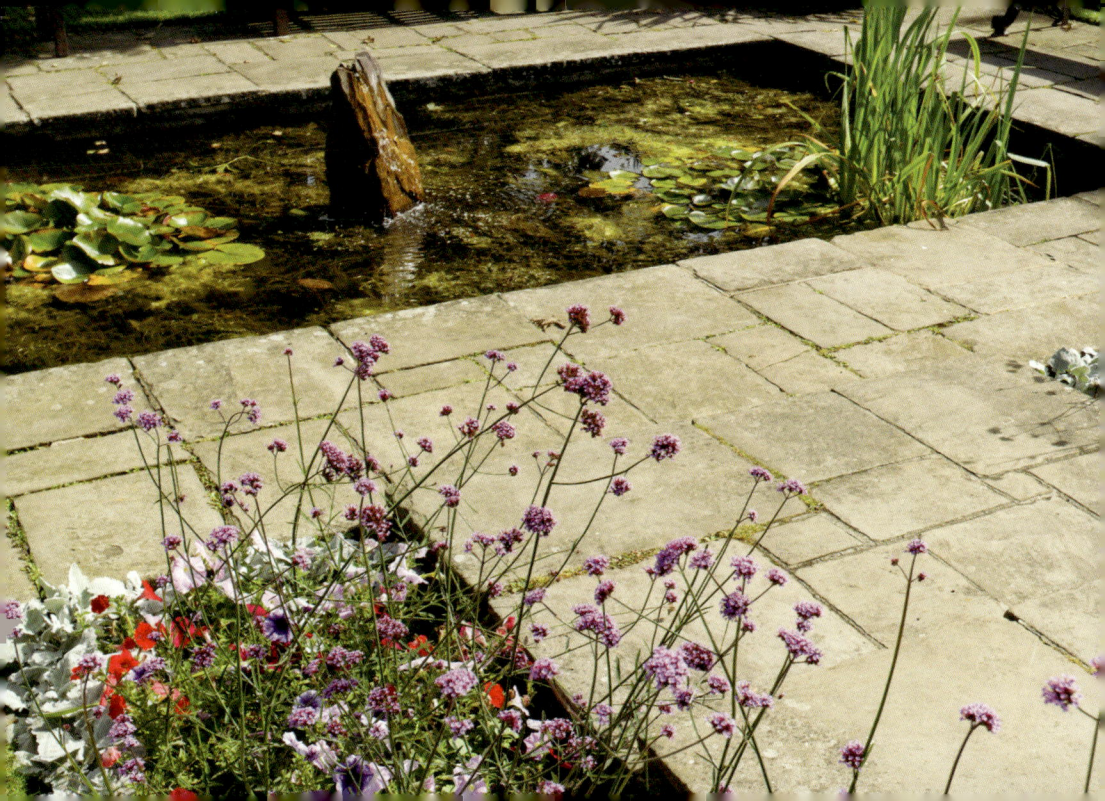

I used to go the Girls' Grammar School in Coolinge Lane in the 1960s and, at that time, The Old High Street had a reputation as somewhere nice girls didn't venture, and we were all banned from going down there in our school uniforms – so as soon as we were out of school, the 'cinema seat' blue crimpolene uniform skirt was rolled up, the blouse pulled out, top buttons undone, and we were straight down the road and into Archie's coffee bar, half way down the High Street, as it was known then. This is supposedly where all the illegal shenanigans went on, what fun!

सन १९६० को दशकमा Old High Street मा राम्रा केटीहरु जादैन थिए । हामीहरुलाई स्कूलको लुगा लगाएर त्यहाँ जान निसेध गरिएको थियो । त्यसैले हामी बाटोमा अर्को लुगा फेरेर Archie को कफि पसलमा जाने गर्दथ्यौं । यो धेरै राम्रो थियो भन्ने हामी सोच्यौं । सुरक्षाको दृष्टिकोणले यहाँ खतरा छ भन्ने भनाई थियो ।

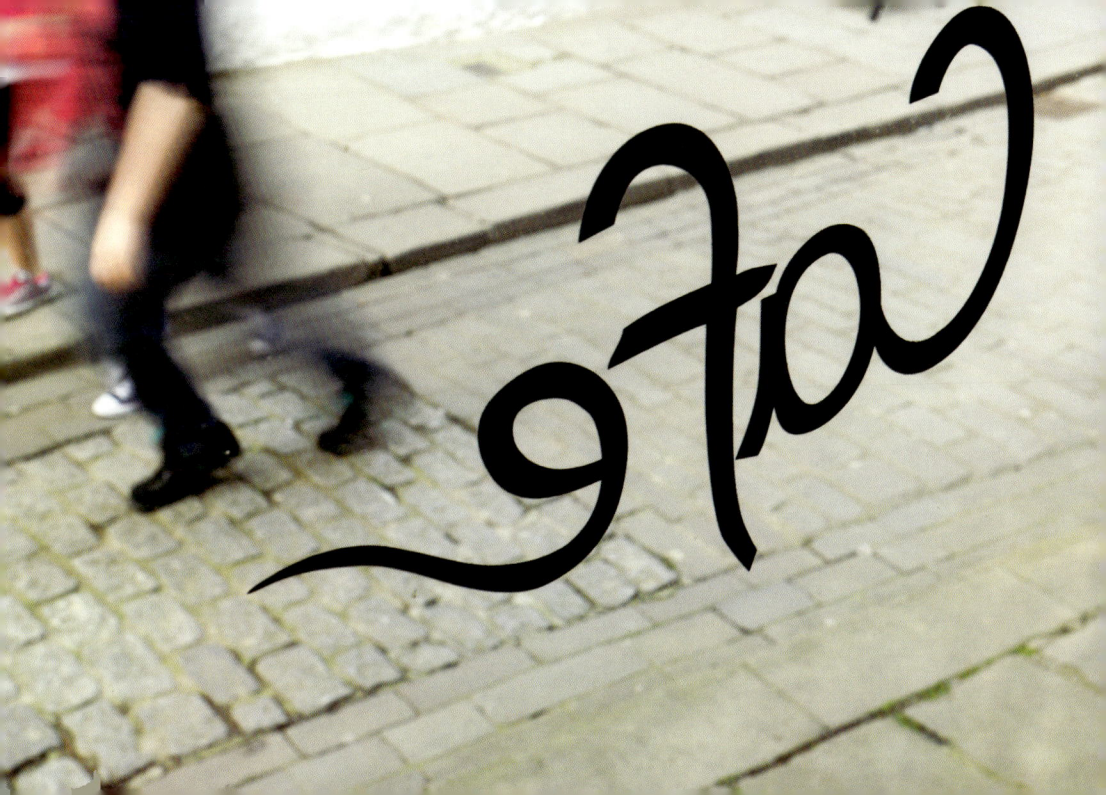

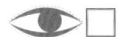

Following a reprinting of James Joyce's book *Ulysses* 500 copies were seized by New York police in 1920; customs men at Folkestone Harbour seized and burned the reprinted copies, because the final chapters were said to contain obscenities.

James Joyce को पुन: प्रकाशित पुस्तक *Ulysses* को ५०० प्रति सन १९२० मा न्यूयोर्कका प्रहरीले कब्जामा लिए पछी फोक्सटन बन्दरगाहका भन्सार प्रमुखले उक्त पुस्तक कब्जा गरी जलाई दिएका थिए किनभने उक्त पुस्तकको अन्तिम अध्यायमा त्रुटिपूर्ण लेख लेखिएको थियो ।

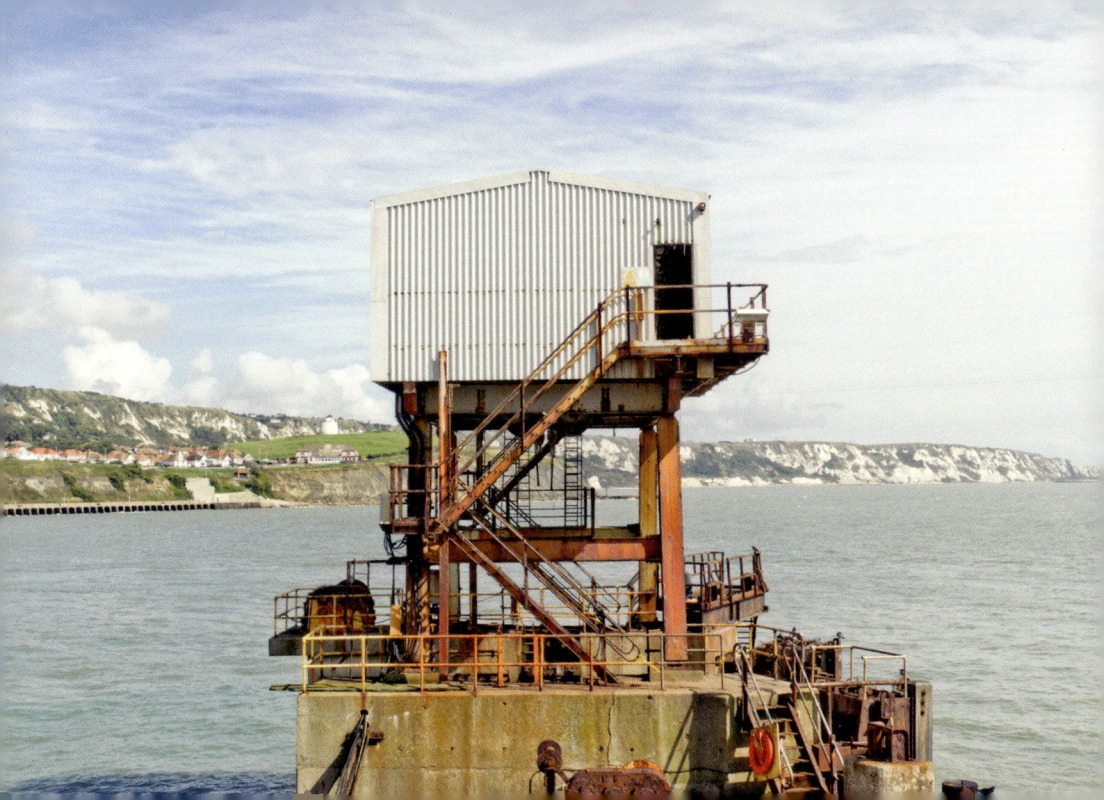

When I was working for the council, two of our employees who had their office at Philippa House became very worried about sightings of a ghost, which kept appearing in a particular corridor. She appeared to be waiting for someone.

It was suspected that she was the spirit of the nursing sister who used to be in charge of the isolation hospital, which had once stood on the site. The sightings became so frequent, and the staff became so anxious, that in the end we had to call in a priest to exorcise the spirit.

It appeared to have worked, as she was never sighted again.

एकान्त स्थानमा भएको यो अस्पतालमा मृतात्माले सताउने गर्दथ्यो । त्यो मृतात्मा सोही अस्पतालमा कामगर्ने एक प्रमुख नर्शको थियो । एकपटक त्यो किचकन्नेलाई अस्पतालको नजिकै उभिएको देखियो । त्यसपछि पटक पटक देखिन थालेपछि कर्मचारीहरु आतंकित हुन थाले । अन्ततः एउटा धामी बोलाएर मृतात्मालाई नष्ट गरियो ।

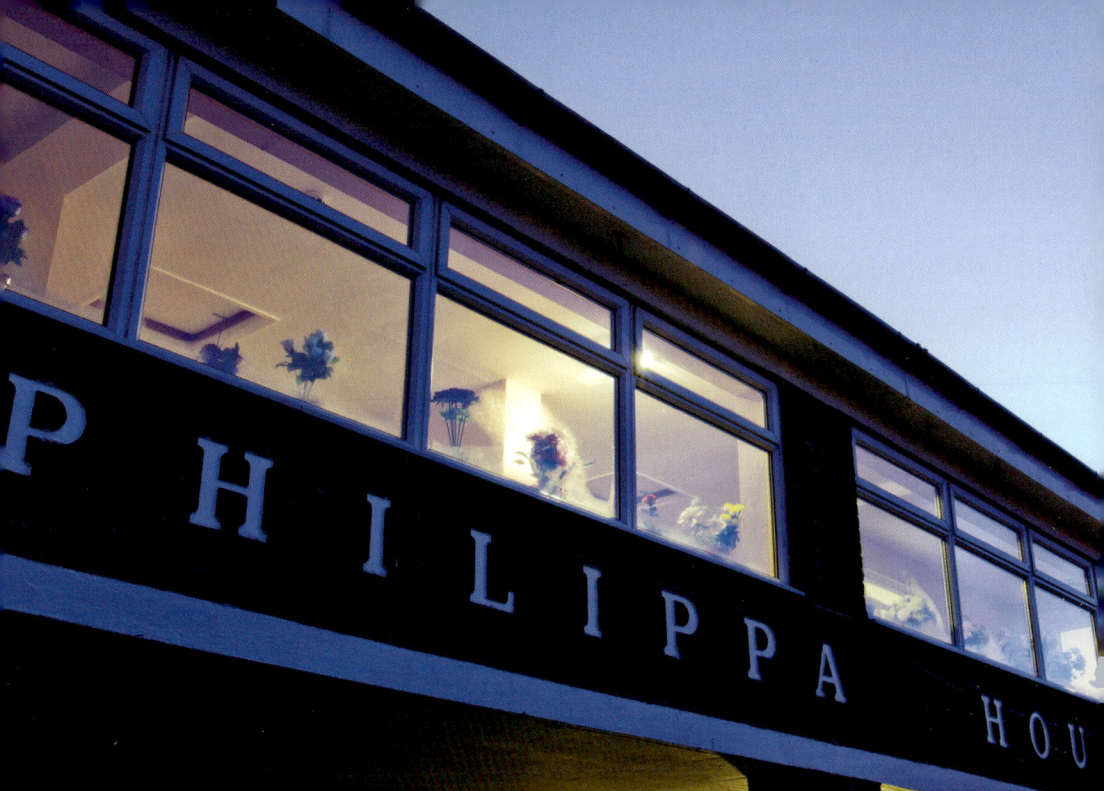

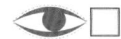
One of my favourite observations on the Old High Street is on the hare and girl statue – it had large pink bubblegum nipples in the summer and blue bubblegum in the winter.

Old High Street मा भएको मुर्ति मलाई मनपर्ने दृश्यावलोकन मध्य एक हो । बसन्त ऋतुमा गुलाफि र ग्रिष्म ऋतुमा निलो रङ्गको ठूलो बबलगम कुनै व्यक्तिले यसलाई दिएको थियो ।

EVERYWHERE MEANS SOMETHING TO SOMEONE

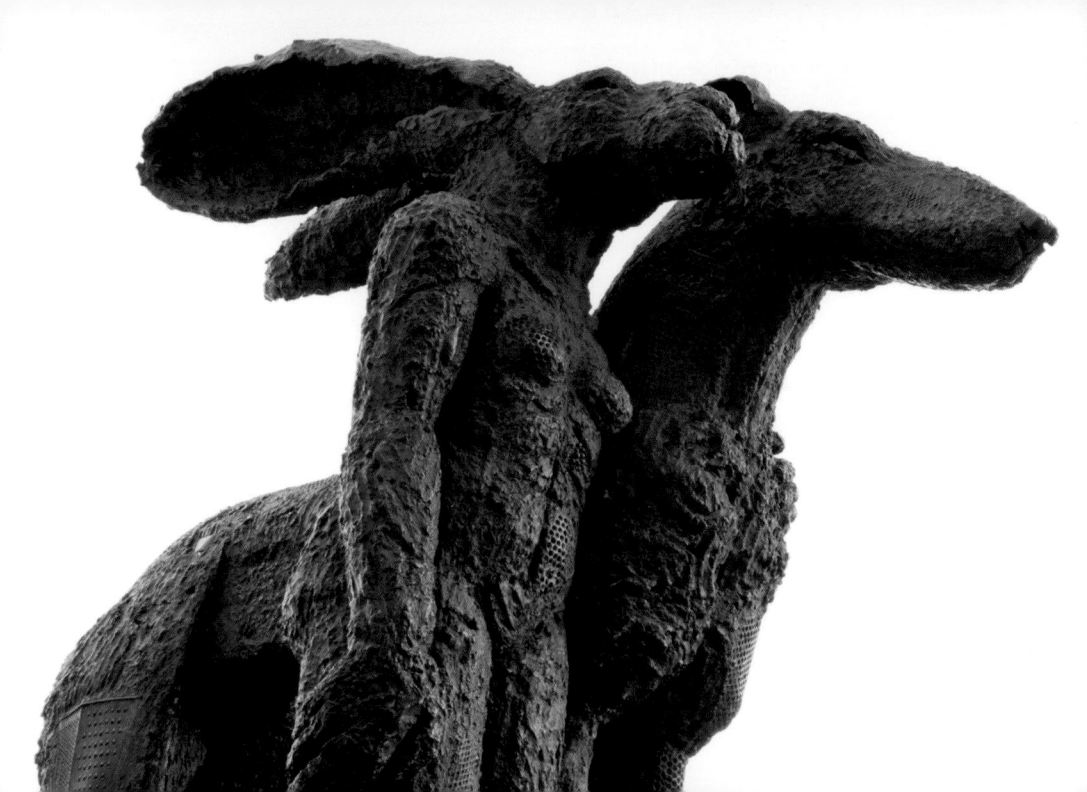

Having left the army years ago, I used to run along the seafront past little Switzerland campsite. Between the end of the campsite and the Samphire Hoe are old walled gardens in the brambles at the edge of the cliff, the houses are just rubble caused by cliff fall or bombing during the war.

There is a rare species of green lizard living on the Warren. When I was little we would find them basking in the sun on the Little Switzerland campsite toilet block walls.

Little Switzerland को क्याम्प क्षेत्रको वरीपरि पुरानो घरहरुको अवशेष छन । समुन्द्रतट भत्किएर वा लडाईमा बलमे गर्दा यस्तो भएको हुनुपर्छ ।

यो ढिस्कनोमा एक प्रकारको हरियो छेपारो बस्ने गर्छ । स्यानोमा म Little Switzerland मा भएको सुची गृहयको भित्तामा मज्जाले घाम तापीरहेको देख्थे ।

Walk up Wear Bay Road past the Martello Tower, pitch & putt golf course and tennis courts. Continue up to where the road bends to the left. Follow the sign to Little Switzerland campsite, down a track that follows the line of the cliffs.

EVERYWHERE MEANS SOMETHING TO SOMEONE

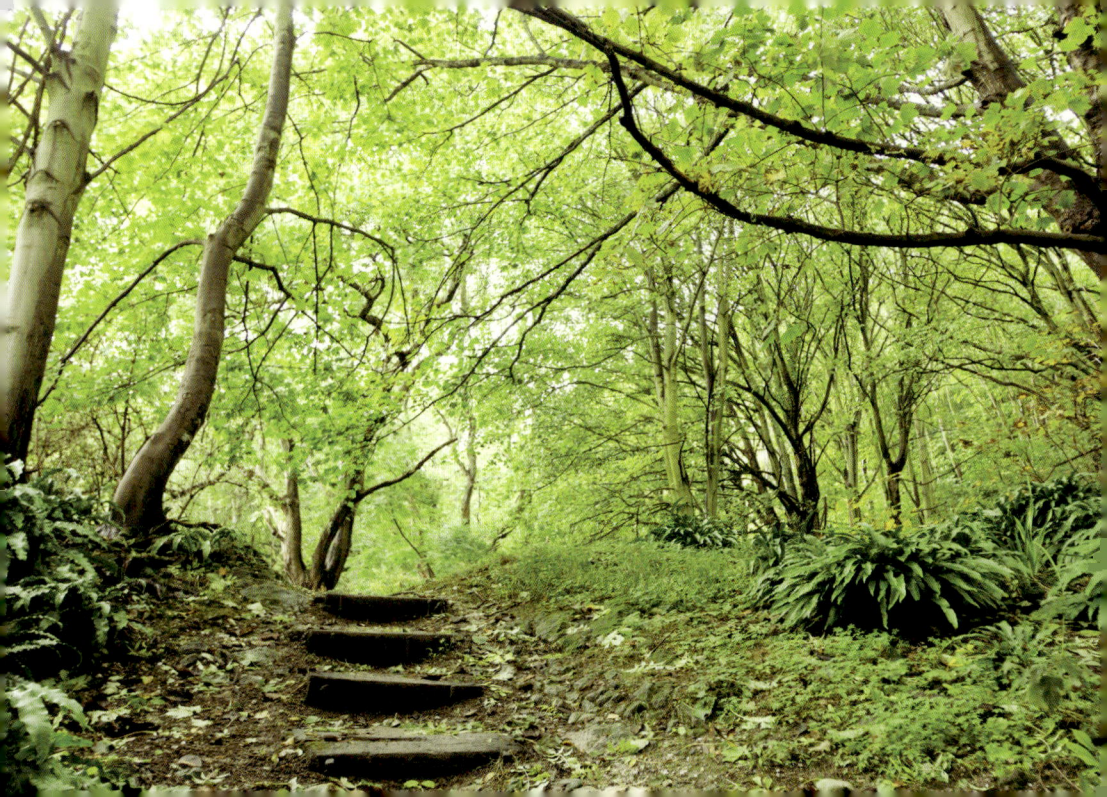

There is a ghost upstairs who appears behind people in their rooms when they are looking in the mirror. She's dressed in a long black Victorian dress.

माथिल्लो तलाको कोठामा मानिसहरुले ऐनामा हेरिरहँदा उनिहरुको पछाडी देखिने एउटा भुत छ । तिनी लामो कालो भिक्टोरि यन लुगामा सजियकी हुन्छन ।

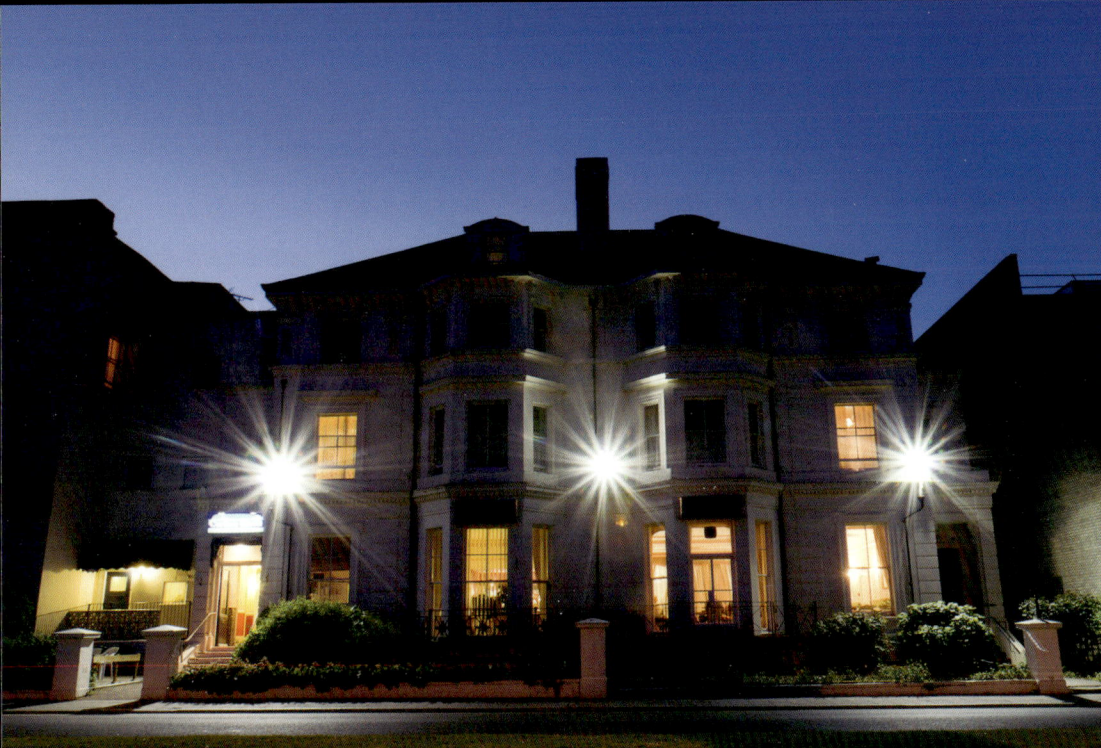

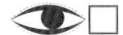

This is all that remains of the two wartime Folkestone East Copt Point Battery sites, which sat alongside each other, facing out to sea, immediately behind the East Cliff Pavilion. These structures are testament to Folkestone's frontline status during the war. One building had a magazine attached where ammunition was stored, but the cliff is crumbling at more than two feet each year, so it's hard to tell how long this will remain intact.

युद्धको समयमा फोक्सटन अग्रिम पङ्क्तीमा थियो । यी भवनहरु सैन्य हातहतियार राख्ने क्षेत्रको अवशेषहरु हुन् ।

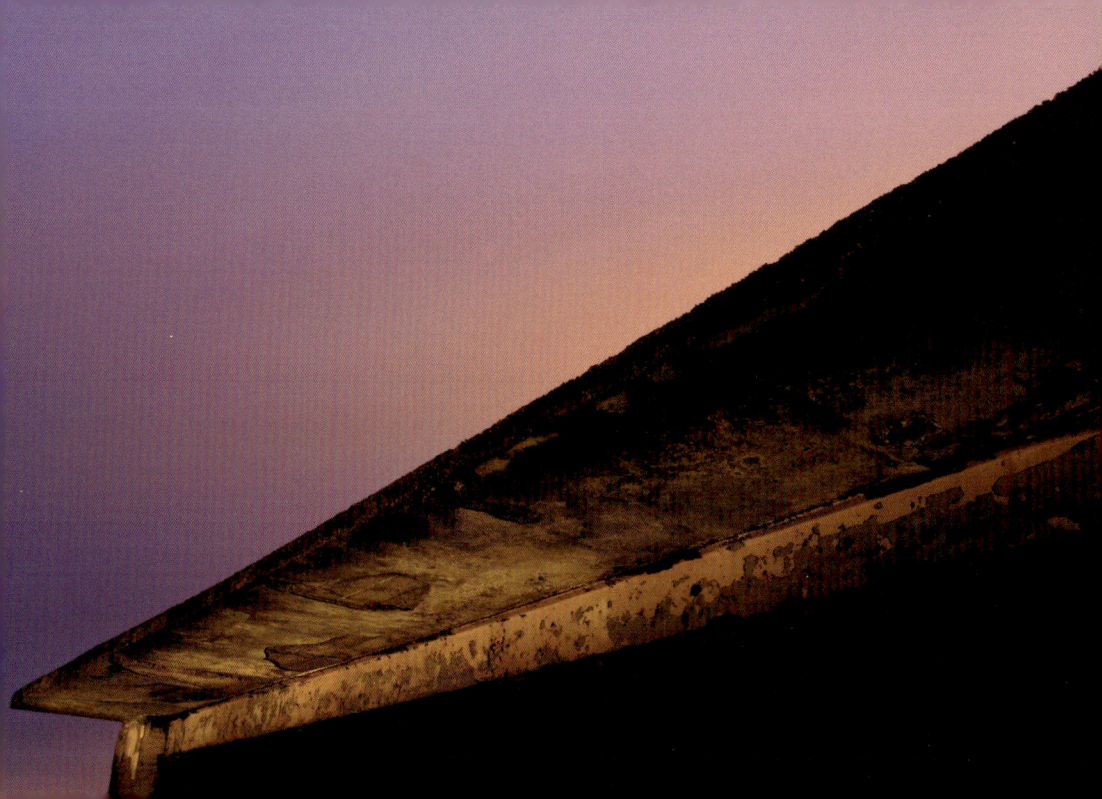

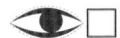

During the war the whole of the beach was mined and out of bounds, so no one was able to go swimming.

युद्धको समयमा समुन्द्रका सम्पूर्ण वगरहरु विस्फोटक पदार्थहरु भरिएको थियो । जसले त्यहाँ पौड़ी खेल्न कोही पनि जान सक्दै नथे ।

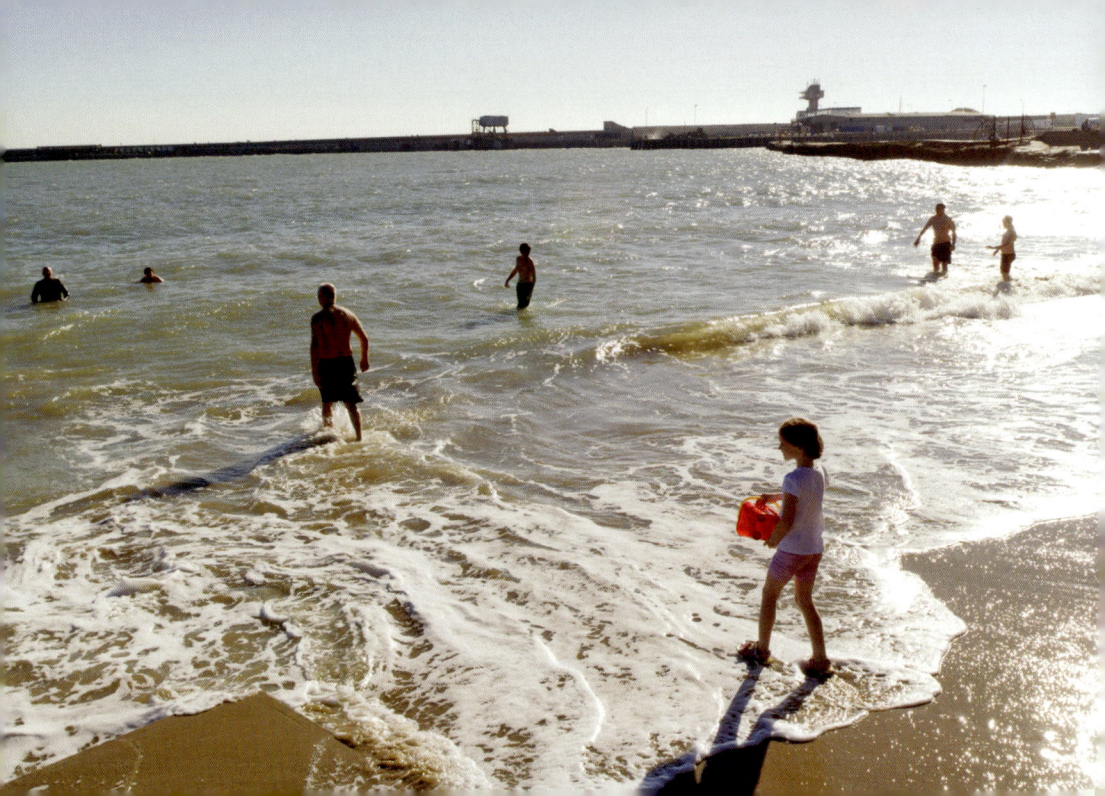

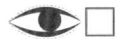

The KFC was once the old Labour Exchange – it is a very austere building and they had very wide counters to stop people climbing over. Some people have memories of times when unemployment was high and huge queues stretched all the way around the corner to the bus station. They were especially busy in the winter, as Folkestone used to have lots of seasonal workers who staffed the hotels and other tourist places, plus people would be laid off over Christmas and holiday periods so that the firms didn't have to pay them.

एक समयमा यो KFC एउटा पुरानो Labour Exchange थियो - बेरोजगारीको संख्या अत्याधिक भएको बेला वस पार्कको छे उछाउ सम्म भिंड लाग्ने गरेको मानिसहरुलाई सम्झना छ ।

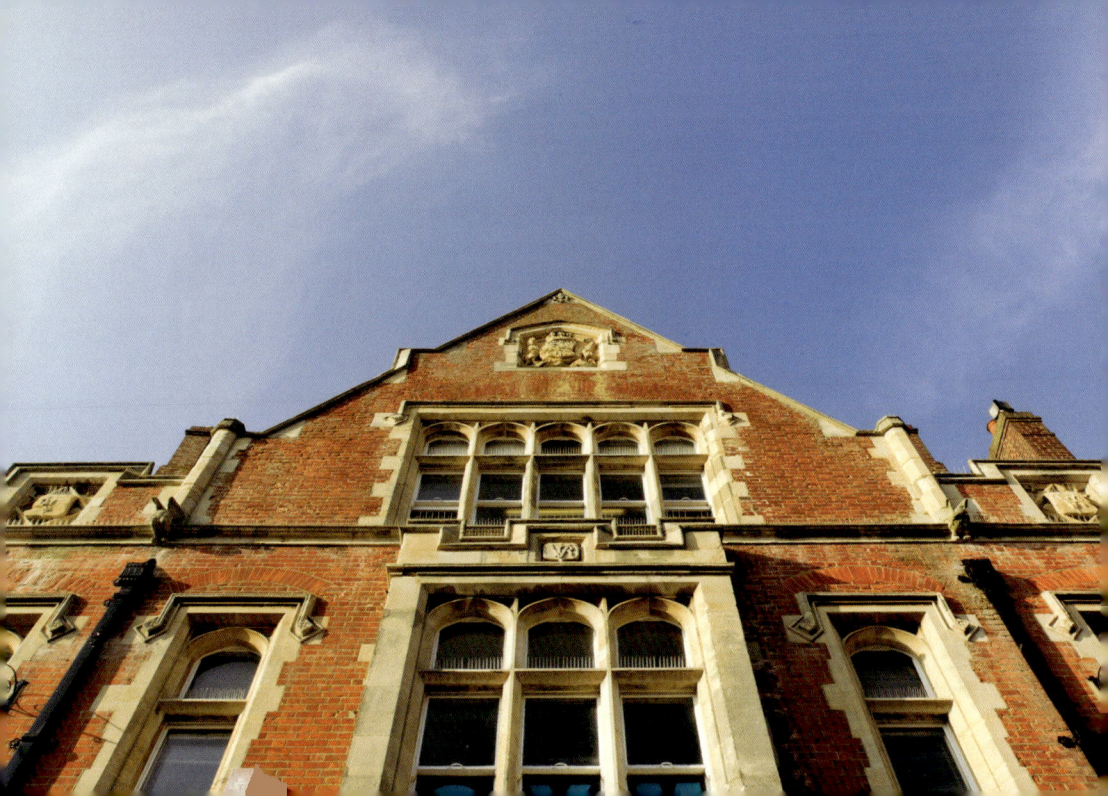

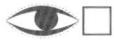

Go to Newington, there's a railway arch there, even though the Newington railway doesn't exist anymore. You can walk to Elham, following the course of the old railway line through all the way to Canterbury – that is where they kept Big Bertha the big gun that was used during the war.

रेल मार्ग नभए पनि Newington मा गयौ भने त्यहाँ रेल छिर्ने पुल छ । यहाँबाट हिंडेर Elham पुग्न सकिन्छ, अझै अगाडी यो पुरानो रेल मार्ग पछ्याउदै गएमा हिँडेर Canterbury पुगिन्छ ।

Drive towards the M20 motorway and take the A20 signposted Newington. After the bridge, turn right and drive through Newington Village. You will see the remains of a bridge over the road, just before the Railway Museum. There are footpaths both sides of the bridge that follow the old tracks.

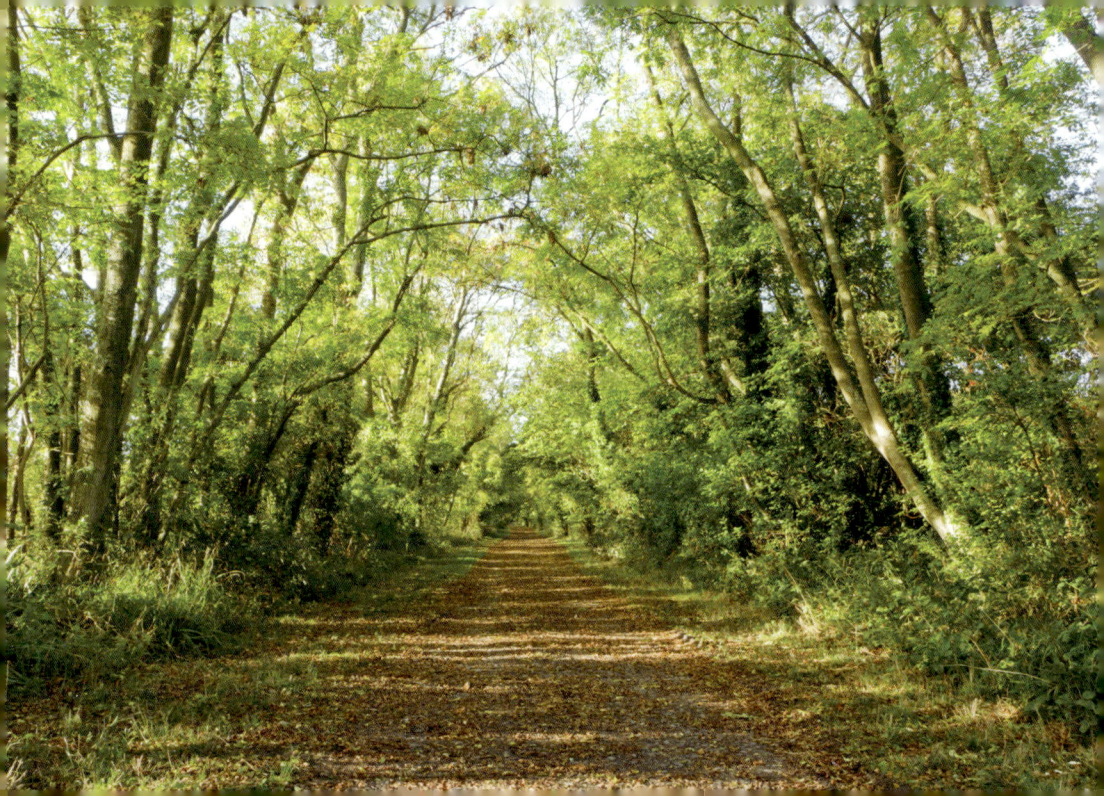

There is a house three doors along from the British Lion that was left in someone's will to two sisters. They fell out and had the house divided in half. That's why the front doors are a little crooked and narrow. It's really quirky inside, the stairs are really twisty and the cottage style garden is split down the middle too. It must be well over 200 years old, looking at the doors.

यी घरहरु दुई दिदी वहिनीहरुका सामुहिक स्वामित्वमा थियो । उनीहरु अलग भएपछि घर पनि दुई भागमा बाँडियो । त्यसले गर्दा घरको अगाडिको ढोका साँगुरो, भित्र पटिको भ-याङ घुमाउरो छन् भने बँगैचालाई पनि मध्य भागबाट विभाजन गरिएको छ । यो २०० वर्ष भन्दा पुरानो हुनसक्छ ।

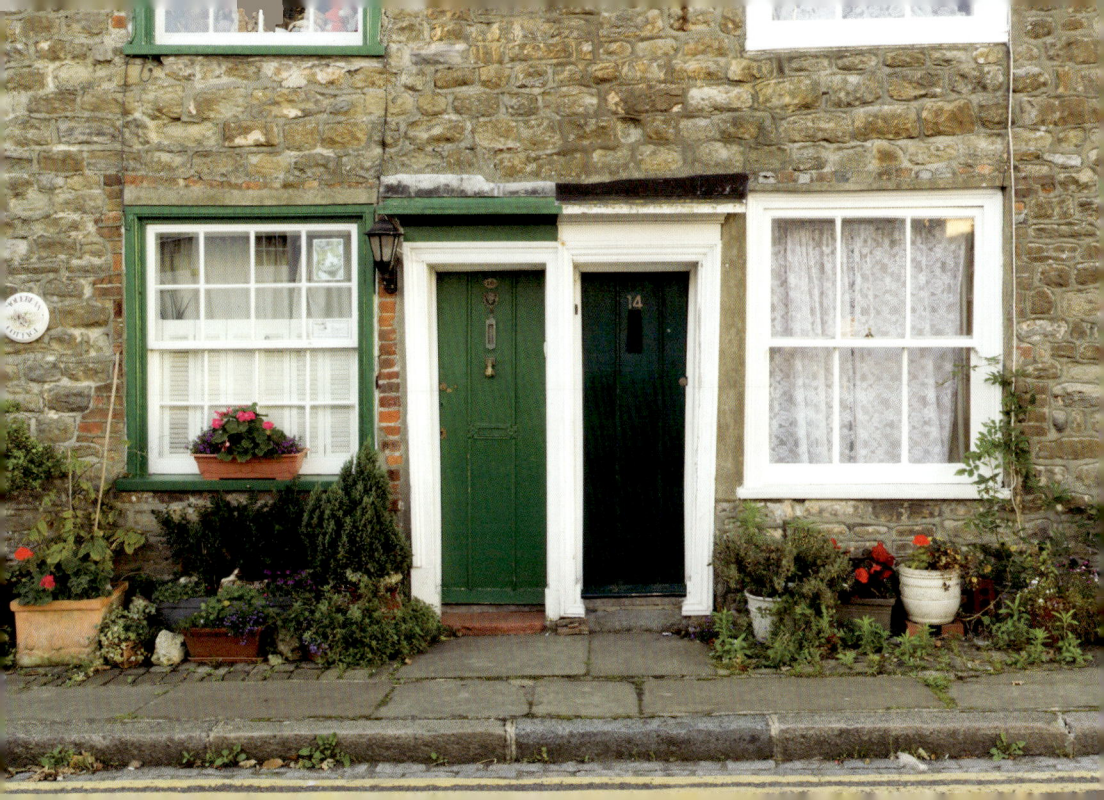

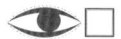

The famous 'Golden Man', who struck the huge gong at the beginning of films by J Arthur Rank was actually the landlord of The Fountain pub in Seabrook. Bombardier Billy Wells had an illustrious life. As well as serving in the army during the war, he was a boxer and was the first man to win the Lonsdale Belt in April 1911. His defence fight, later the same year against American heavyweight Jack Johnson, was cancelled by Home Secretary Winston Churchill, because at the time there was a colour ban. Billy became pub landlord in 1948; the story goes that only a few years earlier, when there was still wartime rationing, The Fountain was only able to open a couple of days a week, because as soon as there was a delivery of beer, the locals would rush in and drink the place dry.

२० औं शताब्दिको मध्यतिर J Arthur Rank को चलचित्रको शुरुमा घण्टी बजाउने एउटा पशिद्ध मानिस थिए । उ सिब्रुकमा भएको Fountain पवका धनी र एउटा मुक्केवाज पनि थिए ।

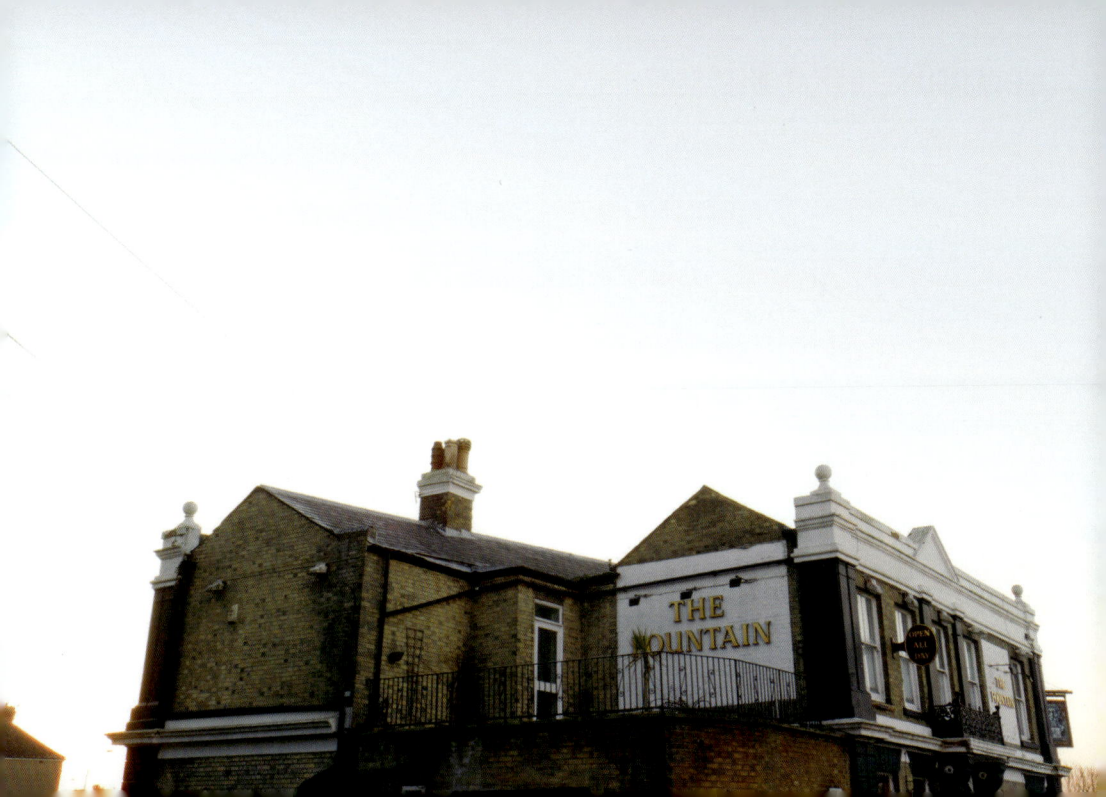

There is a cemetery at the sharp bend in the road at Shorncliffe army camp where 290 Canadian soldiers are buried. On Canada Day, on 1 July, children from the local schools take flowers up and celebrate and commemorate the soldiers who died in the wars by laying flowers on the graves. A number of years ago, a group of children were invited up to meet the Queen at Buckingham Palace because of this important connection.

सर्नक्लिफमा २९० जना क्यानाडाको सिपाही गाडिएको एउटा चिहान घारी छ । १ जुलाईमा क्यानाडा दिवसको दिन स्थानिय केटाकेटीहरु उक्त चिहान घारीमा फुलहरु चढाउने गर्दछन् ।

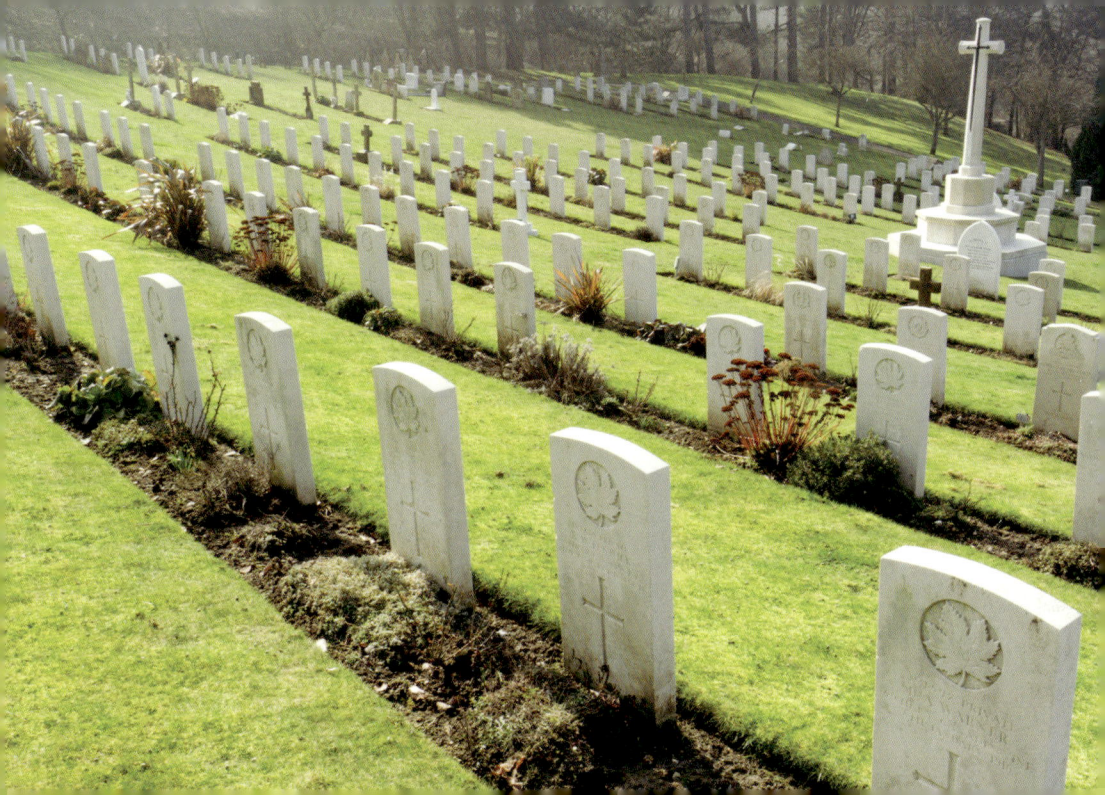

My parents moved to Folkestone in 1972 and bought a town house which straddled Radnor Bridge Road and Ryland Place. The trains still used to run down to the harbour then along Tram Road and their clackety-clack on the tracks would lull me to sleep.

When the fog horn sounded mournfully off the lighthouse through the pea soupers that besieged the coast, I would burrow down into my bed and imagine (as the house was right at the beginning of the row and my room the topmost, front bedroom) that I was at the prow of an enormous ship, sailing across an unknown sea to a distant shore. I had an active imagination and I spent endless, glorious days galloping on an imaginary white horse, across the East Cliff that subsided languorously onto Sunny Sands beach. Here I would build hideouts and catch grass snakes in tin can traps (thankfully never a single adder) and plant grass seeds that grew into hilltop crops for my splendid mount to feed on; here I would survey the curve of the harbour as if I were its Queen. These were without doubt the happiest and most carefree days of my life.

सानो छँदा कुहिरो लागेको समयमा सामुन्द्री जहाजमा बजाईने सांकेतिक आवाज मन पराउँथे । आवाज बजेको बेला म ओछ्यानमा गुटुमुटु भएर जहाजमा भएको कल्पना गर्थें ।

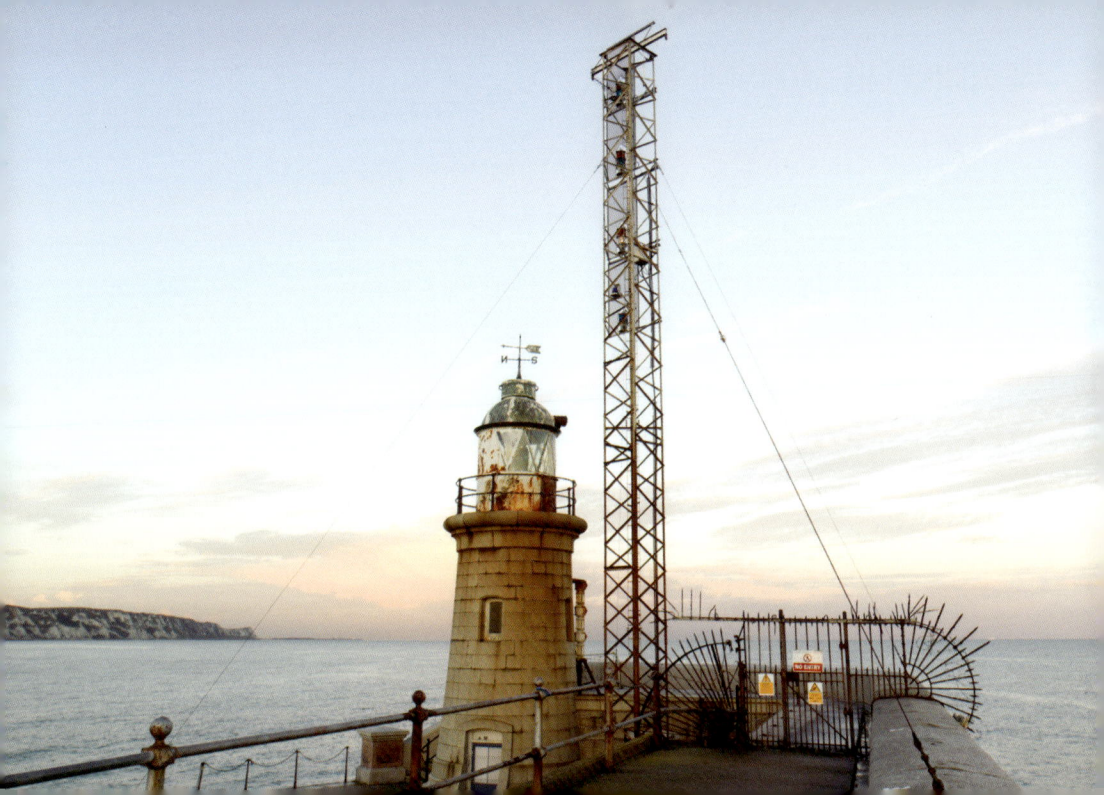

The Mermaid café is part of Folkestone's seaside heritage and has been there forever. My grandmother used to work at the Mermaid Café in the late 1920s. She would sometimes take my mother to work with her, and if the owner came in she would hide her under the counter.

मेरो हजुरआमा १९२० को दशकमा Mermaid Café मा काम गर्नुहुन्थ्यो । कहिले काहिँ मेरी आमालाई पनि काममा लिएर जानुहुन्थ्यो । होटल मालिक आएको वेलामा भने आमालाई टेवल मुनि लुकाउनु हुन्थ्यो ।

EVERYWHERE MEANS SOMETHING TO SOMEONE

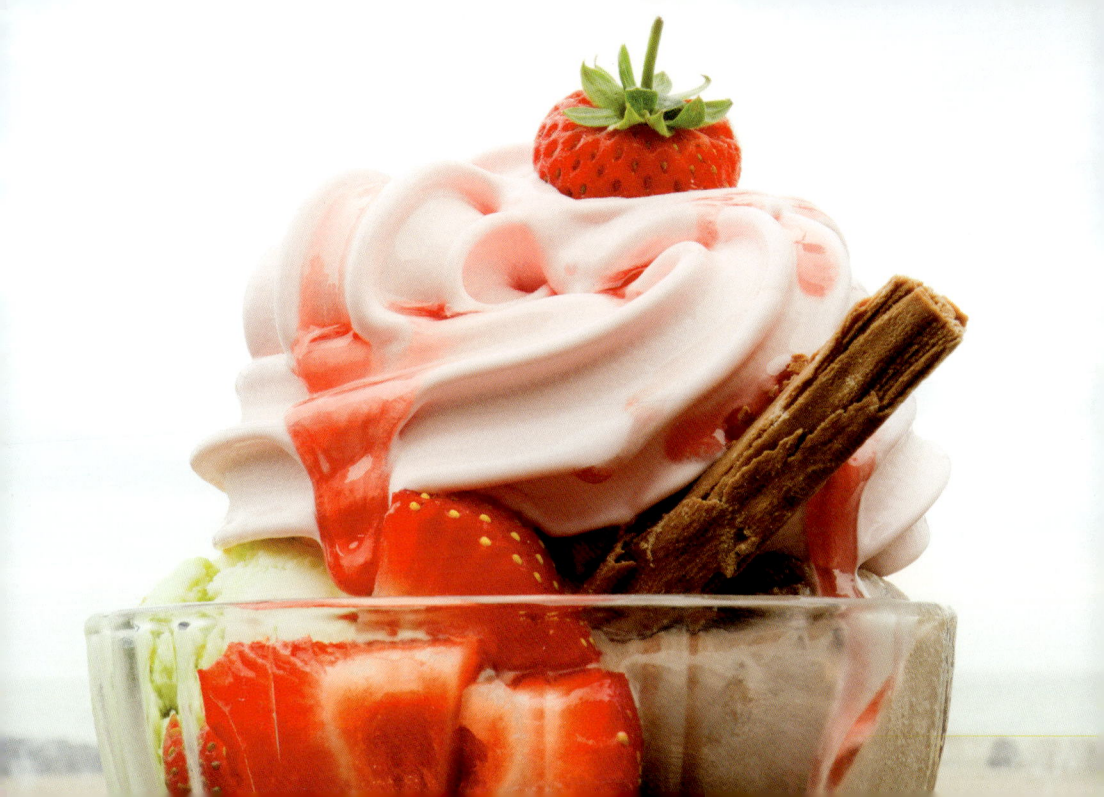

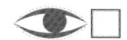

We have a ghost that has been seen on the right hand side of the Hotel, it's believed to be a former occupant, a man who used to own that part of the building before it became a hotel.

यो होटलमा एउटा भूत छ । जो यो होटलको दायाँ पट्टीको भागमा देखा पर्दथ्यो । यो घर होटलमा परिणत हुनु पूर्व त्यो मृतआत्मा उक्त घरको धनी थियो भन्ने विश्वास गरिन्छ ।

EVERYWHERE MEANS SOMETHING TO SOMEONE

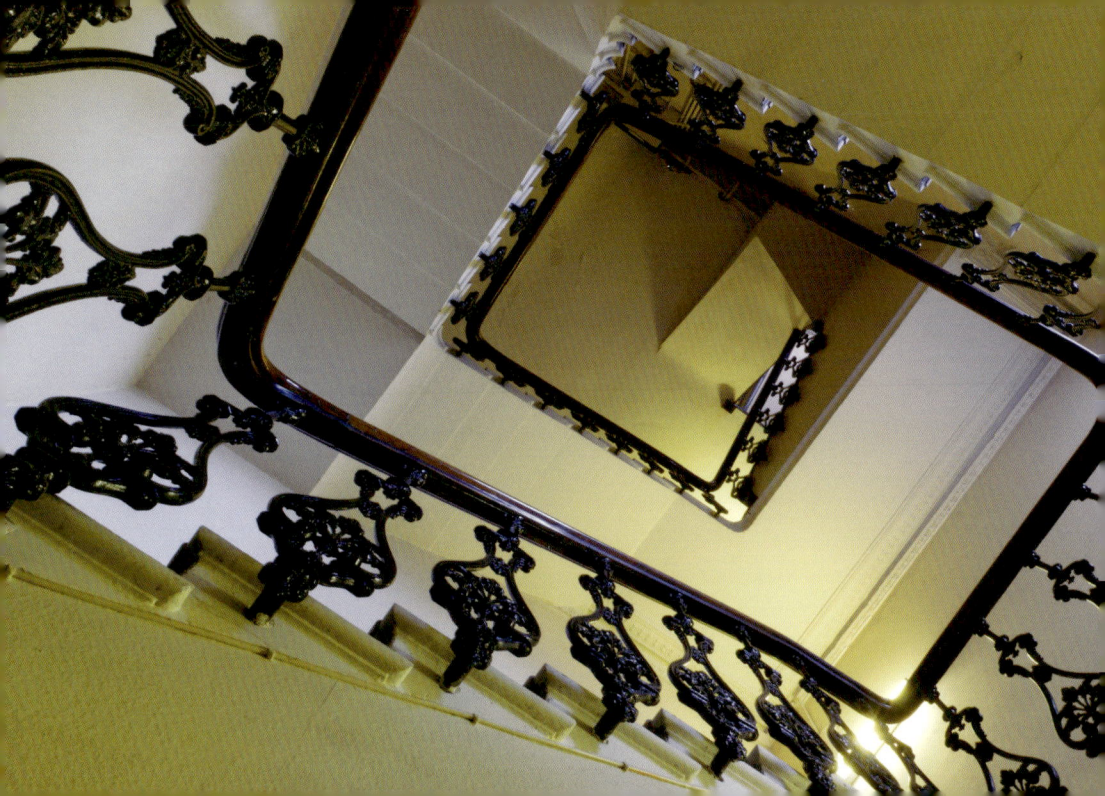

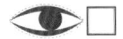

This pub is the oldest pub in Folkestone. The oldest part of the pub is the large beam that runs over the bar and into the cottage next door. It was carbon dated at 460 years old.

यो पव फोक्स्टनको सबैभन्दा पुरानो पव हो । यो पवको सबैभन्दा पुरानो भाग भनेको ठूलो दलिन हो । यो दलिन बारको माथिबाट भएर अर्को घरसम्म पुगेको छ । यस दलिनमा ४६० वर्ष पुरानो भन्ने छापिएको थियो ।

EVERYWHERE MEANS SOMETHING TO SOMEONE

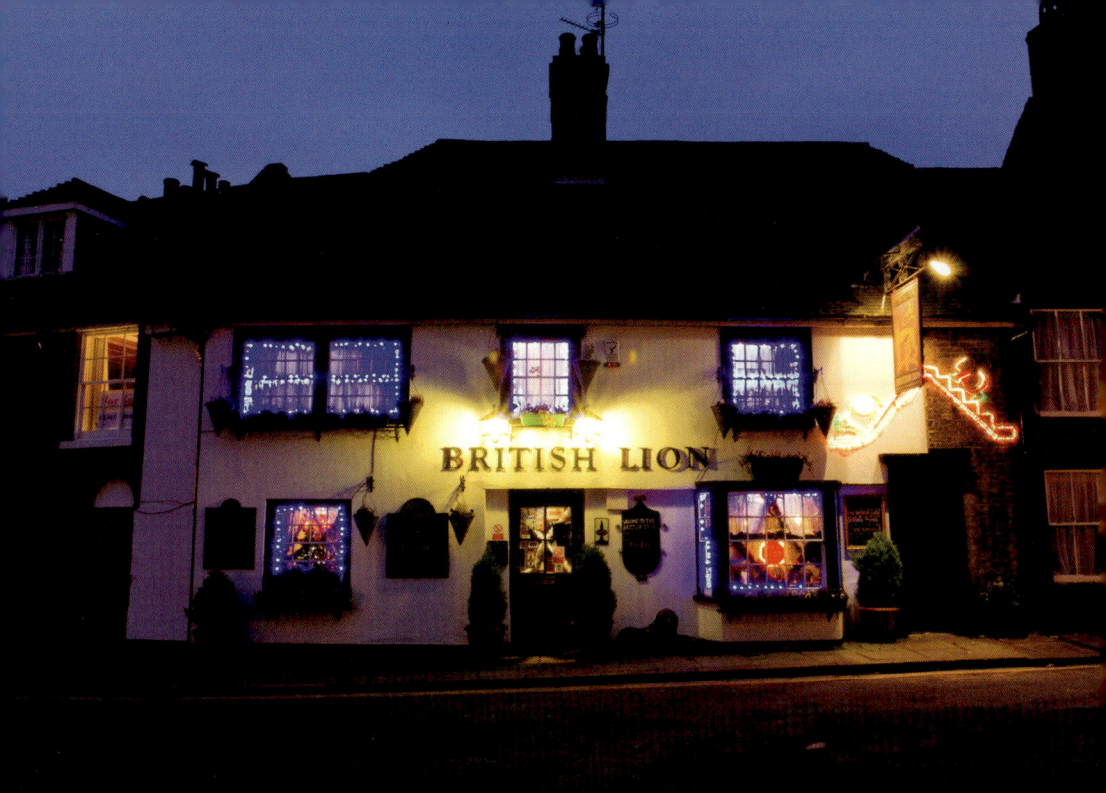

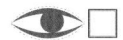

I used to go to the Harvey Grammar School and our cross county run would take us up Cherry Garden Avenue, along the tree lined cart track, up Sugar Loaf Hill, along the tank traps to Caesar's Camp before heading back to school.

I don't know if the tank traps were actually to stop tanks or whether that's just what we called them.

पहिला स्कुले जीवनमा हामी Caesar को क्याम्प सम्म दगुर्ने गर्दथ्यौं । मलाई थाहा छैन, वास्तवमा त्यो ट्यांकरहरुलाई रोक्नको लागि थियो अथवा हामीहरुलाई त्यत्तिकै त्यस्तो भन्ने गर्दथ्यौं ।

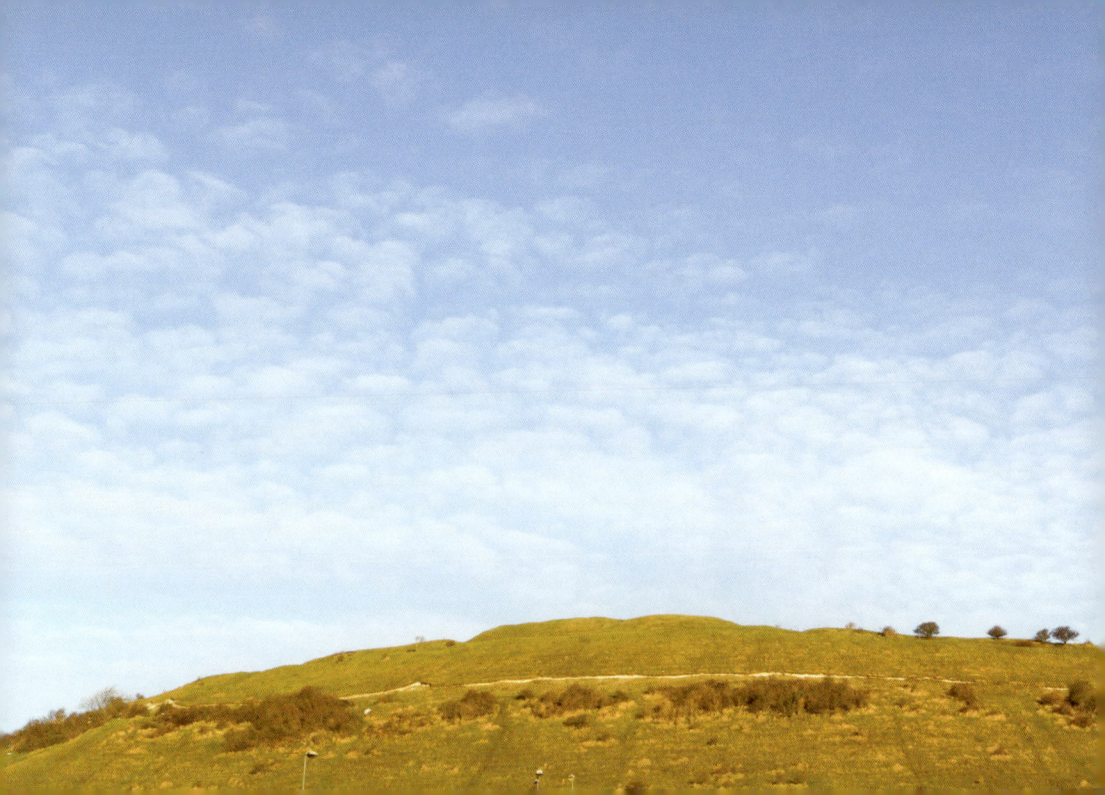

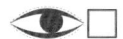

We have lots of sporting groups who return every year. The Essex cricket team, The Freebooters, have been coming to Folkestone for 80 years and staying at The Langhorne Hotel for 20 years. They come in the first week of July and play Folkestone. They keep their Memorabilia here; there are old suitcases full of old photographs, reels of films of past games and beautiful old score books. Coming to Folkestone is a tradition for many of the older men and they love to spend their time looking through the photographs and catching up with each other.

Essex का क्रिकेट समूह Freebooters ८० वर्ष देखि फोक्सटनमा क्रिकेट खेल्न आईरहेका छन् । उनीहरु यहाँ आउँदा २० वर्षदेखि Langhorne Hotel मा नै बस्ने गरेका छन् । उनीहरु एउटा पुरानो बाकसमा पुरानो फोटोहारु, पहिले पहिलेका खिचिएको खेलका रिलहरु र राम्रो अंक प्राप्त गरेको वारेमा लेखिएका कितावहरु होटलमा राख्छन् ।

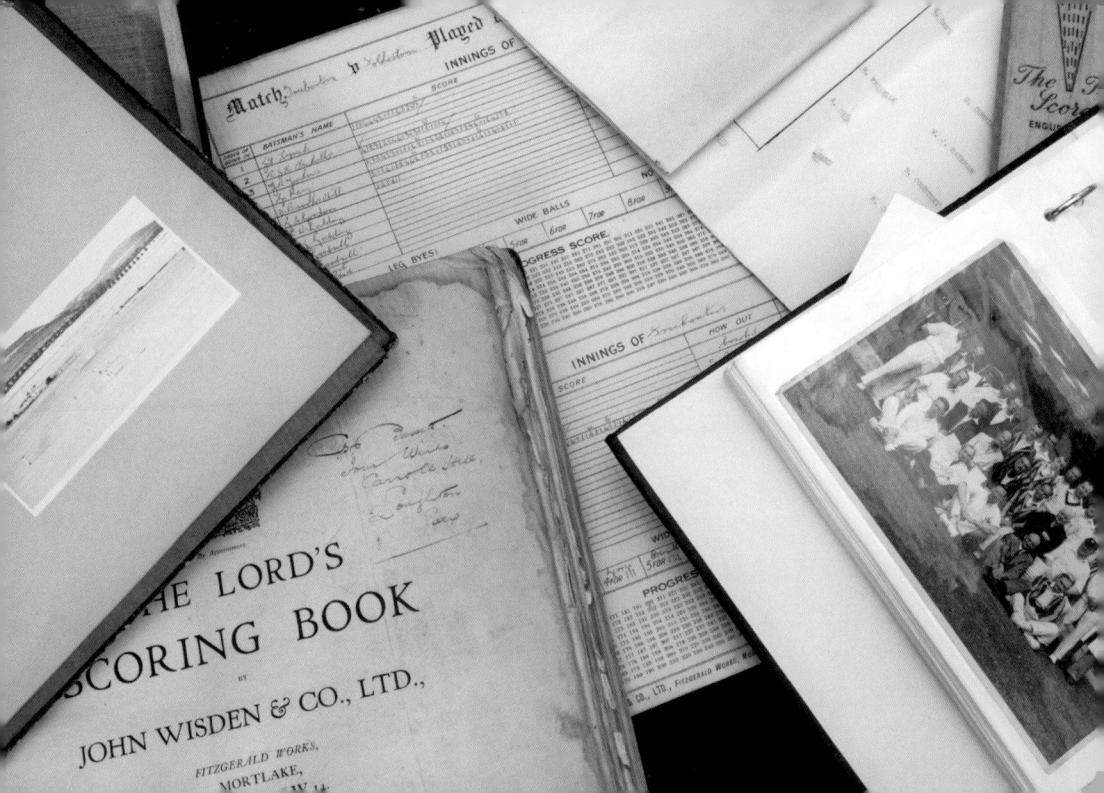

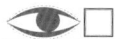

This little plaque is a poignant reminder of the happenings of 25 May 1917. It was a sunny spring day, and the shops in Tontine Street were doing a brisk trade. It was Bank Holiday weekend and many shoppers were purchasing extra provisions for the holiday. An aeroplane circled overhead but few were concerned, as most thought the plane was 'one of ours' from Dover. So the people of Folkestone were taken completely by surprise when the Gotha planes swooped down on the town, dropping their loads of high explosive bombs.

The aeroplanes made their way across from the town centre and dropped a bomb directly outside Stokes Brothers greengrocers causing majority fatalities.

Nearly 60 were killed instantly, many others died later from their injuries and over 100 suffered recorded wounds, although it is thought many more were injured. For those who witnessed it, the carnage was so appalling it could never be forgotten. The land has never been built on permanently since, in memory of those who died.

सन २५ मे १९१७ मा हवाई जहाजहरुले Tontine Street को बाहिरी भागमा बम खसाएका कारण दुर्घटनामा परि महिला तथा बालबच्चाहरुको ठुलो संख्यामा हताहत भएका थिए । उनीहरु सुर्योदयको समयमा खेलिरहेका थिए । झण्डै ७० जनाको तत्कालै मृत्यु भएको थियो । बाँकी रहेका धेरै घाईते मानिसहरु पछि मरे भने १०० जना भन्दा बढी घाउचोटले थलिएका तथ्याङ्क राखिएको थियो ।

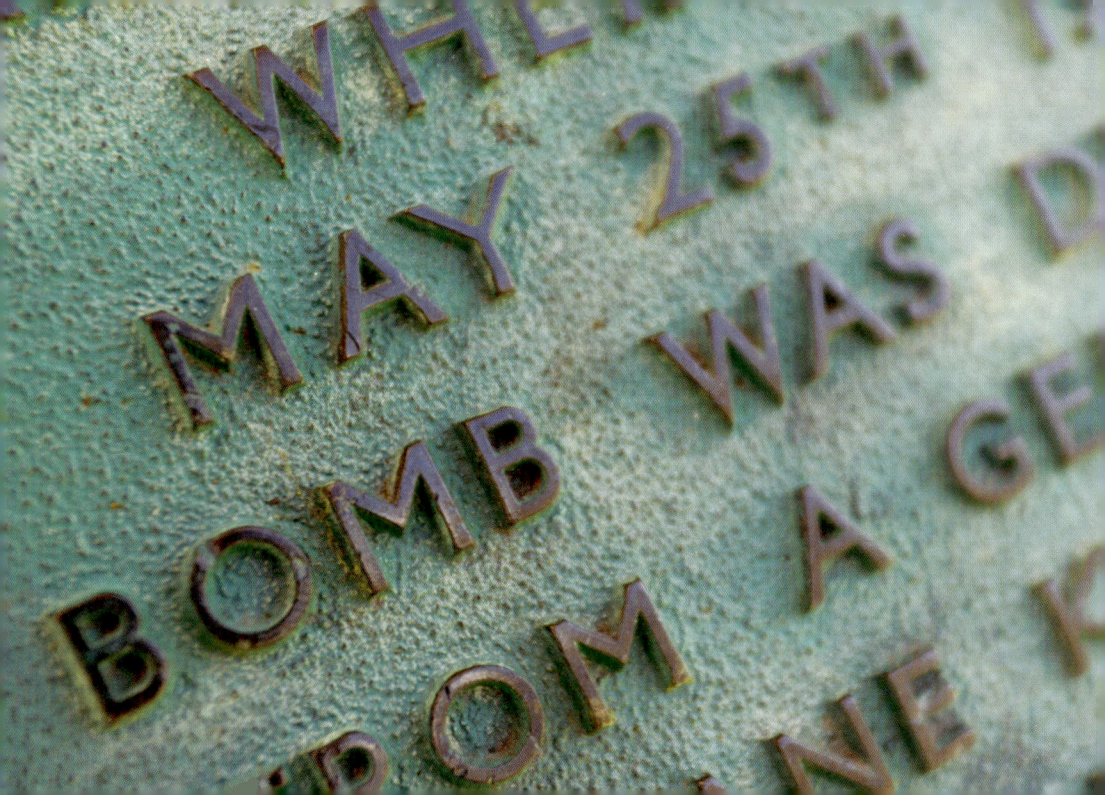

At the root of Folkestone Pier is the old Trinity House Pilot Station, a building with a tall conning tower. From 1514, when they received their charter from Henry VIII, the Cinque Ports Pilots served shipping entering and leaving the Thames & Medway from boats operating close to Dungeness, but based in Dover. During the 60s my uncle, Harry Garner, persuaded Trinity House to build a permanent shore-based Pilot Station at Folkestone. That office was opened in 1971, and continued as the London (South) Pilot Station until 1988 when the national Pilotage Service was dismantled. I was the last Duty Pilot at our Station, and at midnight on September 30 1988 I officially signed off over the radio, switched off the generators, locked the front door, and handed the keys over to the Manager of the Port of Folkestone, to whom we were forced to give the building. Trinity House Pilotage Service ceased to exist after 474 years. The last Pilot to ship inwards from Folkestone to London was Terry Connell.

During the 1987 hurricane the Pilot Station, having its own power generator, played a pivotal role in assisting shipping in our area.

यो निर्देशन गर्ने एउटा टावर हो । यहाँ काम गर्ने मानिसहरुले हावा चलेको समयमा डुंगाहरुलाई बन्दरगाहमा सुरक्षित तरिकाले राख्न जानकारी दिने गर्दथे ।

EVERYWHERE MEANS SOMETHING TO SOMEONE

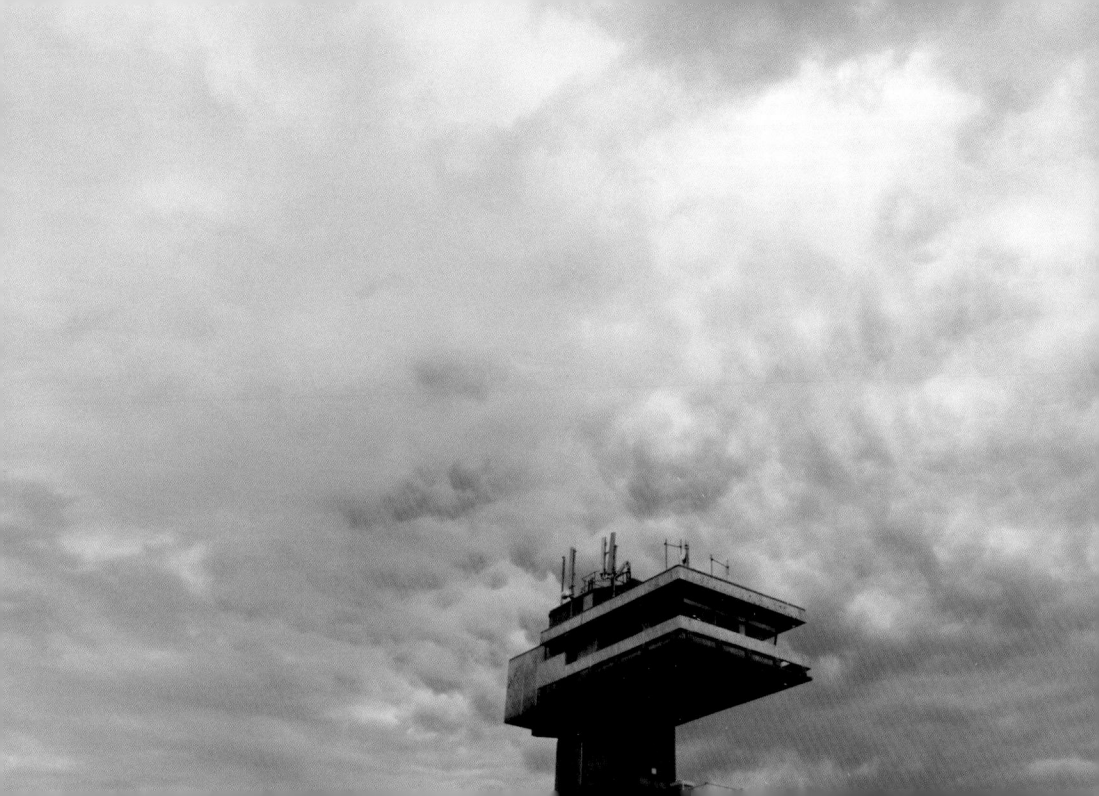

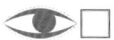

Every October Trafalgar Day is celebrated in a morning service run by the Royal Navy Association at St Peter's Church overlooking the Harbour in Folkestone, and a mid afternoon commemorative parade by East Kent Sea Cadets, from Victory House in Castle Hill Avenue to St Eanswythe's Parish Church. Trafalgar Day is the celebration of the victory won by Vice-Admiral Horatio Nelson's British fleet over the combined French and Spanish fleets at the Battle of Trafalgar on 21 October in 1805.

प्रत्येक अक्टोवर महिनामा St Peter's गिर्जाघरमा Royal Navy Association ले Trafalgar Day उत्सव मनाउने गर्दछन् । यस अवसरमा Castle Hill Avenue देखी St Eanswythe's Parish Church सम्म पैदल यात्रा गरेर मनाईन्छ । Trafalgar Day भनेको २१ अक्टोवर 1805 को Trafalgar को युद्धमा फ्रान्सेली र स्पेनी नौसेनाहरुलाई नेल्सनको वेलायती नौसेनाले पर ाजित गरी विजय प्राप्त गरेको दिनको सम्झना स्वरुप उत्सव मनाईन्छ ।

EVERYWHERE MEANS SOMETHING TO SOMEONE

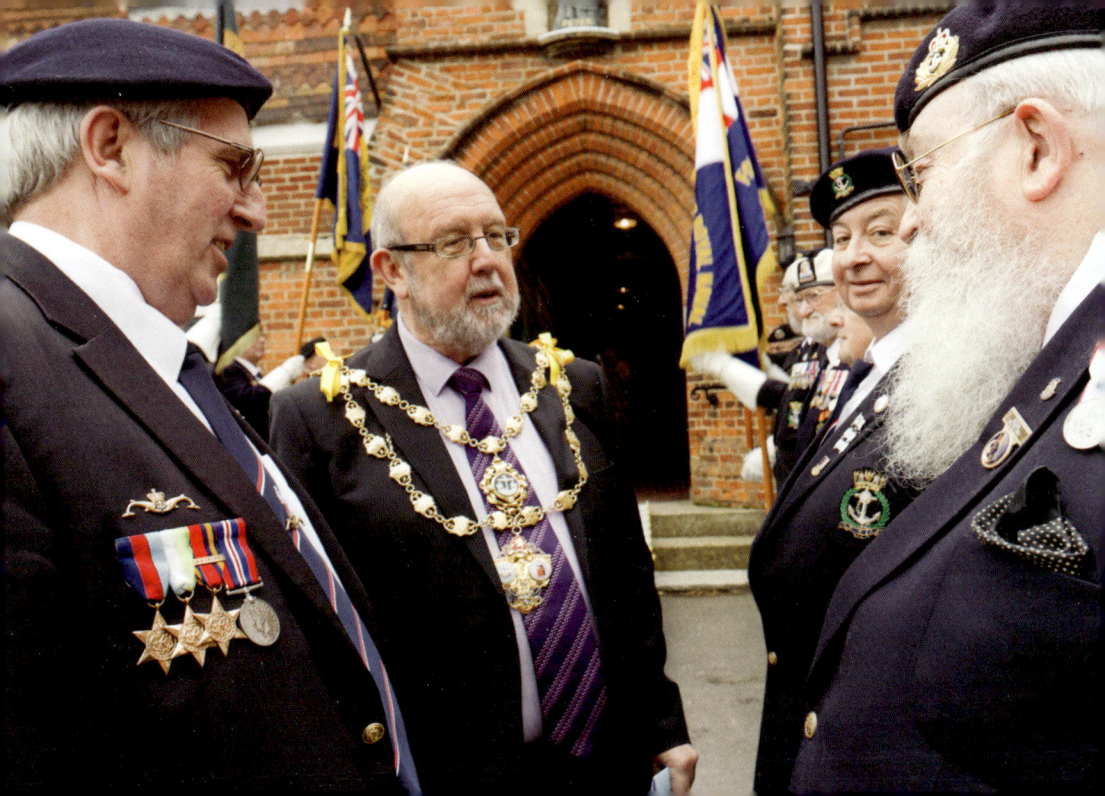

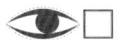

On the 2nd Sunday in June, Folkestone celebrates the life of its most famous citizens. William Harvey, one of seven sons, was born in Folkestone on 1 April 1578. He went to school in Canterbury and studied in Cambridge and Italy before becoming a doctor and lecturer in London. He discovered the circulation of the blood and published a seminal book *Concerning the Motion of the Heart and Blood in Animals* in 1628.

He left money in his will for the founding of the The Harvey Grammar School for Boys in Folkestone, which opened in 1674 and has a continuous history to the present day.

William Harvey को जन्म सन १५७८ अप्रिल १ तारिख फोक्सटनमा भएको थियो । उनले शरिरमा रग्त सन्चारको बारेमा पत्ता लगाए र सन १६२८ मा 'Concerning the Concern of the Heart and Blood in Animals' भन्ने किताव प्रकाशन गरेका थिए । उनले फोक्सटनको Harvey Grammar School for Boys को लागि ईच्छा पत्र मार्फत सहयोग राशि छाडेका थिए । यो स्कुल सन १६७४ सालमा शुरु भएको थियो ।

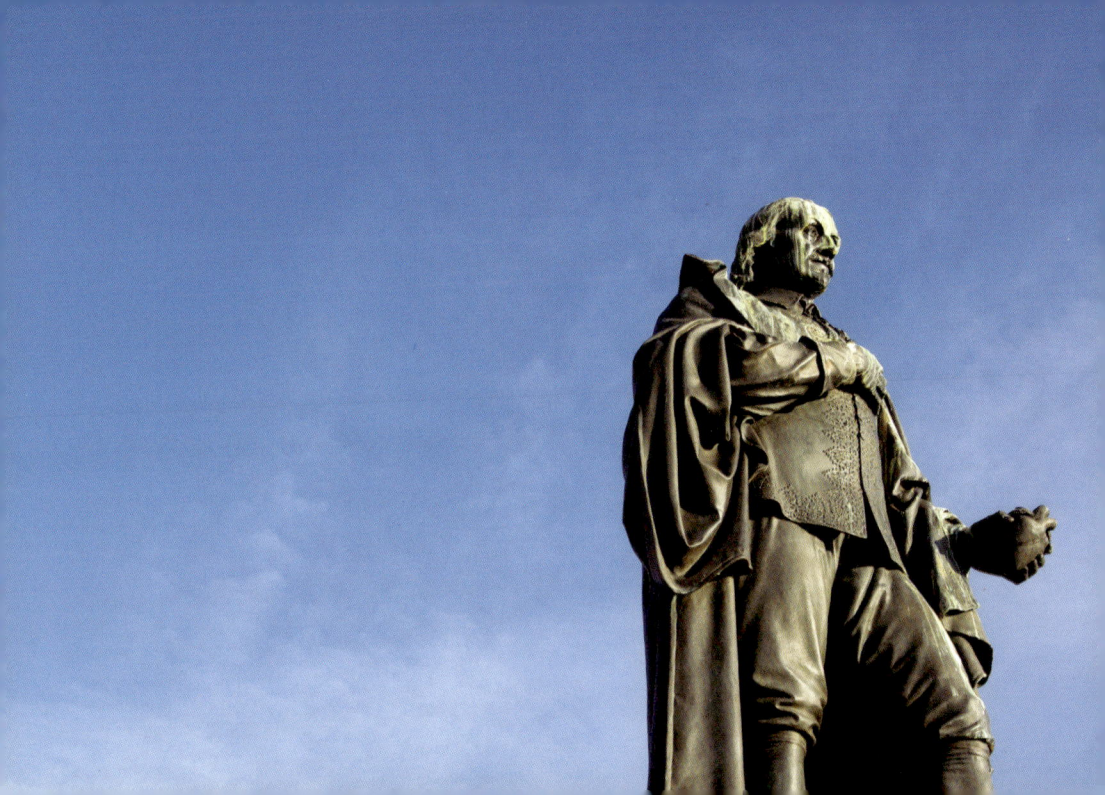

Located in Sandgate Road, with a view of France from the top of the unusual octagonal tower, Holy Trinity Church has a commanding position in the town of Folkestone. It was built by the then Lord Radnor in 1868 as part of the planned expansion of the town, his policy being to build a church every quarter of a mile as the town expanded, so that everyone could walk to church. Does such a policy exist anywhere in the world today?

The church is built of brick with Kentish rag cornerstones, and has clerestory windows, which give it a light feel. It has some exceptional stained-glass windows, including a series depicting the 12 'I am' sayings of Jesus, and an apse, which was magnificently restored for the millennium. The church, which is in excellent repair, can seat 800, and is open every day of the week under the care of a full-time verger. *Songs of Praise* was filmed there in October 2010 and the church hall is part of the homeless hostel scheme that is run with other local churches throughout the winter months.

Lord Radnor ले सन १८६८ मा यो शहर विस्तार गर्ने योजनाले Holy Trinity Church को निर्माण गराएका हुन् । उनले प्रत्येक एक चौथाई माईलमा मानिसहरुलाई चर्चमा जान सुविधा होस भनेर भवनहरुको यो गिर्जा घरको निर्माण गराएका थिए ।

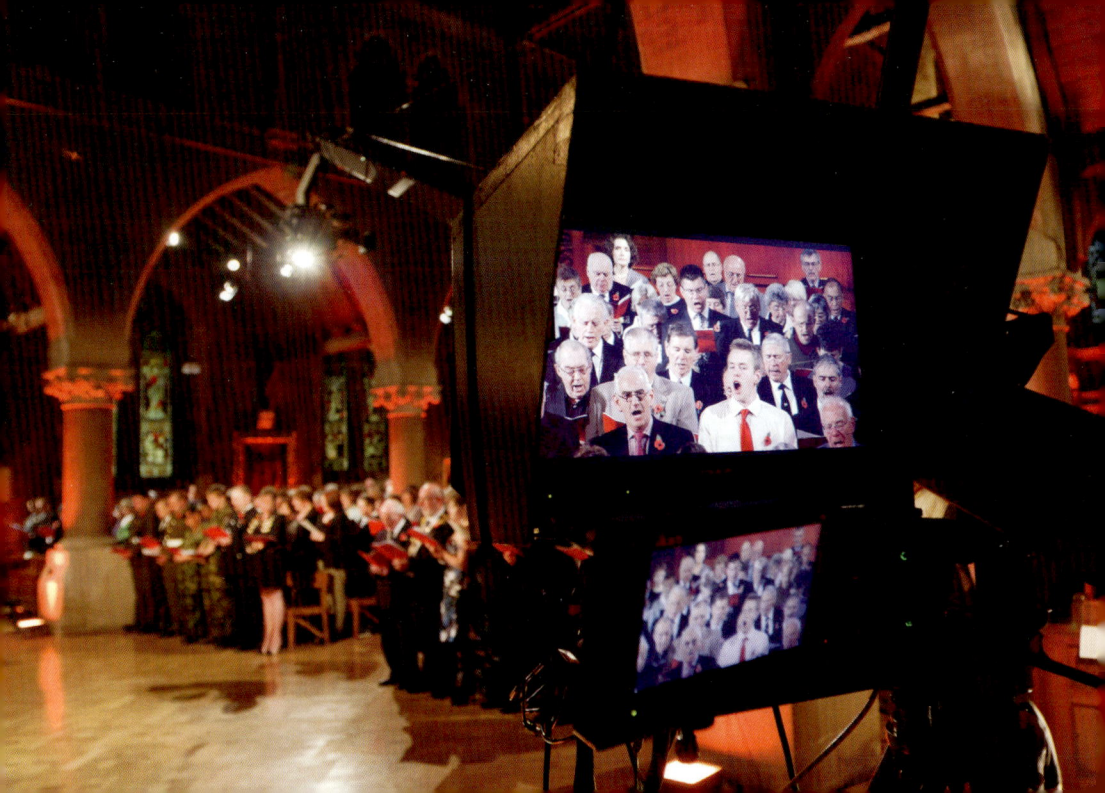

This is such a lovely little commemorative plaque to a dog that for some reason is always left out of guidebooks about Folkestone, so now is its chance to shine. The idea of it always makes me smile. It sounds as if Hector really was man's best friend.

कुनै कारणवश फोक्सटनको बारेमा लेखिएको जानकारी पुस्तिकामा यस्तो राम्रो सम्भनायोग्य कुरा लेख्न सधैं विर्संने गरेको छ । यस्तो कामले मलाई सधैं हसाउँछ । यसले साँच्चिकै Hector पुरुषहरुको मिल्ने साथि थियो भन्ने देखाउँछ ।

In the lobby of Barton House offices

EVERYWHERE MEANS SOMETHING TO SOMEONE

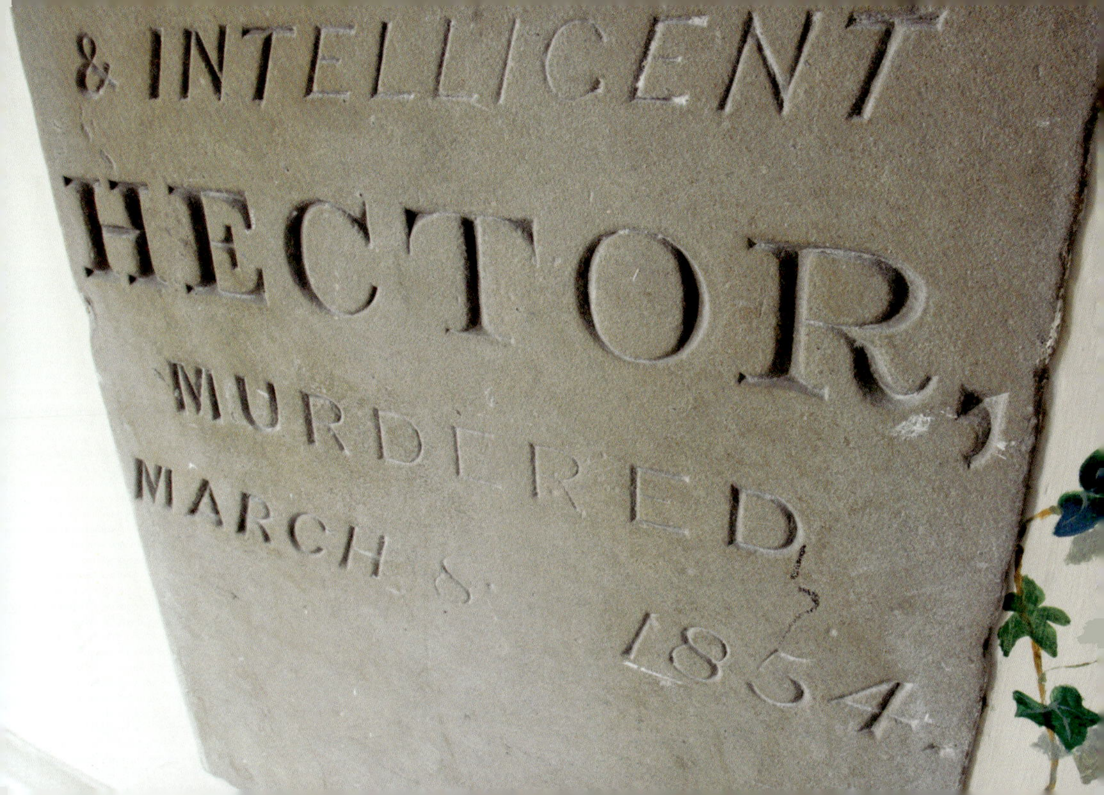

& INTELLIGENT

HECTOR,

MURDERED
MARCH 5
1854

When you walk into town from the bottom of Dover Road, there is one spot where, if you turn around, the word HEAVEN appears above Tontine Street.

It makes me laugh every time I see it… I never really thought of Tontine Street as heaven.

यदी तपाई डोवर रोडको पुछ्छारबाट फोक्सटन बजार तिर लाग्नु भो र Tontine Street को माथी हेर्नैं भयो भने त्याहां स्वांग शब्द लेखिएको छ । यसले मलाई हास उठाउछ, किनभने मैले कहिले पनि सोचिन Tontine Street मा स्वार्ग छ भनेर ।

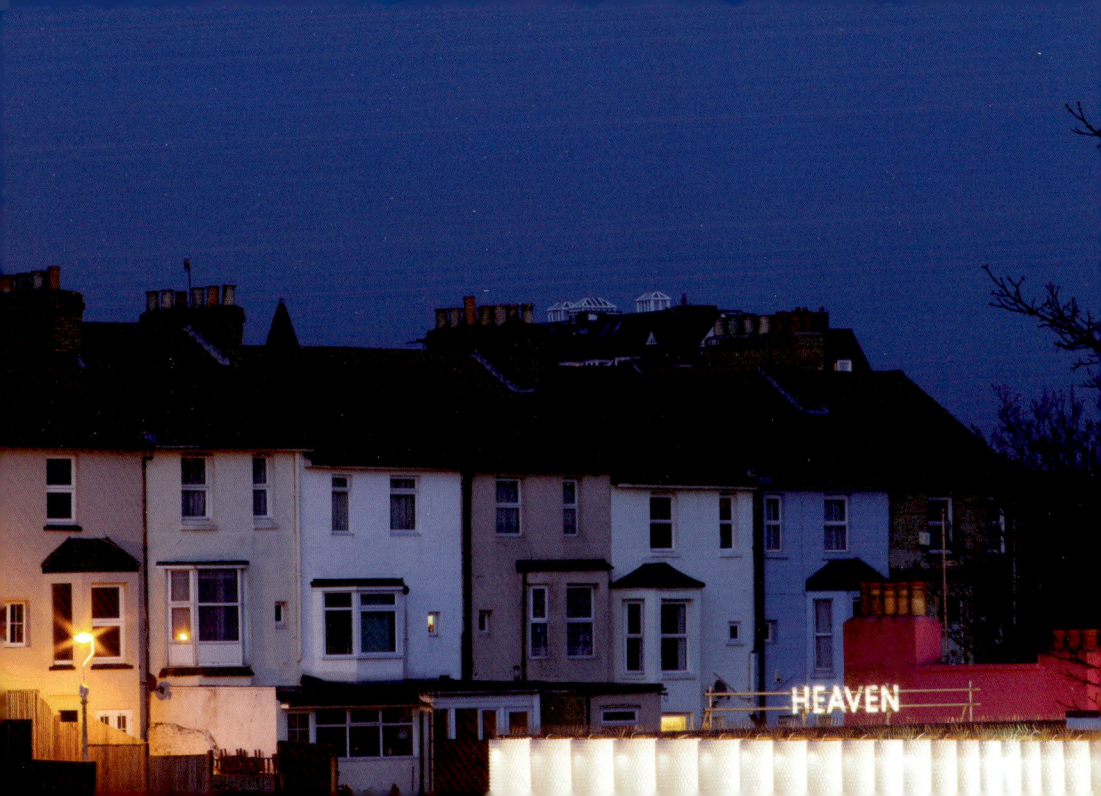

There is a plaque to Folkestone man Walter Tull, who was born in Allendale Street and was a pupil at Mundella Primary. He went on to become the first black officer in the British Army. His achievements also include playing professionally for Tottenham Hotspur football team. His name is recorded on the war memorial at the top of the Road of Remembrance.

फोक्सटन निवासी Walter Tull नामक व्यक्ति बेलायती सेनाका पहिलो कालो अधिकृत थिए । उनको नाम war memorial on the Road of Remembrance को सीरानमा उल्लेख छ । उनी Tottenham Hotspur को व्यवसायिक फुटवल खेलाडी पनि थिए ।

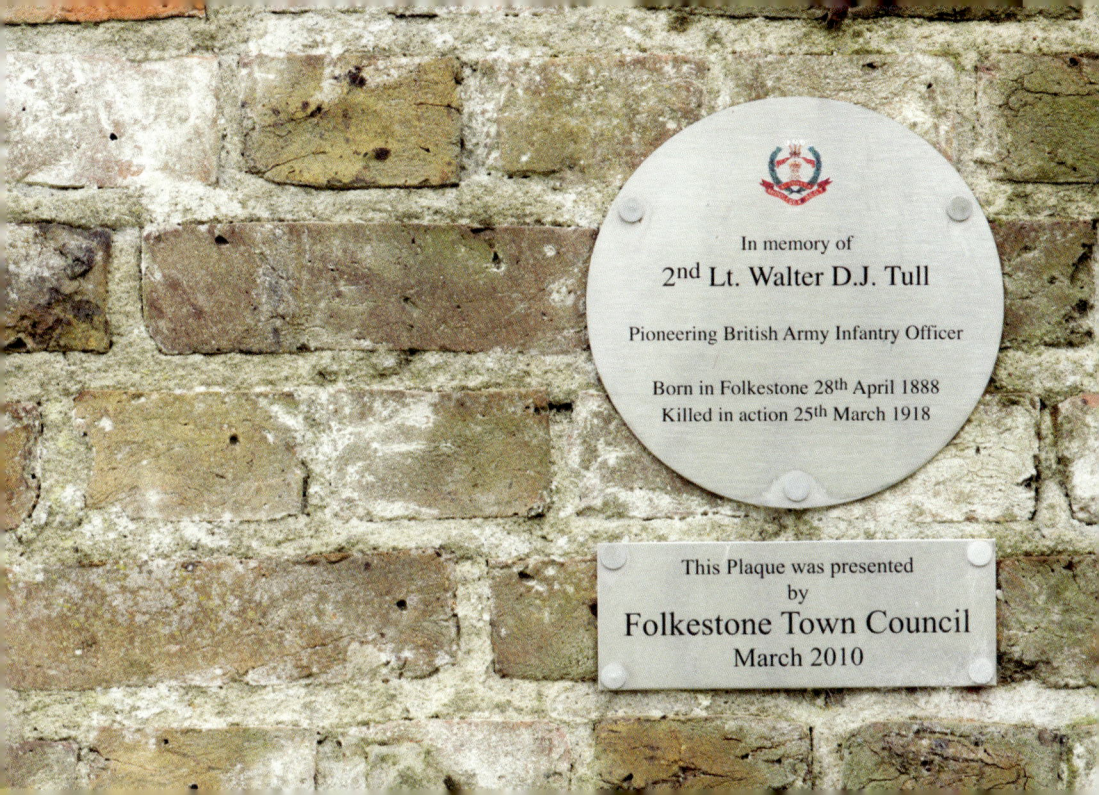

In memory of
2nd Lt. Walter D.J. Tull

Pioneering British Army Infantry Officer

Born in Folkestone 28th April 1888
Killed in action 25th March 1918

This Plaque was presented
by
Folkestone Town Council
March 2010

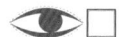

The painting *The Landing of the Belgian Refugees* by Fredo Franzoni shows the scene of 64,000 Belgians who arrived in Folkestone fleeing from the German invasion in August 1914. The refugees were said to have arrived terror stricken with few possessions other than the clothes on their backs. 15,000 of the refugees remained in Folkestone seeking shelter and refuge, and as a consequence the Folkestone Refugee Committee was established to cope with the influx.

Nation-wide appeals were made for food and clothing and the response was immediate and very generous. The Committee was headed by Folkestone's Mayor, Alderman Stephen Penfold, who was later knighted for his war services and those of the town. The painting was restored at the beginning of 2011.

Fredo Franzoni ले बनाएको *The Landing of the Belgian Refugees* चित्रले ६४,००० बेल्जियम नागरिकहरुको दृश्य देखाउँछ । उनीहरु सन १९१४ को अगष्टमा जर्मनको आक्रमणवाट त्रसीत भएर भागेर फोक्सटनमा आएका थिए । यस चित्रलाई सन २०११ को शुरुमा पुननिर्माण गरिएको थियो ।

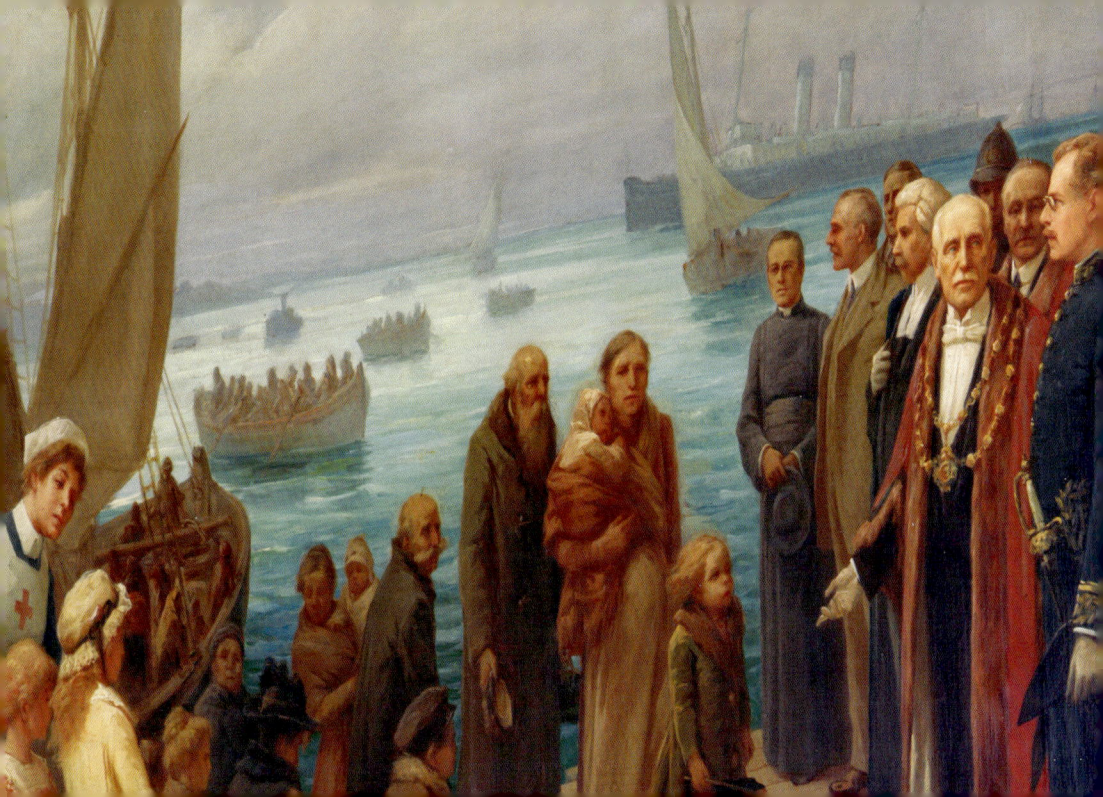

There is a statue of Sir Jeffrey Hudson which stands in Kingsnorth Gardens, he was also known as Lord Minimus. We're not sure why the statue is in Folkestone, but the story goes that he was given to a French queen inside a pie!

Apparently he was an English court dwarf at the court of Queen Henrietta Maria. He was famous as the "Queen's dwarf" and "Lord Minimus", and was considered one of the "wonders of the age" because of his extreme but well-proportioned smallness. He fought with the Royalists in the English Civil War and fled with the Queen to France but was expelled from her court when he killed a man in a duel. He was captured by Barbary pirates and spent 25 years as a slave in North Africa before being ransomed back to England. There is a famous painting of Queen Henrietta Maria with Sir Jeffrey Hudson by Van Dyck.

I am 14 and I have chosen Kingsnorth Gardens, because when my father passed away my mum and me went to Kingsnoth Gardens to lay a wreath for him.

सर जेफरी हड्शनको मुर्ती किडसनर्थ गार्डेनमा राखिएको छ । उनी महारानी Henrietta Maria को दरबारमा रहेको वाउन्ने थिए । सर जेफरी हड्शनले वेलायतको गृह युद्धको समयमा राजतन्त्रको पक्षमा लागेर वोकालत गरेर महारानी संगै फ्रान्स निर्वासीत भए । पछ्छाडी उनले आफुसंग विमती राख्ने मान्छ्को हत्या गरेकोले उत्तर अफ्रिकामा २५ वर्षको सजाय दास भएर भोग्नु पर्‍यो । अन्त्यमा क्षेती पुर्ती वापत पैसा तिरेर जेल मुक्त गरेर वेलायत ल्याईयो ।

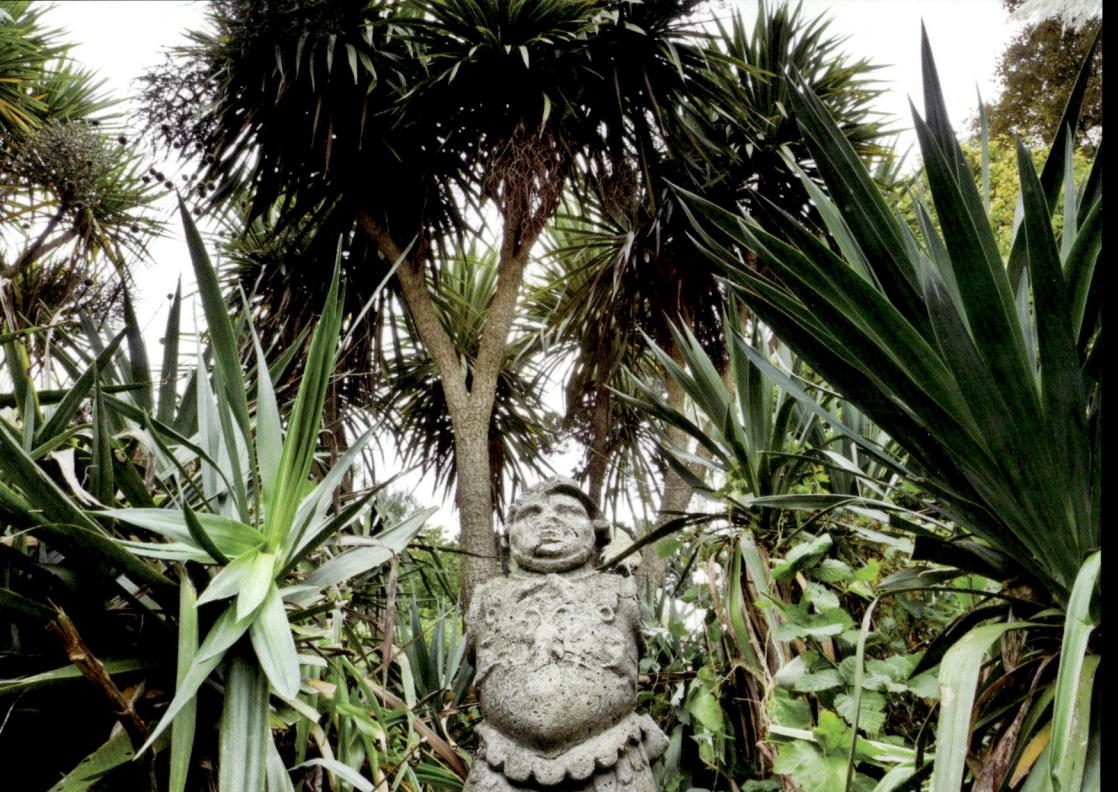

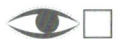

There is a blue plaque on the building in Augusta Gardens where Samuel Plimsoll, who was a British politician and social reformer, lived. He invented the load line for boats called the Plimsoll Line and saved many thousands of lives as a consequence.

He died in Folkestone on 3 June 1898 and is buried in St Martin's churchyard in Horn Street.

Augusta Gardens मा भएको एउटा घरमा राखीएको सिलालेख अनुसार Samuel Plimsoll एउटा अग्रेजी राजनेता तथा समाज सुधारक थिए । उनले डुङ्गाको वजन, जसलाई Plimsoll line भनिन्छ, पत्ता लगाएर हजारौं मानिसहरुको ज्यान बचाएका थिए ।

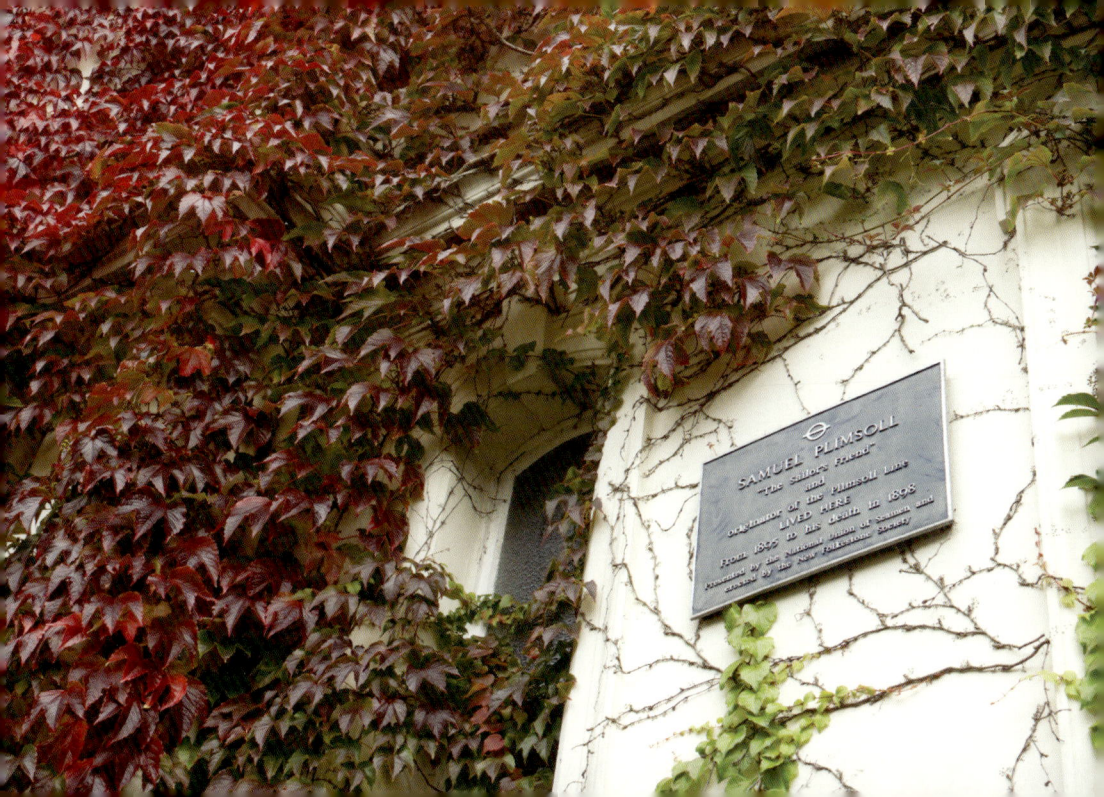

At the eleventh hour on the eleventh day of the eleventh month, the two minute silence is observed on Armistice Day. This day marks the end of the First World War 92 years ago.

The ceremony takes place at the cemetery in Cheriton Road at the Machine Gun Corps (Cavalry) Memorial, which is dedicated to First World War soldiers.

The Mayor and veterans attend a short service arranged by the Cheriton Branch Royal British Legion. After standards have been displayed and wreaths laid, the *Last Post* and *Reveille* are played. All are welcome to pay their respects at this short moving service.

११ बजे, ११ गते र ११ औं महिनाको दिन Armistice Day को उपलक्षमा २ मिनट मौन धारण गरीयो । यो दिनले ९२ वर्ष अगाडीको प्रथम विश्व यूद्धको समाप्त भएको दिनको प्रतिनीधीत्व गर्नछ । यो कार्यक्रमको आयोजना चेरिटन रोडको चिहान घारीमा प्रथम विश्व युद्धमा सहभागी सेनाहरुको संझनामा गरिन्छ ।

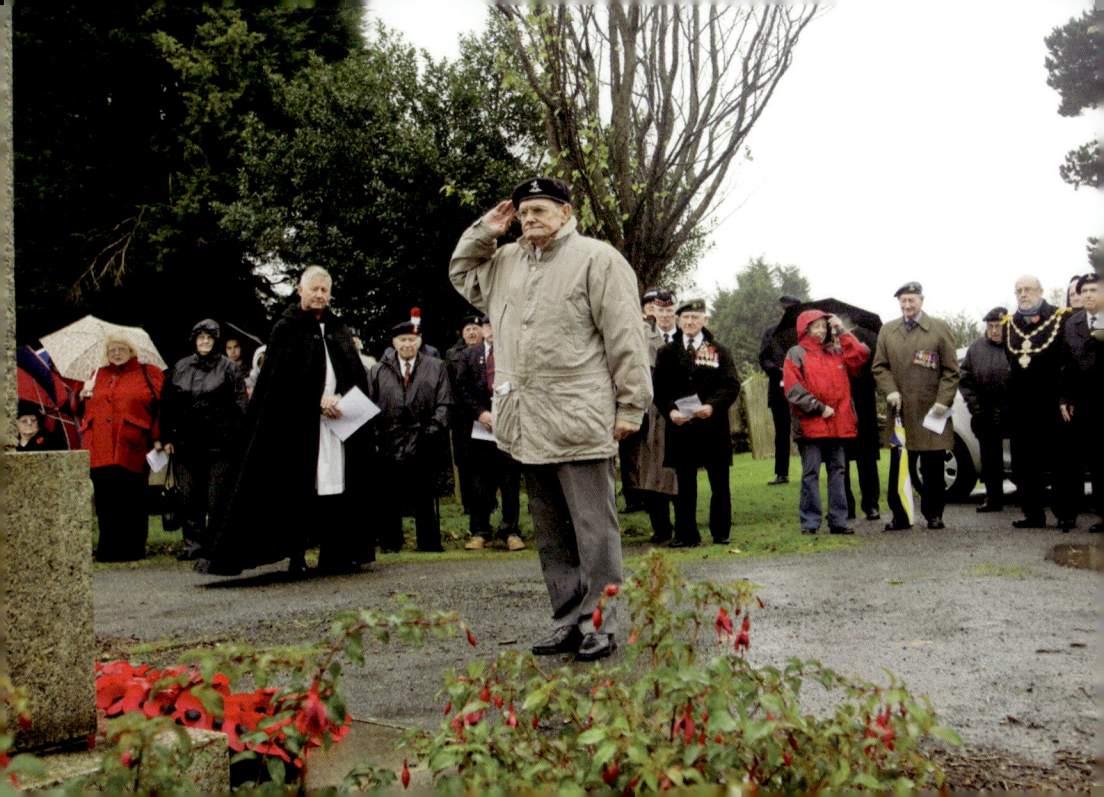

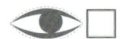

This is the view from my flat – it's generally a very dull view, which is why this graffitied 'SMILE' makes me laugh.

Asking me to smile? You must be joking!

यो मेरो वासस्थानबाट देखिने दृष्य हो र यो सामान्यतः नीरस दृष्य छ । किनभने यो हाँस उठ्दो चित्रले मलाई हसाउँछ। के मलाई हाँस्नु भन्नुको ? तिमीले पक्कै पनि ठट्टा गरेको हुनुपर्छ ।

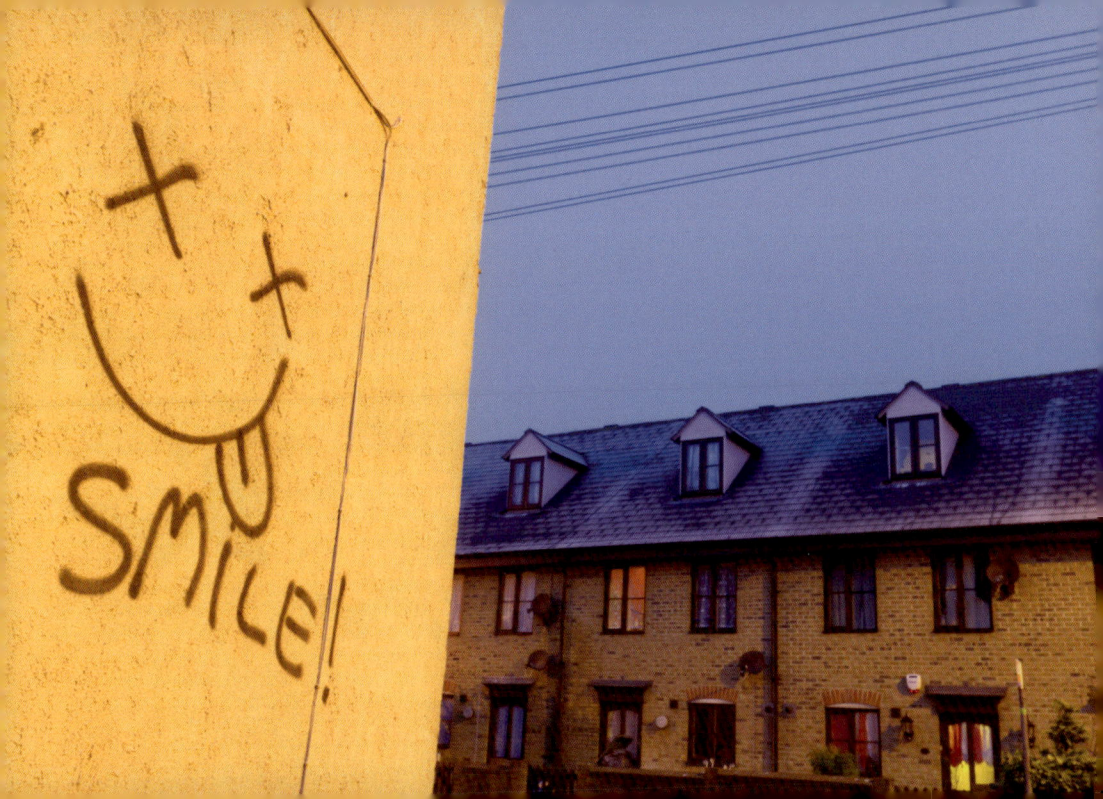

Folkestone Hythe and District Model Railway Club has been a part of Folkestone life for over sixty years, and throughout that period has provided a safe haven for those who don't mind others knowing about their habit.

Club members, as well as producing their own model worlds at home, also find time to work on Club layouts, and many of these personal and joint ventures have featured in the national model railway press, a number winning awards at exhibitions up and down the country as well as abroad.

The highlight of each year is the Model Railway Exhibition hosted by the Club at the Leas Cliff Hall in the first weekend of October, which is now nationally regarded and brings enthusiasts and their families from far and wide to see the best in railway modelling. 2011 will see the 40th annual show. The Club meets at the Broomfield Hall, Broomfield Road, Cheriton on Wednesday evenings from about 7.30pm – www.folkestone-mrc.com

Folkestone, Hythe र District Model Railway Club ६० वर्ष भन्दा पहिले देखि अस्तित्वमा छ । क्लबका सदस्यहरुले उनीहरुको आफ्नै विशेष नमुनाहरु उत्पादन गर्छन । यी मध्ये धेरै नमुनाहरु राष्ट्रिय नमुना रेल्वे प्रेसमा प्रदर्शन गरिएको छ र यसले देश विदेशबाट पुरस्कार पनि जित्न सफल भएको छ ।

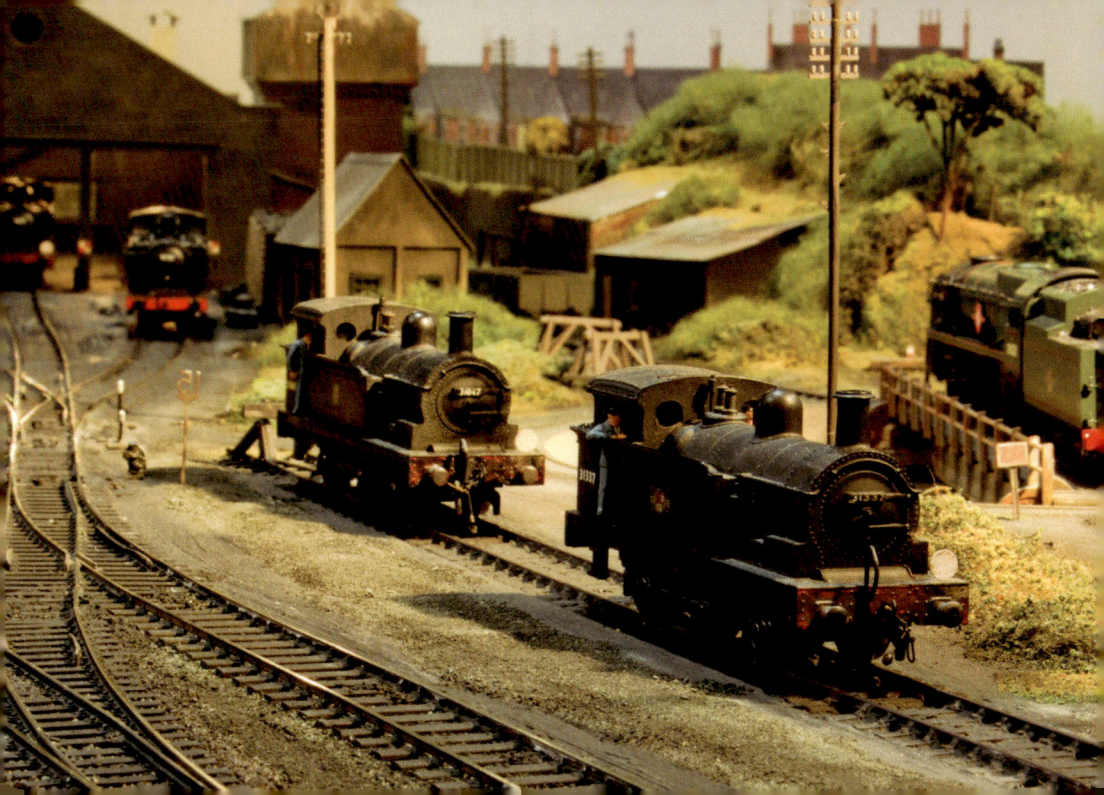

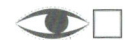

These diagonal rocks have always fascinated me. Apparently, it was Thomas Telford's prototype idea to make the walls stronger against the might of the sea when he built the Harbour in 1809.

It seems to have worked.

 यी विकर्ण आकारका चट्टानहरुको पर्खाल Thomas Telford विचार अनुसार समुन्द्रको छाललाई राख्नको लागी बलियो हुन्छ भनेर फोक्सटनको त्यावरमा १८०९ मा निर्माण गरिएको हो ।

विचारमा यसले राम्रै काम गरे जस्ता छ ।

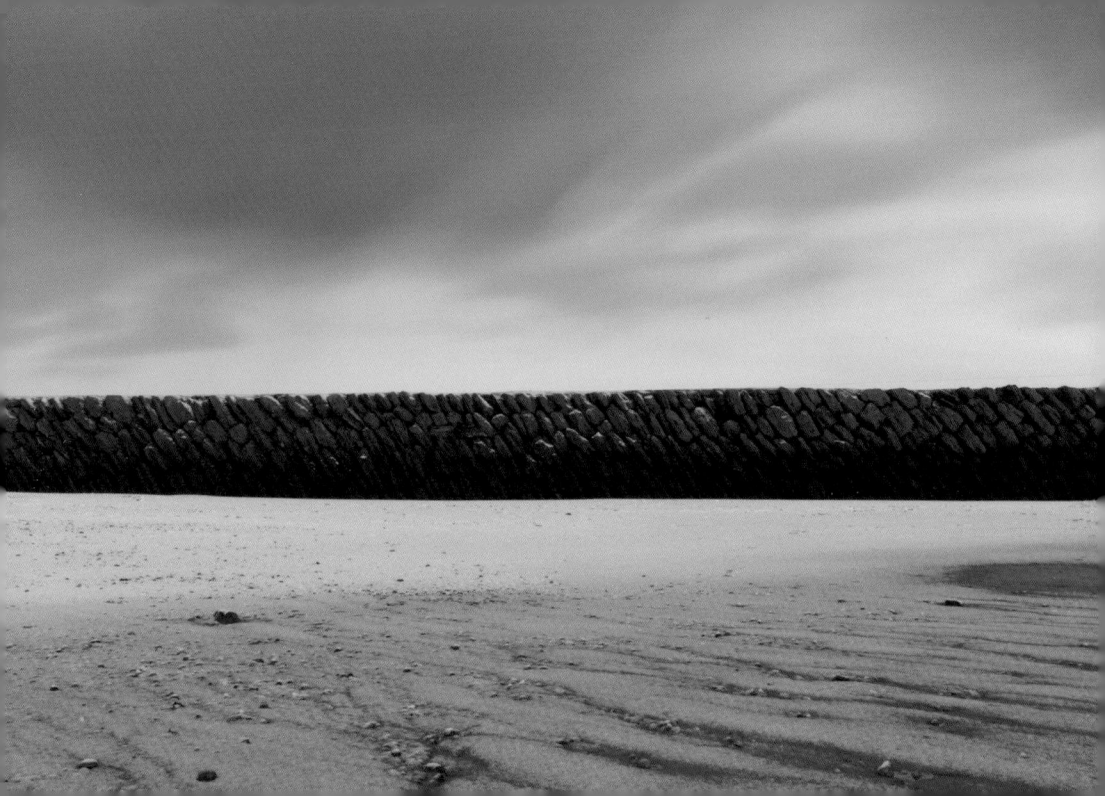

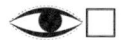

This bit of textured concrete in the centre of a sea of tarmac is all that is left of the huge open air swimming pool that was at the seafront – it was an amazing place!

I clearly remember the rough texture of the concrete underfoot as I ran around the edge of the pool as a child – it seemed to sting your feet. The pool was seawater and when you jumped in, an odd smell of cabbage water went right up your nose.

My parents used to run a B & B in Longford Terrace just on top of the cliff and we used to go there on our own all of the time, travelling up and down in the Leas Lift or climbing the hundreds of steps up from the lower road. It's strange to think that the spectator stands, skating rink, beach huts, and petting zoo, which were next door, together with the changing rooms and café were all bulldozed and used to infill the pool. I like to think of it sleeping just below the surface.

समुन्द्रको किनारमा भएको यो विशाल खुल्ला आकाश मुनी भएको पौडि खेल्ने तलाउको अब भग्नावसेश मात्र बाकी छ । मलाई अहिले पनि सम्झना छ कि, म स्यानो छदा यो पौडि खेल्ने तलाउको वरिपरी दौड्ने गर्दथे । यो बन्द भएपछी यसको छेउमा भएका सवै घरहरु भत्काइयो र त्याहां भएको ठुलो खाल्डो पुरियो ।

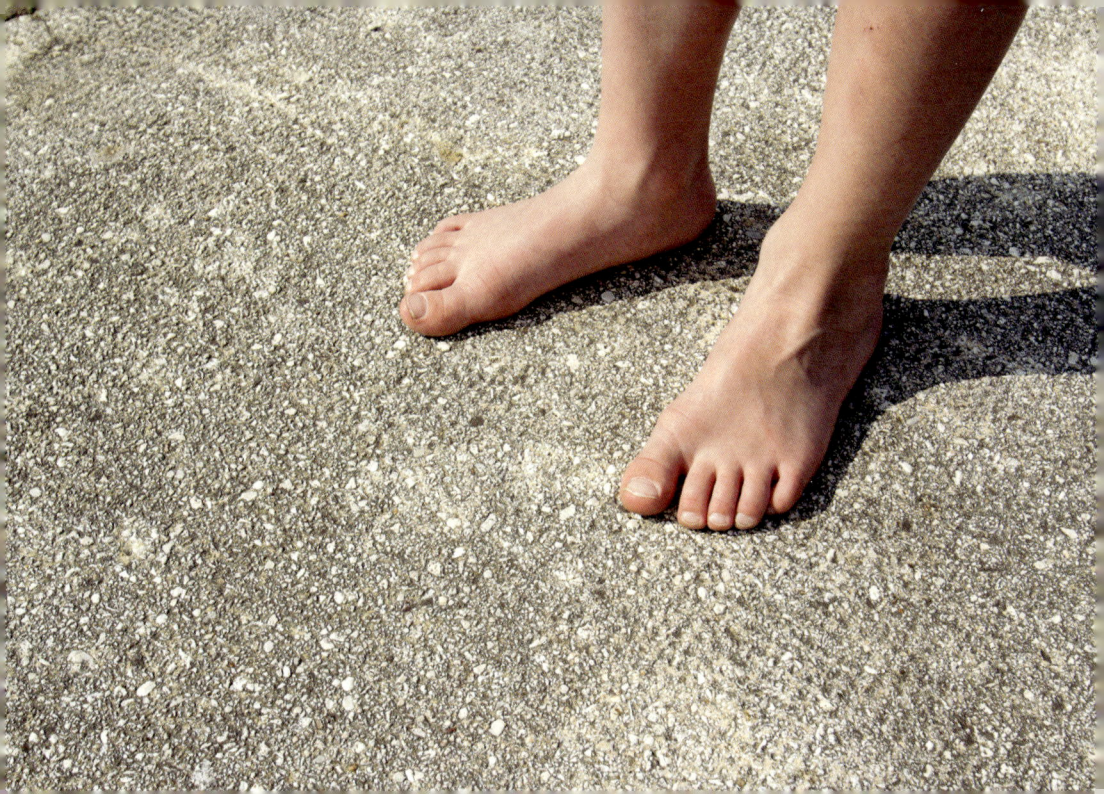

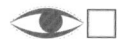

Folkestone changed its name from Folkstone to Folkestone because it was an anagram of Kent Fools!

Folkestone को नाम Folkstone बाट परिवर्तन गरिएको हो किनभने यो Kent Fools शब्द बाट बनेको थियो ।

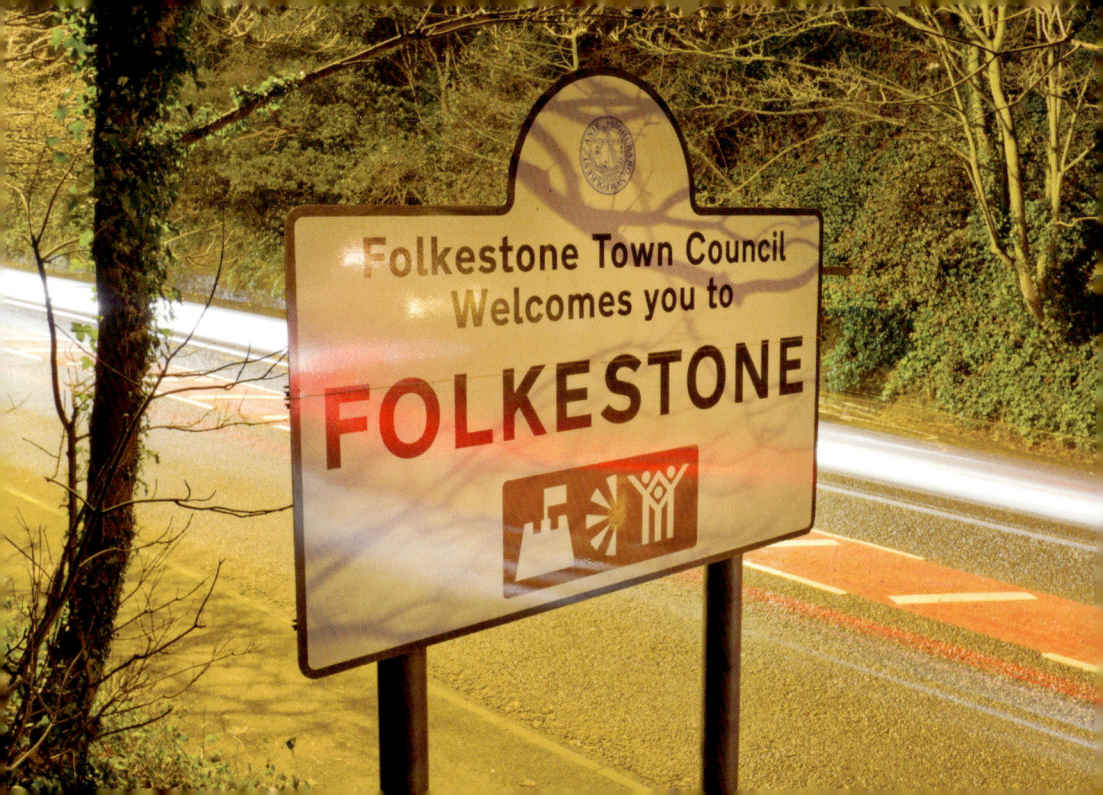

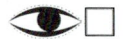

The two-tone grey lampposts situated – amongst other places – on the Leas, bear the crest and words 'Borough of Folkestone'. They are interesting in themselves, attractive to look at and indicate a time when as a Borough, Folkestone took pride in its town.

Leas मा अन्य रमणीय ठाउँहरु मध्ये २ हजार किलोको खैरो रंगको Borough of Folkestone अंकीत बिजुलिका खम्बाहरु पनि हुन् । यी सबै चिजहरु हेर्नमा आकर्षित देखिनुको अतिरिक्त फोक्सटन शहर एउटा Borough को रुपमा गौरावन्वित छ ।

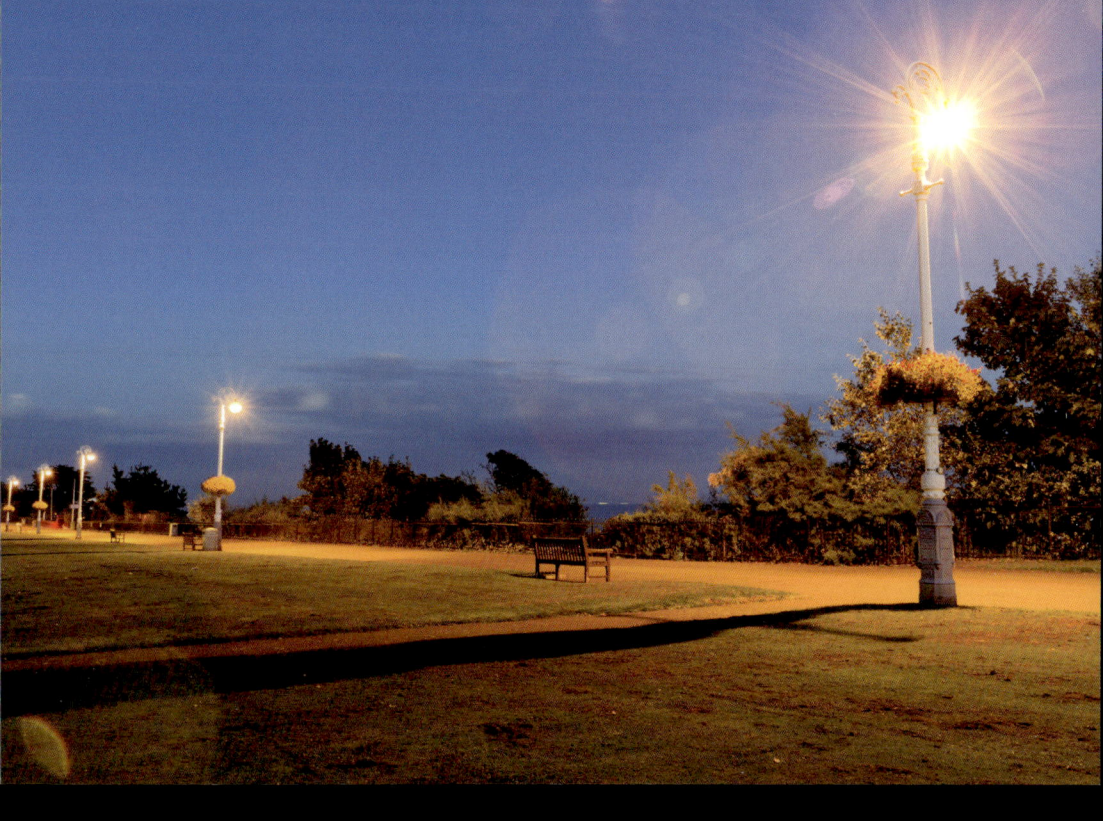

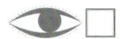

The Marine Pavilion in Marine Gardens is the last remaining Art Deco building in that part of town. Originally from the pier inwards, a Victorian seafront graced the town. Later years saw the replacement, or addition of the Rotunda, outside swimming pool and boating pool. Today the Marine Pavilion, now a nightclub, is the last testimony to what was a bright era of Art Deco architecture.

Marine Pavilion आज रात्रि कल्व भएको छ । कुनै समयमा समुन्द्रि किनारमा जाने यो अति सुन्दर ठाउँ थियो ।

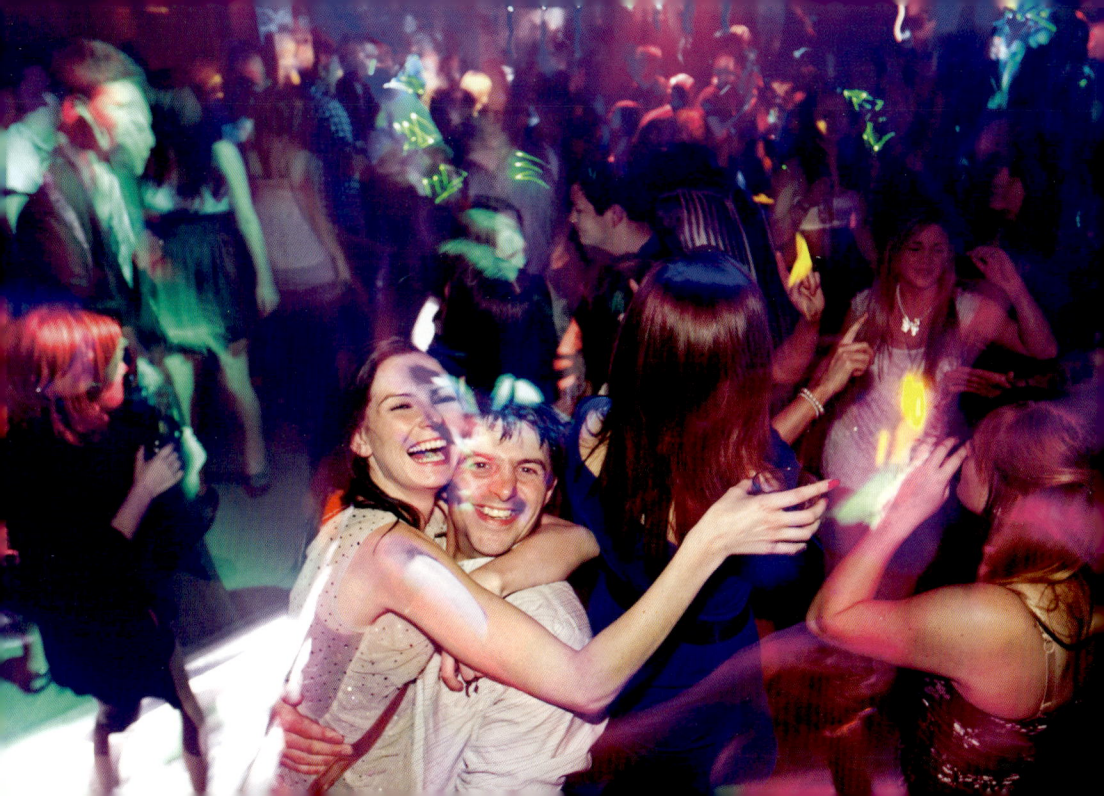

As young girls, my friend Joy and I were offered a job on the Capel Gun Site as it was then known then. There was quite a group of us – men and women – working there. I think Joy and I were about the youngest at the time. There was a big piece of camouflage sacking that had to be sown over the whole of the Gun Site to a wire frame. We loved it and thought we were working on a trampoline! The only thing that worried us was when the big guns fired and we all had to get off and get to the ground, and we were so glad when they stopped and we could get back on the nets again. I remember the NAAFI well, all the bunkers with the big guns dug into the cliffs. We were so proud of ourselves and all the lads on the guns were so friendly.

यो संग्राहालय युद्ध कालमा Capel Gun Site को घर थियो । यहाँ दुश्मन मार्नको लागि शैनिकले प्रयोग गर्ने एउटा ठूलो Camouflaged बन्दुक, NAAFI र पहरा मुनि बंकरमा ठूला-ठूला बन्दुकहरु थिए ।

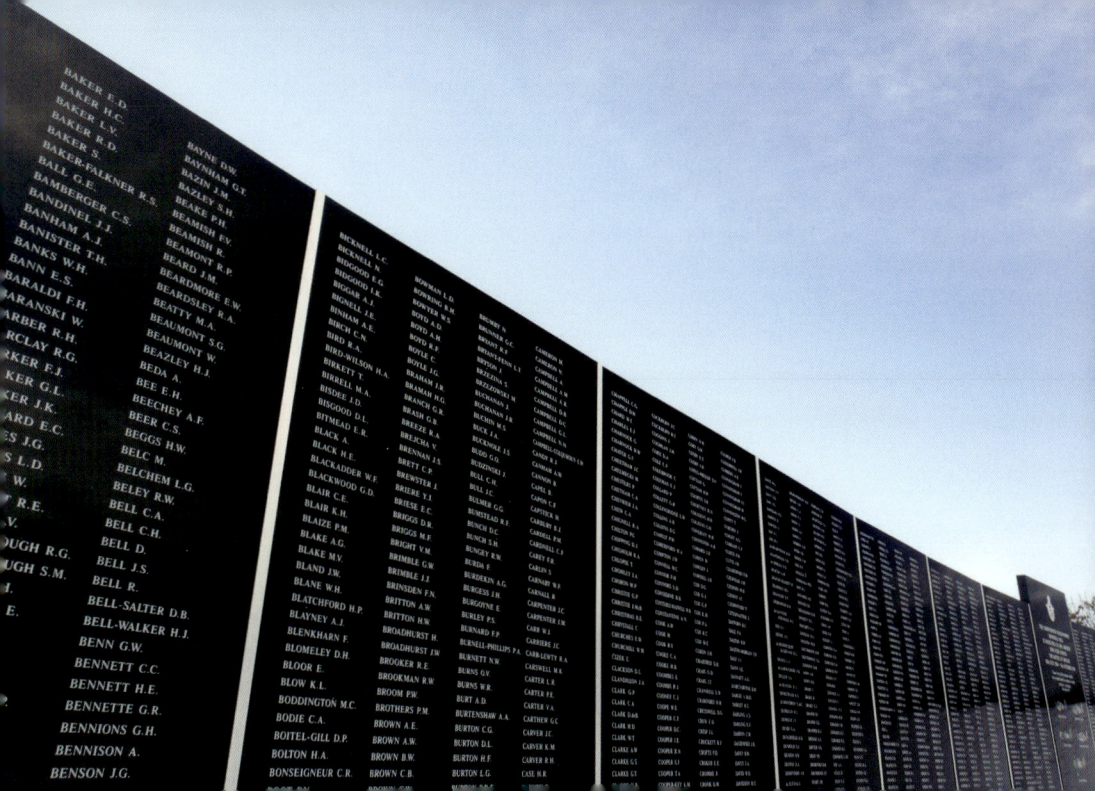

The Sailor's Friend, Samuel Plimsoll, is buried in St Martin's Churchyard in Cheriton. He was called the 'Sailor's Friend' on account of his determination to see the 1876 Merchant Shipping Bill passed which made it compulsory for all ships to carry a mark – the Plimsoll Line – to show when they were fully laden, thus ending the unscrupulous practise of overloading poorly maintained ships which often sank, drowning the sailors and allowing the owner to claim the insurance!

चेरिटनको St Martin's Churchyard मा Samuel Plimsoll लाई गाडिएको थियो । उनलाई नाविकहरुको साथी भनिन्थ्यो किनभने उनले १८७६ मा पानीजहाज सम्बन्धी व्यवसायीक कानून निर्माण गर्न प्रमुख भुमिका निर्वाह गरेका थिए । उक्त कानून अनुसार प्रत्येक जहाजहरुले Plimsoll Line को निशान बोक्नु पर्दथ्यो जसले सम्बन्धित जहाज पूर्ण रुपमा भरिएको छ भन्ने बुभाउँदथ्यो । यसको अतिरिक्त यो कानून लागू भए पछि अनावश्यक सामानहरु थोपरेर पानी जहाजलाई डुब्नबाट बचायो र यसका धनिहरुलाई विमा प्राप्त गर्ने निती पनि वस्यो ।

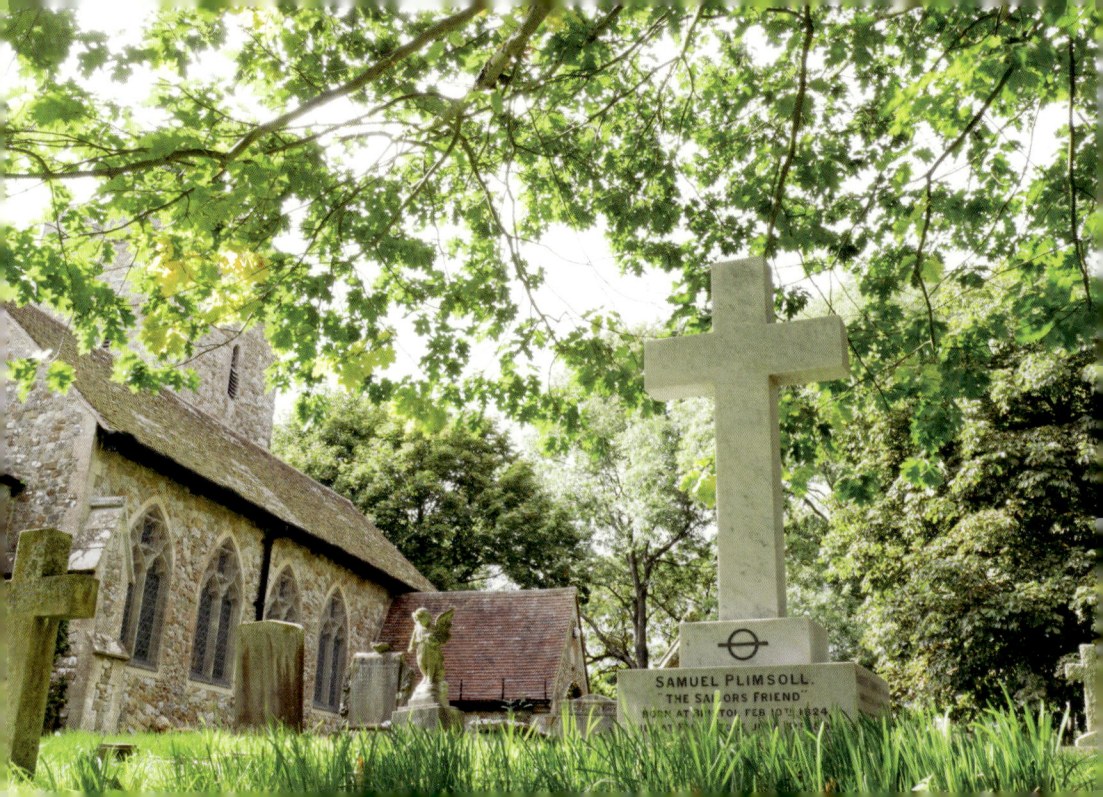

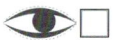

Thomas Fuller Taylor started trading from this shop 86 The Bayle in 1877 as a dairyman. Sometime between 1878 and 1882 he started the pork butchery business. He was succeeded in 1927 by his grandson Thomas Henry Taylor, but Thomas Henry died in 1945 at the age of 56 and his son carried on the business. Tom Taylor's business closed in November 1973 due to the decline in trade. The shop was then occupied by something rather unusual, a witches' 'coven.' The premises was converted into living accommodation in 1997, but still retains the two pigs' heads on the fascia board.

Every Folkestonian knows a house in Bayle Street ornamented with two pig's heads, obviously a former pig-butcher's; likely the adjoining Georges House has jars because it used to sell oil. But why is it called "Hamstede" ? Well, "homestead" means a country house where both people and animals (mainly pigs) lived; but the spelling was very fluctuating in the past, anything from "Hampstead" to "Hamstede". The last spelling was used jocularly to remind of bygone trades.

सन १८७७ देखि १९७३ को विचमा Taylor परिवारकको वंशले यो पसलमा सुँगरको मासु बेच्ने व्यवसाय गर्दथे । यो पसल बन्द भएपछि त्यहाँ एक असामन्य witches' coven ले उपयोग गऱ्यो । सन १९९७ मा यो घरलाई मानिस बसोवास गर्ने वासस्थानको रुपमा परिणत गरिए पनि बितेका दिनहरुको सम्झनाको लागि अझैपनि यहाँ दुईवटा सुँगुरको टाउकाहरु राखिएका छन् ।

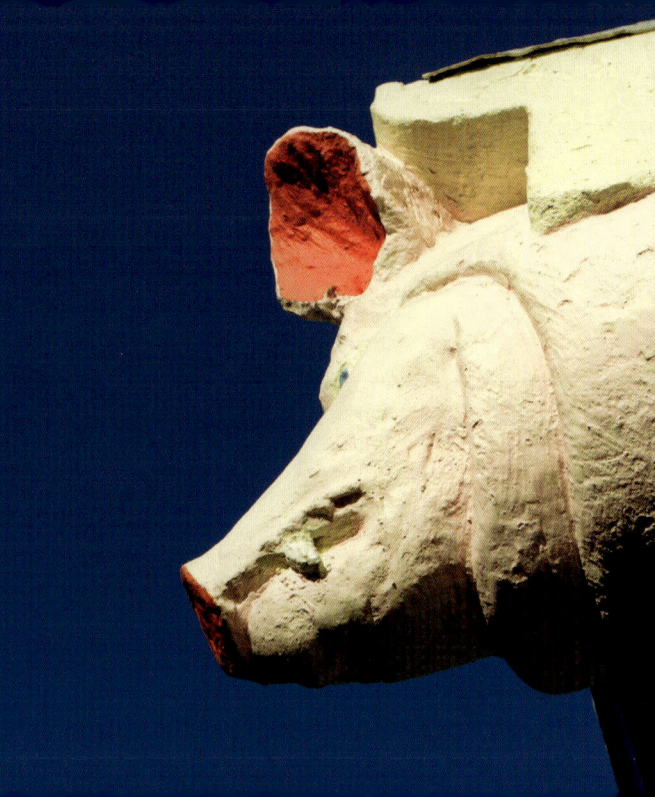

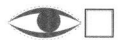

John Logie Baird was born on 14 August 1888 and showed early signs of ingenuity, rigging up a telephone exchange to connect his bedroom to those of his friends across the street. He studied at Glasgow University followed by post WWI service as superintendent engineer of the Clyde Valley Electrical Power Company.

He moved to Folkestone in 1924, where he did his early experimental work at T.C. Gilbert & Co. Limited, Electrical & Radio Engineers at 26 Guildhall Street, where he experimented in the basement, managing to transmit a flickering image across a few feet, thus making Folkestone, *not* Hastings, the birthplace of Television!

My father, Fred Taylor was an apprentice electrician at Gilbert's at the time and he remembered Logie-Baird doing his experimental work there. There is a plaque inside the shop, which was unveiled by his wife to commemorate his work on the premises.

John Logie Baird ले 26 Guildhall Street मा उसको कामको पहिलो प्रयोगात्मक परिक्षण गरेका थिए । त्यहाँ उसले छोटो दुरीमा मधुरो प्रतिमा प्रशारण गर्न सफल भएका थिए । त्यसकारण टेलिभिजनको पहिलो प्रसारण स्थल हेस्टिङ नभएर फोक्सटन हो । मेरो बाबा त्यो समयमा त्यसताका विद्युत प्रविधिकको रुपमा काम गर्ने भएकोले Logie Baird ले गरेको यो प्रयोगात्मक प्रसारणको बारेमा बाबालाई अहिले पनि सम्भना छ ।

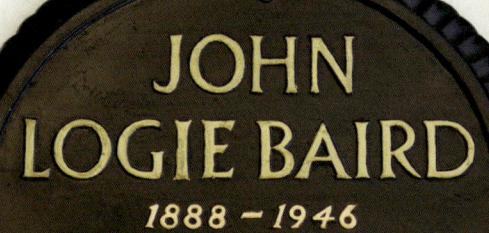

JOHN
LOGIE BAIRD

1888 – 1946

the pioneer of television
conducted some of his
early experiments on
these premises during

1924

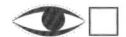

Sea glass; Beach glass; Marine gems; Sea sapphires; Mermaids tears; Baby Soap;

Wrapped up warm on wintery days in the Warren; In search of washed up sea glass, preferably cobalt blue

Strolling hand in hand looking for treasure; Weathered by sand, salt and water

Dodging the tide, walking the beach; Seeking pretty pieces of broken glass

Leaving with pockets full of jewels; And a glow of romance.

1 lb flour
3 oz butter
3 oz lard
3 eggs
1 pint milk
½ oz ground rice
2 oz currants
1 tablespoonful sugar

Make a short crust with flour, butter and lard, roll out, cut into circles and line some breakfast saucers with it. Heat ¾ of the milk in a saucepan. Mix ground rice and sugar in the rest of the milk, turn into the hot milk and stir till it thickens. Leave to cool a little and mix in the eggs slowly, stirring vigorously. Pour over the pastry. Sprinkle the currants over and bake till golden brown.

From Whitbread's Recipes & Relishes

EVERYWHERE MEANS SOMETHING TO SOMEONE

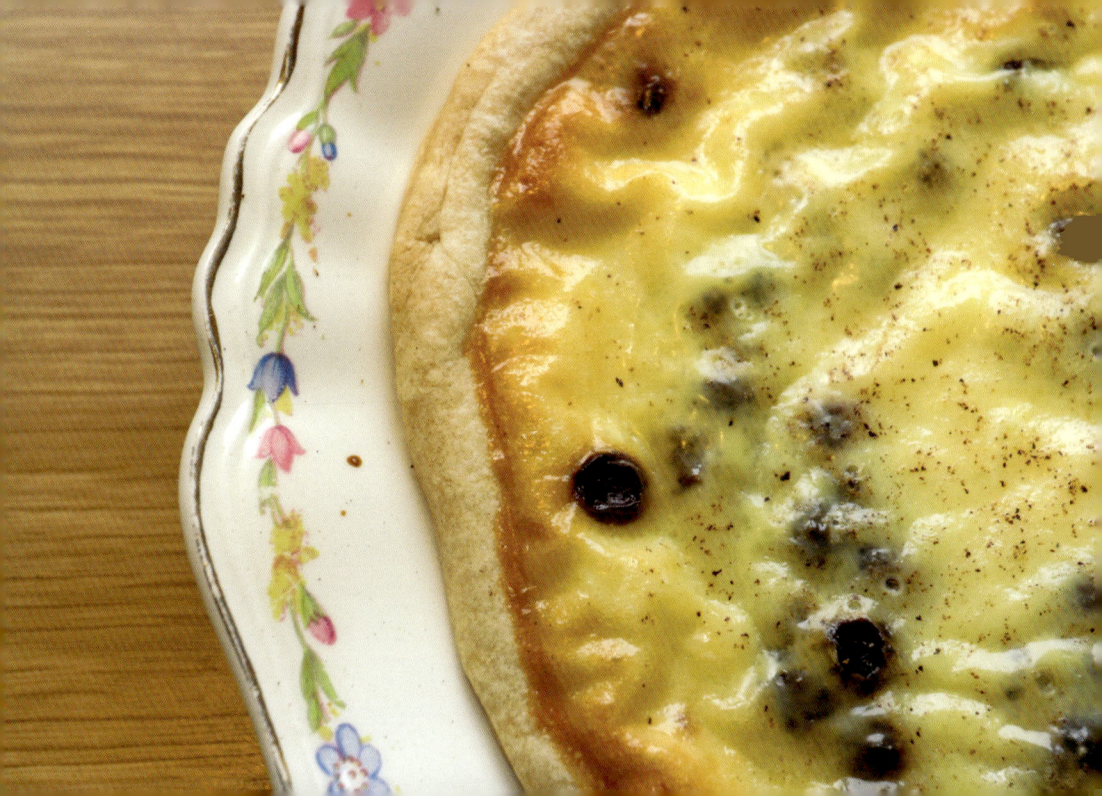

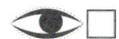

Peter Jurzynski first visited Folkestone in the summer of 1985, prior to the tunnel, when Thatcher and Reagan were in power, the old telephone box was prominent (all around Folkestone) and 'tea shoppes' were plentiful and 'coffee shoppes' were a rarity. Peter came to swim the English Channel, to train for Channel swims but more importantly to meet the wonderful folks of Folkestone. I have successfully swum the Channel 14 times (14 successes/6 failures). I currently hold the record for the most Channel swims by an American. I've visited Folkestone not only in the summer but also at Christmas time; since 1985 I've visited Folkestone 27 times! During the peak of my Channel swimming career, roughly between the mid-1990s and 2005, I would swim nearly every summer day between the first jetty in Folkestone (jetty closest to the Harbour) to the toilets in Sandgate. The tides, depending on day and time, can be extremely strong. My vivid memory is of viewing the beach huts – little yellow-doored beach huts – from the sea on my way to Sandgate. Once I finally passed the huts, I was clear of the strong tide and had an easy swim to Sandgate. Viewing the last beach hut as I glanced back is a keen memory.

सन १९८५ र २००५ सालको विचमा अमेरीकाको Peter Jurzynski ले Channel मा १४ पटक सम्म सफलतापूर्वक पौडी खेलेका थिए । उनी प्रत्येक वशन्त ऋतुमा फोक्सटनको first jetty देखि Sandgate को सौचालय सम्म पौडने गर्थे । उसको सम्झनायोग्य क्षणहरु seafront मा भएको beach huts को yellow doors मा हेर्न सकिन्छ ।

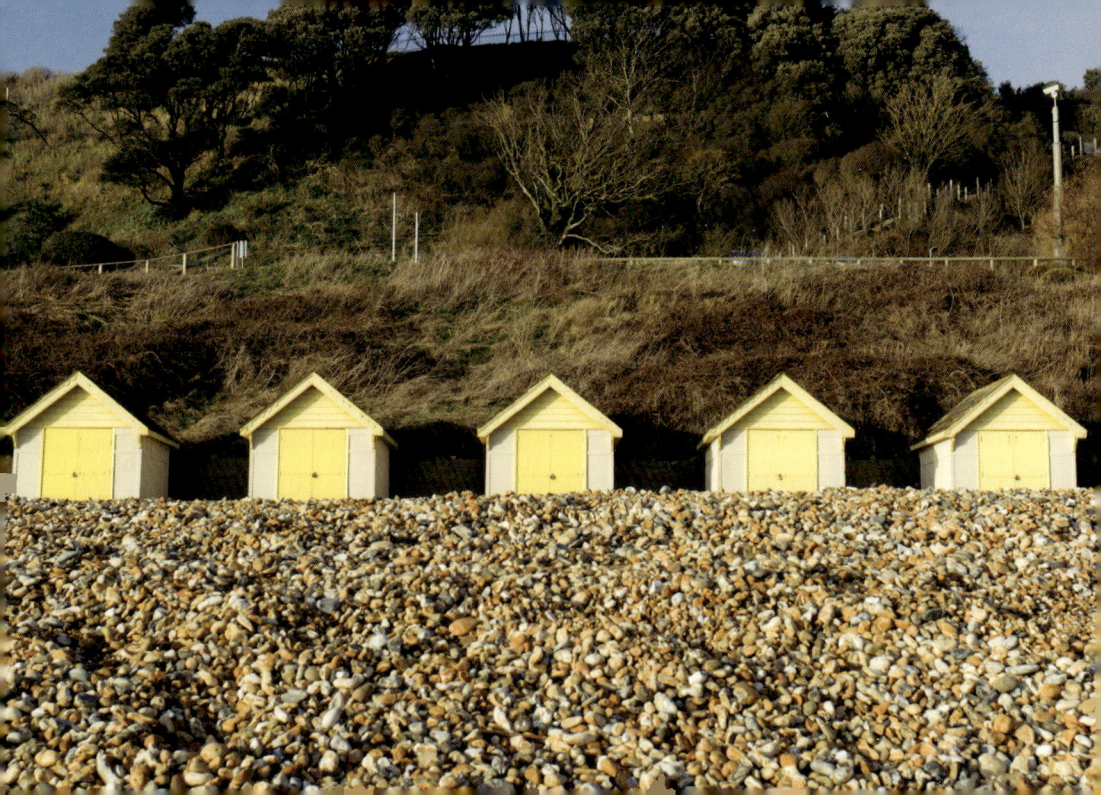

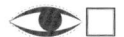

When I first visited England and Folkestone, upon arrival at Folkestone Central RR station, we took a taxi to Marine Terrace where I was staying… while the taxi drove around the Harbour streets I was amazed at the bright colored buildings along the way… a vivid memory.

जब म पहिलो पटक वेलायत तथा फोक्सटनको भ्रमण गर्न आएको थिए, त्यसवेला हामीले ट्याक्सी लिएर Marine Terrace गएका थियौं, जहा हामी वस्दथ्यौ । त्यसवेला टेयाक्सी Harbour streets को वरीपरी घुम्दा त्यहा भएका रङ्गी विरङ्गी घरहरुको रमाईलो दृश्यहरु मनमोहक देखिन्थे ।

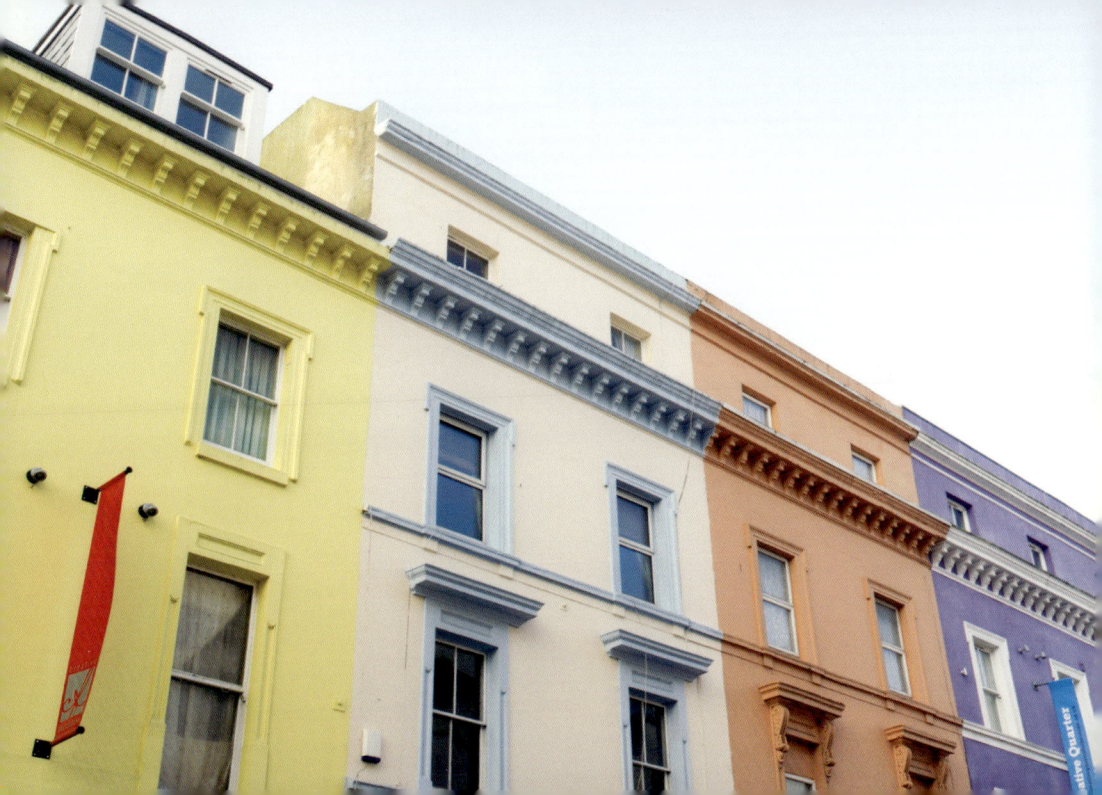

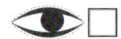

My father worked at the Continental Office, engaged in customs clearance work. The cargo boat *Deal* arrived daily from Boulogne and was unloaded by a steam crane, which moved on rails along the quay. He would obtain the correct tariff from bulky printed volumes, typing the details on various coloured forms. Sometimes he would find time to fish from the end of the cargo pier, and I remember him arriving in our kitchen with a large, slimy conger eel, wrapped in newspaper. It looked alarming and only he would eat it. He would take us along the railway platform and up to the Pier Promenade, to watch the ferries sailing and berthing. We liked to see the large travelling cranes loading cars into the hold and lifting up the gangplank, when all the passengers had boarded. The *Canterbury*, *Isle of Thanet* and *Maid of Orleans* were all familiar to us, but when we travelled abroad for the first time in 1960, it was our favourite, the sleek French *Cote d'Azur* that took us over to Calais, to join the Arlberg-Orient Express to the Tyrol.

मेरो बाबाले बन्दरगाह भन्सार कार्यालयमा काम गर्दा ठुलो क्रेनहरुले पानीजहाजबाट मालसामान उतारेको र यात्रीहरु उत्रिएको देखाउन मलाई त्यहां लाने गर्नु हुन्थ्यो ।

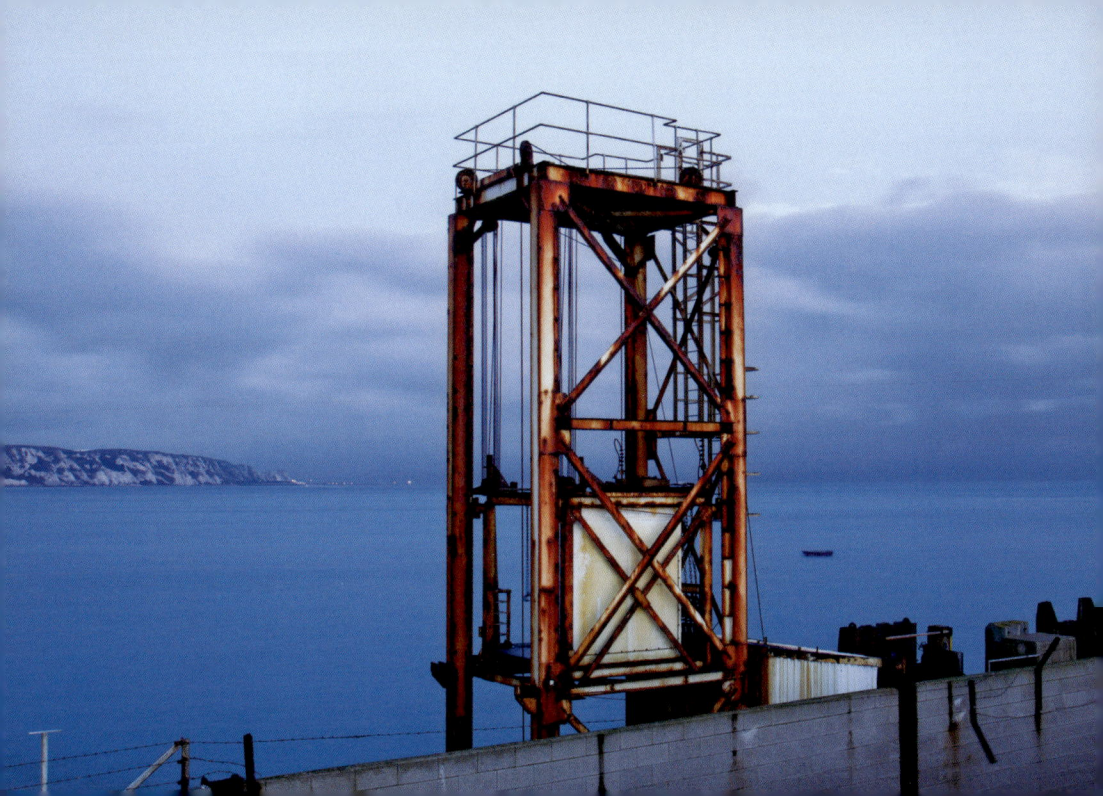

Late one evening I lost my wooden picket fence to the bonfire of a beach party. I was devastated. When considering how I was going to replace it, I remembered the six small fish-shaped Chinese game counters I had recently bought from Rennies in the Old High Street. When repairs to the house next door salvaged a 100 year old pine lintel above the lounge window, I had an idea. I loved the old wood, marked by time and rusty nails and noticed that it was similar in proportion to the Chinese fish counters. I talked to sculptor Mark Sutherland about the possibility of cutting out a simple fish. He liked the idea, but insisted on two fish, not one. So we found another piece of wood from a restored building in Tontine Street and Mark spent weeks carving me two remarkable fish, bringing life to both the wood and the fishy shapes.

I love my new Fish Fence, which has brought me countless opportunities to talk to people as they stand and admire it.

सामुन्द्री किनारमा धुनि बाल्दा मेरो बार जलेपछि एक मुर्तिकारले छिमेकमा भएको पुरानो काठपात प्रयोग गरेर अर्को बनाईदियो । त्यो नयाँ बारलाई मैले भरखरै किनेको माछा आकारको चाईनिज् खेलको सामानले सजाएर राखेको छु ।

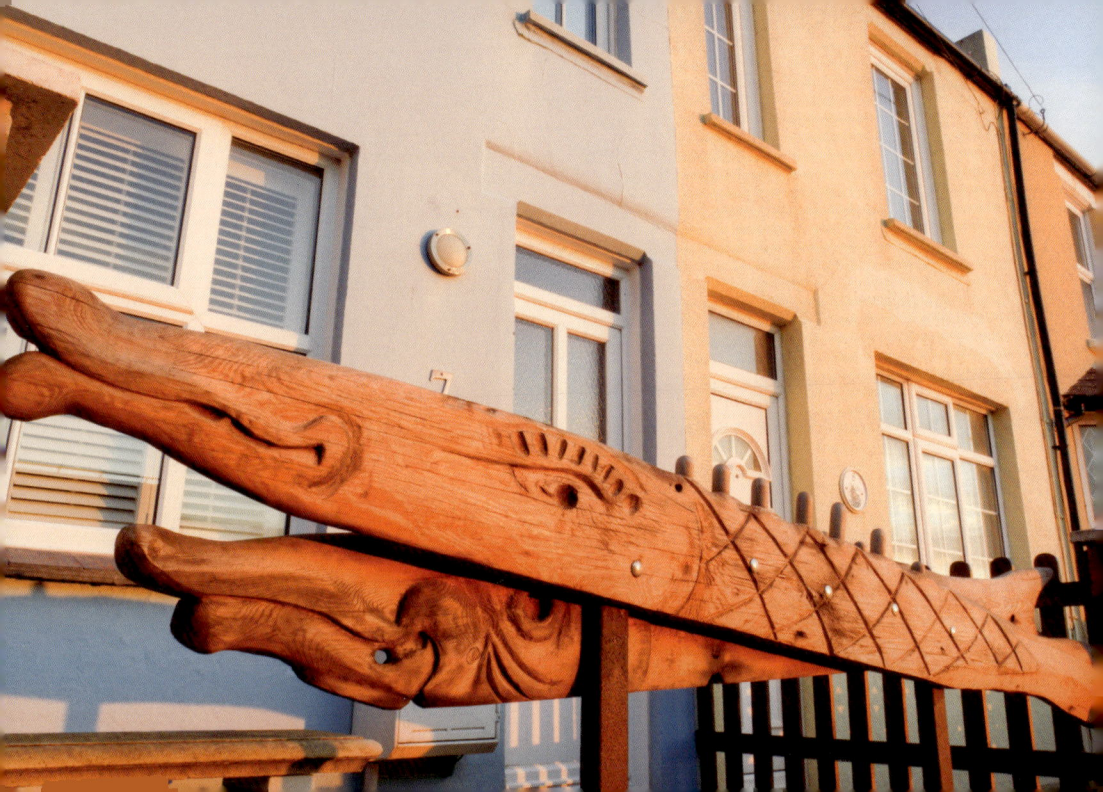

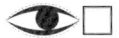

My brother Stewart and I spent many a happy sunny days scrambling on the ruins of the Roman Villa in the 1950s. I had no idea we were causing damage.

Some years later, when people realised it should be preserved, a fence was erected around it. When this precaution failed to keep vandals out, a decision was made to bury it! Recent archaeological excavations revealed it for the first time in many years and unearthed a great deal more information about the extent of Folkestone's long trading history with Europe, which was shown to stretch back much further than had been previous thought.

Visit www.atownunearthed.co.uk for more information on the site.

धेरै वर्ष पछि पहिलो पटक पुरानो रोमनको भत्किएको घर पुनरुत्थान गरिएको छ । यो घट्नाले फोक्सटन र युरोप विचको लामो व्यापारीक ईतिहाँसको बारेमा अझ धेरै जानकारी प्राप्त भयो ।

अन्य जानकारीको लागी वेबसाईट www.atownunearthed.co.uk हेर्नुहोला ।

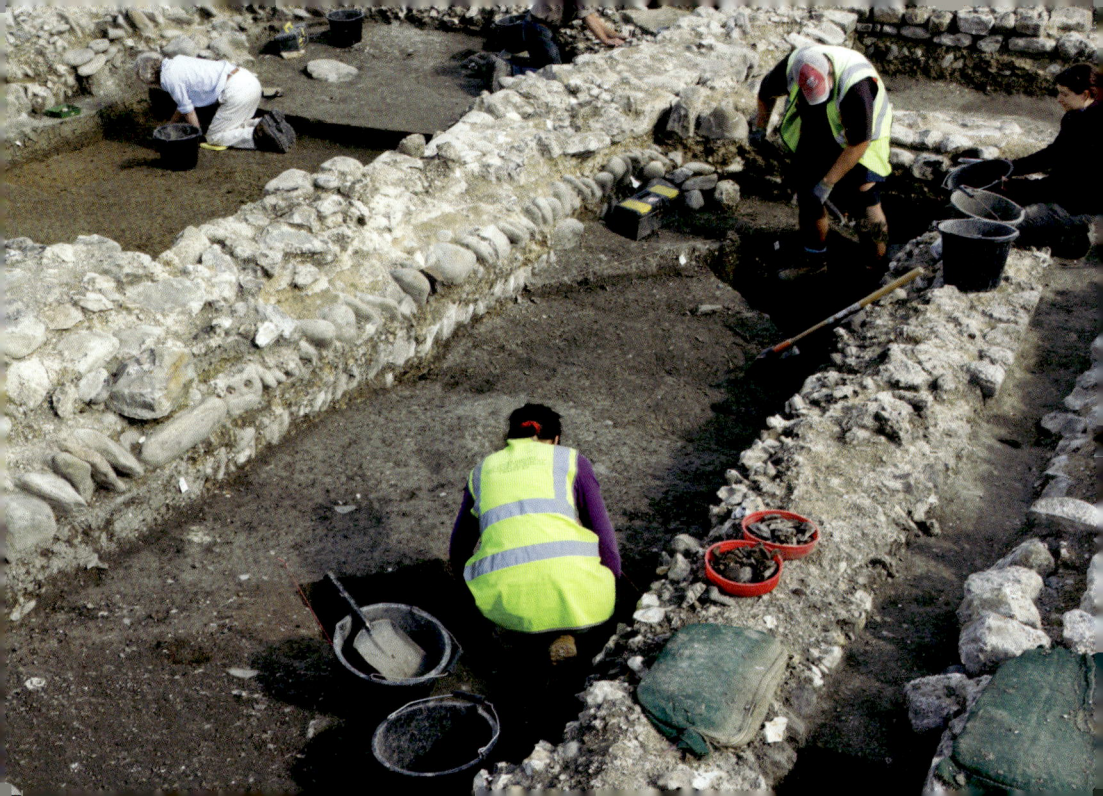

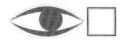

Constructed in 1927 at a cost of £80,000, the Leas Cliff Hall has been the venue for all sorts of entertainment from classical ballet, to Sooty, to Ozzy Osbourne. During the war it held very popular dances. From the Leas it appears to be a fairly ordinary building albeit with some nice ornamental stonework and a great view over the sea. To really appreciate its construction you need to go down to the Lower Leas and admire the way it has been built into the cliff. Apparently it is supported by 51 concrete pillars each 8 foot square and sunk 30 feet into the ground. Quite a feat of engineering.

When I first moved to Folkestone I was told that the Leas Cliff Hall was coveted by Heinrich Himmler who wanted to make this a base of operations for his Gestapo. This is said to be the reason why it was never bombed, despite its size and prominence on the cliffside.

सन १९२७ मा Leas Cliff Hall को निर्माण गरिएको थियो । यहाँ धेरै प्रकारको मनोरञ्जनात्मक सांगितिक कार्यक्रमहरु हुन्छन् । यसका ५१ वटा ठुला सिमेन्टका खम्बाहरु छन् ।

दोश्रो विश्व युद्धको समयमा यसलाई Gestapo को रुपमा उपयोग गर्ने भनेर हल्ला चलेको थियो किन भने यहाँ कहिले पनि बम प्रहार भएन ।

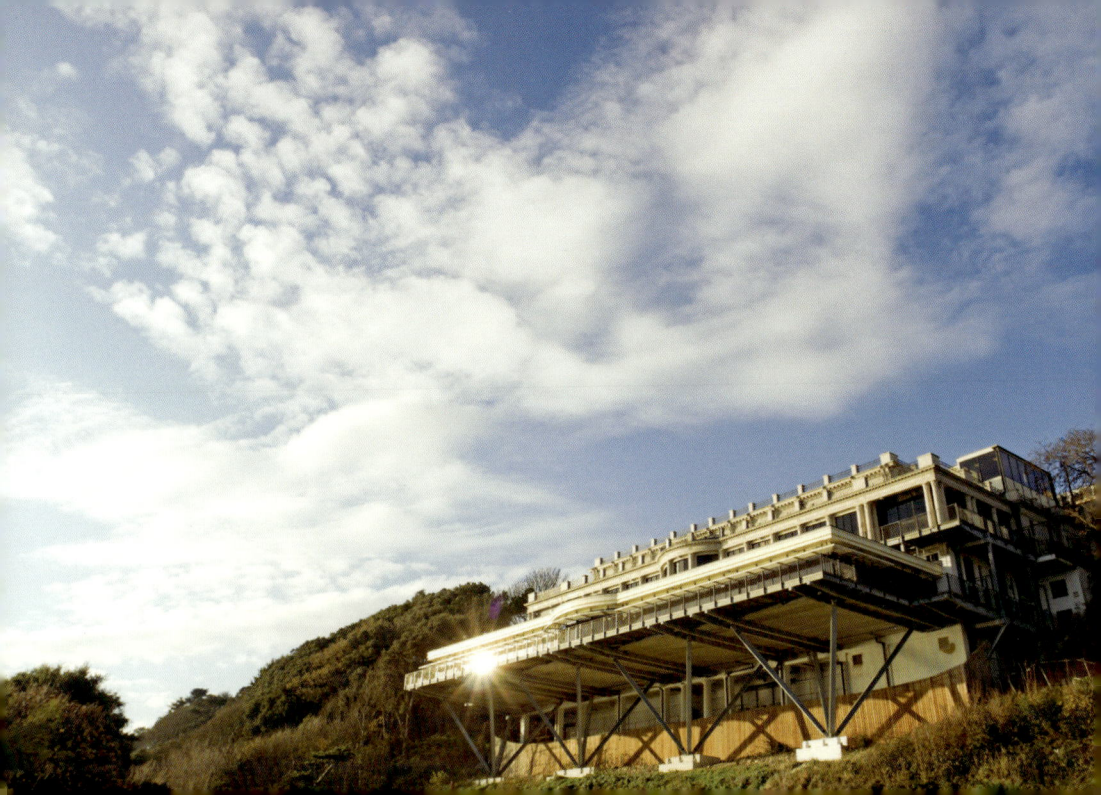

This poignant artwork by Mark Wallinger is so moving. The numbered stones are there to represent the millions of soldiers who marched down from The Leas to the Harbour to sail to the trenches in Europe during the First World War. Many, many thousands of these brave young men did not return.

यो नम्बर लगाएको ढुंगाहरु पहिलो विश्व युद्धमा यूरोप लडाई गर्न गएको सिपाईहरुको प्रतिक हो ।

EVERYWHERE MEANS SOMETHING TO SOMEONE

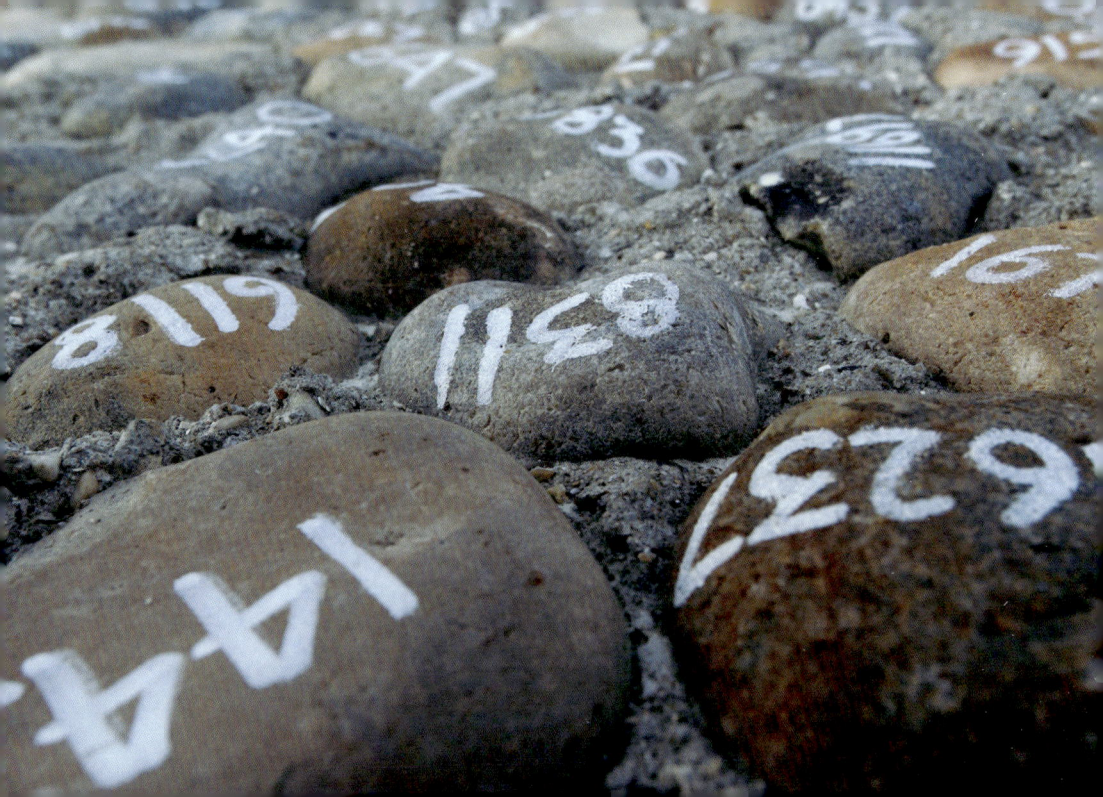

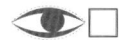

The parish church is very closely linked with Folkestone's history. Henry VIII visited twice and King John also came to Folkestone in 1216 and stayed at the priory, which used to adjoin the church. I always look to see if I can see any signs within the architecture of the building that might indicate where the priory steps would have led out from inside the church, but I haven't spotted anything yet.

William Harvey had a brass plaque for his mother placed in St Eanswythe's parish church.

यो गिर्जाघर फोक्सटनको ईतिहाँससँग सम्बन्धित छ । हेनरी आठौंले यहाँ दुई पटक भ्रमण गरेका थिए । सन १२१६ मा महाराज जोन पनि फोक्सटन आएका थिए र उनि यो गिर्जाघरसँग जोडिएका कुटीमा बसेका थिए ।

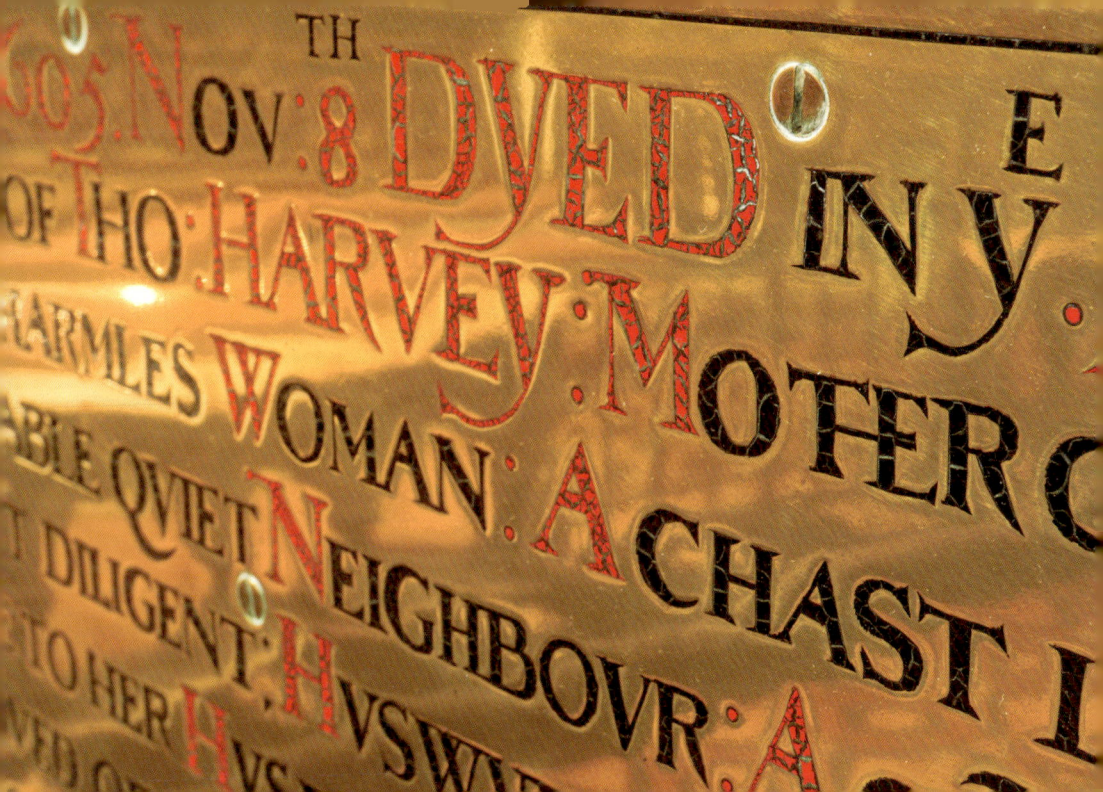

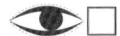

The Foord viaduct, designed by Sir William Cubitt, was completed on 20 November 1843. It is 252 yards and 6 inches long, comprising of nineteen arches each with a span of 30 feet. At its highest point it measures about 88 feet. Quite an achievement, given the building methods available at the time and, unusually, no lives were lost in its construction. When the viaduct was started Foord was a rural hamlet but the coming of the railway led to it becoming very rapidly built up. In fact it was the arrival of the railway that directly led to Folkestone's increase in prosperity during the second half of the nineteenth century.

When I first moved to Folkestone someone told me that when the viaduct was being built, a horse slipped and he and his cart tumbled down inside one of the piers. They couldn't get him out, so he was bricked in to the structure. I always think of him when I go under the viaduct.

William Cubitt ले नक्शाङकन गरेको The Foord viaduct यो रेल हिँड्ने ठुलो पुलको निर्माण सन १८४३ नोभेम्बर २० मा सम्पन्न भएको थियो । यो १९ वटा विशाल खम्बाहरु भएको २५२ गज लामो छ । यसको उच्चाई लगभग ८८ फिट अनुमान गरिएको छ । यो पुलको निर्माण पूर्व फोर्ड एउटा सामान्य गाउ थियो तर रेलमार्गको निर्माणले यसलाई व्यस्त सहरमा परिणत गरेको छ ।

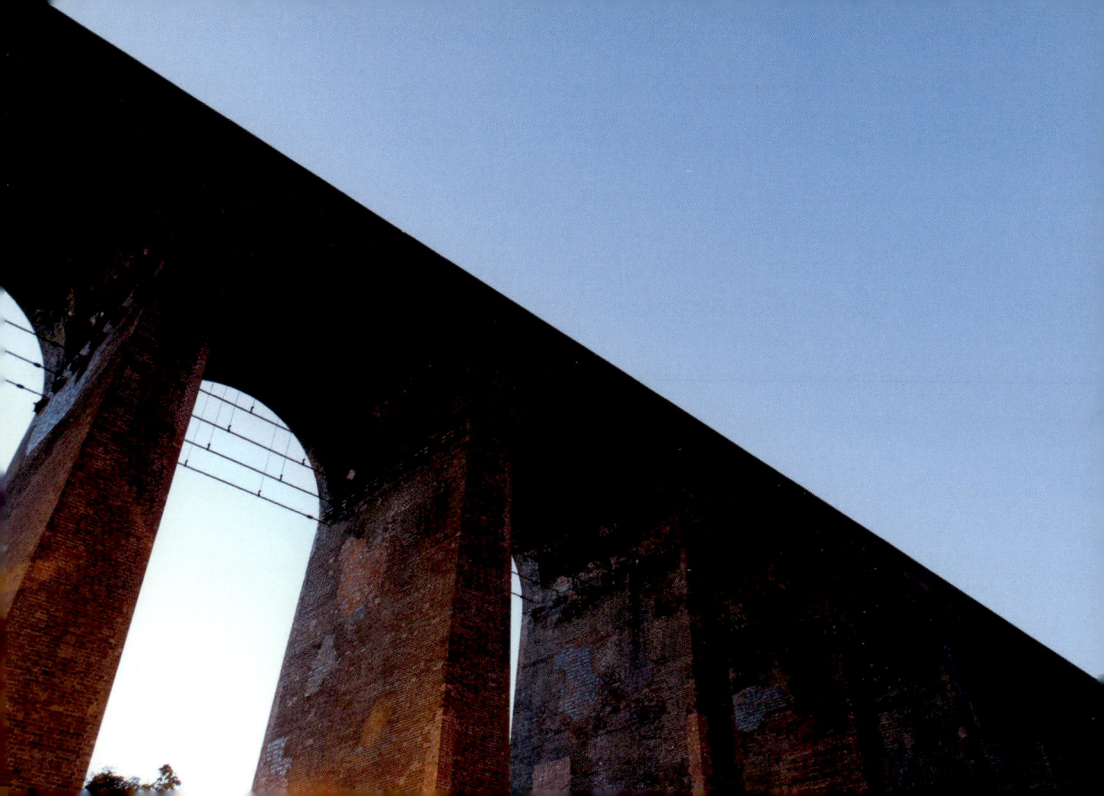

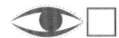

I do have an attraction to the Cold War era Royal Observer Corps nuclear observation point on the hills overlooking Folkestone, having often gone past it walking from Hawkinge to the Harvey Grammar School. As an object of modern history that is almost unknown in the town, it fascinated me that for decades certain local people were on constant alert to receive a phone call, rush to the observation point leaving their families behind, lock themselves down and report nuclear explosions over the English Channel to a central command centre.

म हकिंगसबाट हार्बि ग्रामर स्कुल जाँदा शीतयुद्धको समयमा बनाएको Royal Observtory Corps बाट दृश्यावलोकन गर्ने गर्दछु । यो डाँडाबाट फोक्सटन शहरको चारैतिर हेर्न सकिन्छ । यो आधुनिक ईतिहासको विषय भएकोले शहरमा बस्ने मानिसहरुलाई यसको बारेमा जानकारी थिएन । स्थानिय मानिसहरु बर्षौं वर्ष सम्म फोनको प्रतिक्षा गर्दथे । फोन आएको बेला उनीहरु जति सक्दो चाँडो आफ्नो परिवारहरुलाई छाडेर observation point मा गएर English Channel मा परमाणु विस्फोटन भएको खबर command centre मा गराउँदथे । यो कुराले म प्रभावित हुन्थे ।

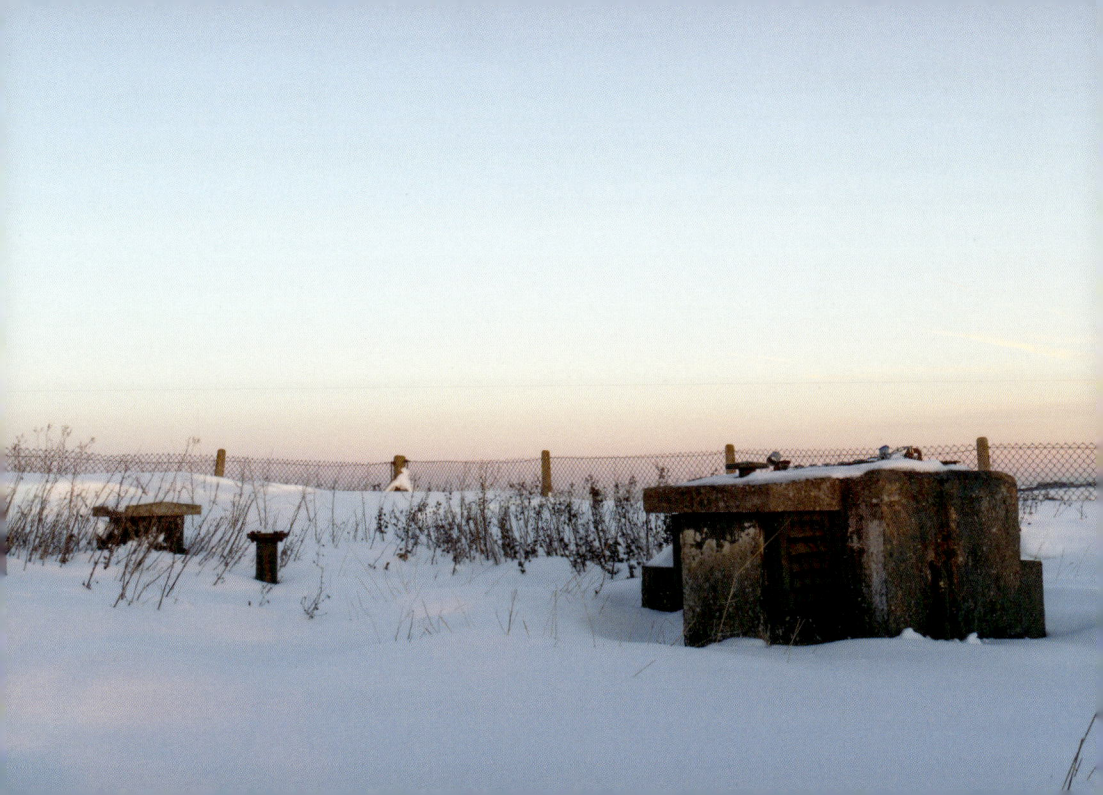

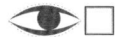

This building was constructed underground, so as not to block the light to the hotels then on either side of it. It opened in 1902 as a tearoom, with luncheons costing two shillings and sixpence and afternoon tea for sixpence. The lease required that it was to be used for "the highest class tea and refreshment trade with a view to securing the best class of visitor only." It had a sprung floor for dancing. In 1928 a stage was built and it began to be used as a theatre, becoming well known for its tea matinées where the actors had to compete with the noise of clattering tea cups. In the 1960s the theatre was home to the Arthur Brough Players. Arthur was a local actor who was best known for his role as Mr Grainger in early episodes of *Are You Being Served*?

One memorable occasion in the 1960s, during one of the plays, an actress got to her feet having previously been seated, and there was a collective inward gasp from the entire (mostly elderly) audience, as she was sporting a mini skirt!

जमिन मुनिको यो भवन सन १९०२ मा होटलहरु र अर्कापटी प्रकाश नछेकोस भनेर बनाईएको थियो । सन १९०२ मा सर्वसाधारणलाई उच्चकोटीको चिया र नृत्यको लागि खोलिएको थियो । सन १९२८ मा यहाँ मंच बनाईयो र सन १९७० को दशकमा बन्द नभए सम्म नाचघरको लागि प्रयोग गरियो । त्यस पश्चात यो सार्वजनिक घरको रुपमा छ ।

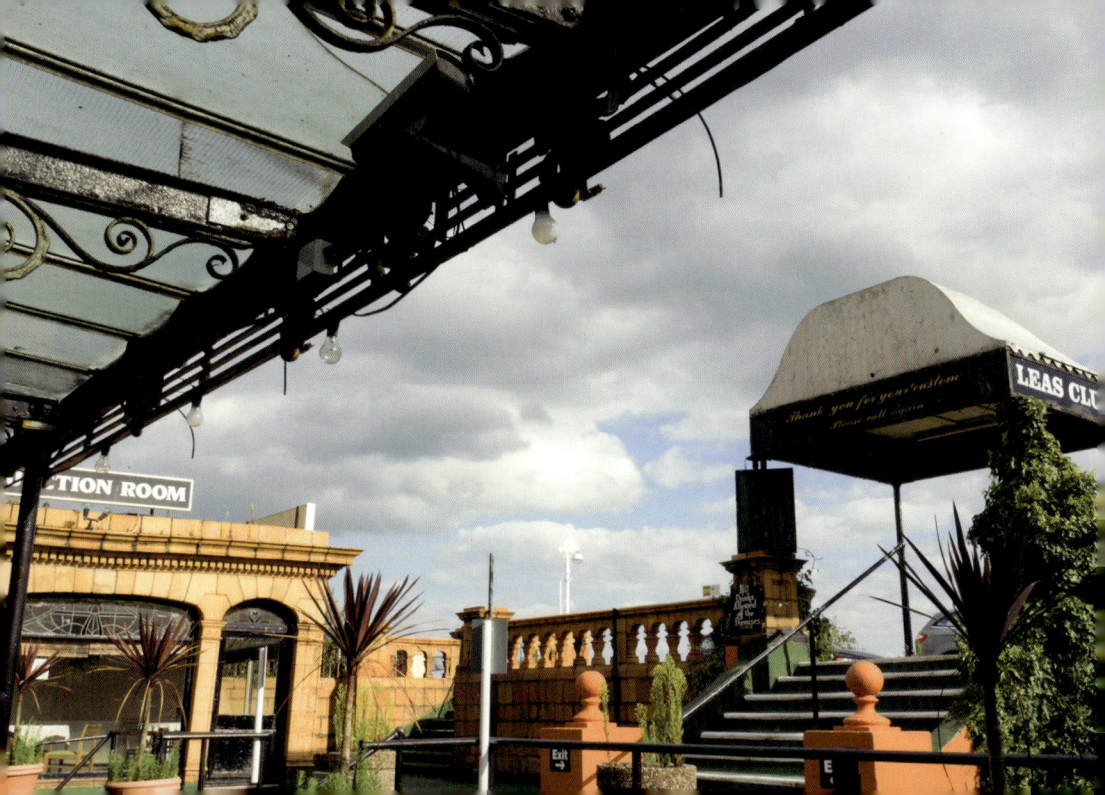

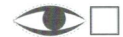

Folkestone's little old fashioned cinema is a real treat to visit, especially if you are a bit of a movie romantic. It feels like you are stepping back into the past and it's a breath of fresh air compared to the multi screen places. One of the really special features is in the back row of the main auditorium: don't go alone, as this is where you will find a row of red velvet 'love seats' that are double width so that you can snuggle up and enjoy the film with your loved one or latest squeeze.

यो फोक्सटनमा भएको स्यानो चलचित्र सुन्दर छ । यसको पछाडी पट्टीको लाइनमा प्रेमी प्रमिकाहरुको लागी केही फराकिलो कुर्सीहरु छन, जहा संगै वसेर आनन्दमयी चलचित्र हेर्दछन ।

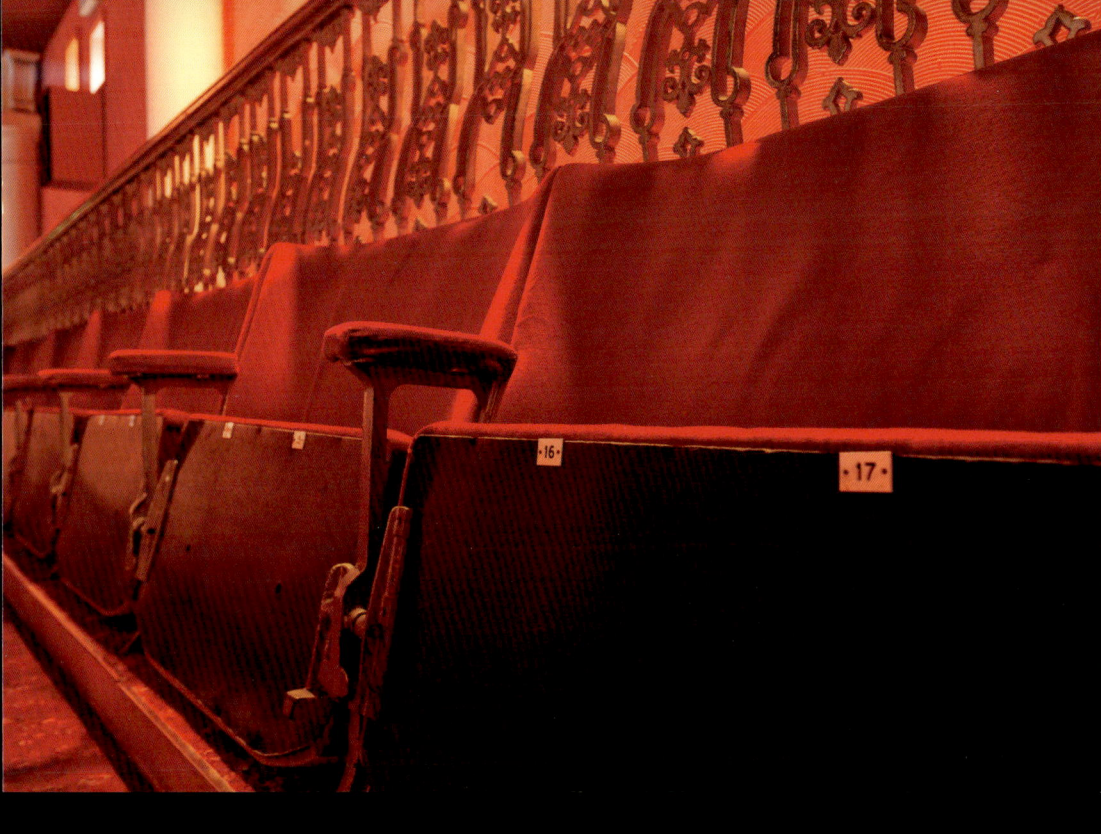

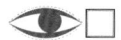

There is much talk about the Leas Lift, yet few folks can better monitor the times it is in operation than can someone swimming in the sea. I have swum many a day along the Folkestone seafront in front of the lift; the lift was my marker – where I put my towel and shoes – during my early morning training for Channel swims. It was my sole companion, it was comforting and reassuring to hear the sounds of the lift in operation when the it began to transport each morning… I knew someone was watching!

म Channel मा पौडी खेलदा पनि Leas Lift बजेको सुन्ने गर्दथ्ये । मेरा जुत्ताहरु यसको ठिक अगाडी पट्टीको बगरमा राखेर यसको वरीपरि पौडी खेल्ने गर्दथ्ये ।

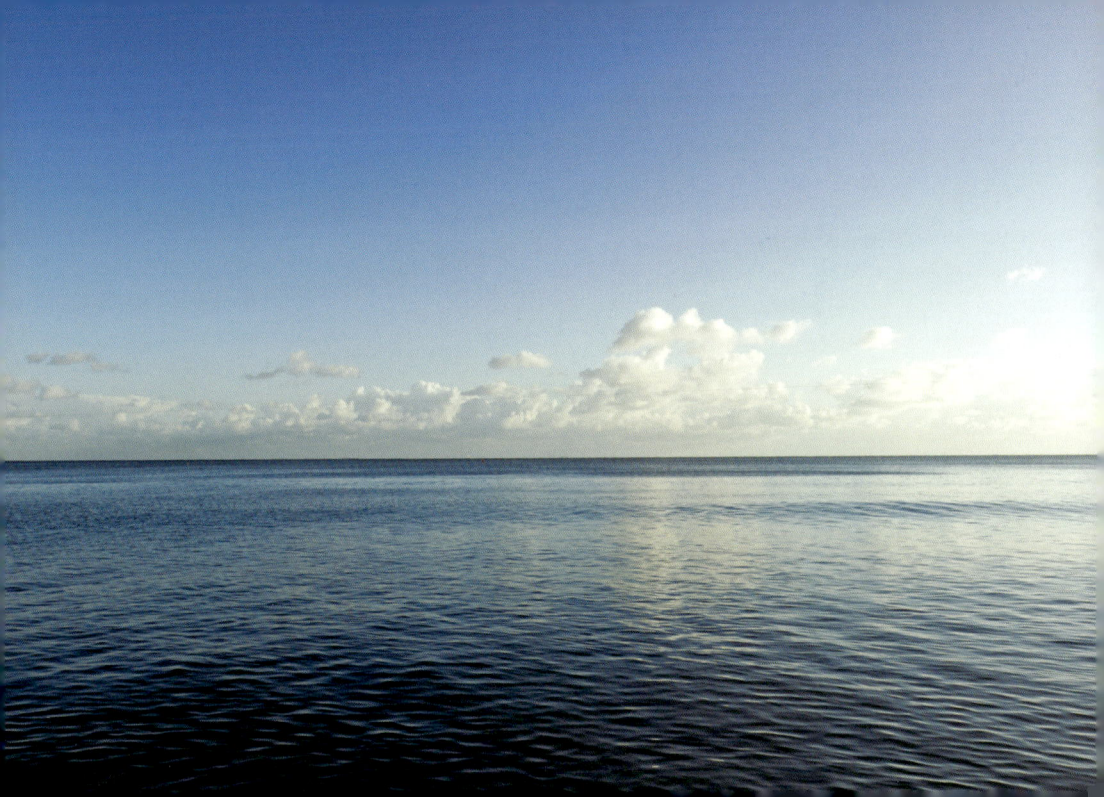

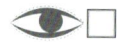

Now a very popular pub, this lovely building used to be a Baptist church. You really need to go inside to fully appreciate it, although the atmosphere has changed a bit! At the back of the building you can still see the pipes from the original church organ. In between being a church and a pub it was for a time a shopping arcade. Several of the traders reported hearing ghostly footsteps on the upper floor and others have heard unexplained whistling up there too. Samuel Peto was a well-known Baptist famous for building railways and Nelson's Column as well as being an MP.

पहिला यो एउटा गिर्जाघर थियो तर अहिले Samuel Peto को पब छ । उनी एउटा Baptist धर्ममधिकारी थिए जसले रेल मार्ग र Nelson's Column निर्माणमा ठुलो भूमिका निर्वाह गरेका थिए । उनी आफैमा उउटा सांसद पनि थिए ।

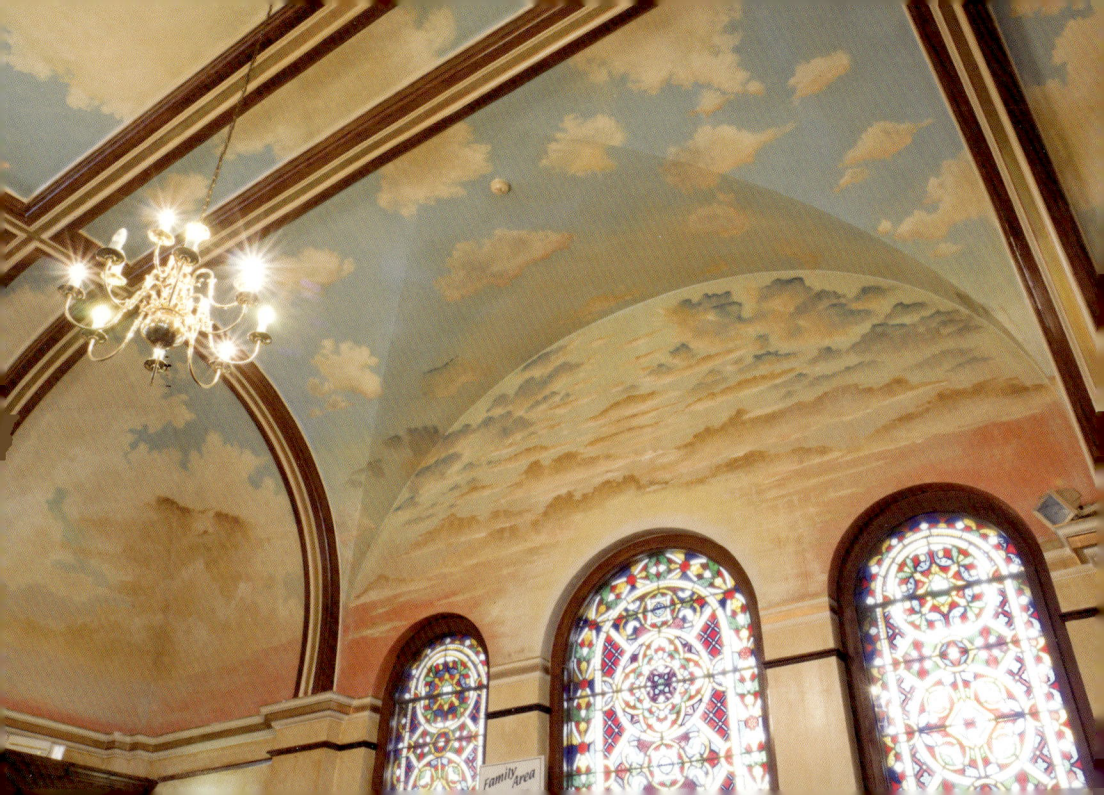

These tram tracks are left over from the mid 19th century, when they served the fish market and the early ferry berth, terminating at the end of the Stade where the South Eastern & Chatham Railway had a marine works. There were a couple of turntables I believe; one of them was under where the Jetty café was near the railway viaduct to the Harbour Station.

The tram tracks were used by horse-drawn trams, which used to go along the Stade to a turntable, leading down alongside the main railway line where fish was loaded on to trains.

घोडाले तान्ने बग्गी यो बाटो हुँदै मुख्य रेलमार्ग सम्म जाने गर्दथ्यो जाहाँ रेलमा माछा भरिन्थ्यो ।

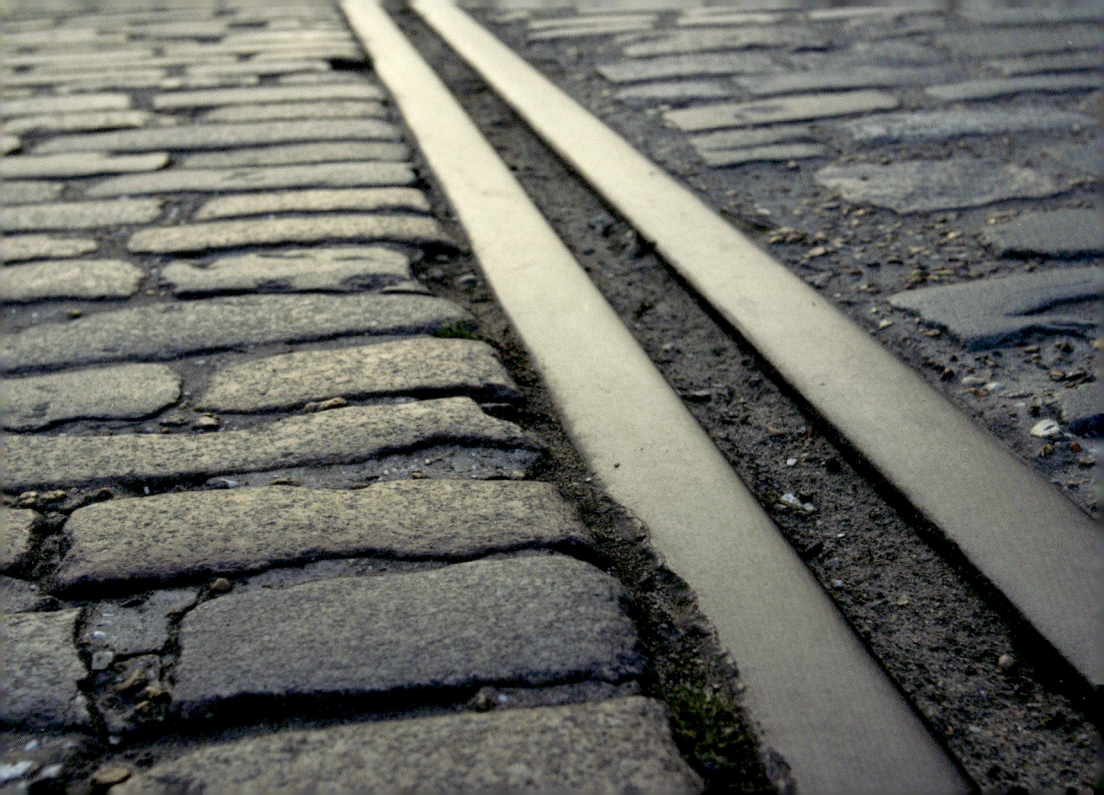

If you look closely you will see that the rocks on the Zig Zag Path are actually man made – known as 'Pulhamite' after the firm of landscape gardeners, James Pulham & Sons, who built the path in the early 1920s. Pulhamite is made from rubble bound together with special concrete and in places you can pick out bit of glass and crockery that were mixed in. The path was built so that bath chairs could be pushed up from the Lower Sandgate Road to the promenade on the Leas. You'd need to be fit! They even added some caves and grottos. The project provided much needed work for local unemployed men and soldiers returning from the First World War.

यो घुमाउरो बाटोको ठुलो ढुंगा वास्तविक होइन । वास्तवमा यो गिटी र सिमेन्टले बनाईएको हो । सायद यसमा बालुवा र सिसाका टुक्राहरु मिसाएको हुन सक्छ । पहिलो विश्व युद्ध पछ्ाडि बनाईएको यो बाटोमा हिंडन नसक्ने मानिसहरुले प्रयोग गने गुड्ने कुसिहरु

तल बाट माथीतिर गुडाउन सजिलो होस भन्ने आषयले बनाईएको थियो ।

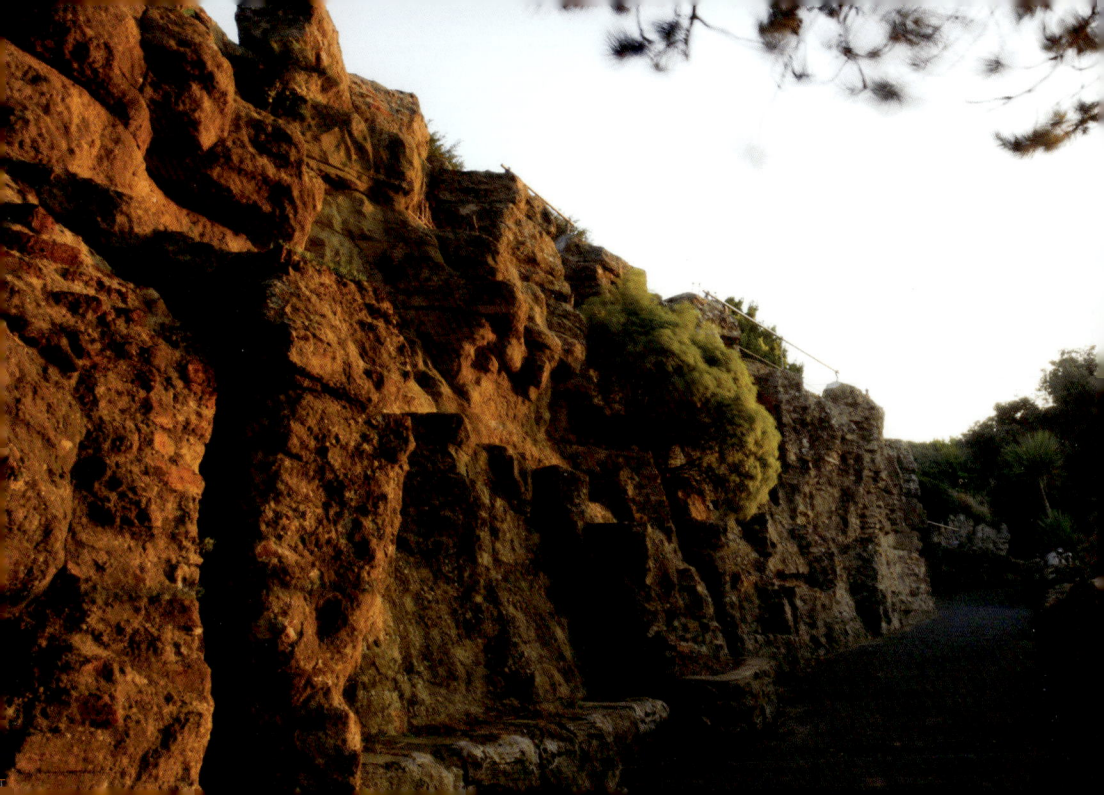

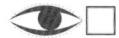

The white line around the hill is apparently the remains of a tank trap, dug by teams of local men, left over from the Second World War. Hard to believe that anyone would consider driving a tank up such a steep hill! If the Germans had made it to the top they would have been rewarded by fantastic views of Folkestone and the surrounding countryside. They would also have been able to explore the earthworks which are all that remains of a castle dating back to the time of wars between Stephen and Matilda. The hill is also known locally as Caesar's Camp but there doesn't seem to be any evidence linking this site to the Romans.

यो डाडाको वरीपरी देखिन्ने सेतो धर्सा दोश्रो विश्व युद्धताका स्थानिय वासिन्दाहरुले बनाएको तबलप धरापको अवशेष हो । तर यसतो भिरालो पाखामा पनि तबलप दगुर्छ भनेर विश्वास गर्न भने गाह्रे छ । यदी यो जर्मनीहरुले बनाएको हो भने फोक्सटन र यसको वरपरको शौदर्य तथा मनमोहक इलाकाको तर्फबाट उनिहरुलाई सम्मान गर्नु पर्दथ्यो ।

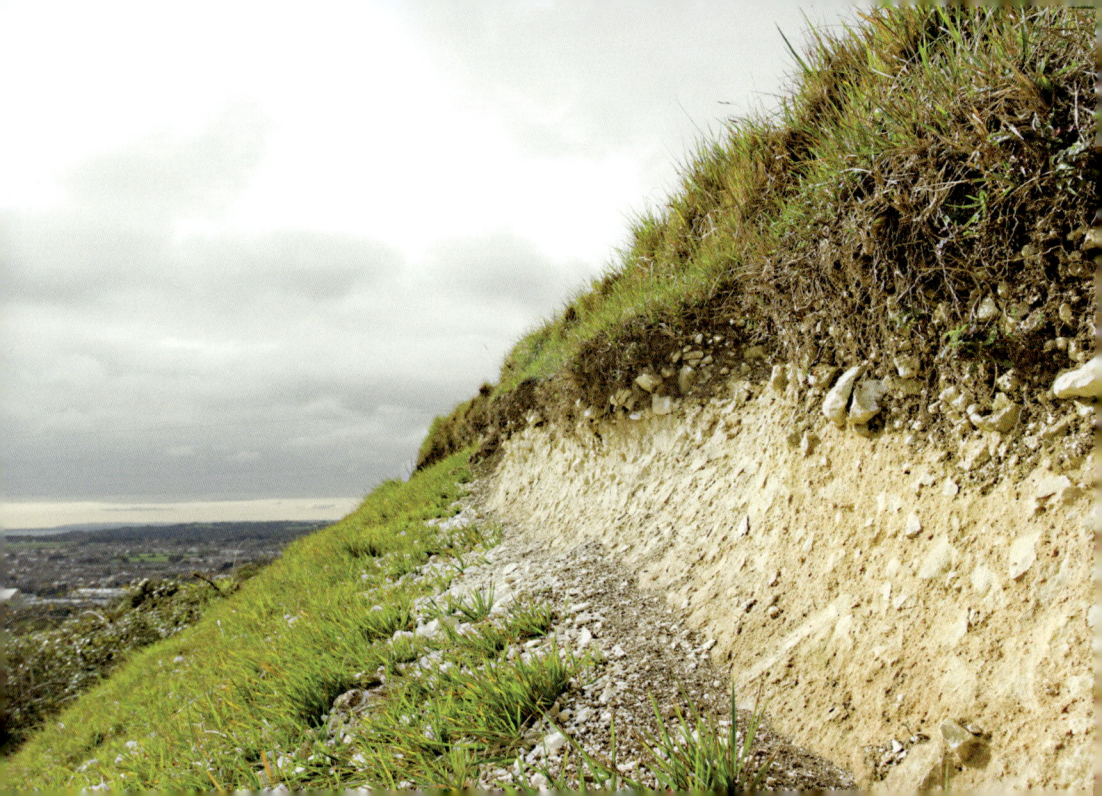

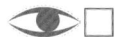

In 1893 the Corporation undertook to provide facilities for public concerts and gave consent to erect bandstands. The first was built in 1893 in the Marine Gardens which had been extensively laid out and planted at the same time. The second was erected on the Leas, opposite Clifton Gardens in 1895 – the only one still standing. The third came about more by accident than by design. The Metropole Hotel was built at the west end of the Leas in 1897 in a setting of gardens, lawns and tennis courts. In the grounds between the wings of the hotel a bandstand was erected for the delectation of guests. Unfortunately the sounds reverberated from the walls and disturbed them. So the proprietors of the hotel (Gordon Hotels Ltd) gave the bandstand to the Corporation, who erected it on the West Leas in front of the hotel in 1902 – the circular flowerbed now in front of it indicates its original location. The bandstands were much appreciated by the fashionable crowds who sat on chairs round the them to listen to A Newman's 'Red Hungarian Band' or, later, Herr Worm's 'Blue Viennese Band'.

Leas मा यो मञ्च सन १८९५ मा निर्माण गरिएको थियो । समुन्द्र किनारमा बनाईएको जम्मा तीन वटा मञ्चहरु मध्ये हाल एउटा मात्र अवस्थित छ ।

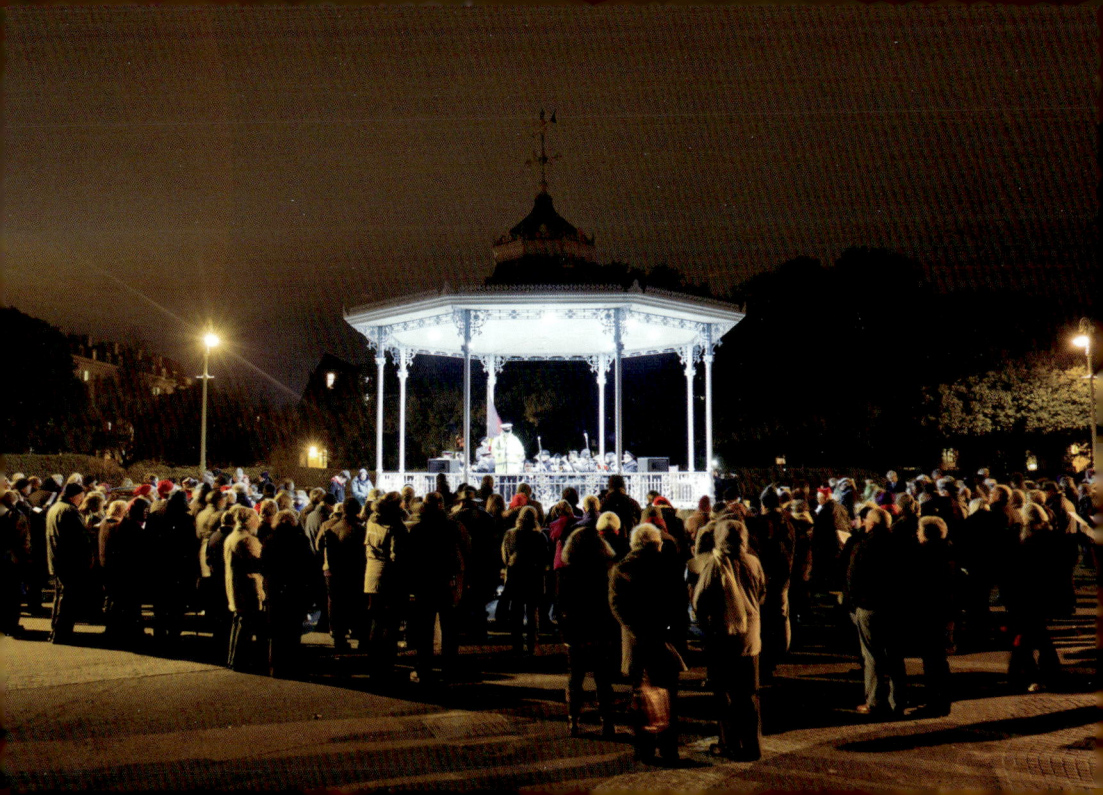

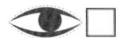

Back in the 19th century this was a toll road, being an easier route between Folkestone Harbour and Sandgate (than going via Sandgate Hill), and this was the old Toll House. You can walk or cycle through and the road has been converted to a children's play area with a zip wire so it's more exciting than the old fashioned playgrounds. Once the children have used up their energy you can have a cup of tea in the Mermaid Café overlooking the sea, or visit the modern day amphitheatre, which is occasionally used for open air performances, before walking up the Zig Zag Path.

The original Toll House was made of wood, but it was only there for two years before the Earl of Radnor built this one – he must have been earning good money from the toll to afford to commission a rebuild in stone. What's really interesting for me is that the architect who built this house, Sydney Smirke, also built the British Library Reading Room, which my father worked in for many years. He was also the architect for Kings College London, which is where my sister lectured. It made buying the place seem like the right move.

१९ औं शताब्दि तिर यो ठाउँमा भएको काठको घरलाई भत्काएर पुरानो दुंगे Toll House को निर्माण गरिएको थियो । फोक्सटन वन्दरगाह बाट सानगेट जाने छोटो बाटो भएकोले सानगेटको डाँडा माथीबाट घुमेर जानुको साटो यहाँ शुल्क तिरेर भएपनि छोटो बाटो जाने गर्दछन मानिसहरु ।

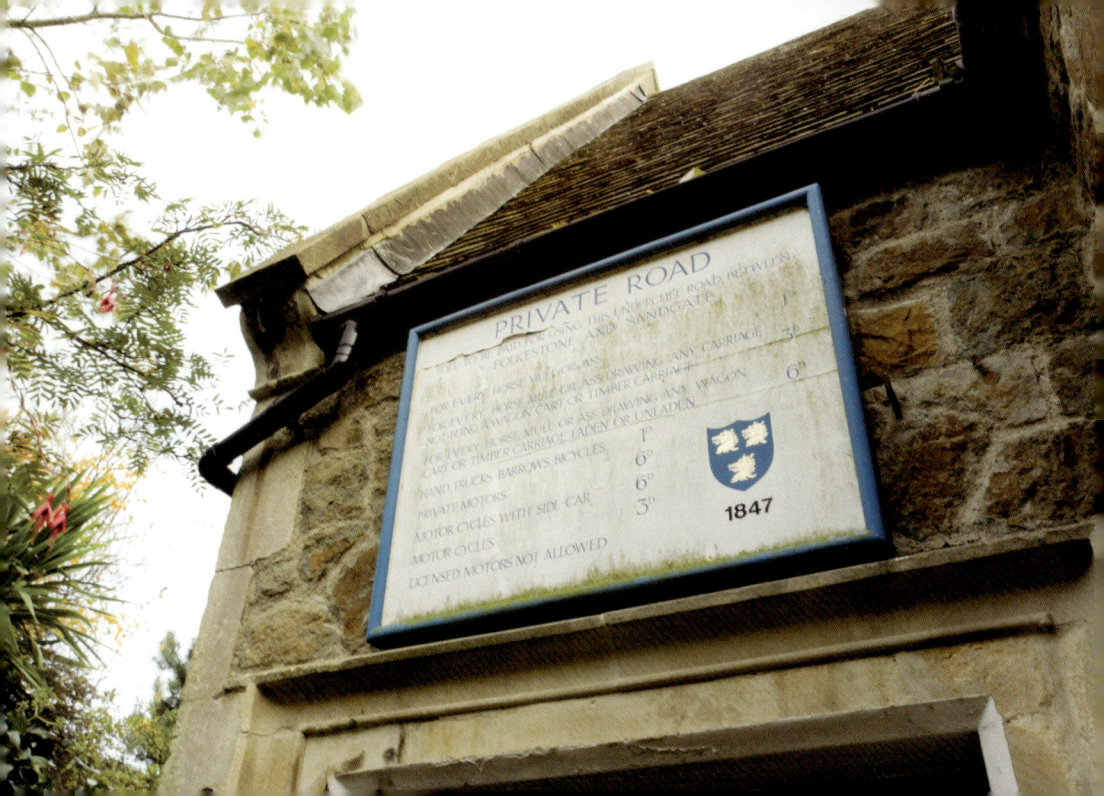

PRIVATE ROAD

TOLLS TO BE PAID FOR USING THE UNDERCLIFF ROAD BETWEEN
FOLKESTONE AND SANDGATE

FOR EVERY HORSE MULE OR ASS	1ᵈ
FOR EVERY HORSE MULE OR ASS DRAWING ANY CARRIAGE	3ᵈ
FOR EVERY HORSE MULE OR ASS DRAWING ANY WAGON CART OR TIMBER CARRIAGE	6ᵈ
NOT BEING A WAGON CART OR TIMBER CARRIAGE LADEN OR UNLADEN	
FOR EVERY HORSE MULE OR ASS DRAWING ANY WAGON	
CART OR TIMBER CARRIAGE LADEN OR UNLADEN	
HAND TRUCKS BARROWS BICYCLES	1ᵈ
PRIVATE MOTORS	6ᵈ
MOTOR CYCLES WITH SIDE CAR	6ᵈ
MOTOR CYCLES	3ᵈ
LICENSED MOTORS NOT ALLOWED	

1847

The magical singing tree, filled with a cacophony of sparrows: a glorious noise that lifts your heart. This little tree, with its seemingly hundreds of residents, is one of my favourite Folkestone landmarks. A place to pause and marvel at another world really. The tree is in such a dull spot – quite unremarkable, close to the road, opposite the police station by a bin. But if you time it right – dusk in spring or autumn is best I think – you find yourself standing in a magical place (it helps if you are dappy about birds).

जादुगर गीत गाउने रुख - भंगेराहरुको बथानले निकालेको चमत्कारिक धुनले सबैको मन छुन्छ ।

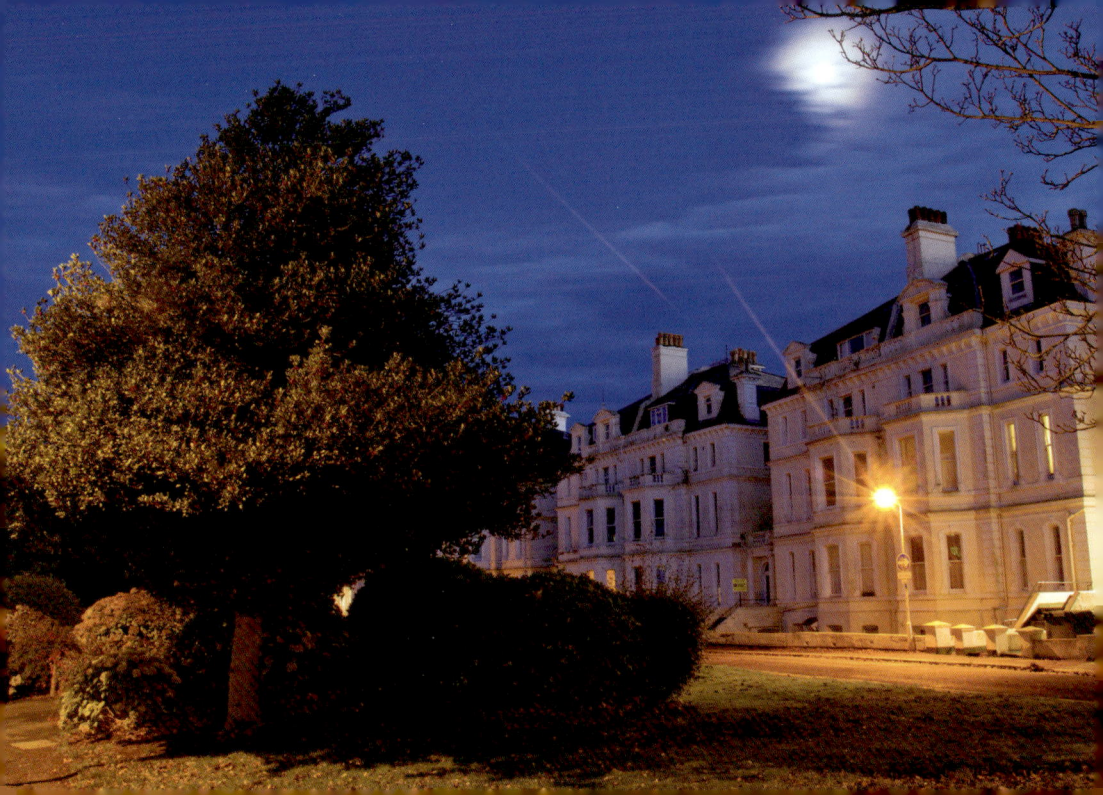

A time-travel of a pub – there's nowhere else like it. Strange compared to every other pub in town. Trapped in time, the 'E.C.T.' is a one-off. The exterior in a row of homes is easily overlooked. Step inside – gas fire (never on); the photo of Joanna Lumley and a pig (!); books to read (romance and historical adventure); the piano (never heard it played)… The glass showcase on the bar contains only aspirin and Curly-Wurlys, and a Walnut Whip if you're lucky. The locals are warm and friendly – I want to say that I find that surprising, but it sounds wrong, yet I can't ever recall walking into an unknown pub and having strangers turn and smile at me, it just never happens.

यो पब एउटा समय बिताउने ठाउँ हो । यसको भित्री भागमा केही पनि परिवर्तन गरिएको छैन र फोक्सटनमा भएको अन्य पबहरु भन्दा यो भिन्न प्रकारको छ ।

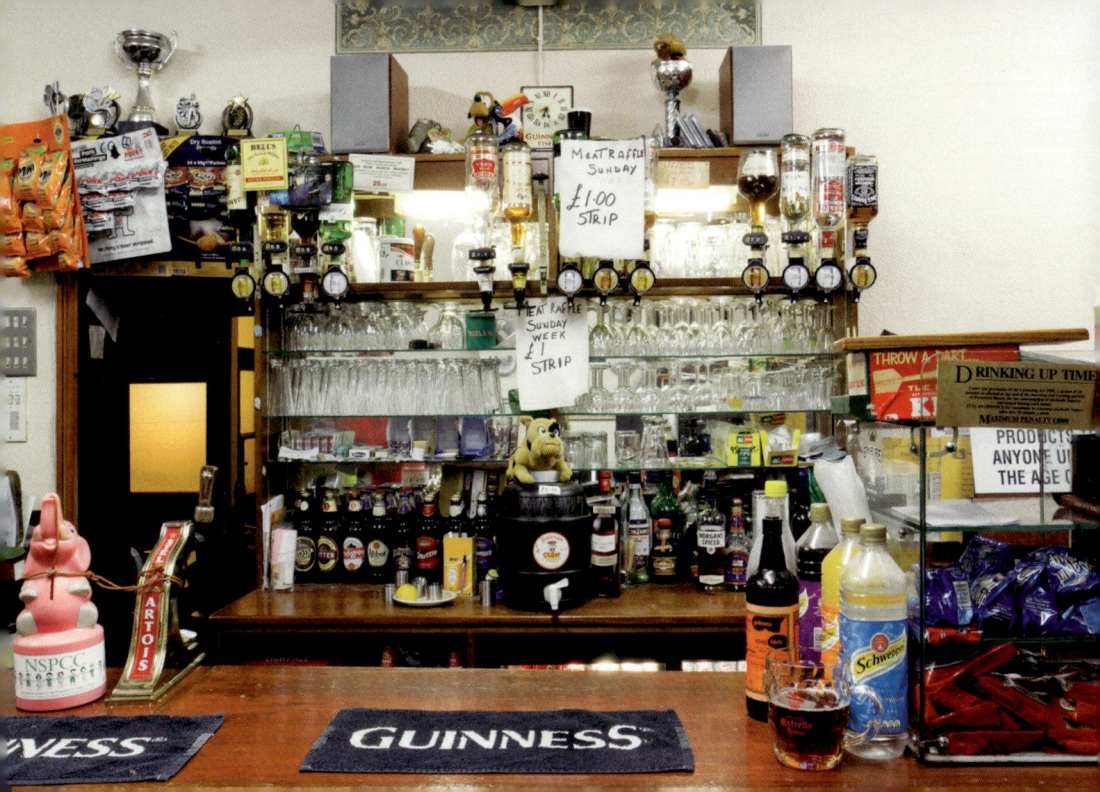

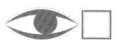

Charles Dickens made several visits to Folkestone. In 1855 he rented this house, which he described as "a pleasant little house with the sea below and the scent of thyme sweetening the breezes from the downs." It was here that he started work on *Little Doritt*.

Slightly further down the coast, HG Wells lived for many years in Sandgate and set his novel *Kipps* in the Folkestone area. He commissioned the architect Voysey to build a house overlooking the sea and many literary figures visited him here including Joseph Conrad, George Bernard Shaw and Henry James.

सन १८५५ मा भिक्टोरियाका पालाका प्रख्यात लेखक Charles Dickens ले तीनवटा Albion Villas भाँडामा लिएका थिए । उसले *Little Doritt* को शुरुवात यहींबाट गरेका थिए ।

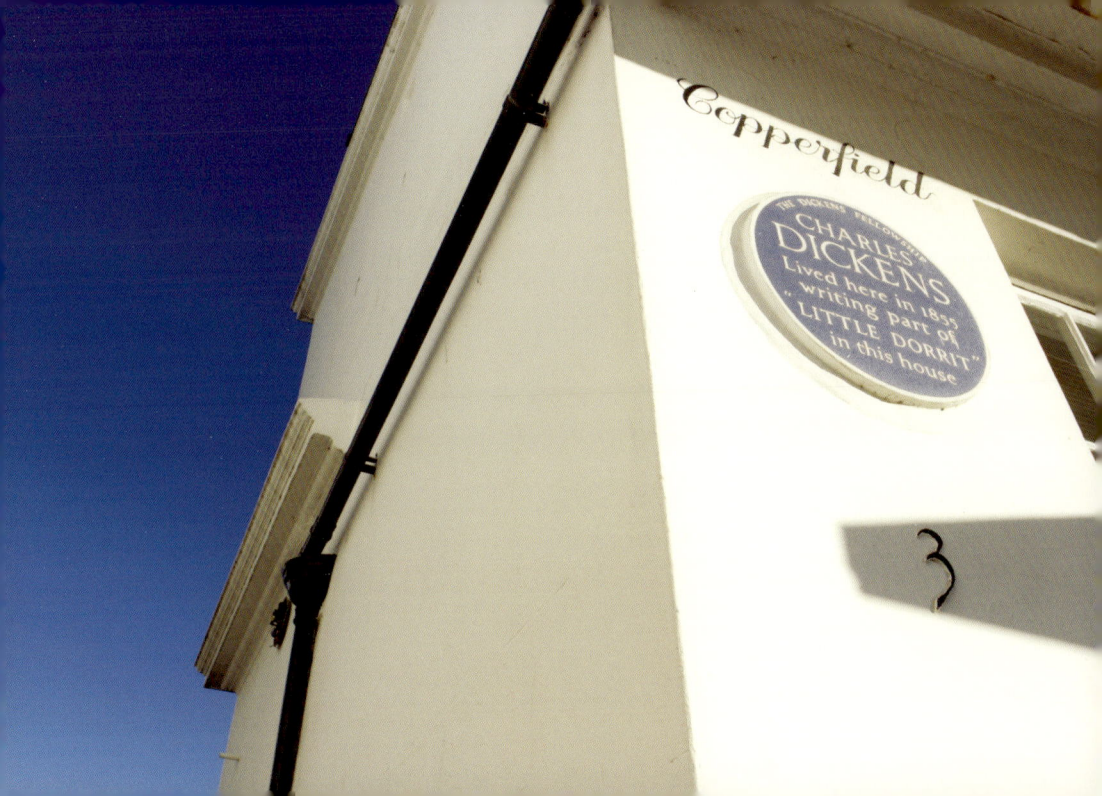

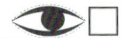

The name 'the Leas' suggests that this was once a meadow. When Folkestone was in its heyday as a popular seaside resort, the Leas was *the* place to be seen and The Grand and Metropole Hotels were *the* places to stay. Edward VII and his lady friend Alice Keppel (great, great grandmother of the Duchess of Cornwall) were regular visitors to The Grand. On a sunny afternoon take a stroll along the Leas and imagine the ladies and gentlemen promenading along in their fashionable clothes. At one time private policemen were employed by Lord Radnor to ensure that no riff raff disturbed the peace.

जुन समयमा फोक्सटन सामुद्रिक दृश्यवलोकनको लागी प्रख्यात थियो, तजभीभबक घुम्न योग्य थियो भने The Grand तथा Metropole Hotel मा मानिसहरु बस्ने गर्दथ्ये । उल्लेखित स्थानहरुमा तल्लो स्तरका मनिसहरुले व्यावधान खडा गरेमा त्यसको सुरक्षाको लागी Lord Radnor ले गैर सरकारी प्रहरीको नियुक्ती समेत गरेका थिए ।

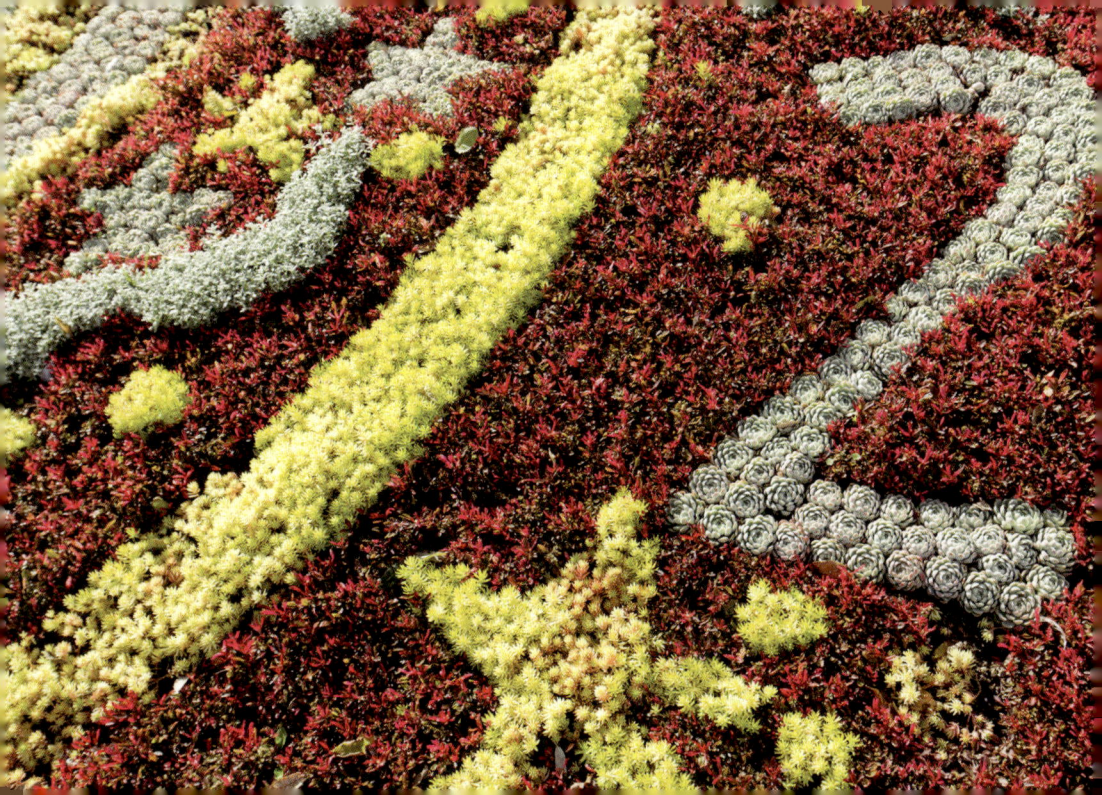

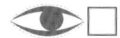

From the top of Castle Hill you can see the reservoir, presumably now the property of Veolia, but formerly owned by the Folkestone and Dover Water Company. Judging by pictures painted in the early nineteenth century, this used to be much more, with a beautiful lake, a tea room and cherry trees. Visitors to Folkestone would walk out to the Cherry Garden for afternoon tea. On special occasions local soldiers would put on a display of their skills on Castle Hill.

Castle Hill को माथीबाट हेर्दा एउटा ट्यांकी देख्न सकिन्छ, त्यो पुरानो नक्साहरुको त्यहा धेरै चिजहरु थिए भन्न सकिन्छ । जस्तै एउटा सुन्दर ताल, चेरीका रुखहरु र एउटा चिया उसल पनि ।

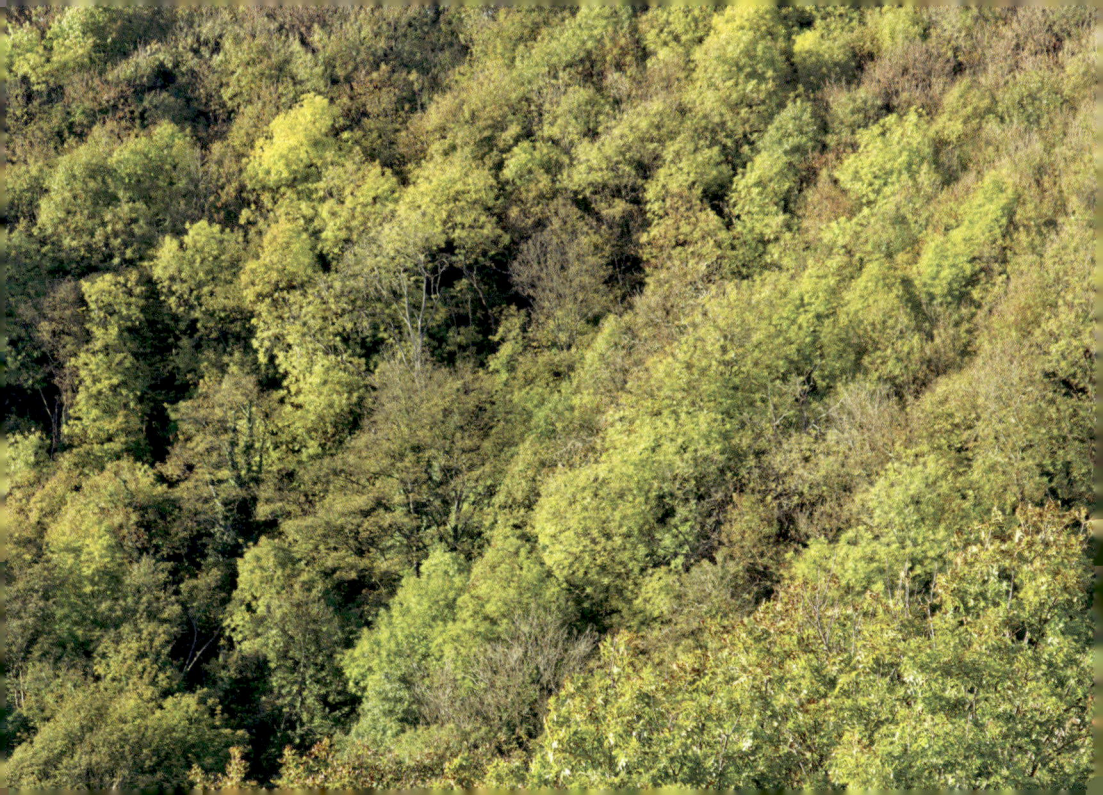

One of my earliest memories is sitting on my Dad's workbench, watching him repair shoes in his boot and shoe repair shop in Foord Road at the bottom of Palmerstone Road, near St John's Church. On the opposite corner was a fish and chip shop. I can still remember the distinctive smell of leather as I watched my dad hammering in tacks, nailing new soles to shoes.

मेरो वच्पन कालको संझनानुसार ययचम च्यबम मा भएको मेरो वाबाको जुत्ता मरमत गर्ने पसलको एउटा वेन्चको छेउमा वसेर उसले छालाको जुत्तामा काटी हमरले ठोकेको हेरिरहन्थे । त्यसवेला गनाएको छालाको गन्ध अझै पनि संझन्छु ।

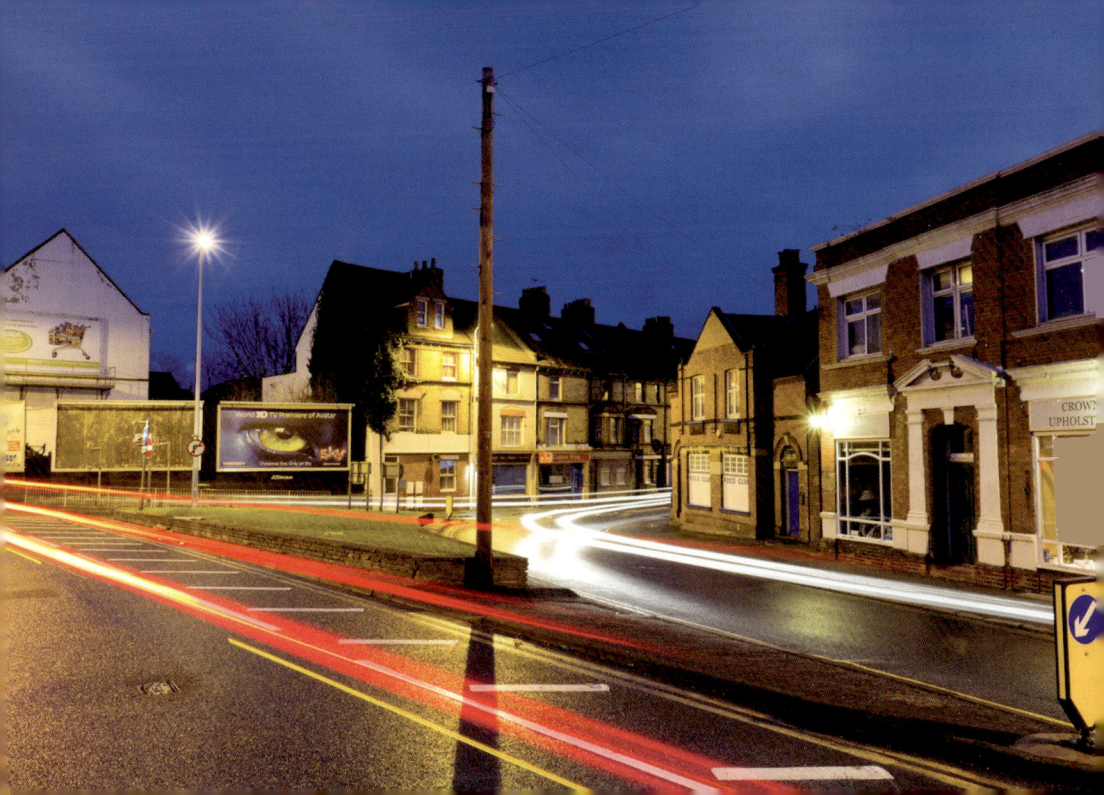

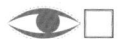

As a boy I used to go 'crabbing' in Folkestone Harbour. My brothers and I would get scraps of fish from the fish market or the whelk stalls, tie them to pieces of string and dangle them in the water in the harbour. We would catch tiny green crabs. I guess we threw them back in again afterwards.

उमेरमा म दाजुसँग बन्दरगाहामा माछा मार्न जान्थे । हामीहरु ससाना माछाहरु जम्मा गरेर त्यसका टुक्राहरु धागोमा बान्थ्यौं र पानीमा डुबाएर राख्थ्यौं । हामी स-साना हरियो गँगटाहरु समात्थ्यौं ।

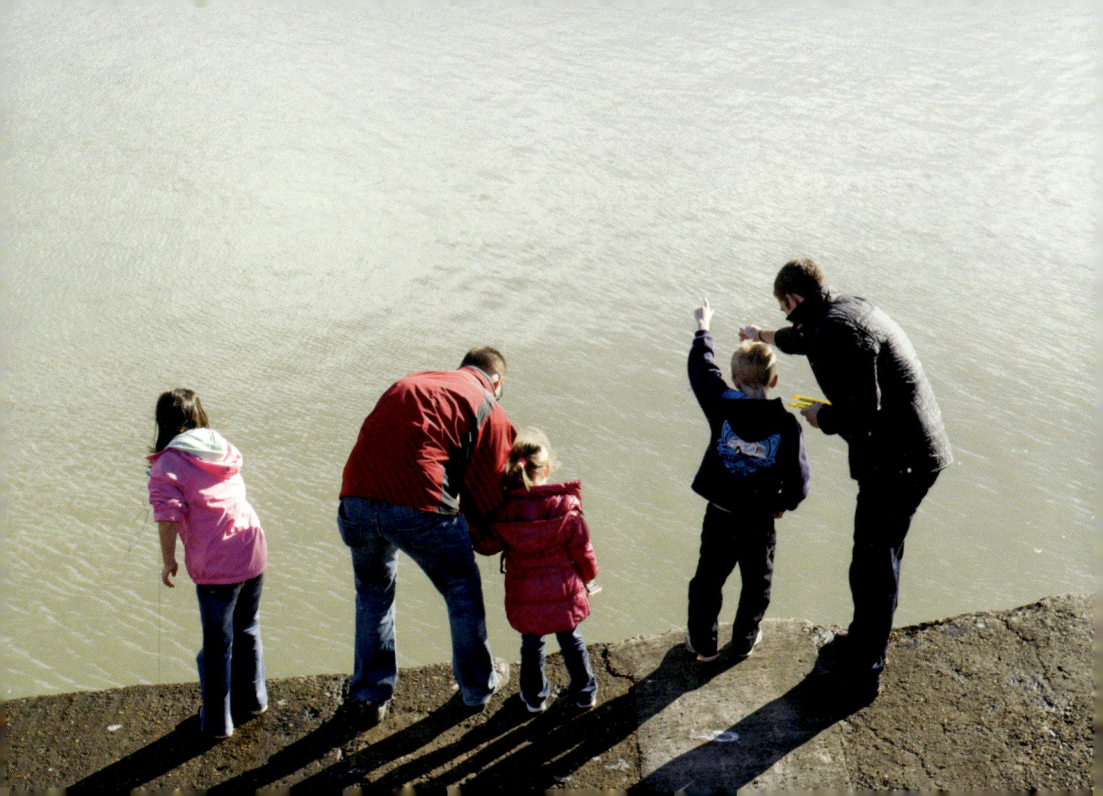

Essential equipment: WD40, broom, dustpan.

Nightmare – crusty padlock, warped door-frame, blistered paint; heroic survivor of rain, spray and deathly cold winds. Apply brute force, cursing, rage and despair, then creak, heave, bang – open at last. Cringe as a million spiders execute random scuttling manoeuvres. Dare to go in. Extreme caution, big ones could be lurking on the ceiling ready to drop. Haul out mould-stained chairs. Examine the umbrella, shake it out over the beach, drag out that bit of stinky old carpet, brush cobwebs off the bike – tyres flat as a pancake. Hasn't been ridden in years but you never know, might come in handy. Flash forward to summer: sunshine, towel drying on the wall, factor 40, salty skin, Crocks (used to be jelly shoes), cool box, crossword, hefty novel. Hutters: "Hello, you here again – marvellous eh." Dog walkers: "Oh naughty boy, sorry he's just being friendly." Dawdling kids: "Stop staring will you, come on I said." Like being on stage or in a museum or a gallery – who can resist a sidelong glance?

Title: *Middle-aged woman reclines by shed*. Mixed media.

"Look at 'er with 'er wine!" Ha ha – nothing beats it – must *try* not to snore…

जाडो मौसम पछि मेरो समुन्द्रिक किनारको कटेरो सफा गरे । गृष्म याममा बाहिर बस्दा संग्रहालय र नाचघरको मन्चमा बसेको जस्तो मलाई अनुभव हुन्छ । मानिसहरु चिने जानेको जस्तै देखिन्छन् तर सहयोग गर्न सक्दैनन् । तर पनि मलाई राम्रो लाग्छ ।

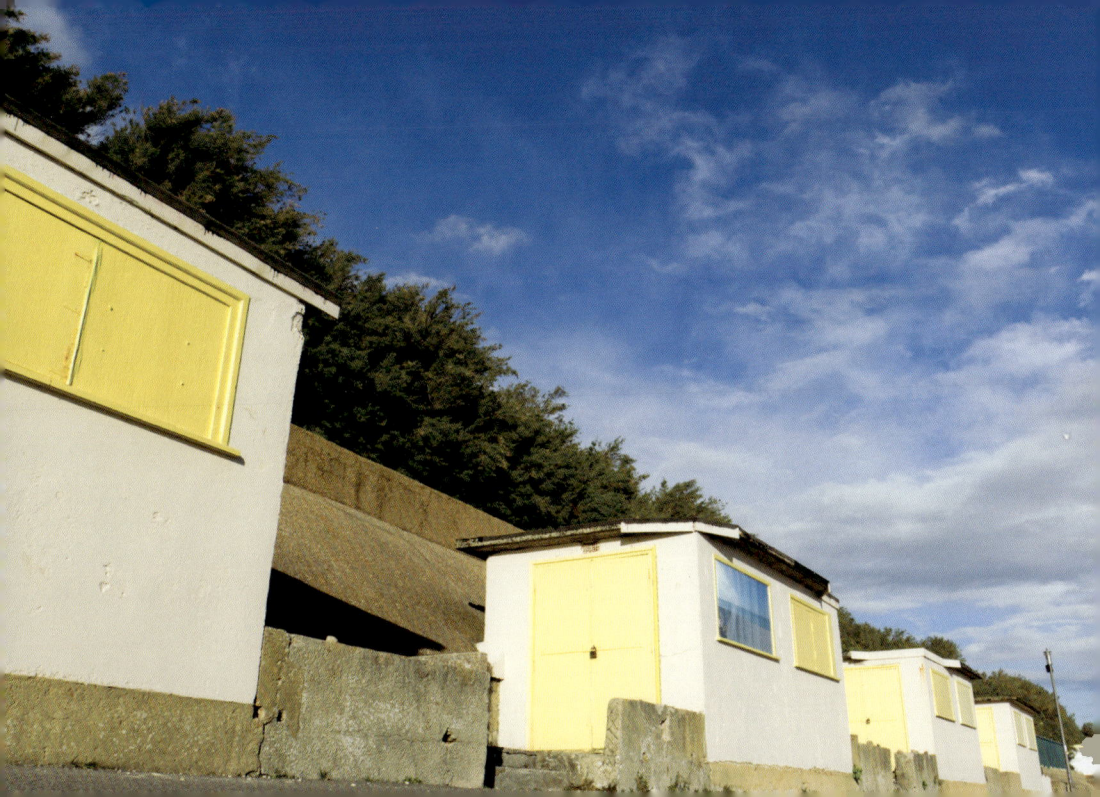

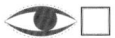

As a young man I spent many happy hours at the Rotunda, on the seafront. It had a slogan, something like – 'You'll wonder what keeps the roof up'! It was a large round concrete domed building full of slot machines, pinball machines etc. I used to love the 'What the Butler Saw' flickergraphs – you turned the handle and got an illicit glimpse of scantily-clad women. In the Rotunda they had a great old jukebox which played old 78s. I remember listening to the new rock'n'roll hits – Presley, Fats Domino, Chuck Berry and the like. Nearby were the dodgems and a roller skating rink – a good place to meet the girls, I seem to remember. Of course the Lower Sandgate Road and the Zig Zag Path up led to the Leas from The Rotunda and were good places to go for walking with the girls you had just met!

युवास्थामा मैले समुन्द्रि किनारको Rotunda को खुल्ला मैदानमा रमाईलो पलहरु बिताएको थिए । यहाँ 'You will wonder what keeps the roof up' उक्ती लेखिएको थियो । यो एउटा ठुलो घुमाउरो परेको भवन थियो । यहाँ विद्युतबाट चल्ने जुवा र अन्य खेल सामग्रीका मशिनहरु थिए । केटीहरुसँग भेटघाट गर्ने यो एउटा राम्रो ठाउँ पनि थियो ।

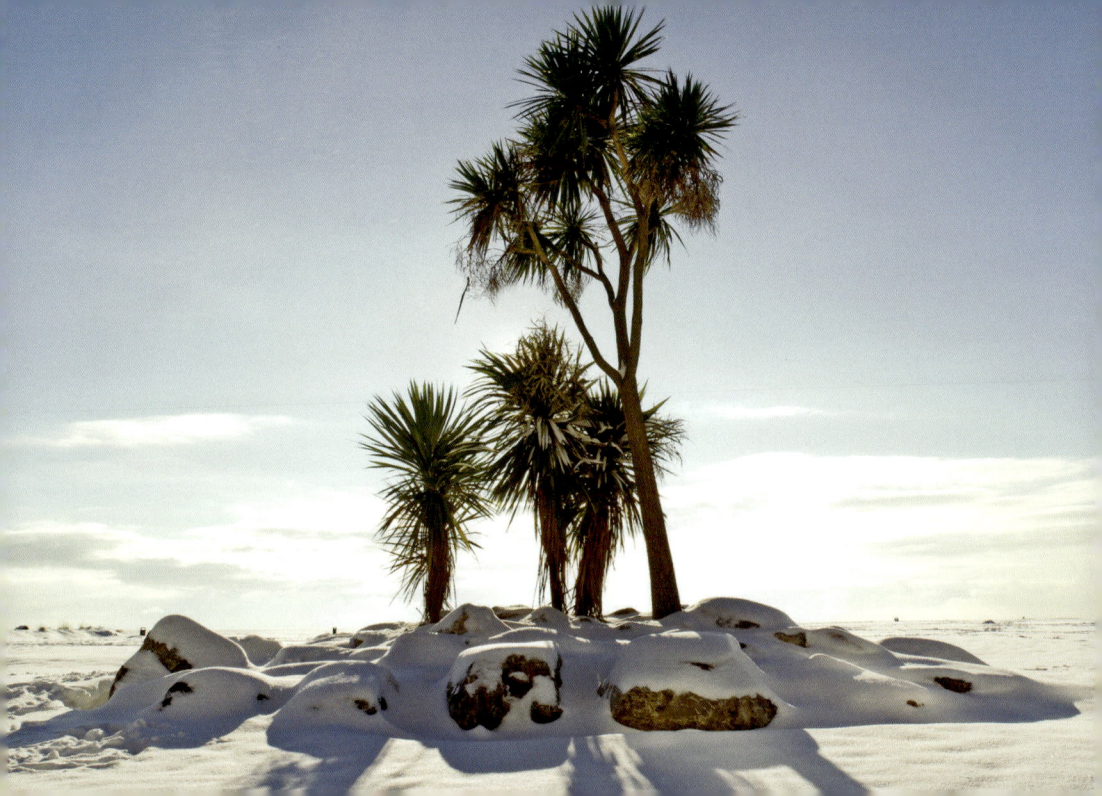

I love all the steps we have in Folkestone. I always look at the steps from half way down The Old High Street, leading to the Bayle, and imagine drunken fishermen, thieves and prostitutes there 200 or, 300 years ago; very evocative.

There are a lot of old stone flights of steps in Folkestone. Many lead in and out of the older areas of town. I remember a story about the ones that lead from The Old High Street up to the Bayle. Back in the early seventies a couple of blokes fell out over something in a nearby pub, one of them left, went home, and got a machete, which he brought back and hid on top of a wall at the top of the steps. He went back to the pub, where the row had started, words were exchanged, then he left the pub and ran up the steps – and waited, machete in hand, in the dark. When the other man ran up the steps he hit him on the head with the machete. Luckily it was only a glancing, bloody blow, but not life threatening. Next day I remember there was a lot of blood on the steps.

हामी हिँडेको फोक्सटनको सबै यात्रा राम्रो लाग्छ । म तिनीहरुलाई Old High Street को बिच देखि तल Bayle जाने बाटो संधै हेर्छु र संझने गर्छु, करिव ३०० वर्ष अगाडी त्यहां भएको मातेको मत्छ्य सिकारी, चोरहरु अनी वेश्याहरुको कल्पना गर्छु ।

EVERYWHERE MEANS SOMETHING TO SOMEONE

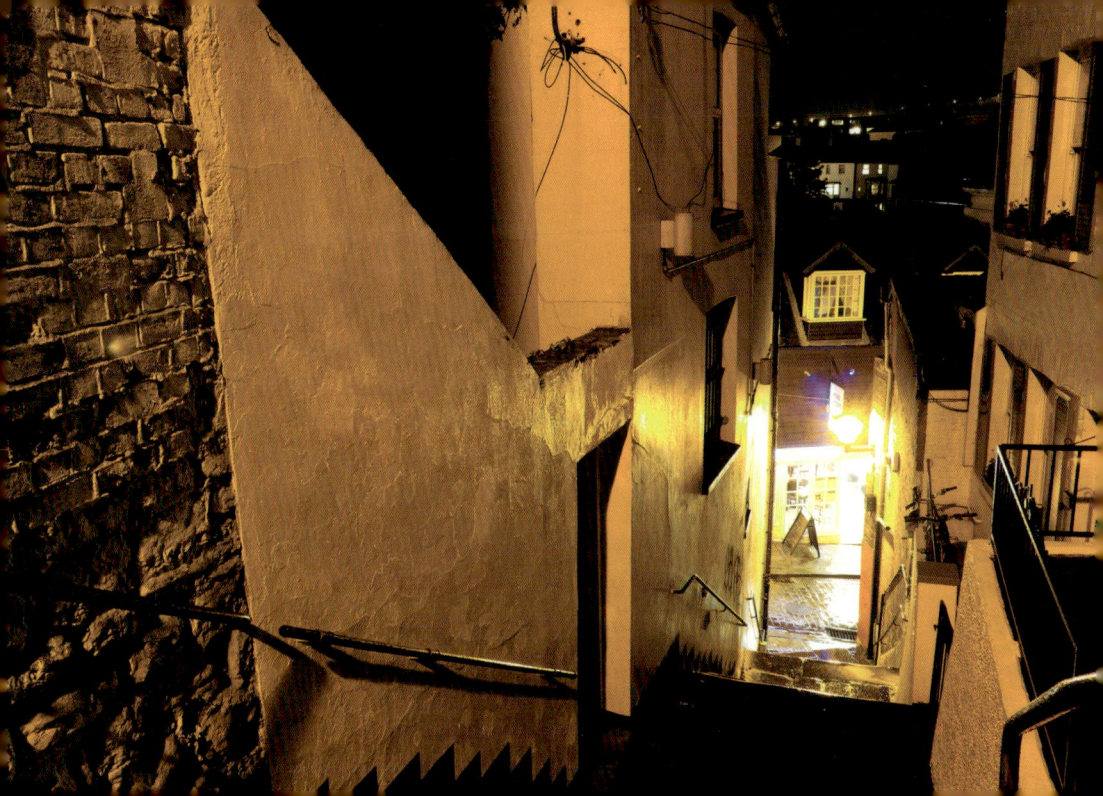

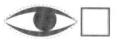

One summer night, we decided to have a bit of a party down on Sunny Sands. Just by the ramp, we managed to collect enough wood for a good fire and chipped in some money for a few bottles of cider. The party was going well, when a young guy drove up in a nice new car, his parents were away on holiday and he had got hold of the car keys. Showing off, he drove the car right down the ramp onto the sands. When the tide started coming in, he tried to drive back up, but the car bogged down. The waves came in really high and were smashing the car against the concrete arch, he stood there crying, probably thinking how he was going to tell his parents what had happened to their nice car.

गरम समयमा हामीहरुले समुन्द्र किनारमा एउटा पार्टीको आयोजना गरेका थियौं । हाम्रो एक साथिले छुट्टी बिताउनु गएको उसको अविभावकको नयाँ गाडी यहाँ ल्याएको थियो । समुन्द्रको सतह बढेपछि उसले गाडी कुदाउन सकेन र नजिकैको पर्खालमा ठोक्कायो । यो घटना आफ्नो अविभावकलाई कसरी सुनाउने भनेर उ धेरै चिन्तित थियो ।

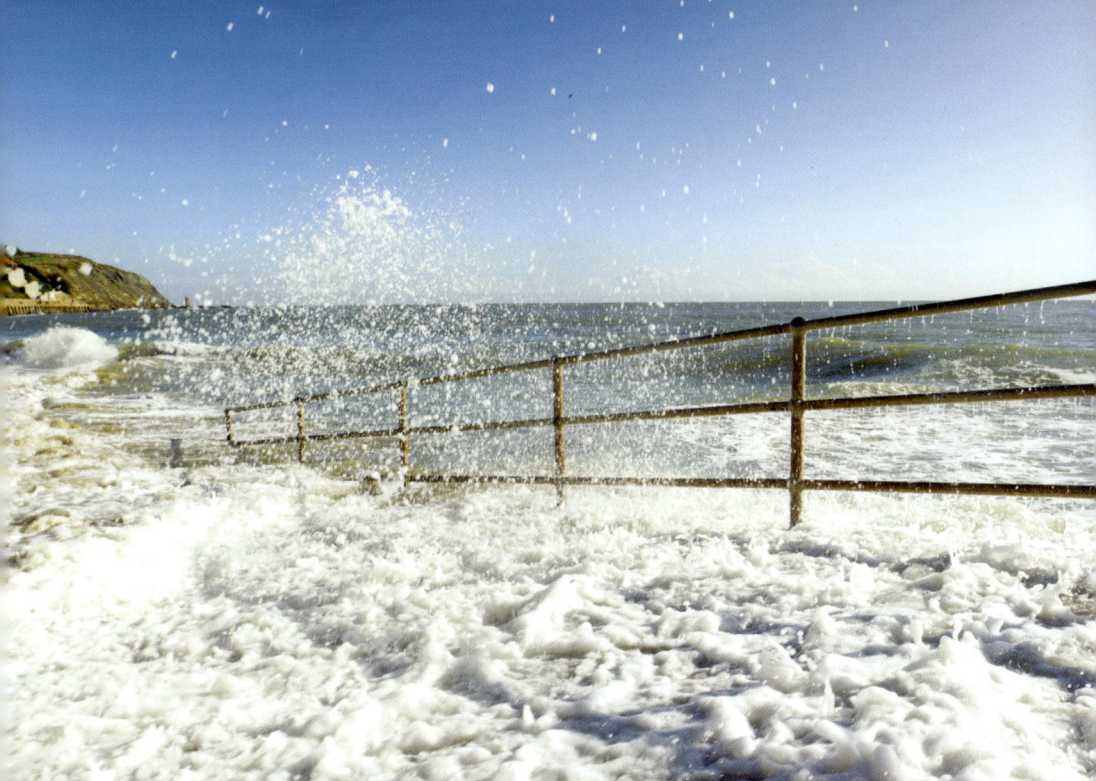

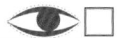

I believe a scene for a James Bond film was filmed at The Grand. I am not sure which one it was.

There was also a James Bond scene filmed at The Warren with Roger Moore and Grace Jones for *A View to a Kill* in the 80s. It's in the last few minutes of the film and has something to do with a bomb and Grace Jones' character May Day saving Silicon Valley from being flooded – The Warren was never so glamorous. Great stuff!

जेम्स बोन्डको चलचित्र The Grand नाम गरेको घरमा छायाइन गरिएको मलाई विश्वास छ तर मलाई पक्का जानकारी भएन यो कुन चाही थियो ।

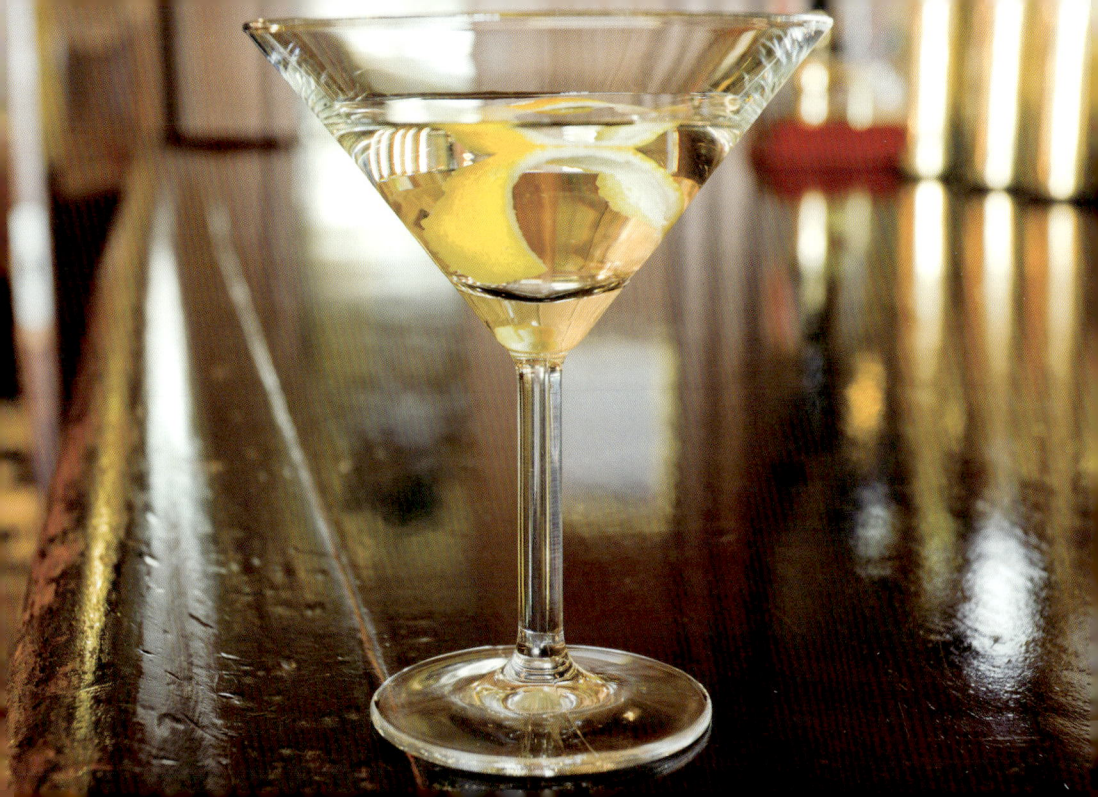

I think this place must be one of the oldest shops in Folkestone and when I moved here, I lived nearby. This tiny café was then called The Sandwich Box and was the only place in Folkestone with a jukebox. At the time none of us had a record player and there wasn't any rock and roll music on the radio, only if you could get Radio Luxemburg.

Every night we would crowd in there; it only had about four stools, so most of the time you stood, and in the winter the windows would steam up, so you couldn't see out. A cup of tea cost 3d, coffee 6d and the jukebox was two plays for 6d or four for one shilling. I spent many happy evenings there with my friends trying to make my cup of tea last all night.

मलाई यो ठाउँ फोक्सटनमा भएको अरु पुरानो पसलहरु मध्ये एक हो भन्ने लाग्छ । ग्रामोफोन भएको यो मात्र एक ठाउँ थियो फोक्सटनमा । त्यहाँ प्रत्येक रात साथिसंग संगीत सुन्न जान्थ्यौं पुरै रातको लागी एक कप चिया बनाउने कोसिश गर्थ्यौं ।

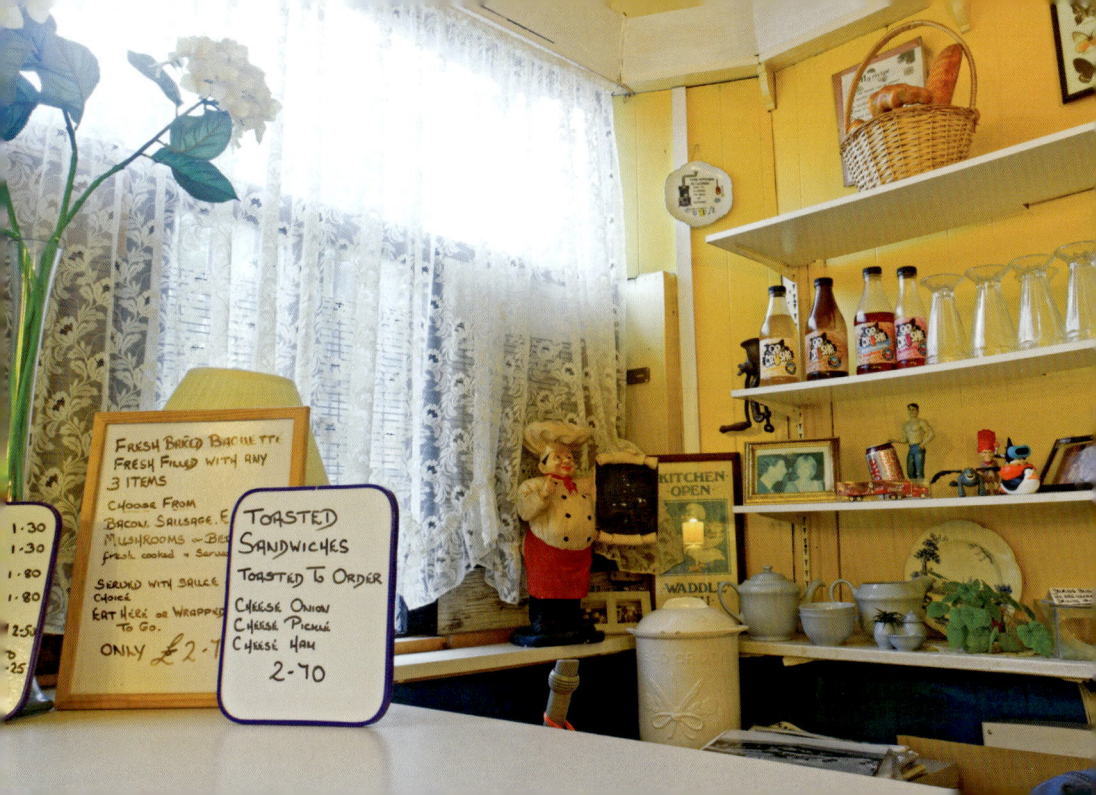

Fresh Baked Baguette
Fresh Filled with any
3 items

Choose From
Bacon, Sausage, E.
Mushrooms or Be
Fresh Cooked + Serve

Served with sauce
Choice
Eat Here or Wrapped
To Go.
ONLY £ 2·7

Toasted
Sandwiches

Toasted To Order

Cheese Onion
Cheese Picnea
Cheese Ham
2·70

1·30
1·30
1·80
1·80

2·5
·25

KITCHEN
- OPEN

WADDL

I was 15 and it was a hot August. My brother and I used to come all the way down from Ashford on our push bikes to watch the rock being made at the Rock Shop and go to the joke shop in The Old High Street. It was a brilliant place and they had a great line in itching powder, nail-through-the-finger bandages, rubber biscuits and fake dog poos. It was great, and amongst other things, I bought a plastic fly, which I put in on my dad's dinner, thinking it was funny and would cause a slight reaction. I hadn't anticipated my mum, she screamed and my dad's dinner went up in the air!

When the Joke Shop closed down, Rennies Seaside Modern acquired some of their old stock, so it's worth a visit for those lovely nostalgic things.

मेरो दाजु र म Old High Street मा भएको हसाउने पुस्तक पसलमा जाने गर्दथ्यौं । यहाँ भएका हसाउँने सामग्रीहरु किनेर आफुनो साथि र परिवारहरु सँग खुब रमाईलो गरिन्यो ।

EVERYWHERE MEANS SOMETHING TO SOMEONE

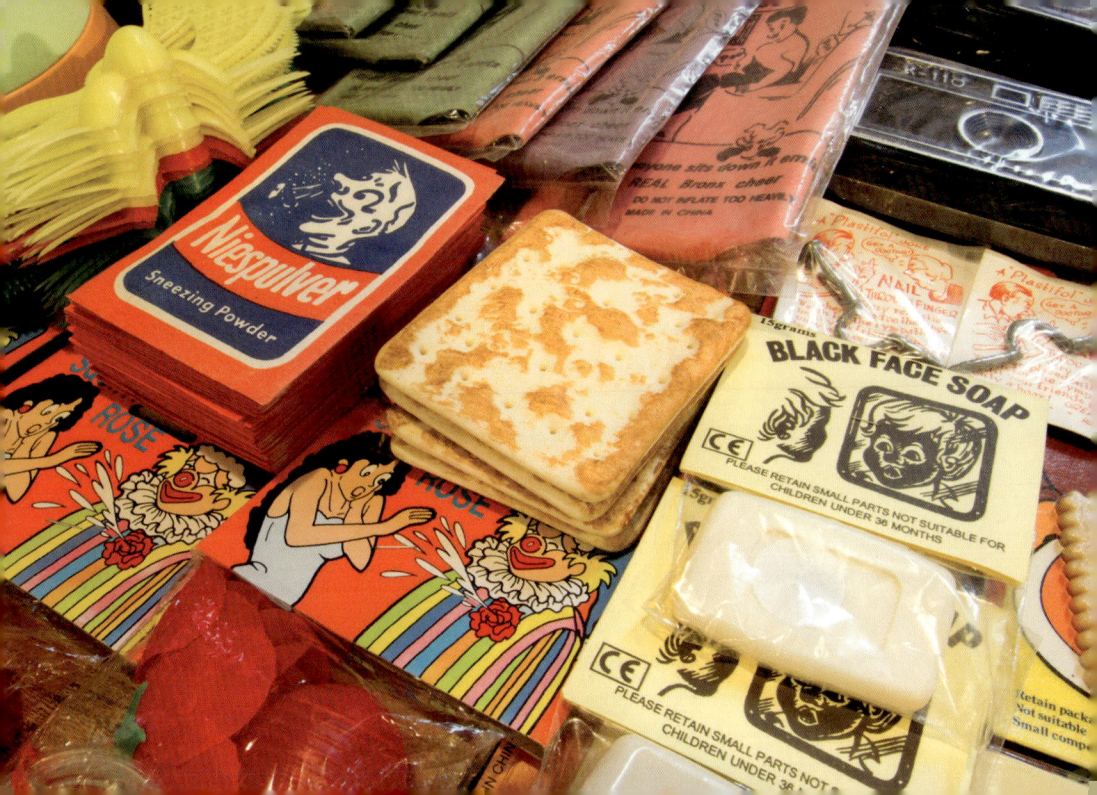

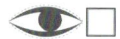

My stay at Folkestone dates from 2003 when I was there as a supporter of the Belgian youth darts team during the Europe Cup. In fact, we bought a supporter-package which included the stay and meals in The Burstin hotel, which is shaped like a ship and can be seen for miles around. I'm sorry to say we did not see much of Folkestone as most of the time we where supporting the darts players.

Our little spare time we spent on pub visits. The few things I recall from the trip was:

a) Holland won the tournament
b) After Shock and Glayva rules
c) Noisy seagulls

When browsing through my photo-database I only find pictures of people getting/or being drunk, darts players or teams posing for the camera.

सन २००३ मा युरोप कपको समयमा बेल्जियमको डार्ट युवा समुहलाई समर्थन गर्न म फोक्सटन आएको थिए । त्यसबेलाको पब र वकुल्लहरु कराएको अभै पनि मलाई सम्फना छ ।

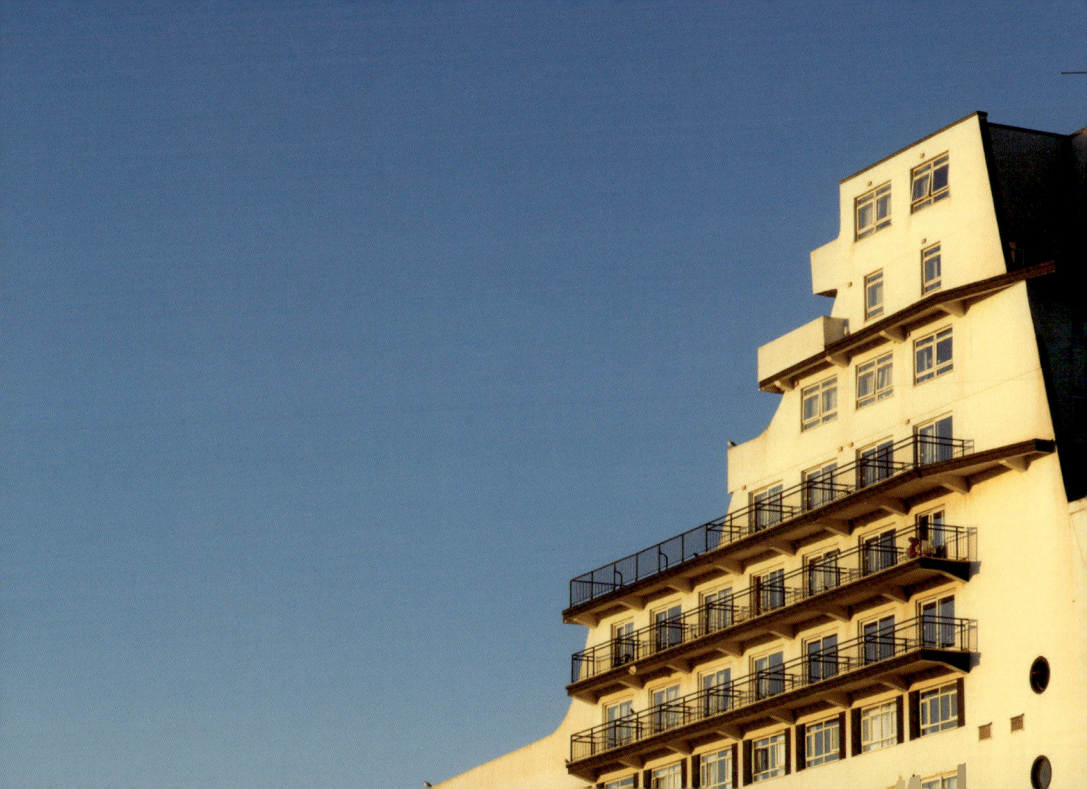

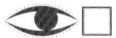

At the top of the Road of Remembrance is a small cairn, made from cobblestones that once covered the slope down to the harbour during the First World War. Nine million men passed through Folkestone during the war, many of them up and down that road, so most families probably have some connection to it. For some soldiers that would have been their last journey in England before heading to the trenches never to return. This story had been largely forgotten, and only the road sign dedicating the 'Road of Remembrance' and this small memorial say something about it. The Folkestone Step Short is working to create a new memorial on this road and to make this story more accessible to people. We also hold an annual memorial walk, which starts at The Grand on the Leas, goes down the Road of Remembrance and on to the harbour. This takes place at 11am on the first Sunday in August.

Road of Remembrance को सिरानमा गुच्छे ढुङ्गाको एउटा स्यानो खम्बा छ । यो ढुंगाहरु एकताका वन्दरगाह जाने बाटो भरी छसिएका थिए । यस बाटो भएर पहिलो विश्व युद्धको समयमा ९० लाख सिपाहीहरुले अन्तिम पटक कवाज खेल्दै युरोप गएका थिए । ति मध्य धेरै सिपाहीहरु कहिले पनि फर्केनन् ।

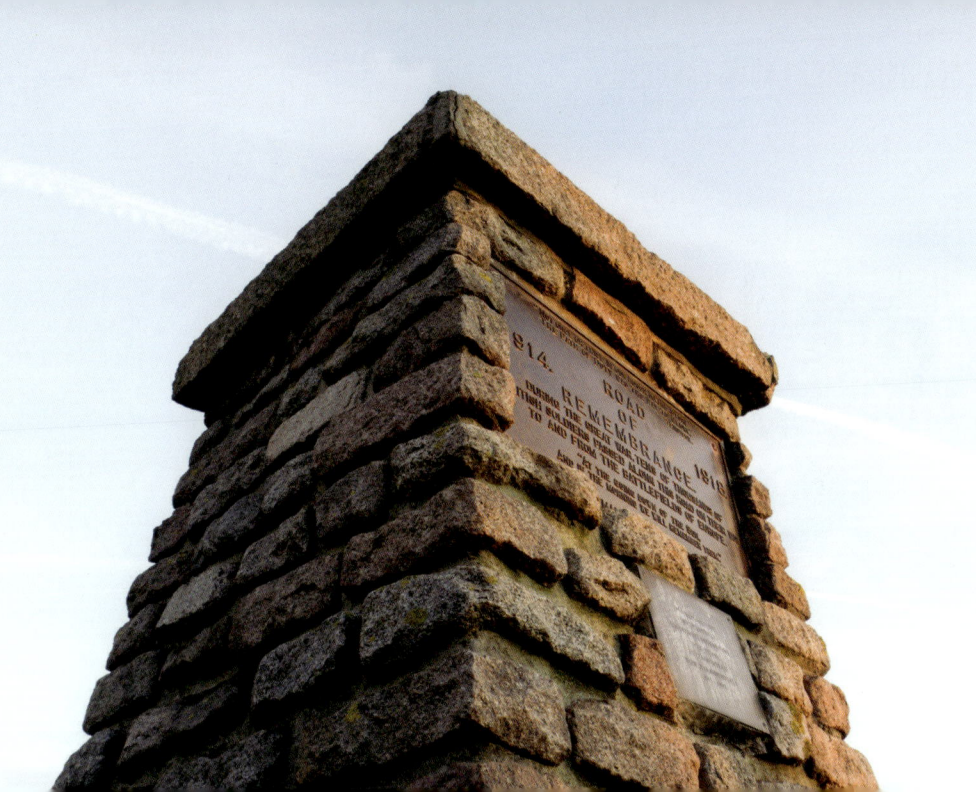

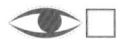

Martello Tower 3 is painted in brilliant white and overlooks the East Cliff and the harbour below. You get one of the best views of the English Channel and France from there, as well as out across Folkestone and along the coast to Dungeness. You can also visit the nearby Coastal Watch, who are a group of volunteers who look out for people and vessels in distress at sea and near the cliffs. From their look out you also get a good view on the ferries slipping in and out of the port of Dover. If you ask them nicely, they might even make you a cup of tea.

Martello तेश्रो सेतो रंगले पोतिएको एउटा टावर हो । यहाँबाट हेर्दा East Cliff र बन्दरगाह देखिन्छ । यहाँबाट Channel र फ्रान्सको राम्रो दृश्य देख्न सकिन्छ । त्यस्तै गरी यहाँबाट फोक्सटनको पारी Dungeness को किनार पनि देखिन्छ ।

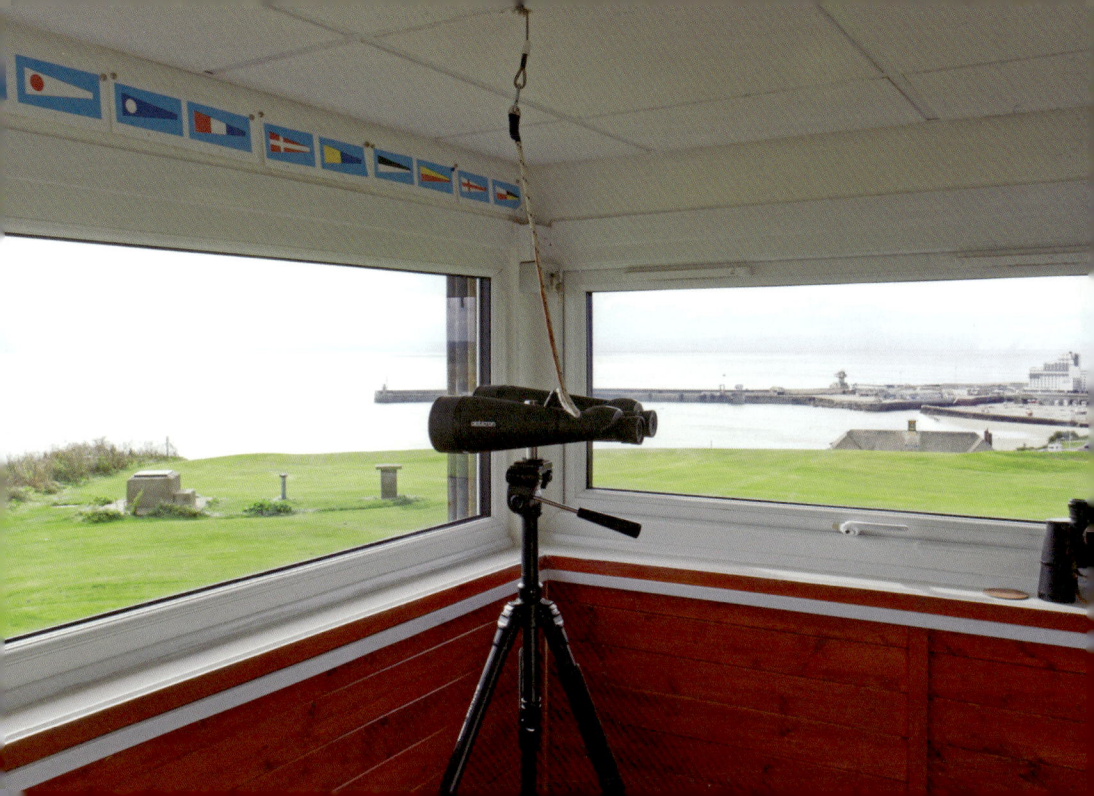

Fifth vine along from the Sandgate End.

When we go dog walking along the Leas, we come back along the Maderia Path, which goes through the Vinery. Wandering through one day, we saw that a vine was missing. I understand that someone might want to steal one of these, but not *vandalise* it, so we looked for the plant… and lo! there it was down the cliff, it had been pulled up and thrown down the cliff. So naughty…

My friend leapt over the wooden balustrade, and whilst hanging on to the balustrade leant out over the cliff, legs disappearing in the bushes and tops of the trees. He grabbed the vine and we hauled it over the balustrade and as he climbed back, I popped it in its hole. The next day we went back with more soil and two litres of water and had a little chat with it.

This vine is talked to on a regular basis and we think it is the tallest, but we are somewhat prejudiced, like proud parents. All the vines are still in place and growing proudly.

एक दिन म मेरो साथीसंग हाम्रो कुकुरको साथ हिँडिरहेको वेलामा लहराको विरुमा उखेलिएको देख्यौं । हामीले त्यसलाई फेरी रोपिदियौं र पानी लगाई संधै हेरचाह गर्यौं । आज यो ठुलो र राम्रो भएको छ ।

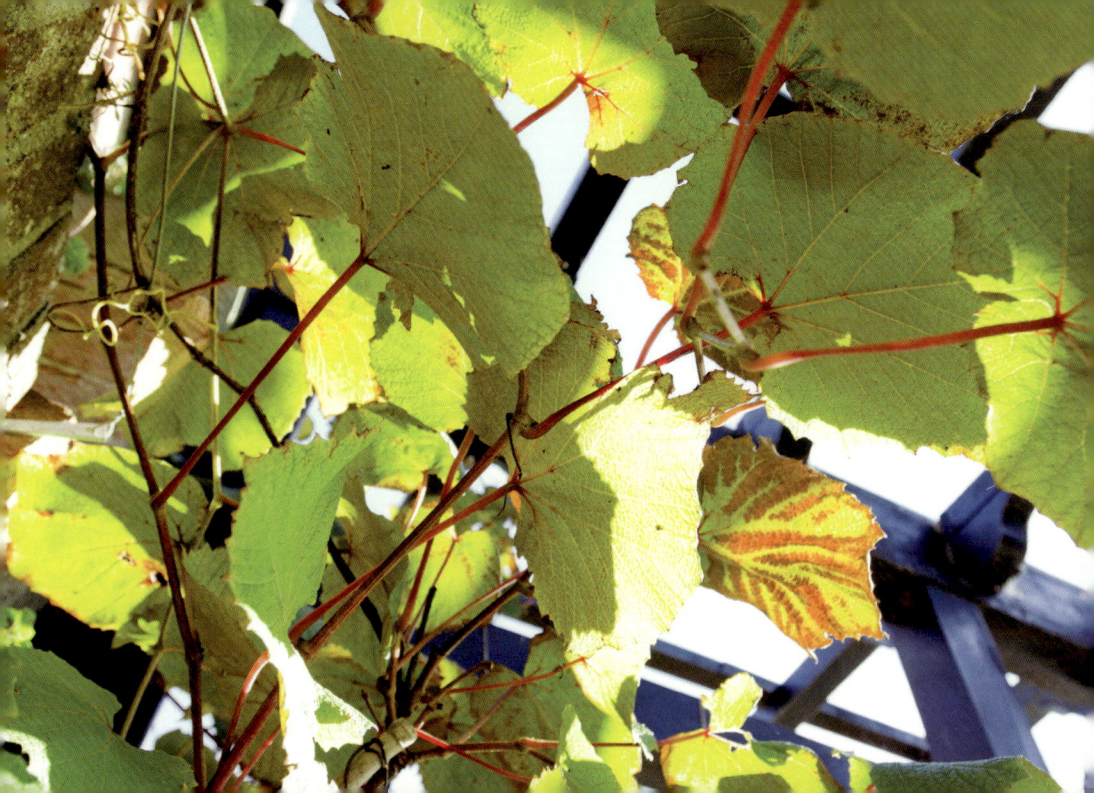

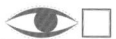

One spring we walked the dogs along the Leas, down to the beach and up the Zig Zag Path, but the path was closed, as they were doing some work on it. We thought that, as it was 5.30, we could walk though as the workman had gone home, but NO the workman there was having none of it and sent us back. We muttered "jobsworth" as we walked back through the Lower Leas Park and up the Metropole Steps, humphing as we went, greatly disgruntled.

The next day the barriers had been taken down and we walked up the Zig Zag Path with the seats newly concreted, looking all smooth and friendly. At the top about halfway along we spotted a little concrete rat, sitting in the lee of the seat. Perhaps that was why he didn't want us up there, as he was still working on this little rat. His ear has now been broken as possibly the concrete mix wasn't quite strong enough; he is a sweet little fella, that rat. We like Mr. Jobsworth now.

बाँगोटिँगो बाटोको लगभग मध्य भागको अन्तिम छोरमा सिमेन्टले बनाएको एउटा सानो मुसा छ । त्यसको कान भाँचिएको छ तर पनि धेरै राम्रो छ ।

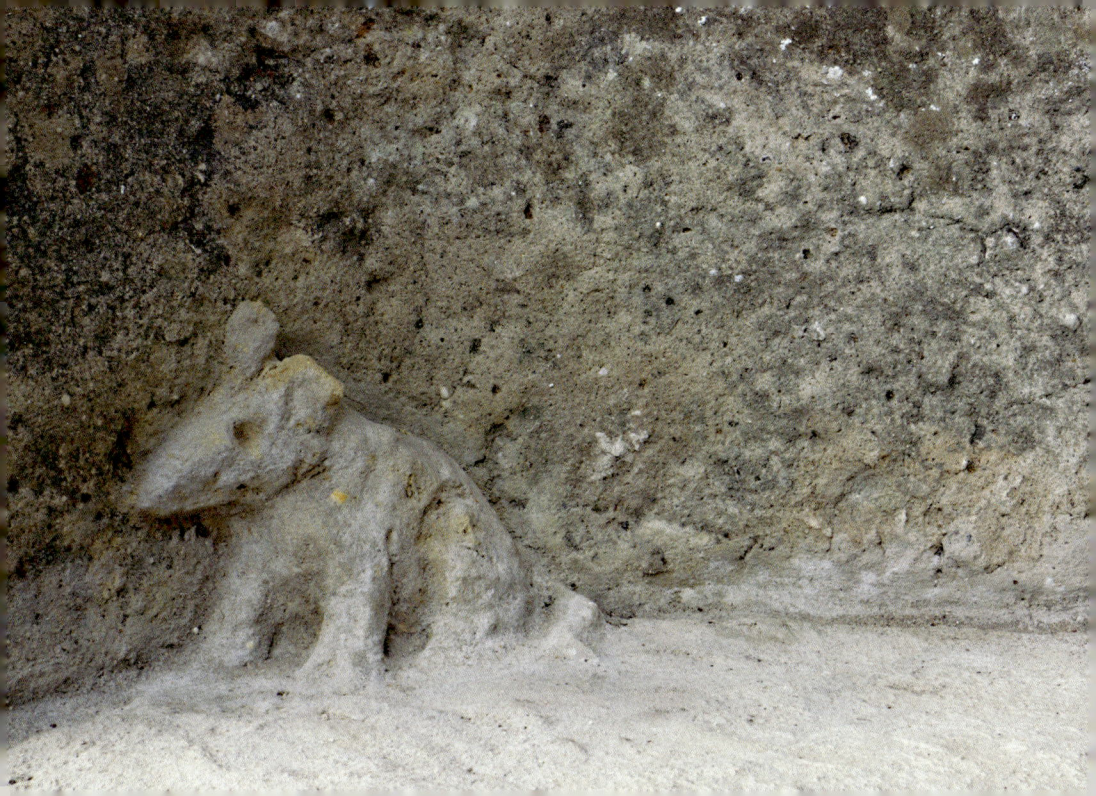

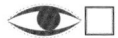

I met my partner Simon when I was working at The Chambers, nine years ago. We were introduced by our mutual friend Darryl who still works there. Darryl pointed Simon out to me, as he was quite drunk, and the next day he came into the coffee shop while I was working and pursued me relentlessly until I moved away to Bristol and we lost touch. I moved back after three years and bumped into him on my first visit back to The Chambers. We got together a few months later and have been together for five years now and have a son called William.

We had our first kiss on the sofa by the door in the Coffee Shop.

मेरो केटासँगको पहिलो चुम्बन Chambers coffee पसलको ढोका छेउको सोफामा भएको थियो । हामी ५ वर्ष देखि सँगै छौं र एउटा छोरा पनि छ ।

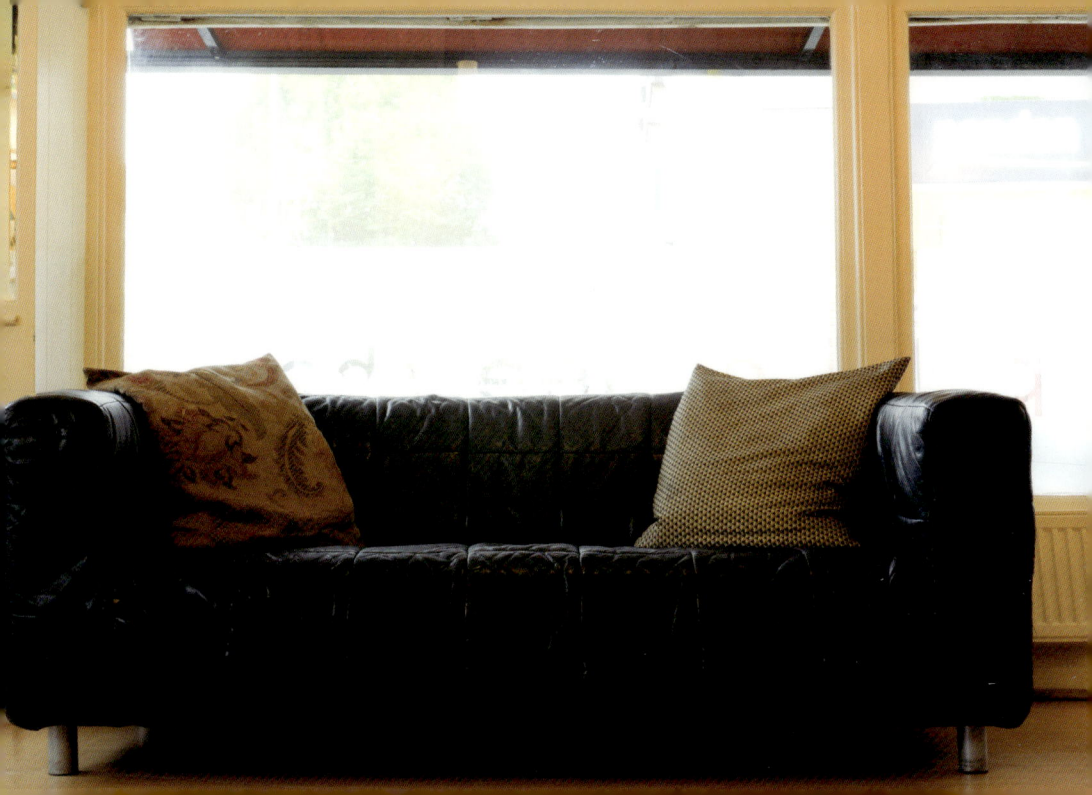

Last January we awoke to find snow having fallen up to one foot high in places! I work in Canterbury and there was literally no way to get into work, unless I physically trudged through the snow for 20 miles. So, we put our wellies on and trekked through the coastal Park, which was completely untouched and picturesque. We made snow angels and had a snowball fight, when we should have been at stinky work.

गत वर्ष हिउँ परेको वेलामा म काममा जान सकिन । हामी Coastal Park मा गयौं र हिउँको डल्ला बनाएर खेल्यौं यद्यपी हामीले दिक्क लाग्ने काममा जानु पर्ने हुन्थ्यो ।

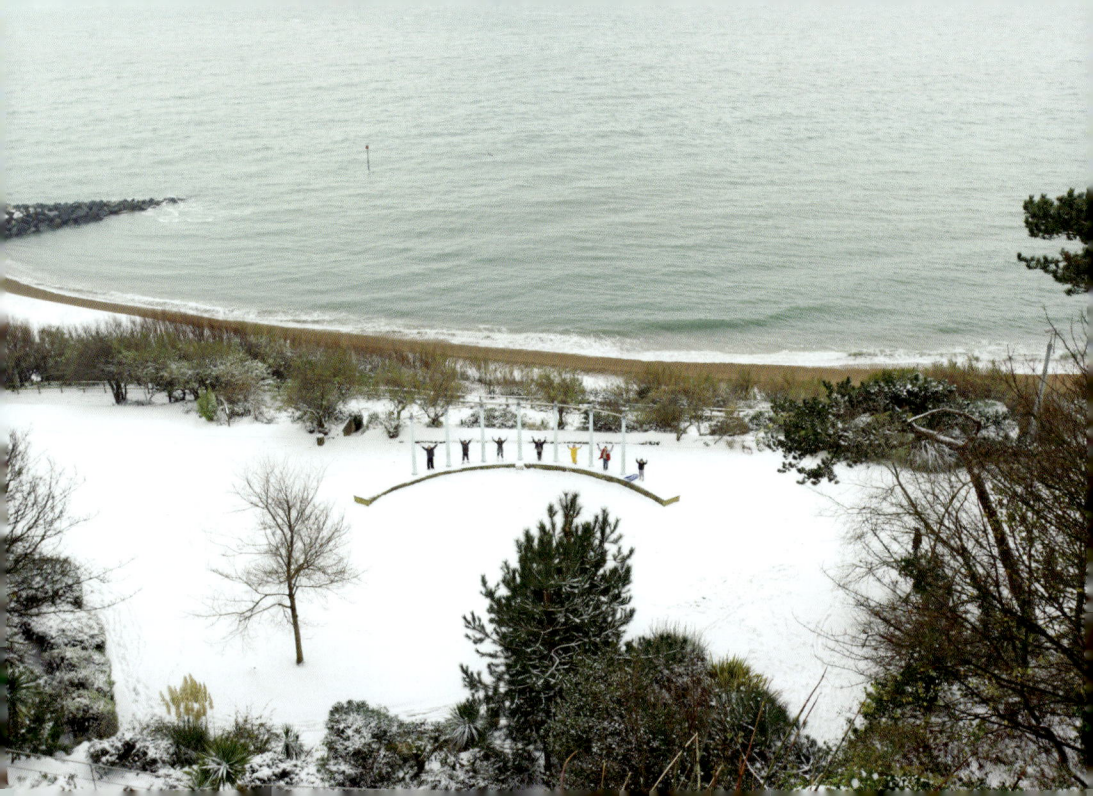

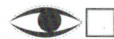

Django's is a great place to go for lunch in Folkestone! :) or a hangover fry up!

फोक्सटनमा खाना खान र थकाई मेटनको लागि Django एउटा राम्रो ठाउँ हो ।

EVERYWHERE MEANS SOMETHING TO SOMEONE

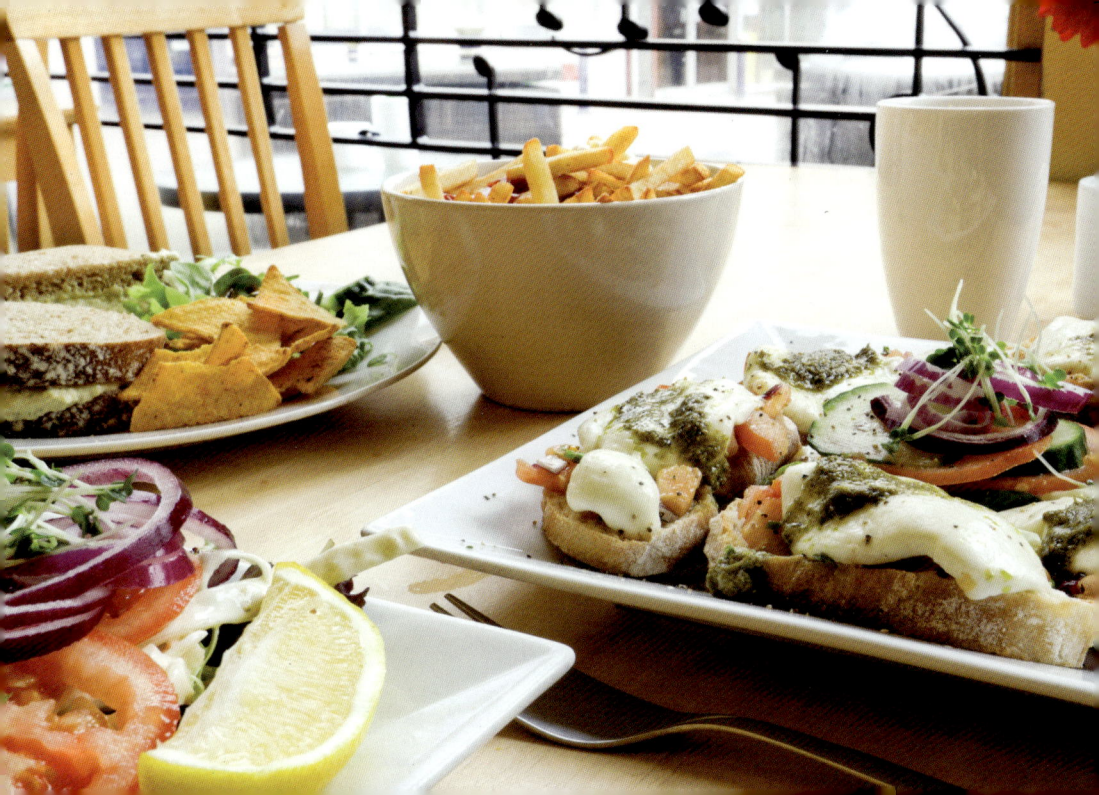

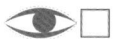

Most days Jocelyn Brooke would walk along the Lower Road on his way from Sandgate to Folkestone. At the Sandgate end near Clare Danstead's spiral, it is still a stunning wilderness that has been enhanced by the landscaping of the shoreline. This quote from Jocelyn Brooke's *The Orchid Trilogy* shows what it meant to him:

"(...the 'Lower Road' which led from our house, along the Undercliff to Folkestone harbour). The Undercliff, a tract of semi-wild land between the Leas and the beach, was for me a kind of substitute for the 'country'. Innumerable small paths traversed the bushy slopes; here and there, where the trees were planted more thickly, one could almost imagine oneself in a real wood. It was a manageable, a half-domesticated wilderness, where one could never wander far enough from the road to feel lonely or frightened."

Metropole मुनिको Coastal Park को नयाँ भर्याडको अन्तिम तलामा Clare Danstead दुंगाको वरीपरी मुर्ति कुदिएको छ ।

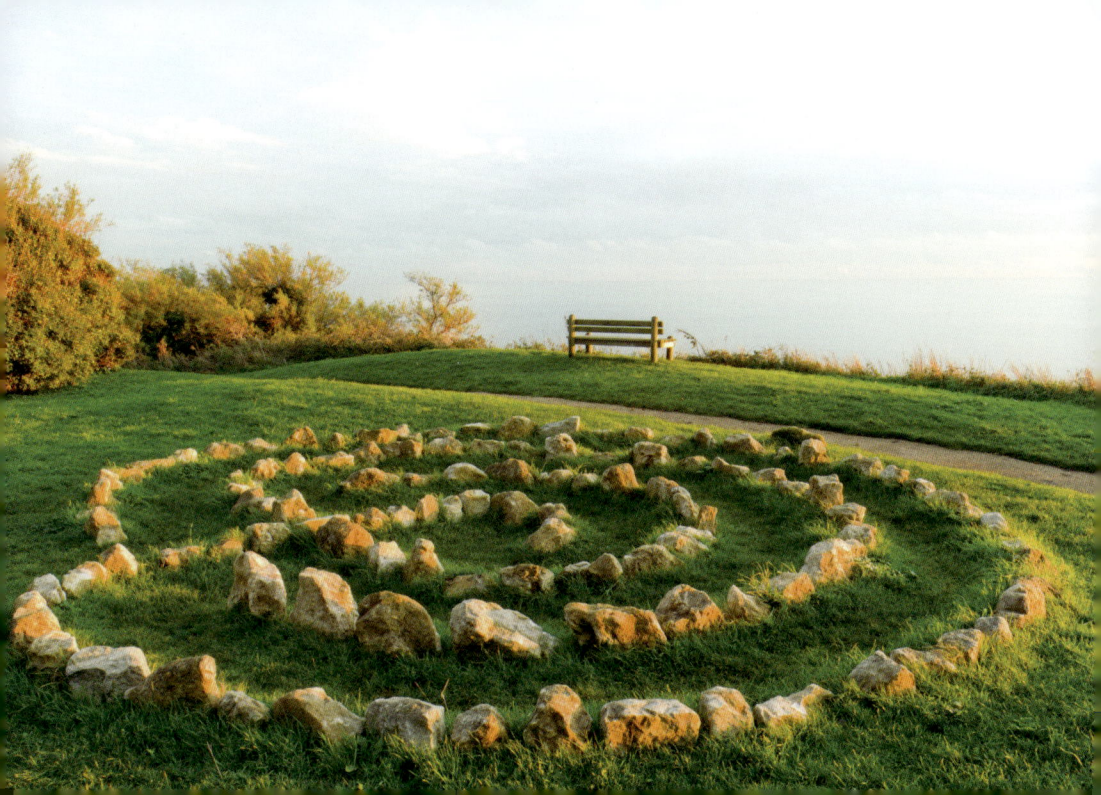

One perfect bright blue sky day, white cliffs ablaze, we were promenading the pier to the lighthouse when a fisherman shouted to his mate, "whoaaaaa!" with a cry that splintered our sun. Wow, we thought he must have caught a whopper. No fish, but a seagull attracted by the wiggling worm bait on the end of the line had been caught as it'd swooped in for the catch, one wing now tangled in the line. The man wound the bird in like a fish, grasped its body, wings splayed, beak threatening to peck, while his mate threw a cloth over its head. It lay still. "They're never harmed," said the fisherman to us, "last week it was a cormorant." When the tangle was loosened, the cloth lifted, the bird flew back into the ether flexing its unscathed muscles, surrendering to thermals like nothing had ruffled its feathers.

मैले एक दिन एउटा वकुल्लालाई माछा मार्ने मान्छेले माछालाई समाए जस्तो गरी समाएको देखें । तर उसले त्यसलाई सुरक्षित साथ पून उडाई दियो ।

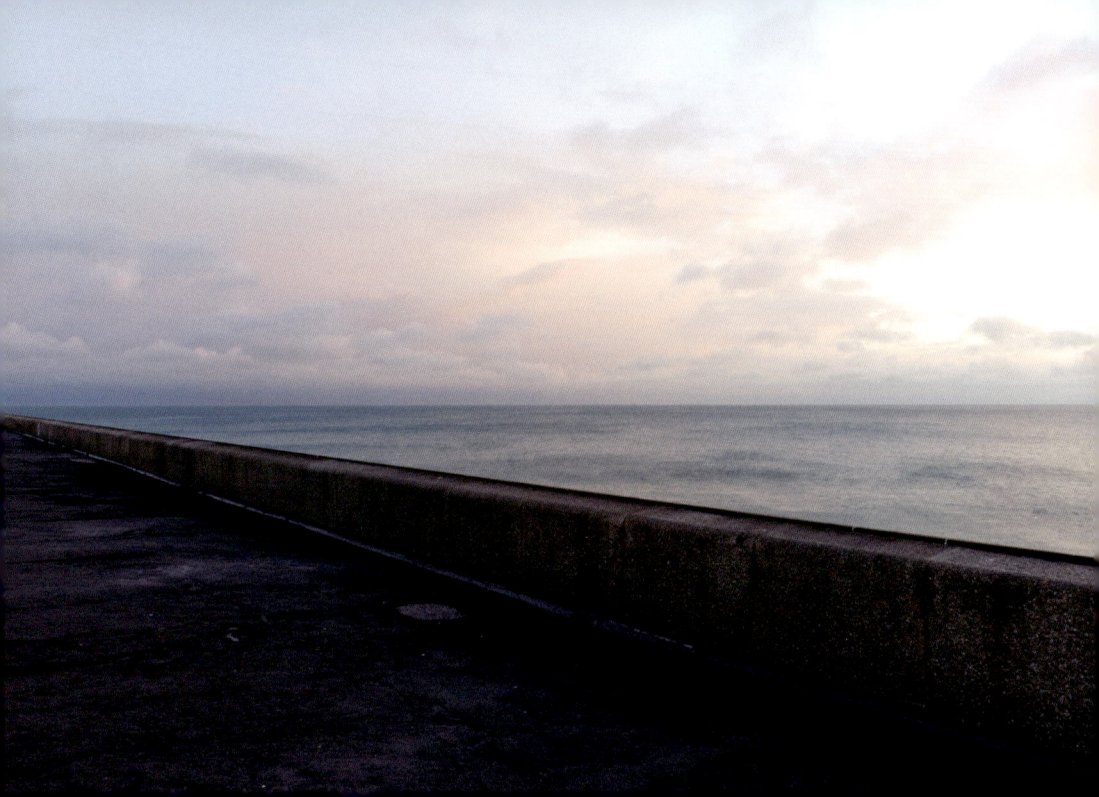

I was cutting through Payers Park, when I spotted a classic burgundy and cream P A Cresta car parked up. I fell in love with it instantly and stuck a note on it to see if it was for sale. That evening the owner popped round, I fell in love with him instantly too! We have been married now for 17 years.

We have happy memories of the Cresta, it was our wedding car, honeymoon car, brought babies home from hospital in her and lots more! Whenever I cut through Payers Park I am reminded how lucky I am and have to smile. Unfortunately she burnt through in the Golden Valley after a fault in the wiring, otherwise we would still have her!

But I do have a fabulous husband, two fabulous boys and I never paid for the car!

म एक दिन Payers Park बाट हिँडिरहेको वेला एउटा राम्रो गाडी भेट्ए जुन मलाई असाध्य मन प-यो । गाडी विक्रीमा राखेको भए मलाई सम्पर्क गर्नँ हाला भन्ने सुचना यसमा टाँसेर छाडे । उक्त गाडी मालिक मलाई भेटन आउँदा उसँग मेरो प्रेम बस्यो । हाम्रो विवाह भएको १७ वर्ष भयो र हाम्रो दुई सन्तानहरु पनि छन् ।

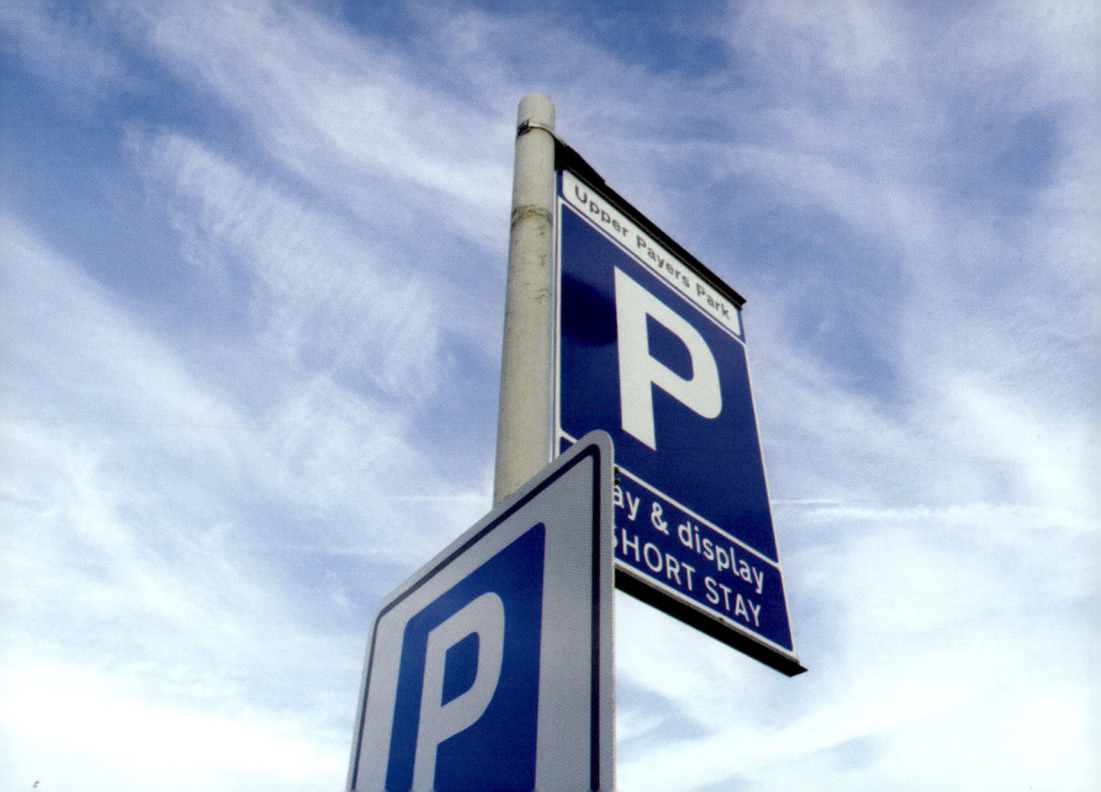

I was born in Folkestone in 1964 and recently moved back after living most of my life on the Romney Marsh. When I was very young my parents often took me and my brothers shopping in Folkestone and we would invariably end up in the harbour area, where we would have cockles from a seafood stall and visit Gi-Gi's café. I remember often looking down over the end of the outside seating area of the café onto the mud if the tide was out and thinking how high I was. The large rusty outlet cover below the café was endlessly fascinating to me, and I believe this is where the famous Pent Stream, which formed much of the Folkestone landscape, now exits to the sea. Ducks would swim in its fresh water as it flowed out into the harbour.

I often visit the harbour at least once a week, and seeing the sad shell of GiGi's café always reminds me of those far off days although I wonder how much longer this building will remain.

बाल्यकालमा मैले Gi-Gi's café को माथिल्लो पटीको कटेरोको पेटी मुनि छोपिएको अवस्थामा खिया लागेको ठुलो फलामो नाली देखेको सम्झना छ । यो खोल्सावाट बगेर आउने पानी समुन्द्रमा मिसिन्छ । यो हार्वरमा समुन्द्र संग मिसिनु भन्दा अगाडि हाँसहरु यो कलकलाउँदो पानीमा पौडन्छन् ।

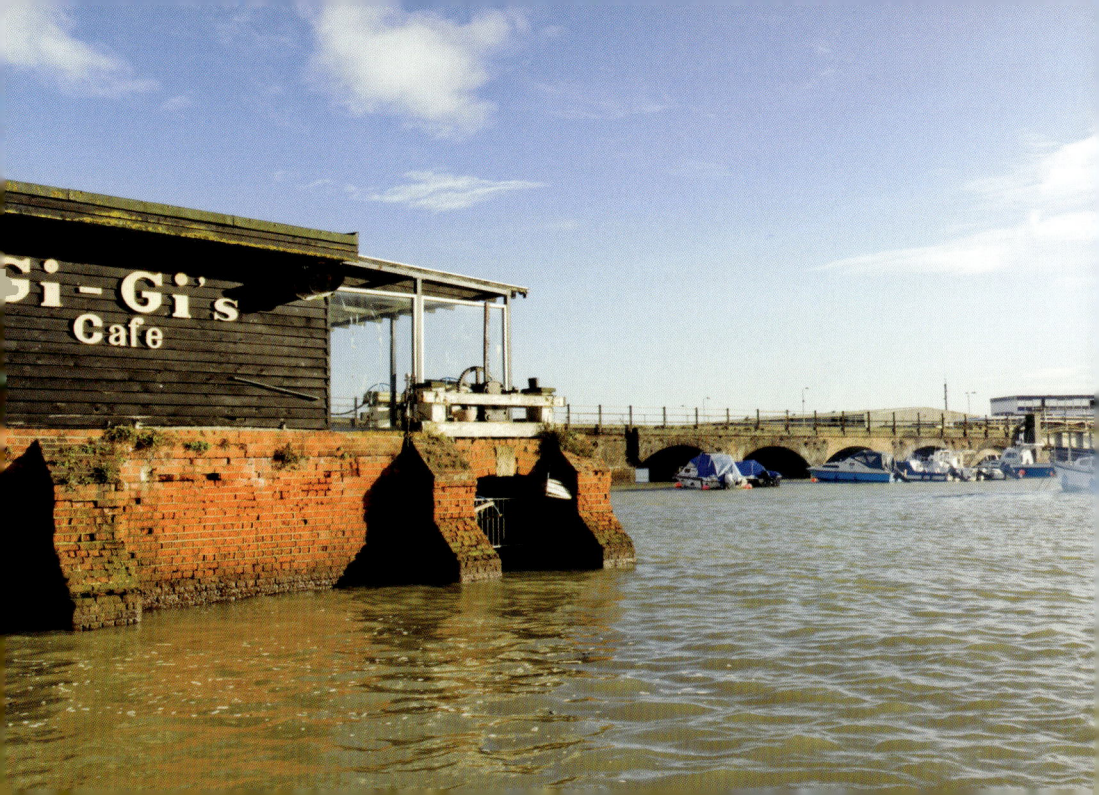

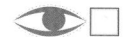

I like the harbour dock Folkestone sign on the pointy out part of the bay where the boats are. I like this because it shows where you are and makes the point that we are proud to be in Folkestone, because we have taken the time to put up this colourful picture. I also think that it's a very social place to be, with fishmongers and gift shops, ice cream stalls and the café above the sands. This, I think, is what is good about Folkestone, that it is a lovely creative place to be.

मलाई यो गित मन पर्छ किनभने यसले हामीलाई कहां छौं भन्ने बुझाउदछ । हामीलाई फोक्सटनमा भएकोमा गौरव छ किनभने यो रंगिन नक्सा बनाउनमा धेरै समय लागेको छ ।

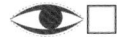

In the park is a brilliant zip wire, you have to practise lots, but you can do a flip on it if you go fast enough.

यो बाबवायर छेकबार गर्नको निम्ति अति उपयोगि हुन्छ । यदि तपाईले बाबवायरद्वारा बनाएको छेकबारलाई छिटो पार गर्ने अभ्यास गर्नै भएको छ भने सजिलै नाघेर जान सक्नुहुन्छ ।

EVERYWHERE MEANS SOMETHING TO SOMEONE

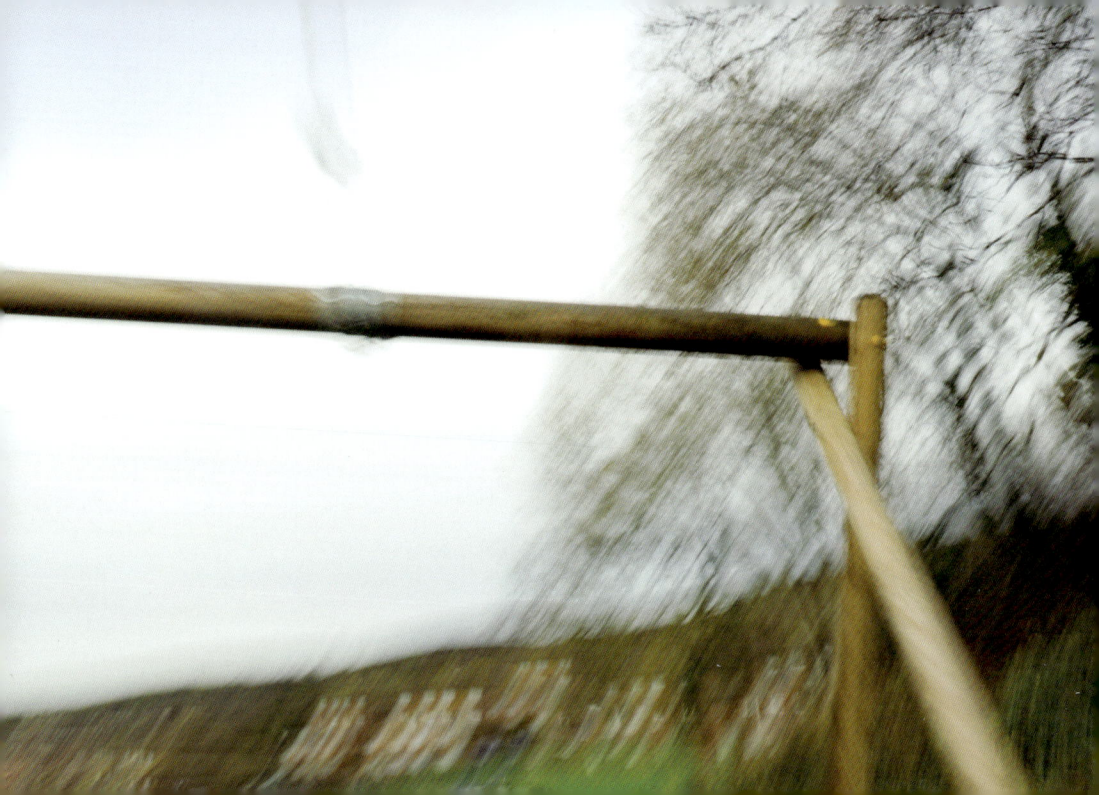

The Orient Express has transported many exotic and famous people from London to Folkestone across this wonderful swing bridge to meet the Boat Train at Folkestone Harbour Station before being whisked off to adventures in Europe. Royalty, film stars, millionaires and television personalities were regular travellers in these wonderful coaches. In addition to real people, there is a huge list of fictitious travellers penned by authors who wanted to add a touch of glamour to their stories, including Bram Stoker's Dracula, Ian Fleming's James Bond and Agatha Christie's Hercule Poirot, who have all had mysterious, romantic and sometimes fatal experiences on board this most famous train.

यो Orient Express ससारकै प्रख्यात रेल हो जुन नियमित लण्डनबाट फोक्सटन चल्ने गर्दछ ।
यसले सधै यो पुलको बाटो भएर Folkestone Harbour Station पुगेर त्यहाको यात्रुलाई यूरोप तिर लैजान्छ ।

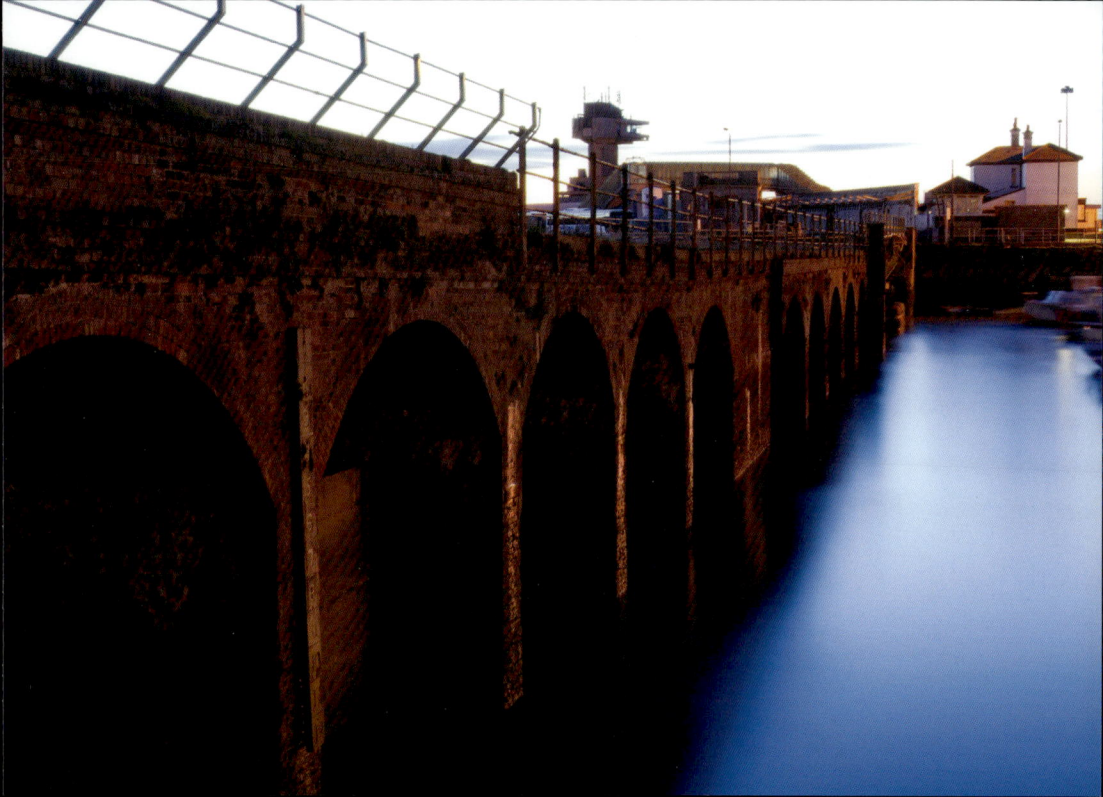

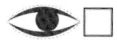

On Sugar Loaf Hill live the 'Boggits'. They are fairy folk that use things around them to dress themselves – seagull feathers, people's old clothes, rubbish from local bins. They are only very small and a local artist, Christine Crane, knows them very well and paints pictures of them.

यहां Boggits वस्ने गर्दछन । यिनीहरुले आइनो वरीपरी रहेका बकुल्लाका प्वांखहरु र थोत्रा झ्याकेका कपडाहरु प्रयोग गरेर आफुलाई सजाउने गर्दछन ।

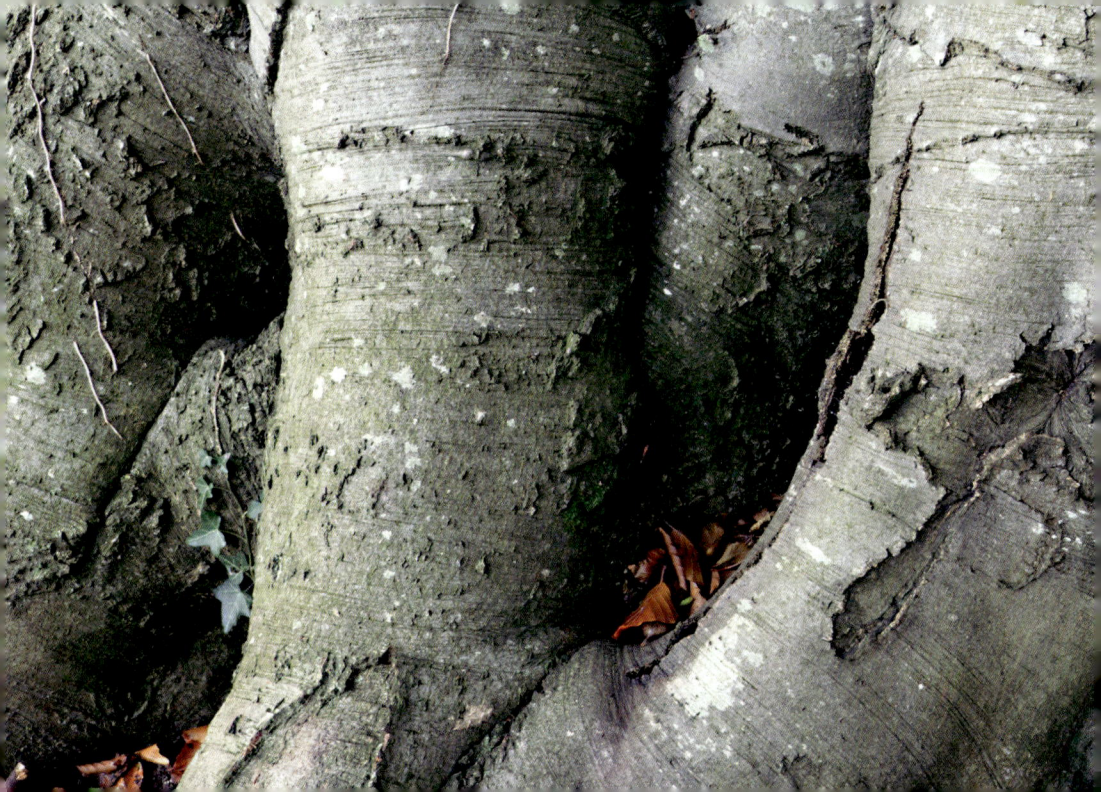

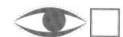

When Queen Victoria came to the town for her holidays, she stayed in the hotel behind the Burstin. She used to go and listen to the music at The Leas. The bandstand is still there today. Half of the hotel is still there but it got bombed in one of the world wars.

महारानी भिक्टोरीया हालीडेको लागि फोक्सटनमा आउनु भएको वेलामा Burstin को छेउमा रहेको होटल Royal Pavilion वस्नु भएको थियो ।

EVERYWHERE MEANS SOMETHING TO SOMEONE

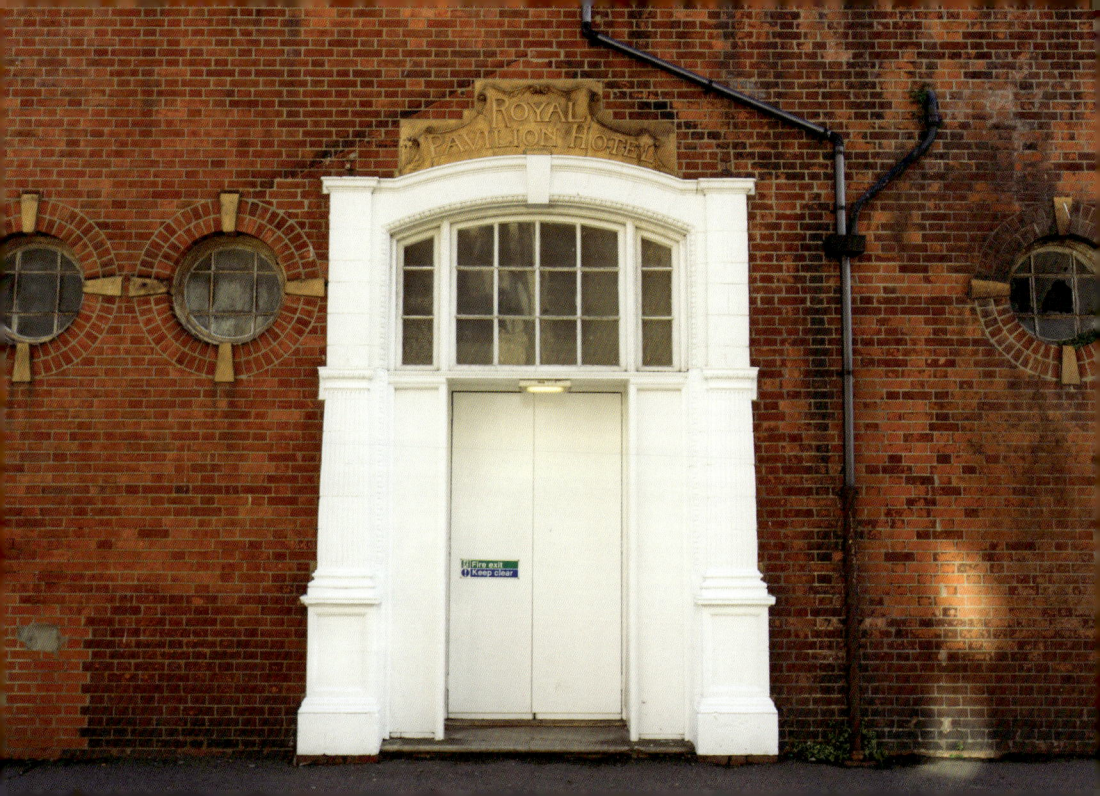

My dad grew up in Folkestone but moved away after he got married. When I was growing up we lived in a lot of different places, but always maintained a link with Folkestone and paid regular visits to aunts, uncles and cousins, that still live here now.

On these visits there is one place that sticks in my mind, because it was when I saw this house that I knew we were just around the corner from my aunt's and uncle's house and the end of the long car journey. This reason that it is particularly noticeable is due it being blue with lots of darker blue paw prints painted all over it!

When I came to live in Folkestone four years ago, after not having visited since I was quite young, I was amazed and pleased to discover that the house was still there adorned with the paw prints. Comforted that some things stay the same, especially one with such personal happy memories.

बाल्य कालमा मेरो बाबाको परिवारलाई भेटन जाँदा यो घरमा कुकुरको पञ्जाको छाप देख्ने गर्दथे । चार वर्ष अगाडी जब म फाक्सटनमा वसाई सरेर आए त्यो छाप अभैपनि त्यहाँ देख्न पाउँदा मलाई साह्रै आनन्द लागेको थियो ।

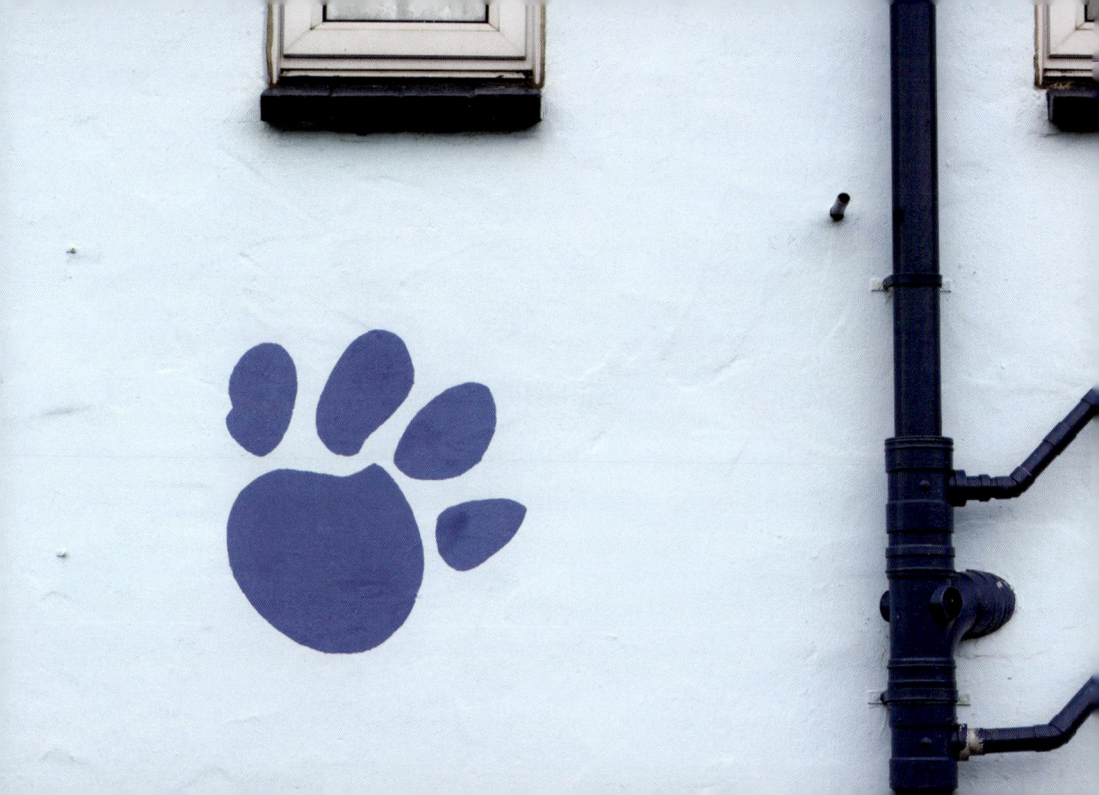

I'm not from Folkestone, but now it feels like 'home' and I would like to tell you why. I live on Tontine Street in a lovely little flat, but when I first moved here it was a bit scary, I didn't really know anyone other than my boyfriend. One day I found a tiny garden just past the Guildhall pub in the Bayle. I sat down on the bench and looked up to the rolling hills in the distance – out of nowhere there was a seagull next to me on the bench, I turned to say 'hello' and off he went walking around the pond over and over again, with one beady eye kept on me! I often visit that tiny garden and I always see a seagull near, sometimes on the bench. As soon as it sees me, off it jumps to walk around and around the tiny pond with one beady eye kept on me! That seagull guards that tiny garden and in a funny sort of way I like to think it's looking out for me too!

त्यहां सधै जसो पोखरीको वरीपरी वकुल्ला हिंडीरहेको हुन्छ । मानौ उ चाही यो वगैचाको पाले हो ।

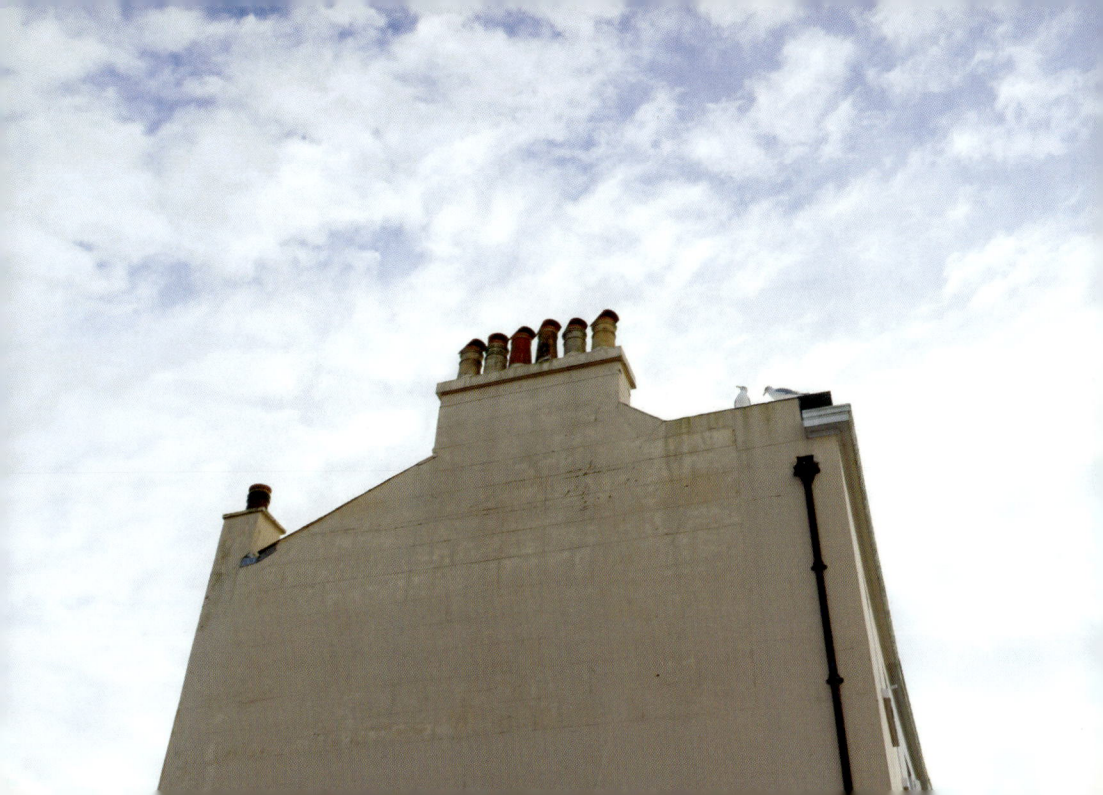

There is the best climbing tree on the rec, it is by the side of the walkway, it is the biggest tree and has loads of branches. It is a really good place to sit.

यो पून निर्माण भइरहेको मैदानमा राम्रो रुख चढ्न पाईन्छ । यो वाटोको छेवैमा छ । यसको थुप्रै हागाहरु छन । यो एकदम ठुलो भएकोले यसमा वस्ने राम्रा ठाउहरु छन ।

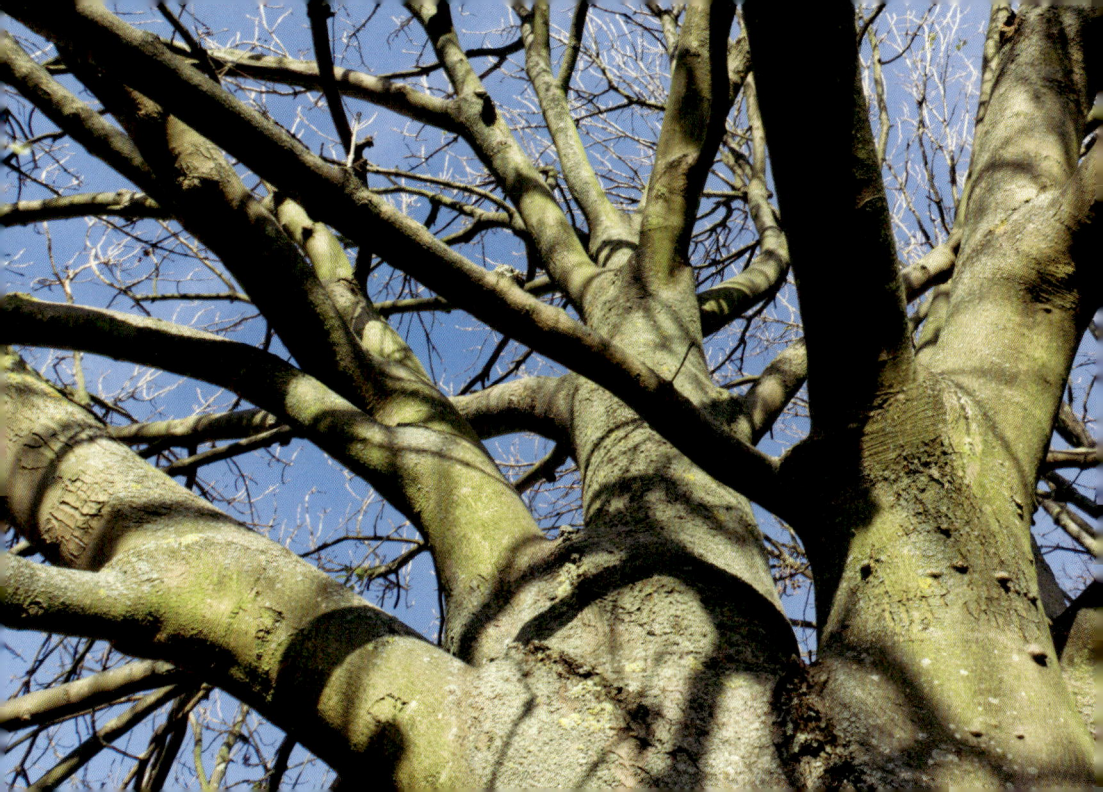

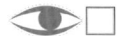

The old part of the school is meant to be haunted by George Spurgeon, the former headmaster of the school. There were noises heard through the floor from the office above, the office that was used by the family liaison officer, but when someone rang the office to complain about the noise, no one was there. There have also been sightings from the street of a figure walking past the window in the night, when there is no one in the school.

The portrait of George Spurgeon is hanging above the stairs, his eyes follow you about everywhere…

यो स्कुलको पुरानो भागमा George Spurgeon को मृतात्माले सताउने गर्दछ । उ यो स्कुलको प्रधान ध्यापक थियो ।

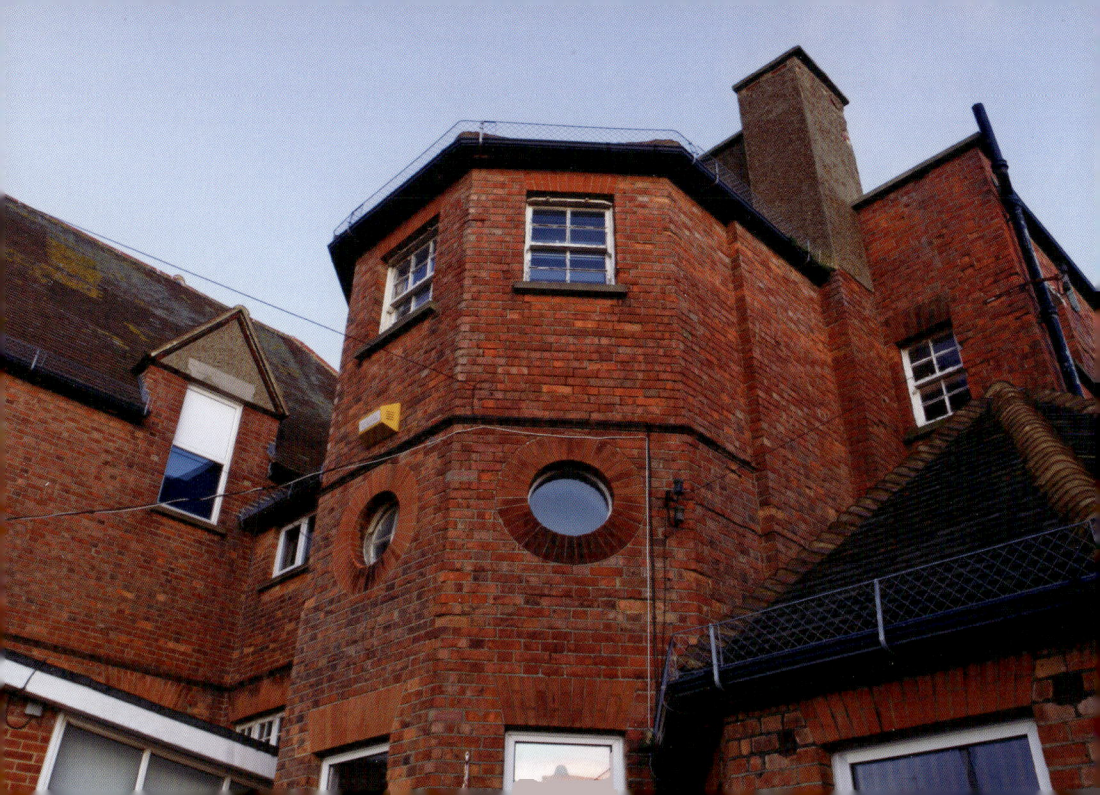

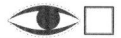

In the woods behind the park we have a base. There is a figure of eight where the motorbikes are ridden, if you go down the slope next to the figure of eight our base is at the bottom hidden and covered by trees.

यो पार्कको पछ्याडी काठमा हाम्रो बस्ने ठाउ छ । यदी त्यो भिरालो तल तिर गयौ भने आठौं तलाको पुच्छारमा रुखहरुले छोपीएको ठाएमा हाम्रो बस्ने ठाउ भेट्ने छौ ।

EVERYWHERE MEANS SOMETHING TO SOMEONE

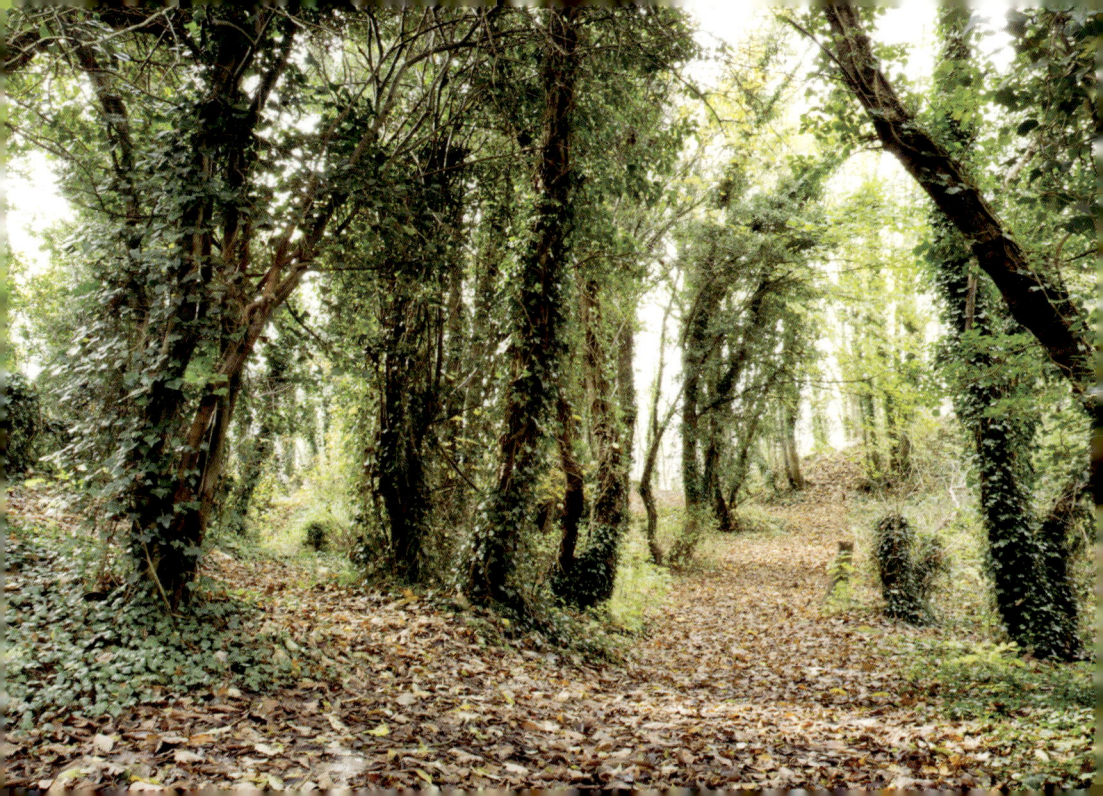

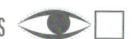
Everybody knows where the modern Channel Tunnel entrance is, however if you walk along the coast to Dover past the Warren and the large concrete apron, you come to a metal door in the cliff. Behind here is part of the system of tunnels that were started way back in the 1860s, over 100 years ago. Every time I go along I find it amazing that the Victorians may have made a tunnel to link England and France, only to have the dream taken away by the army generals who were concerned that the French may invade. It took another 100 years for the famous handshake deep under *La Manche*.

The early Whittaker boring machine was retrieved in 1986 and was on show in the Eurotunnel Exhibition Centre in Cheriton for a number of years before being taken off to the Science Museum.

Whittaker boring machine को माध्यमवाट यो भन्दा अगाडी पनि Channel Tunnel खन्ने पहिलो प्रयास भएको थियो तर यो भल्कीएर उक्त मेसीन समेत पुरीयो । जेहोस १९८६ मा यसलाई पून निर्माण गरीयो, यसको दृश्य Science Museum London मा हेर्न पाईन्छ ।

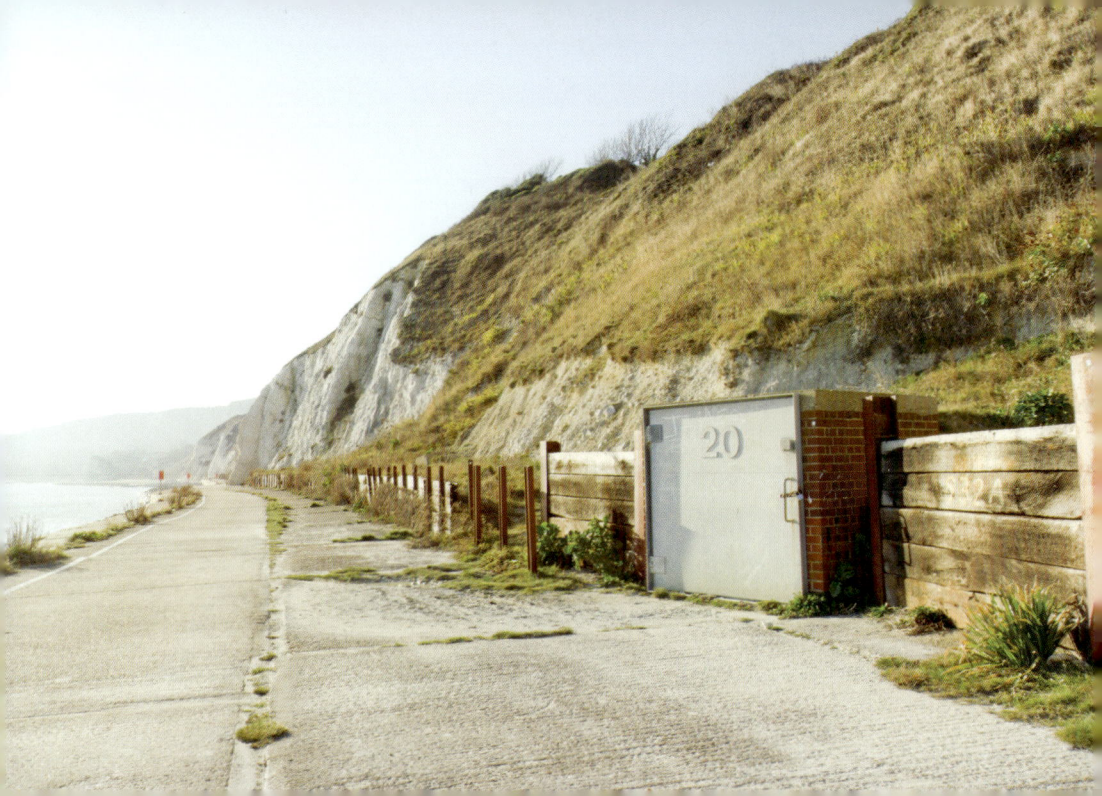

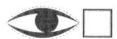

The lollypop lady Jill has been the lollypop lady for thirty five years at least. I remember her when I was a child and I used to cross the road to go to school, and I now teach here!

She had really long white hair and is very well known in the community.

जिल ३५ वर्ष देखी लगातार ललीपप लेडीको रुपमा सेवारत छिन । मेरो बचपन अवस्थामा स्कुल जादा वाटो पारगरेको मलाई अभै संझना छ । आजकाल म यो स्कुलमा पढाउछु ।

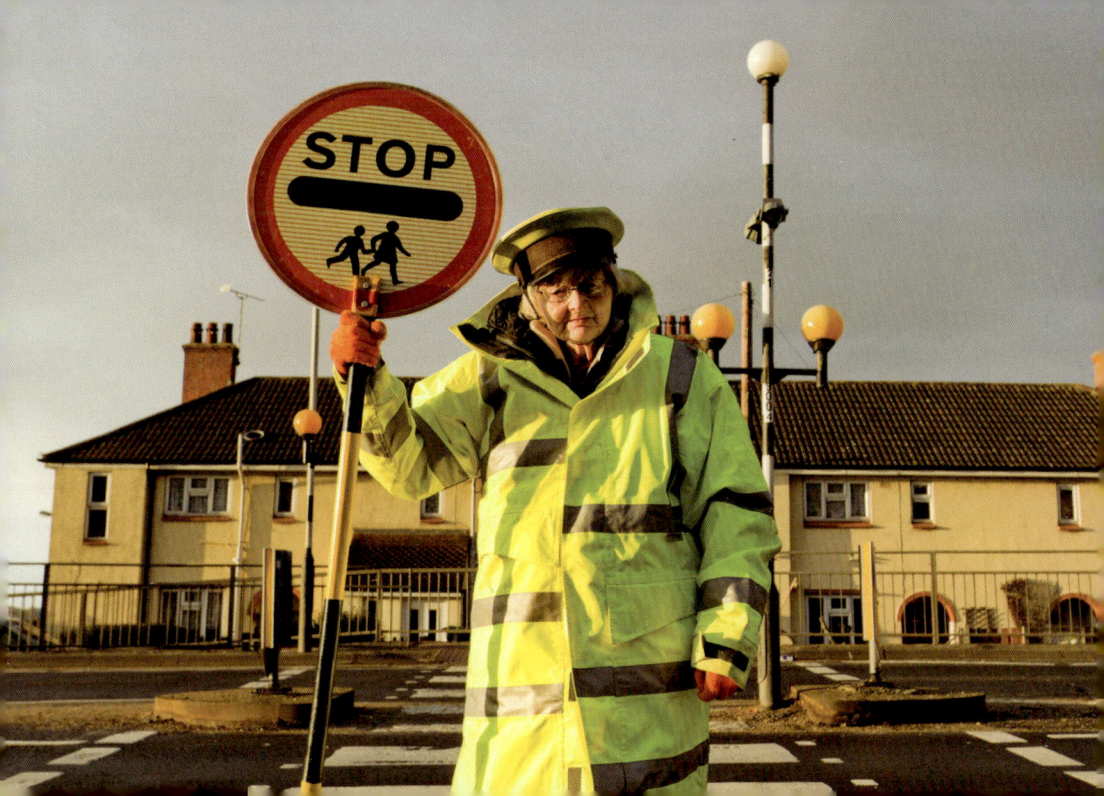

In the early sixties I used to live in a place called Elventon Close, and at the top of our road was the entrance to the council dump. The gate always had a sign on it that said something like Danger, do not enter, and the area of land was called 'The Danger' to us as young boys. It was the easiest way to get to our massive adventure playground, stretching all the way to the hills, before the motorway or Channel tunnel. On a good day (which seemed to be all the time) we could walk to the clay pit, past the brickworks at the top of Ceasar's Way, and hunt for fossils. When we were bored of that, we would strip a strong twig of bark, squeeze a piece of clay on the end and, if you whipped the twig properly, the clay would fly off 50 yards or so, so you could have battles with lumps of 'pug' zooming like real missiles (which stung if you got caught on a bit of bare skin!)

We would always make camps in the holidays. The council used to tip loads of broken paving stones and corrugated iron, and we'd pile these up and make walls and then cover the iron and make snugs, weatherproof houses that looked a bit like the remains of the Viking settlements found in the Orkneys. We would always make a fire and come home stinking of smoke and covered in mud and be put straight in the bath – carefree days!

याहां मोटर वाटो र Channel tunnel निर्माण पूर्व मेरो साथी र म केटाकेटी जस्तै याहां खेल्ने गर्दथ्यौ । हाम्रो लागी यो एउटा रमणिय खेल मैदान थियो ।

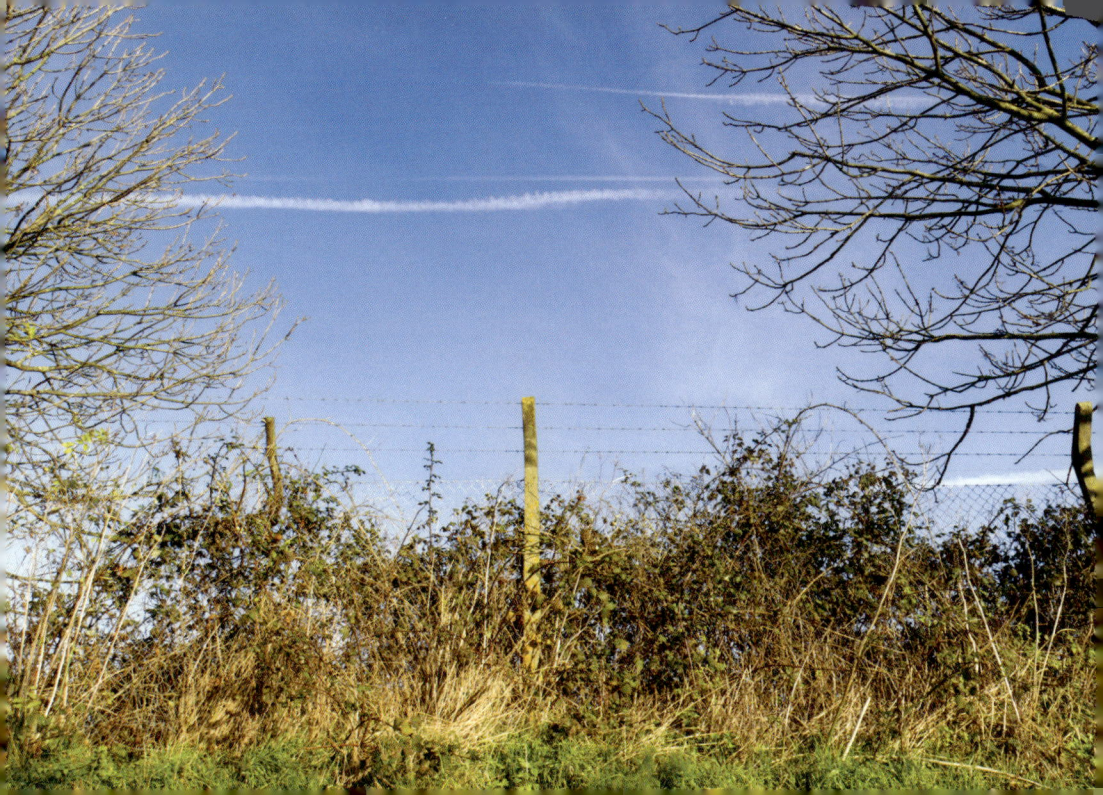

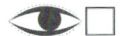

The 'Pitch and Putt' golf course round the Martello Tower has been, and still is, a favourite for me. Sometimes the wind has been challenging, and maybe rain has prevented us from completing all the eighteen holes. And even though once a gull came and stole a ball which was lying in a very promising position to the hole, it's still a great way to spend the afternoon, whatever the weather.

The Martello Towers were constructed around 1805 as part of the defences against Napoleon and his army. Originally there were 74 towers between Folkestone and Seaford. The best place to see them in Folkestone is on East Cliff where you can see no 1 and no 3. No 2 is slightly hidden behind the houses on Wear Bay Road. There are several others in Folkestone but they are not so accessible. The name comes from Cape Mortella in Corsica where there was a strong brick tower which successfully beat off two British ships in 1794.

पहिला यहाँ मैदान, पहाड र तलाउ मात्र थियो ।मेरो आमा र उनको परिवार बल्छी खेल्नेहरुलाई हेर्दै यसको किनारमा घुम्ने र वनभोज खाने गर्दथे ।

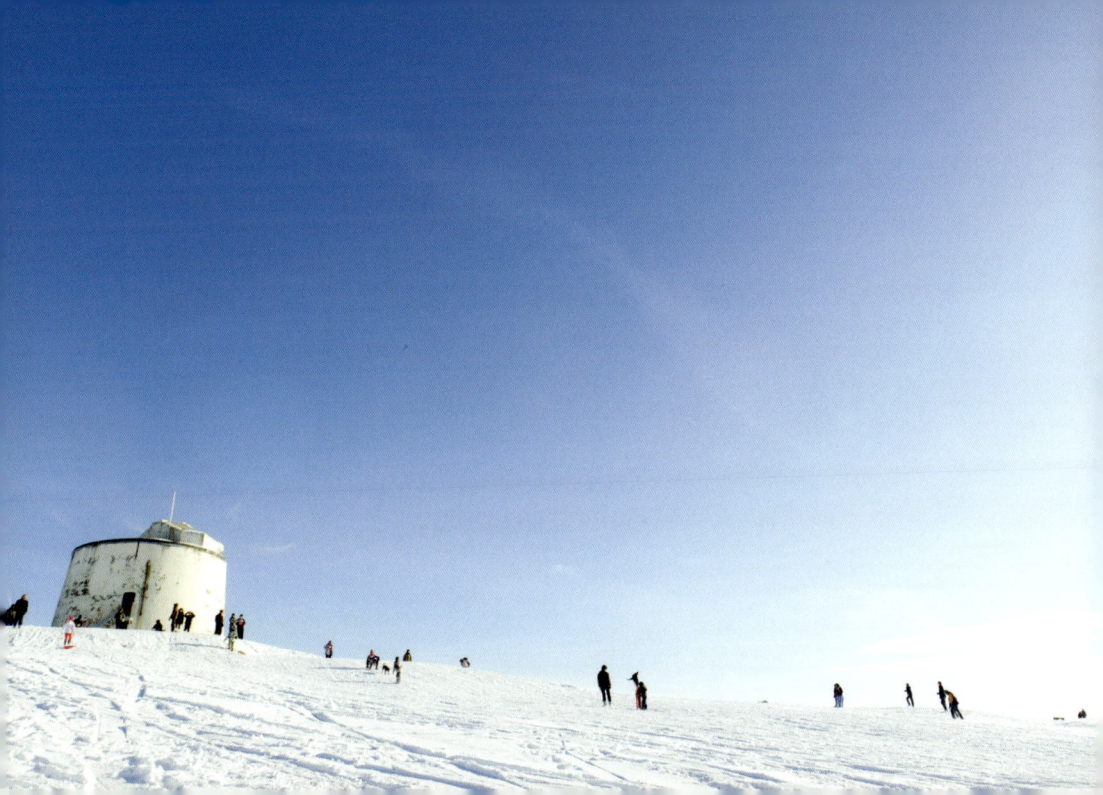

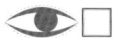

In 2007, I made an enormous decision to sell a much-loved house in Canterbury and move to Folkestone to become part of the emerging art scene. During my first summer I discovered the Coastal Park and in particular the semi circular bench below the Amphitheatre. One evening I was sitting on this bench teaching myself to crochet. The evening sun was hot and all I could hear was the sound of the waves and I thought *this is why I moved to Folkestone.* I return to this bench time and time again, bringing my work with me, chatting with visitors as they pass by and just being happy to enjoy living by the sea.

मलाई अग्लो ठाउमा ईच्छानुसारको वेञ्च मनपर्छ । घमाइलो दिनमा समुन्द्रको छेउमा बसेर छालको आवज सुन्न र नजिकमा आएका घुमन्तेहरु संग गफ गर्न मलाई असाध्य मनपर्छ ।

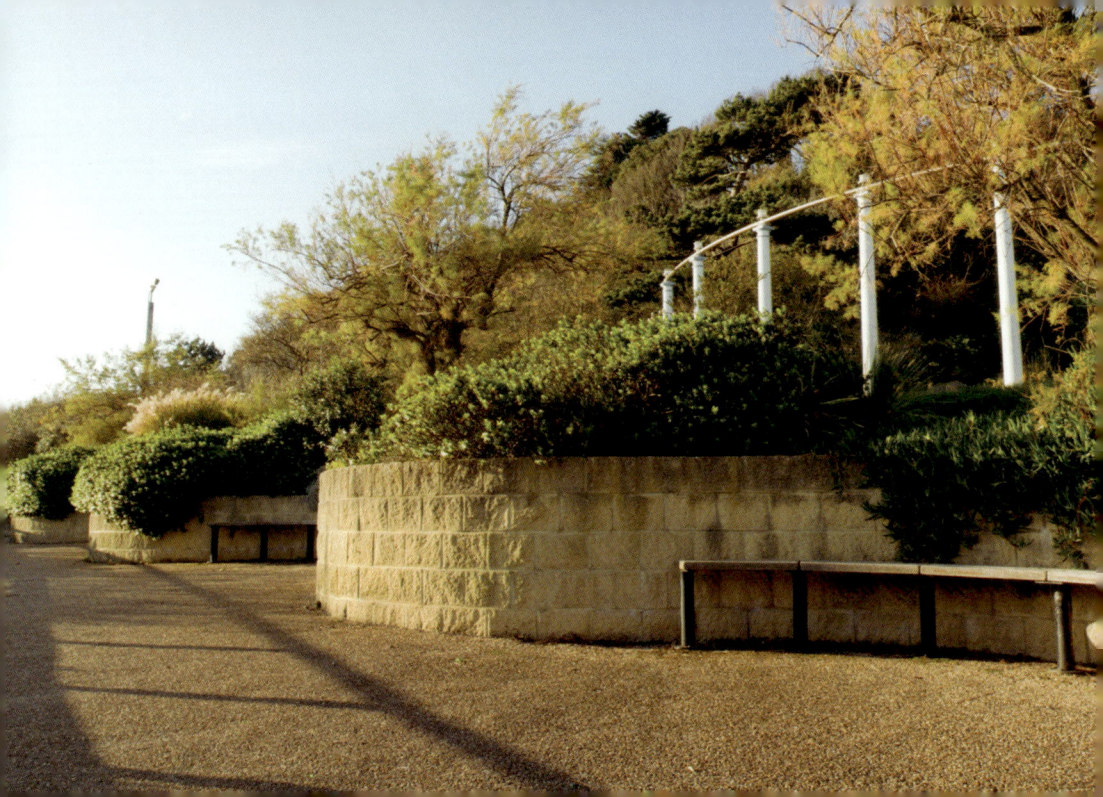

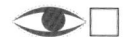

Early in the 17th century the Warren was used for smuggling goods into the town of Folkestone. Hidden within a nearby house were secret passages that led from the Warren. Smugglers brought goods ashore at East Wear Bay and used the passages to reach The Valiant Sailor pub at the top of Dover Hill, before distributing goods to local traders for sale. The government became wise to this and bought the lease to the house, meaning they had to find other ways to smuggle in the goods.

One story tells of a couple from the Warren being confronted by a gang of smugglers that had burst into their house in the middle of the night searching for somewhere to hide their cargo of gold. Choosing the four poster bed where the couple had been sleeping, the goods were concealed and the unwelcome visitors threatened the petrified citizens to say nothing about their visit. Shortly afterwards the authorities arrived to search the house, to see if they could find contraband, but they found nothing and soon left. The following day the smugglers returned to collect their gold.

३ सय वर्ष अगाडी Warren houses सम्मको गोप्य वाटो थियो त्यहा तस्करहरुले गैरकानूनी सरसमानहरु लुकाउने गर्दथ्य । यसतो गैरकानूनी कार्य डोवर हिलको Valiant Sailor नामक सार्वजनिक घरमा पनि गरिन्थ्यो ।

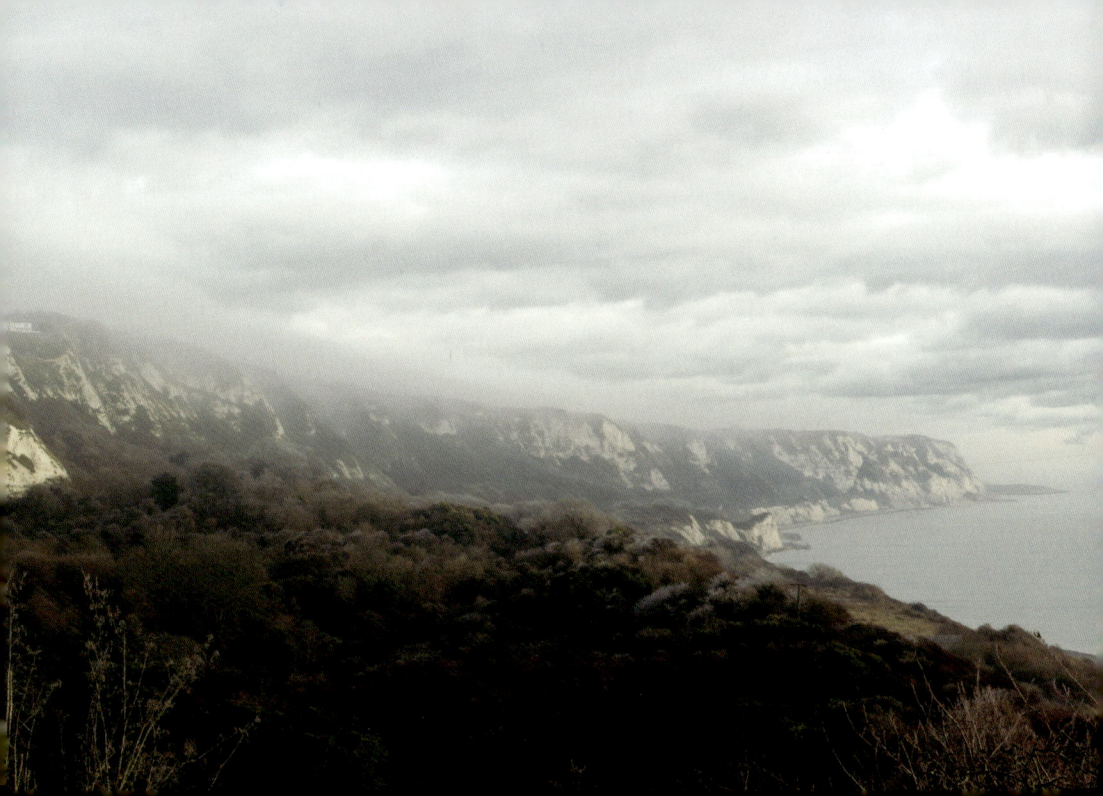

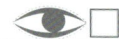

There used to be a row of shops near the railway bridge at the end of Bournemouth Road, and opposite them the long, redbrick wall of the gas works with the huge gasometers rising and falling behind it at different times of day. One of the shops was George's fish and chip shop, run by a Greek family. I remember standing in the queue at the chippy on many occasions and gazing across the road at the wall where someone had graffitied in gloss paint "workers seize power, yours is the rite to rule". I was too young to understand the meaning at the time, but now when I am passing, I can still see the faint trace of the hammer and sickle visible and I wonder who the perpetrator was, and if they ever did seize power!

केही वर्ष अगाडी "सत्ता श्रमिकले लिन्छ, साशन गर्ने अधिकार तिमीहरुको हो" भन्ने वाक्य ठुलो अक्षरले लेखिएको थियो र साम्यवादीहरुको प्रतिक ह्यामर र हशिया भित्तामा थिए । त्यो अक्षरहरु मेटाइयो तर ह्यामर र हशियाको मध्रो आकृती अझैपनि त्याहां देखिन्छ । तर मलाई थाहा भएन, उनिहरुले सत्ता कब्जा गरेकी गरेन्न !

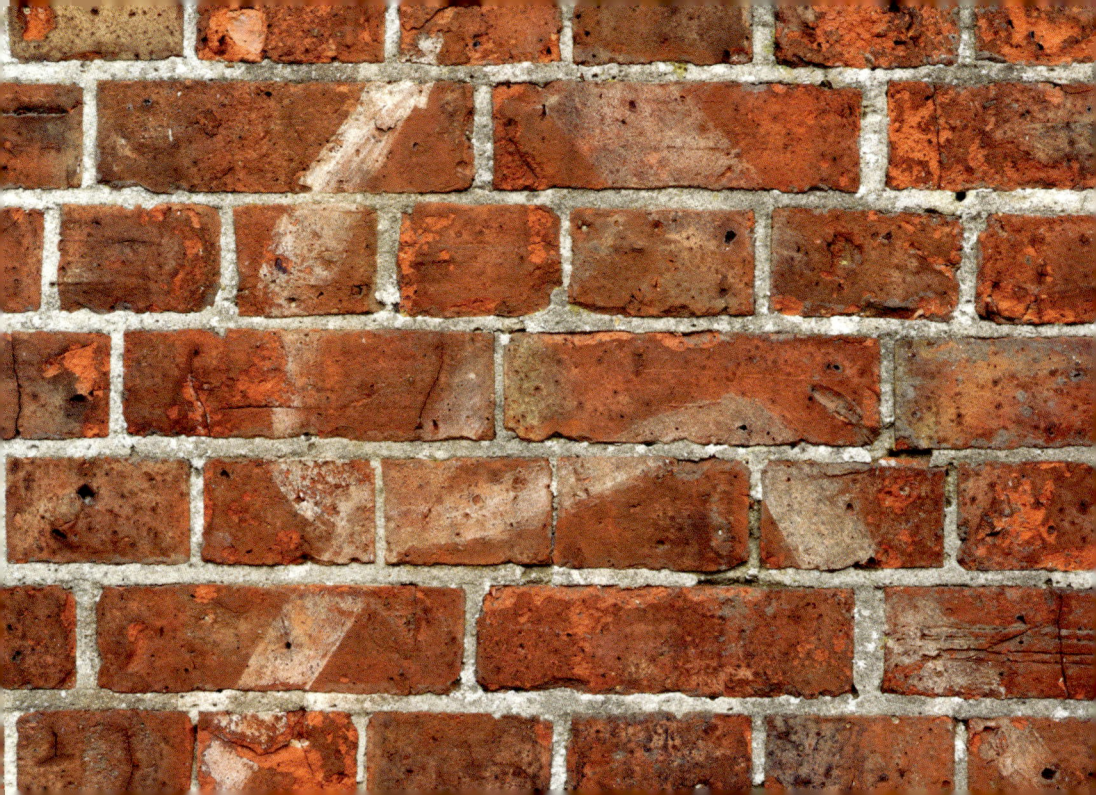

Chummy's has always been at Folkestone Harbour, selling fresh seafood. Many years ago you could actually find Chummy, who was a very charming and good looking man, running the stall himself. He died a few years ago, but his presence is still felt. A few years ago the old barrow was replaced with the architecturally designed stall that you see today. People come from miles away to buy the best jellied eels, whelks, prawns and any other seafood you can imagine, including grilled lobster, garlic prawns, salads and oysters which come from a small bed at Burnham on the Essex coast, which produces fine oysters. Chummy's is known around the world, is part of Folkestone's seaside heritage and has been acknowledged by English Heritage, which recently awarded the stall the title of Best Shellfish Stall in England.

फोक्सटनको ह्यावरमा भएको Chummy's, fresh seafood को लागी संसारकै प्रशिद्ध मानिन्छ ।

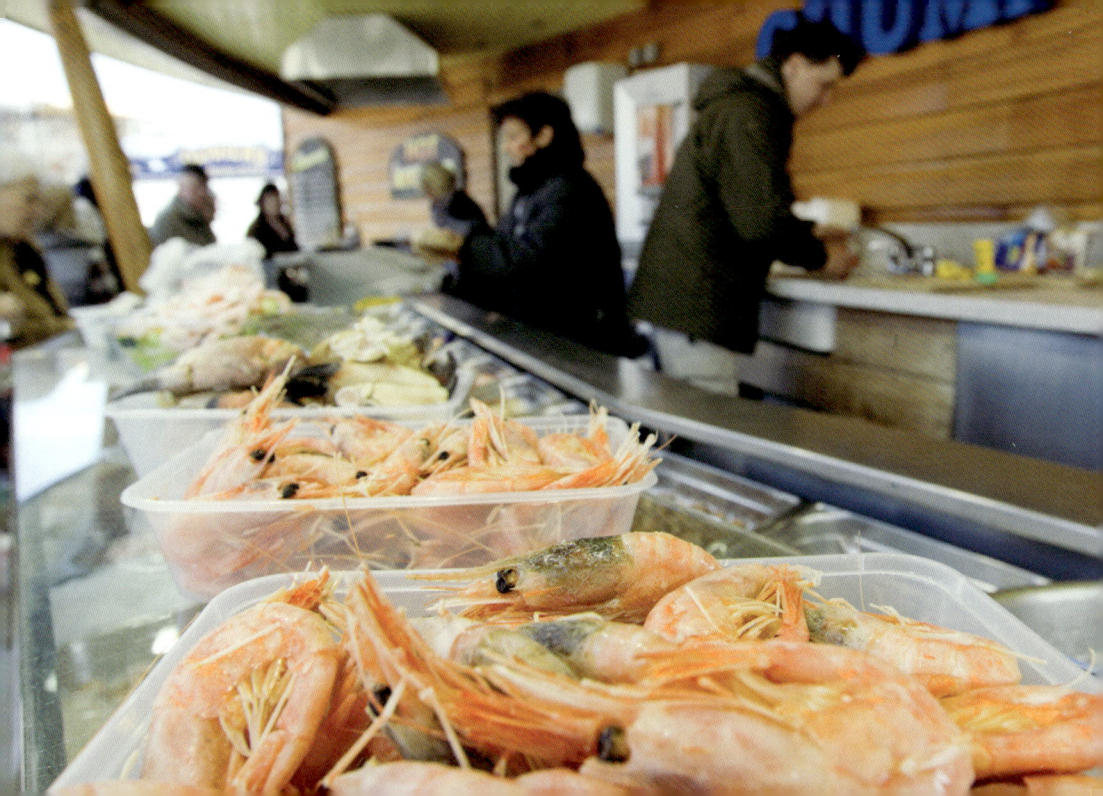

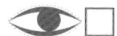

As a girl I remember lots of fishing boats in the harbour. There was an open air auction where the fish were sold, but I never knew where they went. Down near the sands by the arches on The Stade, all the fishermen used to live. Outside there were metal stands to hang the fishing nets out to dry. They used to mend the nets by hand whilst their wives cooked whelks. Once I went down with my big sisters in 1963, the coldest year in Folkestone, when there was snow for three months. We found a frozen fox on the beach and took it home. Our Mum was horrified and the fox didn't live once it had thawed out.

केही वर्ष अगाडी त्यावरमा धेरै माछा मार्ने डुङ्गाहरु थिए । भन्ने ठाउमा माछामार्ने मानिसहरु वस्दथ्य र उनीहरुले मारेको काछ्राहरु सस्तो मुल्यमा वेच्दथ्य । त्याहां भएको धातुको खम्वाहरु माथी सधै माछा मार्ने जालहरु सुकाइरहेको देखिन्थ्यो ।

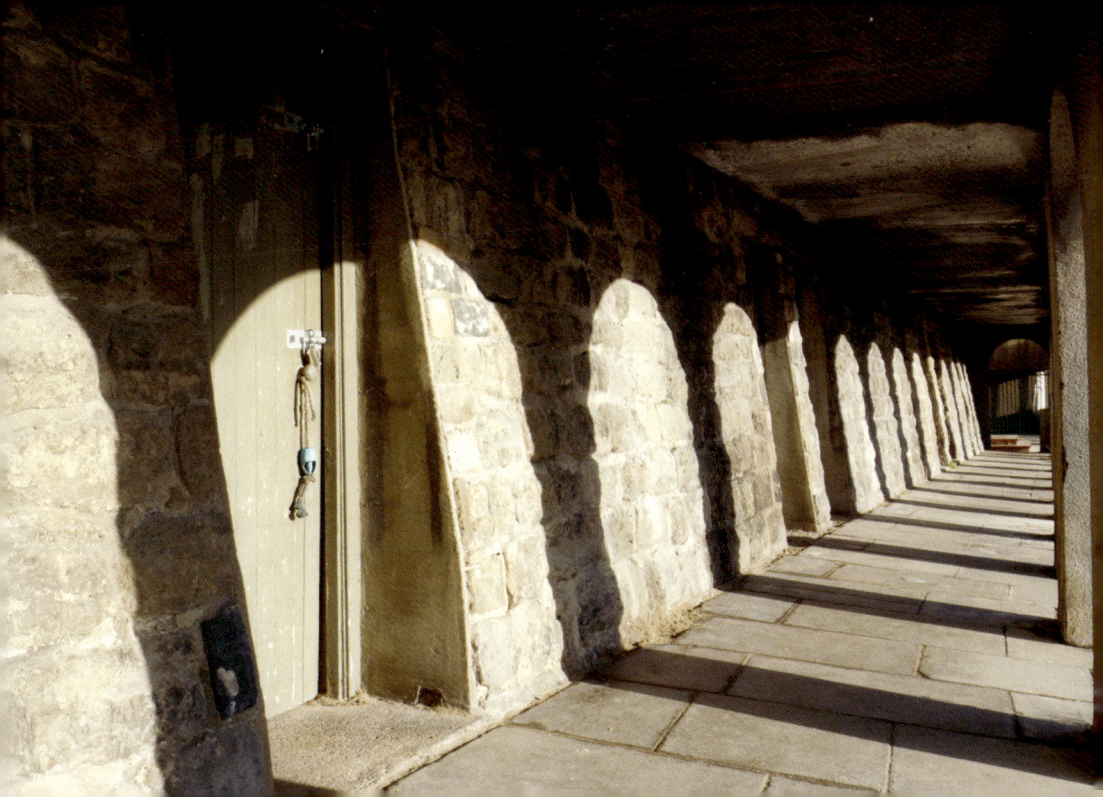

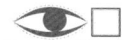

This used to be St Mark's Church built of brick – altogether a fine piece of architecture – but an astonishing feat in 1941! Where did they find the bricks two years into the War? One would have thought too that the skilled builders would have gone off to fight; or was foreign prisoner labour used? The building shows no sign of economy, and its size and provocative position on a hilltop, visible from Nazi-occupied France, and a marker for every passing bombing raid, might well have been conceived as a statement of defiance.

It had the desired effect: within days, Lord Haw Haw's mocking tones were heard announcing the newly completed Church at Shorncliffe was to be bombed, and an unsuccessful attempt was made two nights later. Notice was taken of the threat, for when Archbishop Fisher arrived to perform the Service of Dedication to St Mark, he was given an escort of Spitfires as overhead protection. 57 years later, the final moving service was held at the 11th hour of the 11th month – a significant moment to close a soldiers' church. Afterwards the stained glass was relocated, the organ sold, the books and banners removed. It is now occupied by Folkestone Operatic and Dramatic Society, who hold a great programme of music, drama and events there.

सन १९४१ मा यो चर्च उद्घाटन गर्न धर्म गुरु आउदा उसको सुरक्षाको लागी धेरै चिन्तीत हुनु पर्दथ्यो । आजकाल यो चलचित्र हल भएको छ ।

EVERYWHERE MEANS SOMETHING TO SOMEONE

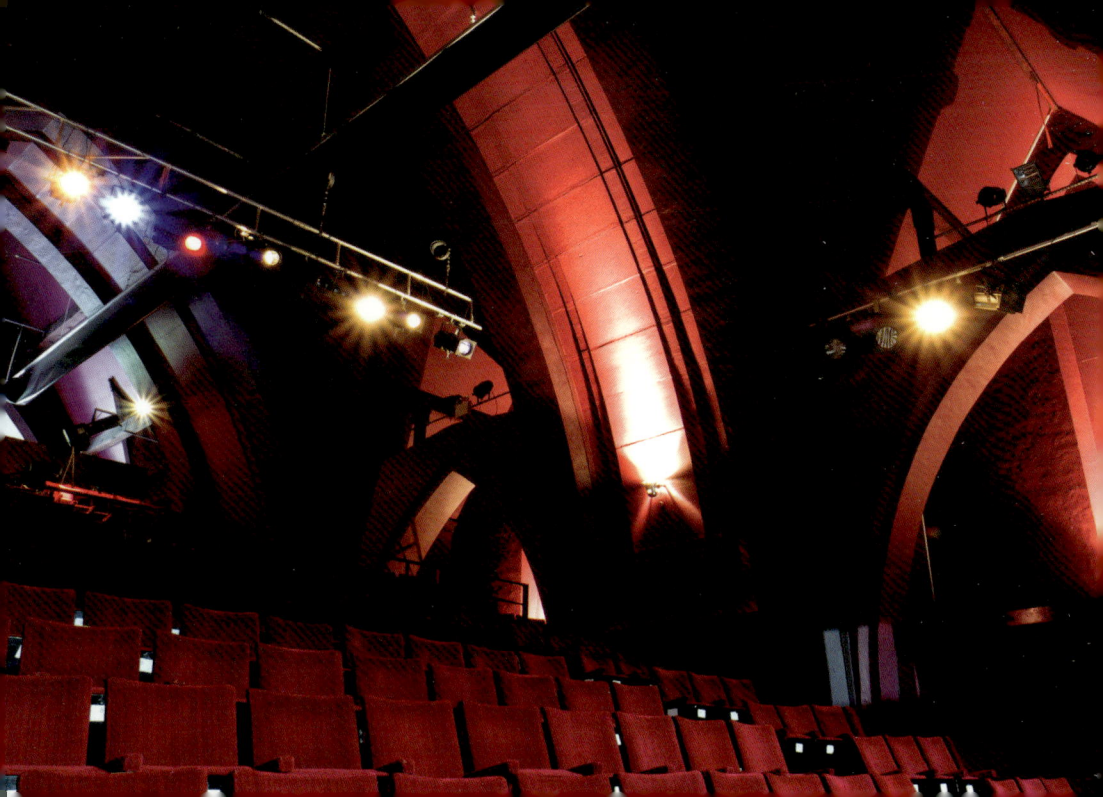

This ceramic horse trough outside 25-27 Plain Road is one of at last two still remaining in the row of houses on the south side of the road from the time that the properties were stables and coach houses for The Grand on the Leas. It was made by Oates & Green Ltd of Halifax, certainly before 1908 when the business was taken over. The firm, manufacturers of brick, tile, earthenware and ceramic products, were world-famous for their urinals. On the brick wall opposite the trough is a heavily rusted ring, still just clinging on, which was used for tying up the horses. Of the other houses, Number 17-19 is the nearest to its original appearance, apart from the replacement of some windows. On the first floor at the front, the door allowing access to the hay loft can still be seen. The original slate roofs had to be replaced after the 1987 storm.

विगत सताव्दीको सुरुवातमा यो तवेलामा The Grand and The Metropole होटलको पाहुनाहरुको घोडाहरु राख्ने गरिन्थ्यो । घोडाहरु मेरो वगैचाको हिडाइन्थ्यो । घोडाहरुलाई वाध्ने जिन काटाहरु अभ्रु पनि त्यहां भ्रुण्डीरहेका छन ।

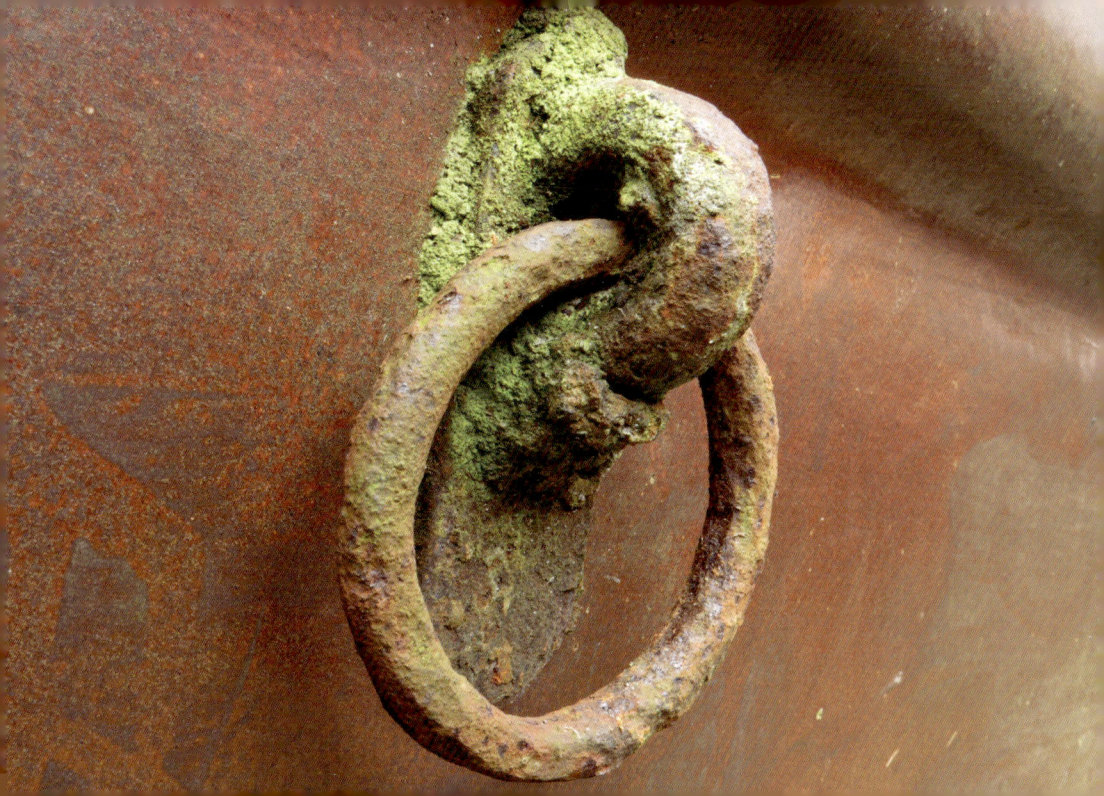

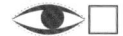

There are numerous examples of these quern stones in museums and private collections, but I am sure many Folkestone residents are unaware of them, or their significance, in the development of Folkestone as a centre of trade, prior to the Roman occupation.

I have several partially-completed stones in my back garden.

त्यहा विभिन्न प्रकारका उत्तर आधुनिककालिन धातुहरु संग्रालयमा राखिएको छ तथापी फोक्सटन वासीहरुलाई यसको महत्वोको वारेमा जानकारी छैन जस्तो छ । रोमनले अधिकरण गर्नु अगाडी फोक्सटन एउटा व्यपारिक केन्द्र थियो ।

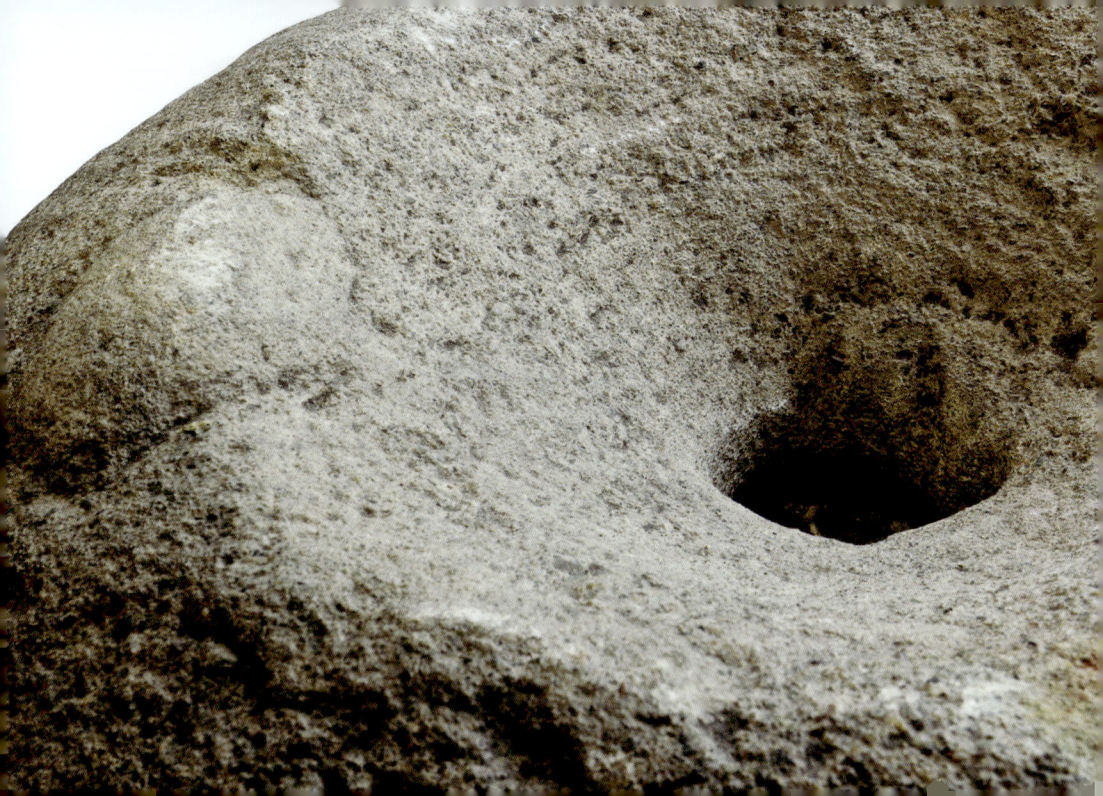

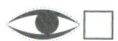

Whilst staying at The Metrople Hotel, Wilfred Owen was happy, writing a letter to his friend Siegfried Sassoon that he just couldn't feel depressed.

"The sun is warm, the sky is clear, the waves are dancing fast and bright… But these are not lines written in Dejection. Serenity Shelley never dreamed of crowns me… Yesterday I went down to Folkestone beach and into the sea, thinking to go through those stanzas and emotions of Shelley's to the full. But I was too happy, or the Sun was too supreme."

He died just over two months later on 4 November 1918 and news reached his family in Shrewsbury just minutes after declaration of the Armistice.

Wilfred Owen नामक यूद्ध कवि Metropole होटलमा अगष्ट १९१४ मा वसेका थिए । उनको मृत्यु २ महिना पछाडि ४ नोभेम्वर १९१८ मा भयो र यो समाचार Armistice घोषणा गरे लगतै उसको परिवारले सुनेको थियो ।

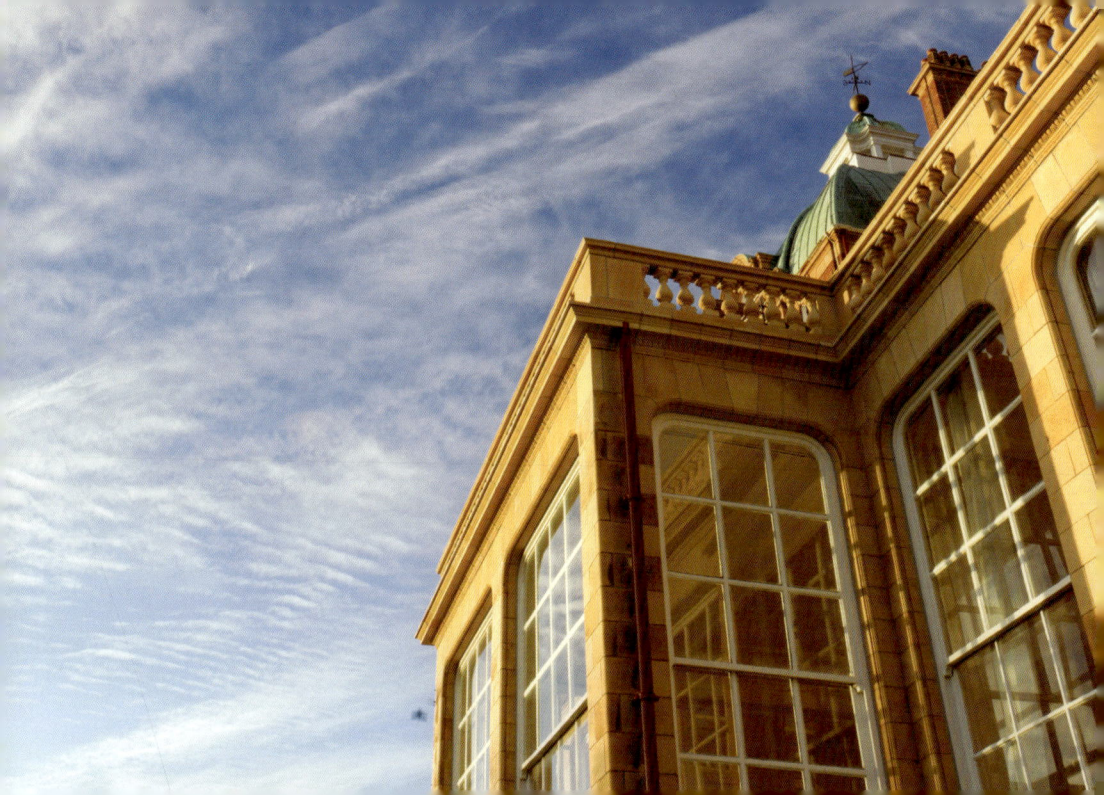

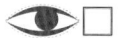

When we used to come down from Tunbridge Wells for a day on the beach, it wasn't important if it was hot and sunny, or grey and damp, I was just as happy beachcombing as playing in the waves. Looking for fossils at Copt Point, I came across small fragments of fossil wood: rich, dark, shot through with veins of glittering pyrite, and so perfectly preserved, that every feature of the grain and figure of the wood is there to see. I still have all the little bits I originally found, but I have since collected many specimens of this beautiful material, and am thinking of writing a book about it, with lots of pictures of the wood in its natural state, as well as cut and polished, and covering every aspect of its origins as trees, the palaeoclimate, geology, fossil formation and modern-day exposure.

Whenever I am on the beach, collecting or studying the fossil beds, I share my enthusiasm with anyone who happens to be there and shows an interest. I am always struck by the fact that so few people seem to know it is there.

क्याप पोईन्टमा धेरै प्रकारका अवशेषहरुको विस्तृत वर्णन गरेर राखिएका पाईन्छन् । तर ति मध्ये काठका टुक्राहरुका आवशेष चाहीं मलाई राम्रो लाग्यो ।

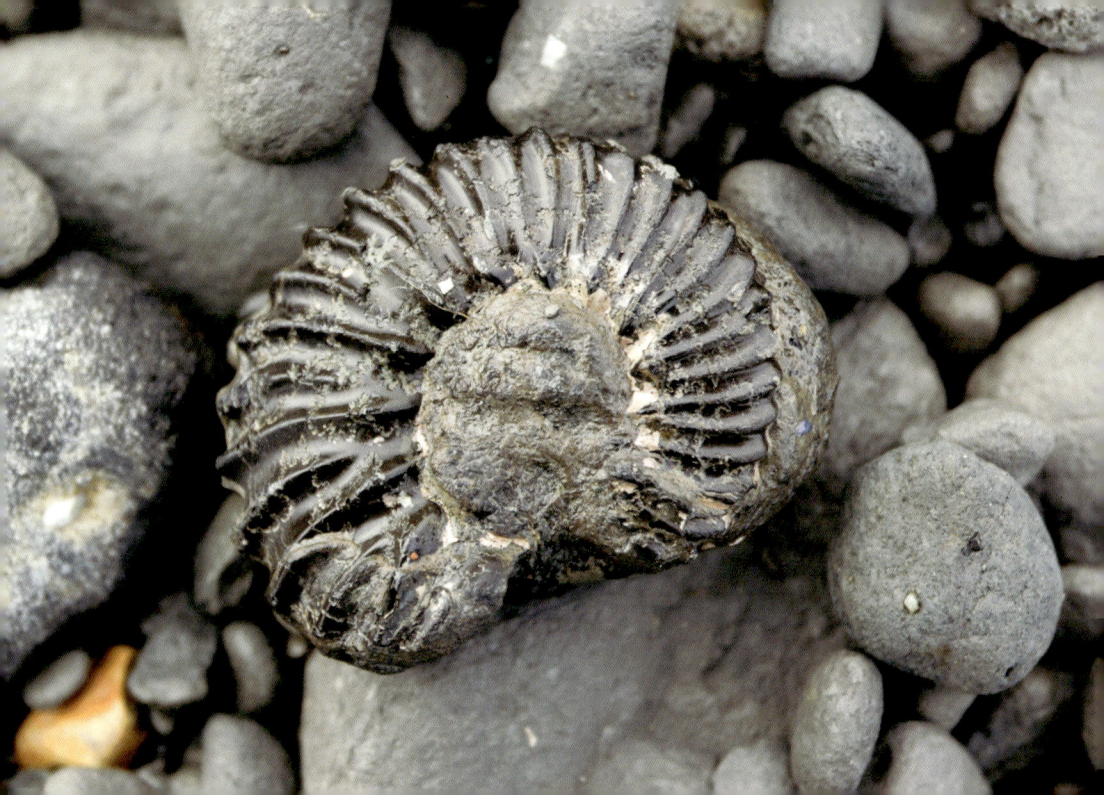

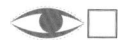

As a child I grew up in London at a time when even day trips to the coast were very special and few and far between, but one of my enduring memories was that I always straightaway headed for any of the seaside telescopes dotted along the coastlines and clifftops. I recall doing just that as soon as the driver had disgorged his coach load by the Water Lift on The Leas on my first visit to Folkestone in the 1950s.

Little did my parents or I know then, that more than 50 years later I would be moving into my own home directly opposite that telescope!

मेरो वचपन अवस्थामा १९५० मा पहिलो पटक लनडनवाट फोक्सटनमा आएको थिए । त्यस वेला मैले लिज लिझ्टको छेउको दुरविनको माध्यमले टाढाको दृश्यलोकन गरेको थिए । आजकाल म त्यसको ठिक अर्को पट्टि वस्दछु तर यो कुरा ५० वर्ष अगाडी मलाई थाहा थिएन ।

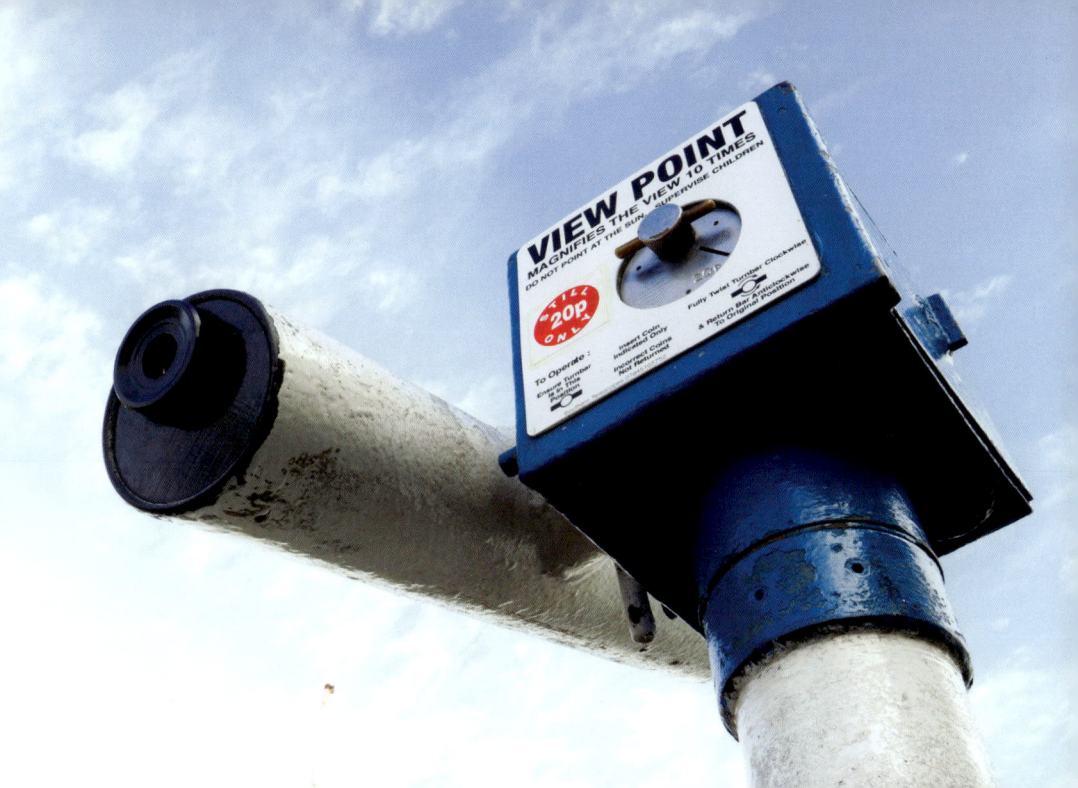

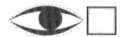

This block of flats is just such a ridiculous structure, it is stuck on to the end of a Victorian crescent with absolutely no regard for its surroundings. It is completely stupid, but I love it!

यो आवासिय कोठाहरु भएको घरको बनावट मलाई अचम्मको लाग्दछ । यसको लम्बाई भिक्टोरियन कृज्यन सम्मा ठोक्कीएको छ र यसको वरीपरी केही छैन । यो ज्यादै रिस उठ्दो छ तथापी मलाई यो मन पर्छ ।

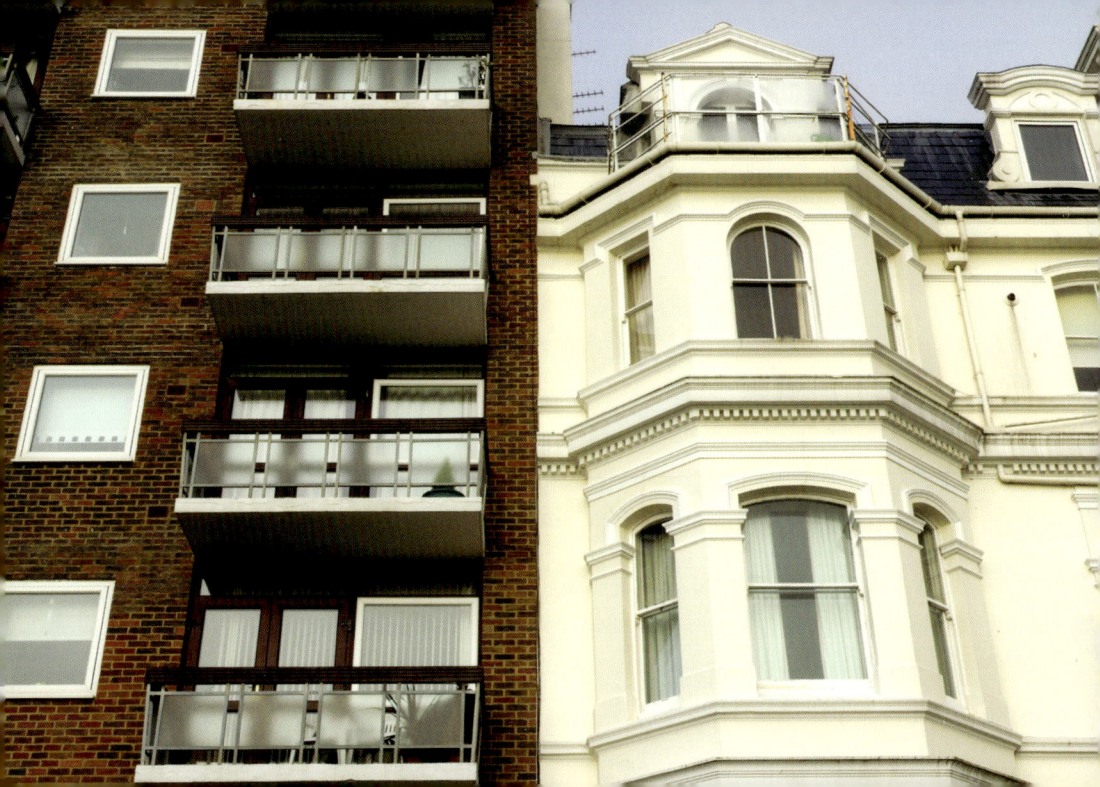

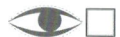

When I first came to Folkestone, I didn't really know anyone but I had dreams of becoming a professional artist. A little lonely and suffering from bouts of insomnia, I found myself one morning walking in the pouring rain past this phone box at 6am as dawn was breaking. This turned into a painting, which led to me, very quickly, becoming known in Folkestone, and opening a gallery, where I have been for nearly six years…

६ वर्ष अगाडी जब म फोक्सटनमा बसाइ सरे, त्यस पछी मलाई रङ्ग कर्मि बन्ने रहर लाग्यो । पहिलो पटक मैले एउटा रातो फोनको वक्सलाई रंग्याउले काम गरेको थिए त्यो सबैले मन पराए पछी मलाई स्थानीय रङ्ग कर्मिको नामले चिनाउन थाल्यो ।

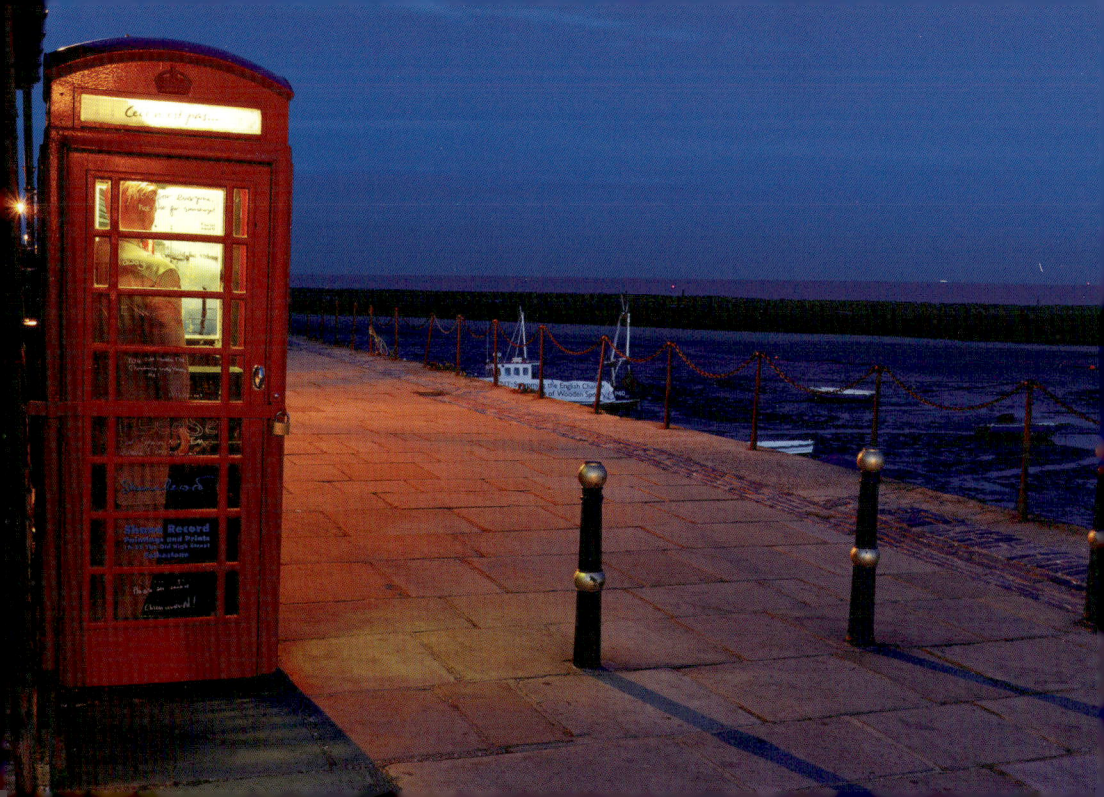

I am so proud that we have what I consider to be Tracey Emin's greatest work, i.e. her casts of baby clothing scattered around the town - it's such fun to point out to visitor friends or even when I'm being taken round on some literary or historical walk… If the speaker has swept past one of Tracey's little baby hats/cardies/woolly booties I just yell out "…and to our left, folks, we have an original Tracey Emin sculpture of a baby bootie/whatever" and it breaks up the monotony and brings a smile to people's faces!

The great thing is, is that they're tucked away in not-so-obvious spots and, amazingly, have survived without vandalism!

मलाई लाग्छ, Tracey Emin ले तयारी गरेका डिजाइनहरु मध्ये little bronze baby clothes उनको सवै भन्दा राम्रो हो । यिनीहरु फोक्सटनमा भएकोमा मलाई गौरव लाग्दछ ।

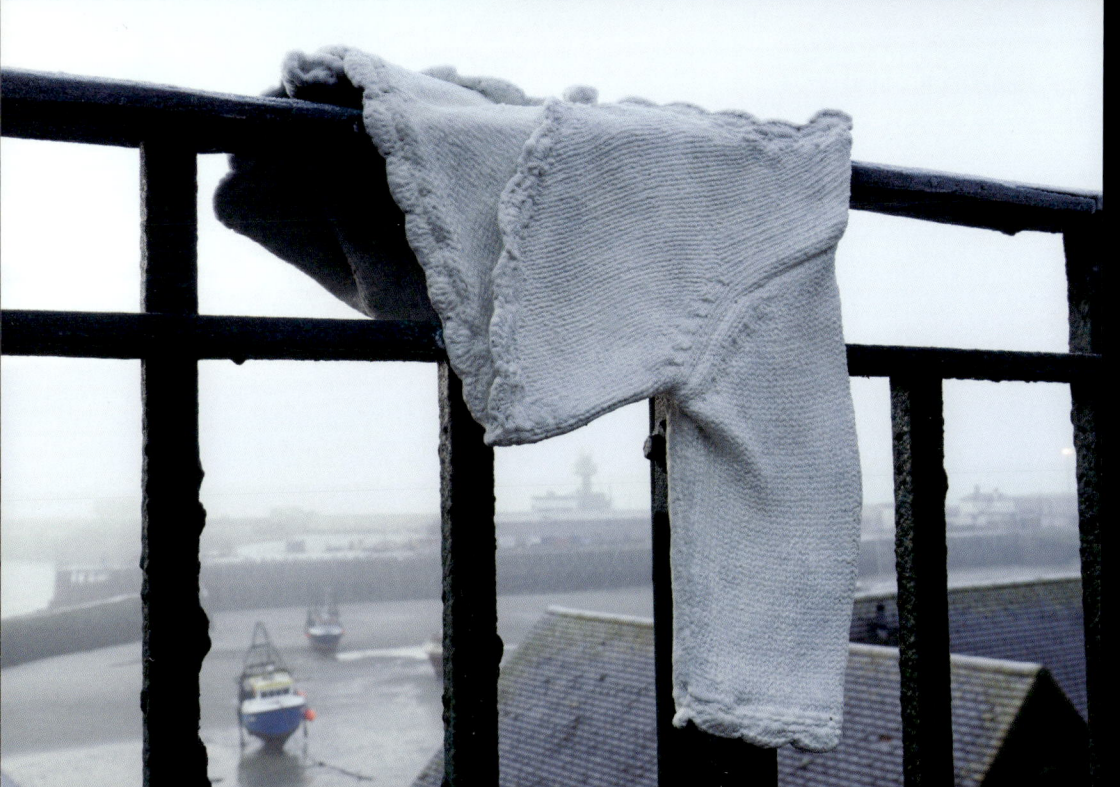

The Marine Crescent, I understand, is a very early example of a building where the shell is constructed of poured concrete, but what I find interesting is that the concrete mix was made from shingle taken off the beach. Truly a building fully integrated with its location!

Marine Crescent मा भएका यी नै हुन सबै भन्दा पहिलो पटक समुन्द्रको बालुवा र गीटी मिसाएर बनाएएका सिमेन्टीको जग भएको पक्की घरहरु ।

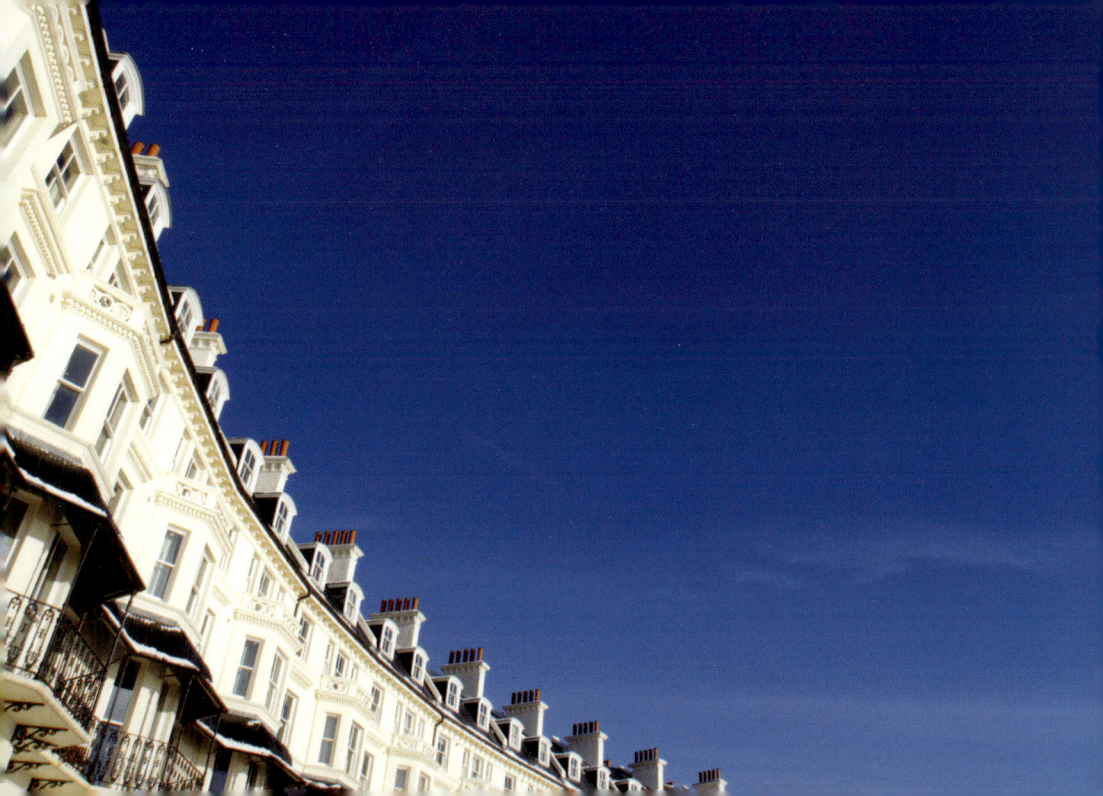

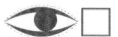

When I was a kid, The Dead End was the whole world. Mums knew that if you weren't at school or in bed you were at The Dead End. The whirring of secondhand BMX's with wonky saddles, and blistering tyres and gravel. A few inches of curbstone incline in the pavement was our bike ramp. Everyone was gong to be a stuntman.

Trains jangled past just beyond the hum of malevolent grey machinery in the electricity works, and the grinding metal screams from the old garage where Joe's hands were black. In rain we'd crawl under the broken down pick-up truck like cats.

The old wreck of a printing workshop had a fence entirely of rust and a great clanking fire escape and it had weeds higher than kids and it had a ghost.

And the main thing was the tree. We each had our own personal branch. When no one else was out I'd just sit right at the top all on my own, in the skinny limbs, swaying. We could climb all over that tree with our eyes closed.

मेरो वच्पन कालमा यस ठाउलाई "The Dead End" भन्दथ्ये । त्यसताका मेरो साथीहरु संग यहां खेल्ने गर्दथ्ये । यो नै हाम्रो संसार थियो त्यस वेला ।

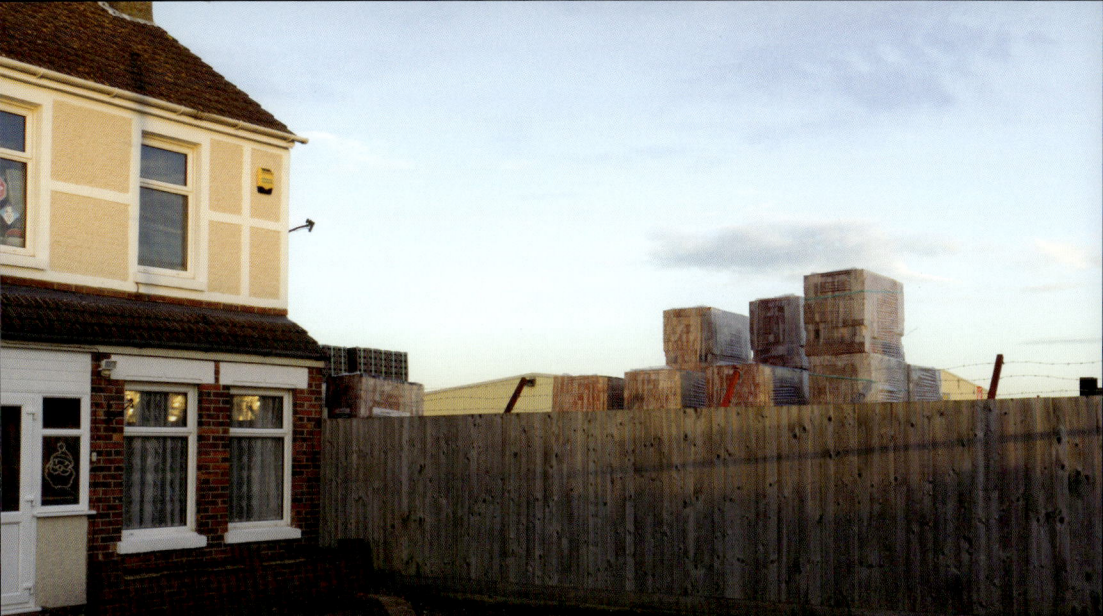

My sister was paid one pound to be an extra in a crowd scene in the 1951 film *Lady Godiva Rides Again*, which was partly filmed in Folkestone. With stars Dennis Price, Kay Kendall and Diana Dors, the film, which was about beauty pageants, used outside locations at the seafront swimming pool, the Leas Cliff Hall and the Metropole Hotel on The Leas. Notorious murderer Ruth Ellis, a friend of Diana Dors, had a walk-on part in the film as a beauty contestant, and was hanged just four years later for shooting her lover David Blakely.

अपराधिक हत्यारा Ruth Ellis ले सुन्दरी प्रतीयोगीको रुपमा भूमिका निर्वाह गरेको चलचित्र फोक्सटनको Metropole मा सुटिङ्ग भएको थियो । त्यसको ४ वर्ष पछ्ाडी उनी सुटिङ्गकै सिसिलामा उनकी प्रेमिका David Blakely संग समर्पित भए ।

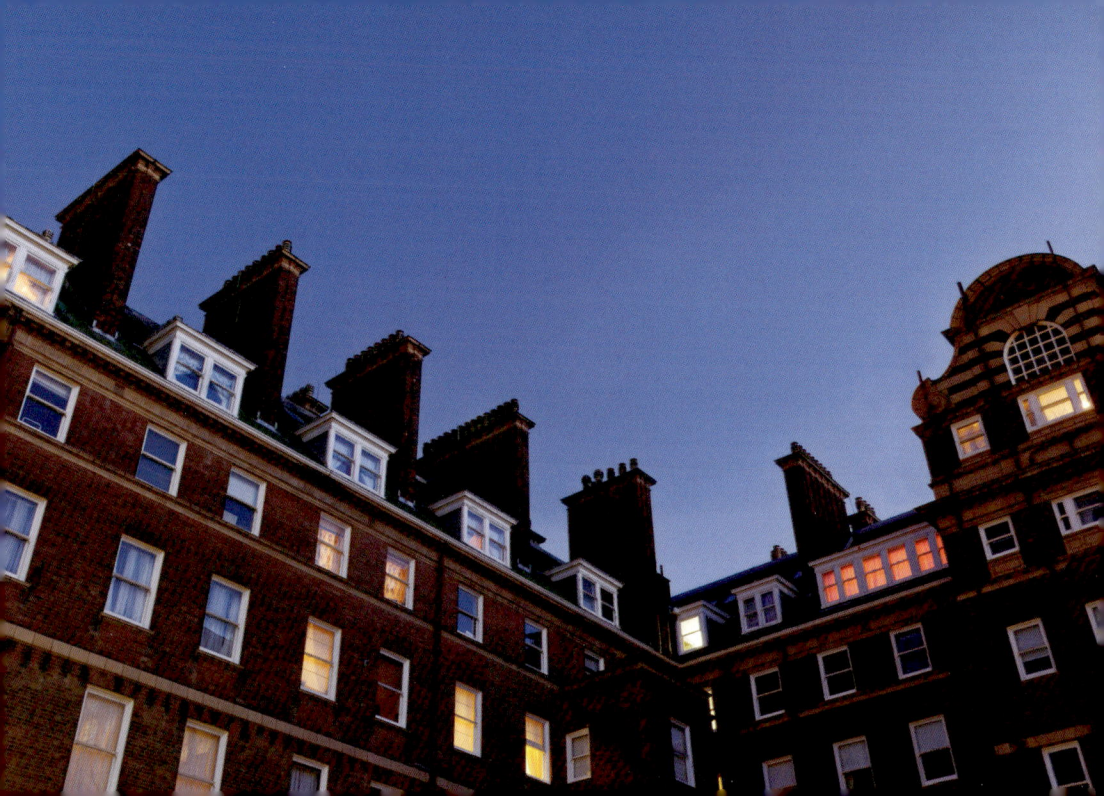

Fisherman, Mr Derek Plum, was featured in *The Sun* after the 46-year-old claimed that on a Thursday evening at Radnor Park Pond, he felt a great tug on his line and the fish he had hooked reeled out 500 yards before he could get a grip. Mr Plum even reckoned that, in the murky water of the pond "...there might even be more specimens like this fish, which is capable of ripping flesh from the bone in seconds... "

What eventually emerged was that he had caught, not a flesh devouring fish, but a Pacu fish, which enjoys sucking fruit!

एउटा राष्ट्रिय पत्रिकामा समाचार प्रकाशन भएको अनुसार फोक्सटनको स्थानिय मक्ष्यसिकारीले एउटा पोखरीमा यसतो माछा समात्यो जुन माछाले फलफुको रस चुस्न मनपराउथ्यो ।

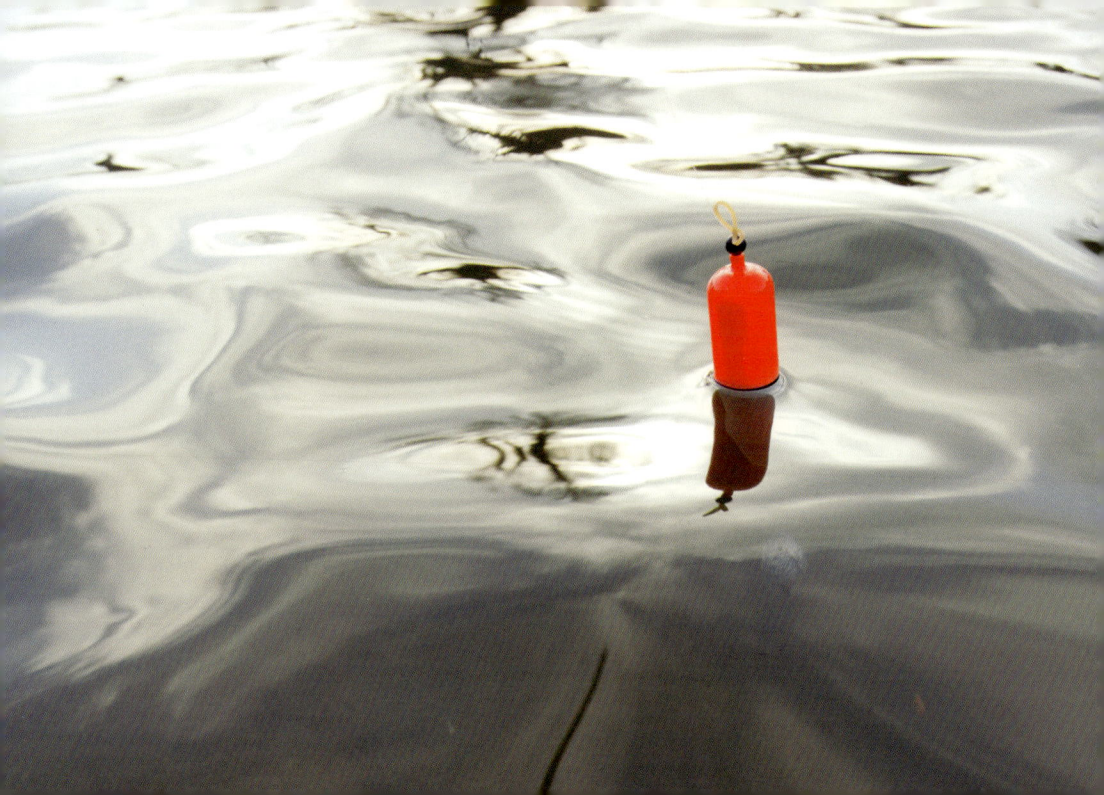

The first day I worked in Folkestone – running the History Centre in The Old High Street, a gentleman came in and said, "Can you help me? I think I remember something, but I'm not sure; I think I remember as a child in the war seeing a Spitfire fly at a tilt through the arches of the viaduct. Can I *really* have seen that? Can you help?"

We were able to find out that the Spitfire could in theory have flown through the arches, but at quite a tilt… but so far we've got no further. Others may know!

त्यहां एउटा अनावश्यक अफवा फैलिएको थियो कि, यूद्धको समयमा अति दुर्त गतिको हवाइ जहाजले Viaduct को गुम्वजहरुको वरीपरी चाहारेर गयो ।

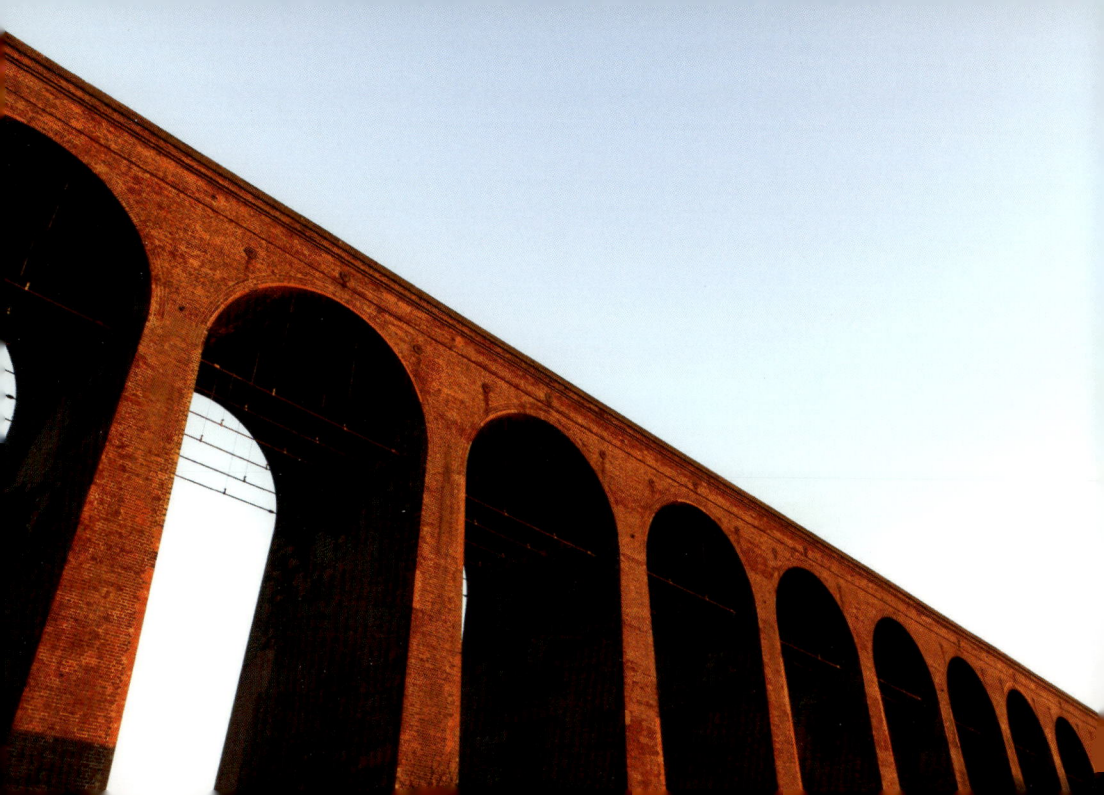

What is now called the Road of Remembrance was originally known as Slope Road, and was the route that 10,000,000 soldiers marched down on their way to Folkestone Harbour and on to the trenches in France and Belgium in WWI. At the top is the war memorial, commemorating the men who died in battle, and a cairn, built from granite blocks. About half way down on the left hand side, is a five room bunker, embedded in the cliff, which was a Naval telecommunications HQ in WWII. Two local ladies set up Mole Café in 1914, on the Harbour Arm, offering free tea to the troops, and 42,000 of them signed a registration book as they embarked.

आजकल यसलाई Road of Remembrance भनिन्छ, यसको वास्तविमक नाम Slope Road हो । प्रथम विश्व यूद्धताका यो वाटो भएर करोडौं सेनाहरु परेड खेल्दै फोक्सटनको ह्यावोर सम्म भरेर फान्स र वेल्जीयमको यूद्ध सुरुङहरु हेर्ने गर्दथ्ये ।

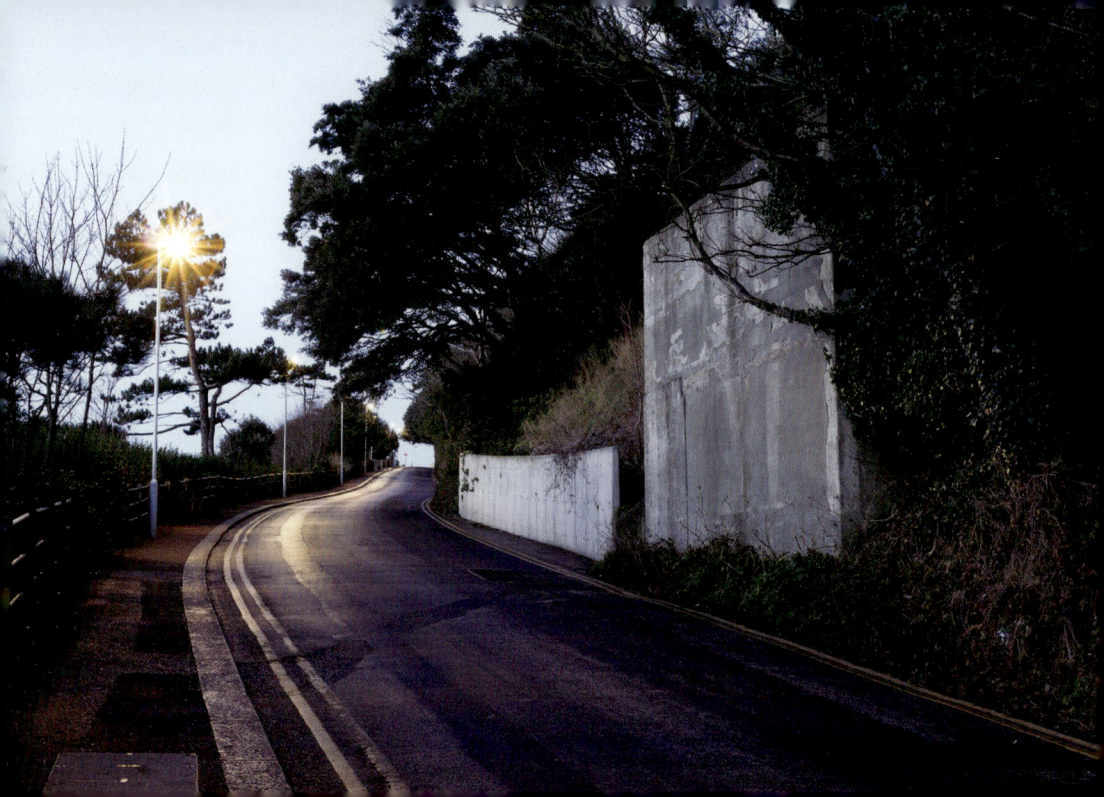

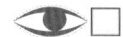

My family have lived in Folkestone for many generations and one of my ancestors, Henry Ullyett, was a headmaster who introduced teaching arts and science to local schools. There is a bronze cast of him in Folkestone Library.

मेरो परिवरहरु फोक्सटनमा धेरै लामो समय देखी वसोवास गर्दै रहेका छन । मेरो पुर्खा, स्थानिय स्कुलको प्रधान ध्यापक थिए र उनले कला र विज्ञान विषय सिकाउथे । फोक्सटनको पुस्तकालयमा उनको एउटा ताम्रा पत्र राखीएको छ ।

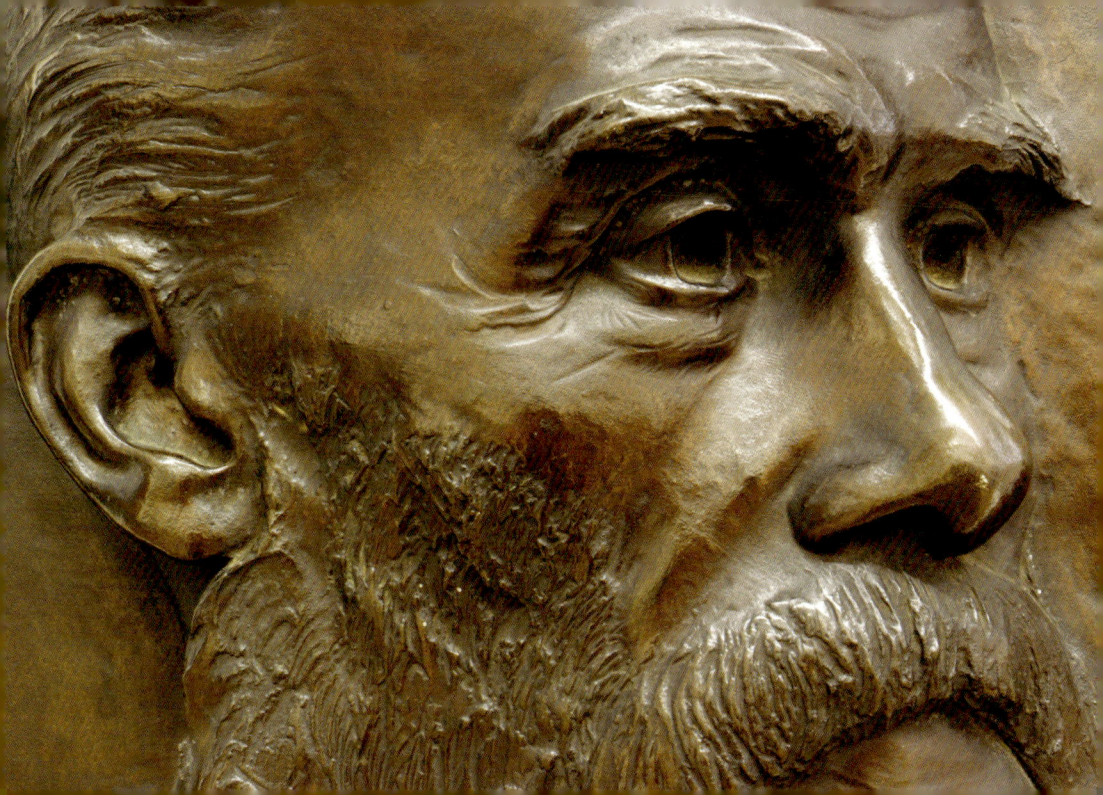

All my life I've lived in Folkestone and most of it close to Radnor Park and I've spent *many* an autumn evening lobbing a stick into the branches of the huge conker tree that stood, until last winter, near the little cottage on the corner of Radnor Park, trying to obtain the conker to end all conkers. That conker never materialised to me – though often it seemed to land right next to the kid standing to my side who was also chucking his stick into the same tree!

My son and I also visited the tree when he was younger, armed with 'a wicked stick that was just right for the job', but still that conker eluded us. It was a very sad day when the tree was too sick to carry on, and even sadder when this mighty icon of Folkestone came down. I passed by often as the team worked over a number of days taking it down and often felt a sadness that something I'd seen almost every day of my life would be gone forever. Another tree has been planted in the same spot. Maybe when my son has a family he can take his son there.

यो रेडनर पार्कको कुनामा भएको स्यानो घर विगतमा सार्वजनिक शौचालय थियो ।

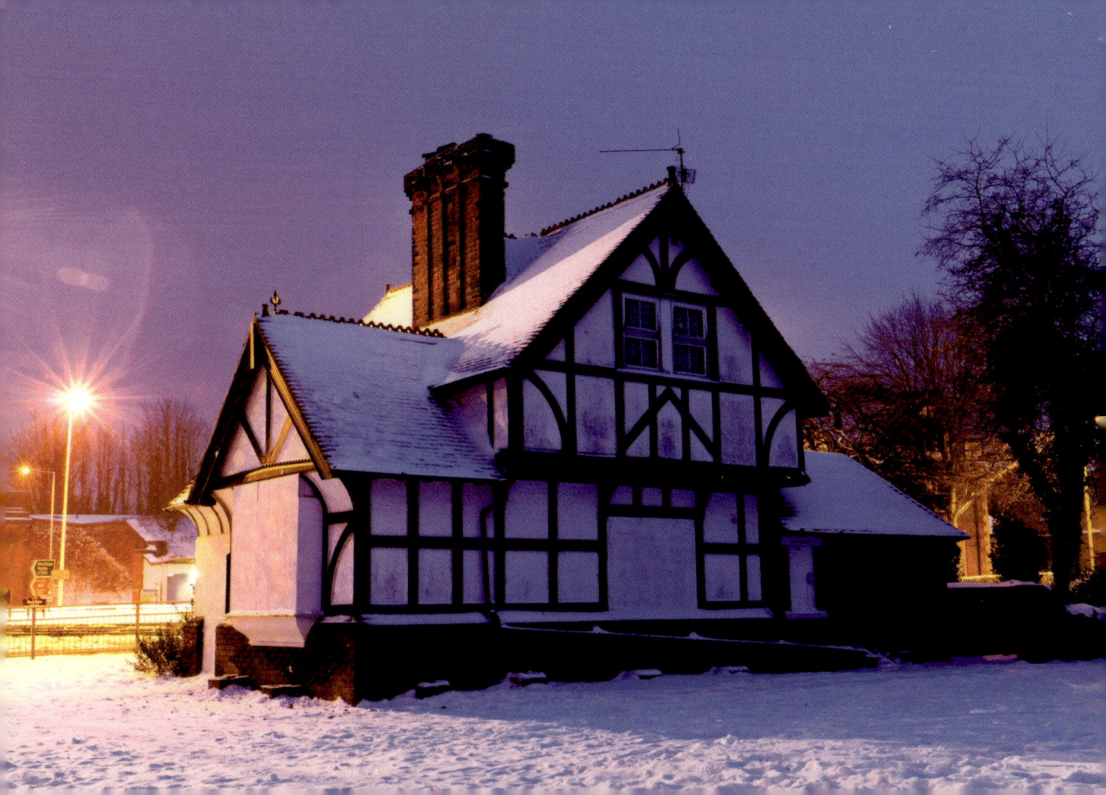

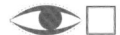

Before Tontine Street became Folkestone's main shopping street in Victorian times, the surface of the street was not cobbled, it was covered in wooden blocks about the size of a house brick, which provided a reasonably firm track for carts to negotiate the muddy conditions.

लगभग सय वर्ष अगाडी सम्म Tontine Street को वाटोमा काठका फल्याकहरु विछ्याईएको थियो जसले गर्दा हिलो वाटोमा जान आउन सजिलो हुन्थ्यो ।

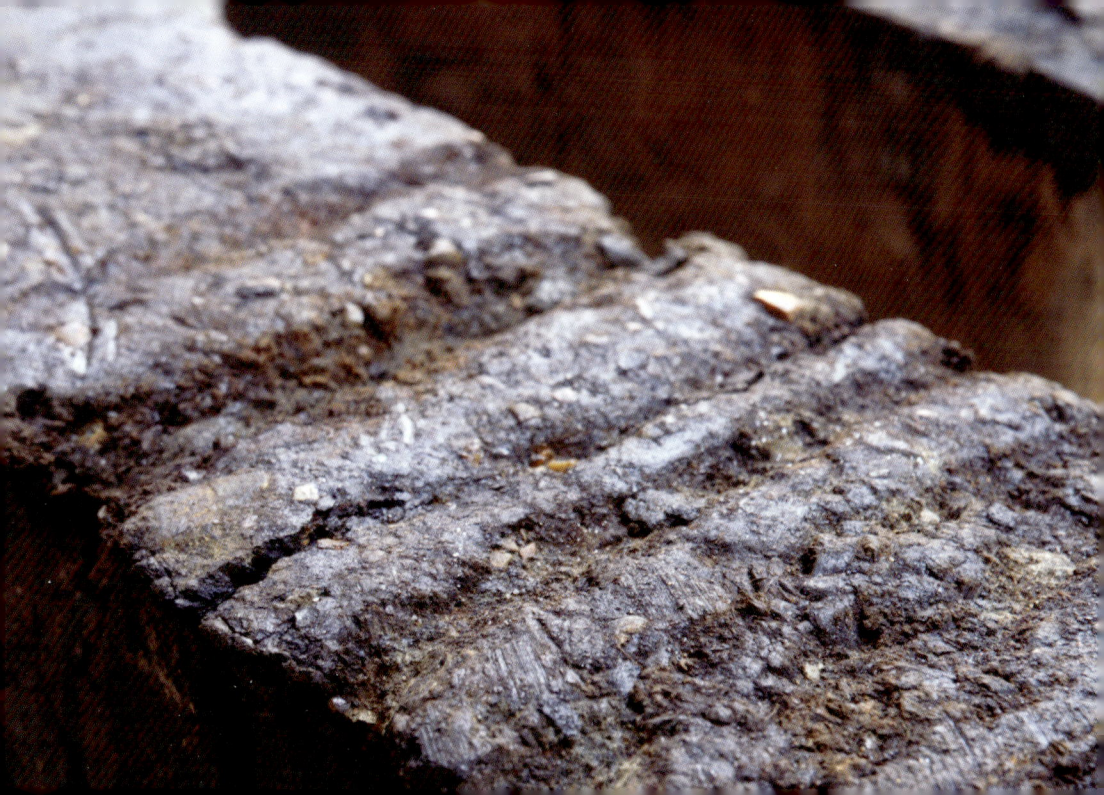

Folkestone sports ground has a long and important local history. It is home to the International Hockey Festival which is organised each Easter by The Folkestone Optimists HC, and has taken place annually for over 100 years. Its celebrations have become legendary throughout the area. During the football season the black and amber of Folkestone FC is regularly seen playing at the ground and the same can be said for the local cricket team. In fact over the years many important cricket matches have taken place here, including games featuring an England XI and with overseas teams visiting from as far as the West Indies. A local claim to fame is that International players such as James Tredwell, and wicketkeeper Geraint Jones have represented Folkestone!

फोक्स्टनमा भएको खेल मैदानले सवै खेलाडीहरु, हक्की, फुटवल तथा किरकेट समुहलाई उत्साहित गर्दछ ।

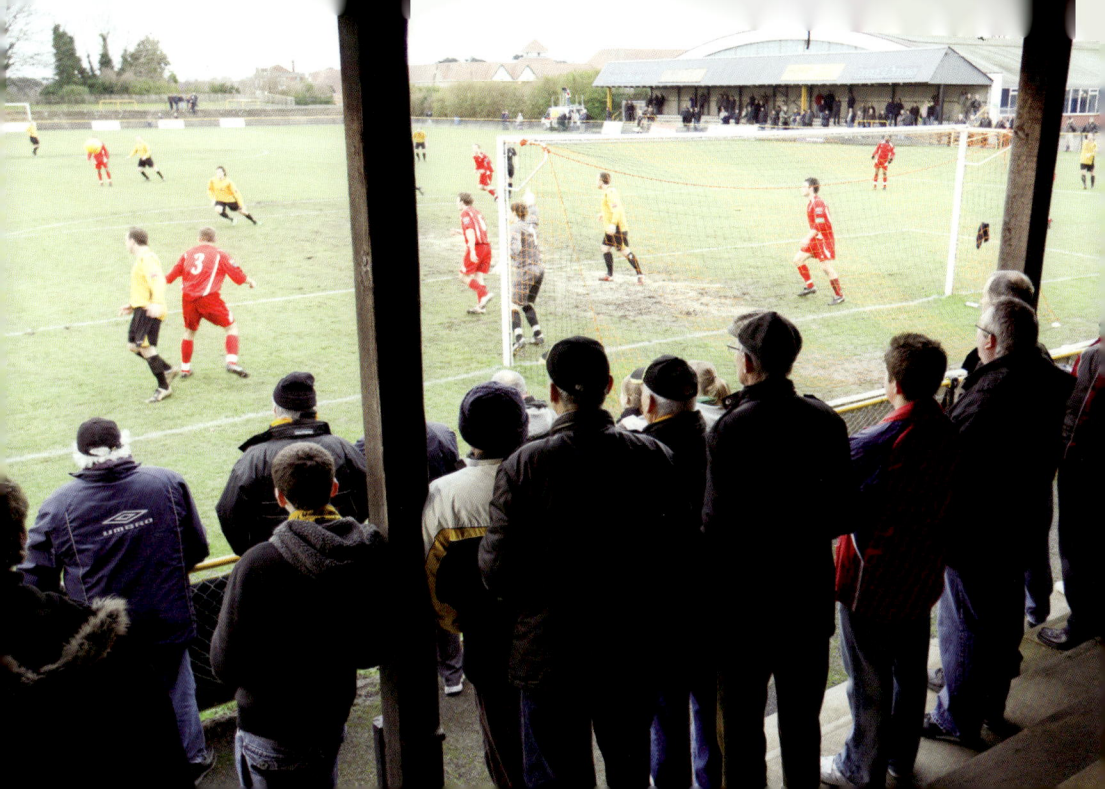

I was a child on the Leas when the first shell to hit Folkestone struck in 1941. It destroyed a house in Millfield, which has been replaced by a modern brick house on the north side of the road, and sticks out as the only modern house in the road. It was fired from mainland France, from Wimereux, I think.

सन १९४१, जुनबेला फोक्सटनमा पहिलो क्षेप्यास्त्र खसेको थियो त्यस बेला म Leas Dff थिए । त्यसले Millfield मा भएका घरहरु भत्काएको थियो । ति भत्कीएका घरहरुको सट्टामा बनिएका सबै नयाँ घरहरु हाल इटाले बनाईएका छन । त्यो क्षेप्यास्त्र चाहीं फान्सको मध्यभागवाट प्रहार गरिएको थियो ।

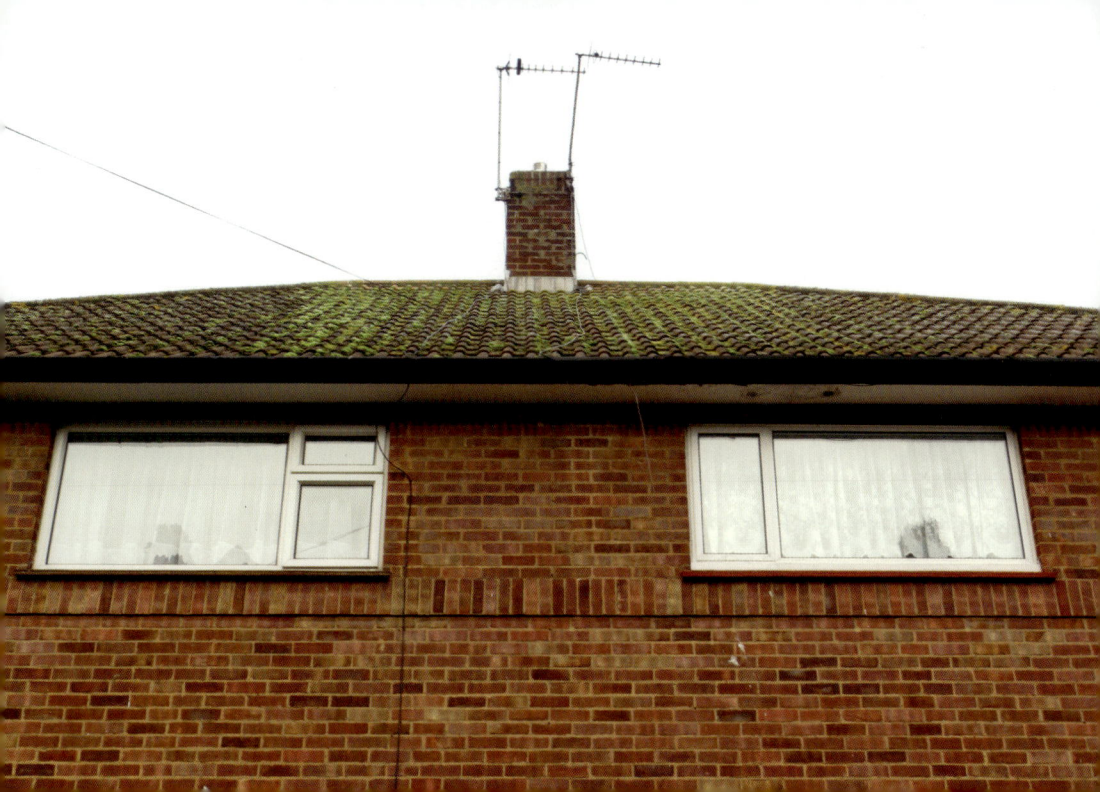

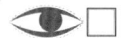

If you visit Folkestone on a *windy* day, go to the lone tower standing on Sandgate Road, with its gargoyles on every corner to scare bad spirits away.

The memorial garden is in the space once occupied by Christchurch before it was destroyed by a German bomb in WWII. It is a space criss-crossed by paths that freeze over in the winter, and in spring is fringed with cherry blossom, with crocuses sprouting rebelliously from the grass. In autumn, the trees shed yellow leaves in golden showers and wooden crosses are placed to honour those lost in war.

But on a windy day, throughout the year, the railings erected protectively around the proud tower *sing*. Whether by accident or design, the uncapped ends at their bases catch the rushing air – a fluid and joyous vibration of molecules – the sound of passing time and souls – the sound of eternity.

जोडले हावा चलेको बेलामा टावरको बार्दलिमा हावाको वेगले आउने आवाज सुमधुर गित जस्तै सुनिन्छ ।

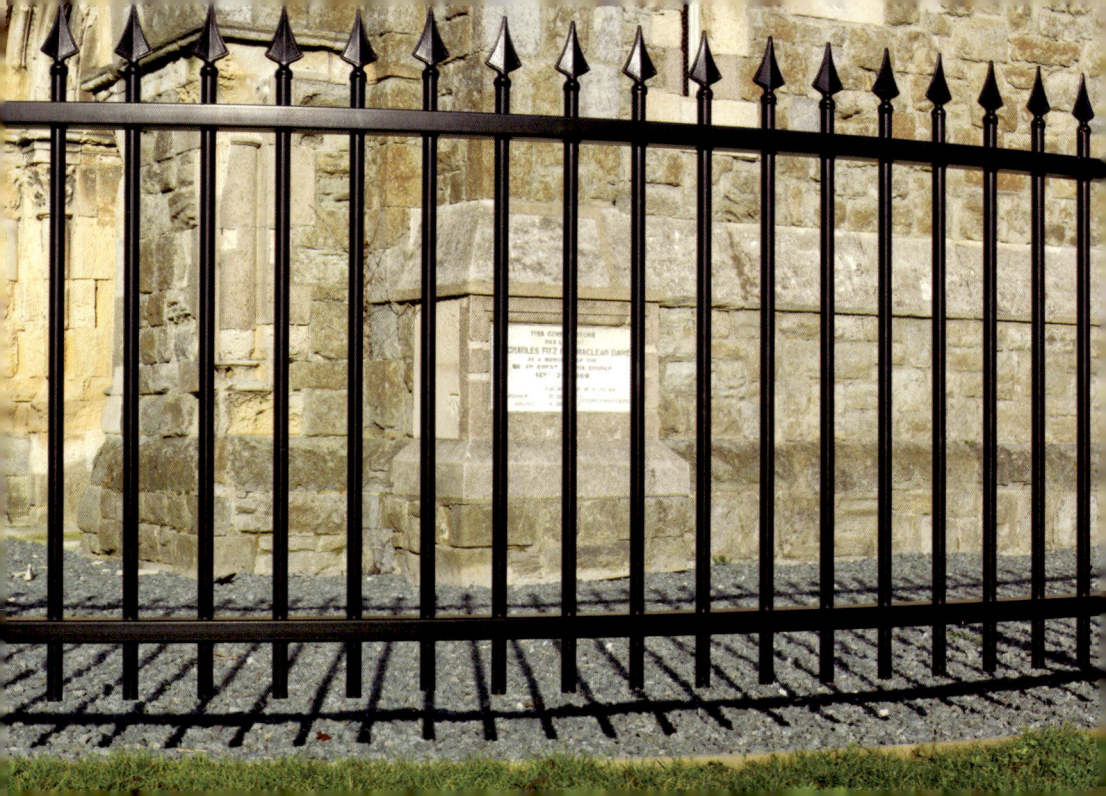

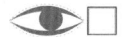

The first baseball game ever played in England was on the cricket ground opposite the Barracks on North Road. The game was introduced through the Canadians based at the barracks during the First World War. There was even a Baseball League set up as a result.

पहिलो पटक वेलायतमा खेलिएको वेशवल North Road को अर्को पट्टी ब्यारेकमा भएको किरकेट मैदानमा हो । यो खेल प्रथम विश्व यूद्धको समयमा क्यवनडियन नियमको आधारमा खेलिएको थियो ।

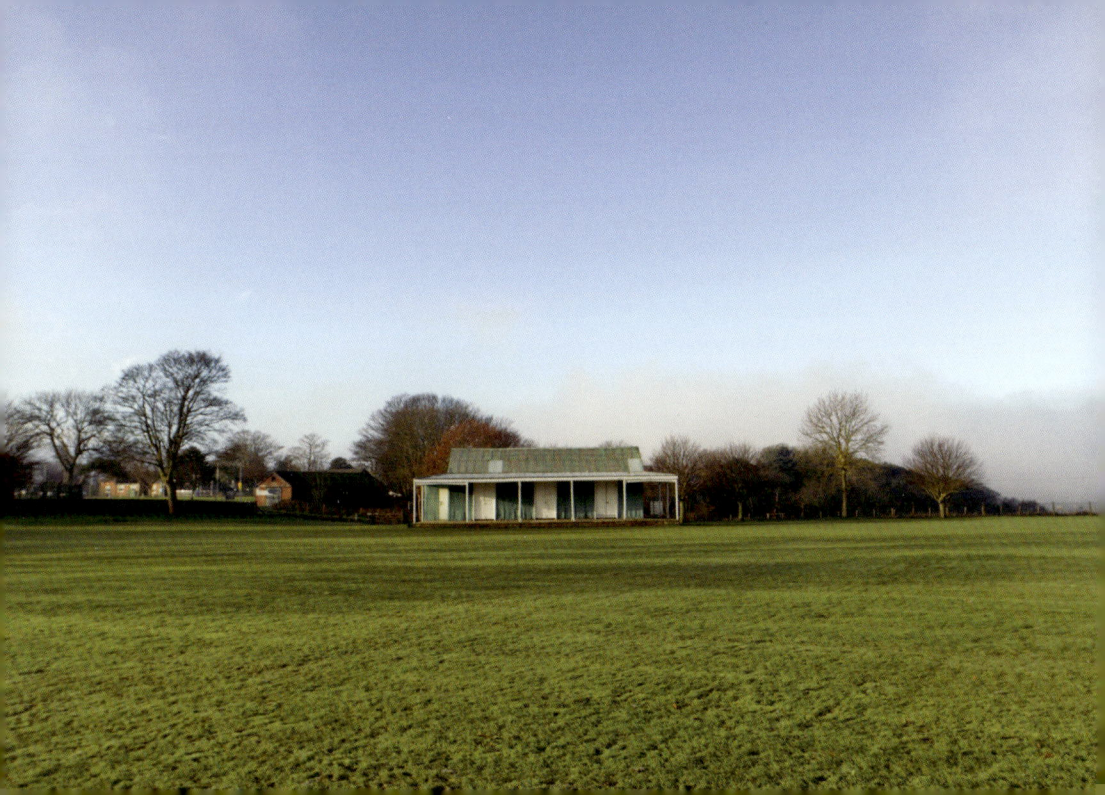

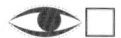

When I was a teenager in 1987, I remember being woken in the early hours to the sound of very strong winds. We lived at the bottom of Dover Hill and there was no traffic coming up or down, because the winds were so strong. In the morning all electricity was out and many schools were closed due to damage – and the wind was still up. I witnessed a greenhouse just take off in the air, luckily it smashed without anyone being hurt.

At the time we didn't realise it was a hurricane, that turned out to cause loads of damage in and around the surrounding area, which included a cross channel ferry that had been blown aground and was stranded down at The Warren with people on board.

फोक्सटनमा सन १९८७ मा खतरनाक हुन्डरी आएको थियो जसले गर्दा व्यापक क्षेती पुर्‍यायो । खास गरेर यसले समुन्द्रमा भएको पानि जहाजलाई यसमा भएको यात्रु सहित समुन्द्रको किनार भरी घुमाएको थियो ।

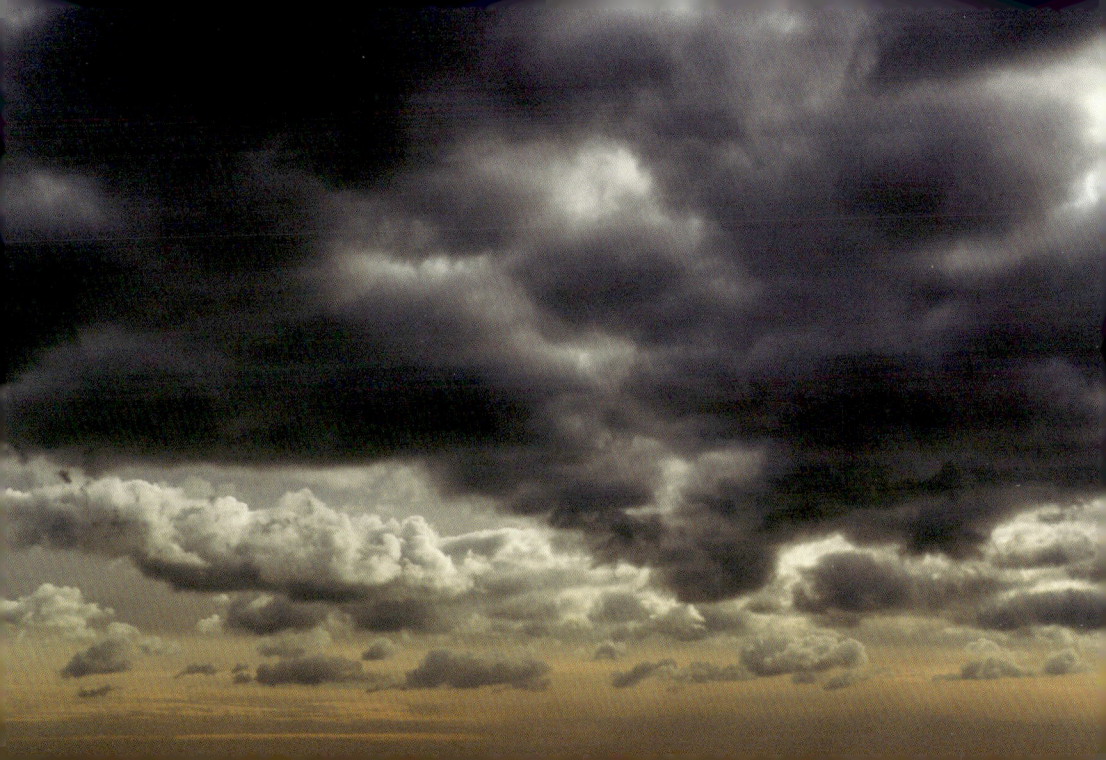

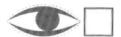

My family used to have a bakery in Canterbury Road and in 1987 the man who lived in the flat above spontaneously combusted. Hardly anything was damaged in the room around him, but only his foot and a small pile of ashes remained to show where he had been. This doesn't happen very often. This story can be found in books about Folkestone.

मेरो परिवारले १९,८७ मा क्याटवरी रोडमा वेकरी दोकान खोलेको थियो । यो दोकानको माथील्लो कोठामा एउटा मानिस वस्दथ्यो । यो मान्छेको छेउछाउको कुनै वस्तुहरु सामान्य अवस्थामानै थिए तर उसको भने सम्पूर्ण सरिर जलेर पैताला र स्यानो खरानीको थुप्रो मात्र भेटीयो त्यहाँ । यसको घटनाहरु प्राय हुदैन ।

EVERYWHERE MEANS SOMETHING TO SOMEONE

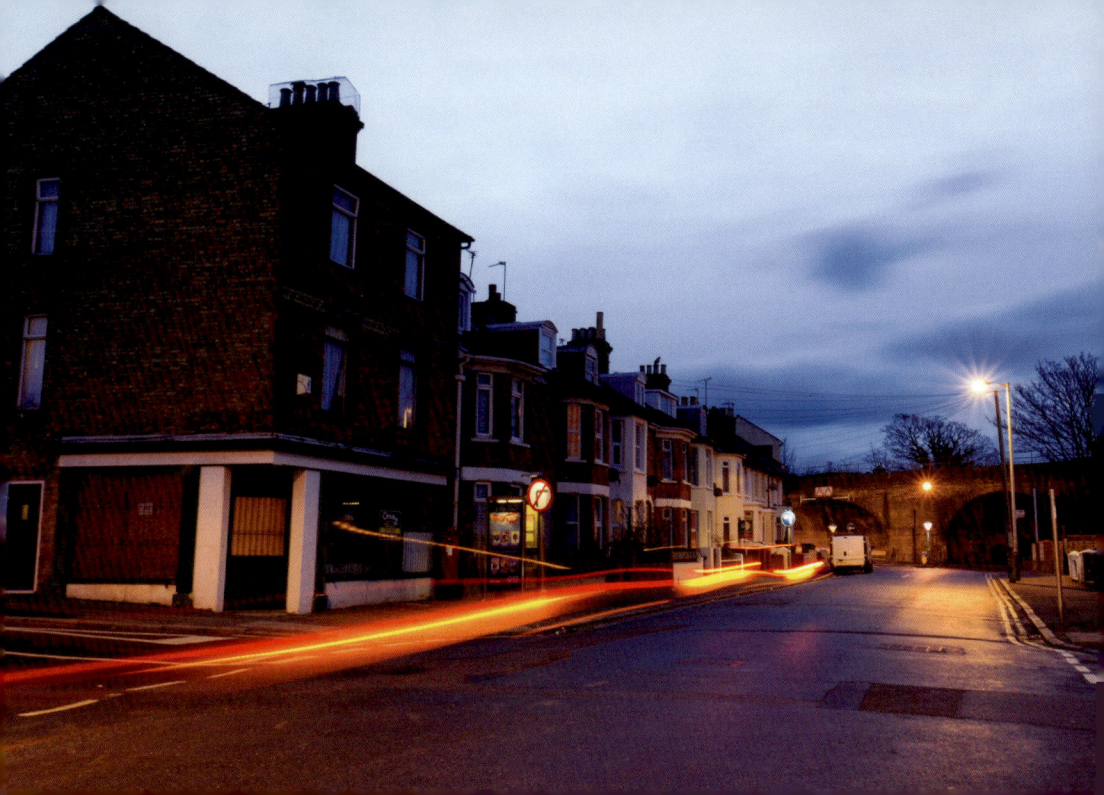

On display in Still in the Trenches is a named bible from a soldier killed in France in 1915 but, very poignantly, alongside it is the bible of his brother, who survived.

I bought it from a military dealer who didn't really appreciate the value of it all. It was very small and is dated 1912; the soldier had it for three years. It would have been picked up and sent back to his family.

यो पसलमा राखिएको वाईबल नामक पुस्तकमा सन १९१५ मा फन्सको यूद्धमा मारीएका तथा जिवीत सिपाईहरुको दुखान्त इतिहासको चित्रण गरिएको छ ।

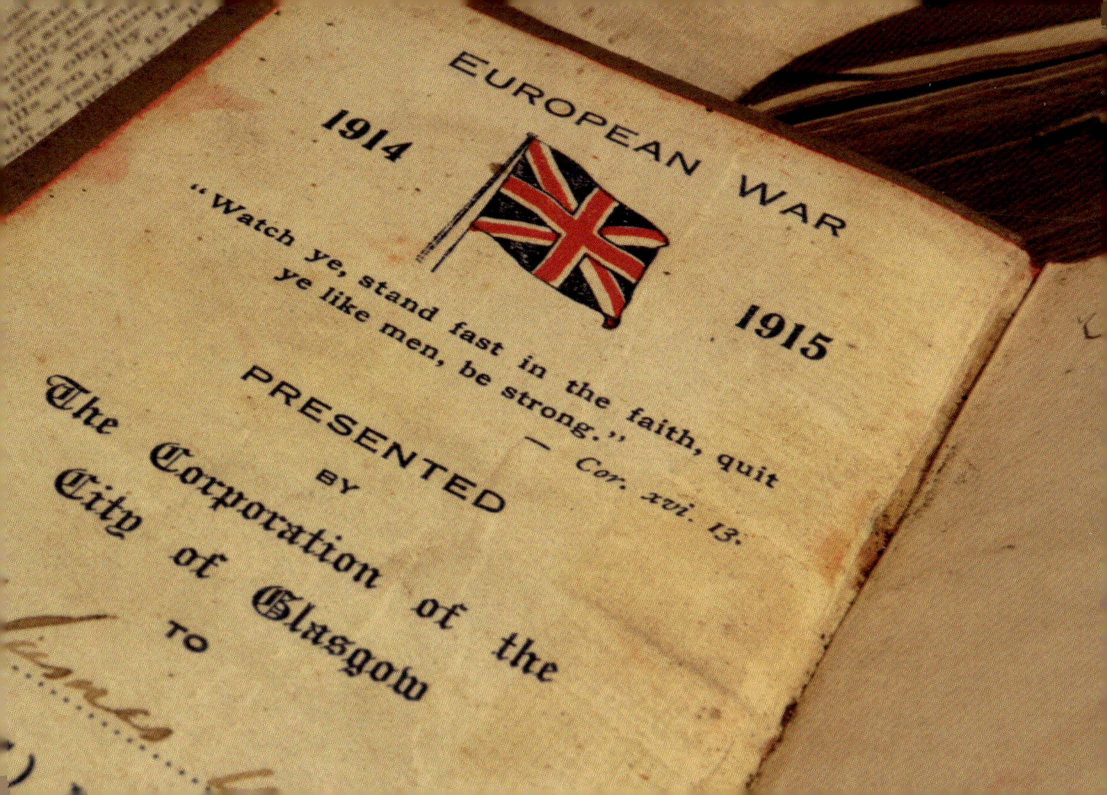

EUROPEAN WAR

1914

1915

"Watch ye, stand fast in the faith, quit ye like men, be strong."
— *Cor. xvi. 13.*

PRESENTED

BY

The Corporation of the City of Glasgow

TO

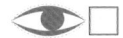

The shelter by Seabrook, I used to play guitar there. One day I was playing and a homeless guy came along with some bongos and we had a jam, he also had some port, which we drank!!

Michael Caine filmed a scene for a film in this shelter a couple of years ago, which provided the locals with a bit of excitement.

म Seabrook मा रहेको टहरोमा बसेर गितार बजाउने गर्दथे । एकदिन मैले उक्त टहरामा गितार बजाई रहेको बेला एक घर बिहिन व्यक्तिले बंगो लिएर आयो र हामी सँगै मिलेर बजाउन थाल्यौं ।

EVERYWHERE MEANS SOMETHING TO SOMEONE

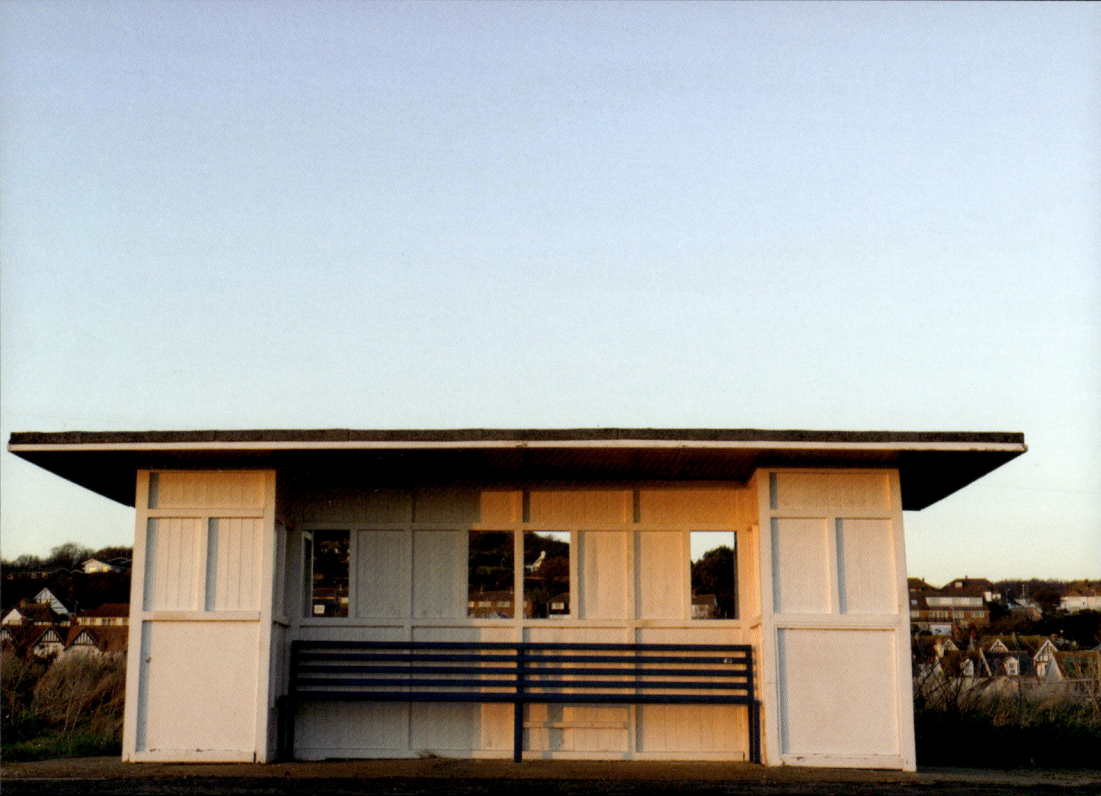

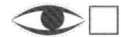

One of the loveliest views is from Nic's bench. The dogs love the woods and they are the nearest ones to us. It's along the path just past one of the Martello towers near the back of the Barracks.

सवैभन्दा राम्रो दृश्य चाहीं Nic's bench बाट देख्न सकिन्थ्यो । हामीहरुबाट नजिक भएको यो काठको फलैंचालाई कुकुरहरुले रुचाउँथे । यस फलैंचा Martello tower जाने बाटोमा पर्दथ्यो जुन सैनिक निवासको पछिल्लो भागमा पर्दथ्यो ।

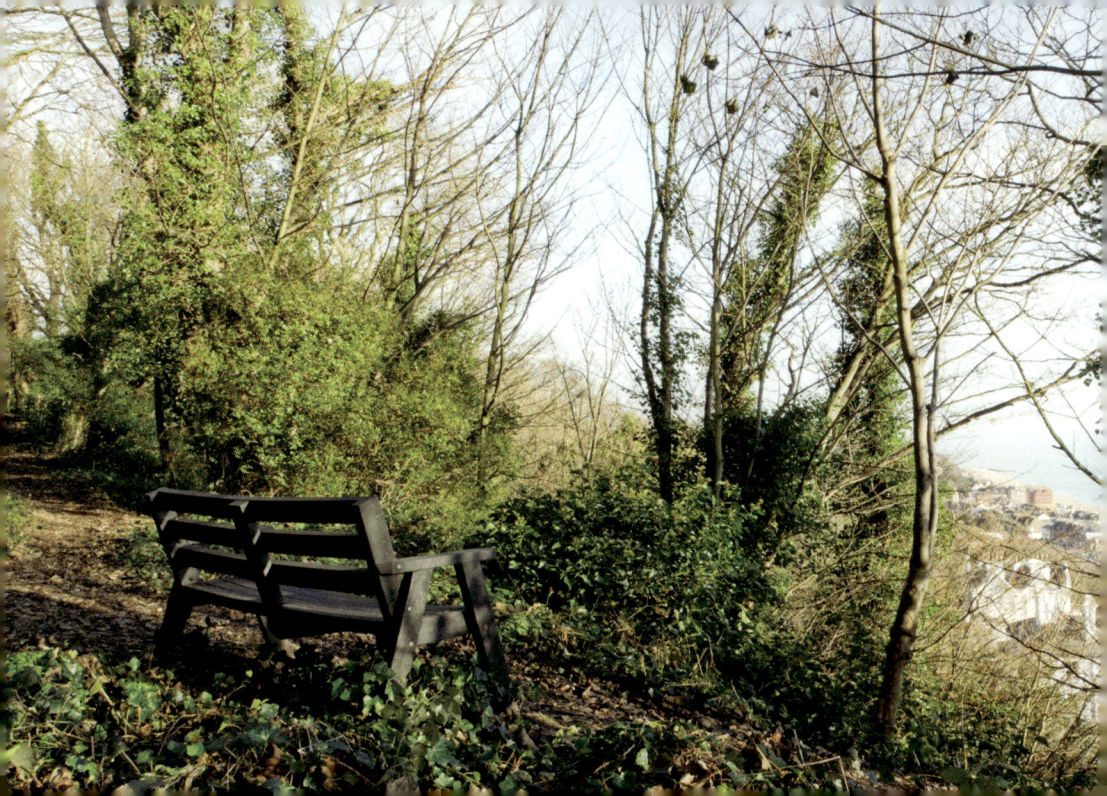

Climb the steps along from the Sunny Sands and find the viewing point. Here you will see the plaque which explains where the site of the landing place for the cross-Channel electricity cables is. This links the French and English electricity grid systems and allows four pairs of cables to transfer 2,000,000 kilowatts of power between the two countries. The cables come from Sangatte to Folkestone. The plaque was unveiled by Shepway District Council on Saturday 19 July 1986. In addition to a bit of history, you also have fabulous views of the Channel and the martello tower behind you.

यो सिलालेखले फ्रान्स र वेलायत विचको विद्युतिय प्रवाहको आदानप्रदानलाई जनाउँछ ।

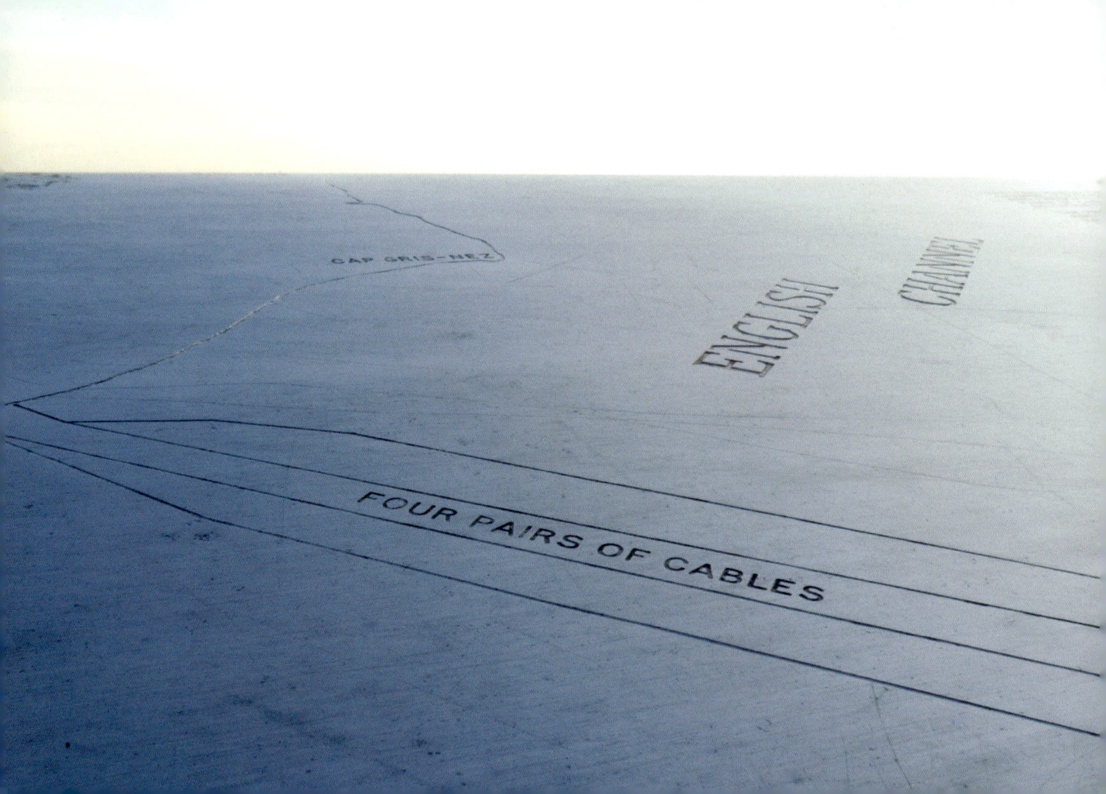

CAP GRIS-NEZ

ENGLISH CHANNEL

FOUR PAIRS OF CABLES

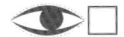

They have a lovely coffee shop with lovely cup cakes. They hire bikes out and you can also get kiddie trailers. They organise mad bike rides into the hills and I've known someone who came back with a broken arm!

त्यहाँ एउटा राम्रो कफि पसल छ जसमा असल कप केककहरु पाईन्छ । उनीहरुले नानी बोक्ने सुविधा भएको साईकलहरु पनि भाँडामा दिने गर्दछन् । उनीहरुले डाडामा साईकल दौडहरुको आयोजना गर्छन् । मैले थाहा पाए अनुसार मानिसहरु उक्त दौडबाट फर्किंदा घाईते भएर आउने गर्दथे । मेरो साथिको पनि उक्त दौडमा पाखुरा भांचिएको थियो ।

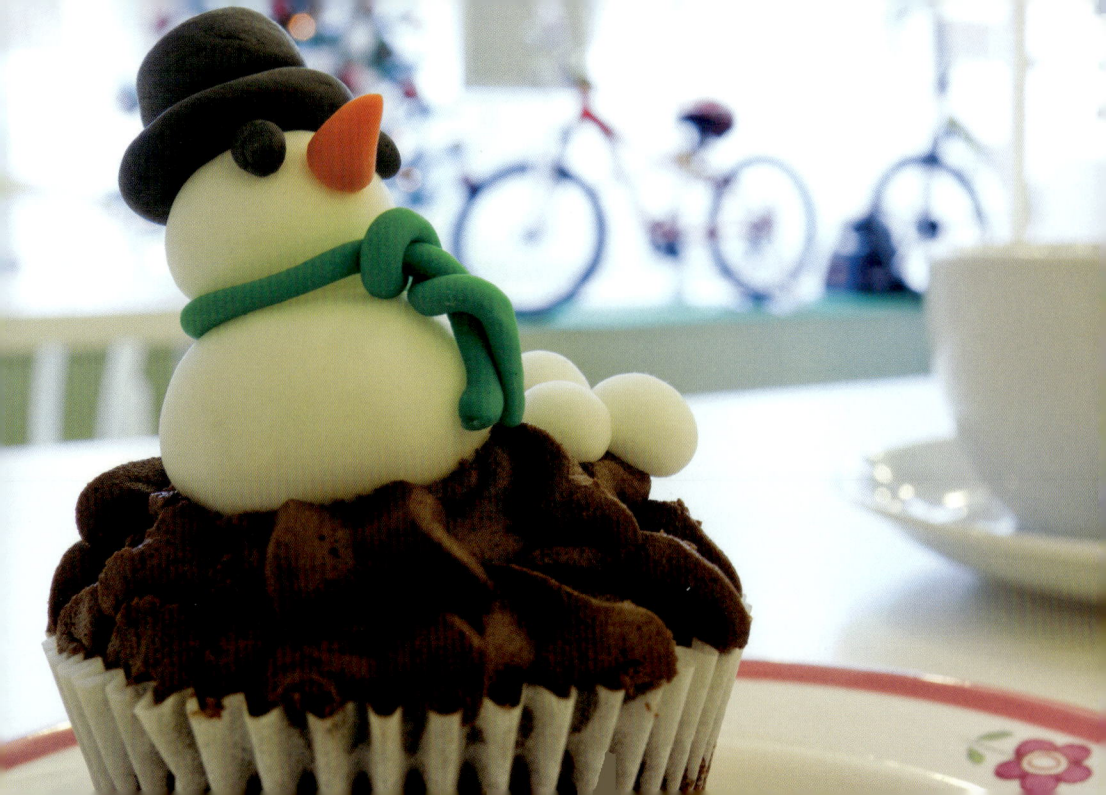

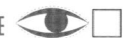

Visitors to the area should all know about the Acoustic Mirrors that are sited all along the south coast. They were first constructed in the 1920s and 30s, as a result of the first world war, before the days of radar and were an early warning system to alert people to incoming enemy aircraft. Someone would sit behind the structure with a listening device and headphones, and the mirrors acted like a big concrete ear amplifying any engine sounds it picked up, giving several minutes vital warning of impending attack.

पहिलो विश्व युद्धको सम्झना दुश्मनको हवाई जहाज आउनु भन्दा अगाडि मानिसहरुलाई सावधान गराउनको निम्ति बजाईने ध्वनिले गराउँदछ ।

Follow the paths along the banks of the Royal Military Canal in the west end of Hythe, and then head up the hill at the stile.

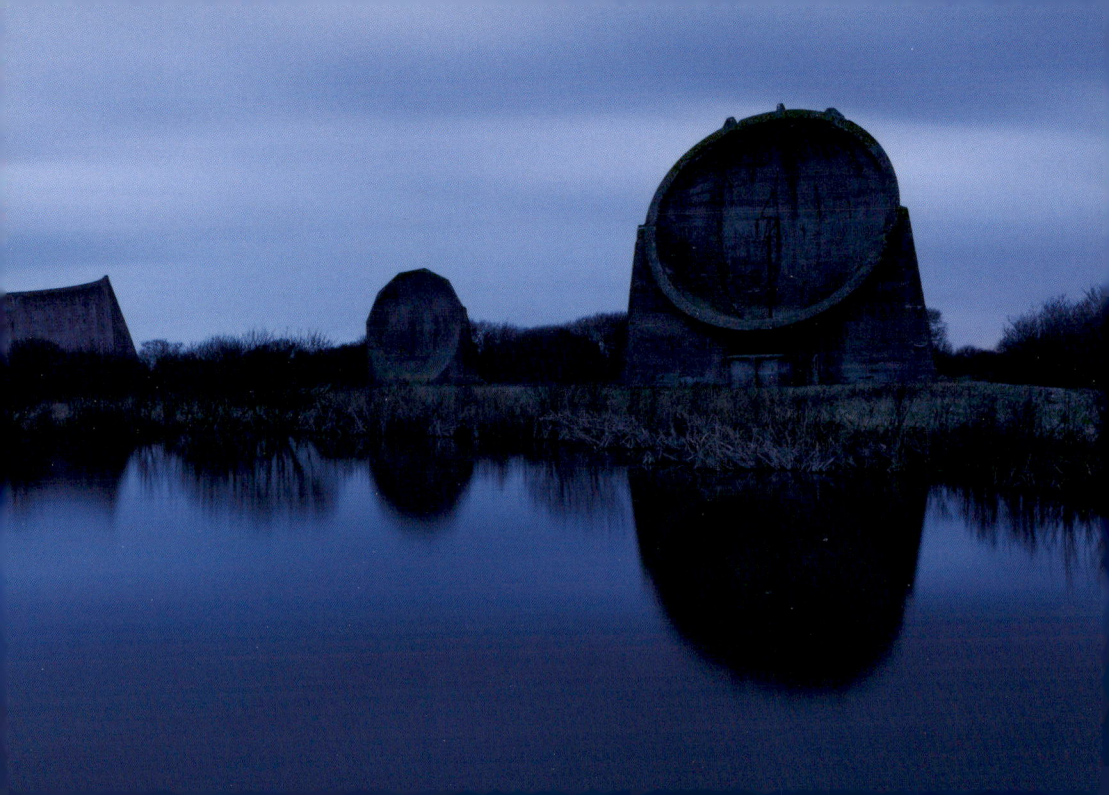

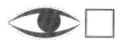

My favourite house in Folkestone is behind the St. Eanswythe's church. There are openings in the brick wall that look through to the garden that is right on the cliff edge. When I first came to Folkestone to see if we might move down from London to be part art scene in the summer of 2006, I walked from Folkestone Central train station and was charmed by all the flowers blooming and lively street activity, but was really intent on seeing the sea. I ended up in the Bayle and sensed that the sea was behind that area. When I came to the wall I peered through the rectangular opening in the brick wall filled with decorative curved roof tiles in a scalloped pattern. Through this opening I could see a beautiful garden, fresh green grass, flowers and a wonderful secret preview of the sea. I was so amazed by the beauty of it. Now, whenever we escape the High Street for a quieter walk home to Rendezvous Street, I stop and look in the third opening from the left for my favourite secret storybook view of the sea that reminds me of my childhood in Hampton, NH which is on the seacoast in New England.

म फोक्सटनमा सरे पछि समुन्द्र बाटको पहिलो दृश्य सुन्दर बगैंचाको पर्खाल थियो । मलाई यसको सुन्दरताले धेरै आकर्षित बनाएको थियो ।

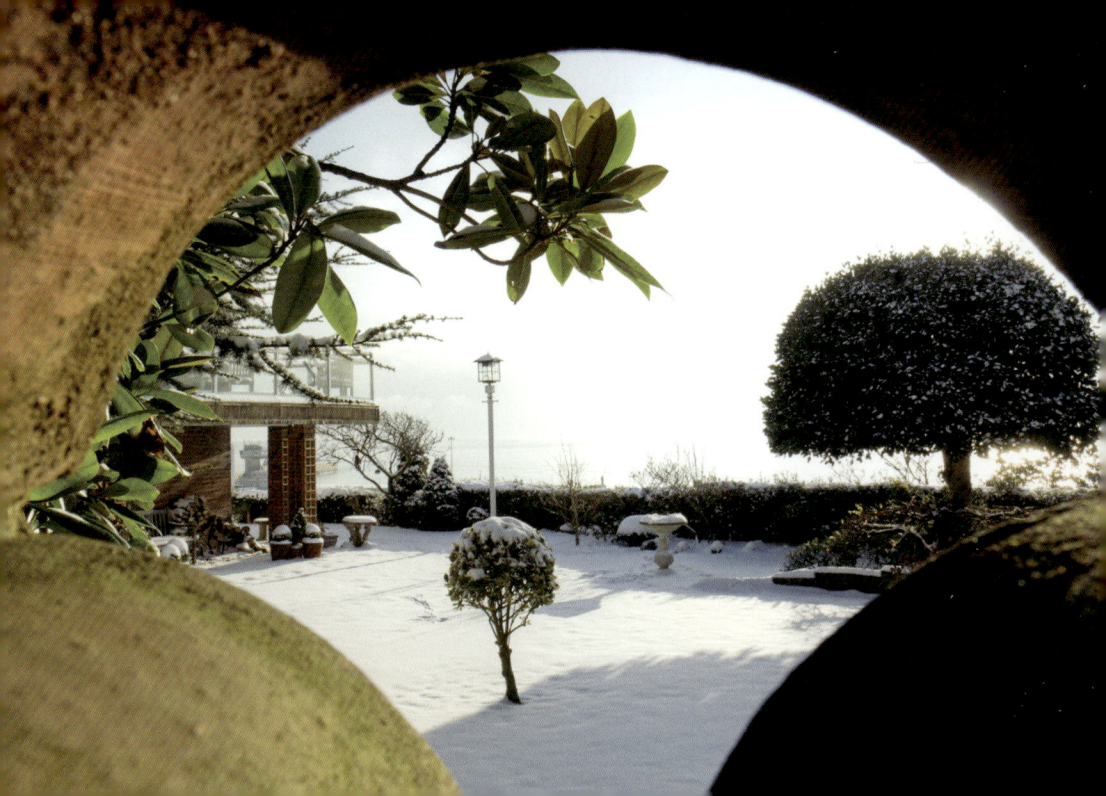

Enjoy the wonderful garden designs and unique seating arrangements in the Lower Leas Coastal Park. A huge amount of work and energy goes into keeping them so attractive throughout the year. At the end, near the Leas Lift and car park are two spyglasses of differing heights. When you look through them you will see the pier and switchback as though they were still in position.

Leas Lift को छेउमा रहेको कोष्टल पार्कमा दुईवटा दुरविनहरु छन् । ति दुरविनबाट हेर्दा तपाईंले समुन्द्रको पल्लो किनारा र बन्दरगाह देख्न सक्नुहुन्छ । यो अहिले पनि त्यस ठाउँमा अवस्थित छ ।

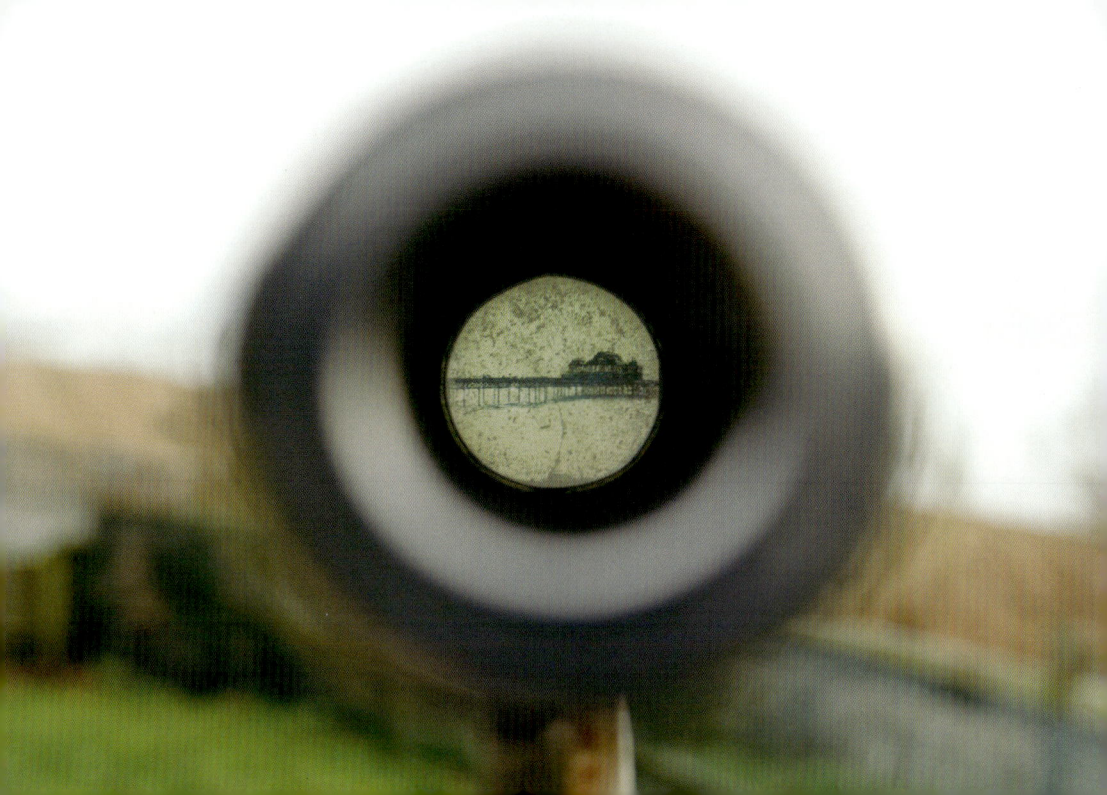

There are many beautiful places in Folkestone. But it is the huge carving of the running white horse, on the hill over the Channel Tunnel, which I like the most. It is so fascinating and beautiful. On a sunny or clear day, from the M20 roundabout at junction 12, when I drive around, I feel like the picture of the horse is running round the roundabout with me, it is so extra-amazing view. This huge horse can be seen on the hill from most parts of the Folkestone. The locally-based regiment of Gurkha soldiers volunteered to help when it was constructed in 2003.

It may be stating the obvious, but in terms of iconic photos the harbour has a multitude of offerings for photo opportunities. The painted FOLKESTONE on the harbour wall to the phone booth with the mannequin is really surreal. Then it goes without saying on a good clear day you have the panoramic views of France, which for me are fantastic. From my attic velux window I have views of the horse on the hillside and when the sun sets the red reflections on my stairwell are sublime.

M20 को roundabout मा गाडी कुदाउँदा त्यो घोडाको तस्विर पनि म सँगसँगै कुदी रहेको छ भन्ने महसुस गर्छुँ । सन २००३ मा स्थानिय पल्टनका गोर्खा सिपाहीहरुको सहयोगमा त्यो घोडाको आकृति निर्माण गरिएको थियो ।

मेरो भ्र्यालबाट डाँडामा घोडा हिँडेको र क्षितिजमा घाम अस्ताएको किरणको दृश्य देख्न सकिन्छ ।

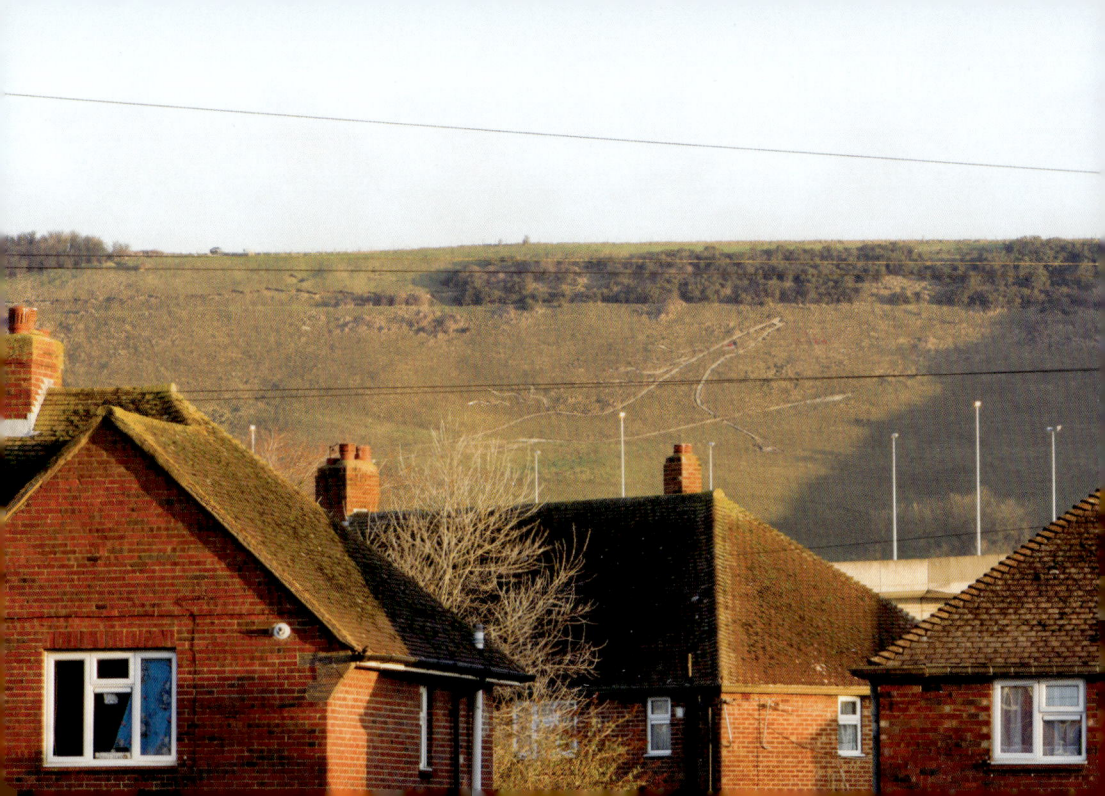

Less than 200 years ago it was common to see sheep grazing on the Leas. This changed in Victorian times when ordinary folk were not welcome to walk along the Leas.

Find the Cow Path along the Leas and walk down it towards the sea to find a whole menagerie of cows and other carved animals at the bottom. Quite delightful.

कम्तिमा २०० वर्ष भन्दा अगाडि सम्म यो Leas क्षेत्रमा भेंडा चराएको देख्न सकिन्थ्यो । भिक्टोरियनको पालामा सामान्य मानिसहरुलाई यस क्षेत्रमा प्रवेश निषेध गरिएकोले यो परिवर्तन भएको हो ।

लिजको छेउबाट गाईबस्तु हिँड्ने बाटोलाई पछ्याउदै समुन्द्र तर्फ जाने बाटो पत्ता लगाउन निकै रमाईलो हुन्छ ।

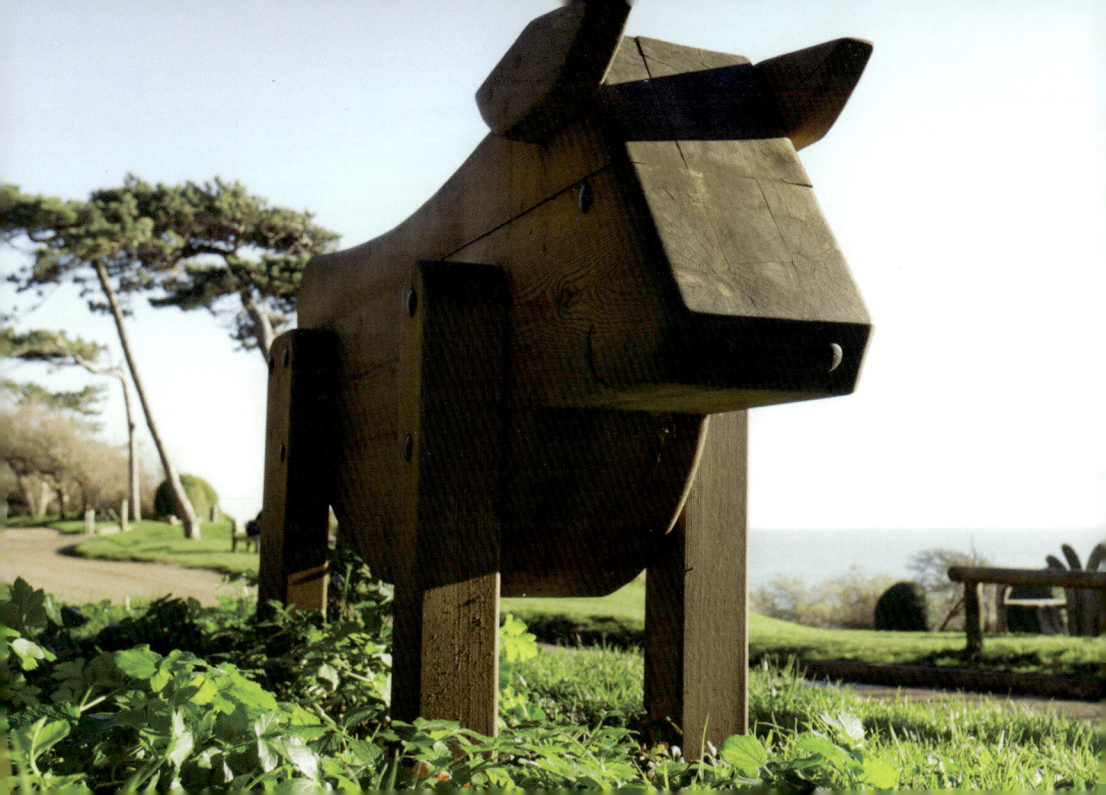

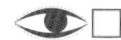

We used to come down to Folkestone in the summer as a family, and my friend and I used to head straight for this slab of concrete, as we always thought it was the best place to spend the day sitting and watching people go by – and it was an especially good place for watching for boys! I have since travelled the world and lived in many countries, but have returned to settle in Folkestone and now live only a few doors away from my childhood friend who used to sit with me on those long hot days.

प्राय ग्रीष्मकालमा म र मेरो साथि परिवार जस्तै भएर फोक्सटनमा आएर सिमेन्टको फल्याकमा ठाडो शिर पारेर बस्ने गर्दथ्यौं । यहा बसेर मानिसहरु आवात जावत गरेको हेदैं दिनको समय बिताउनको लागि यो एउटा राम्रो ठाउँ हो भन्ने हामीलाई लाग्दथ्यो ।

EVERYWHERE MEANS SOMETHING TO SOMEONE

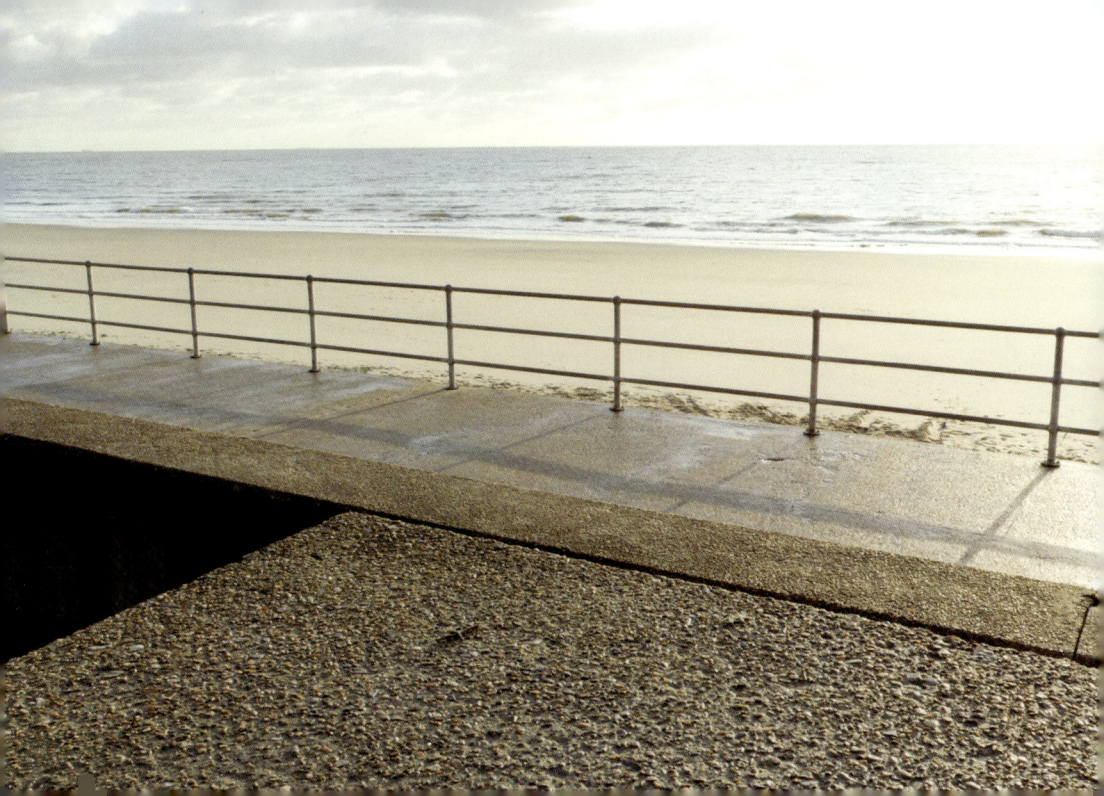

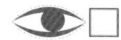

I would certainly direct anyone visiting Folkestone towards the rock pools at the Warren. When I was teaching I would always take my classes down there and we would guarantee to find at least 17 types of creature in the rock pools. We would often camp as a family as well; what is lovely is that you can just pour out of the campsite down on to the beach. It is wonderful and because there is no traffic, it is seldom busy.

यदी कोही फोक्सटनमा घुम्न आउछन भने म तिनीहरुलाई Warren मा भएको ढुङ्गे पोखरीमा जाउन भन्छु । मैले शिक्षण गर्दा वारम्वार त्यहा कक्षा संचालन गर्दथ्ये । त्यसताका हामीले त्यहा जम्मा १७ किसीमको जिवहरु भट्टाएका थियौ ।

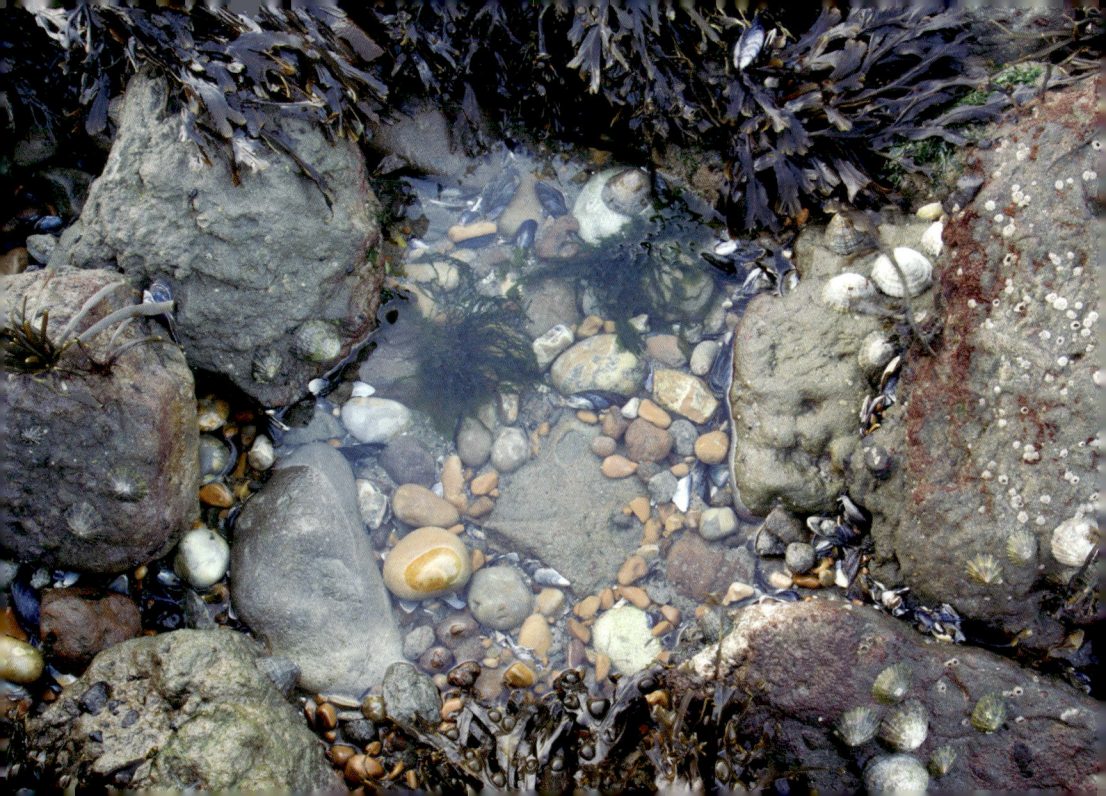

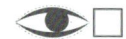

I think visitors should know about The Little Fish Shop in Sandgate. On a sunny evening my wife and I buy our fish and chips and then wander across the road to sit on the seawall and enjoy looking out across the Channel and watch the glorious sunsets.

सानगेटको स्यानो माछा दोकमनमा अलिकति माछा र चिप्स किनेपछि म बाटो पार गर्दै चानेल पारी छितिजमा घाम अस्ताएको रमाईलो दृश्य हेर्दै समुन्द्रको डिलमा बस्छु ।

EVERYWHERE MEANS SOMETHING TO SOMEONE

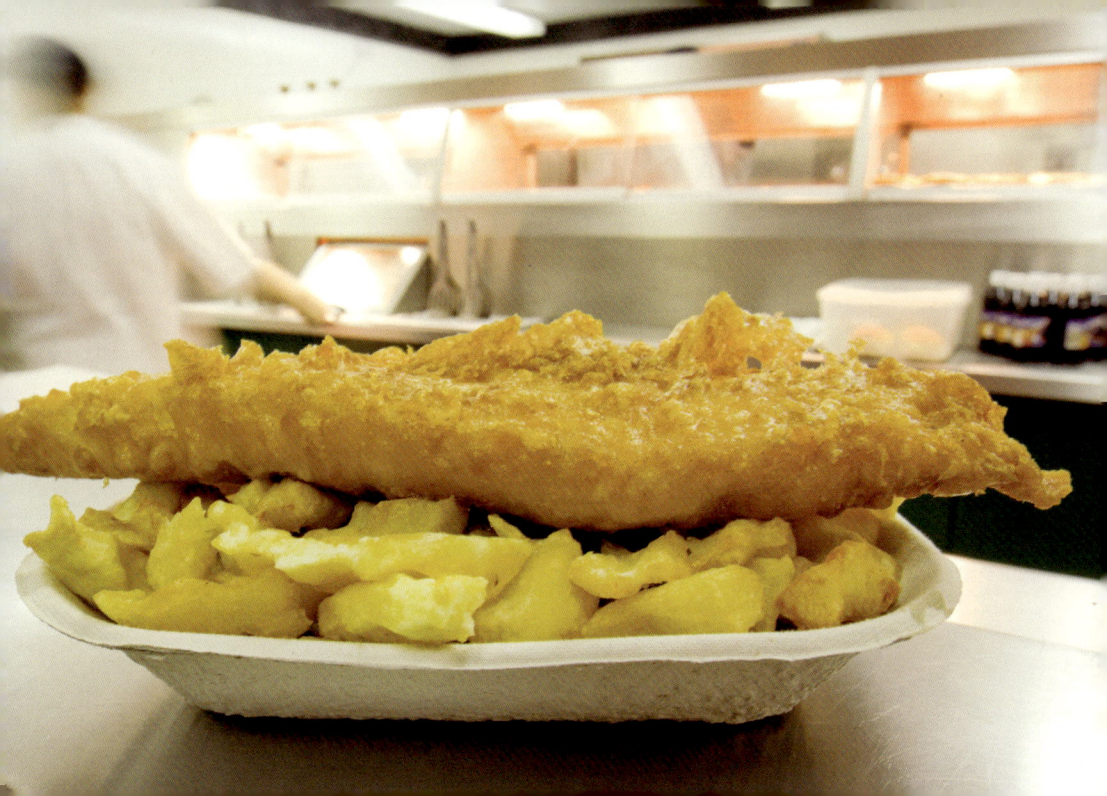

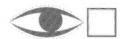

The Leas is a wonderful place for dog walkers. On one of the many benches there is a little plaque dedicated to Phyllis Gibbs and her little black poodles. Isn't that great! It sounds just like a jazz band from Paris in the 1920s.

There are many benches, seating areas and shelters that are the hidden gems of Folkestone. Some with artworks by Tracey Emin, and others that give the best views of our wonderful town.

This summer, at the start of a lovely new 'friendship' and on a budget, I discovered these superb spots and have mapped them. From the Leas to the East Cliff and even up on the hill at Little Switzerland, these shelters are wonderful.

There should be an ice cream van on the Leas!

फोक्सटनमा भएका धेरै फलैचाहरु, बस्नेठाउ र आश्रय स्थलहरु यसको आइनो गहनाहरु हुन् । यसले गर्दा हाम्रो शहरलाई राम्रो देखाउदछ । Leas देखि East Cliff र Little Switzerland को डाँडा सम्म भएका आश्रय स्थलहरु अझ राम्रा छन् ।

फोक्सटनको वरीपरी भएका रमणिय ठाउहरुमा थुप्रै राम्रा विसाउने, खेल्ने, लुकामारी गर्ने र ओत लाग्ने ठाउहरु छन ।

उनीहरुलाई भबक मा एउटा आईसक्रिम भएको गाडी चाहिन्छ ।

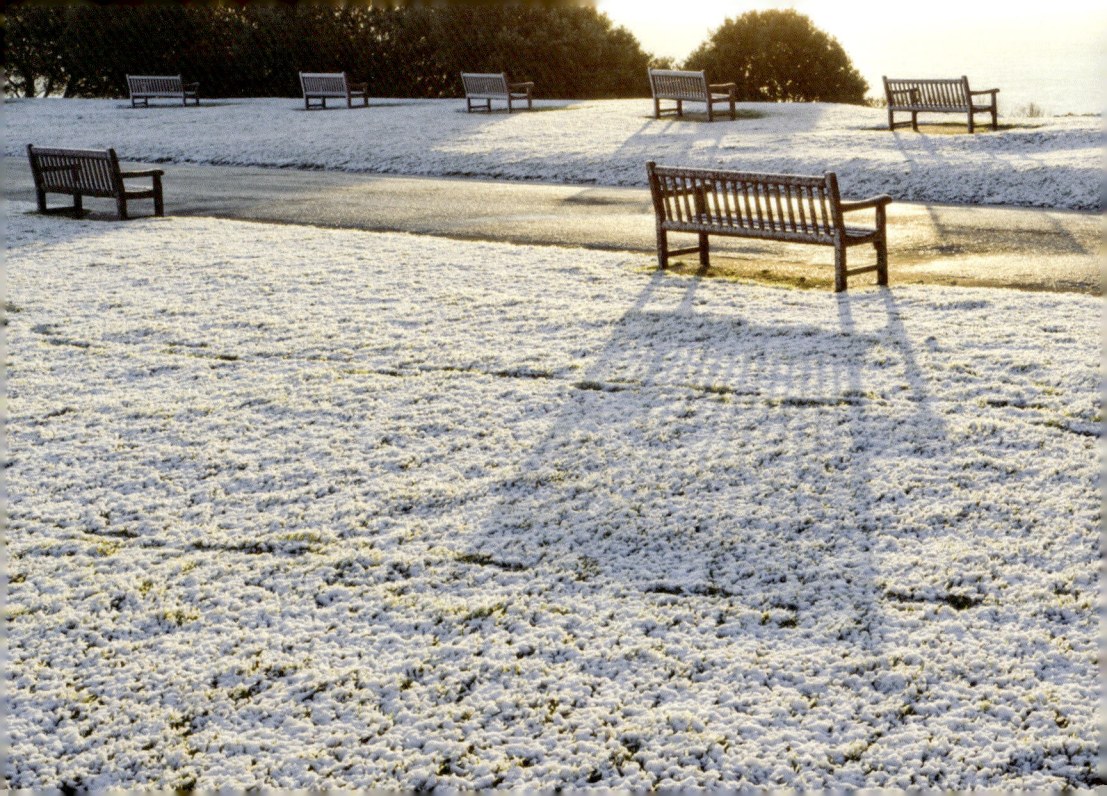

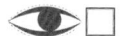

When CCTV was first installed in Folkestone town centre, some of us District Councillors went along to the control room to have a look. Among the clips, we were amazed to see a medium-sized dog on a lead being dragged along on its back by its elderly female owner: when they came to a crossing, the dog got up and walked across – and then lay down again. At one point a passer-by came across, probably to remonstrate, and appeared to receive a robust response!

पहिले नियन्त्रण कोठामा CCTV भरखर मात्र जडान गरिएको थियो । म एक्लै गएर CCTV मा एउटा कुकुरको चर्तिकला देखेर आश्चर्यचकित भएको थिए । त्यो कुकुरलाई उसको मालिक्नी बृद्ध महिलाले पच्छ्राई रहेको थियो । जब उनीहरु बाटो छेउमा पुग्थे, कुकुर उठ्थ्यो अनि बाटो पार गर्थ्यो र त्यसपछि फेरी बस्थ्यो ।

EVERYWHERE MEANS SOMETHING TO SOMEONE

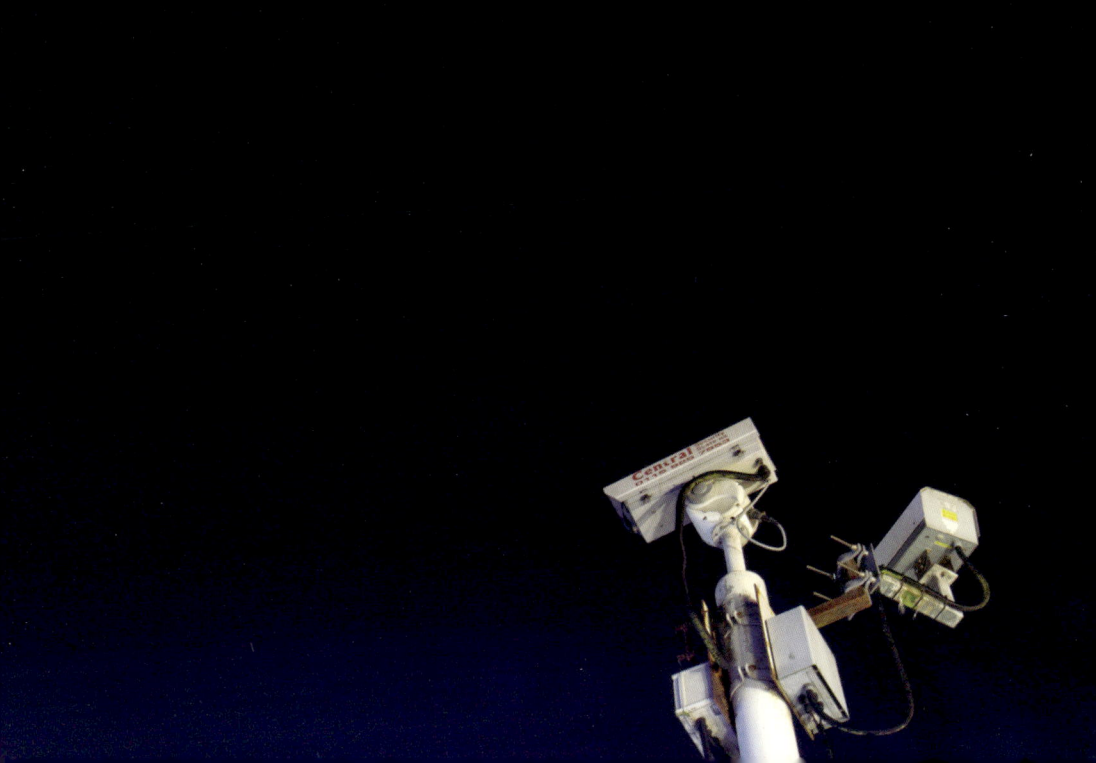

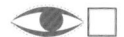

George the ghost sits at the bar. Peter, one of the previous landlords, some years ago felt a tap on his shoulder and heard a voice saying, "Don't change the barrel now!" It turns out that there was a gas leak in the cellar and had he gone down he would have died from the fumes. A week or so later his wife fell down the cellar trap door behind the bar, which she claims she hadn't opened!

There is a 'coffin trap' in the right hand corner of the ceiling as you walk into the bar. You can see where it would have been – one small beam runs at a right angle to the others. The upstairs is so tight that if anyone died, they would not have been able to get the coffin down, so instead they would build the coffin upstairs and the drop it down through the trap door into the bar.

Mike, the landlord, also runs the Lifeboat Rescue Boat.

बारको दाहिने पट्टी कुनामा एउटा 'coffin trap' छ । कुनै व्यक्तिको मृत्यू भएमा शवबाकस भ-याङ्गदेखी तल भ्रार्न सक्दैन थे । त्यसैले यसको सट्टामा उनीहरुले शवबाकस माथिल्लो तलामा बनाउथे र coffin trap को सहारामा मुनि बारमा खसाउँथे ।

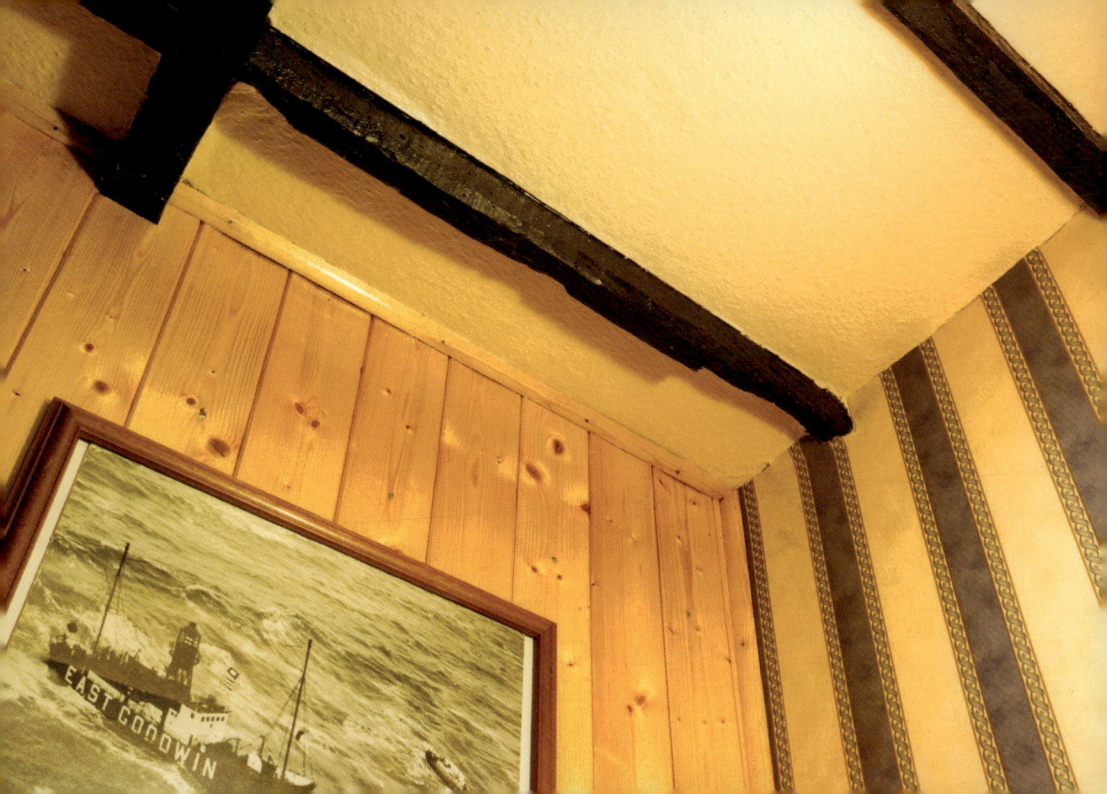

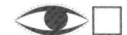

The American Garden was planted by Arch Deacon Croft, who was the vicar of Saltwood in the 1840s, to house his collection of rhododendron bushes that he had travelled the world to collect. The gardens are still open to the public in May.

Arch Deacon Croft भन्ने ब्यक्तिले अमेरिकी बगैंचा बनाएका थिए । उनी सन १८४० मा Saltwood का पादरी थिए । उनको बगैंचा मा भएको गुराँसका बोट विरुवाहरु उनले विश्व भ्रमण गरेर संकलन गरेका थिए । यो बँगैचा अझै पनि सर्वसाधारणको लागि प्रत्येक मे महिनामा खुल्ला हुने गर्दछ ।

EVERYWHERE MEANS SOMETHING TO SOMEONE

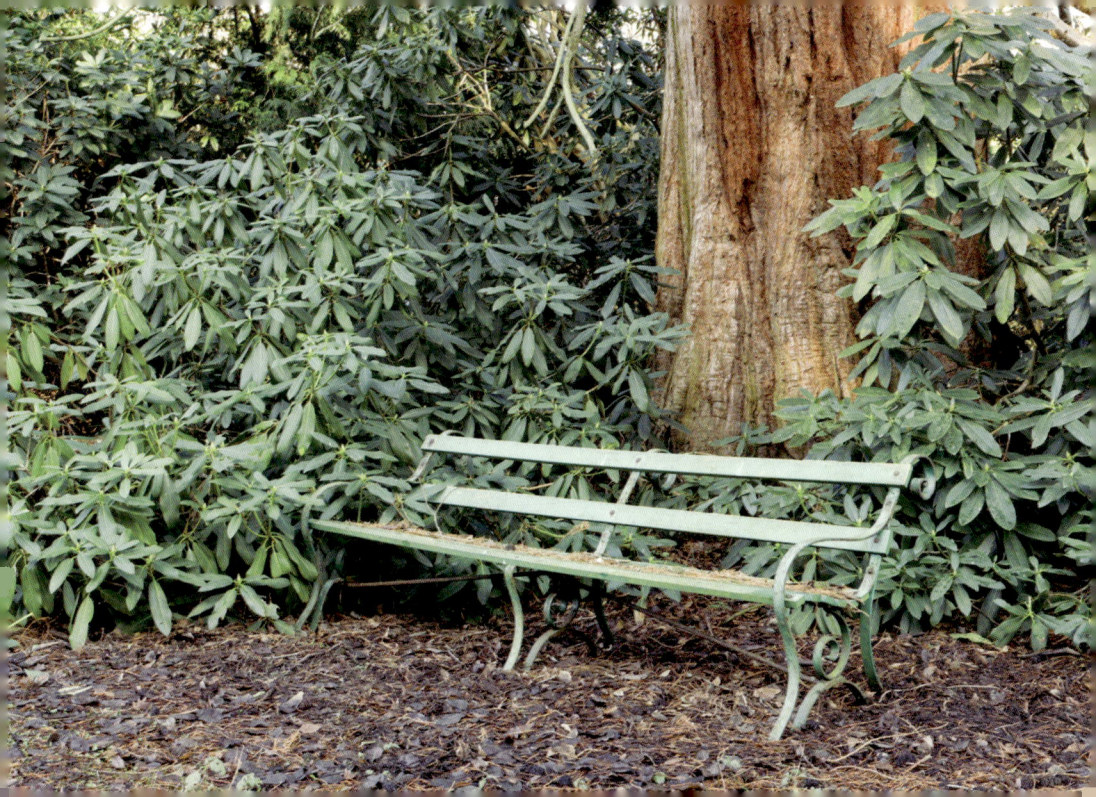

THE SHED SKATEPARK, MARINE PARADE

The Shed youth project and skate park is the best thing about Folkestone, it is always open and offers a safe and friendly place for young people to go. The skate park was recently refurbished, with new ramps and a sculpture, designed by the skaters and bikers and built in collaboration with Strange Cargo. It is now unique, an 'artpark', distinct from any skate park in the area and is featured in the music video *After Dark*.

फोक्सटनको सेड युवा परियोजना र स्केट पार्क सबै भन्दा राम्रो मानिन्छ । युवाहरुको लागि सधै खल्ला अनी परिचीत र सुरक्षित ठाउँ हो यो ।

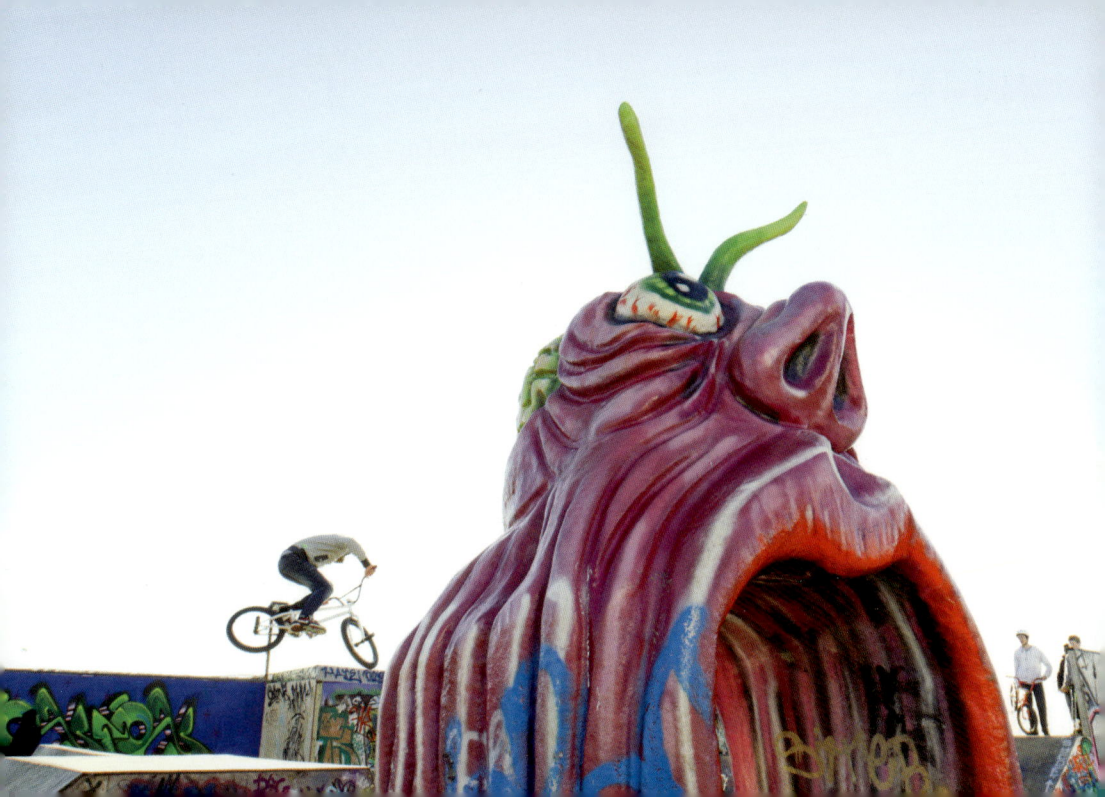

This little road is an ancient route from the west headland on the Bayle, down the valley towards the Pent Stream, which is now Tontine Street. The river could be crossed where the car park now is and the foundations of a mediaeval bridge have been found there… the route then went up behind where the car park is now and along a little road, now known as Harbour Way, on to the eastern headland at the East Cliff.

Folkestone is full of these little routes that cross over the contours and slopes of the valleys.

There's another one just behind Grace Hill in Foord Road South, which in particular is I think very ancient, as is the Old High Street. www.atownunearthed.co.uk

यो Bayle को माथि पश्चिम पटिको साँगुरो ठाउँबाट तल Pent Stream गाउँ तिर जाने प्राचिन मार्गको मुनि आज पानी बग्ने गर्दछ, जहाँ Tontine Street छ । अहिले कार पार्क भएको ठाउँमा पहिले नदी बग्ने गर्दथ्यो । त्यहाँ मध्यकालिन पुलको जग भे टिएको थियो । त्यसपछि यो बाटो कार पार्कको पछाडि हुँदै Harbour Way को सानो बाटो भएर East Cliff सम्म जान्छ ।

EVERYWHERE MEANS SOMETHING TO SOMEONE

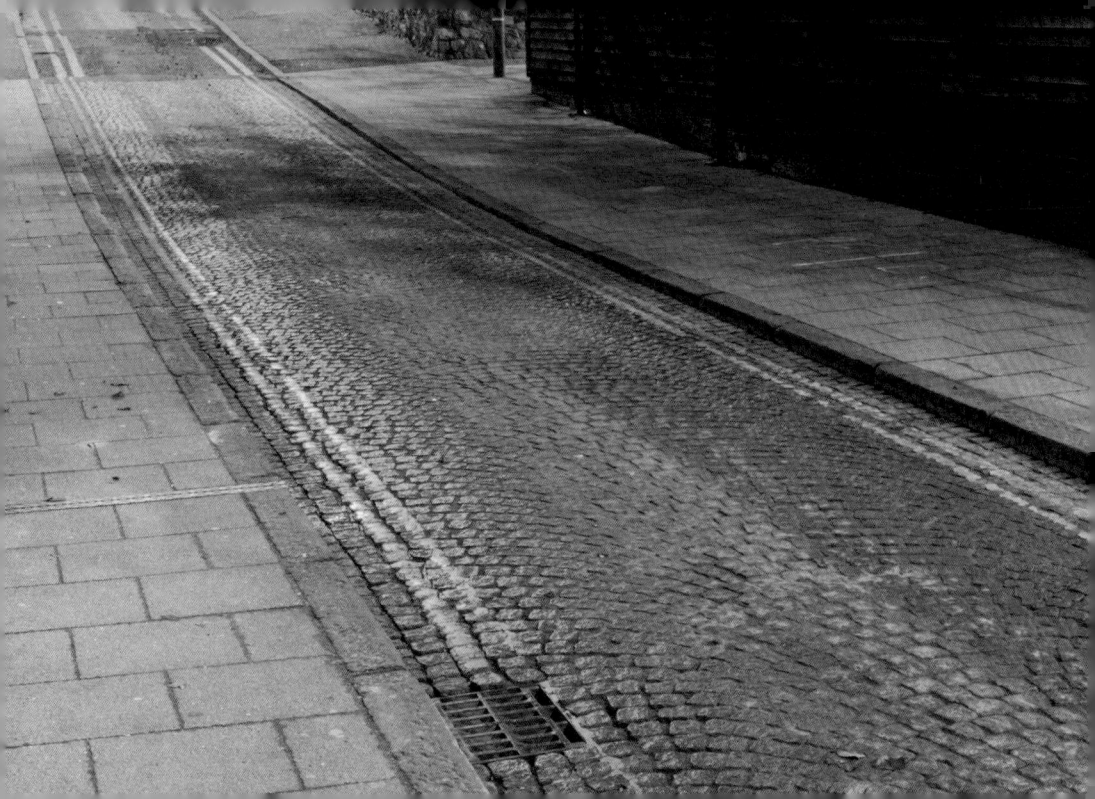

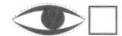

There are concrete structures that look like giant alien eggs on Capel Hill. At The Valiant Sailor, at the top of Capel Hill, turn left and about 20 to 30 metres from the road are the eggs!

हेर्दा ज्यादै ठूलो अण्डाहरुको जस्तो आकार लाग्ने सिमेन्टका यी मुर्तिकलाहरु डोबरको डाँडामा Valiant Sailor पबको नजिकै छन् ।

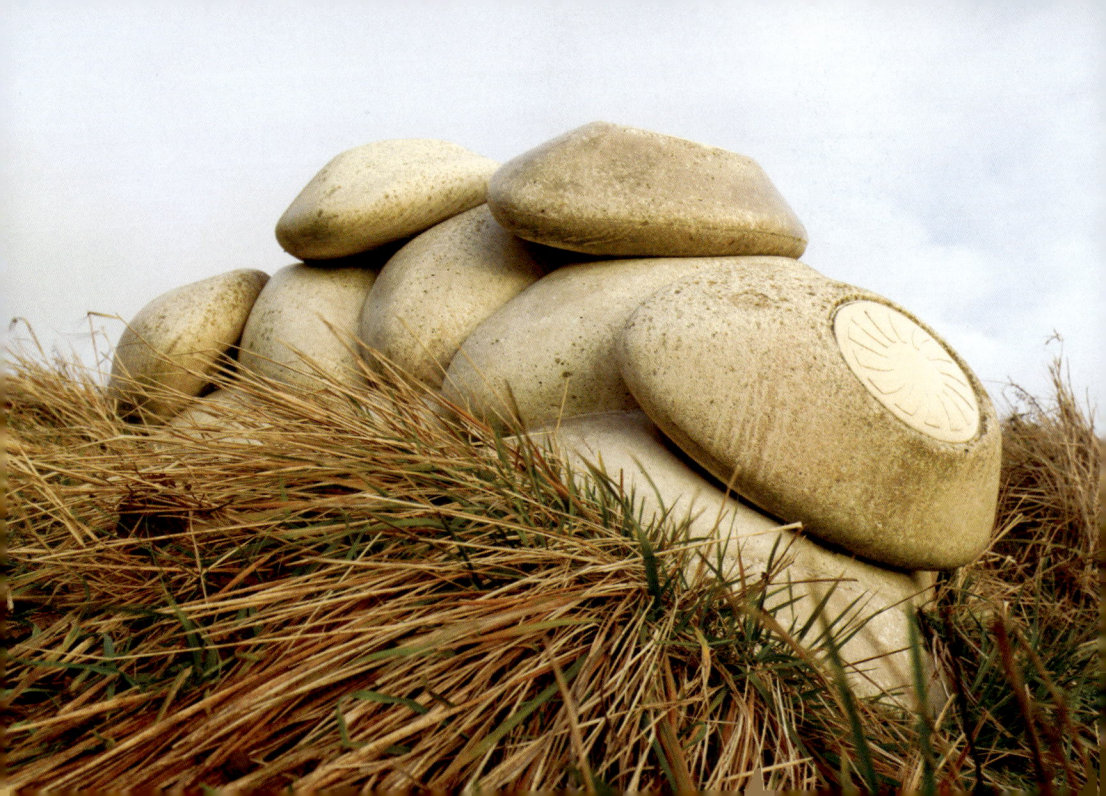

As a child, I scalded myself and spent the next three months in the Royal Victoria Hospital. Unable to get out of bed to play with toys or other children due to the skin grafts, I was given paper and pencil to occupy my time. The three months of continuous drawing hooked me for life and I went on to a career as a professional artist and am now a director of The Chimaera gallery.

When my little brother Chris was admitted to have his tonsils out, I used to stand in the park opposite the hospital and stare up at the children's ward and wave to him. I was only seven, but one day I walked into the hospital, found my way up the endless stairs to the top floor children's ward and gave him his little teddy. I still remember the terror I felt braving this short journey all on my own.

मैले वाल्यकालमा धेरै लामो समय Royal Victoria Hospital मा बिताएको छु । त्यहा कागज र पेनसील दिएर मलाई भुल्याईन्थ्यो किनभने म विस्तरामा नै बसीरहन्थे । मैले पेशाको रुपमा चित्रकार बन्ने ईच्छा गरेकोले हाल म एउटा संघ्रालय संचालन गर्दछु ।

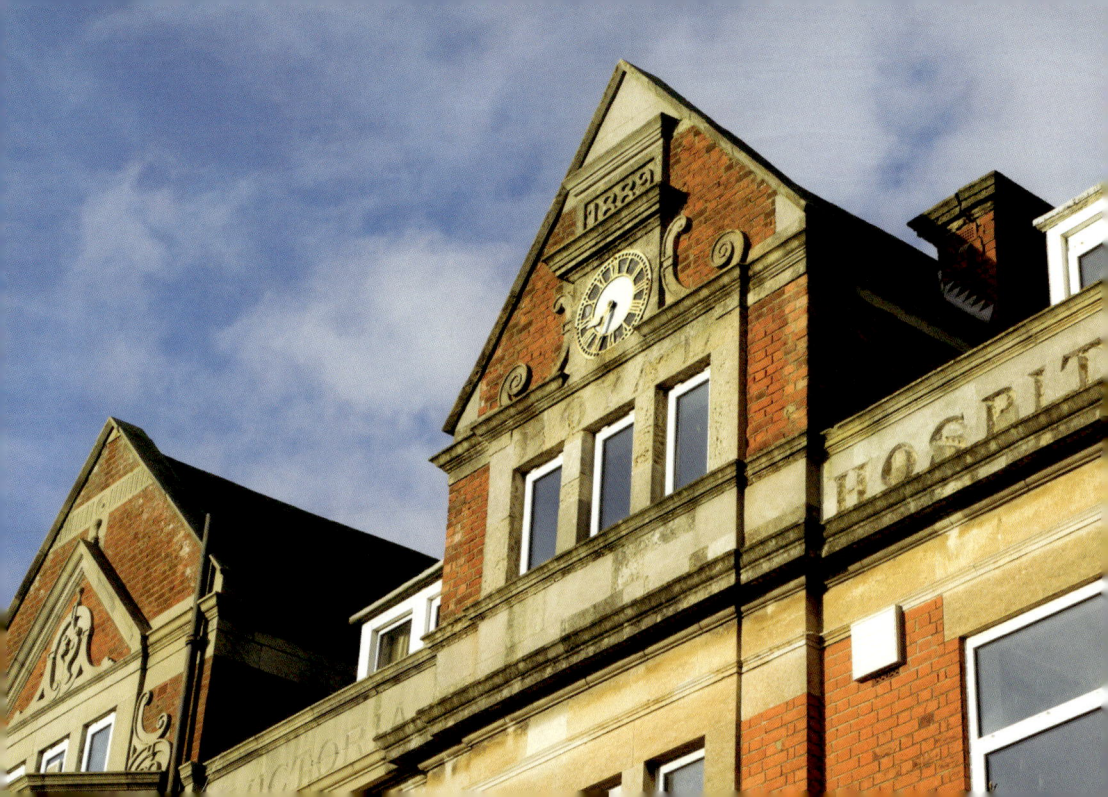

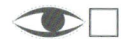

An Art Deco building with a hidden secret – a fabulous ovoid staircase containing a series of engraved and frosted back-lit glass panels featuring marine emblems in the Lalique style. Originally a gas showroom with offices, it was built in 1938 and designed by local architect John Love Seaton Dane. Local papers at that time stated that visitors from miles around flocked to Folkestone to see the building, not only to admire the fabulous interior but also to view the exterior, which was illuminated with neon lighting. Now the Halifax, the building was Grade II listed by English Heritage in 2007.

यो भवनमा भएका भर्‍याङका खुट्किलाहरुमा सिसाका टुक्राहरुले कलात्मक रुपले खोपिएको नौसेनाको चिन्हहरु पाईन्छ ।

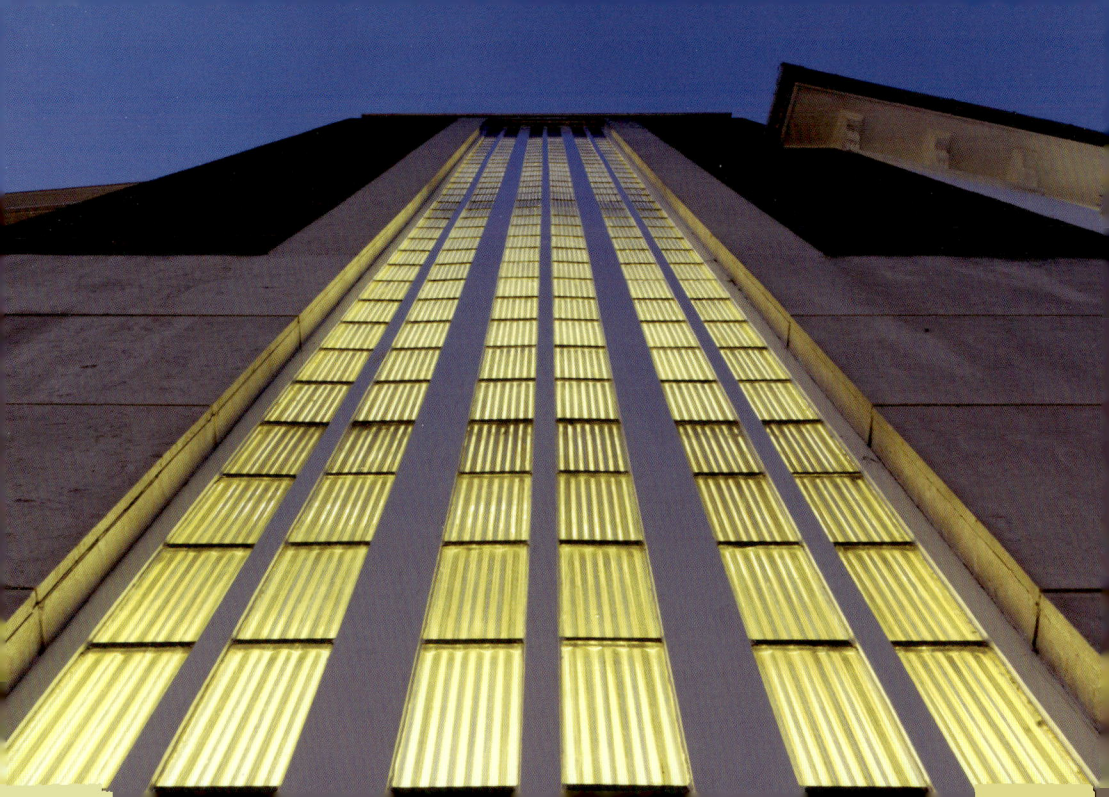

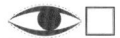

Winter 1963, Folkestone harbour froze over. The fishing boats didn't go to sea for 16 weeks because of the bad weather, with gales of wind from the east for weeks on end and freezing temperatures. There was no fish to catch because the sea was so cold the fish had left this part of the Channel for deeper water. Frost actually killed the conger eels and they were floating on the surface. Crabs and razor fish were also killed by the frost and washed up on the beach. Water mains supplying houses a metre under the ground froze solid. But the main roads and the town were cleared. The snow was loaded onto lorries and dumped in the harbour.

सन १९६३ जाडो याममा फोक्सटन बन्दरगाह पुरै हिउँले जमेको थियो । खराब मौसमले गर्दा माछा मार्ने डुङ्गाहरू १६ हप्ता सम्म समुन्द्रमा जान सकेन । तर मुख्य बाटोहरु र शहरबाट भने हिउँ हटाईएको थियो । मालवाहक गाडीहरु हीउँले पुरेर बन्दर गाहमा थुपारिको थियो ।

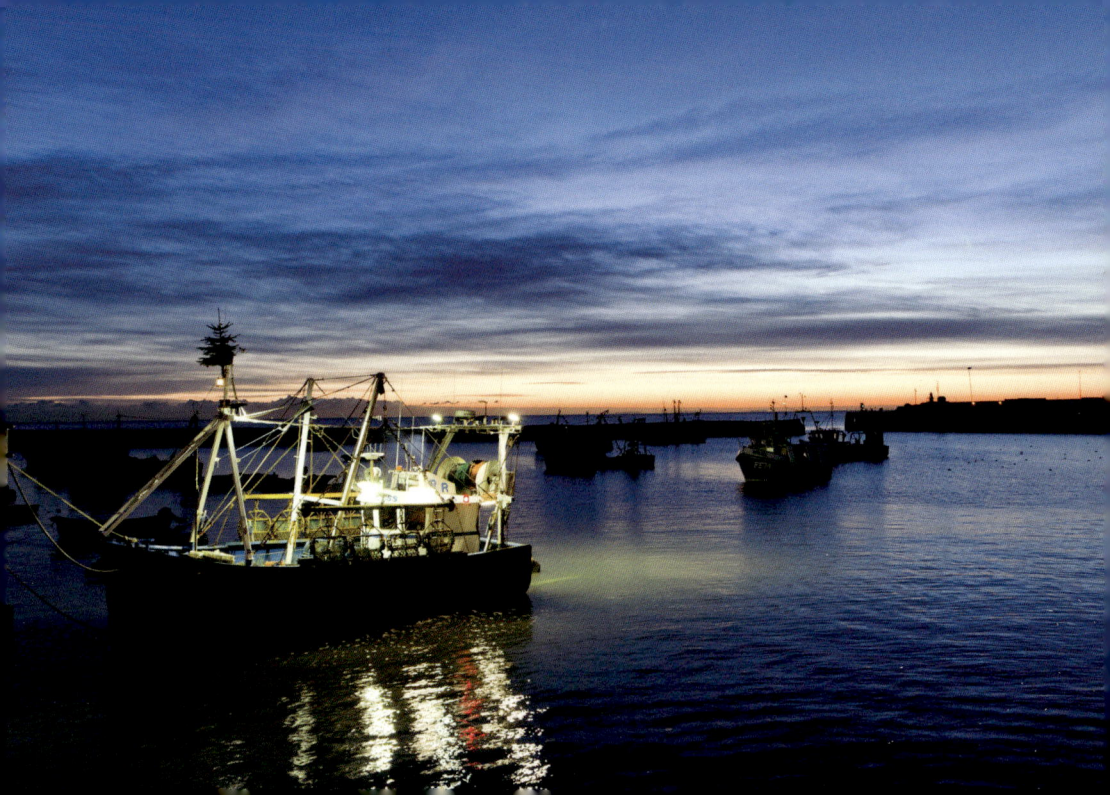

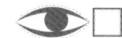

The Royal Standard opened in 1855 and was once three cottages. It has addresses in two streets and is haunted. In the dead of night the cue ball on the pool table rolls backwards and forwards and bounces off the cushions. The landlord only took over the pub six months ago and the family has been woken many times by the noise. There is also a pole in the centre of the pub; tales tell that if you're unlucky it will suddenly become icy cold when you're standing there having a drink. The message on the ceiling beam reads 'If you want to stay here longer, get here earlier'.

Royal Standard सन १८५५ मा तीनवटा घरहरुको एकै साथ स्थापना गरिएको थियो । यस मध्ये दुई घरहरुमा तर्साउने गर्दछ । मध्य रात भएपछि खेल सामग्रीहरु टेबल माथी लडाउन र तकियाहरु यताउता चल्ने गरेको सुनिन्छ ।

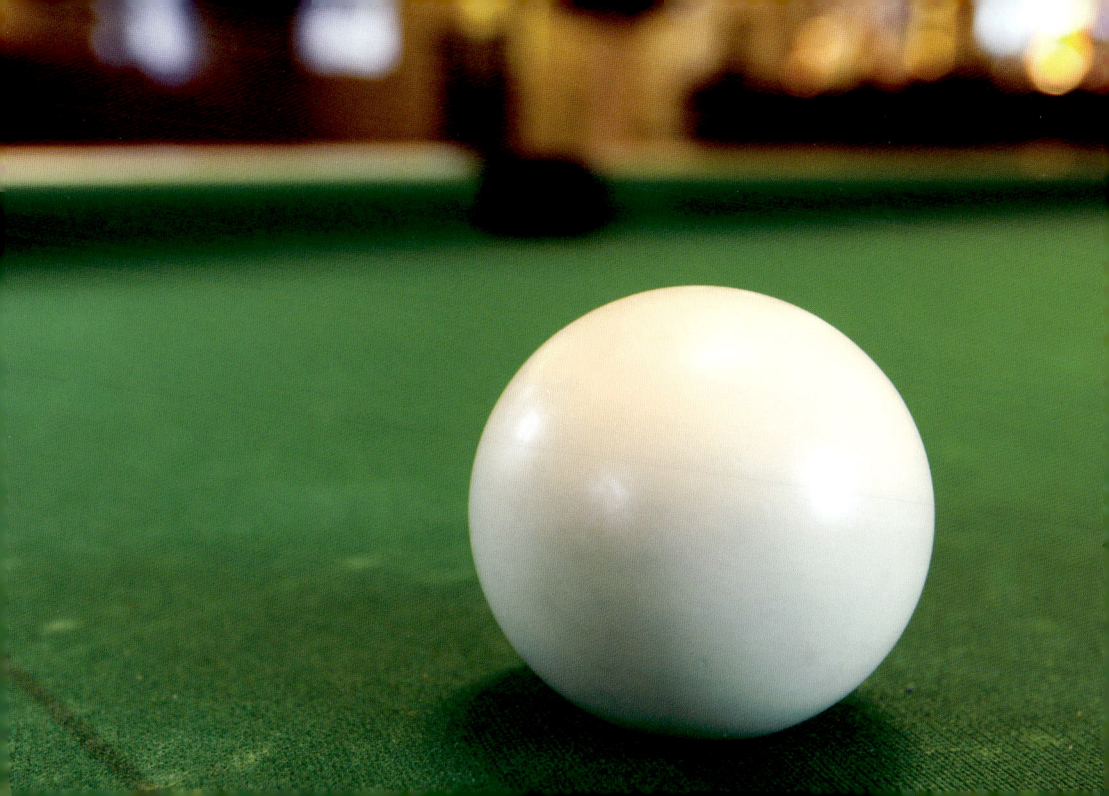

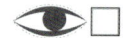

My last visitor got this tour, because it was easily accessible (Warren footpaths not wheelchair friendly unfortunately). For views and snacks go to Cliff Top Café at Little Switzerland, with views across the East Cliff to South Downs! Head down from the Valiant Sailor in Capel, past Little Switzerland, then on to Warren Beach – a short walk to the Apron to look at beach. Then around East Cliff, down through the Durlocks to cobbled harbour area, then on to Coastal Park, all wheelchair friendly! The children's millionaires play-park offers *free* child entertainment and the disposal of any remaining surplus energy, while you sit enjoying yet another cuppa or a beer at the Mermaid, there is wheelchair access here. There's views of the beach and sea air, a perfick day, child friendly and interesting too! The plentiful picnic areas are also all *free*. A perfect day can be spent in our beautiful increasingly accessible Folkestone!

Antique lovers could continue on to Sandgate for olde world English prezzies to take home or take the historic lift up for the promenade on The Leas.

त्यहाँ धेरै गुड्ने कुर्सीहरु छन्, Little Switzerland देखि लामबद्ध भएर सामुन्द्रि किनार हुँदै Coastal Park सम्म हिनेर जाने गर्छन् । त्यहाँ नानीहरुको लागी खेल्ने ठाउँ र वनभोजको लागि कोठाहरु पनि छन् ।

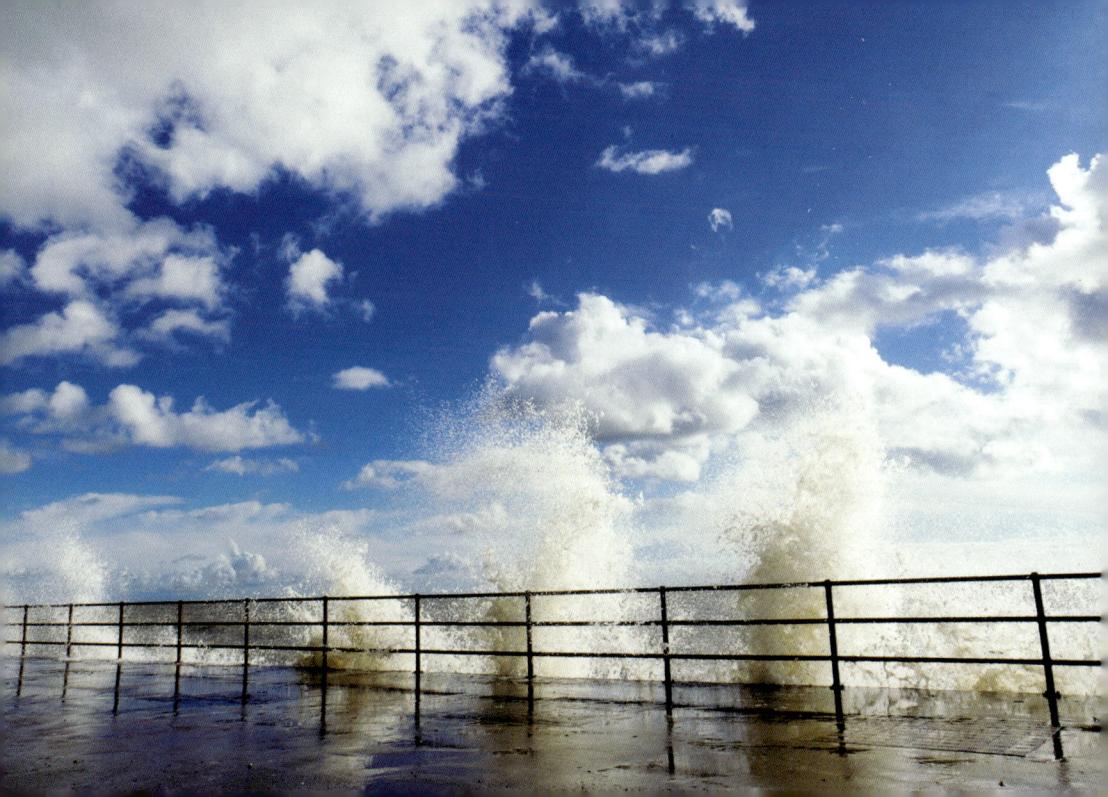

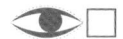

This 16th century pub has a blocked-up archway entrance to smugglers' tunnels that ran down to the other pubs on the Harbour. They led through to the bunker steps that went down to the water's edge at low tide and into the cellar of the Captain's Table pub. It is rumoured that there is a main tunnel that the other tunnels run off, all the way up to St Andrew's on the East Cliff.

Originally the bar was licensed to sell wine and ale, but sometimes spirits would be sold under the counter. To prevent the customs men catching spirits being measured, the tops of the pump handles screw off and the cap is an exact measurement for spirits. They are over 100 years old.

धेरै वर्ष पहिले मदिरा जन्य पेय पदार्थहरु बेच्नेलाई भन्सार अधिकृतहरुले कार्यवाही गर्नबाट वचाउनको लागी वियर तान्ने हेन्डलको विर्को फुकालेर त्यस्ता पेय पदार्थको मात्रा नाप्ने गरिन्थ्यो ।

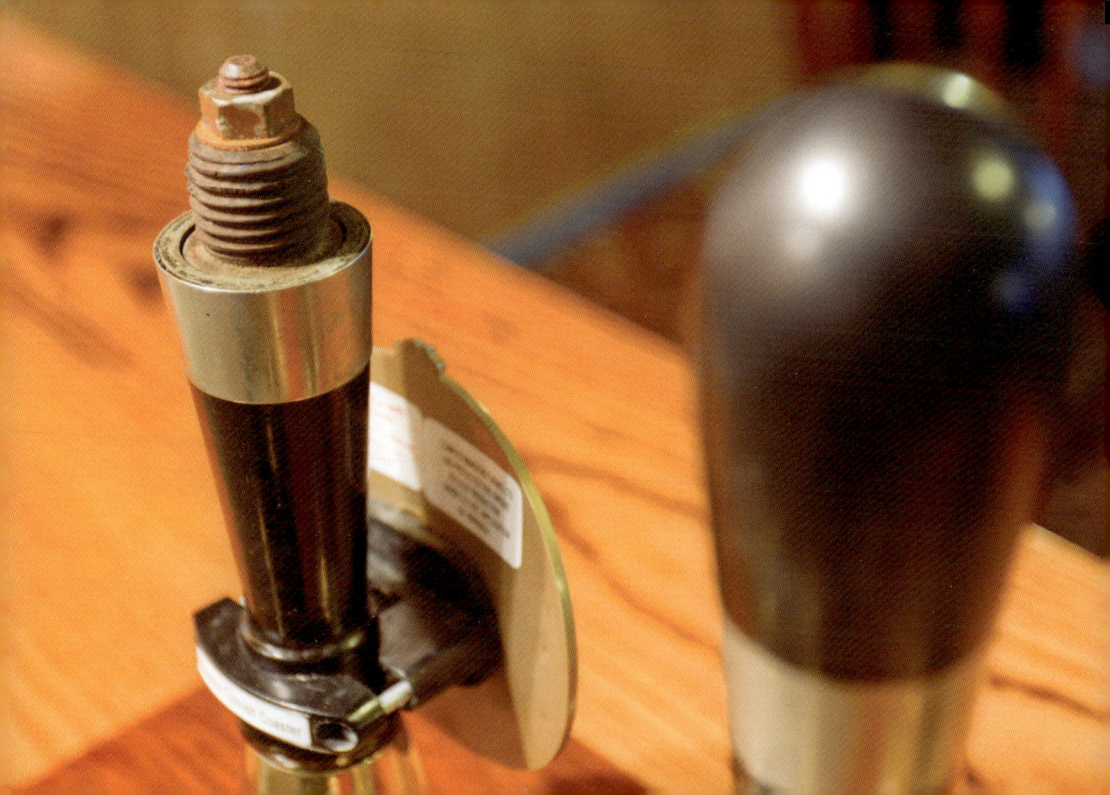

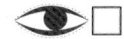

This used to be the Rolls Royce showroom and apparently there were more Rolls Royces in Folkestone than anywhere else at one time. There have been a number of Rolls Royce parades on The Leas over the years.

विगतमा यो Rolls Royce showroom थियो । एक समयमा अन्य ठाउमा भन्दा धेरै Rolls Royce हरु फोक्सटनमा थिए । विगत वर्षहरुमां Leas मा धेरै पटक Rolls Royce प्रदर्शन भईसकेको छ ।

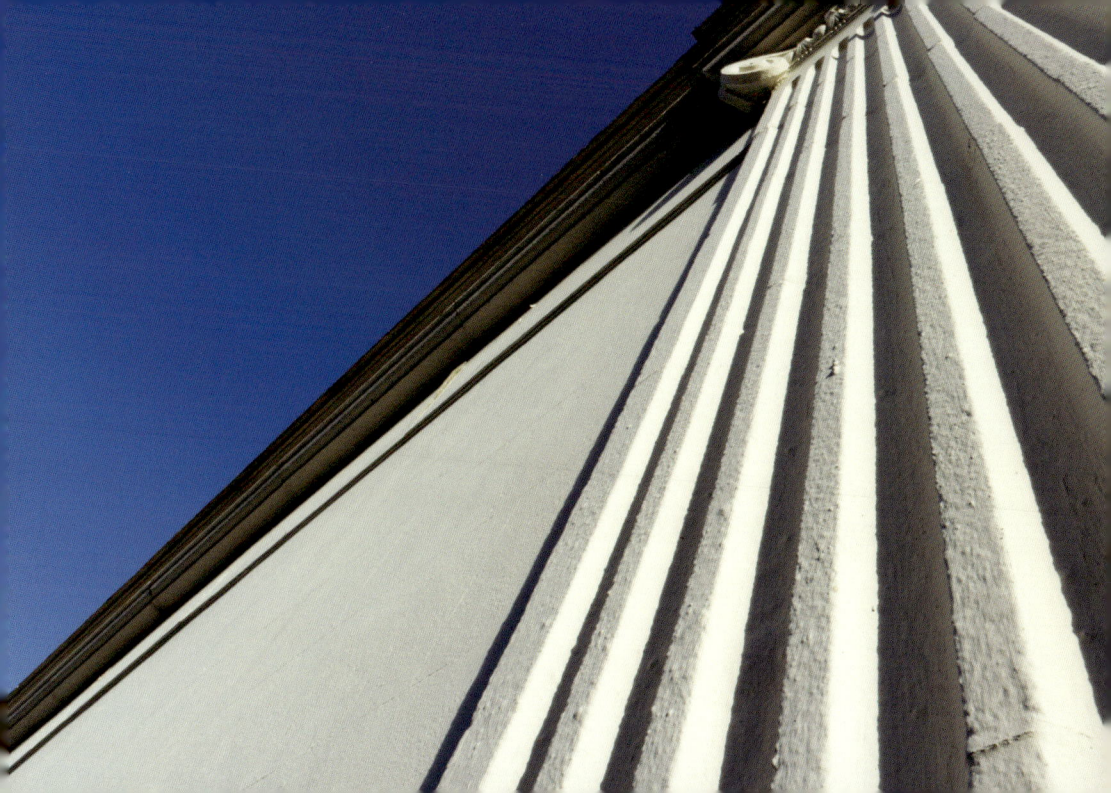

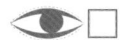

The seashell shop under the arches is a treasure trove for my grandchildren. They don't live locally, so it's a real treat for them and me when they visit. We go to Chummy's first where they have a pot of prawns and I have some cockles. Then they get their £5 pocket money and they are let loose in the shop in command of their spend. There is something for everyone – the glitter fairies, seashells, dolphins…

यो गुम्वजको मुनी भएको खपटा बेच्ने पसल मेरा नातीनातीनीहरुको लागी गाडधन समान हो । तिनीहरु स्थानीय वासिन्दा नभएकोले यहा आउदा यो एउटा राम्रो उपहार हो ।

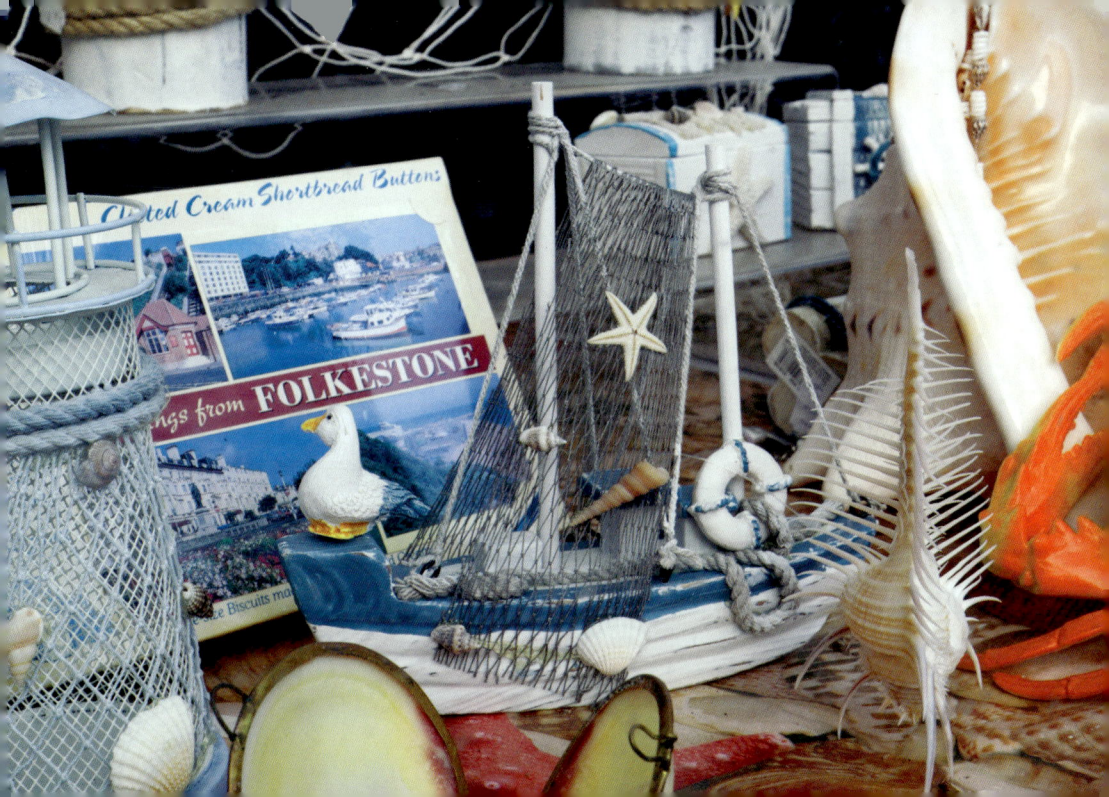

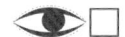

Gerald Holtom lived in Hythe for the last 15 years of his life and is buried in Seabrook cemetery off Horn Street. His famous CND sign is carved on his gravestone.

जेराल्ड हल्टन उसको जिवनमा १५ वर्ष फोकस्टनमा वसेको थियो र मृत्यू पछाडी सिब्रुकको च्यान घारीमा गाडीएको थियो । उसको प्रख्यात सि.एन.डी. अंकित चिन्ह उसको चिहानको ढुङ्गामा खोपिएको छ ।

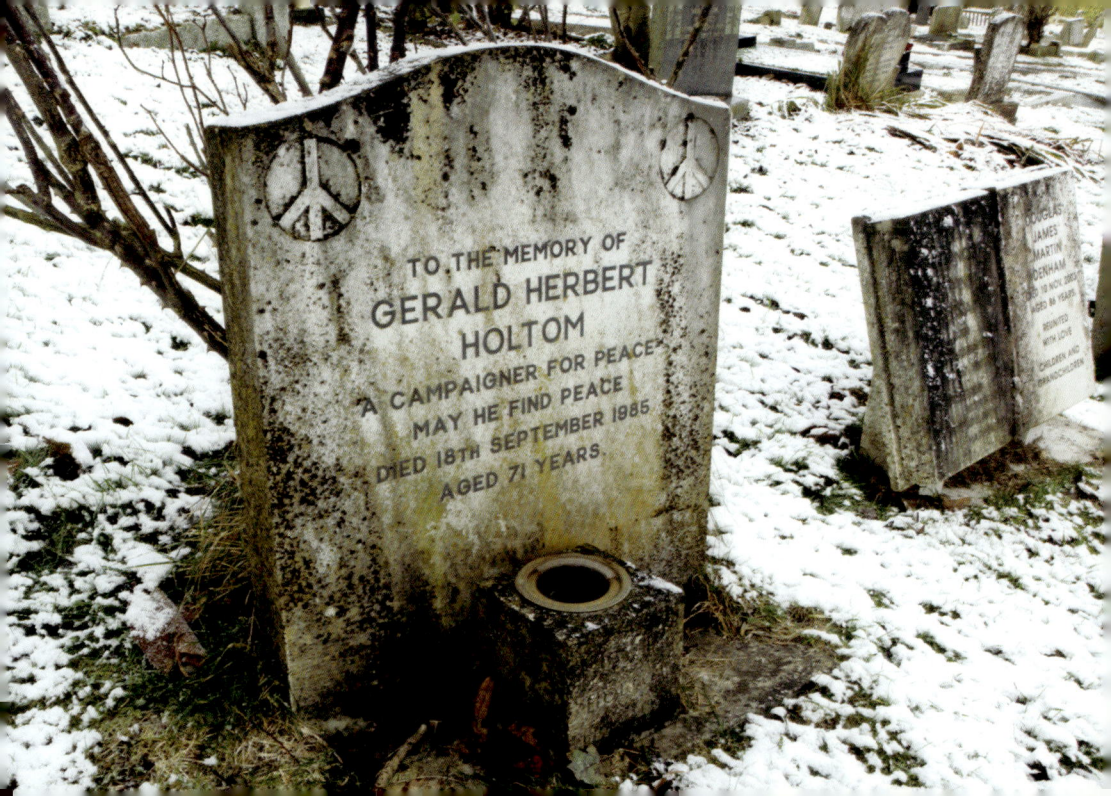

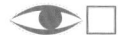

During the First World War the Metropole was home to many officers off to fight in Europe. 'Friendly' ladies from Mayfair came to the Metropole set up a brothel for the officers in the town.

पहिलो विश्व युद्धको समयमा Metropole का धेरै अधिकारीहरुलाई युरोपको लडाईमा भाग लिनबाट वन्चित गराई घर पठाईएको थियो । Mayfair बाट आएका महिलाहरुले Metropole का पदाधिकारीहरुको लागि कोठीको व्यवस्था गरेका थिए ।

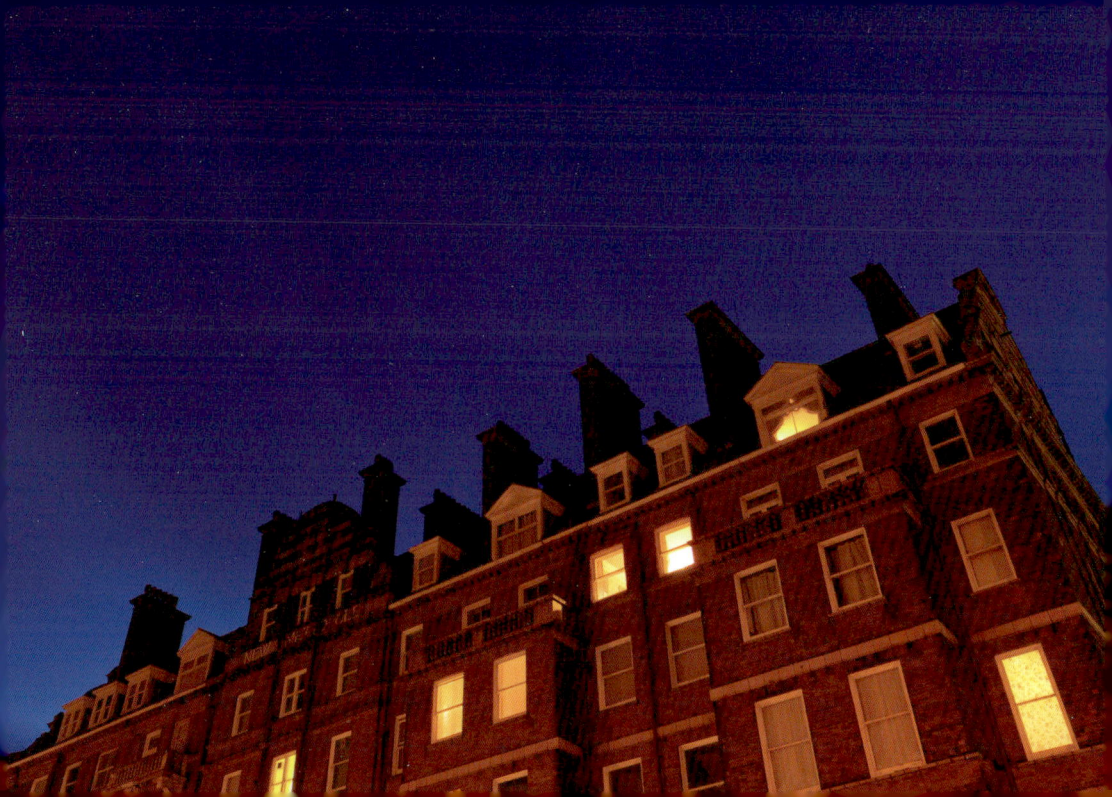

Noel Coward used to live on the Romney Marsh and his film *Blythe Spirit* features ghosts on The Leas. The Leas also features in a chapter of H G Wells' book *The Accelerator*.

Noel Coward को चलचित्र *Blythe Spirit* को विशेषता ीभवक मा भएको भुत सम्बन्धीको थियो । उ रोम्नी मार्शमा बस्ने गर्दथ्यो ।

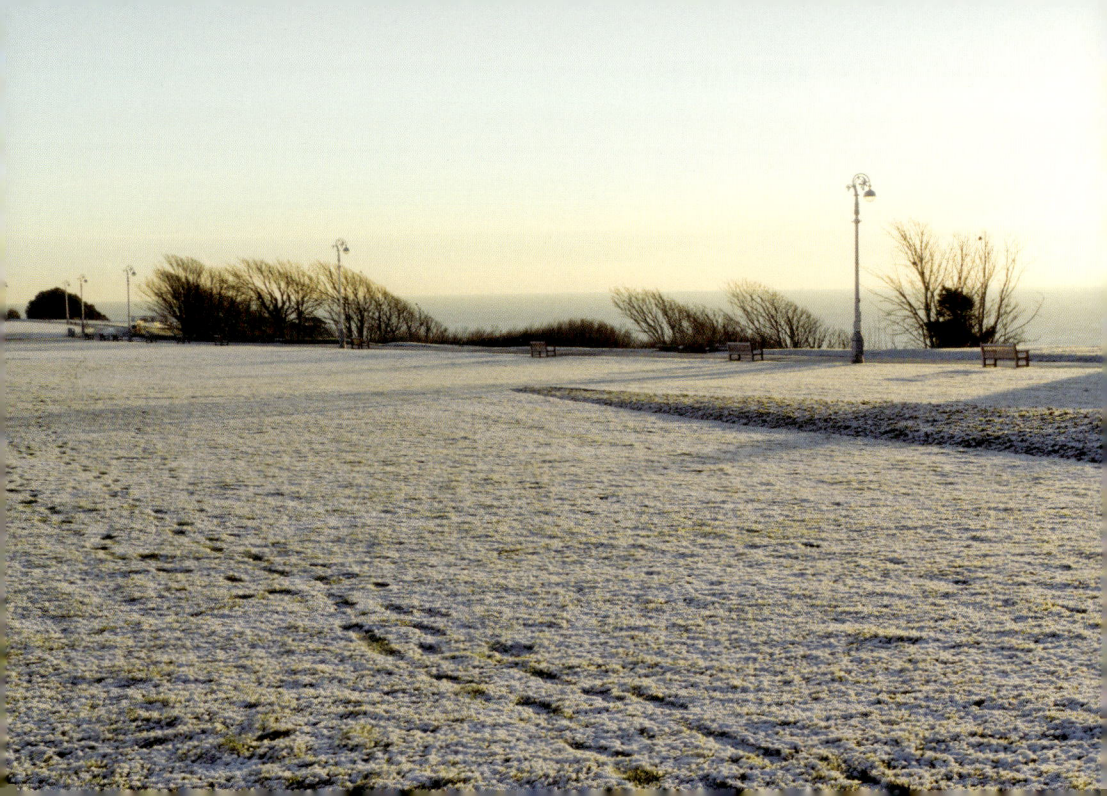

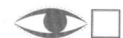

About 100 years ago the Cherry Pickers was originally a house set in amongst an orchard, but there was a tragedy involving a little girl, who fell to her death out of an upstairs window. Shortly after this horrific accident the old house was knocked down, but bizarrely, when the new pub was built, the builders were instructed to build directly on the footprint of the original house, and the rubble of the house where the girl had died was used as hardcore and still sits undisturbed, in the cellar. The ghost of the little girl is still said to walk around the Cherry Pickers at night, especially when there are strong winds or stormy weather.

झ्यालबाट खसेर मृत्यु भएको सानो नानीको मृतात्मा रातको समयमा Cherry Pickers को वरीपरी हिंडेको आवाज सुन्न सकिन्छ ।

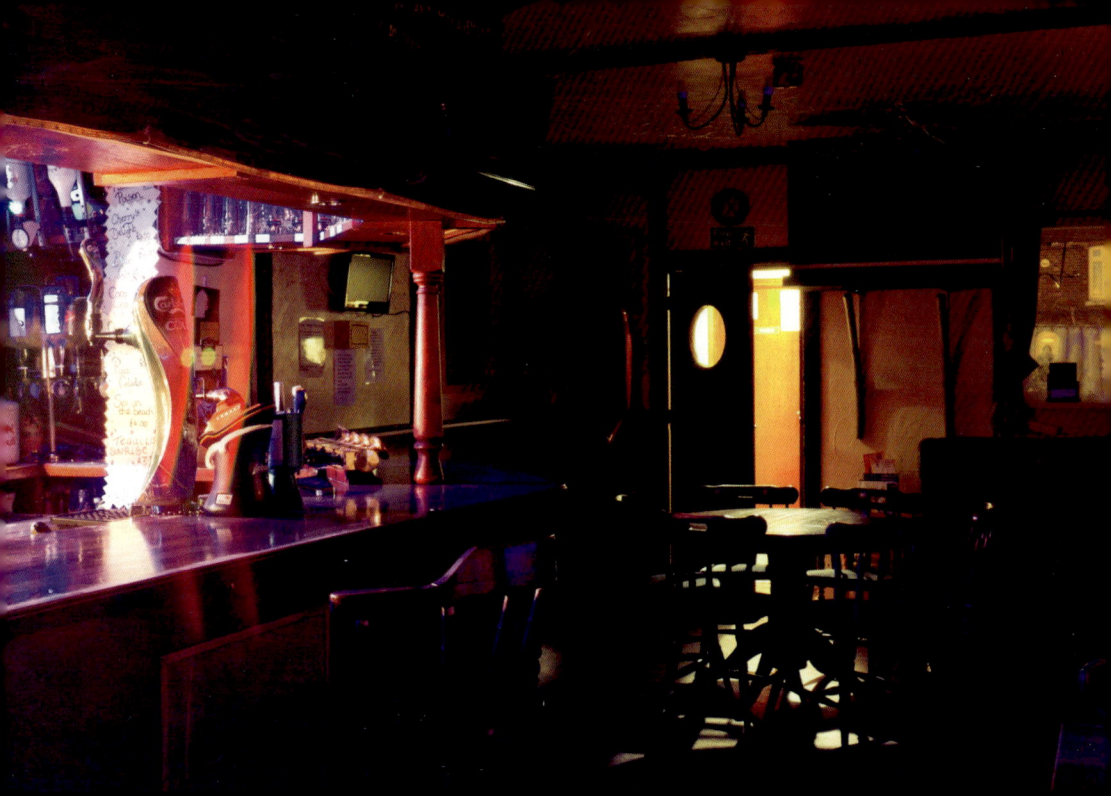

Aged 6, my husband (Nick Jacobs) wondered if his diver Action Man would swim in the pond between Victoria Hospital and Radnor Park, so he threw him in to test his theory. He didn't; and we walk past the pond regularly and wonder if his Action Man is still on the bottom trying to swim his way to the top!

मेरो श्रीमान ६ वर्षको हुदा सोच्ने गर्दथ्यो कि उसको खेलौना हाँसको खेल्ने पोखरीमा पौडिन सक्ने छ । तर वास्तवमा यसो भएन ।

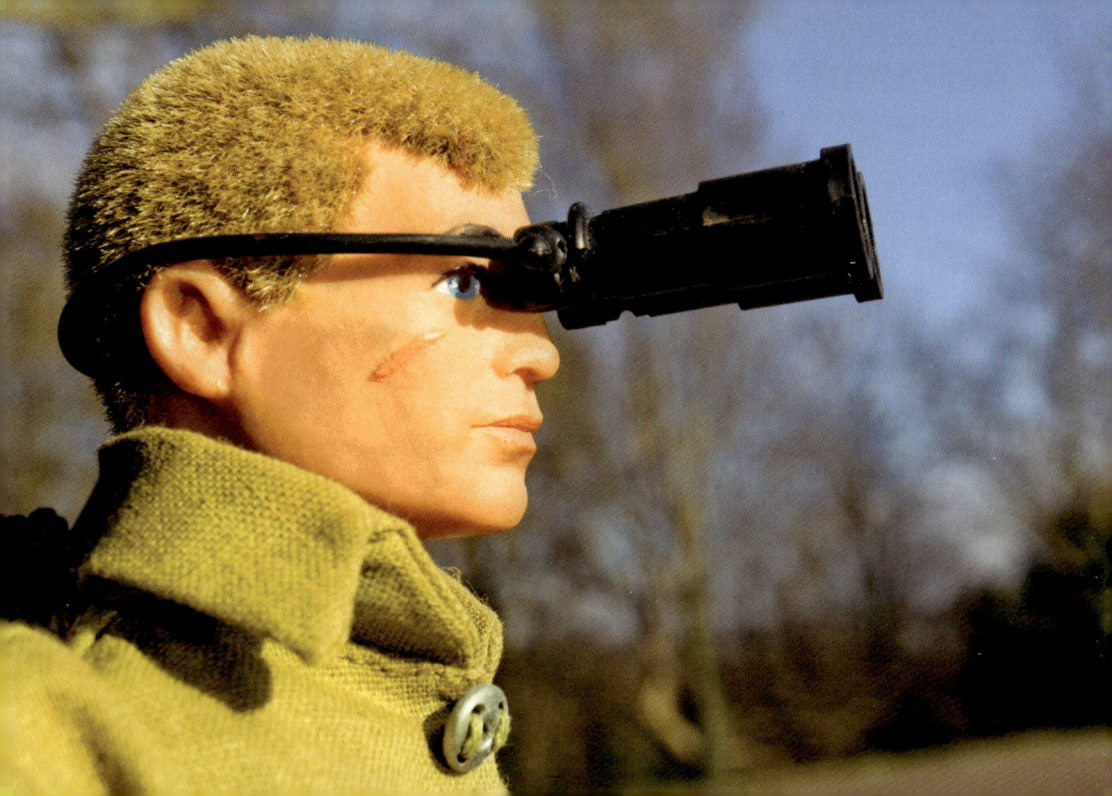

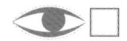

If you walk up Manor Road from the RBS bank on the corner of Sandgate Road, immediately behind the bank there is a narrow footpath that runs along the back of several shops and restaurants. The path comes to an abrupt halt, cut off about two feet above the modern level of the delivery area under Sainsbury's car park. Before Sainsbury's was built, this path led into what must have been one of Folkestone's least-known enclosed gardens, bounded on all sides by the backs of the buildings of Manor Rd, Sandgate Rd, Cheriton Place and Bouverie Road West. The path in the opposite corner of the garden can still be seen near the corner of Cheriton Place and Bouverie Rd West. I discovered the garden as a teenage weekend hippy, and remember it as an oasis of peace and quiet, shielded from the sounds of the streets, a mown lawn of grass shaded by some trees. I think there was a group of trees in the middle, and I guess the big holm oaks outside the entrance to Sainsbury's were also inside the garden. I don't think I went there very often - and I don't recall ever taking anyone with me. I never saw anyone else in the garden either, so for me it seemed like a strange, secret garden. It is only the evidence of the tiny footpaths that confirm to me that I didn't imagine it completely. Or did I?

Sainsbury's को पछाडि एउटा सुन्दर र शान्त बगैंचा थियो । तर त्यो सबै मासियो अब त्यहाँ जाने स्यानो गोरेटोको रुपमा मात्र बाँकी छ ।

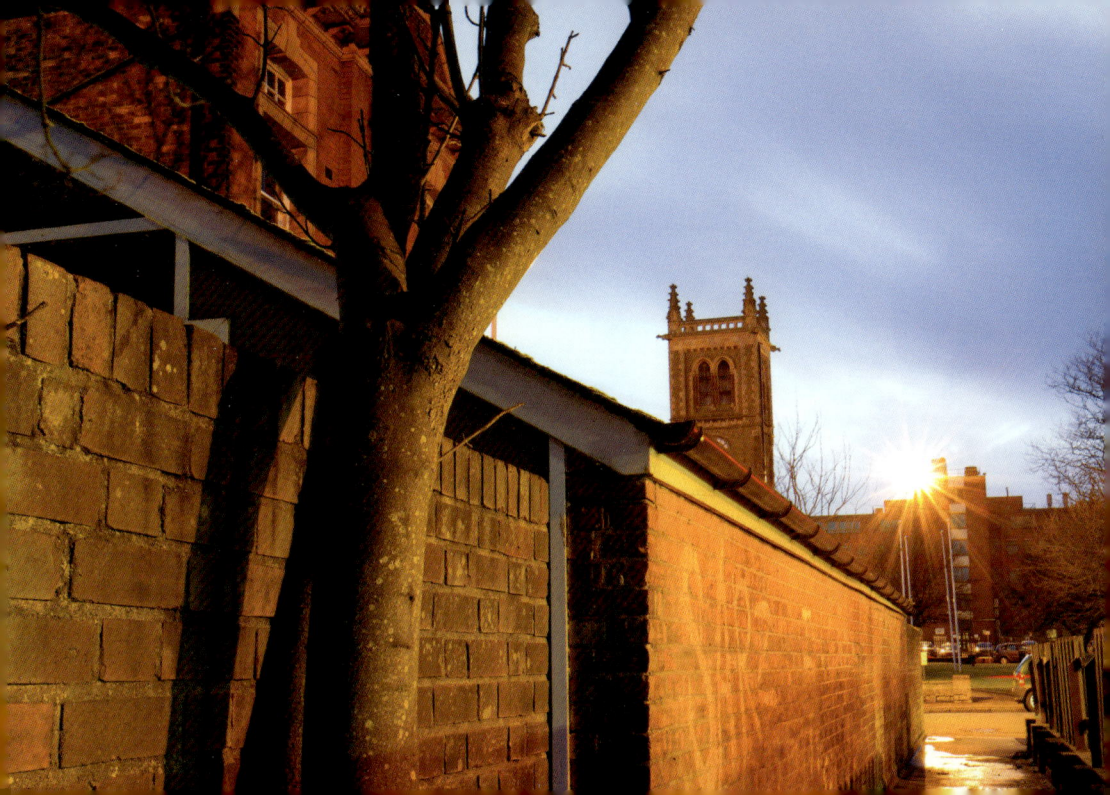

This location bore significance to me in my early years in Folkestone, in the early to mid 70s. A close school friend lived in Southbourne Road, and to get to his house I would have to cross this demarcation line at this heavy old gate. I would have walked from Radnor park, and the crossing meant I was almost at my destination. It was in some way the crossing to safety, like entering a different zone, crossing from west to east, to an area of Folkestone that was safer than the Dover Road and its environs that I, for some reason found threatening on my journey east. The gate itself was held closed by a seemingly huge weight on a pulley, this would take some effort to open. Once on the wooden slatted boards over the tracks the pedestrian would only be yards from the live rails, this added to the sense of danger that was already heightened by the knowledge that trains frequently used the line back then. The crossing was itself somehow both dangerous and reassuring, and always significant.

साथी भेट्न जादा म रेलको लिख माथीवाट पार गर्न ज्यादै उत्साहित हुन्थे । मैले पढ्ने स्कुल रेल चल्ने लिखदेखी अत्यन्तै नजिक थियो ।

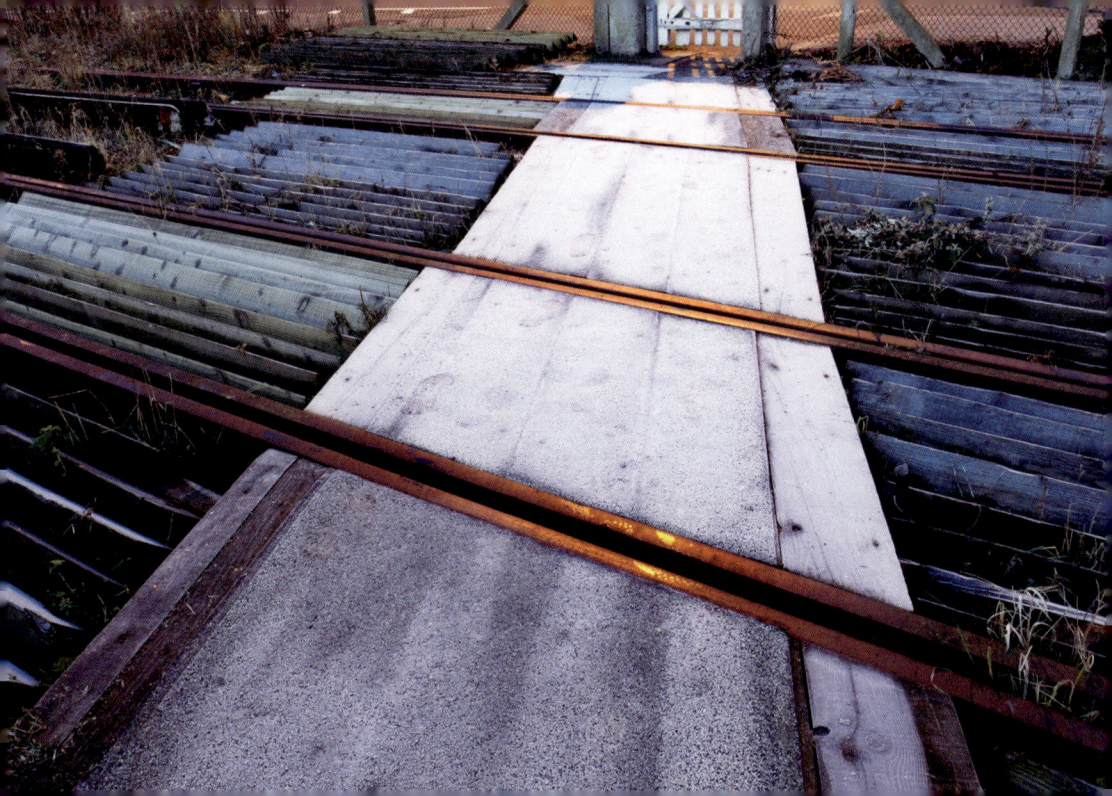

As a child growing up in the Folkestone area I was always puzzled by the name 'Creteway'. I couldn't imagine why our local hills were named after a Greek island!

I used to ponder on whether there was some connection with something that happened in the Second World War? It wasn't until I was working for the White Cliffs Countryside Project and researching local historical landscape, ecology and history that the root of the name became apparent to me.

The word 'Crete' has its root in a word from Old French meaning 'an ancient, hilltop chalk trackway'. So now I could understand the literal meaning of 'Creteway Down' – literally means 'an ancient, hilltop chalk trackway – hill'. The word 'Down' has its root in Anglo-Saxon, I believe, and comes from the word 'Dun' meaning 'hill'. So now every time I see the local 71 bus for 'Creteway Down' I think of that name's very ancient origin!

'Crete' शब्द पुरानो फ्रान्सबाट आएको हो र यसको अर्थ 'an ancient, hilltop chalk trackway' हुन्छ । 'Down' पुरानो शब्द 'मालु बाट परिवर्तन भएको हो र यसको अथ 'जर्षी हुन्छ । त्यसैले Creteway Down को अक्षरश अर्थ 'an ancient, hilltop chalk track' हुन्छ ।

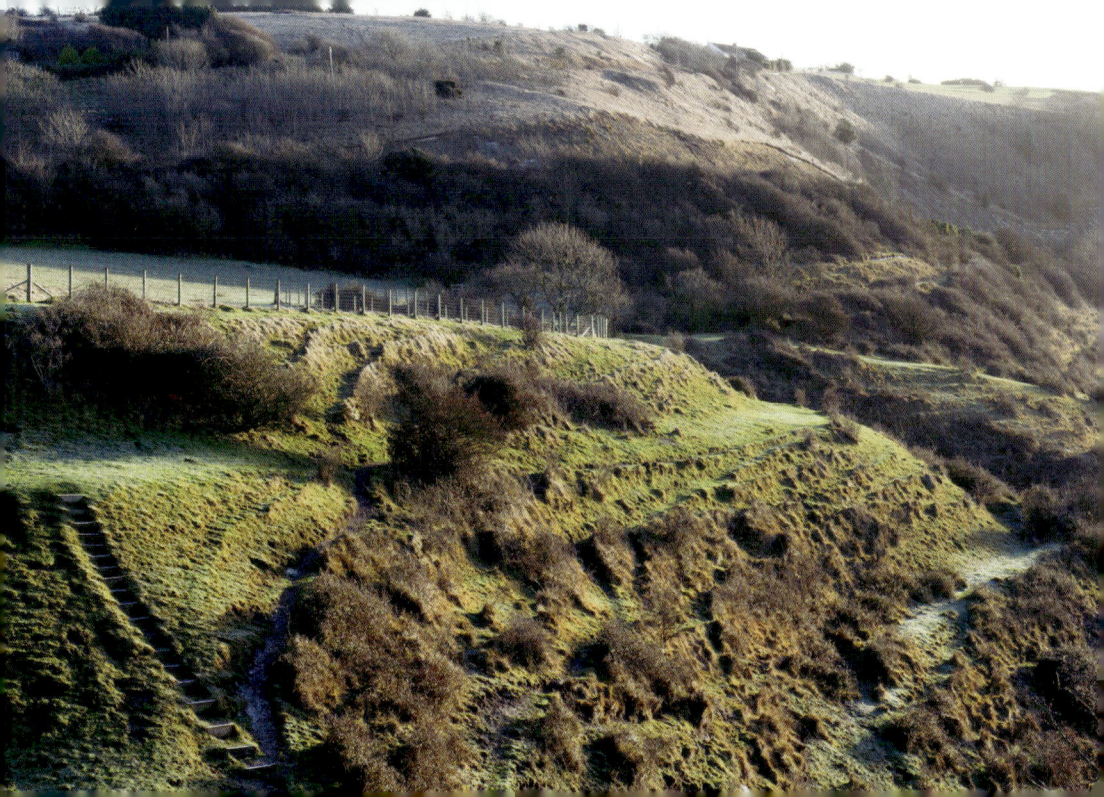

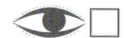

I was made redundant from my job with the LDA in December 2008. Rather than being a negative experience, I felt relieved, freed from the chains that were holding me back.

I had only visited the Warren a few times in the three years I had been living in Folkestone, but that was all about to change during the Summer of 2009. The Warren became an important place for me to relax and formulate ideas. I learned to fish on the beach, discovered fossils, walked and collected the small glass beads that can be found on the sands. The beads of glass are remnants of bottles that have broken into tiny pieces, then worn by the sand and tide. I attempted wind kiting and collected mussels for my tea. Best of all, it was also the year that I made some great new friends in Folkestone, together we had BBQ's on the beach and I finally realised the dream of having my own café. During this summer I found a building, invented the famous Googieburger, and opened Googies for business.

सन २००९ मा मलाई जागिरबाट अवकाश दिएपछि मैले जीवनलाई पूर्ण रुपमा परिवर्तन गर्ने निर्णय गरे । फलत, मैले एउटा उपयुक्त भवन भेट्टाए र त्याहा व्यवसायको रुपमा Googies Café खोले ।

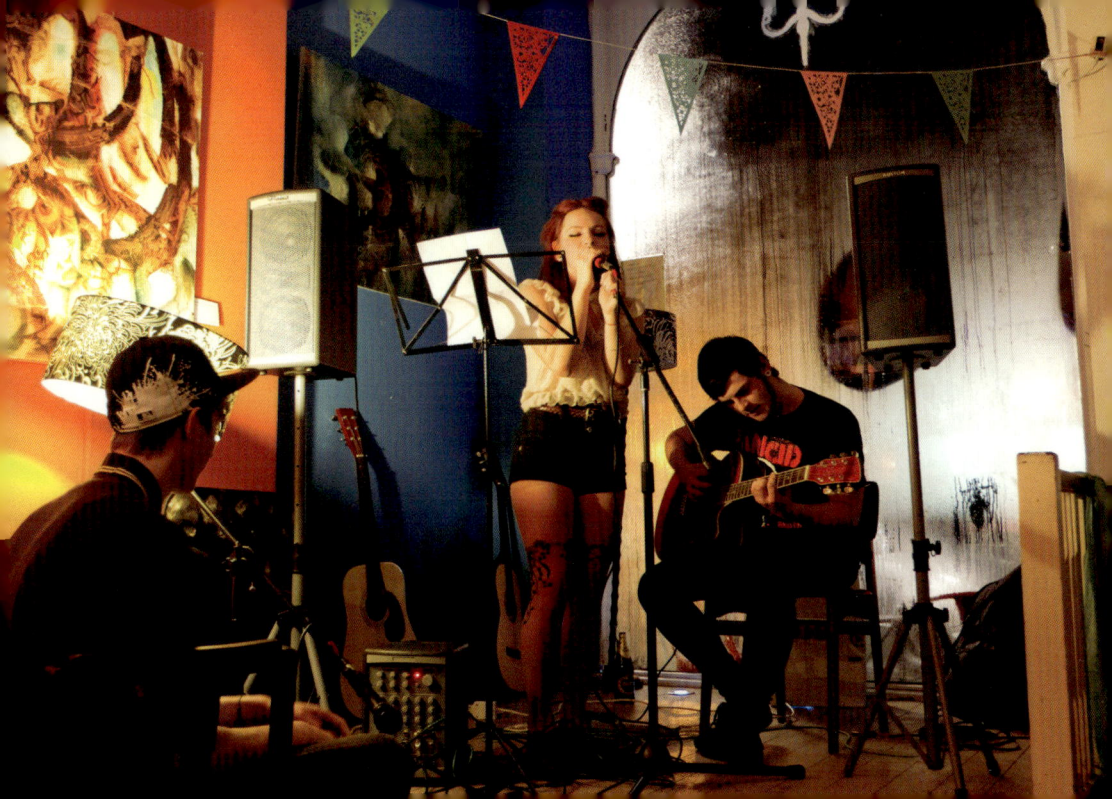

This has been a florist shop continuously for 101 years, opened when Church Street was the most important road in Folkestone. This beautiful florist shop has supplied flowers for generations of weddings, and funerals as well as to all of the local grand hotels.

Legend has it that one previous owner knew Dickens, and that the ancient mulberry tree in the garden is the one that William Harvey famously played in (he was born and lived in the same street).

The shop has some amazing original fittings, including the original Interflora sign and an ancient cellar, which is believed to mark the boundary wall of the old Abbey, this wall can be seen along the alleyways on either side of the street.

यो फुल पसल १०१ वर्ष देखि यहाँ छ । यो पसल पुरानो र ऐतिहासिक कोठामा रहेको छ । यो पुरानो मठको दोसाँधे पर्खालको अवशेष हो भन्ने विश्वास गरिएको छ । यलाई साँघुरो गल्लीको दुवै तर्फबाट देख्न सकिन्छ ।

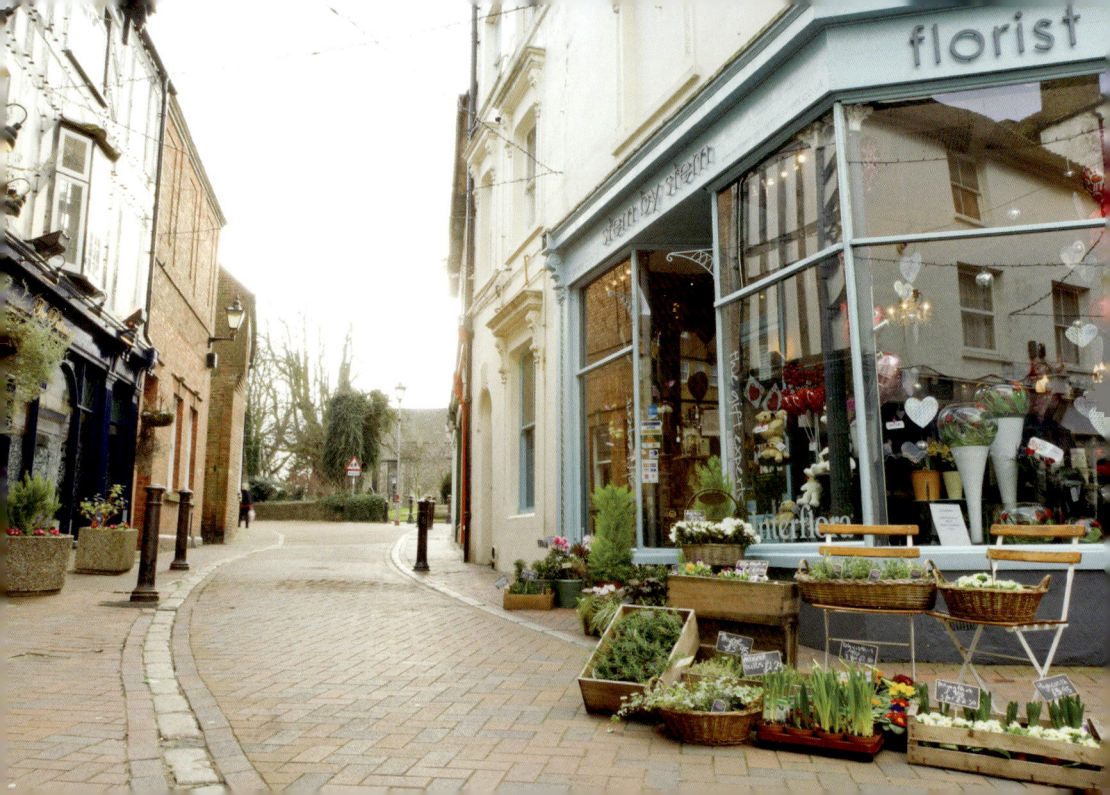

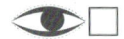

There has been a Christian community in Folkestone since 630 AD. At that time Eadbald ruled the Saxon Kingdom of Kent and built a convent for his daughter Eanswythe, the first women's convent in England. St Eanswythe died whilst still young in 640 and was buried in the church her father had built for her.

In 1885 marble workers working on the church discovered a cavity and an old Saxon coffer containing the remains of a young woman – the long-lost relics of St Eanswythe. If you look to the left of the altar you can see where the cavity is now covered with an elaborate brass grille and engraved door where the relics remain to this day.

St Eanswythe's miracles were lengthening a beam, making the Bayle stream flow uphill to where it was needed, and stopping the birds settling on the nearby fields and consuming the farmers' produce.

वेलायतमा St Eanswythe ले किश्चियन धर्मावलम्बि महिलाहरुको लागि पहिलो संगठन स्थापना गरेका थिए । उनको देनले चराचुरुङ्गीहरुले कृषकको बालिनालीहरु खान बाट बचाएका थिए ।

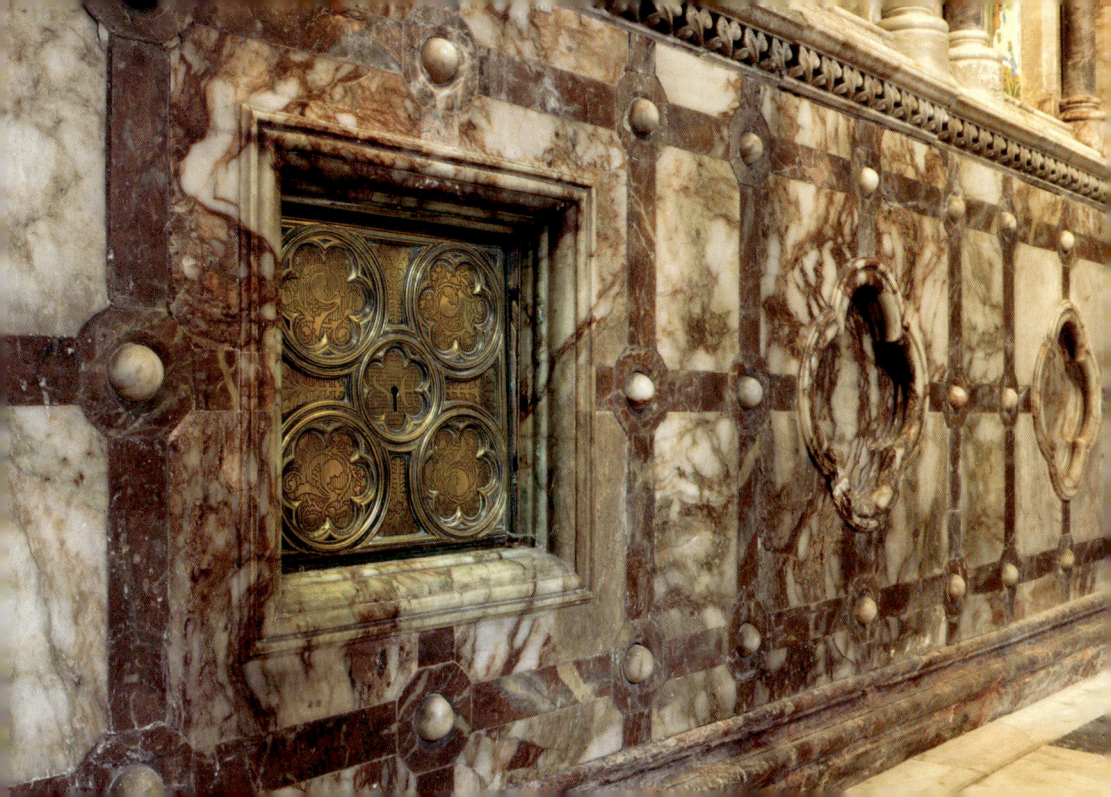

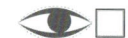

I spent a wonderful week here on this angular, undulating headland situated behind the concrete 'apron' at Folkestone Warren in the glorious summer of 1976. We 'camped' under the stars – in sleeping bags that kept the bugs off. There were three of us, all in our teens, with our whole lives ahead. We drank water from the stream that poured out of a pipe in the 'apron' wall on to the beach (we knew it was fresh – we'd often find fresh water shrimps in our plastic bottles). Beyond the apron, the sea was mysterious milky white due to exploratory channel tunnel workings that rumbled on somewhere nearby unobserved by us. Most days were spent lying in the constant sun listening to the evocative sounds of *Afternoon Delight* or *Forever and Ever* on Radio 1.

At night we told ghost stories and invested the strange lights on the cliff top with supernatural meaning. To add to the sense of other worldliness, in the early hours someone unseen could be heard in the woods behind playing *Amazing Grace* on a flute. A special time in a special place.

म युवावस्थाको हुँदा दुई साथिहरुसंग Warren मा तारा मण्डल मुनी स्लिपिङ ब्यागमा सुतेर एक हप्ता बिताएको थिएँ । यो ज्यादै रमाईलो क्षण थियो ।

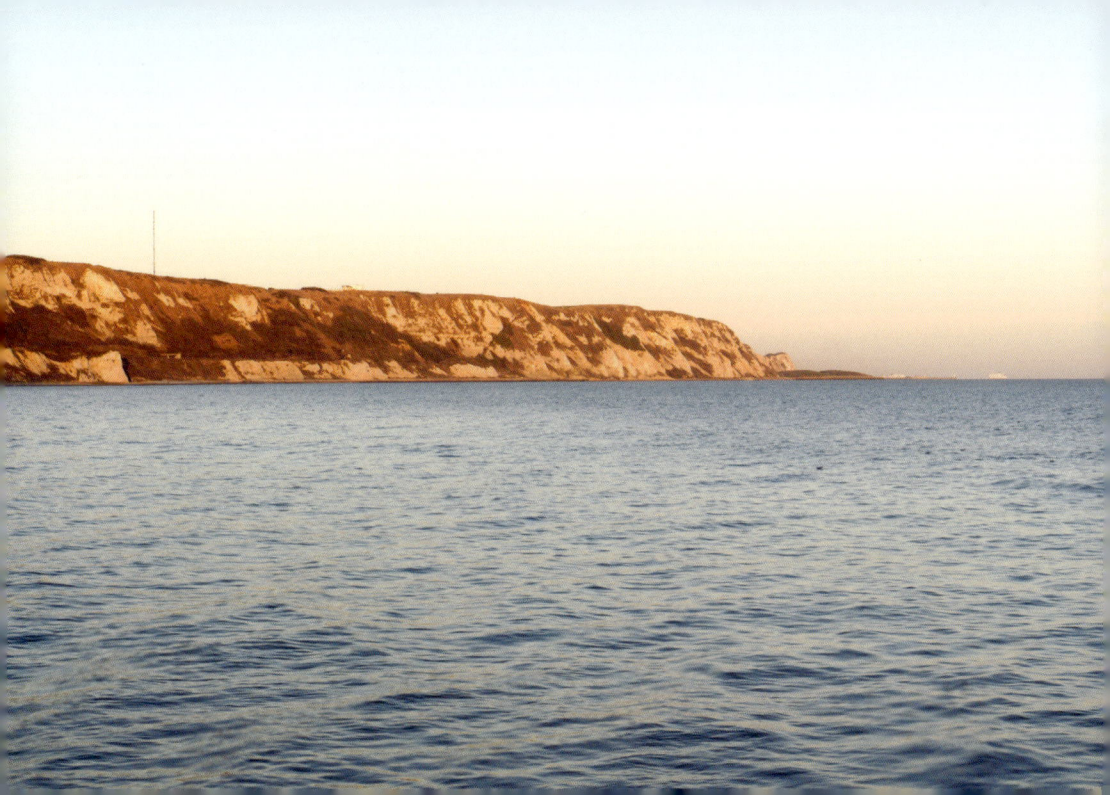

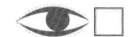

In 1958 I was working for a firm called Demolition and Construction on sea defence work along Folkestone seafront. I remember building a stone wall, and while I was cementing in the stones I decided to leave a reminder of where I had been working and cemented in a farthing in between the large stones. The coin stayed in place for nearly fifty years, but a couple of years ago it disappeared. If you look closely you can still see the outline of where it had once been.

मैले १९५८ साल तिर Channel मा ढगे पर्खाल बनाए तर बाँकी काम सिमेन्टीमा सिक्का गाडेर छाडेको थिए । त्यो सिक्का झण्डै ५० वर्ष जति यहाँ देखिन्थ्यो, हाल हरायो । जेहोस नियालेर हेर्ने हो भने अझैपनि यसको आकार देख्न सकिन्छ ।

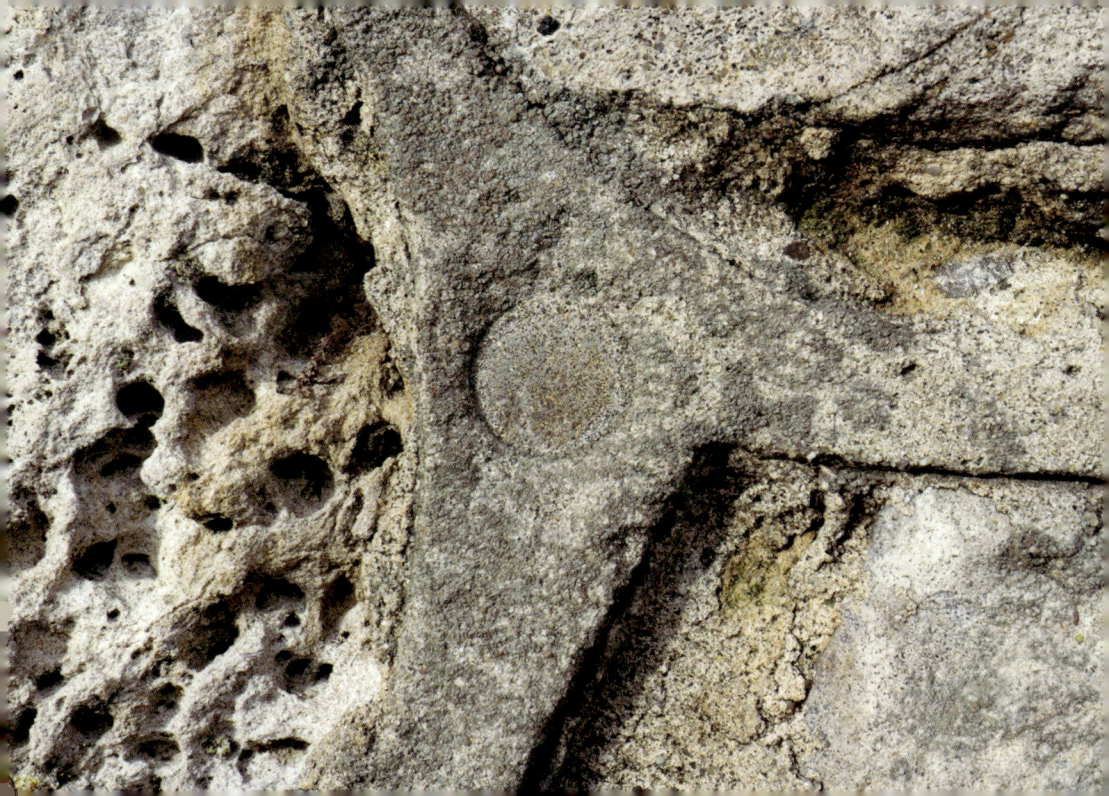

I recently moved back to England after living abroad for many years. I was walking along the lower Sandgate Road with my wife in the Summer of 2010 and noticed a photograph attached to a lamppost. On inspection I said to my wife, "That gentleman looks very much like my Father," to which she agreed. We wondered how we could find out more about it, then recently we noticed an exhibition of old Folkestone photographs was going to be held at the Masonic Hall, Grace Hill. Consequently we went to the exhibition in anticipation of perhaps finding the photo, without success. We were, however, directed to the artists at Strange Cargo, based at Georges House at the top of The Old High Street. They did indeed have a copy, and very kindly offered to print two copies, for myself and my brother.

For more information about Other People's Photographs visit: www.strangecargo.org.uk

धेरै वर्ष पछिको अन्तरालमा म भरखरै मात्र वेलायतमा फर्किएको छु । एक दिन मैले विजुलिको खम्बामा मेरो बाबाको जवानीको फोटा देख्दा छक्क परेको थिए ।

EVERYWHERE MEANS SOMETHING TO SOMEONE

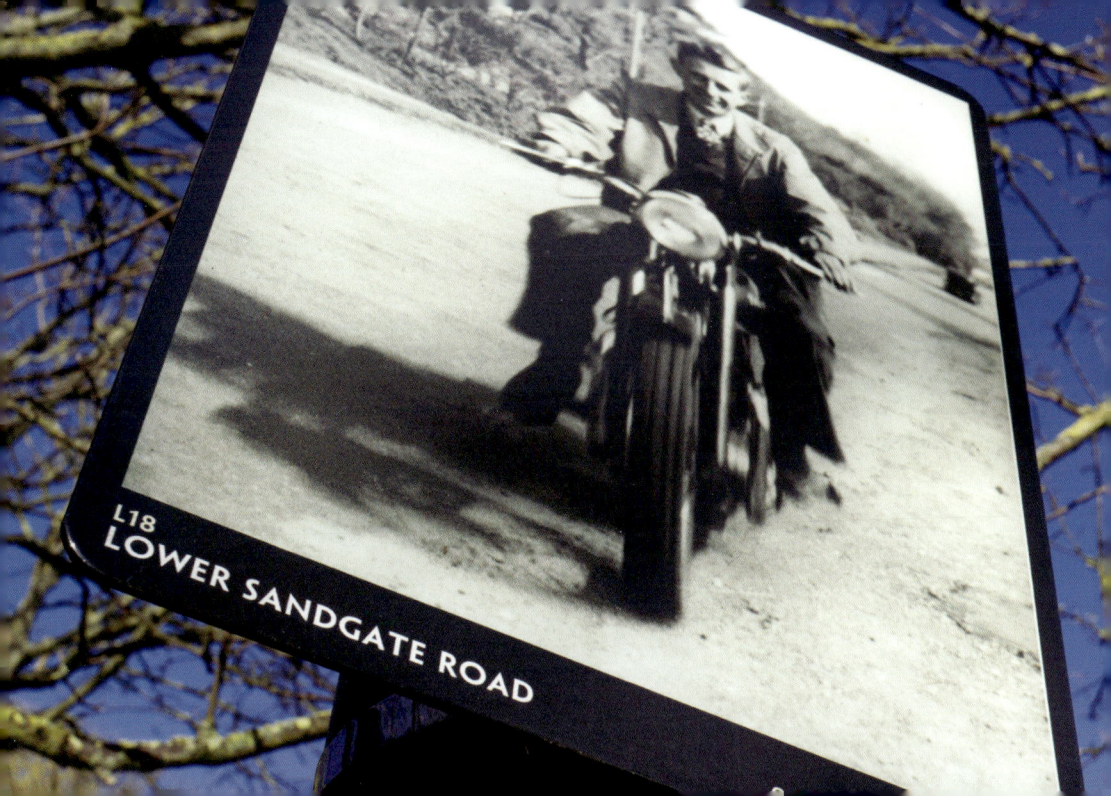

L18
LOWER SANDGATE ROAD

One evening my husband and I were walking along the Leas and we came across an American couple, who were standing looking out to sea. As we passed them the woman, pointing across the Channel, said "What *is* that out there?"

Her husband looked out at the coastline of Boulogne, with its white cliffs and sparkling lights, and knowledgeably replied, "Oh, that's the Isle of Wight."

एक दिन साझमा मेरो श्रीमान र म लिजको वाटो भएर हिड्दै थियौं, त्यहा हामीले एउटा अमेरिकन मानिसले समुन्द्रतिर हेरीरहे को देख्यौं । जब हामीले उनीहरुलाई नाघेर गयौं, ठिक त्यसै वेला ति छोरी मान्छेले भन्यो "त्यहां त्यो के हो ?" उनको श्रीमानले त्यता हेरेर भन्यो " यो Isle of Wight हो" ।

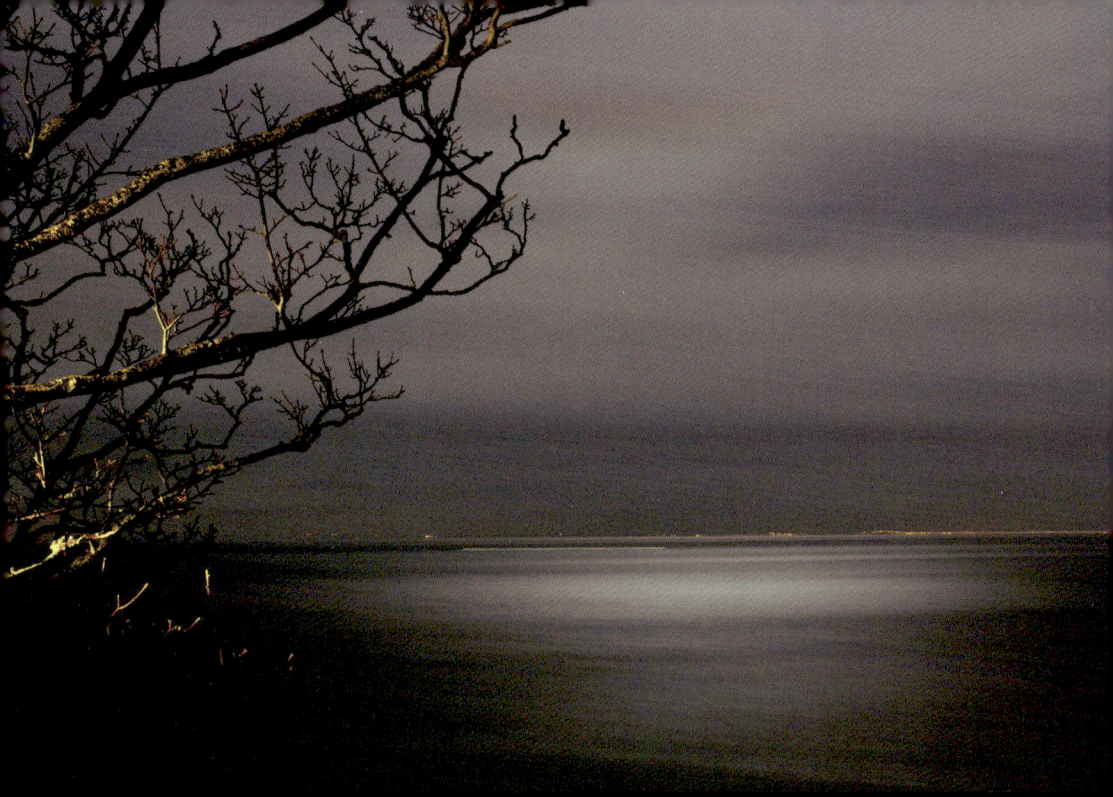

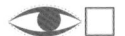

One evening in Sandgate the sea started bubbling. My friend said, "That's the mackerel running." It happens when the sea is flat, the tide is coming in, and the sun is low: that's when the mackerel chases the whitebait. I learned how to cast out and reel in through the boiling sea and caught loads. One morning at sunrise I woke my sceptical brother Adam and my wife Amanda to head to the beach, the sea was full of mackerel as we passed the Hythe Imperial, but when we arrived the tide was going out – so no mackerel. I was depressed I hadn't been able to prove my discovery, but we bought provisions from the garage and had a fry up on the beach as the sun came up. It is one of my favourite memories, and my wife says she fell in love with Folkestone all over again – and I fell in love with her. I still haven't caught mackerel with the family, but even without them, Folkestone is great, isn't it?

सानगेटमा समुन्द्र उम्लेको जस्तो देखिन्छ । वास्तवमा यो म्याकरेल माछाले ह्वाइट विटलाई समुन्द्रको छेउ छेउमा खेदेको हो दृश्य हो ।

DAVE THE DOLPHIN

ADVICE FOR VISITORS

<u>PLEASE!</u>

Respect Dave as a wild and free animal

Do not attempt to touch

Do not attempt to feed - she doesnt need it

Swimmers and Kayaks should avoid overcrowding or surrounding Dave should she come near

Powerboats and Jet Skis are requested to avoid the area around Dave wherever possible, propeller injuries are of great concern, please also be aware of swimmers in the water

Litter especially plastic bags, can be a danger to Dave, please collect them and dispose of them sensibly

Remember that you are being watched by hundreds of people on the shoreline, inappropriate behaviour will be reported and action, if necessary, taken

It is against the law to harass dolphins and all other types of wild animal, we know she likes to play, but we must ask everyone to adhere to the above guidelines

For more information see our leaflets or the website

www.sandgatedolphin.co.uk

Produced with the help of **THE ROGER DE HAAN CHARITABLE TRUST**

Half way along the wall at Folkestone Central Station, among the bronze hand casts is the hand print of Charles Newington, the artist who created the white horse which can be seen on the hills overlooking Folkestone. If you look closely at the hand you will be able to see that the outline of the horse has been drawn into the background. His handprint is one of a 101 prints made of local people who were born in separate years between 1900 and 2000 to celebrate the millennium. At the time the horse artwork wasn't in place. It was installed on the hill in 2003.

फोक्सटन शहरको रेल स्टेहनको पर्खालको विचमा भएको हाते चित्रको चित्रकार Charles Newington ले नै फोक्सटनको डाँडामा देखिने घोडाको नक्शा पनि बनाएका हुन् ।

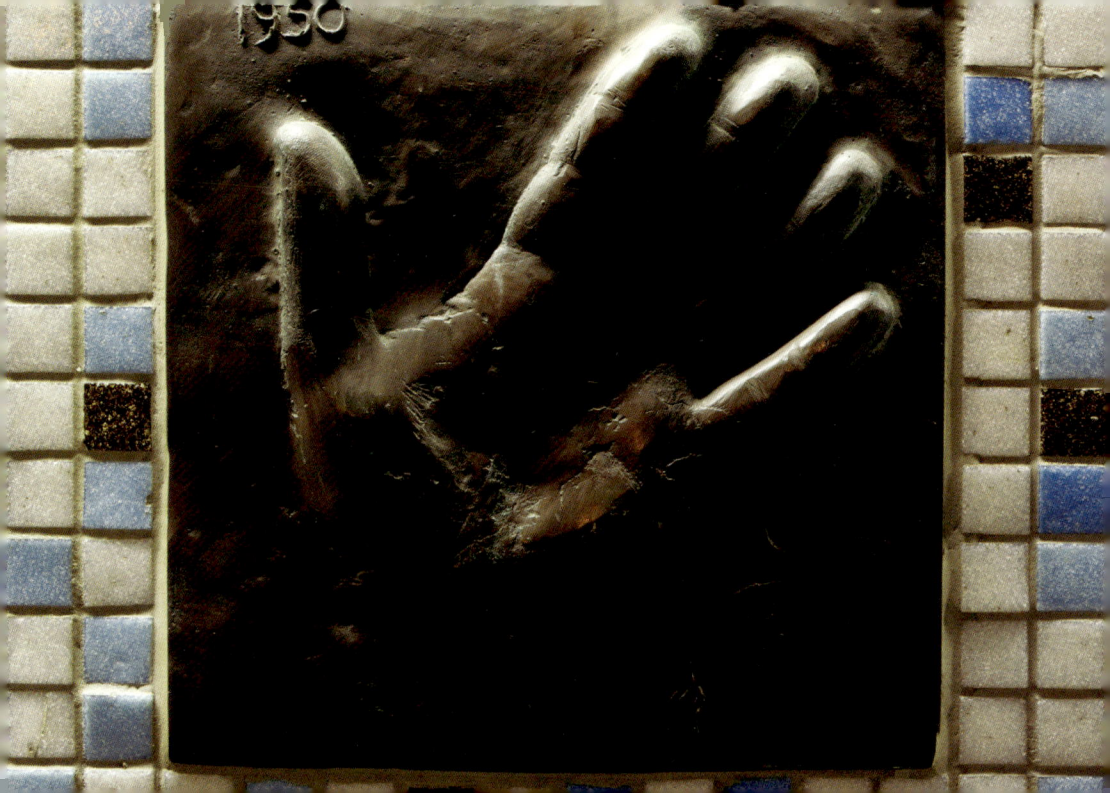

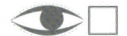

A Hindu temple has been situated in Sir John Moore Barrack since 1999, where the Gurkha Regiment is based. It is mainly for the Gurkha soldiers and their families, but it may be allowed for use by the local community on request.

Sir John Moore Barrack मा हिन्दु धर्मावलम्बीको एउटा मन्दिर छ, जहा १९९९ देखि गोर्खा पल्टन अवस्थित छ । यो मन्दिर सेवारत गोर्खाली सिपाही र उनीहरुका परिवारको लागि मात्र हो । तर अनुरोध गरेमा स्थानिय वासिन्दाहरुले पनि प्रयोग गर्न सक्दछन् ।

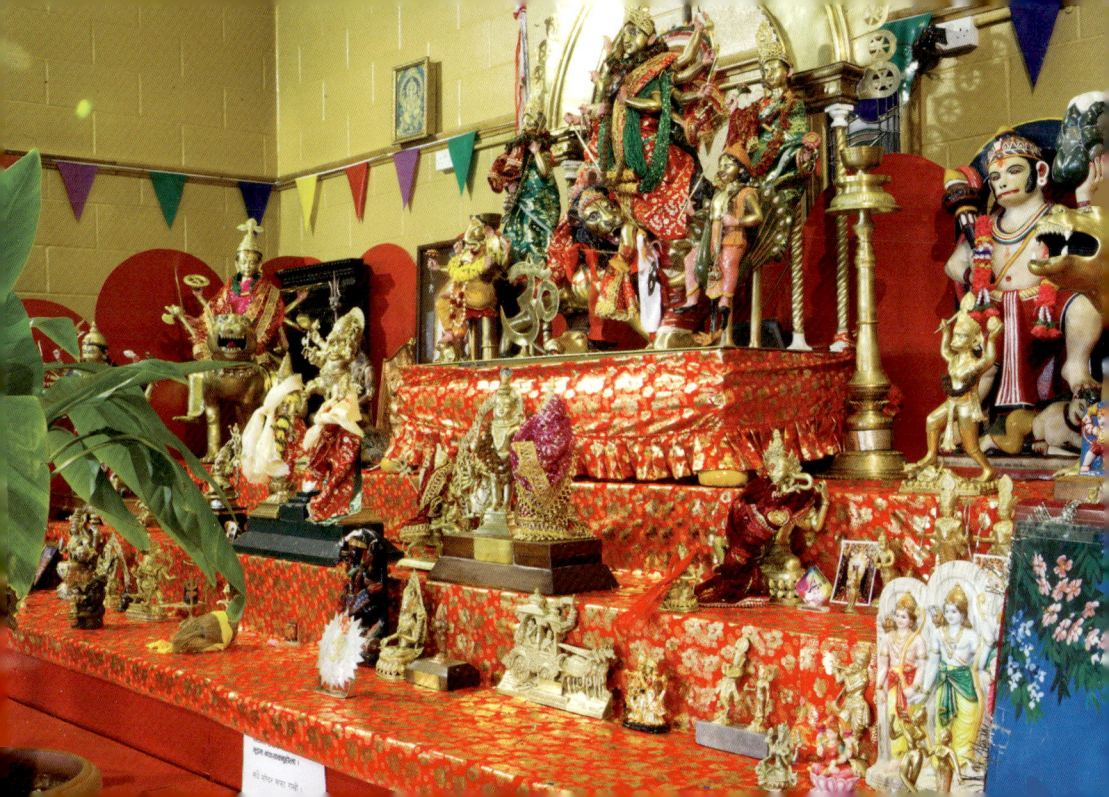

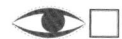

The Donkey Derby is one of those brilliant Folkestone events that just springs up every August in Radnor Park, and everyone goes along to enjoy themselves. I remember years ago a cowboy act, whose whole performance was jumping in and out of his lasso, and doing acrobatics with it. How great is that! There are amusements and all kinds of things to join in and take part in, loads of food and, in my mind, it's always sunny. I have never had the nerve to get on a donkey though.

प्रत्येक अगष्ट महिनामा रेडनोर पार्कमा Donkey Derby को आयोजना हुन्छ । त्यहाँ सवै प्रकारको वस्तुहरु, विभीन्न प्रकारको खाद्य सामग्रीहरुको साथ सहभागिता जनाउँछन र यस वेला सधैं घमाईलो हुन्छ । म कहिले पनि यस कार्यक्रममा सहभागिताको लागि शाहस गर्दिन ।

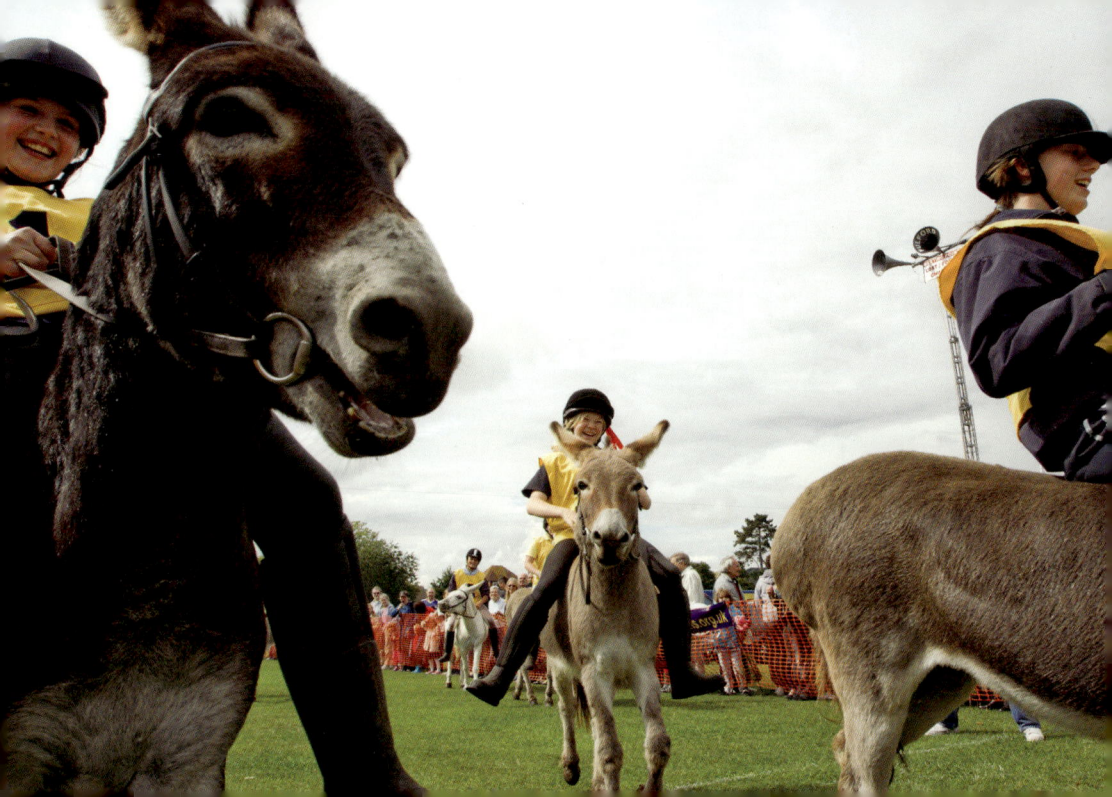

The Blessing of the Fisheries is always held on the Sunday closest to St Peter's Day, and at high tide. I remember the 1955 parade, it was in June and I was asked to help carry the model of the fishing boat at the head of the group with four of my friends from St Peter's School, including G Featherbee, M Jefferies, D Woods and J Fisher. The parade went from the Durlocks, down North Street, along Radnor Street onto The Stade, overlooking the Harbour and the fishing boats. The parade included St Peter's Sea Scouts, pupils from the school and a military band. The Bishop of The Windward Isles officiated at the blessing ceremony. The Blessing of the Fisheries still continues to this day.

When the sea mist rolls in, I've heard the bell at St Peter's Church rings out to help the fishermen find their way back to port. It's a very eerie, mournful sound, and reminds us how tough and dangerous it must have been in the days before radar and GPS, and how many fishermen have lost their lives in the fog.

सामुन्द्रिक सतह बढेको बेलामा Sunday Closest देखि St Peter's Day सम्म माछा मार्नेहरुको प्राथनाको आयोजना गरिन्थ्यो । यो खतरनाक काममा जाने स्थानिय सवै मच्छय सिकारीहरुको सुरक्षाको लागि आशिर्वाद लिने एउटा समारोह हो ।

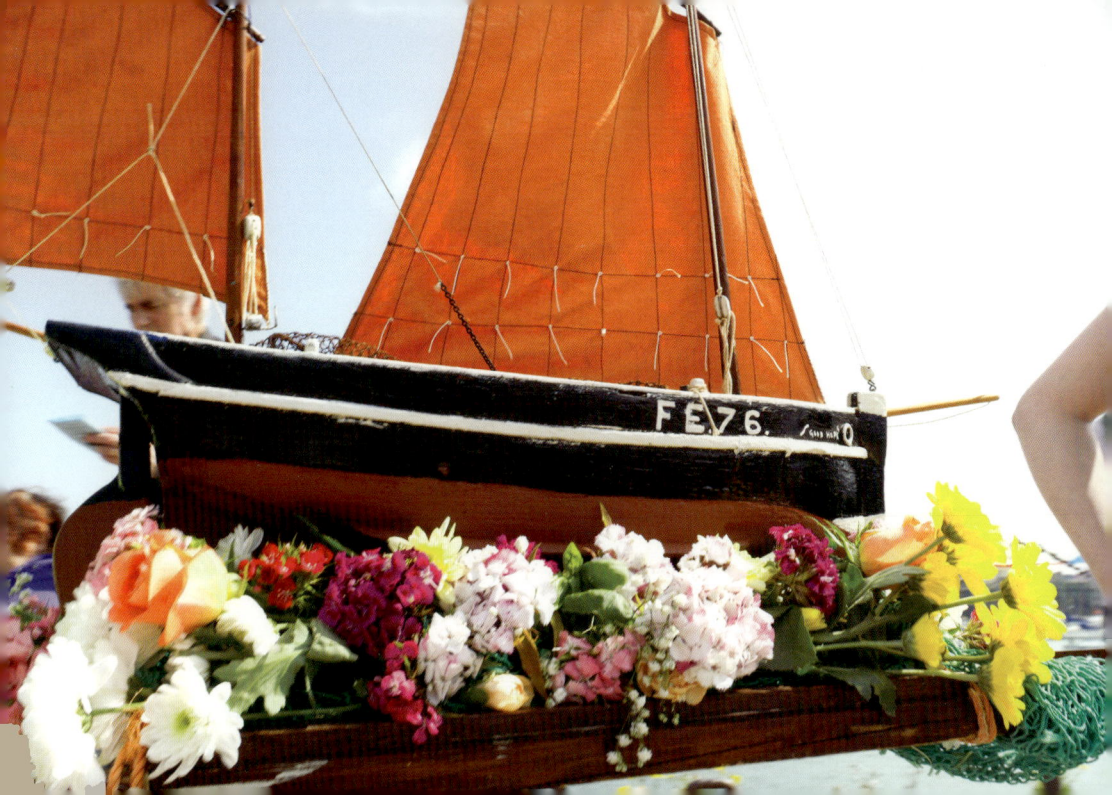

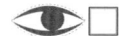

Coming out of the cold and into the Harbour Fish Bar down at the harbour, I sat down at a table and started to look around; there on the wall next to one of those amazing modern art paintings of dolphins is a very faded picture of Princess Di beaming out at you. You can't help but smile at the oddity of it all.

जाडोको समयमा Harbour Fish Bar को टेबलमा बसेर ऐताउता हेर्दा त्यहांको भित्तामा एचष्ल्अभकक म्ऽ को आश्चर्य चकित मुद्रामा डल्फिनको नक्शाको छेउमा देख्न सकिन्छ ।

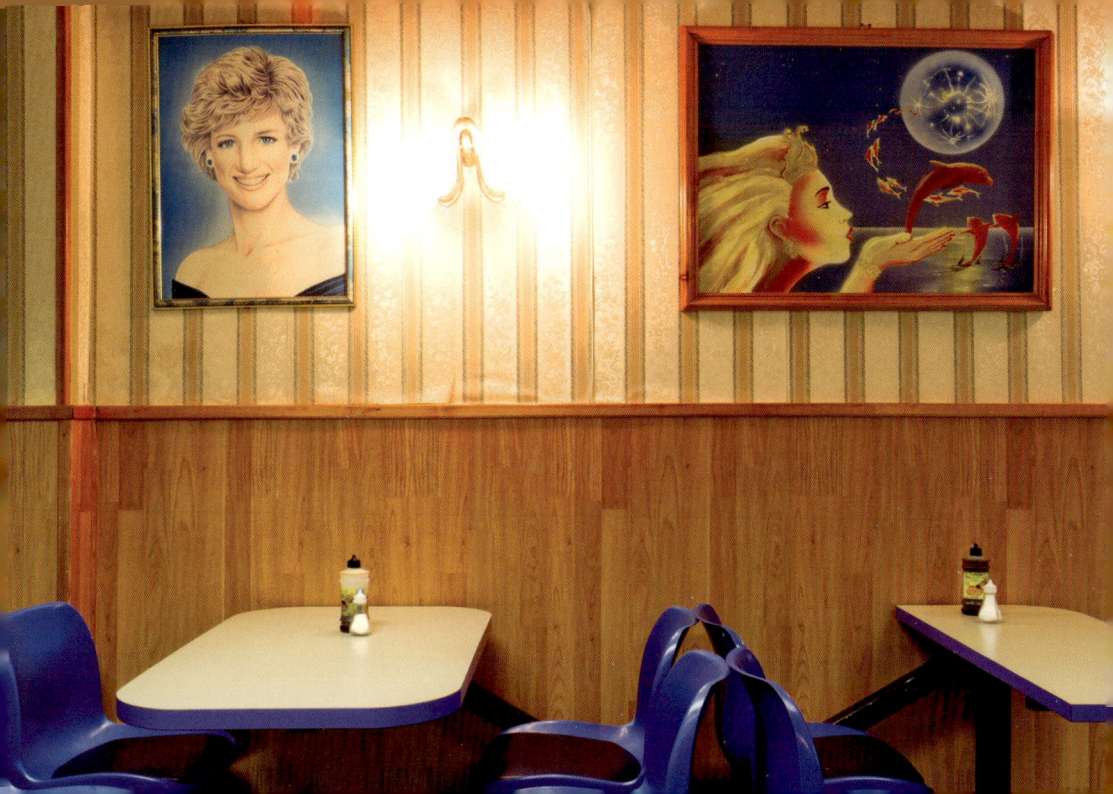

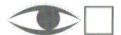
The First Footguards are a locally-based historical re-enactment group, who portray the footguards as they were in 1815, now renamed – after the Battle of Waterloo – the Grenadier Guards.

We provide a full living history camp and take part in battle re-enactments of the period, both in the UK and in Europe. The unit drills are held on the first Sunday of each month unless 'on campaign' and anyone who has a love of this period in history is welcome to come along. For more details of drill venue and times please see the website www.firstfootguards.org. Who knows, you may be tempted to take the King's shilling and join the regiment.

We love to take part in local events such as the Hythe Festival and Euromilitaire, which is held at the Leas Cliff Hall. There are many soldiers in the group, which also includes musicians, a regimental surgeon and camp followers.

पहिलो थल सेनाहरु स्थानिय रुपमा पुनर्व्यवस्थि भएका थिए । उनीहरुले सन १८१५ मा सैनिक द्वारा खेलिने कवाजहरु आजपनि हरेक महिनाको पहिलो आईतवार खेलिन्छ ।

EVERYWHERE MEANS SOMETHING TO SOMEONE

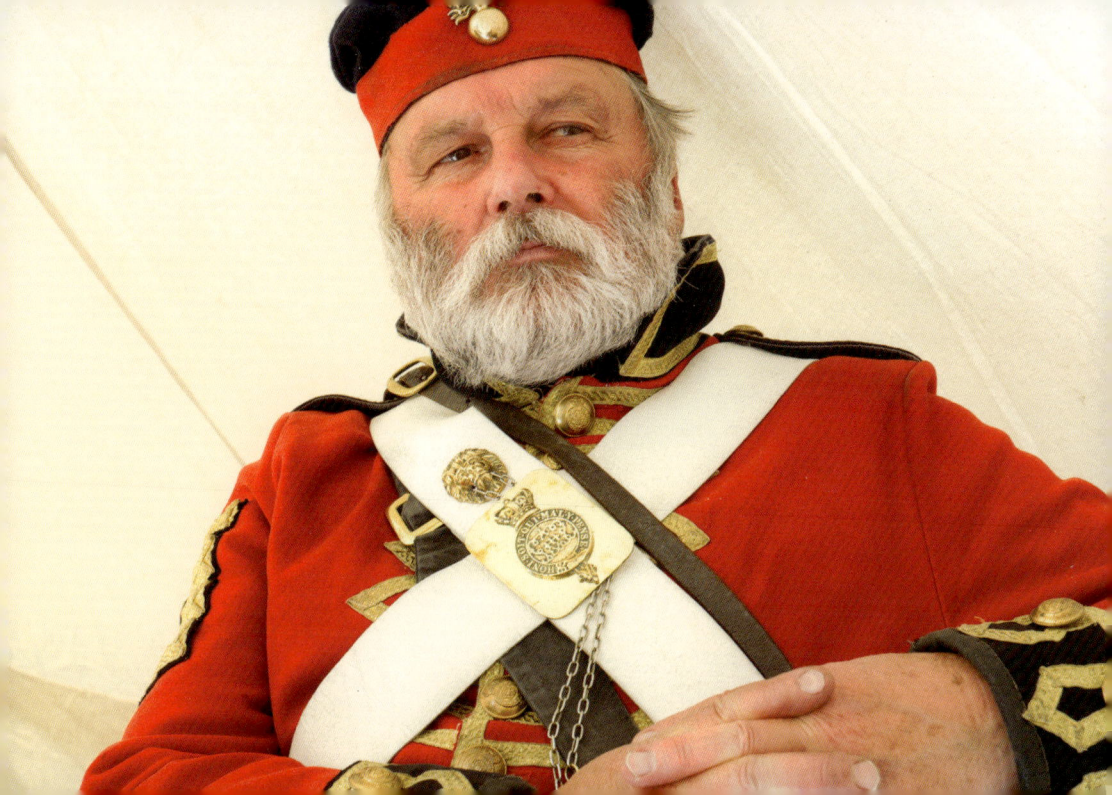

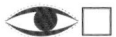

I often wondered about the small figure of the lady in the corner of the Chambers cellar bar – she is downstairs, inside a glass cabinet and she has very real eyes that seem to be watching you wherever you sit. Apparently when the staff take food orders, the table beside the cabinet is always referred to as 'the scary lady table'. I recently found out that she had been made some years ago for an exhibition about carnival, and has been living in the pub ever since. She is based on the figure that appears in German artist Max Beckmann's painting *Carnival* and is of his friend Fridel Battenberg in fancy dress to celebrate the end of the carnival season. The Chambers has lots of interesting things like that, plus you can also get great food, real ale and regular live music – top visit!

Chambers को एक कुनामा हेर्दा महिलाको सानो स्वरुप देखिन्छ जस्को आखा हेर्दा साच्चे सजिव जस्ते लाग्दछ । यो स्वरुप प्रदर्शनीको लागि केही वर्ष अगाडि बनाईएको थियो र त्यसपछि यसलाई पवमा सधैको लागि राखिएको हो ।

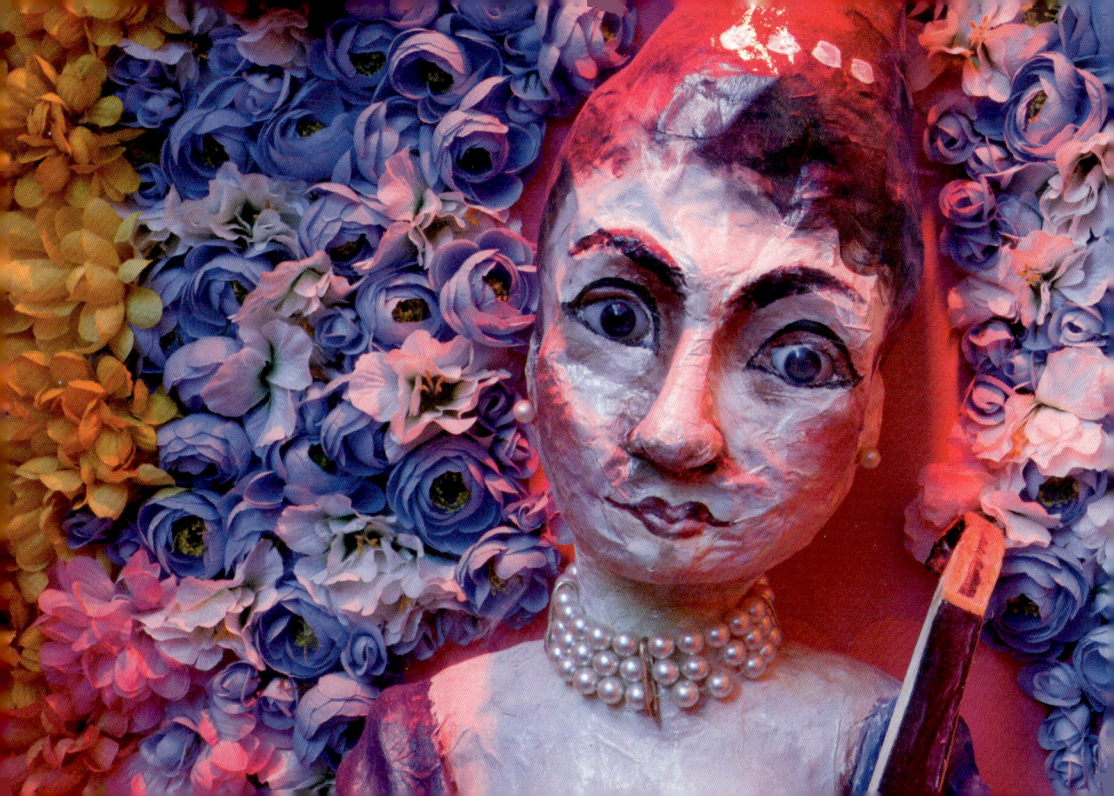

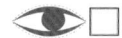

A Nepali theme park is located in Cheriton Park where Nepalese games Bag Chal (tiger movements) and Tap tape (draught, similar to chess game) can be played on the picnic bench. There is also a model of the Mountain Everest.

चेरिटनको पार्कमा एउटा नेपाली पार्क बनाईएको छ । त्यहा picnic bench मा नेपाली खेल वागचाल र Tap-Tape खेल्न सकिन्छ । उक्त स्थानमा नेपालमा अवस्थित सवोच्च शिखर सगरमाथाको नमुना पनि देख्न सकिन्छ ।

EVERYWHERE MEANS SOMETHING TO SOMEONE

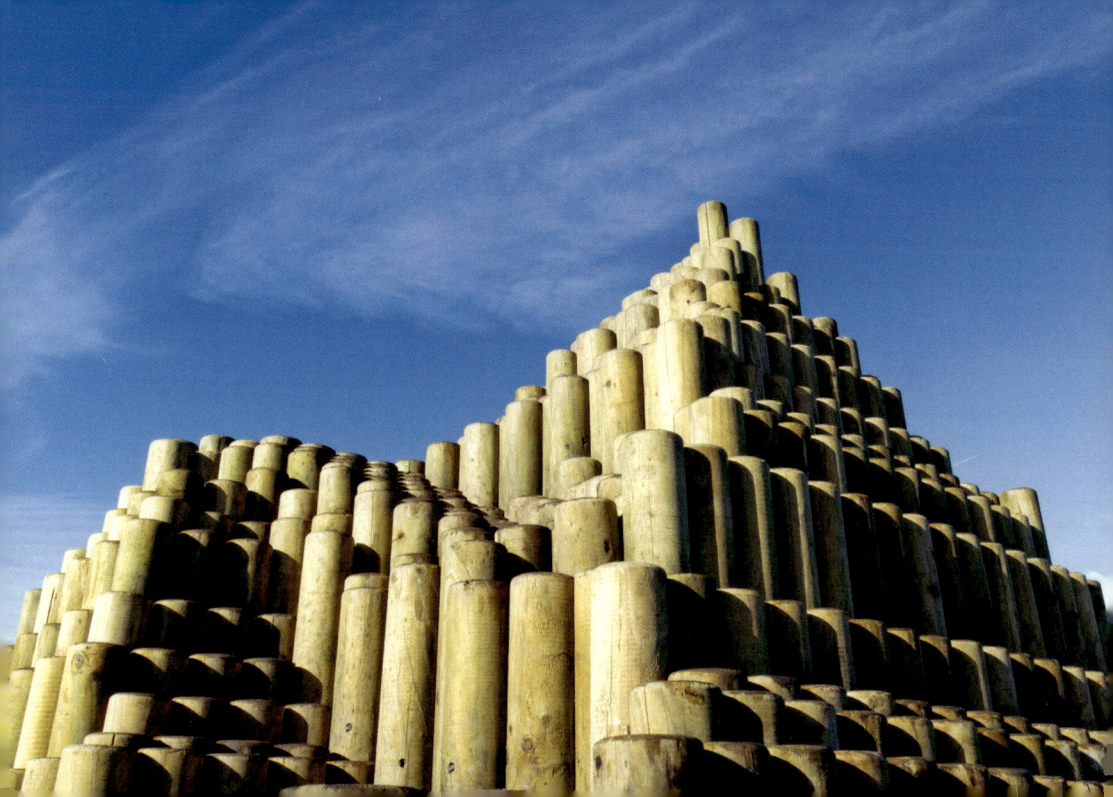

When I stand on the platform my mind goes back to the 1940s and 50s when we would wait with excitement for the train to take us to London for the Festival of Britain, and later, The Coronation. The station was called Shorncliffe in those days and was much more attractive than now; it was double the present size with wood canopies all round.

I was at Morehall School in 1951 and it went round school that they were making a film, *Lady Godiva Rides Again,* at the station. In our lunch break we went to see the filming; various starlets who were playing beauty queens were arriving by train. Among them were Diana Dors, a very young Joan Collins and, although we did not know it then, the last woman to be hung, Ruth Ellis.

Shorncliffe was the station I went from with trepidation to do my National Service. The date was 4 December 1957, the morning after the Lewisham train crash in which many Folkestone people were killed and injured.

सन १९५० को दशकमा यो स्टेशनलाई सोर्नक्लिफ भनिन्थ्यो । यो स्टेशन त्यतिवेला वरिपरि काठले छोपिएको, दोब्बर ठूलो र अहिलेको भन्दा धेरै आकर्षक थियो ।

EVERYWHERE MEANS SOMETHING TO SOMEONE

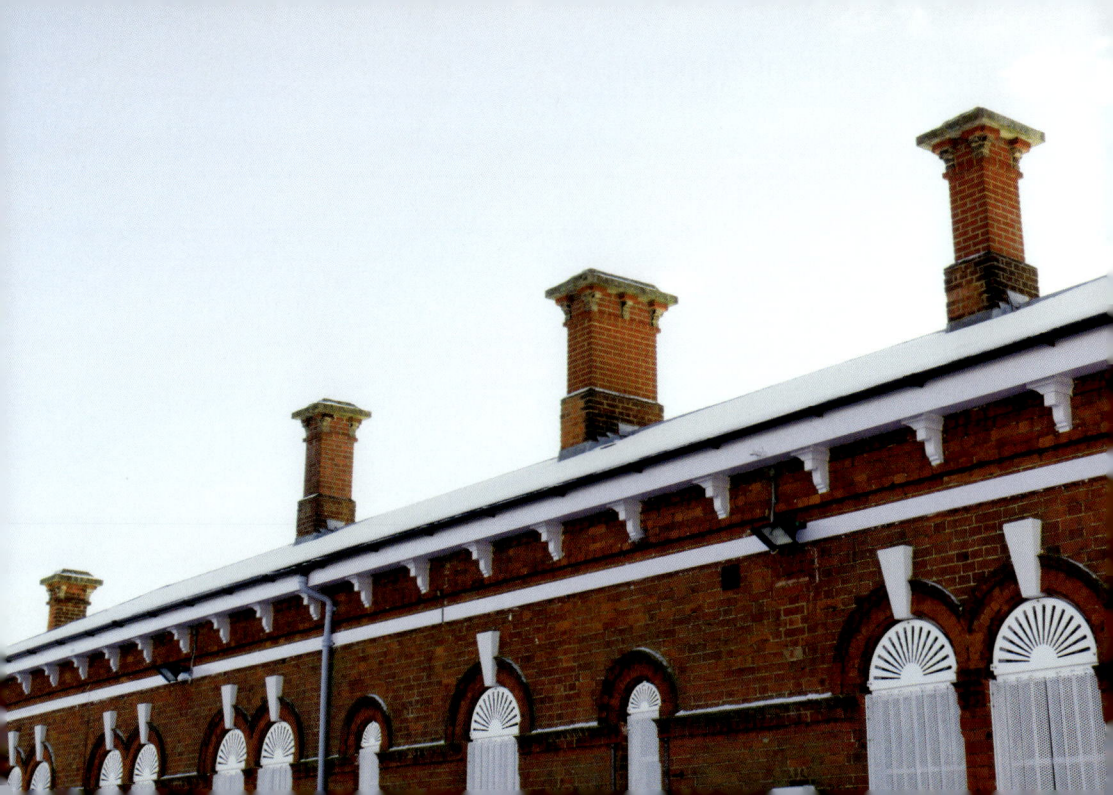

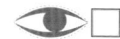

On the seafront at Sandgate is a small piece of wall, the last remnant of the Victorian Alhambra Music Hall, locally called 'the Bricks'. Evidently the clientele were pretty rough, consisting of the Military from Shorncliffe and local fishermen. The building later became The Rex Cinema. When there was a storm at high tide, the screen on the back wall would vibrate! After the war the cinema was incorporated into Rayner's Beach Club. I was then a member of 18+, a very successful local young people's group. One of our members was part of the Rayner family, so we had many a good night at the club. Rayners was demolished in the 1970s and the present flats built on the site.

को सामुन्द्रिक किनारमा पर्खालको एउटा सानो भाग छ । यो पर्खाल Victorian Alhambra Music Hall को अन्तिम अवशेष हो । यो हल सिपाहीहरु र स्थानिय मच्छ्य सीकारिहरुले प्रयोग गर्ने गर्दथे ।

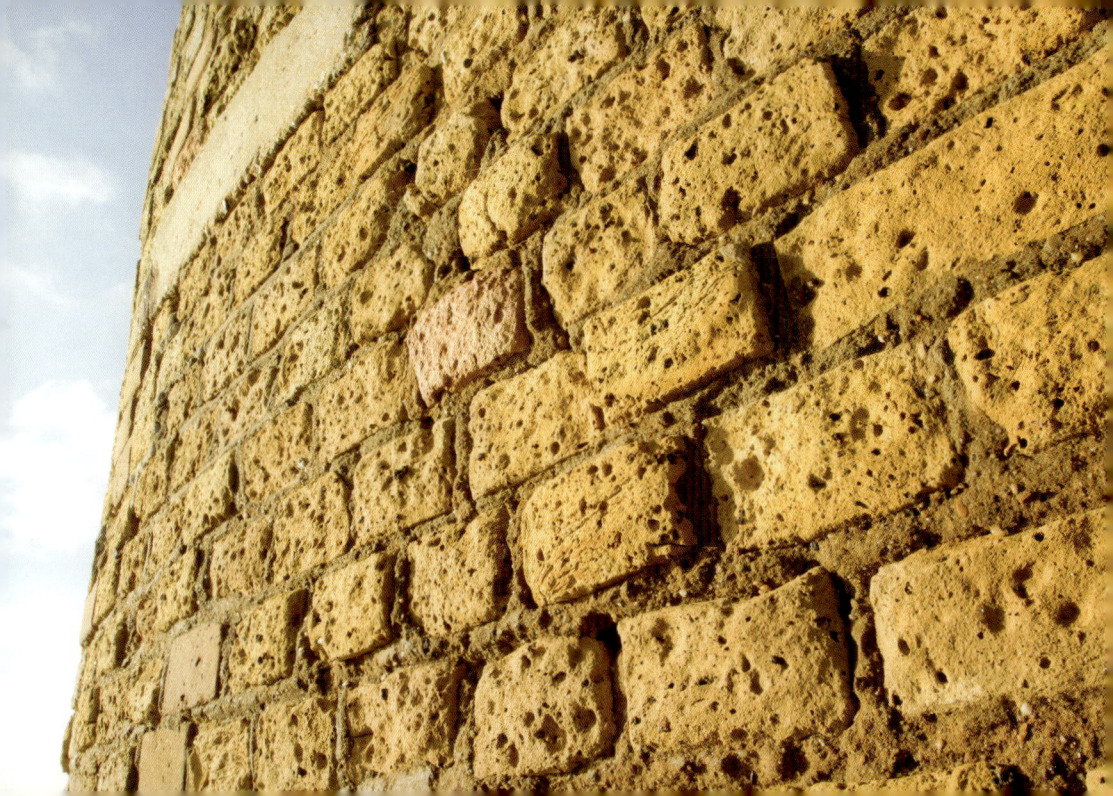

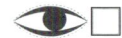

If you want to wander a bit further during your visit, the Romney, Hythe and Dymchurch small gauge steam railway is not to be missed. It is known locally as the Light Railway and there is a station in Hythe where you can board this wonderful miniature train and travel the 13.5 miles around the bay to Dungeness on Romney Marsh. It's absolutely brilliant; there are request stops along the way, a bit like bus stops, but beside the track. Several of the locomotives include buffet cars in their rolling stock, and the main stations at Hythe, Lydd and Dungeness have cafés. The railway has been open since 1929 and was famous for being the 'smallest public railway in the world'. Following its wartime service it was reopened to the public by Laurel and Hardy and has been running ever since. A little bit of local history not to be missed. www.rhdr.org.uk

For an extra special treat, the great model railway – including dinosaurs – upstairs at New Romney station is highly recommended!

The Romney, Hythe र Dymchurch मा बाफले चल्ने रेलगाडी देख्न सकिन्छ । हाईथमा एउटा स्टेशन छ, जहाँबाट यो र माईलो रेल चढेर १३.५ माईल टाढा रहेको Dungeness on Romney Marsh को यात्रा गर्न सकिन्छ ।

Follow the A259 through Sandgate and into the town of Hythe. Drive through Hythe to a set of traffic lights; turn right towards the Canal and the Station's on your left.

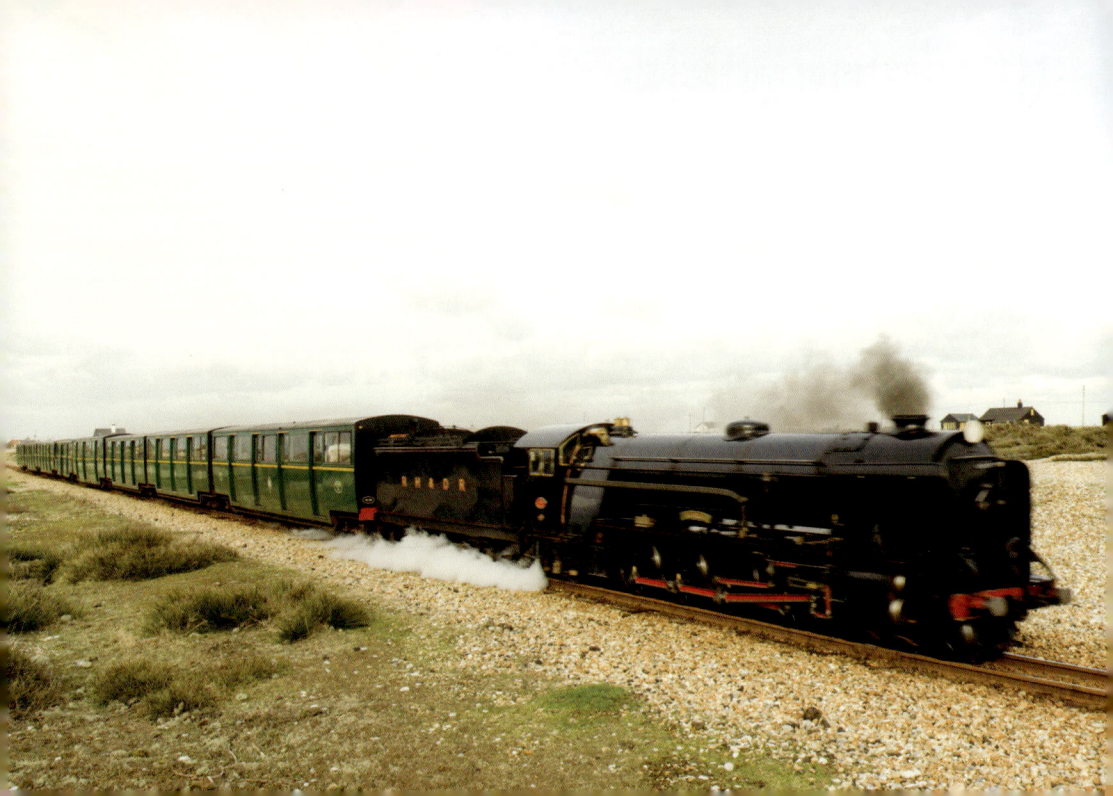

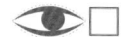

If you get fed up with the film you are watching in one of the auditoriums at the Silver Screen cinema in Sandgate Road, you can always entertain yourself reading the names of Folkestone's past mayors which are written on the back wall. This is one of the remnants of the building's old Town Hall days, and snippet of the town's long history.

यो चलचित्र घर फोक्सटनको वजारमा थियो र यसको पछाडी पट्टीको भित्तामा सम्पूर्ण पुर्व मेयरहरुको नाम स्वर्ण अक्षरले लेखिएको थियो ।

1885-6.	JOHN BANKS
1886-7.	JOHN SHERWOOD
1887-8.	JAMES PLEDGE
1888-9.	STEPHEN PENFOLD
1889-90.	JOHN HOLDEN
1890-1.	GEORGE SPURGEN
1891-2.	STEPHEN PENFOLD
1892-3.	JOHN BANKS
1893-4.	THOS. J. VAUGHAN
1894-5.	STEPHEN PENFOLD
1895-6.	GEORGE SPURGEN
1896-7.	JOHN BANKS
1897-8.	STEPHEN PENFOLD
1898-9.	WILLIAM SALTER
1899-1900.	W. C. CARPENTER
1900-1.	DANIEL BAKER
1901-2.	THE Rt. HON. THE EARL OF RADNOR

1928-9.	ALBERT CASTLE
1929-30.	
1930-31.	JOHN WARD STAINER
1931-32.	
1932-33.	
1933-34.	ALBERT CASTLE
1934-35.	RICHARD WHITE
1935-36.	
1936-37.	ALBERT CASTLE
1937-38.	
1938-39.	GEO. ALBERT GURR
1939-40.	
1940-41.	Died by enemy action
1941	JOSEPH SEYMOUR GURR
1941-42.	ALBERT CASTLE
1942-43.	

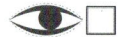

Boxing Day is my birthday and I always feel strangely compelled to do fairly daft things to mark the occasion. I'm not a regular Boxing Day Dipper because, if I'm in Folkestone for Christmas, I like to do the annual Saltwood cross country run, which unfortunately usually clashes with the Dip. But I have done it a few times. A couple of years ago some friends and I invented the Folkestone Crap Triathlon. We did the run up at Saltwood, cycled the five miles down to Sunny Sands and threw ourselves into the sea. Lovely! We rounded it off with a pint or two of Guinness in the Royal George. Magic!

बक्सिङ डे को दिन मेरो जन्मदिवशमा साथि र म विहानै साईकलमा चढेर Saltwood हुँदै पाँच माइल तल घमाईलो वगर तिर गयौं र समुन्द्रमा हाम फाल्यौं । हामीले त्यहाँ चक्कर लगाए पछि भट्टीमा एकदुई पाइन्ट वियर पियौं । रमाईलो भयो ।

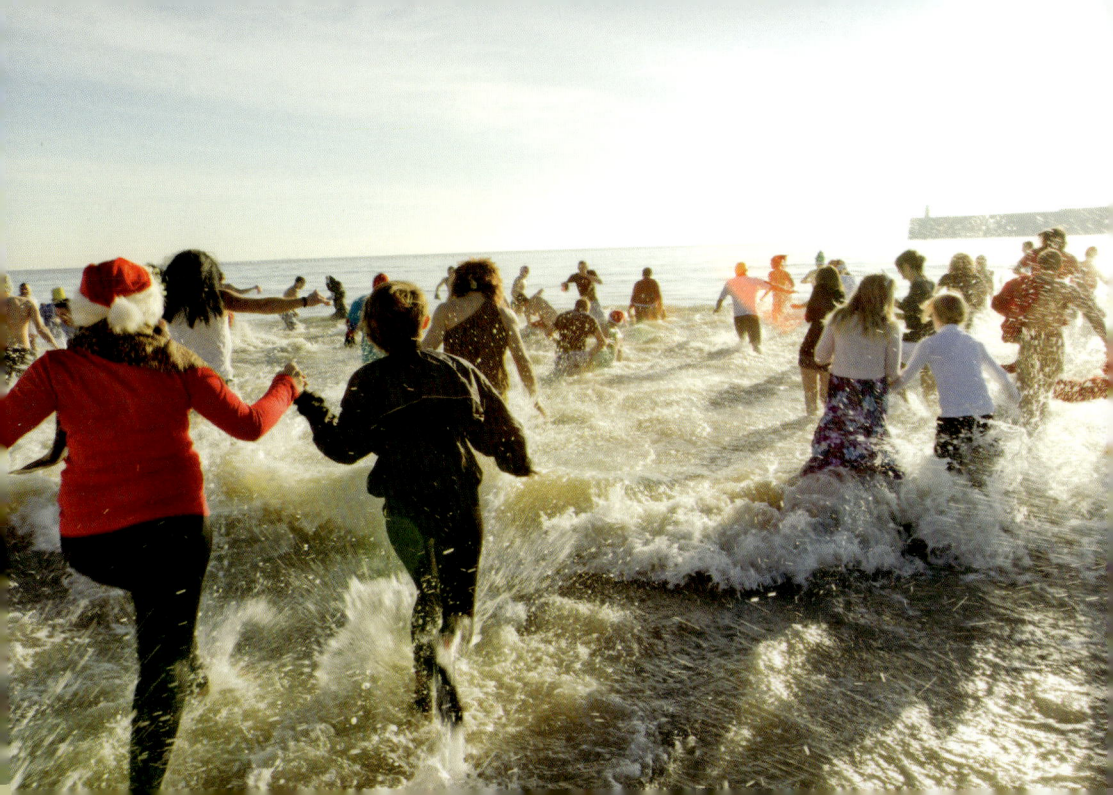

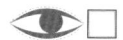

My husband's grandmother ran the corner shop on the corner of Canterbury Road and Green Lane from 1870; it is now a Chinese takeaway. There was a lot of poverty in the town (no social services) – if you didn't work you didn't eat! She saw lots of big families unable to cope. This was when she started her business. She bought rags from people, paying 1d or 2d for a bag of rag, which she bundled up into large quantities and sold on. The business expanded and they started taking other materials like metal, paper, rubber, rabbit skins, bones, and glass, including jam jars. I suppose it was the first kind of recycling! Jam jars were bought for 1/2d for a 1lb jar or 1d for a 2lb jar. These were very much sought after during the war years, as we were often given a tray of jam, which was very acceptable, as it was natural. When I was a little girl this place was like a magical hatch that opened and a hand popped out and just gave people money, like a cash machine! When the buses got to that stop they used to call out, "Anyone for Jam Jar Alley?"

मेरो श्रीमानको हजुर आमाले क्यान्टबरी रोड र ग्रिन लेनको विचमा सन १८७० देखी एउटा दोकान चलाउथ्यो, जहा आजभोली चाईनिज Takeaway छ । त्यस समयमा धेरै गरीव मानिसहरु सहरमा वस्ने भएकोले काम नगरेमा खान पनि पाउदैनथ्ये। उनले विभिन्न प्रकारका सरसमान उदाहरणको लागी धातु, कागज तथा वक वबच हरुको पुन रपान्तरण गरेर वेच्ने गर्थ्ये । म स्यानो छदा त्यहा एउटा ढोका थियो । त्यो भित्रबाट हात निकालेर मानिसहरुलाई पैसा दिईन्थ्यो । गाडीहरु त्यो स्टेशनमा पुग्दा "Anyone for Jam Jar Alley!" भन्ने गरिन्थ्यो

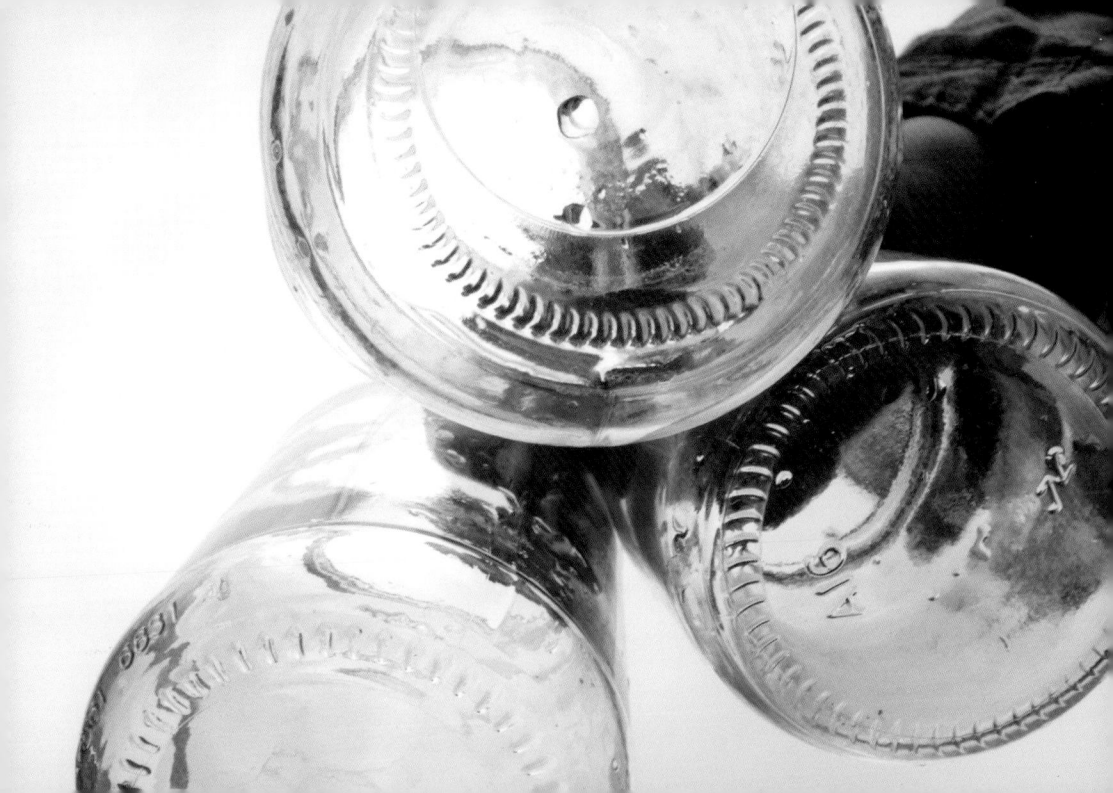

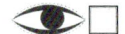

She is made from sheets and recycled building materials. Although not complete and suffering from frostbite in places, I hope to complete and make repairs when the weather gets warmer. The motivation for making the statue came from the Panasonic camera advert where she dances.

यो मूर्ती कपडा र भवनमा प्रयोग गरिएका सामग्रीहरुबाट बनाईएको हो । अझै यो पुरा वनी सकेको छैन । मलाई आशा छ, मौसम न्यानो भएपछि यसको उचित मर्मत भई निर्माण पुरा हुने छ । यो मुर्ति बनाउनमा पानासोनिक क्यामेराको विज्ञापनमा नाचेको दृश्यले प्रेरणा मिलेको हो ।

EVERYWHERE MEANS SOMETHING TO SOMEONE

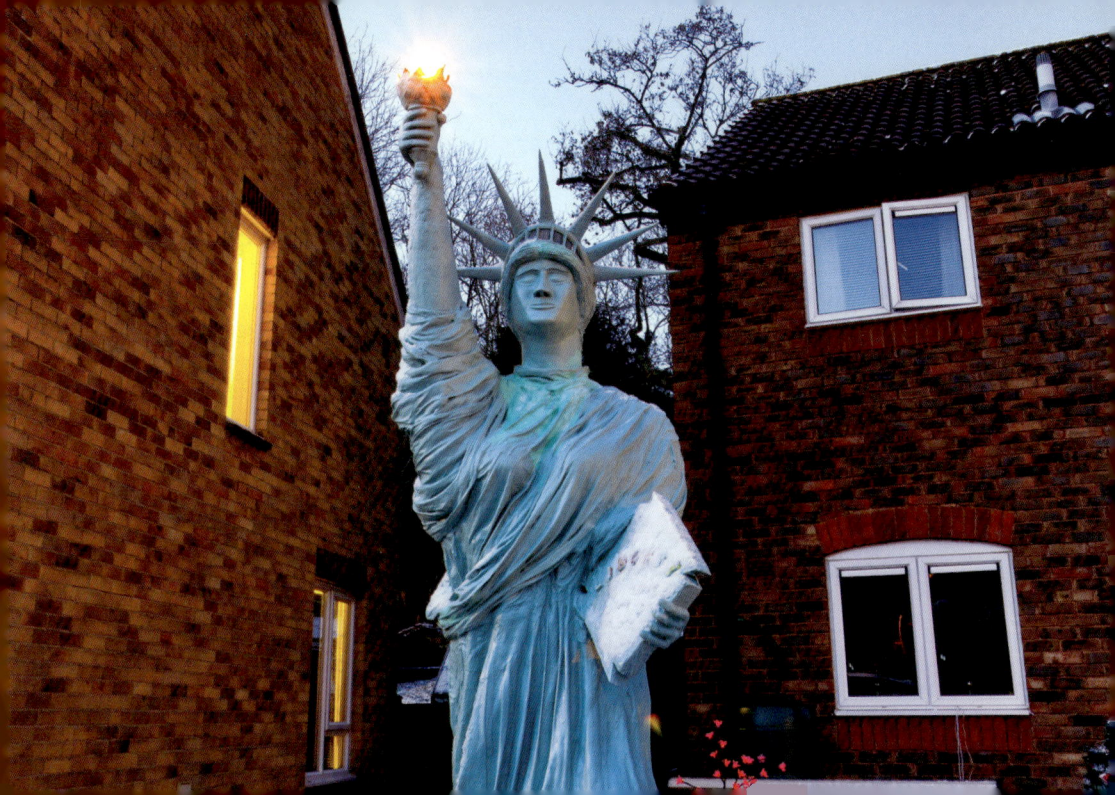

Perched above Sandgate, overgrown and all but forgotten, lies Shorncliffe Redoubt. Originally a substantial earthwork fort, the remains of two of the walls can still be seen and, from them, a view across the English Channel to the coast of France. Built at the end of the eighteenth century, the Redoubt was crucial during the Napoleonic Wars in defending he Kent coast from the anticipated invasion by French forces. In 1802, General John Moore took command of the defence of Kent, and this is where he set about creating an elite brigade of soldiers, the Light Infantry. On the land around the Redoubt the men trained to such exacting standards that the methods introduced by Moore are still used by today's British Army. Although Moore died in battle in 1809, his men played a central part in the ultimate defeat of Napoleon at Waterloo in 1815. Today, there is nothing to signify the importance of the site, whereas, in Boulogne, where Napoleon amassed 200,000 troops for the invasion of England – an invasion which never took place – there is a tall column set in a formal park with a museum. Perhaps it is time that a similar memorial should be erected at Shorncliffe Redoubt.

सन १८०२ मा यस ठाउँमा General John Moore ले उच्च वर्गका सिपाहीहरुलाई सरल तरकाले तालिम गराउँथे । यो विधीलाई आज पनि वेलायती सेनाहरुले प्रयोग गर्नें गर्दछन् ।

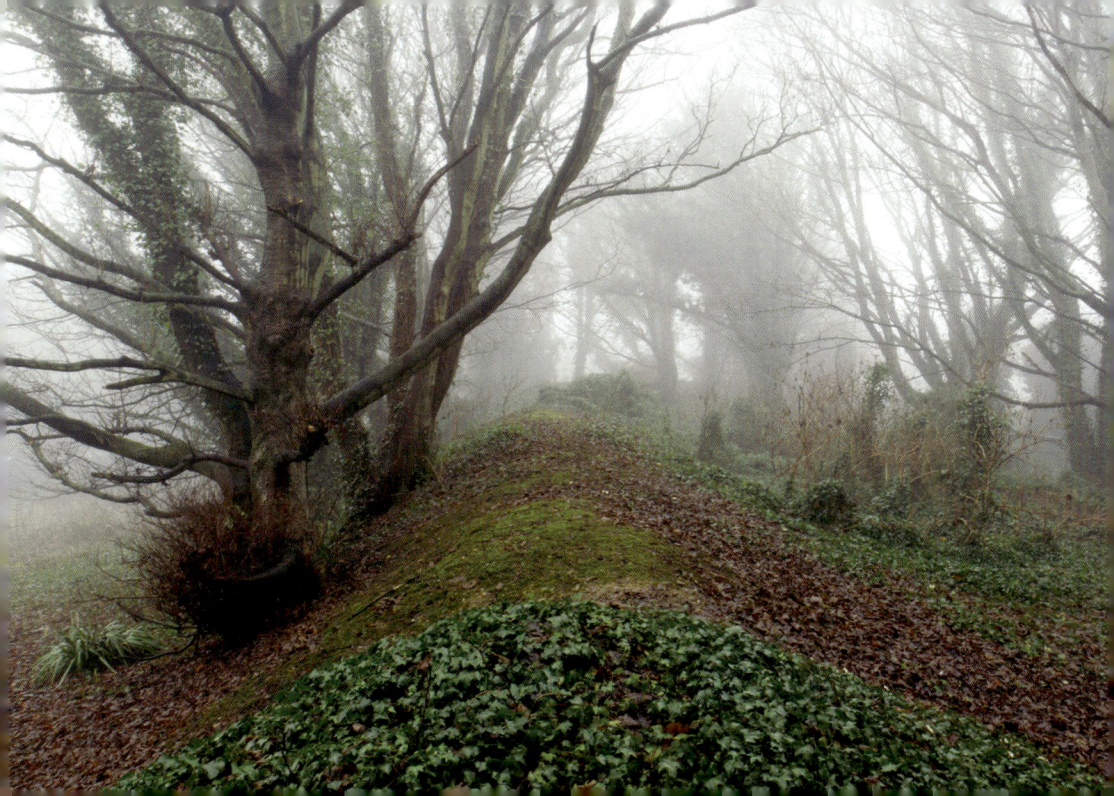

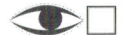

There are so many stories about the Grand. Edward VI often met his mistress Alice Keppel there, who is the great great grandmother of The Duchess of Cornwall. The bearded King and his entourage were a familiar sight in the Grand, and onlookers called the glasshouse on the front of the building the Monkey House – the expression *monkey business* was coined at the time, because of the rumoured goings-on inside. Other famous visitors included the Edward VII and Agatha Christie, and the building was used as a military hospital during the war. These days it's a great place to take afternoon tea and enjoy views across the Channel.

दिनमा कफि र केक खादै Channel पारीको दृश्य हेरेर मनोरञ्जन लिन The Grand असाध्यै राम्रो ठाउँ हो ।

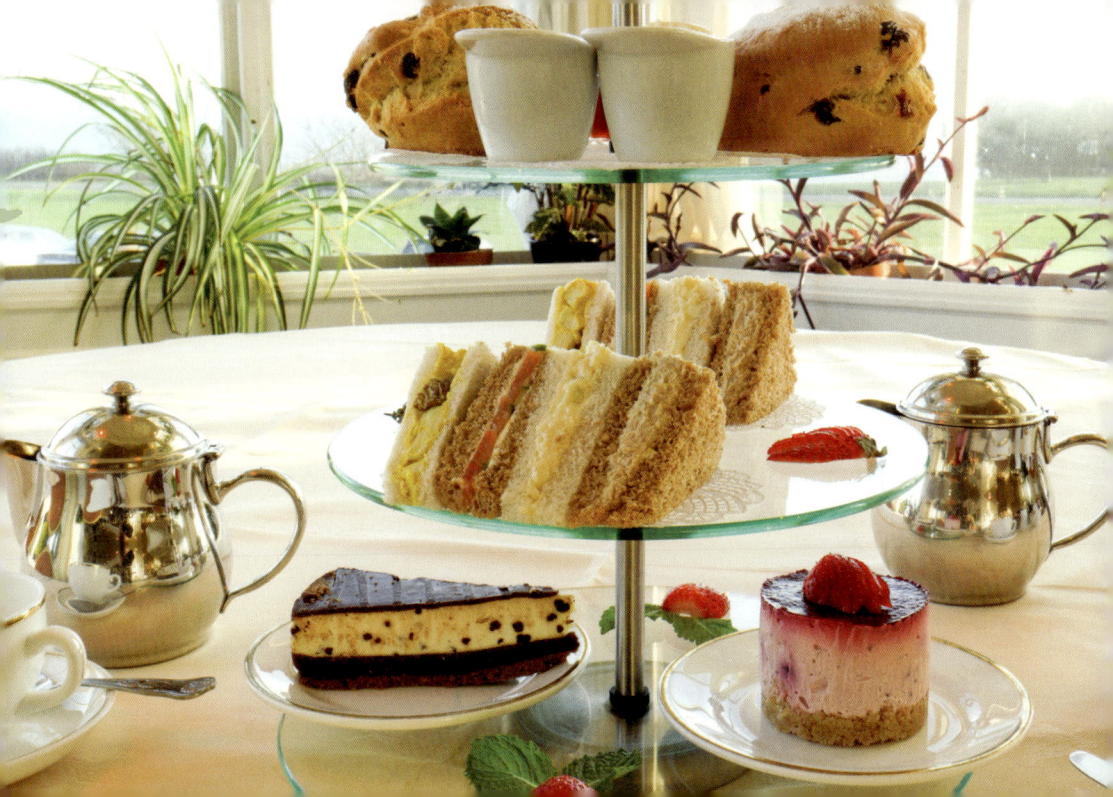

My mother grew up just round the corner from the Cherry Pickers pub in Cheriton. On the weekends when her dad was home from his job in London, my Mum, her parents and her baby sister would pack a picnic and head down to Tile Kiln Lane, past the allotments and into the fields beyond, where there is now the Channel Tunnel, the motorway roundabout and the round hill tunnels. There used to be nothing but fields, hills and a giant sparkling lake. My mother and her family would then wander up the bank and set up their picnic while watching the men try their luck at fishing.

My mother's parents moved down to Cheriton from London many years ago to bring up their family in, what was then, the countryside. Little did they know that the hustle and bustle of city life would soon follow them with its busy roads, fast food restaurants and the gateway to Europe via the Channel Tunnel just round the corner from their old house.

पहिला यहाँ मैदान, पहाड र तलाउ मात्र थियो ।मेरो आमा र उनको परिवार वल्छी खेल्नेहरुलाई हेर्दै यसको किनारमा घुम्ने र वनभोज खाने गर्दथे ।

EVERYWHERE MEANS SOMETHING TO SOMEONE

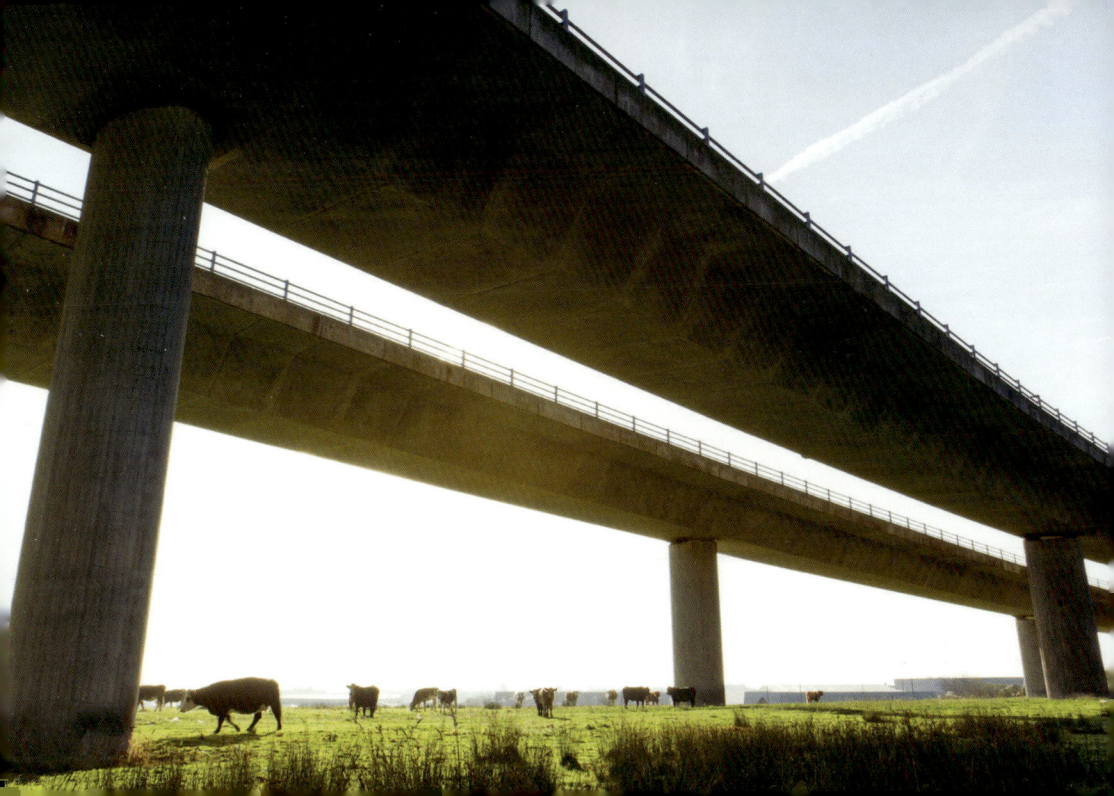

Folkestone Baptist Church was founded in 1750. It was a group of people who believed that baptism into the Christian faith should only be for believers and that the local members should decide how a church should be run, rather than priests and bishops. These doctrines made the Church of England treat Baptists as though they were heretics and so they were not allowed to be buried with 'normal' people. The Baptists met in the parlour of Mr Stace, the miller, and members were buried in his back garden. Over time, the ground around Mr Stace's garden was cut away to construct New Street and Bradstone Road, leaving the Baptist Burial ground twenty feet above ground. By the 1850s, there was a rapprochement between the churches and everyone was able to be buried in state cemeteries. The last burial in the Bradstone Road burial ground was in 1855. A local story suggests the graveyard was for viaduct workers who died of cholera. Quite a lot of them were children. Some of the gravestones mention cholera and bear a skull and cross-bones.

यो पुरानो चिहान घारी स्थानिय Baptist धर्मावलम्बिहरुको लागि थियो । वेलायतको गिर्जाघरले क्रिश्चनहरुको चिहान घारीमा उनीहरुको लास गाड्न दिदैन थियो । त्यसैले यो जमिन चिहान घारीको रुपमा प्रयोग गरियो जुन वास्तवमा यो स्थानिय व्यवसायि Mr. Stace को घर पछाडिको बँगैचा थियो ।

EVERYWHERE MEANS SOMETHING TO SOMEONE

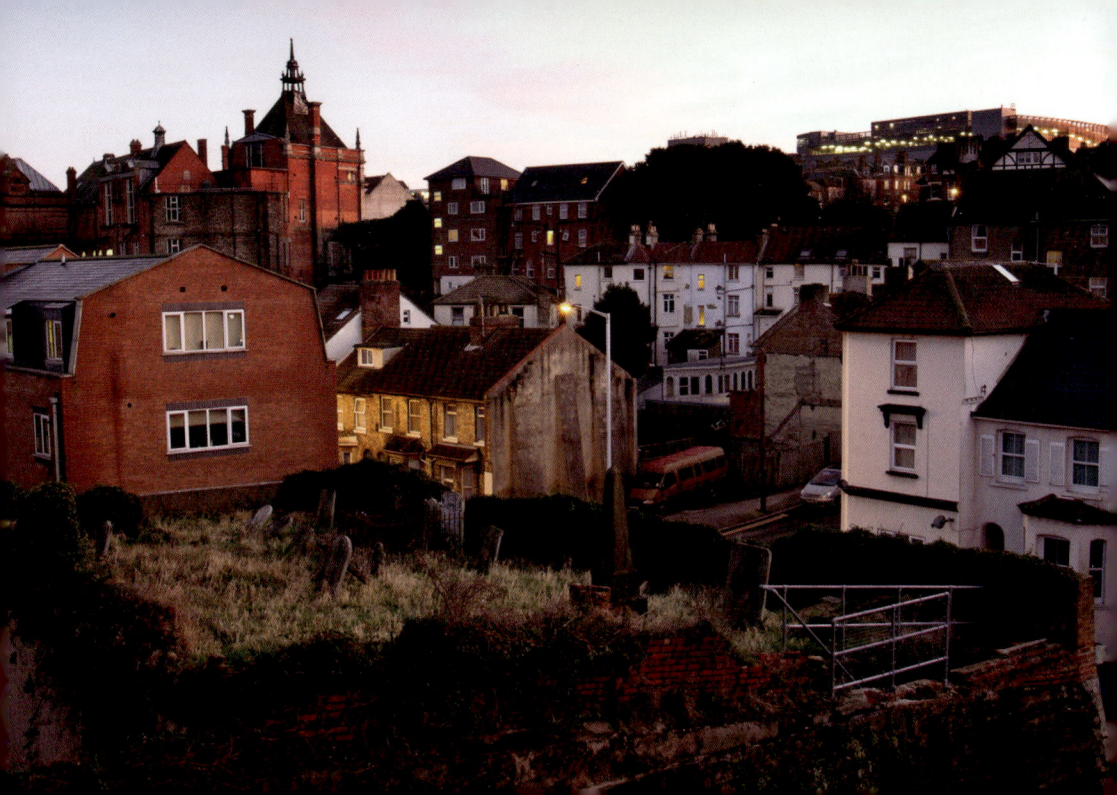

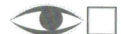

The Visitor Centre is a branch of the Gurkha Museum. Displayed items in the Centre are about the history of the Gurkhas and their service to the British Crown. The main Gurkha Museum is located in Winchester town.

यो विन्चेस्टरमा भएको गोर्खालीको संग्राहालयको एउटा शाखा मात्र हो । यसमा संरक्षण गरिएको सम्पूर्ण सामानहरुले गोर्खाली सेनाले वेलायति सरकार प्रति पु-याएको सेवाको बारेमा जानकारी दिन्छ । गोर्खालीको मुख्य संग्राहालय चाही विन्चेस्टर शहर मा छ ।

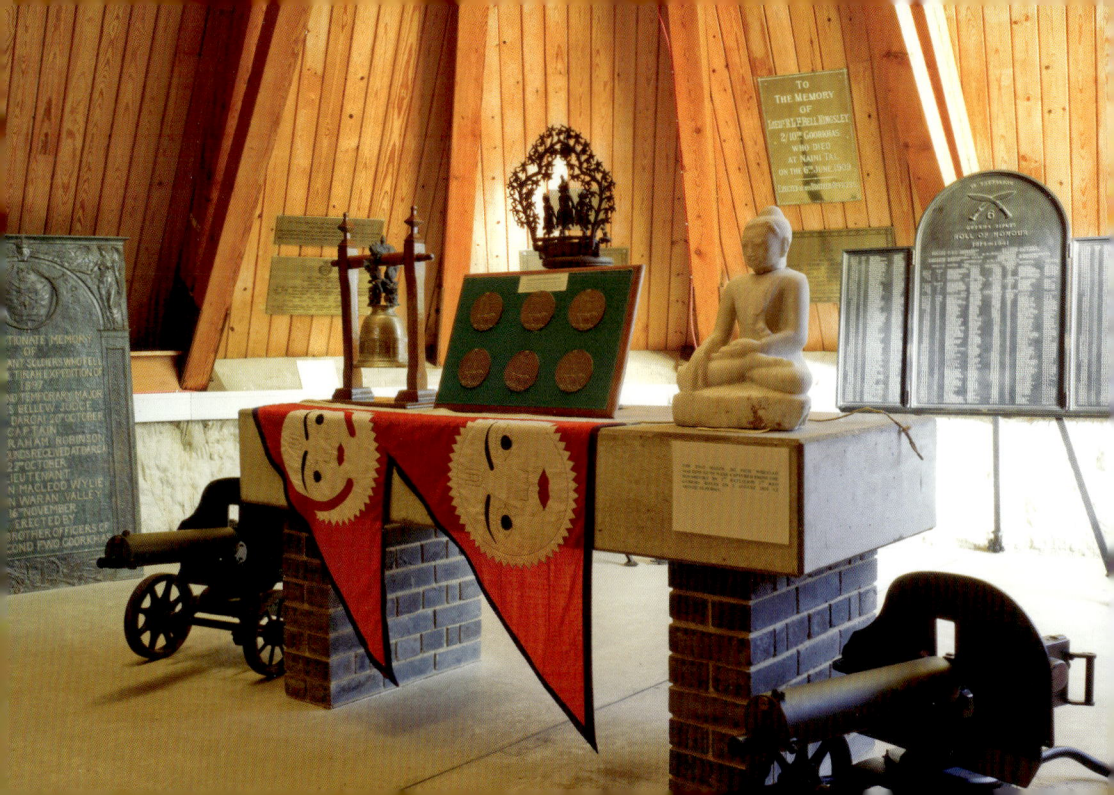

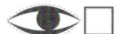

There are two sights that I look forward to seeing every day on my way to work in Folkestone. The first is the sky over the Channel that I see as I drive down Canterbury Road, it is always surprising and always breathtaking. The second is the window at number 13, The Bayle. This is the smallest and most beautiful gallery in Folkestone and has a window full of creations, the like of which you will never have seen. It's hard to have a favourite, but I loved the Passed Pussies exhibition with real cats' whiskers, and the Action Man real ale pub, with an actual working fire! It is always changing and always clever and beautiful.

The Bayle चाही फोकस्टनमा भएको मध्य सबै भन्दा स्यानो र सुन्दर संग्राहलय हो । यो १३ नम्बरको भ्याल अत्यन्त उत्कृष्ट नमुना हो, यस्तो सायदै तपाईले देख्नु भको होला ।

EVERYWHERE MEANS SOMETHING TO SOMEONE

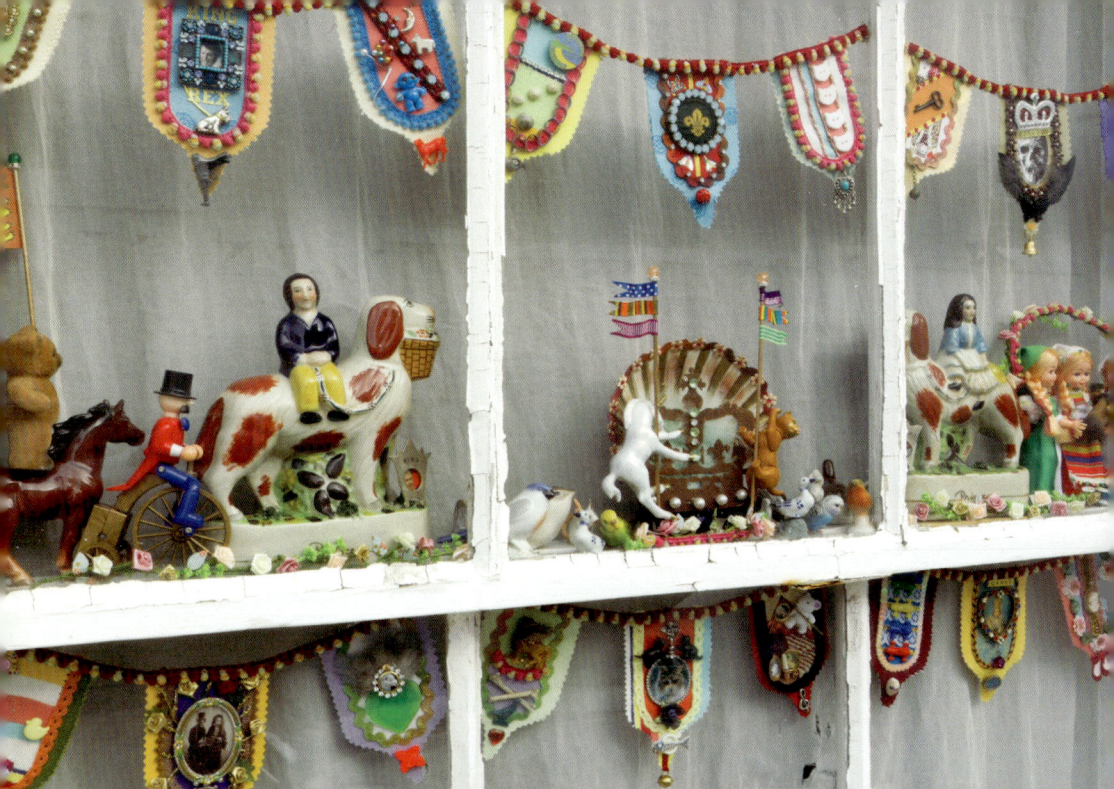

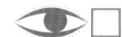

This gallery has been here for years and is a great place for people to visit. The exhibitions change regularly, so you are never sure what you will see, as there can be paintings one week, an installation the next and film or performance shortly afterwards. Quite often you will find the artist in the gallery, which means you can have a chat and find out more about them and their work. I know lots of artists who have shown there and they all love its quirky proportions, big windows and open space. A must for anyone who likes a gallery visit.

यो संग्रालय यहां वर्षौं देखी छ र यो घुम्नको लागी असल ठाउ हो । यहां भएको चित्रहरु बारम्बार परिवर्तन भइरहन्छन । प्राय यहा सधै रङ्गकर्मिहरु आउने भएकोले तिनीहरु संग कुरागर्न पनि सक्नुहुनेछ ।

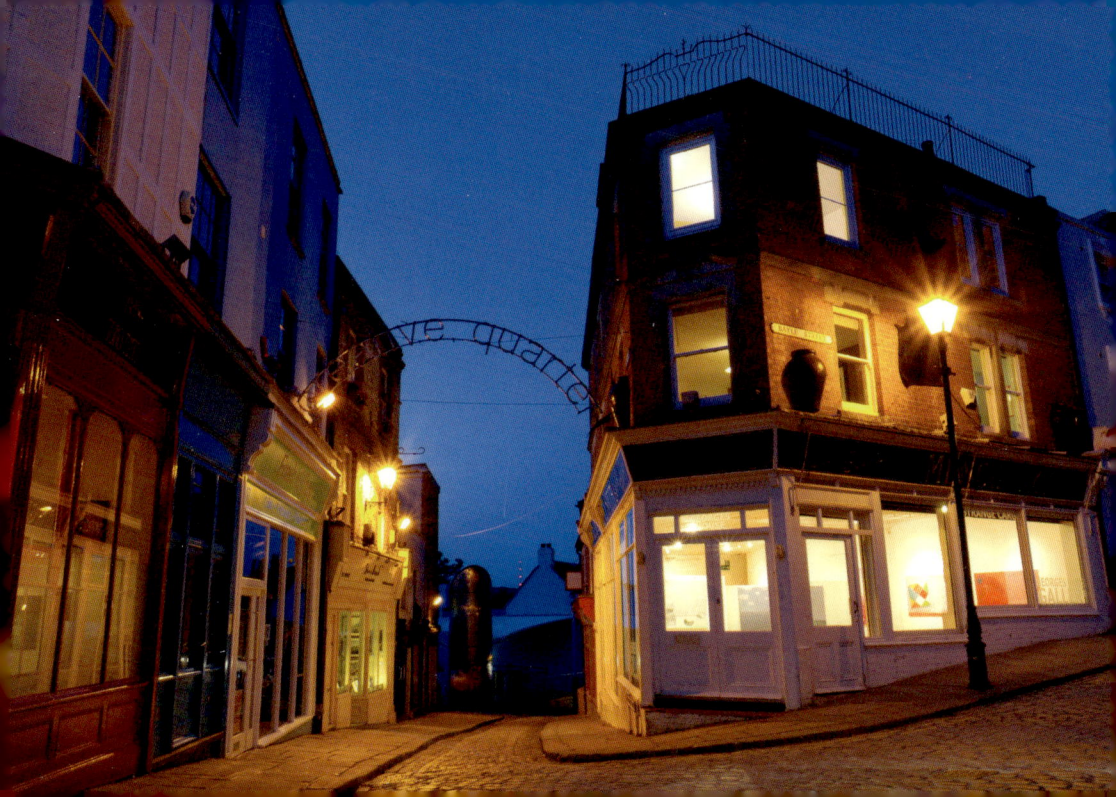

The Folkestone Channel Rotary Club organises Santa's Giant Charity Fun Run every Christmas through the streets of Folkestone, starting in the pedestrian precinct on Sandgate Road. In its first seven years it has already raised over £70,000 for charities and good causes. Even in Siberian winter weather conditions over 500 Santas usually register to take part. The Santas come from all corners of the globe – from China and Hong Kong to the Czech Republic and Nepal. It's becoming a great local tradition.

प्रत्येक वर्ष क्रिसमसको समयमा फोक्सटनको सहरमा Channel Rotary Club ले Santa Fun Run को आयोजना गर्दछ । हाल सम्ममा यसले ७० हजार पैण्ड सहयोग रकम संकलन गरिसकेको छ र यो एउटा परम्परा चएको छ फोक्सटनको लागी ।

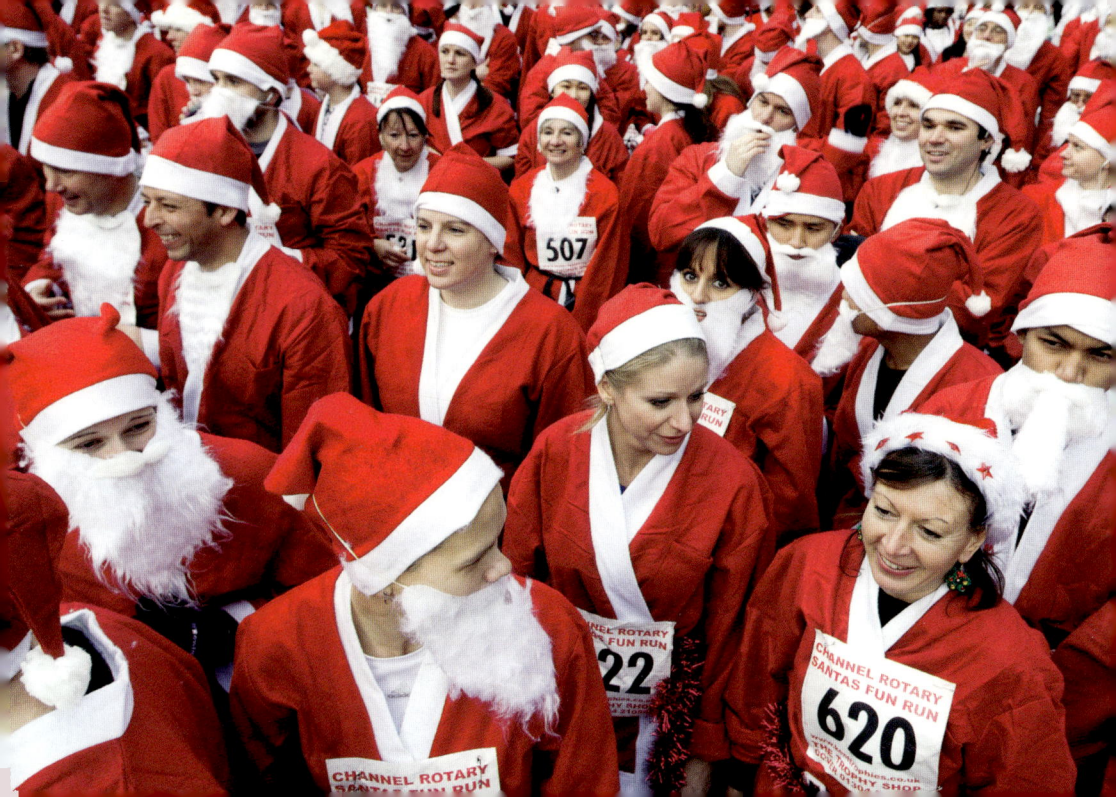

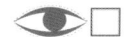

There's a place off the Zig Zag Path, leading down to the Coastal Park, which always stirs a lovely memory for me. When my two children Vanessa and Christopher were young, we came up with a special Christmas present for their father, which was to create a storybook featuring the two of them, together with pictures. The story was called *Bearnapped* and it told the tale of the kidnapping of their treasured teddies. The storyline included footprint clues that led the reader from our home in Coolinge Lane to The Leas and down the Zig Zag Path. There, in a concrete structure which was a resting place and sea viewing point (now just an uncovered flat area), the children confronted the bearnapper – who was none other than our friend Gabrielle, who was forced to 'put 'em up' and hand over the teddies! Her reason for taking the toys? She had been worried that the children loved their teddies more than her, which was nonsense and everyone was happy to be together again and, of course, everyone lived happily ever after!

जब मेरा दुई छोराछोरीहरु युवा अवस्थामा थिए, हामीले उनीहरुका बाबाको लागी एउटा कथाको किताब बनाएका थियौ । यो कथामा फोक्सटनको हाम्रो घर देखि पैदल यात्रा गर्दै घुम्ति बाटोसम्म पुग्दा नानीहरुका हराएका खेलौनाहरु भेटिन्छ । यो एउटा खुशीको कथा हो ।

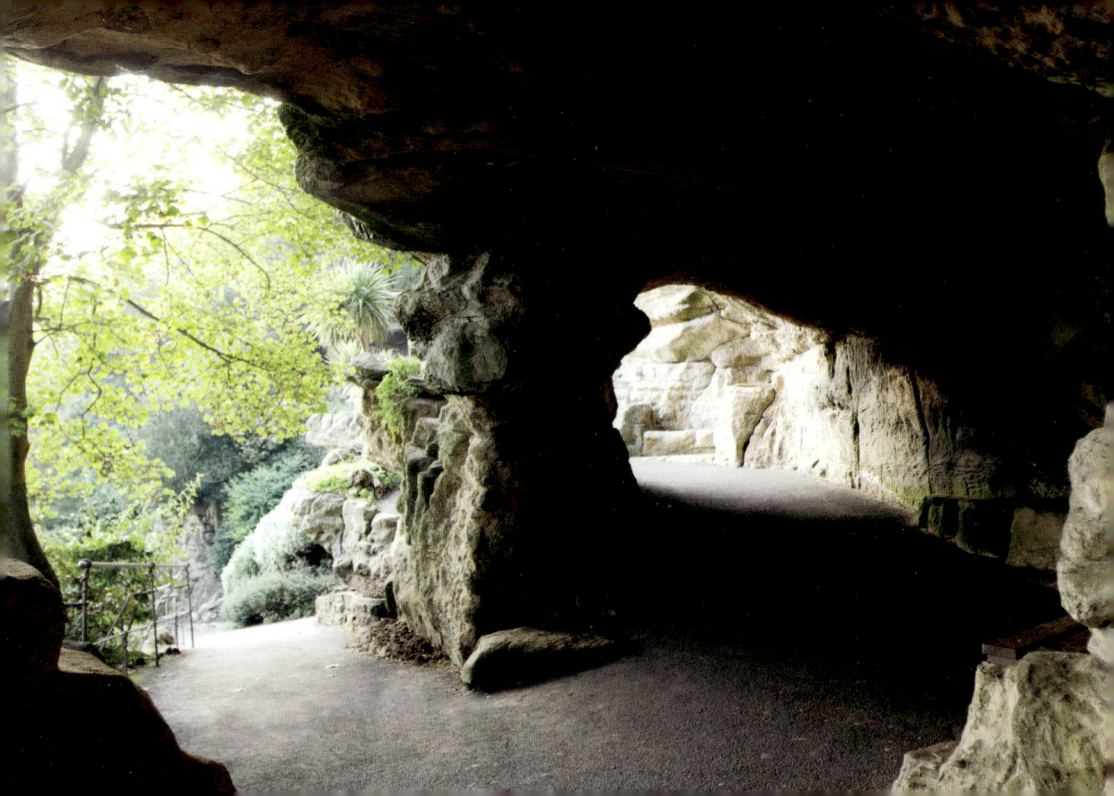

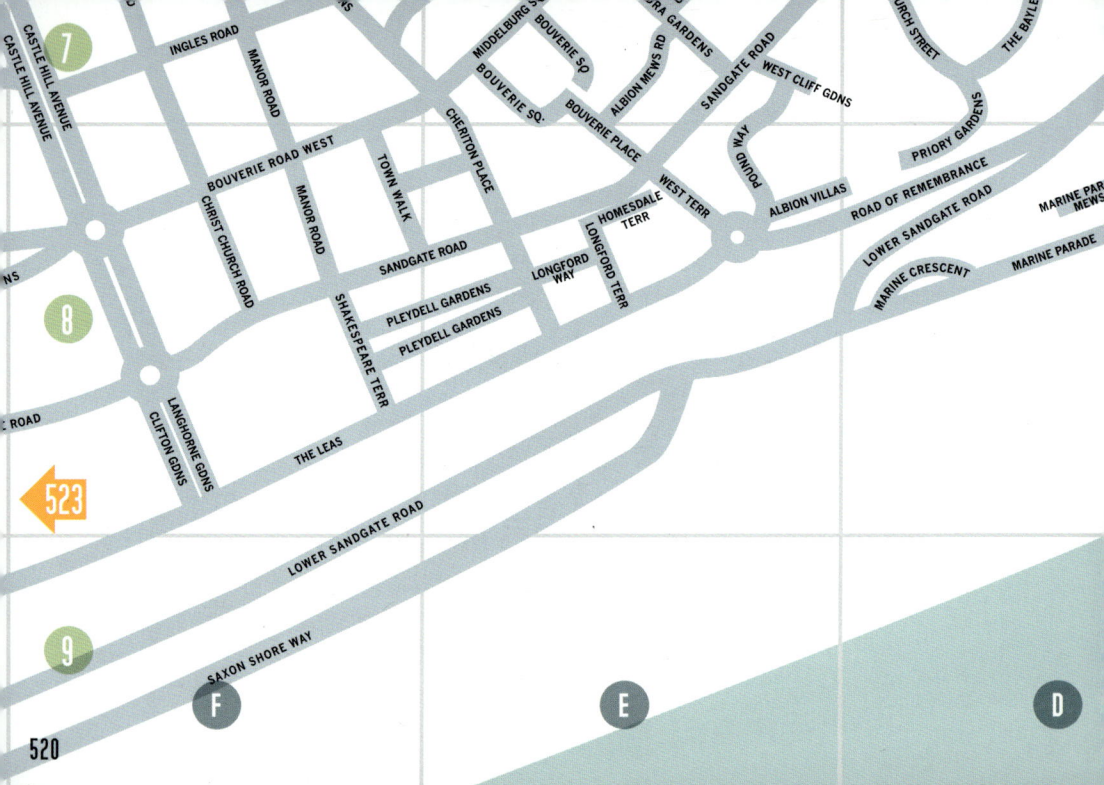

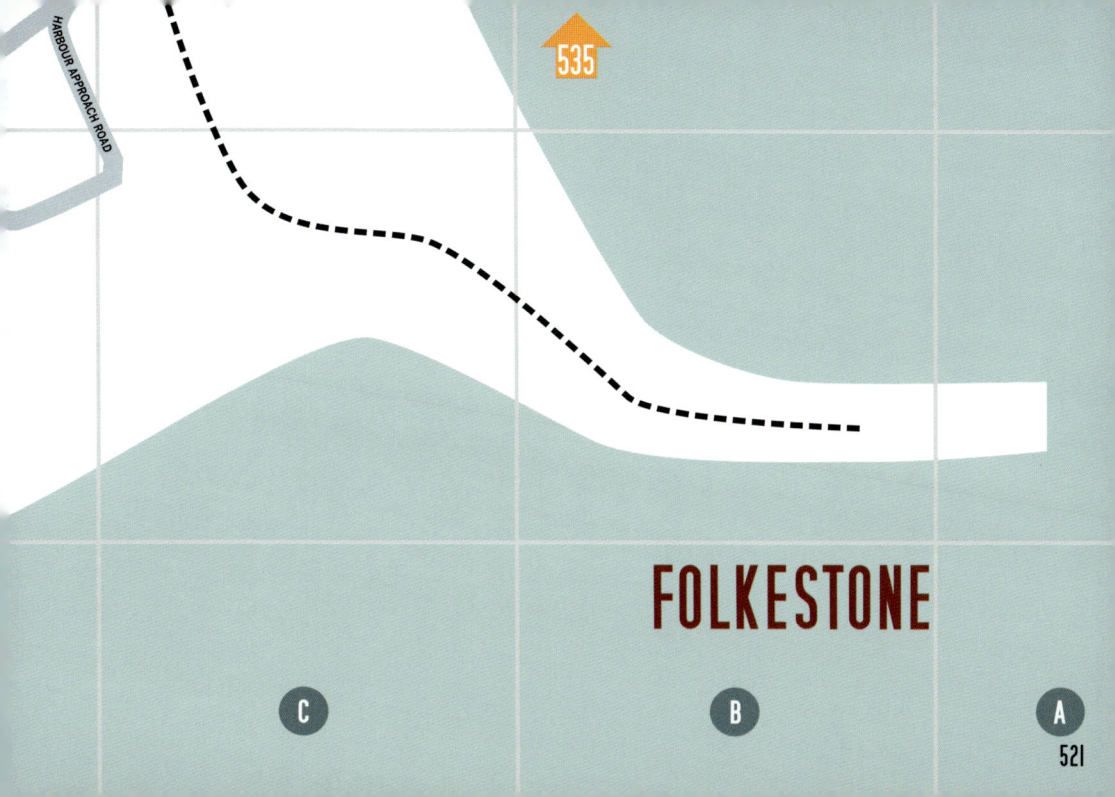

HARBOUR APPROACH ROAD

535

FOLKESTONE

C

B

A

521

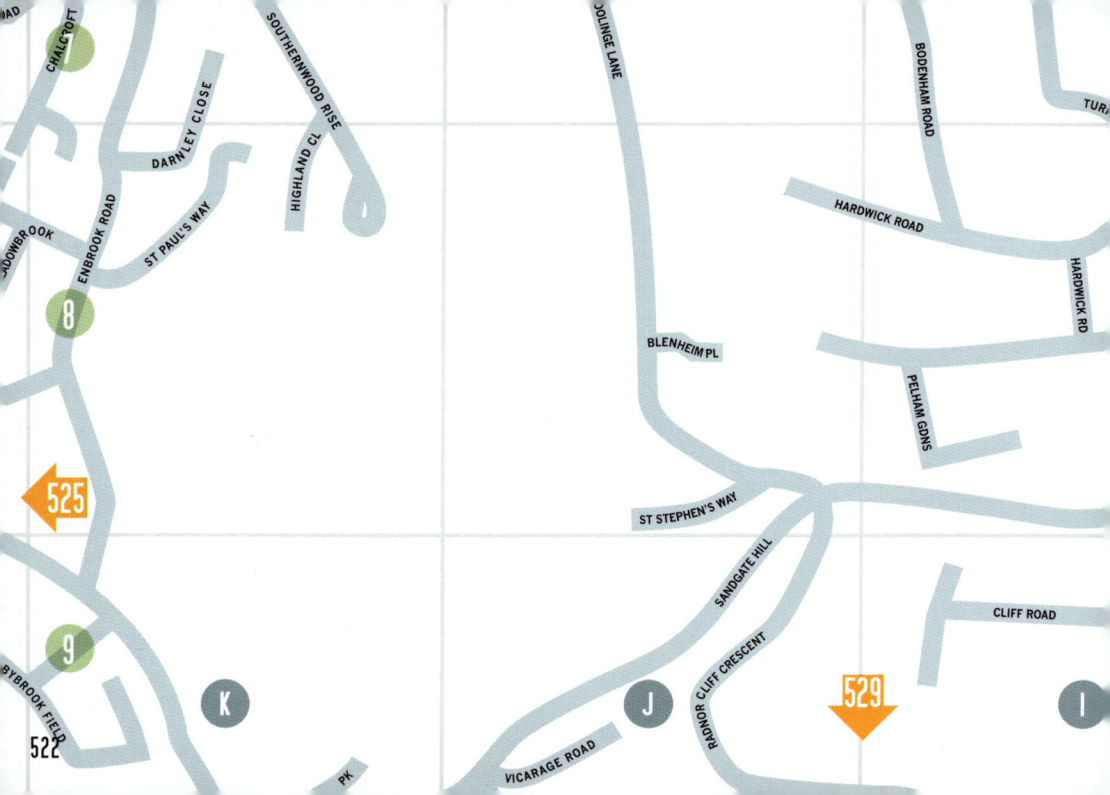

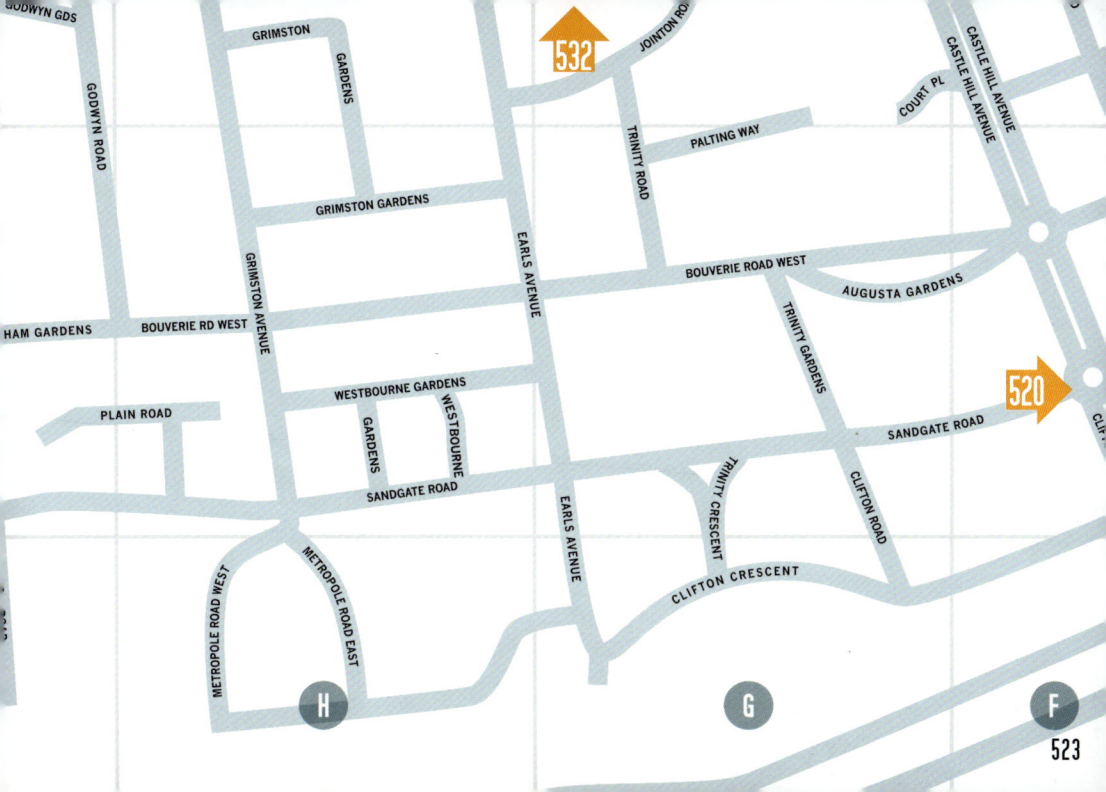

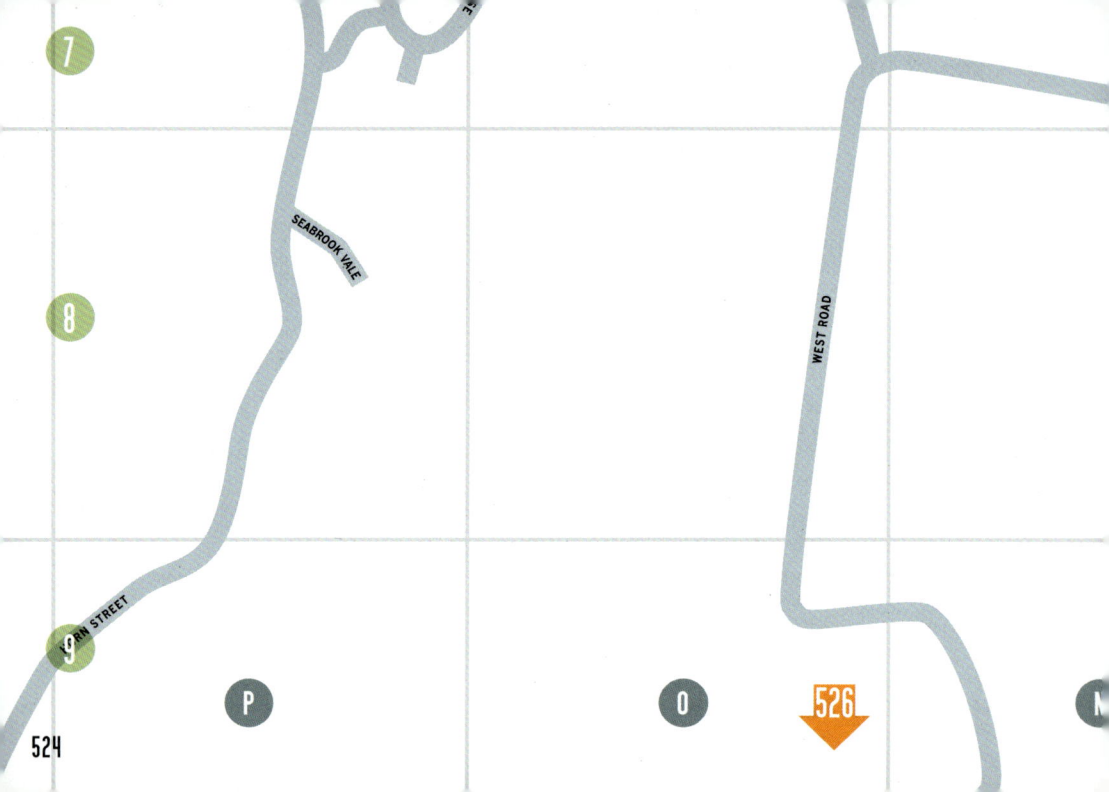

SEABROOK VALE

WEST ROAD

YARN STREET

P

O

526

N

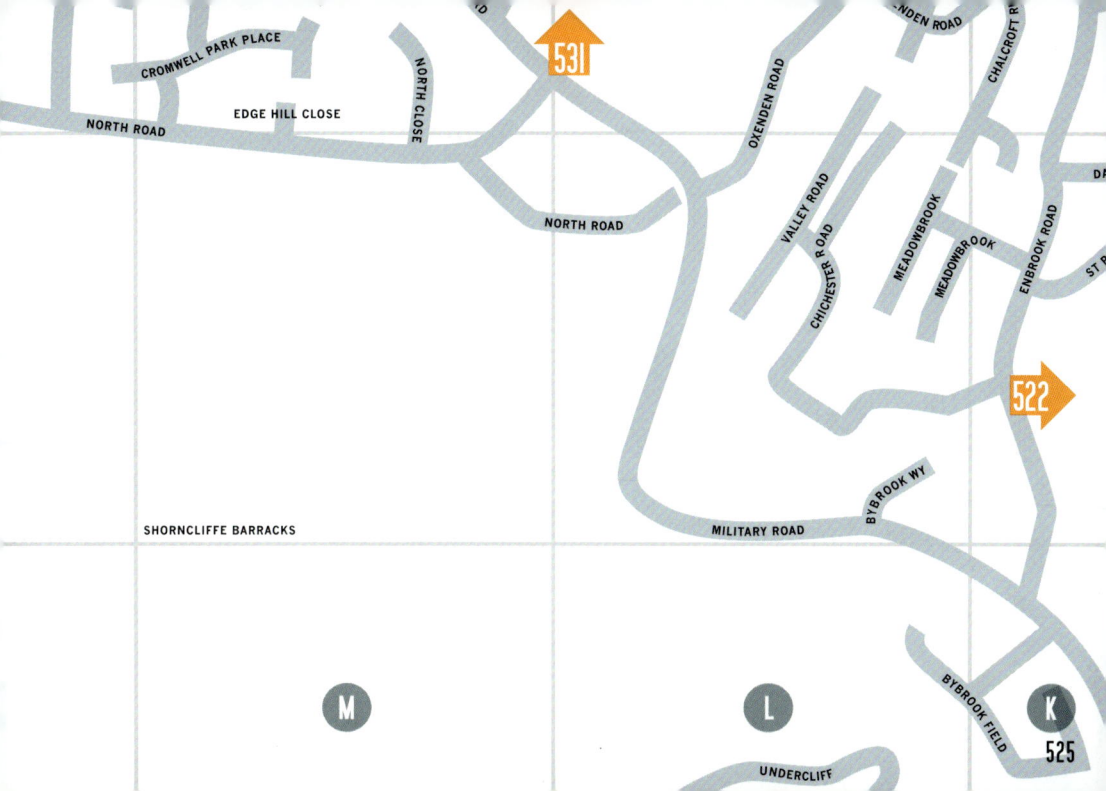

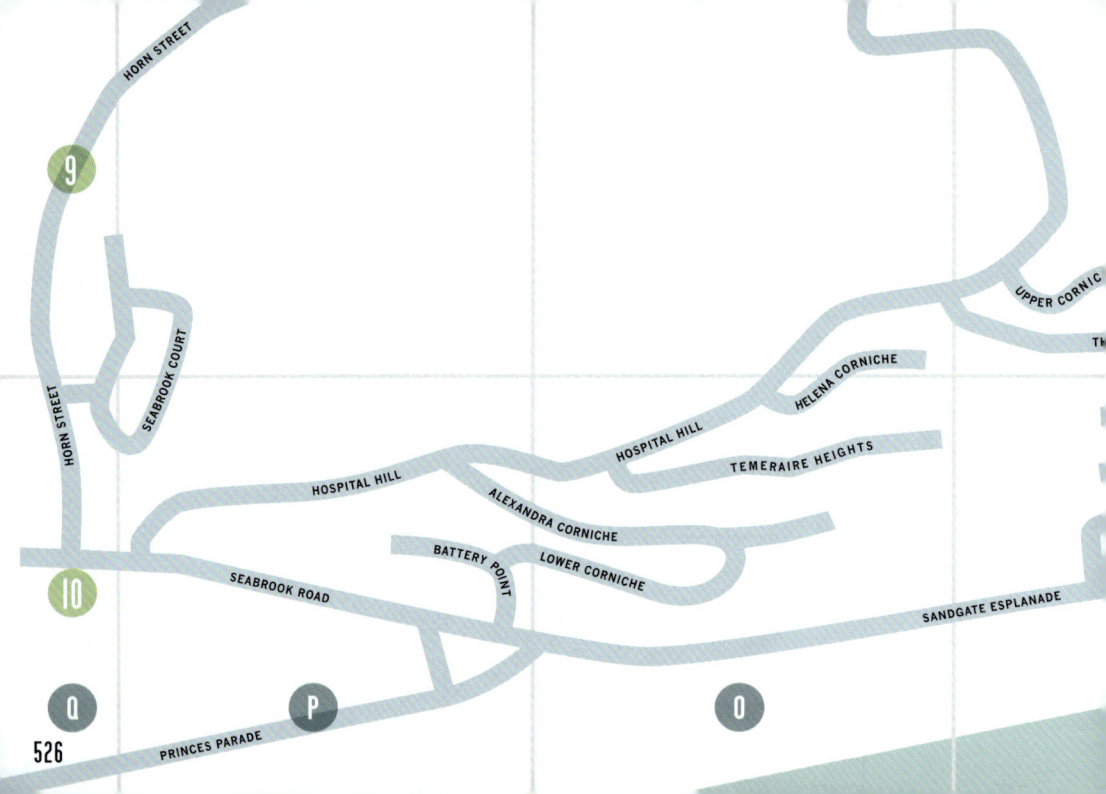

HORN STREET

SEABROOK COURT

HORN STREET

SEABROOK ROAD

HOSPITAL HILL

HOSPITAL HILL

ALEXANDRA CORNICHE

BATTERY POINT

LOWER CORNICHE

TEMERAIRE HEIGHTS

HELENA CORNICHE

UPPER CORNIC

SANDGATE ESPLANADE

PRINCES PARADE

9

10

Q

P

0

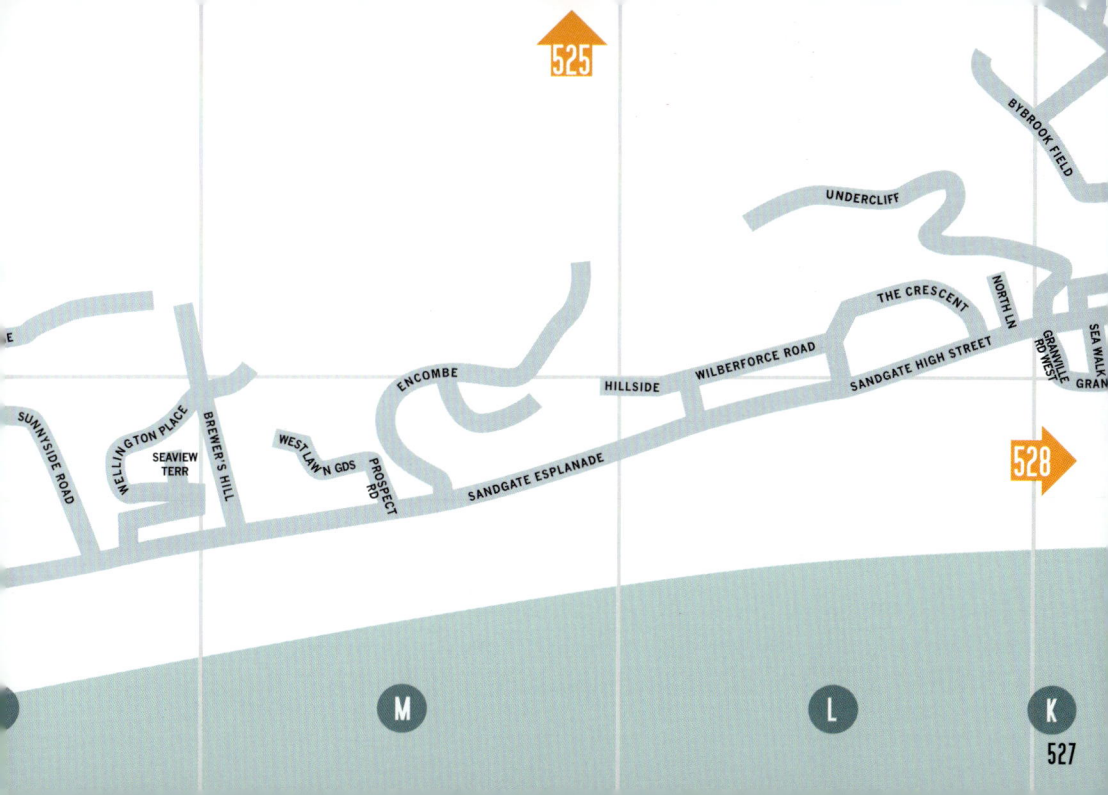

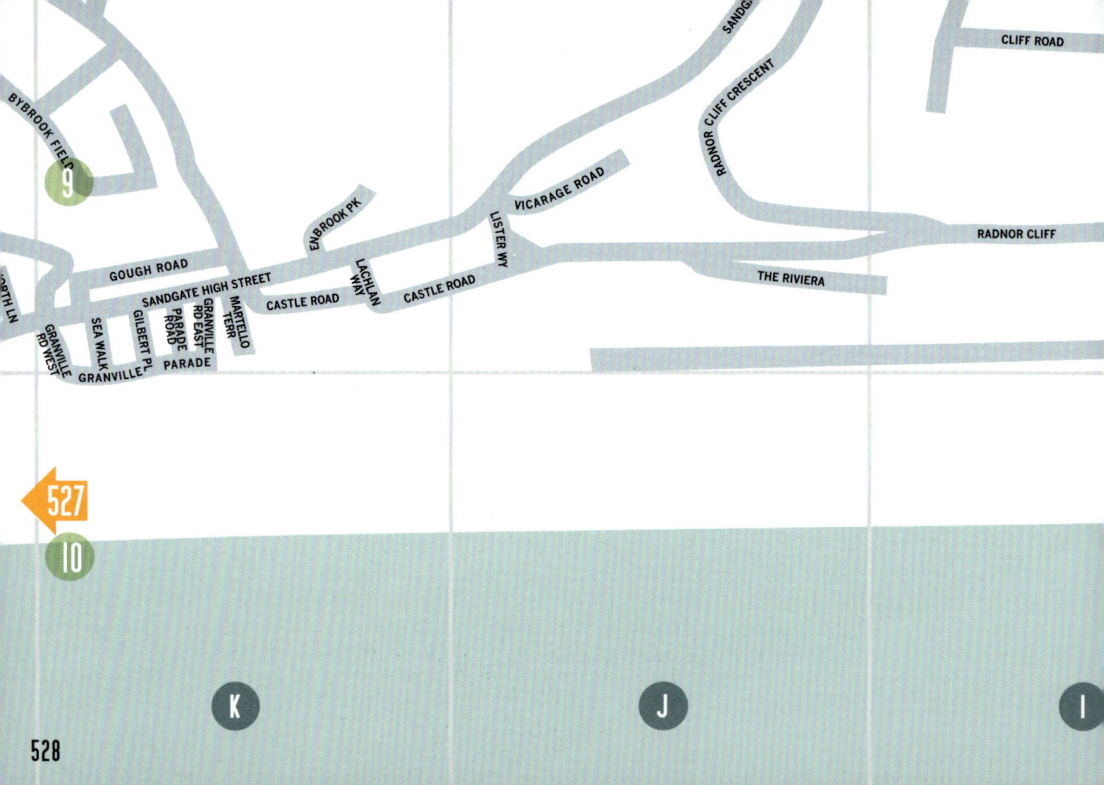

CLIFF ROAD

BYBROOK FIELD

SANDG

RADNOR CLIFF CRESCENT

9

EV BROOK PK

VICARAGE ROAD

RADNOR CLIFF

GOUGH ROAD

LISTER WY

LACHLAN WAY

SANDGATE HIGH STREET

CASTLE ROAD

CASTLE ROAD

THE RIVIERA

RTH LN

GRANVILLE RD WEST

SEA WALK

GILBERT PL

PARADE ROAD

GRANVILLE RD EAST

MARTELLO TERR

GRANVILLE

PARADE

527

10

K

J

I

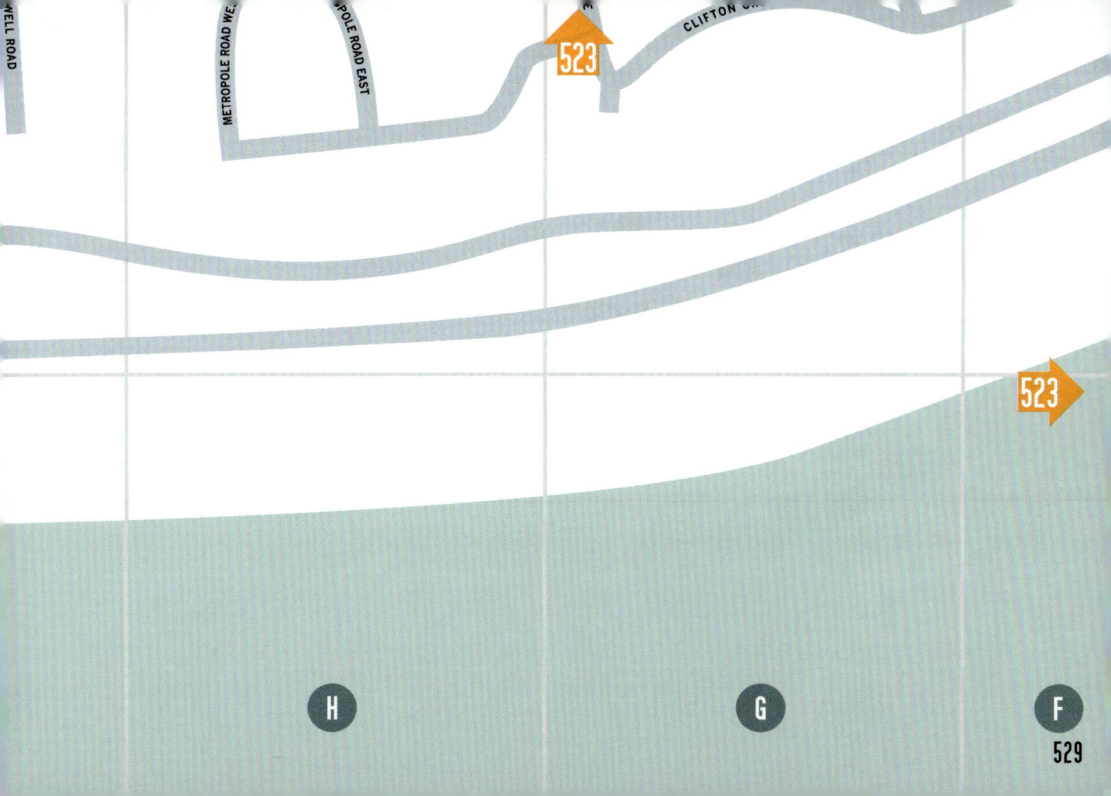

METROPOLE ROAD WE...

...POLE ROAD EAST

...ELL ROAD

CLIFTON C...

523

523

H

G

F

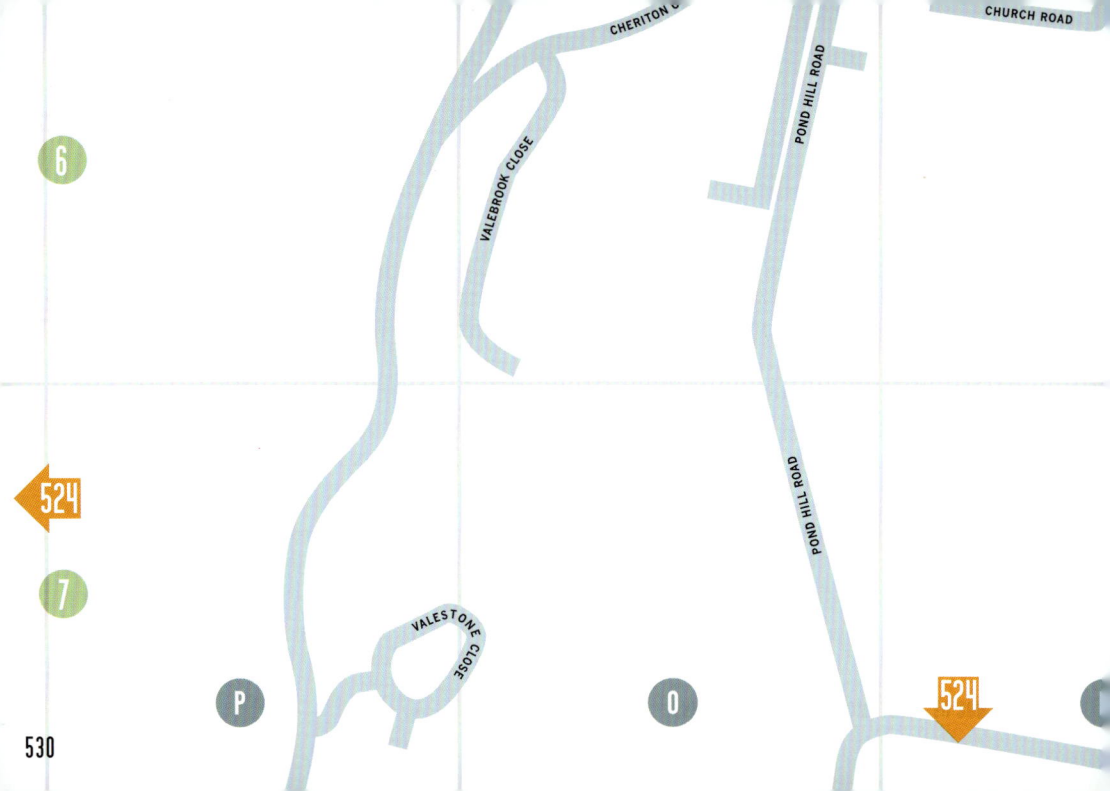

CHURCH ROAD

CHERITON C

VALEBROOK CLOSE

POND HILL ROAD

POND HILL ROAD

VALESTONE CLOSE

6

524

7

P

O

524

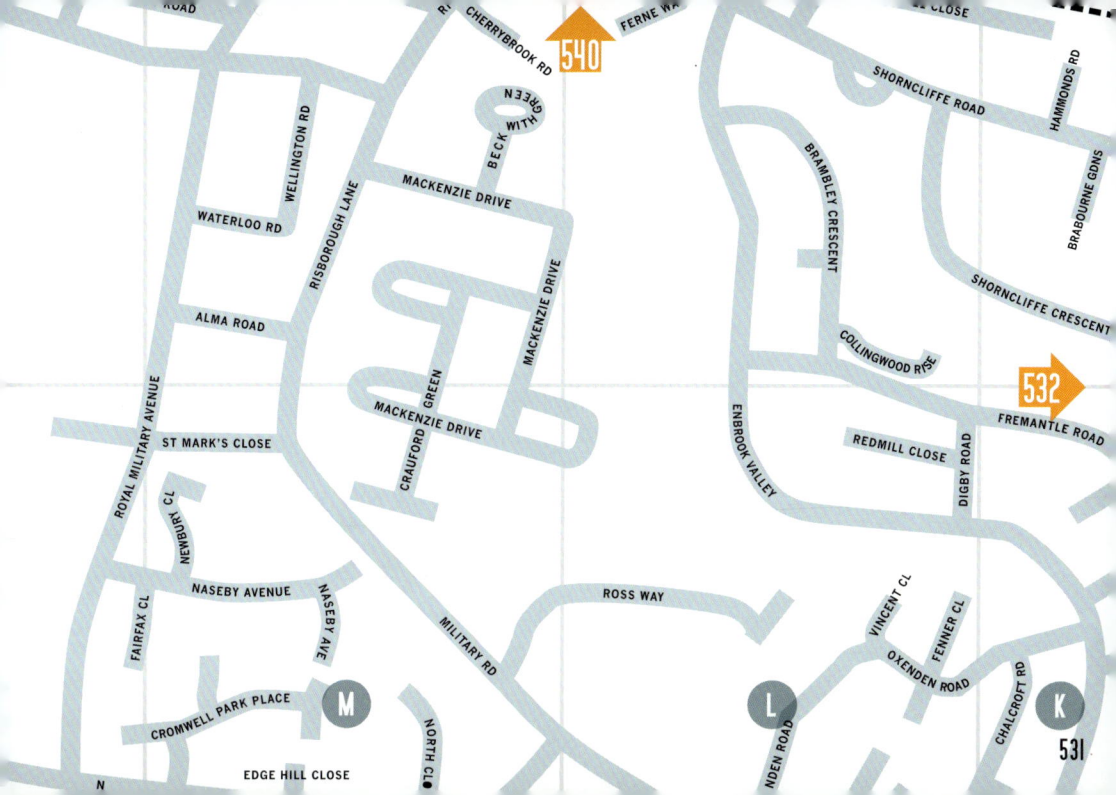

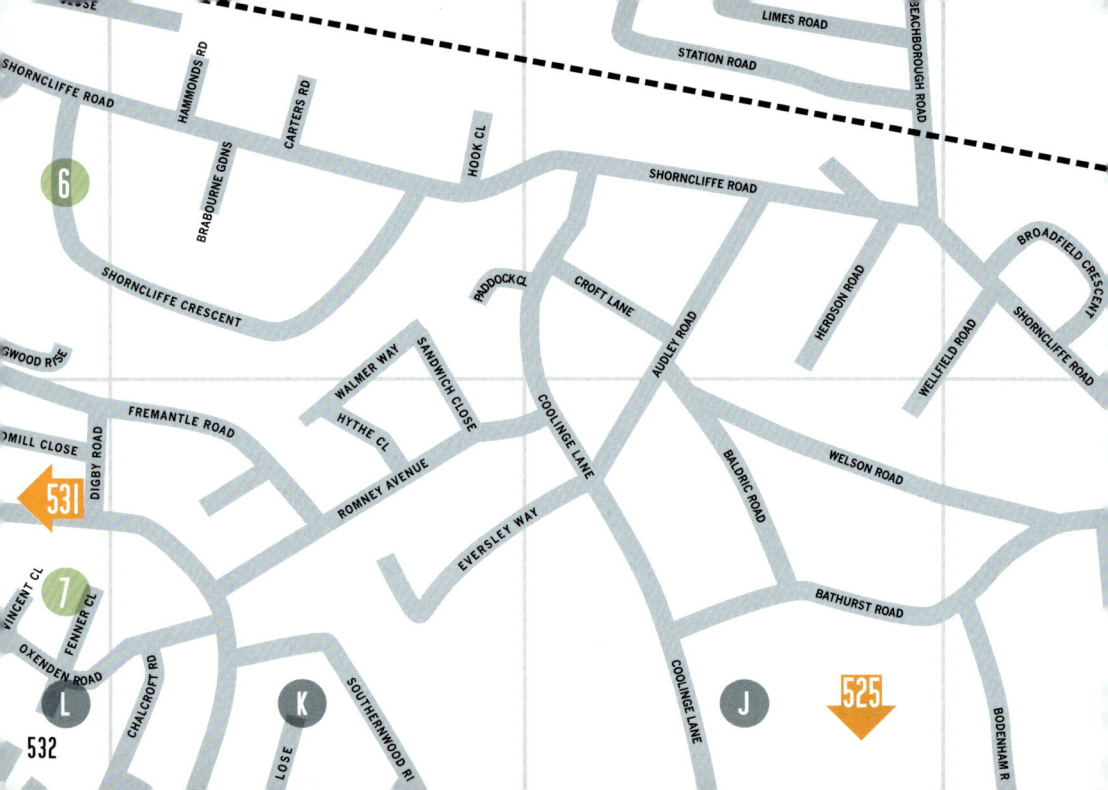

LIMES ROAD

STATION ROAD

BEACHBROUGH ROAD

SHORNCLIFFE ROAD

HAMMONDS RD

CARTERS RD

HOOK CL

BRABOURNE GDNS

6

SHORNCLIFFE CRESCENT

SHORNCLIFFE ROAD

BROADFIELD CRESCENT

HERDSON ROAD

WELLFIELD ROAD

SHORNCLIFFE ROAD

PADDOCK CL

CROFT LANE

AUDLEY ROAD

GWOOD RISE

WALMER WAY

SANDWICH CLOSE

HYTHE CL

COOLINGE LANE

FREMANTLE ROAD

DIGBY ROAD

OMILL CLOSE

531

ROMNEY AVENUE

BALDRIC ROAD

WELSON ROAD

EVERSLEY WAY

VINCENT CL.

7

FENNER CL

OXENDEN ROAD

CHALCROFT RD

K

SOUTHERNWOOD R

L

LOSE

J

COOLINGE LANE

BATHURST ROAD

525

BODENHAM R

532

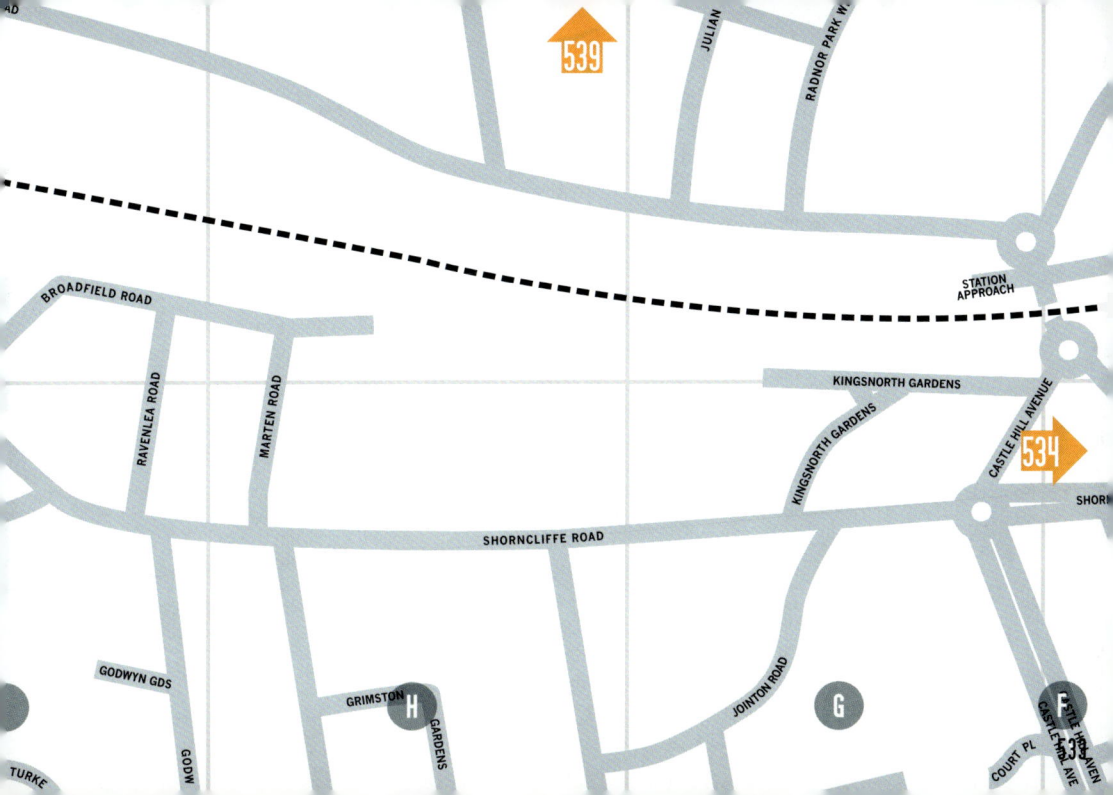

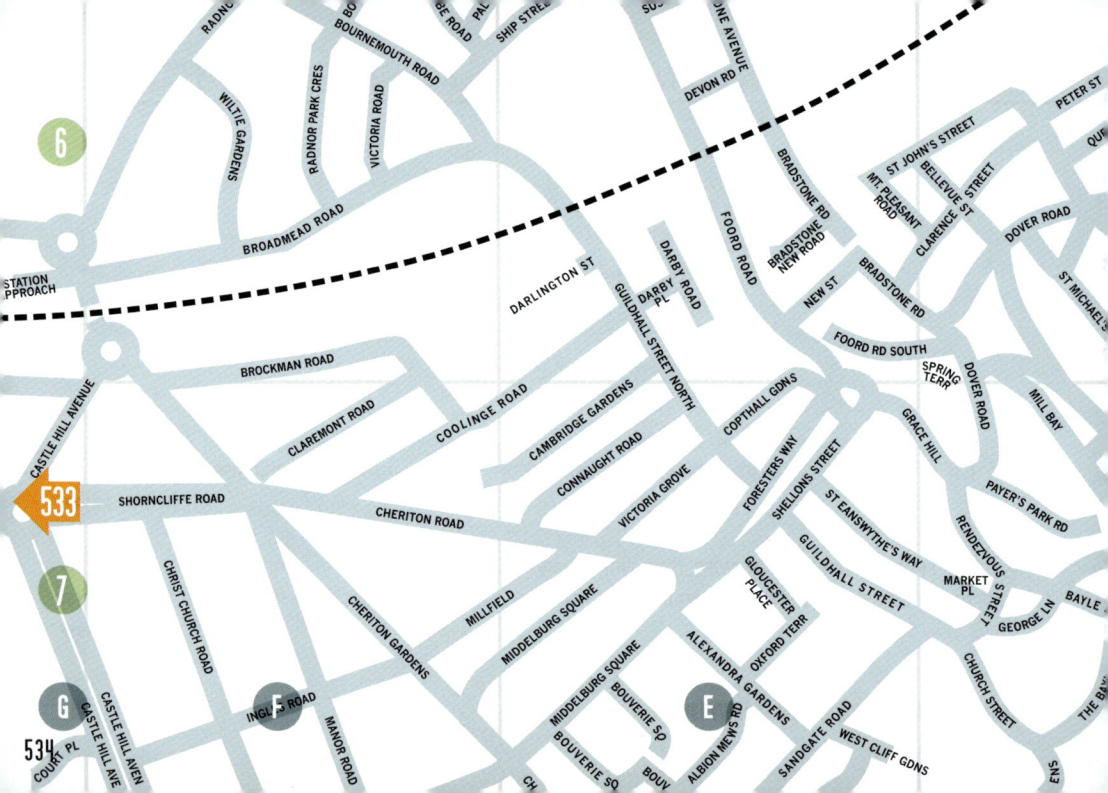

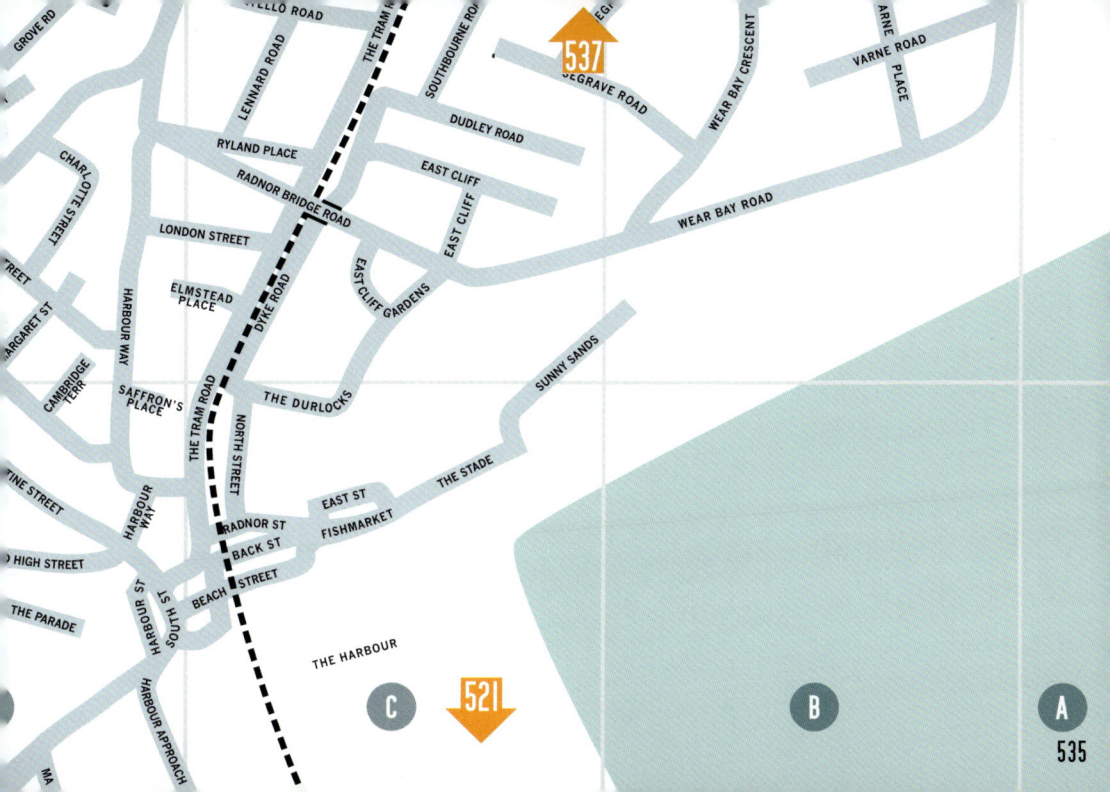

GROVE RD

'TELLO ROAD

THE TRAM ROAD

SOUTHBOURNE ROAD

537

EGI

SEGRAVE ROAD

WEAR BAY CRESCENT

ARNE ROAD

VARNE ROAD

PLACE

LENNARD ROAD

DUDLEY ROAD

RYLAND PLACE

EAST CLIFF

CHARLOTTE STREET

RADNOR BRIDGE ROAD

EAST CLIFF

WEAR BAY ROAD

LONDON STREET

DYKE ROAD

ELMSTEAD PLACE

EAST CLIFF GARDENS

'REET

HARBOUR WAY

MARGARET ST

SUNNY SANDS

CAMBRIDGE TERR

SAFFRON'S PLACE

THE DURLOCKS

THE TRAM ROAD

NORTH STREET

'TINE STREET

THE STADE

HARBOUR WAY

EAST ST

FISHMARKET

RADNOR ST

HIGH STREET

BACK ST

BEACH STREET

ST

SOUTH ST

HARBOUR ST

THE PARADE

THE HARBOUR

521

C

B

A

HARBOUR APPROACH

MA

535

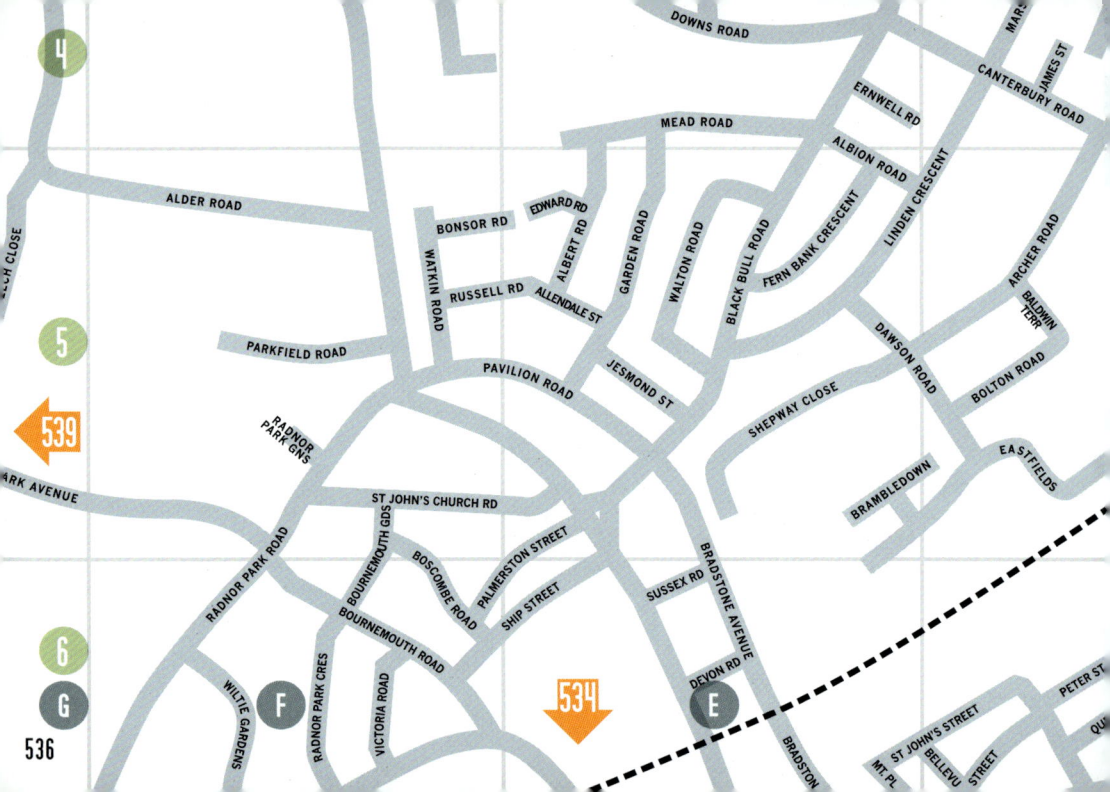

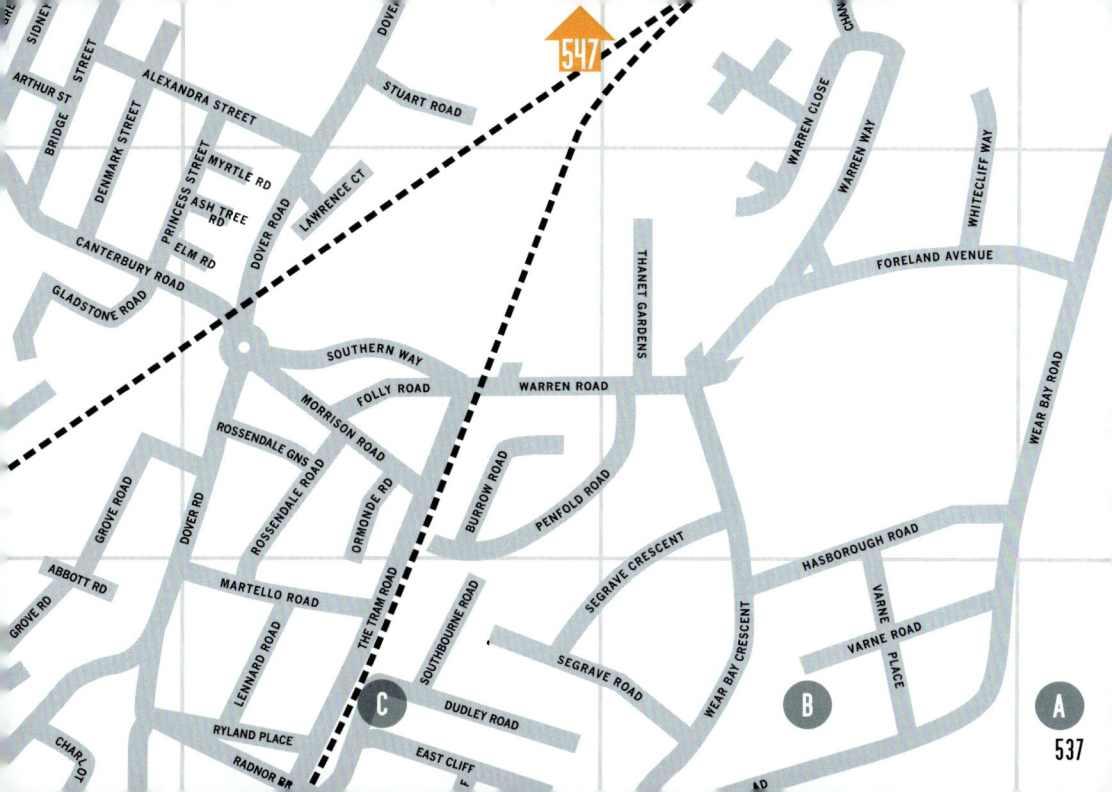

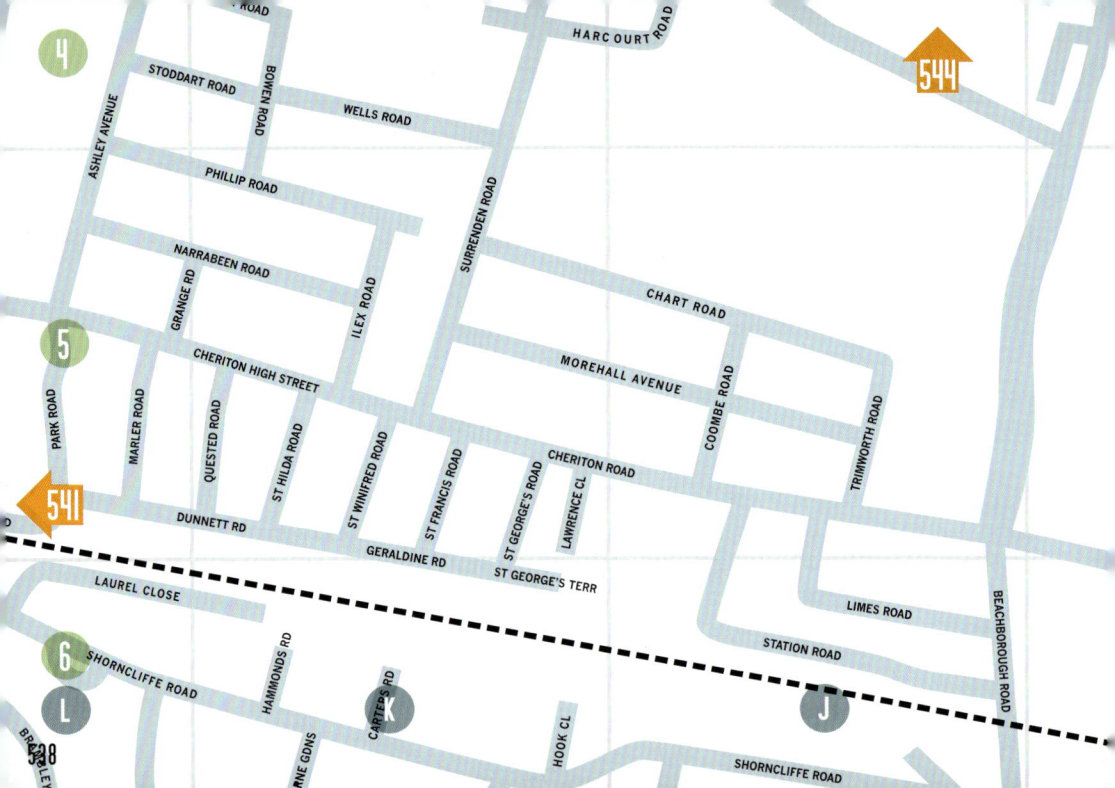

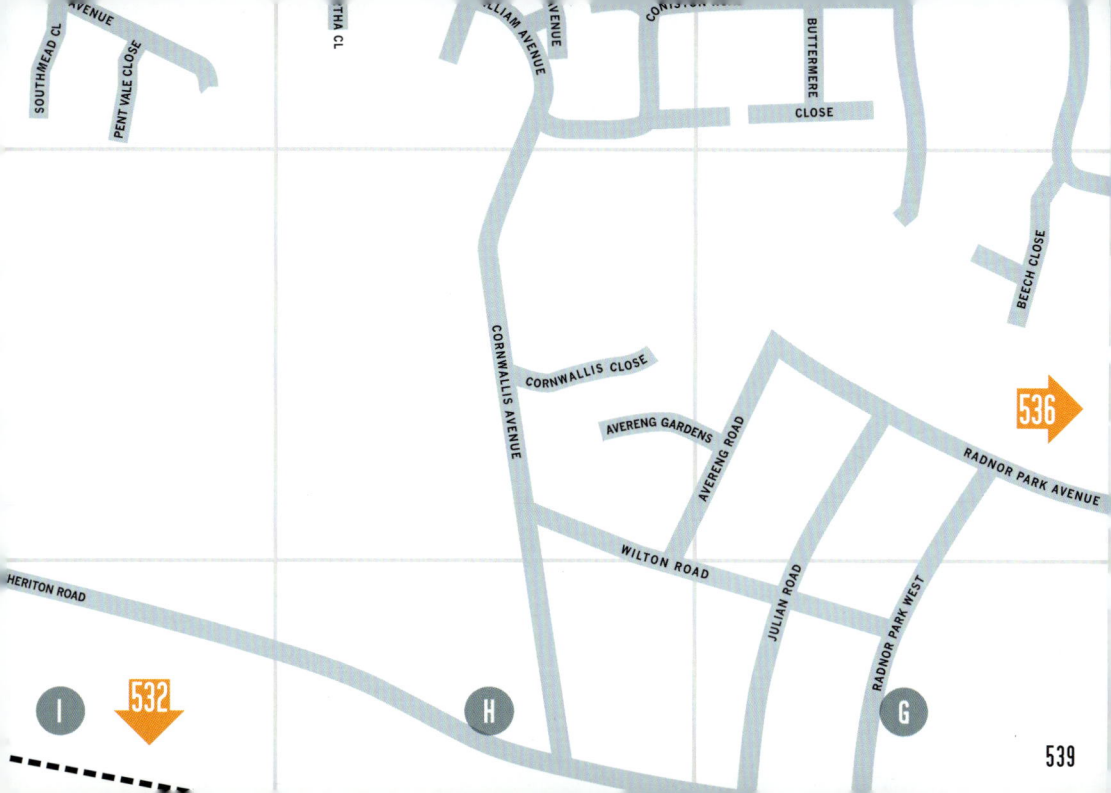

SOUTHMEAD CL

PENT VALE CLOSE

AVENUE

THA CL

LLIAM AVENUE

AVENUE

CONISTON RO

BUTTERMERE

CLOSE

BEECH CLOSE

CORNWALLIS AVENUE

CORNWALLIS CLOSE

AVERENG GARDENS

AVERENG ROAD

RADNOR PARK AVENUE

536

WILTON ROAD

JULIAN ROAD

RADNOR PARK WEST

HERITON ROAD

I

532

H

G

539

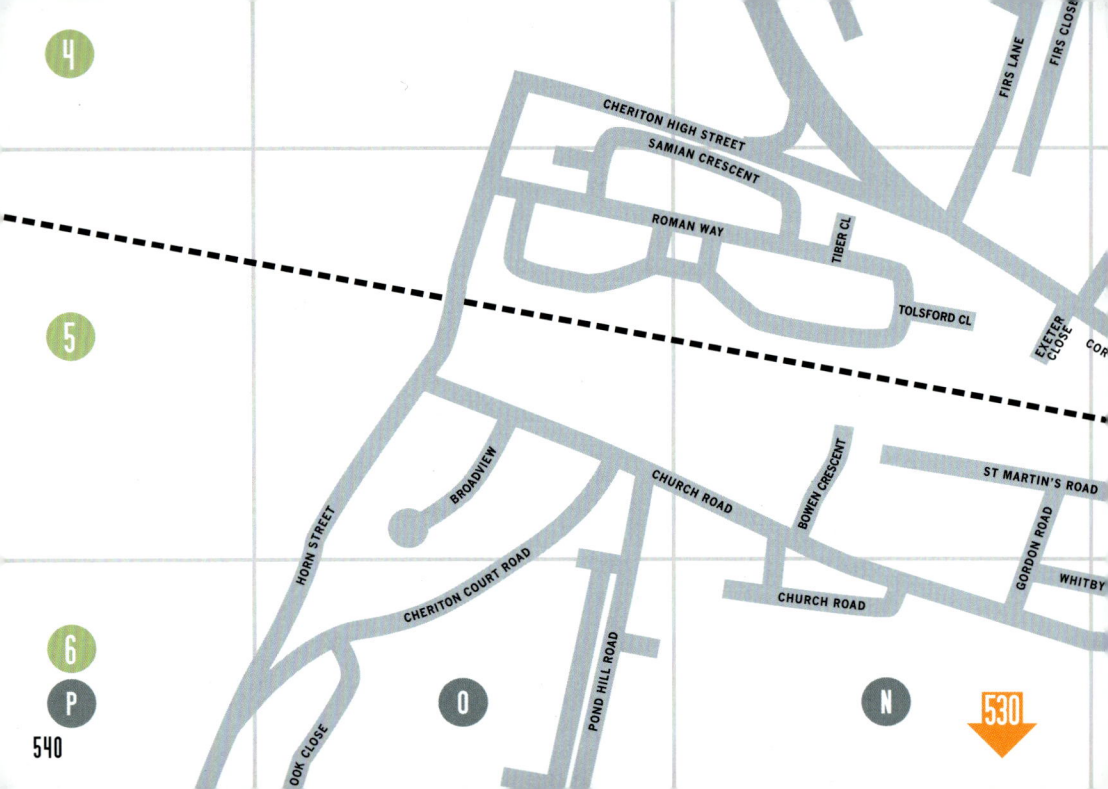

FIRS LANE

FIRS CLOSE

CHERITON HIGH STREET

SAMIAN CRESCENT

ROMAN WAY

TIBER CL

TOLSFORD CL

EXETER CLOSE

COR

ST MARTIN'S ROAD

BOWEN CRESCENT

CHURCH ROAD

GORDON ROAD

WHITBY

CHURCH ROAD

BROADVIEW

HORN STREET

CHERITON COURT ROAD

POND HILL ROAD

OOK CLOSE

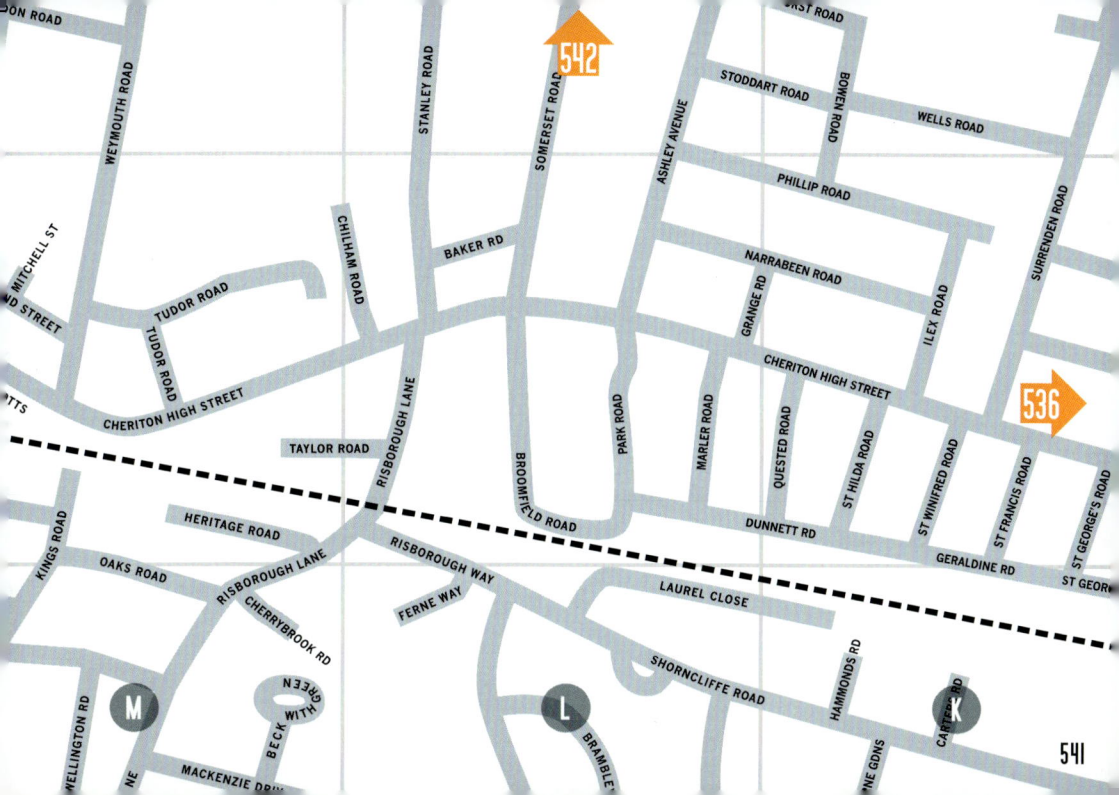

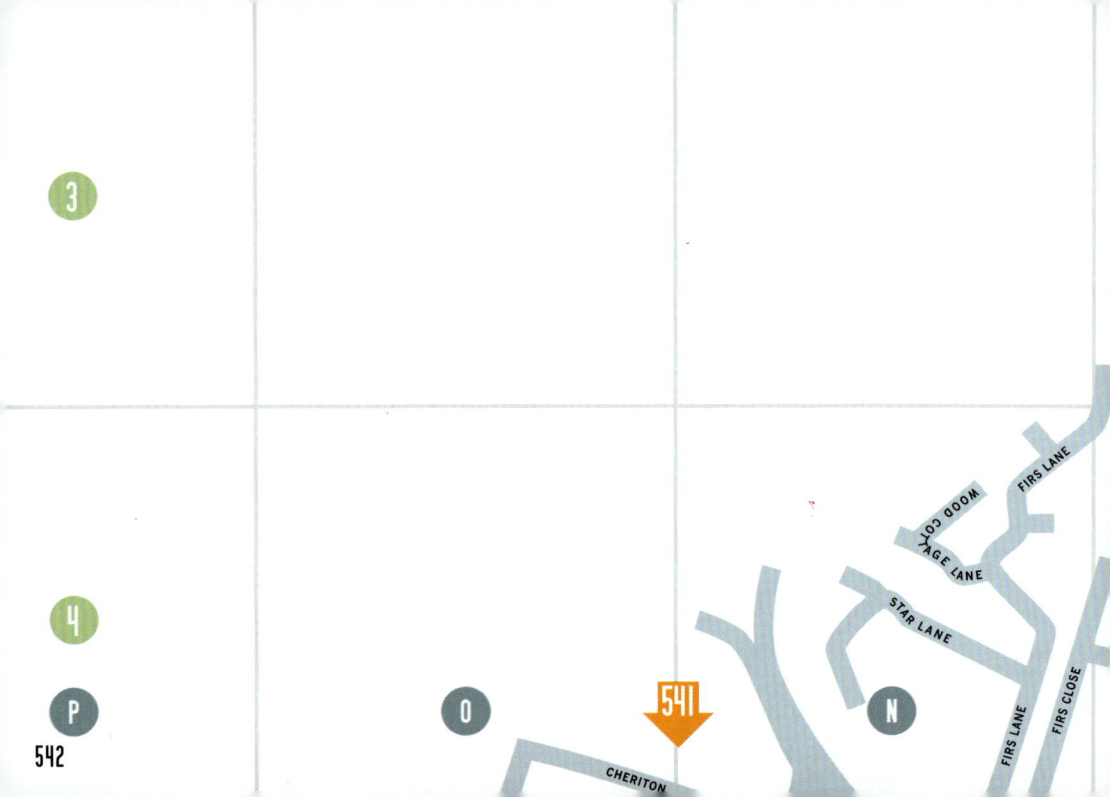

P

542

O

541

N

CHERITON

FIRS LANE

WOOD COL...

...AGE LANE

STAR LANE

FIRS LANE

FIRS CLOSE

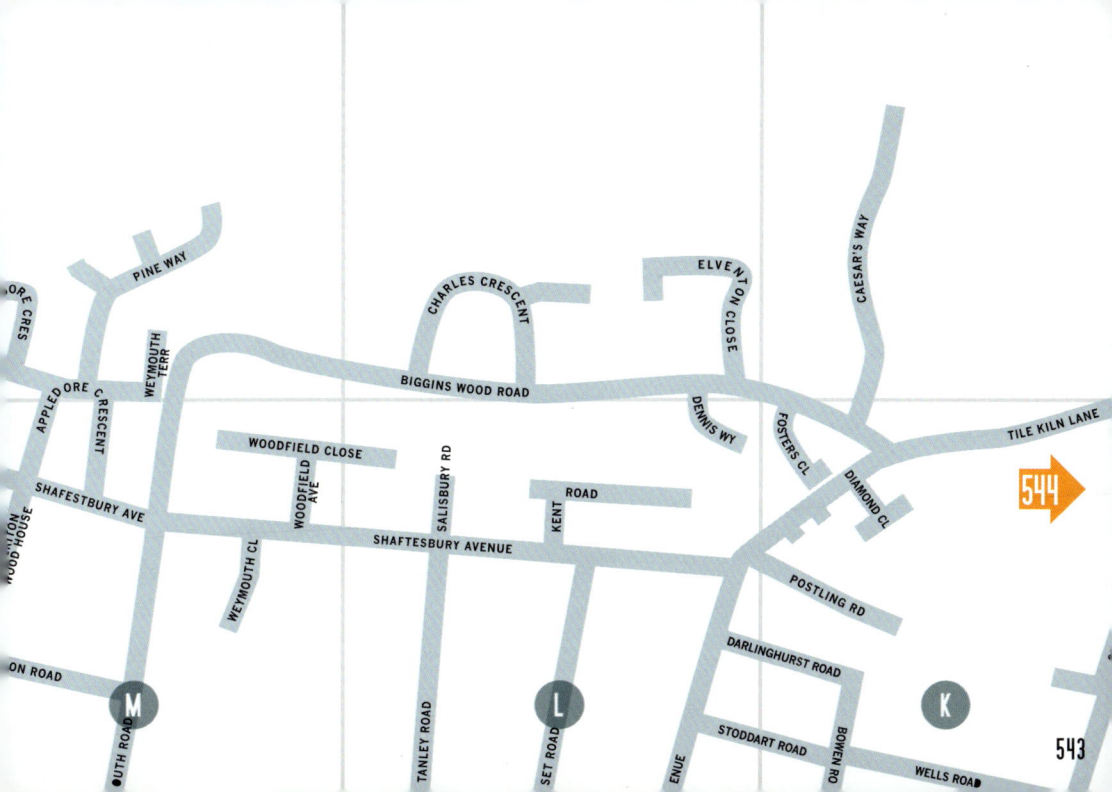

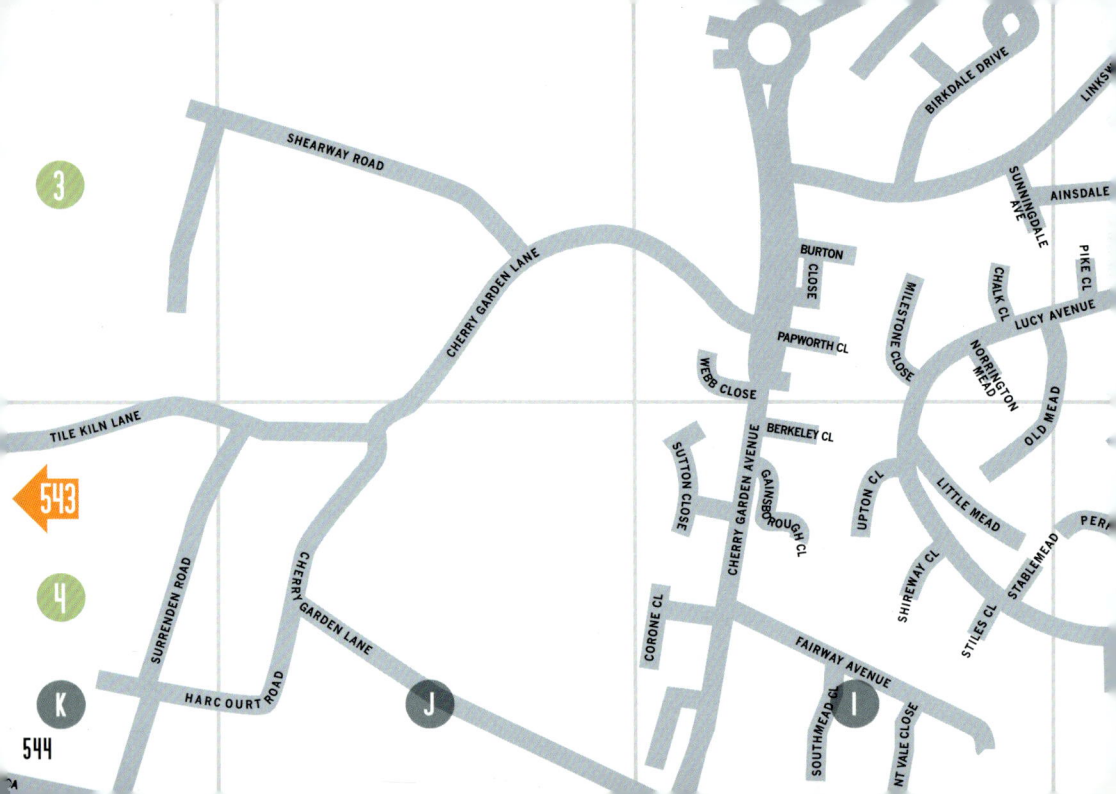

SHEARWAY ROAD

BIRKDALE DRIVE

LINKS

SUNNINGDALE AVE

AINSDALE

CHERRY GARDEN LANE

BURTON CLOSE

MILESTONE CLOSE

PIKE CL

CHALK CL

LUCY AVENUE

PAPWORTH CL

NORRINGTON MEAD

OLD MEAD

WEBB CLOSE

TILE KILN LANE

BERKELEY CL

SUTTON CLOSE

LITTLE MEAD

PERI

543

UPTON CL

STABLEMEAD

SURRENDEN ROAD

CHERRY GARDEN LANE

CHERRY GARDEN AVENUE

GAINSBOROUGH CL

SHIREWAY CL

STILES CL

4

CORONE CL

HARCOURT ROAD

K

CHERRY GARDEN LANE

J

FAIRWAY AVENUE

SOUTHMEAD CL

NT VALE CLOSE

I

544

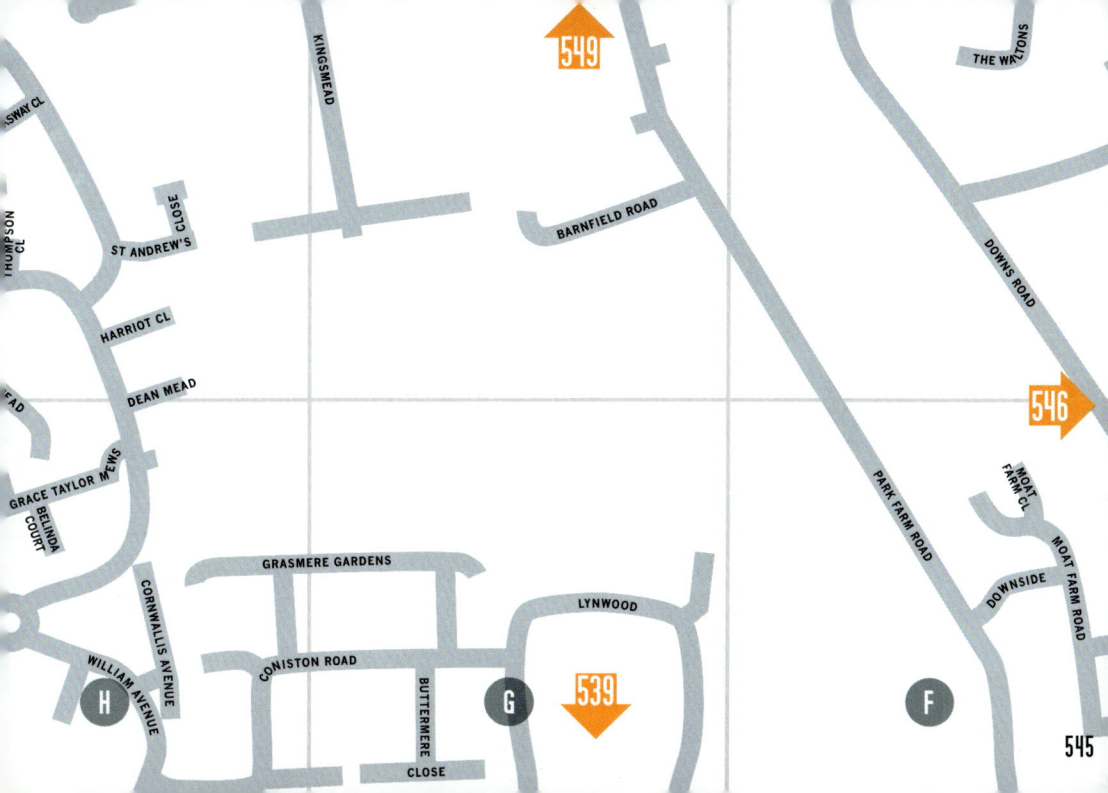

549

KINGSMEAD

THE WATSONS

S'WAY CL

CLOSE

ST ANDREW'S

THOMPSON CL

BARNFIELD ROAD

DOWNS ROAD

HARRIOT CL

DEAN MEAD

EAD

546

MOAT FARM CL

GRACE TAYLOR MEWS

PARK FARM ROAD

BELINDA COURT

GRASMERE GARDENS

LYNWOOD

MOAT FARM ROAD

CORNWALLIS AVENUE

DOWNSIDE

WILLIAM AVENUE

CONISTON ROAD

BUTTERMERE CLOSE

H

G

539

F

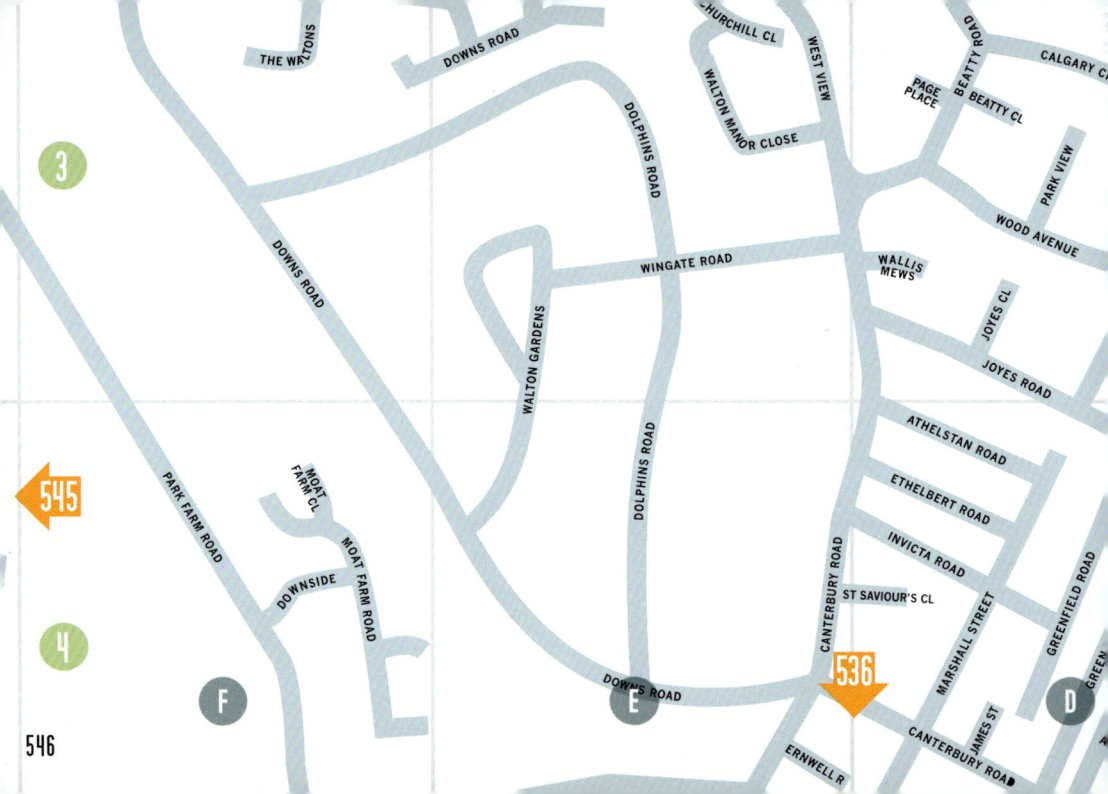

THE WALTONS

DOWNS ROAD

CHURCHILL CL

WEST VIEW

CALGARY C

BEATTY ROAD

PAGE PLACE

BEATTY CL

WALTON MANOR CLOSE

PARK VIEW

WOOD AVENUE

DOLPHINS ROAD

DOWNS ROAD

WINGATE ROAD

WALLIS MEWS

JOYES CL

JOYES ROAD

WALTON GARDENS

ATHELSTAN ROAD

ETHELBERT ROAD

INVICTA ROAD

GREENFIELD ROAD

PARK FARM ROAD

MOAT FARM CL

DOLPHINS ROAD

CANTERBURY ROAD

ST SAVIOUR'S CL

GREEN

MOAT FARM ROAD

DOWNSIDE

MARSHALL STREET

JAMES ST

DOWNS ROAD

CANTERBURY ROAD

ERNWELL R

3

545

4

F

E

536

D

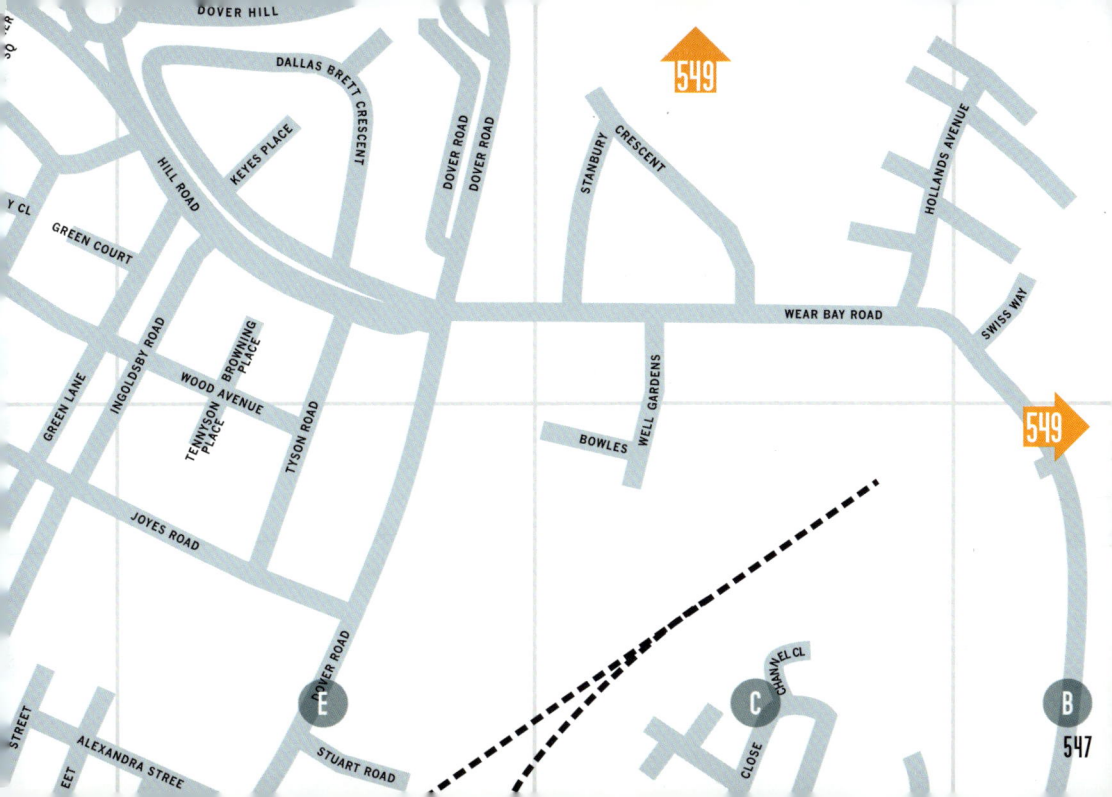

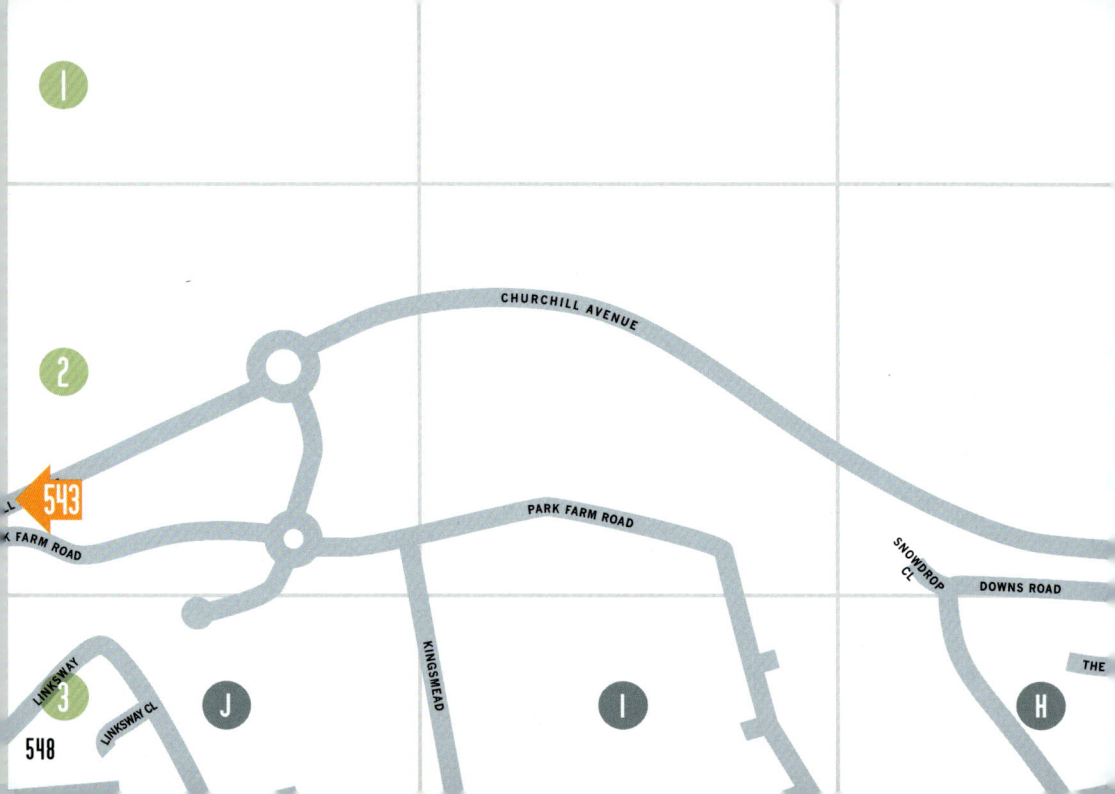

CHURCHILL AVENUE

PARK FARM ROAD

K FARM ROAD

SNOWDROP CL

DOWNS ROAD

THE

LINKSWAY

LINKSWAY CL

KINGSMEAD

543

548

1

2

3

J

I

H

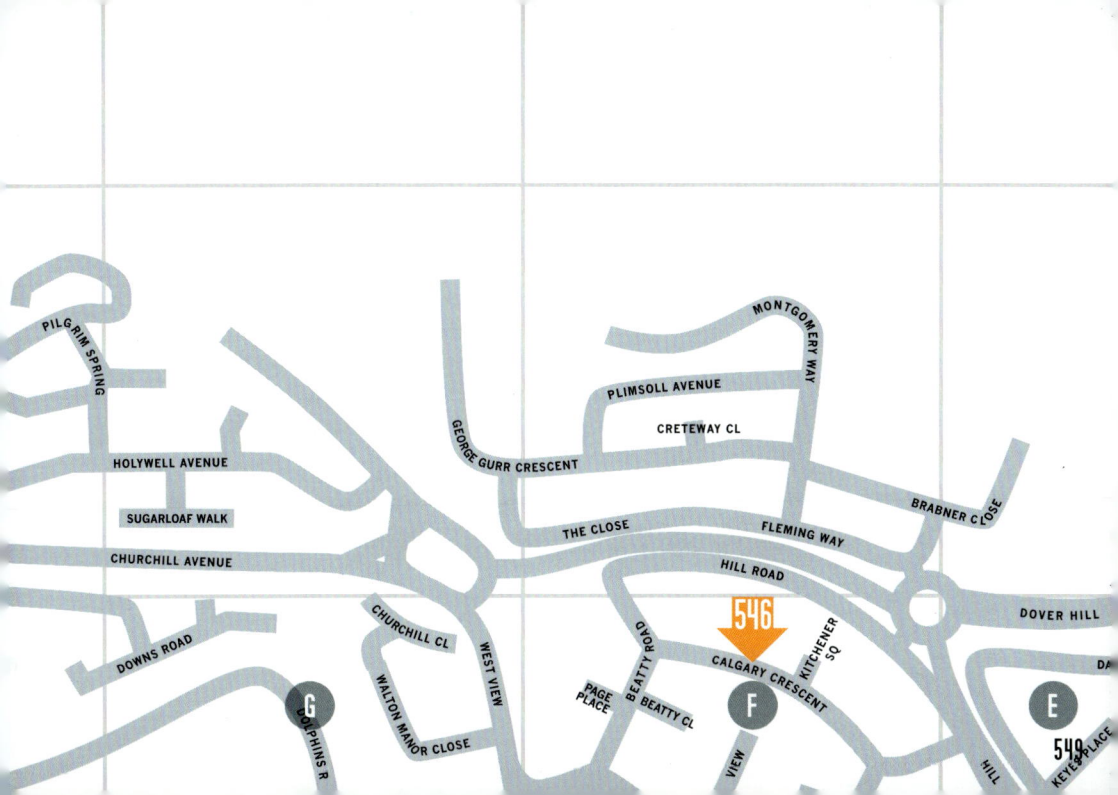

INDEX OF PLACES

EVERYWHERE MEANS SOMETHING TO SOMEONE

EVERYWHERE MEANS SOMETHING TO SOMEONE